संक्षिप्त

हिन्दी-अंग्रेजी शब्दकोश

प्रतियोगी परीक्षा अभ्यर्थियों, सभी आयु वर्ग के छात्र-छात्राओं तथा अन्य पाठकों के लिए विशेषतः उपयोगी

वी एण्ड एस पब्लिशर्स

प्रकाशक

वी एण्ड एस पब्लिशर्स

F-2/16, अंसारी रोड, दरियागंज, नई दिल्ली-110002
☎ 23240026, 23240027, 23240028
info@vspublishers.com • www.vspublishers.com

Online Brandstore: amazon.in/vspublishers

क्षेत्रीय कार्यालय : हैदराबाद
5-1-707/1, ब्रिज भवन (सेन्ट्रल बैंक ऑफ इण्डिया लेन के पास)
बैंक स्ट्रीट, कोटी, हैदराबाद-500 095
☎ 040-24737290
vspublishershyd@gmail.com

ISBN 978-93-505714-4-6

नवीन संस्करण

मुद्रक : परम ऑफसेटर्स, ओखला, नई दिल्ली-110020

प्रकाशकीय / Publisher's Note

विज्ञान सम्बन्धी शब्दकोशों को प्रकाशित करने के बाद हिन्दी से अंग्रेजी में अनुवाद के लिए एक मानक शब्दकोश की आवश्यकता महसूस करते हुए वी एण्ड एस पब्लिशर्स अपनी नवीनतम पुस्तक संक्षिप्त हिन्दी-अंग्रेजी शब्दकोश प्रस्तुत करते हैं। शब्दकोशों की परम्परा को ध्यान में रखते हुए लेखक ने प्रस्तुत शब्दकोश में अधिक से अधिक साहित्यक शब्दों के साथ देशज, आंचलिक, विज्ञान, भूगोल, बैंकिग तथा खगोलीय शब्दों के साथ उसके व्याकरणीय क्रम की जानकारी दी है। शब्दकोश में वर्तनी की एकरूपता और शुद्धता का भी विशेष ध्यान रखा गया है। आजकल बहुत-सी पुस्तकों में अनुनासिक स्वर (ँ) की जगह अनुस्वार (ं) का प्रयोग देखने को मिल रहा है लेकिन इस शब्दकोश में अनुनासिक शब्दों का विधिवत प्रयोग किया गया है। शब्दकोश के अन्त में सामान्य जनजीवन में प्रचलित व्यवहारिक शब्दों, मापतौल के मानकों, हिन्दी अंग्रेजी मुहावरे, बैंकिग, भारतीय संविधान में प्रयुक्त हिन्दी के पारिभाषिक शब्दों आदि को विशिष्ट परिशिष्ट के तौर पर दिया गया है।

हमें विश्वास है कि यह शब्दकोश छात्र-छात्राओं के लिए बेहद उपयोगी होने के साथ अन्य पेशेवर लोगों जैसे डाक्टर, वकील, इंजीनियर तथा शिक्षकों के लिए सहायक सिद्ध होगी। हालाँकि शब्दकोश में कोई त्रुटि न रहे इस बात का विशेष ध्यान रखा गया है लेकिन फिर भी भूलवश कोई त्रुटि रह गयी हो तो पाठकों से निवेदन है कि वे इस ओर हमारा ध्यान जरूर आकर्षित करें ताकि अगामी संस्करण में इस त्रुटि का निवारण किया जा सके।

A perceptibly good response given by readers to our previously published (Ten in number so far) concise dictionaries on science and commerce subjects has encouraged us to undertake publication of another dictionary in high demand - A Hindi-English Dictionary. Like previous dictionaries this again is a concise version. This edition is expected to fulfil the academic and writing requirements of students, researchers, scholars, translators, educationists, and writers. This dictionary is quite different from others in that the 'Terms' defined have been drawn from all resource attributes - *tatsam, ardhtatsam, tadbhav*, *deshaj* and *videshaj*, besides those used currently in literature, vernacular &

regional languages, science, geography, commerce & business etc. Terms used in common parlance, compound words, syntax and other grammatical details to improve writing also are explained.

One more special point that needs mentioning! Computerization has led to many notable changes in writing Hindi words. *Anunahasik* symbol (ँ) has given way and is replaced by a nasal sound (*anuswar*). It has become a fashion to use *anuswar's symbol* (ं) by writers, litterateurs, educationists and publishers without any qualm in their works. However, this dictionary has stayed true to Hindi way of writing – the original style of writing.

In the Appendices section, body parts, common ailments, apparel, cereals, fruit & vegetables, herbs & spices, household items, professions, idioms & phrases, foreign words have been included. Scientific symbols & notations, terms used in administration, management, economics, science, mathematics etc, besides other important facts, help make this dictionary more useful for readers.

It is hoped that this dictionary will be found useful by student community besides others such as, educationists, writers, translators as well as doctors, lawyers, and engineers.

Every effort has been taken to keep this dictionary error-free. However, should you come across any mistake, misprint, unsatisfactory annotation or explanation, please intimate us. We would incorporate your valuable suggestion while acknowledging your contribution.

संक्षिप्त हिन्दी-अंग्रेजी शब्दकोश में शब्दों का क्रम विन्यास

इस शब्दकोश में शब्दों का क्रम विन्यास स्वरवर्ण (अ से औ) तथा बाद में व्यंजनवर्ण (क से ह) तक रखा गया है। स्वरवर्ण में अनुस्वारयुक्त शब्दों को जैसे अं, अंक, अंकि, अंकी, अंकु, अंकू, अंकृ, अंके, अंकै, अंको, अंकौ इत्यादि के क्रम में रखा गया है। इसके बाद व्यंजन एवं इसके युग्मवर्ण का समावेश किया गया है जैसे– अ, अक, अका, अकि, अकी, अकु, अकू, अकृ, अके, अकै, अको, अकौ, अक्क, अक्य, अक्ट, अक्त, अक्र, अक्ल, अक्ष इत्यादि उपरोक्त क्रम विन्यास में स्वरवर्ण में अ से लेकर औ तक तथा व्यंजनवर्ण में क से लेकर ह तक सरल एंव यौगिक शब्द समूह की रचना की गयी है।

स्वरवर्ण का क्रम– अ, आ, इ, ई, उ, ऊ, ऋ, ए, ऐ, ओ तथा औ।

व्यंजनवर्ण का क्रम– क, ख, ग, घ, च, छ, ज, झ, ट, ठ, ड, ढ ण, त, थ, द, ध, न, प, फ, ब, भ, म, य, र, ल, व, श, ष, स तथा ह।

शब्दकोश देखने की विधि

मान लिया किसी पाठक को यदि 'अंग' शब्द का अंग्रेजी अर्थ देखना है तो वह शब्दकोश में अंग शब्द की तलाश के लिए अंक शब्द से शुरू होने वाले शब्द के नीचे आठवें शब्द में अंग शब्द को पृष्ठ संख्या 13 पर देखें।

यहाँ अंग शब्द का अर्थ–

अंग [*nm*] a limb; member; body; part; component; organ;–भंगिमा/भंगी [fascinating or inviting] physical gesture or posture, graceful manner or carriage; ~ रक्षक a bodyguard; ~ हीन maimed; limbless; disabled;–फूले न समाना to be in a rapture.

लिखा है यहाँ पर–

nm[1] का अर्थ - noun male

;–[2] भंगिमा/भंगी का अर्थ– चिह्न वाले जगह पर मूल शब्द अंग के बाद भंगिमा/भंगी को पढ़ें अर्थात् अंग भंगिमा का अंग्रेजी में शब्दार्थ physical gesture or posture है।

~[3] रक्षक का अर्थ अंगरक्षक है जिसका अंग्रेजी में अर्थ bodyguard है।

–[4] हीन का अर्थ चिह्न की जगह मूल शब्द अंग के बाद हीन शब्द को जोड़कर इसे अंगहीन अर्थात् maimed; limbless; disabled पढ़े।

–[5] फूले न समाना को – अंग फूले न समाना अर्थात् to be in a rapture पढ़ें।

युग्म अक्षर जैसे क्ष का प्रयोग क व्यंजन वर्ण के साथ किया गया है। पृष्ठ संख्या 68 में देखें। क+ष = क्ष। इसी प्रकार ज्ञ = ज्+ञ पृष्ठ संख्या 100 में देखें।

त्र त्+र का प्रयोग शब्दकोश के पृष्ठ संख्या 116 में त्यौरी शब्द के पश्चात् -

त्रपा [*nf*] shame, an unchaste woman, fame, renown [*adj*] ashamed देखें।

How to Read this Dictionary

Words in this dictionary have been placed in alphabetical order of the Devnagri script of Hindi– first the vowels (from अ to औ) and then the consonants (from क to ह). Within the vowels, the first syllable अ is followed by words beginning with a nasal sound and is symbolized with a dot on the top of letters (अं, अंक, अंकि, अंकी, अंकु, अंकू, अंकृ, अंके, अंकै, अंको, अंकौ) etc. Words beginning with (अ, अक, अका, अकि, अकी, अकु, अकू, अकृ, अके, अकै, अको, अकौ, अक्क, अक्य, अक्ट, अक्त, अक्र, अक्ल, अक्ष) (but without nasal sound) are written in the order of vowels, consonants and composites.

The words have been arranged in this order. Identical method has been used for arranging words of all other vowels, consonants and their component words (अ से लेकर औ तक तथा व्यंजनवर्ण में क से लेकर ह तक) etc.

Order of Vowels (In Hindi अ, आ, इ, ई, उ, ऊ, ऋ, ए, ऐ, ओ तथा औ)

Order of Consonants (In Hindi क, ख, ग, घ, च, छ, ज, झ, ट, ठ, ड, ढ ण, त, थ, द, ध, न, प, फ, ब, भ, म, य, र, ल, व, श, ष, स तथा ह)

The lead words have been marked in a darker shade throughout the dictionary. The lead word mentioned at the top on left and right corner in each page give an idea about the arrangement of the words in order. The lead word on the left top corner of the page indicates the first word in the left column of the page. The lead word on the top right corner of the page indicates the last word on that page.

Each lead word is followed by the part of speech in *italics*. This is followed by the meaning in English. Sub-entries in its continuation are shown with their proper meaning. This facilitates the reader to know the application of words in different forms and uses. For example, in the word दल on 120 page the part of speech [*nm*]. is shown in *italics*. Its English meanings are given; this is followed by sub-entries i.e., दलदल, दलाल, दलित, दलील page 121 etc. with their proper meanings in English.

How the meaning of a word is searched: Suppose the meaning of the word कमनीय is to be seen. In the dictionary please go to the page 58 you will find the word कमनीय with all its parts of speech, meanings etc.

Abbreviations used in the Dictionary

adj.	—	adjective.	*adv.*	—	adverb.
arith.	—	arithmetic.	*conj.*	—	conjunction.
e. g.	—	for example.	*fem.*	—	feminine.
i.e.	—	that is.	*ind.*	—	indeclinable.
interj.	—	interjection.	*mas.*	—	masculine.
math.	—	mathematics.	*n.*	—	noun.
prep.	—	preposition.	*pron.*	—	pronoun.
pl.	—	plural.	*p.p.*	—	past participle.
p.t.	—	past tense.	*sing.*	—	singular.
sup.	—	superlative.	*usu.*	—	usually.
v. aux.	—	verb auxiliary.	*v. i.*	—	verb intransitive.
v. t.	—	verb transitive.	*a.*	—	adjective
पु०	—	पुल्लिग	स्त्री०	—	स्त्रीलिंग
क्रि०	—	क्रिया	वि०	—	विशेषण

भूमिका

हिन्दी शब्द का अर्थ भारत में आर्य, द्रविड़ तथा अनार्य के द्वारा बोली जाने वाली भाषा के लिए होता है। यूँ तो हिन्दी भाषा पूरे भारतवर्ष में बोली जाती है लेकिन उत्तर भारत के मध्य भाग में हिन्दी भाषा प्रमुखता से बोली जाती है। इसके सीमावर्ती क्षेत्रों मैथली, मारवाड़ी, ब्रज, छत्तीसगढ़ी और अवधी भाषा को भी हिन्दी भाषा का ही अंग समझा जाता है। हिन्दी भाषा की उत्पत्ति और उसके अब तक के विकास को मुख्यतः तीन श्रेणियों में बाँटा जा सकता है। (1) आर्य भाषा में प्रचलित शब्द (2) अनार्य भाषा में प्रचलित शब्द (3) विदेशी भाषाओं से आये शब्द।

हिन्दी के शब्दों में सबसे अधिक संख्या वैसे शब्दों की है जो प्राचीन आर्य भाषाओं से लेकर मध्यकाल होते हुए वर्तमान में भी विद्यमान हैं। ऐसे शब्दों को तद्भव कहते हैं। क्योंकि इन शब्दों की मूल उत्पत्ति संस्कृत शब्द से हुई है। कुछ ऐसे भी शब्द मिल सकते हैं जिसकी उत्पत्ति ऐसे शब्दों से हुई हो जिसका व्यवहार प्राचीन आर्य भाषा के ऐसे शब्दों से हुआ हो जो शायद प्राचीन आर्यभाषा के साहित्य (संस्कृत) में नहीं होता था। अतः ऐसे शब्दों का संस्कृत से सम्बन्ध निकल आना आवश्यक नहीं है। हिन्दी बोलचाल में तद्भव शब्द अत्यधिक संख्या में मिलते हैं। सही मायने में ये हिन्दी के मूल शब्द हैं। साहित्यक हिन्दी में संस्कृत के विशुद्ध शब्दों की संख्या सबसे अधिक है। भारत की अन्य भाषाओं बांगला, मराठी, उड़िया, पंजाबी आदि शब्दों का हिन्दी शब्दों पर कम प्रभाव पड़ा है।

हिन्दी के तत्सम या तद्भव शब्दों में अधिकांश शब्द ऐसे हैं जो प्राचीनकाल में अनार्य भाषाओं से मिल गये थे। अब ये शब्द हिन्दी के लिए आर्यभाषा के समान हैं।

आर्य एवं अनार्य भाषाओं के अतिरिक्त भारत में लम्बे समय तक विदेशी शासकों का शासन था। भारत में विदेशियों के शासन को मुख्यतः दो भागों में बाँटा जा सकता है। (1) इस्लामी (2) यूरोपीय।

इस्लामी शासनकाल में वैसे शब्द जिसका प्रयोग उस दौरान की शासन व्यवस्था, कचहरी, फौज, स्कूल तथा विदेशी संस्थाओं में किये जाते थे। दूसरे वे शब्द जो प्रभाव के कारण आयी हुई नवीन वस्तुओं तथा नये ढंग के पहनावे या शौक से सम्बन्धित विदेशी शब्द होते थे। तुर्क, अफगान और मुगलों के शासन के दौरान प्रचलित शब्दों के प्रभाव को समकालीन कवि की कविताओं में साफ देखा जा सकता है। मुगलों के पतन के बाद भारत में यूरोपिओं का आगमन हुआ। अंग्रेजी शासनकाल के दौरान भारत में हिन्दी शब्दों के साथ अंग्रेजी शब्दों का भी चलन आरम्भ हो गया, ऐसे सभी प्रचलित विदेशी शब्दों को हम लोगों ने संक्षिप्त हिन्दी-अंग्रेजी शब्दकोश में उचित स्थान दिया है।

मुसलमानों के शासनकाल में अधिकतर फारसी शब्दों का प्रयोग होता था क्योंकि यहाँ की राजकीय भाषा फारसी थी। जैसे- कैंची, तोप, गलीचा, बीबी आदि। अंग्रेजों के शासनकाल में हिन्दी भाषा में अंग्रेजी शब्दों का व्यापक प्रभाव पड़ा। जैसे- कलक्टर, गजट, अस्पताल, ऑफिस, कॉपी, किताब, जज, जेल आ. दि। इसी प्रकार पूर्तगाली फ्रांसीसी और डच भाषाओं के कुछ शब्द हिन्दी भाषा में ऐसे घुलमिल गये कि वह अब हमें विदेशी प्रतीत नहीं होते हैं। इन शब्दों में अलमारी, कमरा, तौलिया, मेज और सितार आदि प्रमुख है। आज जब हिन्दी को राष्ट्रभाषा का गौरव मिल चुका है ऐसे में हिन्दी के शब्द भण्डारों को अंग्रेजी में बदलने की नितात आवश्यकता है।

परम्परा को देखते हुए किसी भी हिन्दी की अंग्रेजी होनी चाहिए। प्रस्तुत **हिन्दी-अंग्रेजी शब्दकोश** में लेखक ने शब्दकोश लेखन की आधुनिक पद्धति का इस्तेमाल कर हिन्दी शब्दों के साथ उस शब्द की अंग्रेजी में व्याकरण की जानकारी तथा सामानार्थक अर्थ को विस्तारपूर्वक समझाने का प्रयास किया है। शब्दकोश को पाठकों के लिए अत्यधिक उपयोगी बनने हेतु हमने इसमें हिन्दी के सिर्फ आवश्यक शब्दों को ही सम्मिलित करने का निर्णय लिया है। वर्तमान समय में हिन्दी भाषा का स्तर प्रायः गिरता जा रहा है। थोड़ी समस्या हिन्दी की देवनागरी लिपि की शुद्ध वर्तनी को लिखने को लेकर भी है। देवनागरी लिपि में कवर्ग, चवर्ग, टवर्ग, तवर्ग के पंचम वर्ण की मात्राओं का उपयोग नहीं के बराबर हो रहा है। अनुनासिक (ँ) को तिलांजलि देकर उसकी जगह अनुस्वर (ं) की मात्रा का बहुत से लेखक, विद्वान और प्रकाशक धड़ल्ले से उपयोग कर रहे हैं। यथा चाँदी की जगह पर चांदी, तथा खाँसी की जगह खांसी का प्रयोग जगह-जगह देखने को मिलता है। लेकिन हमने प्रस्तुत शब्दकोश में अनुनासिक

चिह्न का विधिवत इस्तेमाल कर हिन्दी की गरिमा बनाये रखने की भरसक कोशिश की है। शब्दकोश में तत्सम तथा तद्‌भव विदेशी भाषाओं के साथ परिशिष्ट में खासतौर पर अर्थशास्त्र, विज्ञान, गणित, प्रशासनिक शब्द, प्रचलित मुहावरे और लोकोक्तियों को यथोचित स्थान देकर इसे पाठकों के लिए अत्यन्त उपयोगी बनाने की कोशिश की गयी है।

प्रस्तुत शब्दकोश का संकलन विशेषतौर पर उन पाठकों को ध्यान में रखकर किया है जिनकी अंग्रेजी भाषा पर अच्छी पकड़ है, और वह हिन्दी भाषा का अंग्रेजी में अर्थ जानना चाहते हैं। दूसरे पाठक उस वर्ग से हैं जो हिन्दी और अंग्रेजी भाषाओं को सामान्यतौर पर जानते हैं लेकिन दोनों में से किसी एक भाषा में प्रवीण नहीं है। ऐसे लोगों के बीच आजकल हिंग्लिश भाषा का प्रयोग धड़ल्ले से हो रहा है। आमतौर पर ऐसे लोगों के बीच बातचीत के दौरान ऐसी स्थिति आ जाती है। जब वे हिन्दी और अंग्रेजी दोनों भाषाओं की मिली-जुली भाषा का प्रयोग करने लगते हैं ऐसे शब्दों को आजकल हिंग्लिश कहा जाता है। जैसे कुंजीपटल को हिन्दी भाषा में कीबोर्ड के रूप में प्रयोग करना। दोनों तरह के पाठक और छात्र प्रस्तुत संक्षिप्त हिन्दी अंग्रेजी शब्दकोश पढ़कर अपने मनोवांछित शब्द को आसानी से तलाश कर सकते हैं।

अ

अ the first letter and the first vowel of the Devanagri: alphabet; a prefix signifying negation.

अ – देवनागरी और संस्कृत कुटुंब की अन्य वर्णमालाओं का पहला अक्षर और स्वर वर्ण है। इसका उच्चारण स्थान कंठ है। व्यंजन वर्णों का उच्चारण 'अ' वर्ण की सहायता के बिना नहीं हो सकता। यथा क+अ = क, ख+अ = ख आदि वर्ण अकार के साथ बोले और लिखे जाते हैं। उपसर्ग के तौर पर 'अ' का प्रयोग करने से यह रहित, हीन या उलटा के अर्थों में प्रयुक्त होते हैं। उदाहरण : स्वस्थ-अस्वस्थ। स्वस्थ के पूर्व 'अ' वर्ण का प्रयोग करने से इसका अर्थ उलटा हो जाता है।

अंक [*nm*] a number, numeral, figure, digit; marks; a mark; an act [of a drama or play]; lap, embrace; ~ गणित [the science of] Arithmetic.

अंकन [*nm*] stamping; plotting; marking.

अंकित [*adj.*] marked; inscribed, written; endorsed.

अंकुर [*nm*] a sprout; an off-shoot; a seed-bud.

अंकुरित [*adj.*] sprouted, germinated.

अंकुश [*nm*] a hook, elephant-driver's iron hook; hamulus; control.

अँकोड़ा [*m.*] a large hook.

अंग [*nm*] a limb; member; body; part; component; organ;–भंगिमा/भंगी [fascinating or inviting] physical gesture or posture, graceful manner or carriage; ~ रक्षक a bodyguard; ~ हीन maimed; limbless; disabled;–फूले न समाना to be in a rapture.

अंगड़-खंगड़ [also अंगड़-भंगड़] [*nm*] disorderly stuff; scraps; junk.

अँगड़ाई [*nf*] twisting or stretching of the body for relaxation.

अंगार, अंगारा [*nm*] an ember, live coal, burning charcoal; –उगलना to be fierce and fiery in speech; –बरसना to be excessively hot [said of the weather] to rain hot coals.

अँगिया [*nf*] a pair of bodice.

अंगीकार [*nm*] adoption; acceptance; undertaking.

अँगीठा [*nm.*] fire stand.

अँगीठी [*nf*] a grate, portable oven, fire pot.

अंगुल [*nm*] [measurement equal to] a finger's breadth, thumb, big toe.

अँगूठा [*nm*] the thumb; –दिखाना to defy and deride; to evade in defiance.

अँगूठी [*nf*] a finger-ring.

अंगूर [*nm*] a grape; अंगूरी vinous; –खट्टे होना to decry something that has proved inaccessible.

अँगौ (गो) छा [*nm*] a towel, any piece of cloth for wiping [the body] dry.

अँग्रेज [*n*] an Englishman; ~ जियत Englishion, Anglican, अँग्रेजी [*n*] the English language; [*adj.*] English; Anglican.

अंचल [*nm*] the outward fringe or portion of a etc.; a region, border region, tract, zone

अंजन [*nm*] collyrium, an eyesalve; ~ हारी a sty.

अंजर-पंजर [*nm*] the physical frame, skeleton; the joints of the body;–ढीले होना slackening of the body [on account of excessive physical strain or sudden heavy jerk or impact].

अंजरा [*nm.*] a nettle.

अंजलि [*nf*] cup-shaped hollow formed by the joining of the two palms together.

अंजाम [*nm*] the conclusion, end; result; completion.

अंजीर [*nm*] a fig-tree; its fruit.

अंट-शंट [*adj.*] absurd; incoherent, irrelevant, inconsistent; meaningless.

अंटी [*nf*] fold of the loin cloth on the waist; space between any two fingers of a hand; a spool; a knot.

अंड [*nm*] an egg; ~ कोश testicles.

अंत:करण [*nm*] the conscience, inner self.

अंतर [*nm.*] interior, middle, midst.

अंत:कालीन [*adj.*] provisional.

अंत:पुर [*nm*] the women's apartment in a royal household, harem; a thalamus.

अंत:प्रज्ञा [*nf*] intuition.

अंत:प्रेरणा [*nf*] intuition; inspiration, inner urge.

अंत:स्थ [*adj.*] intermediate, situated in between; [*nm*] the traditional semi-vowels य, र ल and व.

अंत [*nm*] the end, termination; conclusion; ~ हीन unending, endless;–भला सो भला all is well that ends well.

अंततः [*adv.*] lastly, finally, at last; eventually.

अंतरंग [*adj.*] internal, interior; intimate; private.

अंतर [*nm*] difference; distance; interval; spacing; margin interior; the heart.

अंतरा [*nm*] any verse of a song, etc. excepting the first. (अँतरा)–next but one.

अंतरात्मा [*nf*] the soul, inner self, spirit.

अंतराल [*nm*] an interval, intervening time or space, gap; inner space.

अंतरिक्ष [*nm*] space, sky.

अंतरिम [*adj.*] interim.

अंतर्गत [*adj.*] included, hidden, conceived.

अंतर्जातीय [*adj.*] inter-caste.

अंतर्ज्ञान [*nm*] intuition.

अंतर्दृष्टि [*nf*] insight.

अंतर्देशीय [*adj.*] inter-state; inland.

अंतर्द्वंद्व [*nm*] inner conflict.

अंतर्धान [*nm*] disappearance; reduction to invisibility.

अंतर्निहित [*adj.*] implied; understood; included.

अंतर्प्रांतीय [*adj.*] inter-provincial [correct form **अंतःप्रांतीय**]-

अंतर्प्रादेशिक [*adj.*] inter-regional, inter-state.

अंतर्भाव [*nm*] inclusion.

अंतर्मुख [*adj.*] introvertive.

अंतर्मुखी [*adj.*] introversive, introvertive.

अंतर्यामी [*adj.*] pervading the interior or inner self; [*nm*] the Supreme Spirit.

अंतर्राष्ट्रीय [*adj.*] international.

अंतर्राष्ट्रीयता [*nf*] internationalism.

अंतर्वस्तु [*nm*] the content.

अंतर्वासी [*adj.*] instaying; indoor; –रोगी indoor patient.

अंतर्विरोध [*nm*] self-contradiction, inner contradiction.

अंतर्विवेक [*nm*] the conscience.

अंतर्हित [*adj.*] latent, concealed; rendered invisible.

अंतस्थल [*nm*] the heart of hearts; mind.

अंतिम [*adj.*] last, final, ultimate, concluding/ conclusive.

अंत्य [*adj.*] the last; the lower-most; ~ ज belonging to the lowest class/caste.

अंताक्षरी [*nf*] a verse-reciting competition in which the following participant recites a couplet beginning with the last letter of the couplet recited by the foregoing participant.

अंत्येष्टि [*nf*] last/funeral rites.

अंदर [*adj.*] in, inside, within.

अंदरूनी [*adj.*] internal, internecine; inward.

अंदाज़ [*nm*] an estimate, a guess; mode, style; gesture; characteristic manner; ~ न roughly, approximately.

अंदाजा [*nm*] an estimate, a guess.

अंदेशा [*nm]* misgiving, misapprehension; suspicion.

अंध [*adj.*] blind; unthinking.

अंधकार [*nm*] darkness; gloom.

अंधड़ [*nm*] a violent dust-storm.

अंधविश्वास [*nm*] superstition, blind trust.

अंधा [*adj.* and *nm*] blind; unenlightened;–कुआँ a blind well; ~ कुप्प pitch dark; black out; अंधे की लकड़ी/लाठी a helpless man's only support; अंधे के आगे रोये अपने दीदा खोये throwing pearls before the swine; अंधों में काना राजा a figure among ciphers.

अंधाधुंध [*adv.* and *adj.*] indiscreetly; indiscriminately, recklessly, at random; wild, reckless, rash.

अंधानुकरण [*nm*] blind/mechanical imitation or emulation.

अंधापन [*nm*] blindness; recklessness; folly.

अँधियारी [*adj.*] see अंधकार [*nf*] blinkers.

अंधेर [*nm*] outrage; wrong; anarchy, complete lawlessness or mismanagement; ~ खाता/गर्दी anarchical state of affairs, complete lawlessness or mismanagement;–नगरी a maladministered and lawless state or town, etc.; चौपट राजा a confused ruler, a chaotic state.

अँधेरा [*nm* and *adj*] darkness; dark;–गुप्प/घुप्प pitch dark; black out.

अँधेरी [*nf*] darkness.

अंबर [*nm*] the sky; cloth/clothes, garment.

अंबार [*nm*] heap, pile, bulk; ~ खाना a junk-house, godown.

अंश [*nm*] a part; share; division; fragment; ingredient; contribution; numerator [of a fraction]; degree.

अंशत: [*adv*] partly; partially.

अकड़ [*nf*] stiffness, rigidity; intractability; airs, affectation, show; strut, haughtiness, conceit; ~ फूं airs, arrogance, arrogant behaviour; ~ बाज haughty, arrogant.

अकड़ना [*v*] to be stiff, rigid or intractable; to assume airs, to be affected; to be haughty or conceited.

अकथ, अकथनीय [*adj.*] ineffable, indescribable.

अकबक [*nf*] wish-wash; disconnected utterances, nonsense; – मारी जाना to be nonplussed, to be flabbergasted, to be at one's wit's end.

अकर्मक [*adj.*] intransitive [*verb*].

अकर्मण्य [*adj.*] idle, indolent; inert.

अकल्पनीय [*adj.*] unimaginable; unthinkable, inconceivable.

अकस्मात् [*adv.*] unexpectedly, accidentally, all of a sudden.

अकाट्य [*adj.*] irrefutable, incontrovertible, indisputable.

अकार [*nm*] the letter a *(v)* and its sound; ~ रांत [a word] ending in a (अ).

अकारण [*adv.* and *adj.*] without any reason or cause, without any pretext, needlessly, causelessly; wanton, causeless, groundless; unprovoked.

अकारथ [*adj.* and *adv.*] futile, useless, ineffectual; in vain.

अकारादि क्रम [*nm*] alphabetical order.

अकाल [*nm*] famine; scarcity; [*a*] premature; untimely; –मृत्यु untimely demise; –वृष्टि untimely rains.

अकिंचन [*adj.*] poor, pauper; destitute; ~ ता poverty, pauperism; destitution.

अकुलाना [*v*] to feel uneasy/restless, to be fidgety.

अकूत [*adj.*] immeasurable, unfathomable.

अकृतज्ञ [*adj.*] ungrateful, thankless.

अकेला [*adj.*] single; lonely, lonesome; solitary; [*adv*] by oneself, singly, alone; अकेले-अकेले all alone, without a companion; ~ पन a feeling of loneliness, lonesomeness; solitude, solitariness.

अक्खड़ [*adj.*] headstrong; stiff-necked, rude and rough, haughty; ~ पन headstrongness, haughtiness.

अक्तूबर [*nm*] [the month of] October.

अक़्ल [*nf*] common sense; intellect; wisdom; – काम न करना,–मारी जाना to be in a fix or dilemma; – के घोड़े दौड़ाना to indulge in mental gymnasium; –के पीछे लाठी लिए फिरना to indulge in stupidity all the time; to demand a tribute to the dead; –चकराना,–चक्कर में आना to be nonplussed; –चरने जाना,–का चिराग गुल होना to lose the faculty of reasoning, to lose power of discrimination; – पर पत्थर/परदा पड़ना, –गुम होना to be bereft of senses or intellect, to lose one's wits; –बड़ी (या) कि भैंस knowledge predominates over mere strength; –सठियाना to suffer senile decay, to suffer from mental paralysis.

अक़्ल/मंद [*adj.*] prudent, sagacious; intelligent; wise; sensible; ~ मंदी prudence, sagacity; intelligence; wisdom; sensibility.

अक्ष [*nm*] an axis.

अक्षम्य [*adj.*] unpardonable, inexcusable.

अक्षय [*adj.*] imperishable, undecaying; perennial.

अक्षर [*nm*] any letter of the alphabet; syllable; [*adj*] imperishable, undecaying; intact; ~ गणित Algebra; ~ माला the alphabet.

अक्षरश: [*adv.*] literally; in toto; verbatim.

अक्षांश [*nm*] latitude.

अक्षुण्ण [*adj.*] unimpaired, unbroken, intact; entire, complete.

अक्स [*nm*] a shadow, reflected image, reflection.

अक्सर [*adv*] often; generally, usually.

अक्सीर [*adj.*] unfailing, sure; –दवा a sure/sovereign remedy.

अखंड [*adj.*] the whole, complete; undivided; ~ **नीय** indivisible; –पाठ non-stop recitation.

अखंडता [*nf*] indivisibility; integrity; completeness.

अखंडित [*adj.*] unbroken, undivided; unimpaired; irrepudiated.

अख़बार [*nm*] a newspaper; ~ री pertaining to news or newspaper [*s*].

अखरना [*v*] to make one feel sore; to be disagreeable or unpleasant.

अखाड़ा [*nm*] an arena, wrestling arena; place for exercise; a congregation of sadhus or their abode.

अखाड़िया [*nm* and *adj.*] a master fighter; skilled mano-euvrer; strategist.

अखिल [*adj.*] whole, all, entire, pan–.

अख़्ख़ा [*int*] oh! [an exclamation of surprise or wonder in case of an unexpected appearance or meeting, etc.]

अख़्तियार [*nm*] power; right; authority.

अगड़म-बगड़म [*nm]* junk, a disorderly heap of scraps.

अगम [*adj.*] inaccessible, unattainable; incomp-rehensible.

अगम्य [*adj.*] see अगम in-cohabitable.

अगर [*conj.*] if, in case; ~ बत्ती an incense stick.

अगर-मगर [*nf*] if and but; wavering, hitch; dilly-dallying.

अगल-बगल [*adv.*] on both sides; side by side; nearby.

अगला [*adj.*] next, following; coming, approaching; the other [person].

अगस्त agast [*nm*] (the month of) August.

अगहन [*nm*] the ninth month of the Hindu calendar.

अगाड़ी [*nf*] the front part; facing; the rope used for tying a horse's neck; [*adv.*] in front of; in future.

अगाध [*adj.*] unfathomable; profound, deep.

अगुआ [*nm*] a leader; pioneer, forerunner; guide; ~ ई leadership; guidance.

अग्नि [*nf*] fire; the god of fire; appetite; digestive faculty.

अग्र [*adj.*] first; foremost; chief; [nm] the fore-part of anything; the head; ~ गण्य leading, prominent; ~ ज an elder brother; ~ दूत herald, forerunner; ~ लेख an editorial, a leading article.

अग्रणी [*adj.*] leading, pre-eminent, outstanding.

अग्रसर [*adj.*]–करना to forward, to move ahead; –होना to proceed, to go ahead.

अग्रिम [*adj.*] first; foremost; chief; [*adv.*] in advance; [*nm*] an advance.

अघाना [*v*] to be satiated, surfeited or satisfied (with), to have abundance (of something).

अघोरी [*adj.* and *nm*] filthy, uncouth and unclean (man), one who indulges in indiscriminate eating; a member of the order of mendicants called 'aghor panth'.

अचंभा [*nm*] wonder, surprise, astonishment.

अचकचाना [*v*] to be taken aback or astonished, to be confounded/dumbfounded.

अचकन [*nf*] a kind of tight fitting long coat.

अचर [*adj.*] immovable; constant; invariable; [nm] an invariant.

अचरज [*nm*] surprise, astonishment, wonder.

अचल [*adj.*] immovable/immobile; stationary, motionless, still; firm, sessile.

अचानक [*adv.*] all of a sudden, suddenly, unexpectedly.

अचार [*nm*] pickles.

अचूक [*adj.*] infallible; unfailing, unerring; sure.

अचेत [*adj.*] devoid of consciousness, unconscious, senseless.

अचेतन [*adj.*] unconscious; inanimate.

अच्छा [*adj.*] good; excellent; genuine; fine; pleasant; righteous; sound; [*adv.*] well; correctly; granted; [int] all right, well done! so long! –खासा fairly good; adequate; अच्छे-अच्छे big guns, those who matter, significant people.

अच्छाई [*nf*] goodness; virtue; merit.

अच्छापन [*nm*] goodness.

अछूत [*adj.*] untouchable; [*nm*] an untouchable; ~ तोद्धार uplift of the untouchables.

अछूता [*adj.*] fresh; untouched; unpolluted.

अजगर [*nm*] a python, a huge snake.

अजनबी [*adj.*] unknown, unfamiliar; alien; [*nm*] a stranger.

अजब [*adj.*] strange; peculiar.

अजान [*adj.*] ignorant, innocent; – में unknowingly, unwittingly.

अजायब/घर, ~ खाना [*nm*] a museum, a curio-collection centre.

अज़ीज़ [*adj.*] dear; [*nm*] a near relative, kith and kin.

अजीब [*adj.*] strange, peculiar, arousing a sense of wonder; अजीबोगरीब unique, peculiar.

अजीर्ण [*nm*] indigestion [caused by overeating].

अजूबा [*nm*] a curio, wonder.

अजेय [*adj.*] invincible, uncon-querable.

अज्ञात [*adj.*] unknown.

अज्ञान [*nm*] ignorance, paucity of knowledge.

अटकना [*v*] to get stuck up; held up.

अटकल [*nm*] a conjecture, guess; ~ बाज one who is given to making conjectures or guesses.

अटकलपच्चू [*adj.*] random; fanciful, imaginary, uncertain; [*nm*] a random guess, mere conjecture.

अटपटा [*adj.*] odd; absurd, incongruous.

अटल [*adj.*] firm; irrevocable; resolute, unwavering, steadfast.

अटाटूट [*adj.*] immense, immeasurable; crammed full.

अटारी [*nf*] a small garret, an attic.

अटूट [*adj.*] unbreakable; firm; incessant; immense.

अट्टहास [*nm*] a horse-laugh, peal of loud laughter.

अट्ठाईस [*adj.*] twenty eight.

अट्ठानवे [*adj.*] ninety eight.

अट्ठावन [*adj.*] fifty eight.

अट्ठासी [*adj.*] eighty eight.

अठन्नी [*nf*] an eight-anna coin.

अठहत्तर [*adj.* and *nm*] seventy eight.

अठारह [*adj.*] eighteen.

अड़ंगा [*nm*] an obstacle, obstruction, impediment;

अड़ंगेबाज an obstructionist;

अड़ंगेबाजी obstructing tactics, obstructionism.

अड़चन [*nf*] hindrance; hitch; difficulty.

अड़तालीस [*adj.* and *nm*] forty eight.

अड़तीस [*adj.* and *nm*] thirty eight.

अड़ना [*v*] to stick [to a position] ; to insist; to halt; to be restive [as a horse].

अड़सठ [*adj.* and *nm*] sixty eight.

अडिग [*adj.*] unflinching; firm, steady.

अड़ियल [*adj.*] inflexible; stubborn, mulish.

अड़ोस-पड़ोस [*nm*] neighbourhood, vicinity; अड़ोसी-पड़ोसी neighbours.

अड्डा [*nm*] a stand; base; meeting place, resort, perch; chopping block.

अणु [*nm*] a molecule, an atom, minute particle; [a] molecular; atomic; ~ वीक्षण यंत्र a microscope.

अतः [*adv.*] hence, therefore, thus, on this accounts.

अतएव [*adv.*] hence, so, therefore.

अतरसों [*adv.*] the day prior to the day-before-yesterday or next to day-after-tomorrow.

अतल [*a*] bottomless, fathomless; also ~ स्पर्शी. very deep.

अति ati a prefix expressive of extremity, beyond, over, surpassing, extra, intense, excessive, etc; [nf] excess.

अति/क्रम, ~ क्रमण [*nm*] infringement; contravention, violation.

अति/चार [*nm*] transgression, trespass; profanation, outrage; violation.

अतिथि [*nm*] a guest; –सत्कार/सेवा hospitality.

अति/प्राकृत, ~ प्राकृतिक [*adj.*] supernatural.

अति/मानव [*nm*] a superman; ~ मानवीय superhuman.

अतिरंजना [*nf*] exaggeration; overstatement.

अतिरिक्त [*adj.*] additional; extra; spare; auxiliary; besides; except.

अतिरेक [*nm*] plenty, abundance; surplus; excess; redundancy.

अति/वाद [*nm*] extremism; excess; ostentation; exaggeration boastfulness; ~ वादी an extremist; extremistic; boastful; ostentatious.

अतिवृष्टि [*nf*] excessive rains, unusually heavy downpour.

अतिव्याप्ति [*nf*] over-extension (of a rule, etc.); over-permeation.

अतिशय [*adj.* and *adv.*] exceeding/exceedingly, excessive/excessively.

अतिशयोक्ति [*nf*] exaggeration [a figure of speech].

अतिसार [*nm*] dysentery.

अतीत [*adj.* and *nm*] [the] past; [*adv.*] beyond.

अतुल [*adj.*] unparalleled, unequalled; immense.

अतृप्त [*adj.*] unsatisfied, unfulfilled; frustrated.

अत्तार [*nm*] a perfumer; druggist, pharmaceutical chemist.

अत्यंत [*adv.* and *adj.*] very much, much; excessively, exceedingly; extremely.

अत्याचार [*nm*] atrocity, tyranny; excess; outrage.

अत्याचारी [*adj.*] atrocious, tyrannous; excessive; outrageous; [*nm*] a tyrant, despot.

अथ [*nm*] the beginning, commencement; an auspicious and inceptive particle, now, then;– से इति तक from beginning to end.

अथक [*adj.*] untiring; unceasing.

अथवा [*conj.*] or; that is.

अथाह [*adj.*] unfathomable, bottomless; very deep.

अदद [*nf*] a piece; number; a figure.

अदना [*adj.*] insignificant; low, inferior; trifling.

अदब [*nm*] respect; respect-fulness; politeness.

अदम्य [*adj.*] irrepressible; irresistible.

अदरक [*nf*] ginger.

अदला-बदली [*nf*] ex-change; interchange; mutual transfer.

अदा [*nf*] coquetry blandish- ment; graceful manner or carriage, mien; performance.

अदायगी [*nf*] payment; fulfilment.

अदालत [*nf*] a court of law; अदालती judicial; litigious; ~ बाजी litigation; litigiousness.

अदावत [*nf*] animosity; enmity; estrangement; hostility; hence अदावती [*adj.*] inimical, unfriendly.

अदृश्य [*adj.*] invisible, imperceptible; not worth seeing.

अदृष्ट [*nm*] fate, fortune; [*adj.*] unforeseen.

अद्भुत [*adj.*] marvellous; fantastic; singular; supernatural.

अद्यतन [*adj.*] up-to-date; modern.

अद्वितीय [*adj.*] sui generis; unique, unparalleled.

अध:पतन [*nm*] downfall, fall; degradation, degeneration.

अधकचरा [*adj.*] immature; incomplete; half-baked; unassimilated.

अधम [*adj.*] mean, base, vile.

अधमरा [*adj.*] half-dead, near-dead.

अधमुआ [*adj.*] half-dead, near-dead.

अधर [*nm*] the underlip; a lip; mid-air, empty space, space between earth and sky; –में झूलना/लटकना to hang in mid-air, to be without a prop.

अध/र्म [*nm*] vice; wrong; sin, sinful act; unrighteousness, immorality; ~ र्मी sinful; vicious; an evildoer, a sinner.

अधार्मिक [*adj.*] irreligious; unrighteous, profane.

अधिक [*adj.*] more; much; many; plenty; surplus; abundant; ~ तम maximum; ~ तर most; mostly; ~ ता excess, abundance.

अधिकरण [*nm*] the locative [case]; an organ, agency; instrumental organisation [as न्यायाधिकरण].

अधिकांश [*adj.*] more than half; most; [nm] a major portion; ~ त:, ~ में mostly; generally.

अधिकाधिक [*adj.*] more and more; progressively increasing; utmost.

अधिकार [*nm*] right; authority; command; possession; occupation; entitlement;–क्षेत्र jurisdiction; – पत्र a letter of authority; charter. अधिकार क्षेत्र : area of authority or competence, jurisdiction.

अधिकारी [*nm*] an officer; authority; a title-holder; an owner; [*adj.*] vested with or possessing authority; autho-ritative; occupying, in occupation.

अधिकृत [*adj.*] occupied [as –क्षेत्र]; authorised, vested with authority [as–प्रतिनिधि] authorised representative.

अधिनायक [*nm*] a dictator; supreme leader; –तंत्र dictatorship; ~ त्व dictatorship.

अधिपति [*nm*] a ruler, king, master; chief.

अधिमान्य [*adj.*] preferable; preferential.

अधिमास [*nm*] a leap month.

अधिवेशन [*nm*] a session; meeting.

अधीक्षक [*nm*] a superintendent.

अधीन [*adj.*] dependent; subordinate, subject to the authority of; under, ~ ता subordination; subjection; dependence, subjugation.

अधीर [*adj.*] restive, fidgety; impatient; petulant; nervous; ~ ता impatience, petulance; nervousness.

अधुना [*adv.*] now, at present; ~ तन modern, up-to-date.

अधूरा [*adj.*] incomplete, unfinished.

अधेड़ [*adj.*] middle-aged, verging on old age.

अधेड़पना [*nm.*] middle age.

अधोगति [*nf*] fall, downfall; degradation.

अधो [*pref.*] downward, below.

अध्यक्ष [*nm*] president; chairman; head; speaker; ~ ता chairmanship; headship; speaker-ship.

अध्ययन [nm] study; कक्ष study room.

अध्यवसा/य [*nm*] enterprise, diligence; volition; ~यी enterprising, diligent, industrious.

अध्यात्म [*nm*] spiritual contemplation; ~ वाद spiritualism; –विद्या/शास्त्र metaphysics.

अध्यादेश [*nm*] an ordinance.

अध्या/पक [*nm*] a teacher, master; an educator; ~पन teaching; instruction.

अध्याय [*nm*] a chapter.

अध्येता [*nm*] a student; scholar.

अनंत [*adj.*] endless, unending; eternal; infinite; [*nf*] infinity.

अनंतर [*adv.*] after, afterwards; in the wake of.

अन a Hindi prefix used to denote a negative sense, as ~ मेल, ~ होनी

अनख [*nm*] 1 anger; displeasure. 2 envy. 3 malice.

अनखना [*v*] to be angry or displeased with anyone.

अनगढ़ [*adj.*] crude, un-wrought; unpolished; natural.

अनगिनत [*adj.*] innumerable, numberless, countless.

अनजान [*adj.*] unknown, un-acquainted; ignorant.

अनदेखा [*adj.*] unseen, un-foreseen.

अनधिकार [*adj.*] unauthorised; [*nm*] want of right; –चेष्टा unauthorised attempt.

अनन्नास [*nm*] pineapple tree or its fruit.

अनन्य [*adj.*] identical; unique; close, intimate [as मित्र]; completely loyal; ~ता identity, sameness; uniqueness; exclusiveness; –भाव sole loyalty/devotion; ~सामान्य unique, typical.

अनपचा [*adj.*] undigested.

अनपढ़ [*adj.*] illiterate, unlettered.

अनबन [*nf*] discord, estrangement, rift.

अनभिज्ञ [*adj.*] ignorant; unaware; unapprised; ~ता ignorance; unawareness.

अनमना [*adj.*] indisposed; out of sorts, in low spirits; absent-minded.

अनमिल [*adj.*] discordant; irrelevant.

अनमेल [*adj.*] inharmonious, discordant; dissimilar, heterogeneous; unmixed.

अनमोल [*adj.*] invaluable, precious, priceless.

अनर्गल [*adj.*] unrestrained, unbarred; absurd; ~ता absurdity.

अनर्थ [*nm*] calamity; absurdity; grievous wrong; contrary meaning; ~कर/कारी calamitous, devastating.

अनल [*nm*] fire.

अनवरत [*adj.*] continuous, incessant, unremitting.

अनविच्छिन्न [*adj.*] unbroken, continuous.

अनशन [nm] fast; starvation.

अनश्वर [*adj.*] immortal, immutable, imperishable.

अनसुना [*adj.*] unheard [of]; –करना, सुना-अनसुना करना to ignore [deliberately], not to pay any attention [to].

अनहोनी [*nf*] the improbable, the impossible; [*adj.*] unusual; improbable.

अनागत [*adj.*] the future, not come, not attained; unknown.

अना/चार [*adj.*] misconduct, lasciviousness, licentiousness; immorality; malpractice; wrong doing.

अनाज [*adj.*] grain corn.

अनाड़ी [*adj.*] inexperienced, unskilful; [*nm*] a novice, tyro, bumpkin, an ignoramus.

अनाथ [*nm*] an orphan; [*adj.*] orphan, without any protector; helpless.

अनाथालय, अनाथाश्रम [*nm*] an orphanage.

अनादर [*nm*] insult; disrespect, disregard.

अनादि [*adj.*] having no beginning, ever-existent, eternal.

अनाप-शनाप [*adj.* and *nm*] slipslop, nonsense, absurd [talk], prattle, babble.

अनामिका [*nf*] the ring finger.

अनायास [*adv.*] without effort, with ease; suddenly; spontaneously.

अनार [*nm*] a pomegranate; ~ दाना dried seeds of pomegranate.

अनार्य [*nm* and *adj.*] a non- Aryan; [*adj.*] not noble, not respectable; inferior.

अनावरण [*nm*] exposure.

अनावर्ती [*adj.*] non-recurring [as expenditure]; a periodic [as a circuit].

अनावश्यक [*adj.*] unnecessary; unimportant.

अनावृत्त [*adj.*] open, uncovered.

अनिंद्य [*adj.*] irreproachable, flawless.

अनिच्छा [*nf*] reluctance, unwillingness.

अनित्य [*adj.*] transient, transitory; variable; fleeting.

अनिमिष, अनिमेष [*adj.*] unwinking, without a wink.

अनियंत्रित [*adj.*] uncontrolled, unrestrained, unrestricted; arbitrary.

अनियत [*adj.*] indefinite, occasional; unallotted; erratic; casual; ~कालिक aperiodic; casual.

अनियमित [*adj.*] irregular; disorderly.

अनिर्वचनीय [*adj.*] indescribable; ineffable.

अनिवार्य [*adj.*] inevitable; unavoidable; essential, compulsory; irresistible, obligatory; mandatory.

अनिश्चय [*nm*] indecision, uncertainty.

अनिश्चित [*adj.*] uncertain undecided, indefinite, vague; unsettled; ~ता indefiniteness; uncertainty; vagueness.

अनिष्ट [*nm*] harm, calamity; ~कर/~कारी [*adj.*] evil, harmful, calamitous; ominous.

अनीति [*nf*] impropriety, ine-quity; high-handedness.

अनु a prefix meaning after, afterwards, like, along with, repeatedly, towards, etc. [as **अनुयायी**, अनुकरण].

अनुकंपा [*nf*] kindness, compassion.

अनु/करण [*nm*] imitation; emulation; ~ करणीय exemplary; imitable, worth emulating or imitating.

अनुकूल [*adj.*] favourable; agreeable; well-disposed; conformable; ~तम optimum; ~न conditioning; adaptation.

अनुक्रम [*nm*] sequence, succession.

अनुक्रमणिका [*nf*] a list of contents, an index.

अनु/गत [*adj.*] obedient, prone to obey or follow; [*nm*] a follower.

अनु/गमन [*nm*] following; self-immolation by a widow.

अनुगृहीत [*adj.*] obliged, grateful.

अनुग्रह [*nm*] obligation, favour, kindness.

अनु/चर [*nm*] an attendant; a hanger-on; follower.

अनुचित [*adj.*] improper, unbecoming, unseemly; wrong.

अनु/ज [*nm*] a younger brother.

अनुज्ञा [*nf*] permission.

अनुताप [*nm*] remorse; repentance.

अनुदान [*nm*] a grant.

अनुदार [*adj.*] not liberal, conservative; parochial; parsimonious, stingy.

अनुदेश [*nm*] instruction; ~क instructor.

अनु/नय [*nm*] persuasion, propitiation, mollification.

अनु/नाद [*nm*] resonance, echo.

अनुनासिक [*adj.*] nasal; [*nm*] a nasal sound.

अनुप/म [*adj.*] matchless, unparalleled; ~मेय unparalleled; matchless.

अनुपयुक्त [*adj.*] inexpedient; unfit, unsuitable.

अनुपयो/गी [*adj.*] useless, unavailing; ~योगिता uselessness, the state of being of no utility.

अनुपस्थित [*adj.*] absent.

अनुपस्थिति [*nf*] absence.

अनु/पात [nm] proportion; ~पाती proportional.

अनुपान [*nm*] a vehicle, anything taken with a medicine after it..

अनुपूरक [*adj.*] supplementary.

अनुपूर्ति [*nf*] supplementation; compensation; subsidy.

अनुपूर्वी [*adj.*] successive; consecutive.

अनुप्राणित [*adj.*] imbued, inspired, informed.

अनुप्रास [*nm*] alliteration; rhyme.

अनुबंध [*nm*] contract; addendum; appendage; stipulation; suffix.

अनुभव [*nm*] experience; ~वाद empiricism.

अनुभवी [*adj.*] experienced, veteran, seasoned.

अनु/भाव [*nm*] ensuant response, suggestion [by look or gesture].

अनुभूत [*adj.*] tried; experienced.

अनुभूति [*nf*] emotional experience, realisation; sensibility.

अनु/मति [*nf*] assent, approval, leave.

अनुमान [*nm*] guess; estimate, surmise; supposition; inference; ~तः approximately, about.

अनुमो/दन [*nm*] approval, approbation; ~दित approved, approbated.

अनुयायी [*nm*] a follower, an adherent.

अनु/रक्त [*adj.*] attached, in love [with], fond; ~रक्ति attachment, dotage, fondness.

अनुरा/ग [*nm*] love, affection, attachment, fondness; ~गी affectionate, loving, fond.

अनुरूप [*adj.*] like; fit; conformable, beseeming; according to; analogous.

अनु/रोध [*nm*] request; entreaty.

अनु/वाद [*nm*] translation; repetition; ~ वादक a translator.

अनु/शासन [*nm*] discipline; ~ शासक a disciplinarian.

अनुशासित [*adj.*] disciplined.

अनुशीलन [*nm*] constant study or practice; investigation.

अनु/श्रुत [*adj.*] traditional; ~ श्रुति tradition.

अनुष्ठान [*nm*] ritual, ceremony; religious performance; undertaking; exercise; solemnisation.

अनुसं/धान [*nm*] research; investigation; ~ धाता a researcher.

अनुसरण [*nm*] [the act or process of] following pursuance.

अनुसार [*adj.&prep.*] according to, in conformity with.

अनुस्यूत [*adj.*] intertwined, interwoven.

अनुस्वार [*nm*] lit. after-sound–the nasal sound [in some of the Indian scripts] which is marked by a dot above the line and always follows the preceding vowel.

अनूठा [*adj.*] unique; unparalleled, unprecedented.

अनूदित [*adj.*] translated.

अनूद्य [*adj.*] translatable; worthy of translation.

अनूप [*adj.*] unequalled, unparalleled, singular, unique.

अनेक [*adj.*] many, numerous; several; ~ता/त्व diversity; ~मुखी emerging into different directions, versatile [as प्रतिभा].

अनैतिक [*adj.*] immoral; depraved; ~ता immorality; depravity.

अनोखा [*adj.*] peculiar, queer; novel; ~ पन peculiarity, novelty.

अनौचित्य [*nm*] impropriety; indecency.

अनौपचारिक [*adj.*] informal; unofficial; unceremonious; ~ ता informality.

अन् a Sanskrit prefix to words beginning with vowels, signifying negation [e.g.] अनभिज्ञ, अनाचार, अनन्त.

अन्न [*nm*] corn, food, [usu. cooked]; ~ देव spirit corn.

अन्न-जल [*nm*] bread and butter; subsistence.

अन्नदाता [*nm*] master; patron, benefactor; one who provides subsistence; a form of address used by subjugated and subordinated people for their masters and patrons.

अन्य [*adj.*] other, another; different; –पुरुष the third person [in Grammar].

अन्यत्र [*adv.*] elsewhere.

अन्यथा [*adv.*] otherwise; [*adj.*] contrary, against.

अन्य/मनस्क, ~ मना [*adj.*] out of sorts; absent-minded, mentally elsewhere; indisposed.

अन्याय [*nm*] injustice, wrong; inequity.

अन्यायी [*adj.*] unjust, inequitable; [*nm*] a wrong-doer; persecutor.

अन्योक्ति [*nf*] an allegory; ~ परक allegorical.

अन्योन्य [*adj.*] reciprocal.

अन्व/य [*nm*] the natural order or sequence of words in a sentence; logical syntactical concordance of words in a sentence; logical connection of cause and effect or proposition and conclusion; lineage.

अन्विति [*nf*] unity [esp. dramatic]; syntactical sequence [of words].

अन्वी/क्षण [*nm*] investigation, thorough/microscopic examination.

अन्वे/षण [*nm*] exploration, enquiry; investigation; hence ~ षक, ~ षी.

अपंग [*adj.*] cripple, maimed.

अप a Sanskrit prefix denoting–away, off, base, down, deterioration or inferiority; as an allomorph of आप in Hindi it also denotes 'self' as ~ काजी selfish; ~ स्वार्थी selfish.

अपकर्ष [*nm*] downfall; degeneration, degradation, debasement.

अपकार [*nm*] harm, ill-turn, damage; disservice; wrong.

अपकारी [*adj.*] detrimental, hurtful/harmful, damaging; [nm] one who inflicts harm, one who does an evil turn.

अपच [*nm*] indigestion, dyspepsia.

अपढ़ [*adj.*] unlettered, illiterate.

अपथ्य [*adj.*] insalubrious, unwholesome, unhealthy.

अपदस्थ [*adj.*] deposed; dismissed, relieved of one's post.

अपना [*adj.*] one's own, pertaining to oneself; -तेरी [a feeling of] thine and mine, a parochial outlook; ~पन cordiality, [a feeling of] ownness, affinity; –पराया kindred and alien; –मकान कोट समान every man's house is his castle;–सा मुँह लेकर रह जाना to face discomfiture, to be chagrined; अपनी-अपनी ढपली अपना-अपना राग each one blowing one's own trumpet; अपनी-अपनी पड़ना to be keen each after his own interests or affairs; अपने मुँह मियाँ मिट्ठू self-praise is no recom-mendation; बनना to indulge in self-praise.

अपनाना [*v*] to [treat as one's] own; to adopt; to appropriate.

अपभ्रंश [*nm*] a corrupt form of a word, corruption; one of the middle Indo-Aryan languages.

अपमान [*nm*] insult, disgrace, affront.

अपयश [*nm*] ill-repute, disrepute, infamy.

अपरंच [*ind*] moreover, furthermore, besides.

अपर [*adj.*] other, another, different; later; latter; following; inferior.

अपराध [*nm*] crime; offence; fault, guilt; ~ विज्ञ criminologist; –विज्ञान criminology.

अपराधी [*adj.* and *nm*] [*adj.*] criminal, guilty; offending/offender.

अपराह्न [*nm*] afternoon, post-midday.

अपरिचित [*adj.*] unacquainted; [*nm*] a stranger.

अपरिमित [*adj.*] measureless; limitless; enormous; infinite; indeterminate.

अपरिमेय [*adj.*] immeasurable, infinite; irrational.

अपरिष्कृत [*adj.*] unrefined; crude.

अपरिहार्य [*adj.*] indispensable; inevitable, unavoidable.

अपरूप [*adj.*] ugly, grotesque; unparalleled.

अपर्याप्त [*adj.*] inadequate, insufficient.

अपलक [*adv* and *adj.*] without a wink/blink, unwinking, unblinking.

अपवचन [*nm*] slander, calumny.

अपवर्त्य [*nm*] a factor; divisor.

अपवाद [*nm*] exception; slander, calumny; hence ~क, अपवादी.

अपविचार [*nm*] mistrial; a mischievous/bad idea.

अपवित्र [*adj.*] unholy, impure; desecrated, profane.

अप/व्यय [*nm*] waste, wastefulness; extravagant expenditure, squandering; ~व्ययी a squanderer; wasteful, extravagant.

अपशकुन [*nm*] ill/bad omen; inauspicious omen, an occurrence or event portending evil.

अपशब्द [*nm*] an abuse; abusive language or word, a vulgar word.

अपस्मार [*nm*] epilepsy; catalepsy.

अपस्वार्थी [*adj.*] selfish, concerned about own ends.

अप/हरण [*nm*] abduction; kidnapping; usurpation.

अपादान [*nm*] the ablative case.

अपार [*adj.*] boundless; shoreless; immense.

अपारगम्य [*adj.*] impermeable.

अपारदर्शी [*adj.*] opaque.

अपार्थिव [*adj.*] unearthly, celestial; spiritual.

अपाहिज [*nm* and *adj.*] a cripple/crippled; disabled.

अपि [*ind.*] also; and; though, although; ~तु but, on the other hand.

अपील [*nf*] an appeal.

अपूर्ण [*adj.*] incomplete, unfinished; imperfect, deficient; ~भूत past imperfect [tense].

अपूर्व [*adj.*] unprecedented; novel; unique.

अपेक्षा [*ind*] [generally preceded by की or the relative case meaning] in comparison with; [*nf*] expectation, requirement; ~ कृत comparatively, comparatively speaking.

अपेक्षित [*adj.*] expected; requisite.

अप्रकाशित [*adj.*] unpublished; unexposed, undisclosed.

अप्राकृत [*adj.*] abnormal; unnatural.

अप्रचलित [*adj.*] obsolete, [gone] out of currency; out of date, antiquated.

अप्रत्यक्ष [*adj.*] in-apparent; invisible; indirect.

अप्रत्याशित [*adj.*] unexpected; sudden.

अप्रधान [*adj.*] secondary, subsidiary; minor.

अप्रयुक्त [*adj.*] not used, unused; obsolete [word].

अप्रसन्न [*adj.*] unhappy; displeased; out of sorts.

अप्रस्तुत [*adj.*] indirect, accidental or extraneous; not principal, not being the main subject matter; irrelevant; [*nm*] the object of comparison [in Rhetorics].

अप्राकृ/त, ~ तिक [*adj.*] unnatural; abnormal; uncommon.

अप्राप्य [*adj.*] unattainable, unobtainable; rare.

अप्रामाणिक [*adj.*] unauthoritative; inauthentic.

अप्रासंगिक [*adj.*] irrelevant, out of context.

अप्रिय appriy [*adj.*] unpleasant, disagreeable; offensive.

अप्रैल [*nm*] [the month of] April.

अप्सरा [nf] a celestial damsel; fairy; nymph.

अफरा [*nm*] swelling of stomach due to overeating, indigestion or accumulation of wind.

अफ़रा-तफ़री [*nf*] confusion, hurry-skurry; commotion; panic.

अफ़लातून [*nm*] a person of overweening pride; boaster [based on the corrupt form of the name of one of the earliest and greatest Greek thinkers–Plato].

अफ़वा/ह [*nm*] a rumour.

अफ़स/र [nm] an officer; ~ री the post, function or air of an officer; officialism; officialdom.

अफ़साना [*nm*] a story, tale.

अफ़सोस [*nm*] sorrow, grief; [int] alas!

अफ़ारा [*nm*] tympanitis.

अफ़ीम [*nf*] opium.

अफ़ीमची [*nm*] ān opium-addict.

अब [*adv*] now; –की/के this time; next time; –जाकर at long last; –तब करना to evade, to dilly-dally;–तब होना to be in the verge of death; –से now onwards, in future.

अबरक [*nm*] mica.

अबरी [*nf*] marble paper; [*adj.*] variegated.

अबला [*nf*] a member of the weaker sex–a woman.

अबाध [*adj.*] without restraint; free, smooth.

अबूझ [*adj.*] unintelligible; insolvable; inane.

अबे [*ind*] an address expressive of disrespect or intimate relationship; you fellow!; –तबे करना to use contemptuous or rude language.

अबोध [*adj.*] innocent; ignorant; ~ गम्य unintelligible; inconceivable.

अभागा [*adj.*] unfortunate, accursed, unlucky, ill-starred.

अभा/व [nm] want, dearth, deficiency, shortage, lack; ~ वात्मक negative.

अभि a Sānskrit prefix denoting towards, over, near, above, repeated, excessive, etc.

अभिचार [*nm*] incantation, employment of spells for a malevolent purpose, sorcery, black magic.

अभिजात [*adj.*] aristocratic, well-born; classic; [nm] an aristocrat, noble; ~तंत्र aristocracy; –वर्ग aristocracy, nobility; ~ वाद classicism; aristocracy.

अभिज्ञ [*adj.*] well-conversant [with], knowing all [about something].

अभिधा [*nf*] denotation, the literal power or sense of a word.

अभिधान [*nm*] a name; noun nomenclature.

अभिधेय [*nm*] literal meaning.

अभिनंदन [*nm*] greeting, reception, a ceremonious welcome; applause; –ग्रन्थ a commemoration volume; –पत्र an address of welcome.

अभिनय [*nm*] acting, performing [on the stage].

अभिनव [*adj.*] novel, new; recent.

अभिनिवेश [*nm*] concentration, deliberation; perseverence.

अभि/नेता [*nm*] an actor; ~ नेत्री an actress.

अभिन्न [*adj.*] identical; not different; close, intimate; integral; ~ ता identity; sameness, oneness,

अभिप्राय [*nm*] intention; implication; purport; design, import, purpose.

अभिभावक [*nm*] a guardian.

अभिभाषण [*nm*] an address [speech delivered by a dignitary].

अभिभूत [*adj.*] overwhelmed; overpowered; overawed.

अभि/मान [*nm*] pride; vanity, arrogance; ~ मानी proud; vainglorious, arrogant.

अभिमुख [*adv.*] directed towards, facing; disposed to, intending to.

अभियान [*nm*] a campaign; an expedition.

अभियुक्त [*nm* and *adj.*] [*an*] accused.

अभियोग [*nm*] accusation, charge; lawsuit, case; indictment.

अभिराम [*adj.*] beautiful, lovely; delightful.

अभिरुचि [*nf*] taste, liking.

अभिलाषित [*adj.*] cherished, desired, longed for.

अभिला/षा [*nf*] desire, yearning, longing, craving, wish.

अभिवादन [nm] deferential salutation; greeting.

अभिवृद्धि [*nf*] prosperity; development, progress.

अभिव्यंजना [*nf*] expression; manifestation; ~ वाद expressionism.

अभिव्यक्ति [*nf*]: expression; manifestation.

अभिशाप [*nm*] a curse.

अभिषेक [*nm*] inaugurating or consecrating [by sprinkling water]; inauguration of a king, royal function.

अभिसार [*nm*] meeting; rendezvous [of lovers].

अभिसारिका [*nf*] a woman who goes to meet her lover or keeps an assignation.

अभिहित [*adj.*] named, designated; called.

अभी [*adv.*] just now, this moment.

अभीष्ट [*adj.*] desired, cherished.

अभूतपूर्व [*adj.*] unprecedented; [that has] never existed before.

अभेद [*nm*] identity, oneness.

अभेद्य [*adj.*] indivisible; indistinguishable; impregnable, impenetrable.

अभ्यर्थना [*nf*] welcome reception; supplication; request.

अभ्यर्थी [*nm*] a welcomer, suppliant; candidate.

अभ्यागत [*nm*] a guest, visitor.

अभ्यास [*nm*] practice; exercise; habituation.

अभ्यु/त्थान [*nm*] rise, rising; elevation.

अभ्यु/दय [*nm*] rise, rising [of luminaries]; rising [to prosperity, happiness, etc.]; advent; aggrandizement.

अमचूर [*nm*] dried mango parings [used as spice].

अमन [*nm*] peace, tranquillity

अमर [*adj.*] immortal, eternal, undying; [*nm*] a god, deity.

अमर/ता [*nf*] immortality; also ~ त्व [*nm*].

अमरूद [*nm*] guava.

अमर्त्य [*adj.*] immortal, deathless, eternal.

अमल [*nm*] action, execution; application; addiction;–में लाना to execute, to implement.

अमलदारी [*nf*] rule, authority; sway.

अमला [*nm*] staff; paraphern-alia.

अमली [*a*] practical; [*nm*] an addict;–जामा पहनाना to translate into action, to put into practice.

अमानत [*nf*] something given in trust, a deposit.

अमानती [*adj.*] deposited or given in trust.

अमानी [*nf*] casual labour; time/daily wages.

अमानुषिक [*adj.*] inhuman; beastly; cruel.

अमाव/स, ~ स्या [*nf*] the last day of the dark fortnight.

अमिट [*adj.*] indelible, ineffaceable; indestructible.

अमित [*adj.*] unmeasured, boundless; immense, enormous.

अमीर [*adj.*] rich, wealthy; [nm] a rich man; a chieftain; अमीराना lordly, princely.

अमीरी [*nf*] richness, wealthiness.

अमुक [*adj.*] such and such, so and so.

अमूर्त [*adj.*] abstract; intangible, incorporeal.

अमूल्य [*adj.*] valuable, precious; priceless.

अमृत [*nm*] nectar.

अमृतबान [*nm*] a jar.

अमोघ [*adj.*] unfailing, unerring; infallible.

अम्माँ [*nf*] mother.

अम्ल [*nm*] acid; [*adj.*] sour; ~ ता acidity; sourness.

अयोग्य [*adj.*] incompetent; unworthy; unqualified; unfit; ~ ता unfitness; disqualification; inability.

अरक्षित [*adj.*] insecure; unprotected, undefended.

अरगनी [*nf*] clothesline, a rope wire or bamboo used for hanging clothes on.

अरथाना [*v*] to explain [the meaning of]; to make explicit.

अरब [*adj.*] a thousand million; [*nm*] an Arab; the Arab country.

अरमान [*nm*] an aspiration, longing; –निकालना to have it out, to have one's fulfilment; –रह जाना not to have one's aspirations materialised.

अरवी [*nf*] a kind of taro.

अरसठ [*adj.* and *nm*] see अड़सठ.

अरसा [*nm*] period, duration, interval.

अरसिक [*adj.*] dry, prosaic; inaesthetic.

अराजकता [*nf*] anarchy, chaos; ~ वाद anarchism; ~ वादी [*an*] anarchist.

अरारोट [*nm*] arrow-root.

अरावल [*nm*] the vanguard.

अरि [*nm*] an enemy, a hostile person.

अरुचि [*nf*] dislike, aversion; distaste; ~ कर disgusting, loathing; unpalatable.

अरुणिमा [*nf*] reddish brown tinge/colour.

अरुणोदय [*nm*] day-break, early dawn.

अरे [*int*] O !, a form of address [used for inferiors or juniors].

अरोचक [*adj.*] uninteresting; boring.

अर्क [*nm*] essence; extract.

अर्ग/ल, ~ ला [*nm, nf*] a log for fastening a door, draw-bar.

अर्घ [*nm*] libation [in honour of a deity]; value, price; ~ दान offering of libation.

अर्घ्य [*nm*] things worth offering [to deity, etc.] as argha [see].

अर्च/न, ~ ना [*nm, nf*] worship, adoration.

अर्ज़ [*nf*] request, supplication; width.

अर्जित [*adj.*] acquired; earned.

अर्ज़ी [*nf*] an application; petition

अर्ज़ीदावा [*nm*] a plaint, a petition submitted by the plaintiff in a court of law.

अर्थ [*nm*] meaning; import, sense; wealth, money; [*ind*] for, for the sake of; ~ गर्भित significant, pregnant with meaning; ~ वत्ता significance.

अर्थव्यवस्था [*nf*] economy; economics; economic set up/system.

अर्थ/शास्त्र [*nm*] Economics; ~ शास्त्री an economist; ~ शास्त्रीय/-सम्बन्धी economic.

अर्थहीन [*adj.*] meaningless, absurd; moneyless.

अर्थात् [*adv.*] that is, that is to say, namely [viz.].

अर्थालंकार [*nm*] meaning-based figure of speech.

अर्थी [*nf*] a bier; [*nm*] a petitioner; [*adj.*] desirous; suppliant.

अर्दली [*nm*] an orderly, attendant.

अर्ध [*adj.*] semi-, demi-; half.

अर्धचन्द्र [*nm*] the crescent, half-moon; अर्धचंद्राकार crescent-shaped; semi-lunar.

अर्ध/वृत [*nm*] semi-circle; ~ वृत्ताकार semi-circular.

अर्धव्यास [*nm*] radius.

अर्धांगिनी [*nf*] wife, better half.

अर्धाली [*nf*] two successive feet of a चौपाई.

अर्पण [*nm*] an offering; surrender [ing]; assignment; cession.

अर्राना [*v*] to crash down, to tumble down; to fall down with a violent noise.

अर्वाचीन [*adj.*] modern, new, recent.

अर्हंत [*a*] qualified; competent; [*nm*] names of Lords Jin, Buddh and Shiv.

अर्ह [*adj.*] qualified; competent; ~ ता qualification; competence.

अलं/कार [*nm*] embellishment; ornament; figure of speech; hence ~ करण ~ कार-शास्त्र Rhetorics.

अलक [*nf*] a curl, a lock of hair.

अलकतरा [*nm*] coaltar, tar.

अलग [*adj.* and *adv*] separate, apart, aloof; distinct; -अलग individually, separately; -थलग aloof; isolated.

अलगनी [*nf*] see अरगनी.

अल/ग़रज़ [*adj.*] careless, negligent; ~ ग़रज़ी carelessness, negligence.

अलगाव [*nm*] isolation, separation; breach; cessation, segregation.

अलता [*nm*] a lac-dye used by Hindu women for staining their feet red.

अलबत्ता [*adv.*] nevertheless; of course, certainly, truly.

अलबेला [*nm*] a dandy, beau; [*adj.*] dandy; foppish, frivolous.

अलभ्य [*adj.*] rare; unattainable, unobtainable.

अलमबरदार [*nm*] a standard-bearer.

अलमस्त [*adj.*] carefree, sprightly, gay.

अलमारी [*nf*] an almirah, a cupboard.

अलमूनियम [*nm*] aluminium.

अलर्क [*nm*] a rabid dog; –रोग rabies.

अललटप्पू [*adj.*] see अटकलपच्चू.

अलवान [*nf*] a kind of woollen shawl.

अलसाना [*v*] to be slack or sluggish, to feel lazy, to be overtaken by inertia.

अलसी [*nf*] linseed;–का तेल linseed oil.

अलह/दा [*adj.*] separate; aloof; ~ दगी separation; aloofness.

अलापना [*v*] to tune the voice, to pitch or raise the voice; to sing.

अलामत [*nf*] sign, symptom.

अलाव [*nm*] a bonfire for warming up the body; camp-fire.

अलावा [*ind*] besides, in addition to; apart from; except.

अलिखित [*adj.*] unwritten, unrecorded.

अलील [*adj.*] indisposed.

अलोना [*adj.*] without salt; tasteless; insipid.

अलौकिक [*adj.*] unearthly, heavenly, celestial; phenomenal; transcendental, supernatural.

अल्प [*adj.*] a little, small; minute; short; few; ~ ता smallness, minuteness; insignificance; ~ प्राण unaspirated; vigourless, lacking vitality; ~ भाषी taciturn; reserved; ~ बुद्धि a nitwit, idiot; silly; ~ मत minority; ~ विराम comma; ~ संख्यक minority [group, party, community, etc.]; o वर्ग minority group; ~ संख्या minority; अल्पायु of young age; short-lived, ephemeral; अल्पाहारी abstemious, abstinent [in respect of food].

अल्लाह [*nm*] God.

अल्हड़ [*adj.*] carefree, having carefreeness reinforced by child-like simplicity and a touch of innocence; ~ पन carefree and innocent nature.

अव a Sanskrit prefix denoting after, downwards, smallness or diminution, decay, determination, etc.

अवकाश [*nm*] leisure; leave of absence; recess; space; –प्राप्त retired.

अवगत [*adj.*] apprised; informed.

अवगाहन [*nm*] immersion, bathing; profound study, deep delve.

अवगुंठन [*nm*] veil[ing].

अवगुण [*nm*] defect, demerit; vice; fault.

अवचेत/न [*nm* and *adj.*] [the] sub-conscious; ~ ना subconscious mind.

अवज्ञा [*nf*] contempt, disregard; defiance; insubordination.

अवतरण [*nm*] descent; a passage; quotation; -चिह्न quotation marks [" "].

अवतरित [*adj.*] descended; become incarnate; quoted.

अवतार [*nm*] an incarnation; ~ वाद the theory of incarnation; अवतारी incarnate, the source of incarnation; superhuman.

अवतीर्ण [*adj.*] descended; incarnated.

अवधारणा [*nf*] a concept.

अवधि [*nf*] period; time; limit; term; duration.

अवधूत [*nm*] a [peculiar type of] religious mendicant; [*adj.*] rough and rugged [man].

अवयव [*nm*] a part, portion; member; limb; component; ingredient; a member or component, part of logical argument of syllogism.

अवर [*adj.*] low; inferior; under; puisne; junior.

अवरुद्ध [*adj.*] obstructed, hindered, impeded; restrained; impounded; arrested.

अवरोध [*nm*] an obstruction, hindrance, impediment; restraint; taboo.

अवरोह [*nm*] a descent; act of descending.

अवर्णनीय, अवर्ण्य [*adj.*] indescribable, defying description; ineffable.

अवलंब [*nm*] support, stay; dependence; prop.

अवलि, अवली [*nf*] row; range; continuous line; series; set.

अवलो/क, ~ कन [*nm*] seeing, beholding, viewing; perusal; scanning; ~ कनार्थ for perusal.

अवशिष्ट [*adj.*] left; remaining; residuary; residual; [nm] residue, remnant.

अवशेष [*nm*] remnant, remains, residue, residium; vestige; relics; [a] remaining, residual.

अवशोषक [*nm*] absorbant; [*adj.*] absorbing.

अवश्यंभावी [*adj.*] certain; inevitable.

अवश्य [*adv.*] certainly, definitely; necessarily; ~ मेव without fail, certainly; undoubtedly.

अवसर [*nm*] opportunity, chance; occasion; scope; ~ वादी opportunist [ic].

अवसाद [*nm*] lassitude, languor; dejection, despondency, depression.

अवसान [*nm*] end; death; terminal, termination.

अवस्था [*nf*] condition, state; age; stage; phase.

अवस्थान [*nm*] a phase.

अवहेलना [*nf*] neglect; disdain, contempt.

अवांछनीय [*adj.*] undesirable; unwelcome.

अवांछित [*adj.*] unwanted, unwelcome; undesired.

अवांतर [*adj.*] secondary; intermediate, intermediary.

अवाक् [*adj.*] speechless; stunned.

अविकल [*adj.*] intact; unabridged.

अविकारी [*adj.*] immutable, not subject to mutation or variation; direct [form].

अविकृत [*adj.*] unimpaired; not mutilated, not deformed; intact.

अविचल [*adj.*] steady; motionless; firm, unswerving.

अविनाशी [*adj.*] immortal; indestructible, imperishable.

अविनीत [*adj.*] impertinent, pert, impolite, immodest.

अविभक्त [*adj.*] undivided; unsplit; intact; also अविभाजित.

अविभाज्य [*adj.*] indivisible.

अविलंब [*adv.*] at once; without delay; forthwith.

अविवाहित [*adj.* and *nm*] unmarried; bachelor, celibate.

अविवे/क [*nm*] absence of reason, indiscretion; imprudence; injudiciousness; hence ~ की [*adj.*] rash.

अविश्वसनीय [*adj.*] unreliable, untrustworthy.

अविश्वास [*nm*] distrust, disbelief; lack of confidence; suspicion, doubt; –प्रस्ताव no-confidence motion.

अविश्वासी [*adj.*] distrustful, suspicious; [nm] an unbeliever.

अविहित [*adj.*] forbidden [by law]; not prescribed.

अवैज्ञानिक [*adj.*] unscientific; unsystematic.

अवैतनिक [*adj.*] honorary.

अवैध [*adj.*] illegal, unlawful; illegitimate, illicit; invalid, ~ ता illegality; illegitimacy.

अव्यक्त [*adj.*] not manifest/apparent; imperceptible; indistinct.

अव्यय [*nm*] an indeclinable [generally used in grammatical context].

अव्यवसायी [*adj.*] amateur; non-professional.

अव्यव/स्था [*nf*] unlawlessness, disorder, disarray, chaos; ~ स्थित disorderly; chaotic; unsystematic.

अव्यवहार्य [a] unsociable; unusable; unactionable; impracticable.

अव्यावसायिक [*adj.*] non-professional; amateur [ish].

अव्यावहारिक [*adj.*] impractical; not feasible.

अव्वल [*adj.*] first; foremost.

अशकुन [*nm*] see अपशकुन.

अशक्त [*adj.*] weak, feeble; unable; incompetent; invalid, disabled.

अशक्य [*adj.*] impossible, impracticable; unmanageable; invincible.

अशर्फ़ी [*nf*] a gold coin; अशर्फियों की लुट, कोयले पर मोहर penny wise pound foolish.

अशांत [*adj.*] restless, agitated; unquiet, disturbed, perturbed.

अशांति [*nf*] unrest, disquietitude, agitation; disturbance; want of tranquillity.

अशिक्षित [*adj.*] uneducated; unlettered, illiterate.

अशिष्ट [*adj.*] ill-mannered, rude; indecent, indecorous, impolite; ~ ता indecency, impoliteness; ill manners, rudeness.

अशु/द्ध [a] incorrect, erroneous, wrong; impure; ~ द्धता incorrectness, impurity; ~ द्धि an error, a mistake; ~ पत्र errata.

अशुभ [*adj.*] inauspicious, ill- omened; evil; bad; [*nm*] the evil.

अशोभन [*adj.*] unseemly, unbecoming; indecent.

अश्रु [*nm*] a tear; ~ पात shedding of tears.

अश्रुत [*adj.*] unheard [of]; ~ पूर्व unheard of [before]; unique, novel.

अश्लील [*adj.*] obscene; indecent, vulgar; ~ ता obscenity, vulgarity.

असंख्य [*adj.*] innumerable, countless; also ~ क.

असंग/त [*adj.*] incoherent; irrelevant; inconsistent; absurd; irrational; anomalous, incompatible; discordant;~ तता,~ ति incoherence; irrelevance; absurdity; irrationality; incompatibility; anomaly.

असंतुलित [*adj.*] unbalanced; erratic.

असंतुष्ट [*adj.*] dissatisfied, discontented, disgruntled; malcontent; aggrieved.

असंतो/ष [*nm*] dissatisfaction, discontent, discontentment; ~ षी insatiable, one who is temperamentally discontented, greedy.

असंदिग्ध [*adj.*] indubitable; certain, definite.

असंबद्ध [*adj.*] disconnected, irrelevant; incongruous.

असंभव [*adj.*] impossible, impracticable.

असंयत [*adj.*] unrestrained; intemperate, immoderate.

असंयम [*nm*] unrestraint; intemperance; absence of moderation.

असंस्कृत [*adj.*] uncultured; unrefined; raw.

असत् [*adj.*] evil, bad; non-existent, illusory.

असत्य [*nm*] a lie, falsehood; untruth; [*adj.*] untrue, false; ~ ता falsehood, untruth.

असफल [*adj.*] unsuccessful; ~ ता failure.

असबाब [*nm*] luggage, baggage; goods and chattels.

असभ्य [*adj.*] uncivilized, uncivil; discourteous; indecent; ill-bred; rustic; ~ ता uncivility; indecency; vulgarity; rusticity.

असमंजस [*nm*] a dilemma, fix, suspense.

असमत [*nm*] an oven, a cooker.

असमता [*nf*] inequality; disparity; unevenness.

असमय [*adv.* and *adj.*] untimely, out of season; [nm] time of adversity; unseasonableness.

असमर्थ [*adj.*] incapable, incompetent; ~ ता incapability, incompetence, incapacity, inability.

असमान [*adj.*] unequal; dissimilar; ~ ता disparity, inequality; dissimilarity.

असर [*nm*] effect; influence; impression.

असल [*adj.*] real; true; original.

असलियत [*nf*] reality; truth.

असली [*adj.*] real; true; pure, unadulterated.

असह [*adj.*] unbearable, unendurable.

असहमति [*nf*] disagreement, dissent; discordance.

असहयोग [*nm*] non-cooperation.

असहाय [*adj.*] helpless; lonesome.

असहिष्णु [*adj.*] intolerant, unenduring; ~ ता intolerance, lack of endurance.

असह्य [*adj.*] intolerable, unbearable.

असाढ़ [*nm*] the fourth month of the Hindu calendar.

असाधारण [*adj.*] extraordinary; unusual; uncommon; ~ ता extraordinary quality; uniqueness; unusualness.

असाध्य [*adj.*] incurable; impracticable, unfeasible.

असामयिक [*adj.*] untimely; inopportune.

असामी [*nm*, sometimes *nf*] a tenant; client; victim.

असाम्य [*nm*] inequality; disparity; disequilibrium; imbalance.

असार [*adj.*] worthless; unsubstantial; unreal; illusory; immaterial.

असावधान [*adj.*] careless, uncautious; negligent.

असावधानी [*nf*] carelessness; negligence; absence of caution.

असीम [*adj.*] limitless, boundless.

असीमित [*adj.*] unbounded, unlimited.

असीस [*nf*] see आशीष.

असुर [*nm*] a demon.

असुविधा [*nf*] inconvenience.

असैनिक [*adj.*] civil, non-military; [*nm*] a civilian.

अस्त [*adj.*] set [as the sun]; sunk; ~ प्राय almost set or sunk; dying.

अस्तबल [*nm*] a stable.

अस्तर [*nm*] the lining of a garment; inner coating of colour or varnish; base [in painting].

अस्त-व्यस्त [*adj.*] confused; scattered; helter-skelter.

अस्ताचल [*nm*] the western mountain [behind which the sun is supposed to set].

अस्तित्व [*nm*] existence, being, entity; ~ वाद existentialism; ~ वादी an existentialist; existentialistic.

अस्तु [*interj.*] however; well, now; be it so!

अस्त्र [*nm*] a weapon [especially a missile].

अस्त्र-शस्त्र [*nm*] armament, weaponry; arms, weapons.

अस्त्रागार [*nm*] an arsenal, armoury.

अस्थायी [*adj.*] temporary, labile, unstable; provisional.

अस्थि [*nf*] a bone.

अस्थिर [*adj.*] unstable, unsteady; variable; vacillating; fickle, wavering; ~ ता inconstancy; instability; unsteadiness; vacillation.

अस्पताल [*nm*] a hospital.

अस्पष्ट [*adj.*] not clear; indistinct; vague; dim, obscure; blurred.

अस्पृश्य [*adj.*] untouchable; ~ता [the system and practice of] untouchability.

अस्फुट [*adj.*] indistinct, not clear; blurred; impalpable.

अस्मिता [*nf*] ego; vanity, pride.

अस्वस्थ [*adj.*] unhealthy; morbid; hence ~ ता. morbidity.

अस्वाभाविक [*adj.*] unnatural; artificial; hence ~ ता [nf].

अस्वी/कृत [*adj.*] unaccepted; refused, rejected; denied; ~ कार, ~ कृति non-acceptance; refusal, rejection; denial.

अस्सी [*adj.*] eighty; [nm] the number eighty.

अहं [*nm*] ego; -भाव ego, egoism; ~ वाद egoism; ~ वादी egoist [ic]; -वृत्ति ego-instinct.

अहंका/र [*nm*] vanity; egotism; vainglory; ~ री egotist, vainglorious.

अहंता [*nf*] ego; egoism.

अहम [*adj.*] important, significant.

अहमक् [*nm* and *adj.*] a blockhead, an idiot, a fool; most foolish; stupid.

अहमियत [*nf*] importance, significance.

अहम्मन्य [*adj.*] vainglorious, pretentious, overweening, conceited.

अहा, अहा हा [*interj.*] an exclamation expressing surprise or delight; how excellent, well done! wonderful! etc.

अहाता [*nm*] a compound; precincts; enclosure.

अहिंसक [*adj.*] non-violent, [person].

अहिंसा [*nf*] non-violence; ~ वाद the creed of non-violence; ~ वादी a follower of the principle of non-violence; non-violent by creed.

अहेर [*nm*] hunting, chase, game.

अहेरी [*nm*] a sportman, a fowler, a hunter.

अहित [*nm*] harm, damage, injury; evil; ~ कर harmful, injurious, detrimental.

अहो [*interj.*] Oh! O!

अहोई name of a rite held before Diwali, when women pray for children.

आ the second letter and the second vowel of the Devanagri: alphabet; a Sanskrit prefix used to denote up to, until, from, throughout, along with, well, etc.

आ - देवनागरी वर्णमाला का दूसरा (स्वर) वर्णं और 'अ' का दीर्घ रूप है।

आँक [*nm*] a plant also called सेंहुड़

आँक [*nm*] spot, mark

आँकड़े [*nm*] data; statistics, figures.

आँकना [*v*] to assess, to reckon; to evaluate; to appraise; to mark.

आँख [*nf*] an eye; the eye of a needle; the sprout at the joint of a sugarcane; ~ मिचौनी the game of hide and seek; also ~ मिचोली –उठाकर देखना, –उठाना to cast a hostile look; –ओट पहाड़ ओट out of sight, out of mind; –का तारा, –की पुतली the apple of one's eye, iris; darling, pet, beloved; ~ का पानी उतर/ढल/मर जाना to be lost to shame, to become shameless; –की किरकिरी an eyesore; –के अंधे नाम नयनसुख to name a dunce as Plato; (से) –चुराना/छिपाना to avoid being sighted by, to avoid catching one's eye; –टेढ़ी करना to frown, to cast a hostile/wrathful look; –डबडबाना to be on the verge of tears; to have the eyes filled with tears; –तरेरना to look with angry eyes; –निकालना to cast a wrathful glance; –पड़ना to sight per chance; –फूटी पीर गई the eye lost, the pain gone; better the eye out than suffer persistent pain; –बचाना to avoid being sighted; –बदलना, to bring about a sudden change in one's favourable attitude, to withdraw favour or regard all of a sudden; –मिलाना –में आँख डालना to look squarely in the face, to look straight into somebody's eyes; –में खून उतरना to have one's blood up, to have the eyes reddened with extreme rage; –लड़ाना to meet stare with stare, to interchange glances, to cast amorous glances; आँखें चुराना to avoid taking notice of; to avoid an exchange of looks; आँखें दिखाना/निकालना to look [at] angrily or menacingly, to cast a threatening look; आँखें नीची करना to cast eyes downward [out of shame, modesty, etc.]; आँखें फाड़कर or फाड़-फाड़कर देखना to stare [at] with bewildered eagerness or astonishment; आँखें फेरना or फेर लेना to adopt an attitude of indifference towards someone dearly loved, to withdraw one's affection; आँखें बिछाना to give a very cordial welcome; आँखें भर आना or डबडबाना to have the eyes filled with tears, to be almost in tears; आँखें लाल-पीली करना to become livid with anger; आँखों के आगे अँधेरा छाना to faint [on account of a sudden fit of weakness, etc.]; आँखों देखा self-witnessed; माना कानों सुना न माना seeing is believing and hearsay is no evidence; आँखों पर परदा पड़ना to be under an illusion, not to see the obvious; आँखों पर बिठाना/बैठाना to extend a hearty welcome, to receive and treat with utmost affection and reverence; आँखों में खटकना to be an eyesore, to arouse unpleasant feelings; आँखों में धूल झोंकना/डालना to throw dust in the eyes [of], to cheat; आँखों में रात काटना to pass the night awake, not to have a wink throughout the night.

आँगन [*nm*] a courtyard.

आँच [*nf*] the heat of flame, fire; [fig.] harm.

आँचल [*nm*] the extreme part of a sari enveloping the upper part of a woman's body; region.

आँत [*nf*] intestines.

आंतरिक [*adj.*] internal, intra; innate, inner.

आंदोलन [*nm*] a movement, agitation, campaign.

आँधी [*nf*] a dust-storm –के आम a windfall.

आँव [*nf*, used by some as *nm*] mucus.

आँवन [*m.*] iron band round the nave of a wheel.

आंशिक [*adj.*] partial; fractional.

आँसू [*nm*] tear; **–पोंछना** to console.

आइंदा [*adv.*] in future; [*adj.*] future; ensuing.

आईना [*nm*] a looking glass, mirror.

आकर [*nm*] a mine; source; storehouse, treasury; -ग्रंथ a source book.

आकर्ण [*adj.* and *adv.*] [stretching or stretched] up to the ear.

आकर्षक [*adj.*] attractive, charming, alluring.

आकर्षण [*nm*] attraction, charm, allurement; –शक्ति the power of gravitation; attraction.

आकर्षित [*adj.*] attracted, charmed, allured.

आकलन [*nm*] reckoning, calculation.

आकस्मिक [*adj.*] sudden, abrupt; contingent, accidental; fortuitous, casual.

आकांक्षा [*nf*] aspiration.

आकांक्षी [*adj.* and *nm*] [an] aspirant.

आकार [*nm*] form, shape, size; the vowel आ [a:] and its sound; –प्रकार size and shape; –विज्ञान, morphology.

आकारांत [*adj.*] [a word] ending in a: (आ).

आकारिकी [*nf*] morphology; ~ य morphological.

आकाश [*nm*] the sky; the space; ~ कुसुम lit. a flower of the sky, meaning an impossibility, a fanciful thing; ~गंगा the milky way; ~ मंडल the celestial sphere; –पाताल एक करना to leave no stone unturned, to put in Herculean efforts; –पाताल का अंतर as wide asunder as the sky and the nether world, a tremendous difference; –से बातें करना to be sky high, to be as lofty as the sky.

आकाशवाणी [*nf*] an oracle; a proper name given to All India Radio.

आकीर्ण [*adj.*] crowded; full of diffusion; diffused; scattered.

आकुल [*adj.*] restless, uneasy; distracted; distressed.

आकुलता [*nf*] restlessness, uneasiness; mental distress.

आकृति [*nf*] shape, figure, form; structure; appearance; features; ~ मूलक morphological, structural; ~ विज्ञान morphology.

आकृष्ट [*adj.*] see आकर्षित.

आक्रमण [*nm*] attack, aggression, incursion, invasion.

आक्रामक [*nm*] an invader; aggressor; attacker; [a] aggressive; ~ ता aggressiveness, hostility.

आक्रोश [*nm*] acrimony, acerbity; wrath. गुस्सा।

आक्षेप [*nm*] allegation; accusation, invective; charge.

आख़िर [*nm*] the end; [*adv.*] at last, after all; ~ कार ultimately, after all, at long last.

आख्यान [*nm*] telling, communication; a tale, legend; fable; description.

आख्यायिका [*nf*] a fable, short episodic narrative.

आगंतुक [*nm*] a comer, visitor.

आग [*nf*] fire; –खाना अंगार उगलना to eat fire, to emit fumes; –पर पानी डालना to pacify/cover down [all infuriated persons]; –बरसना lit. shedding of fire, meaning to have scorching heat, [also see–बरसाना]; [for something] to be scarce and expensive; –बरसाना to bombard, to cannonate [also see–बरसना]; –में घी डालना to add fuel to the fire; –में पानी डालना to extinguish the fire, to cause a quarrel to end; –होना to be furious, to be in a rage.

आगज़नी [*nf*] arson.

आगत [*adj.*] arrived, come; occurred, happened; –स्वागत welcome [to a guest], warm reception.

आगबबूला [*adj.*] violently enraged, wild with rage.

आगम [*nm*] coming near, approaching; an augment [in grammar]; birth, origin; scripture; traditional doctrine or precept; collection of such doctrines; anything handed down and fixed by tradition; induction; proceeds.

आगमन [*nm*] arrival, approach; induction.

आगमनात्मक [*adj.*] inductive; –तर्कशास्त्र inductive logic.

आगा [*nm*] front, frontage, the fore part of anything; face; the future, the morrow; –पीछा pros and cons.

आगामी [*adj.*] next; future; coming, ensuing.

आगाह करना [*v*] to warn against or notify.

आगाही [*nf*] information, knowledge; foreknowledge.

आगे [*adv.*] ahead, in front of, before; in future; –दौड़ पीछे छोड़ haste makes waste; –पीछे one behind the other, front and rear, sooner or later; ~ कोई न होना to be without any kith and kin; –से in future.

आग्रह [*nm*] insistence, pertinacity; persistence.

आघात [*nm*] blow, stroke, hit; shock; trauma; impact; accent.

आचमन [*nm*] sipping water from the palm of the hand [for self-purification]; to swallow [as a liquid]; to assimilate.

आचरण [*nm*] conduct; behaviour; practice.

आचार [*nm*] conduct; custom, practice; ethos; behaviour, –विचार manners and morals.

आचारशास्त्र [*nm*] ethology, ethics.

आचार-संहिता [*nf*] moral code.

आचार्य [*nm*] a teacher, preceptor; professor; founder or leader [of a school of thought]; an initiator.

आचार्या [*nf*] **1** a spiritual preceptress or guide **2** the wife of an acharya.

आज [*adv.*] today;

आजकल [*adv.*] nowadays, these days; –का modern; –में in a couple of days, soon, without delay.

आजन्म [*adv.*] since birth.

आज़माइ/श [*nf*] trial, test; ~ शी on trial, experimental.

आज़माना [*v*] to try, to [put to a] test.

आज़ाद [*adj*] independent, free.

आज़ादी [*nf*] independence, freedom.

आजीवन [*adv.*] throughout life, for a whole lifetime.

आजीविका [*nf*] livelihood; calling.

आजू-बाजू round about, about, nearby.

आज्ञा [*nf*] order; ~ पत्र a writ, written order.

आज्ञप्ति [*nf*] an order, decree.

आज्ञाका/री [*adj.*] obedient; ~ रिता obedience.

आटा [nm] flour; (कंगाली में)–गीला होना to be plunged into complications when already afflicted; आटे के साथ घुन पिसना to undergo an undeserved suffering on account of association; आटे दाल का भाव मालूम होना to be confronted with unwelcome realities of practical life.

आठ [*adj.*] eight; [nm] the number eight; –आठ आँसू रोना to shed floods of tears.

आडंब/र [*nm*] ostentation, affectation; showing off; tinsel, hypocrisy; ~ री ostentatious, tinsel, showy.

आड़ [*nm*] a cover, screen; a barricade; shield, strut; block.

आड़ा [*adj.*] oblique; horizontal; transverse; –वक्त trying or difficult time; आड़े वक्त पर काम आना to do a good turn when one is in difficulty; आड़े हाथों लेना to rebuke, to put to shame by sarcasm; to tick off.

आड़ू [*nm*] a peach.

आढ़त [*nf*] commission agency; brokerage, commission.

आढ़तिया [*nm*] a commi-ssion agent; broker.

आतंक [*nm*] terror, panic; ~ वाद terrorism; ~ वादी a terrorist; आतंकित terrorised.

आततायी [*nm* and *adj.*] an oppressor; tyrant; oppressive.

आतशक [*nm*] syphilis.

आतिथेय [*nm*] a host, one who extends hospitality.

आतिथ्य [*nm*] hospitability.

आतिश [nm] fire; ~ बाज a fire-works manufacturer; pyrotechnist; ~बाज़ी fire-works, display of fire-works, pyrotechnic display.

आतुर [*adj.*] rash, hasty; restless.

आतुरता [*nf*] rashness, hastiness; restlessness.

आत्म [*nm*] self; [*adj.*] pertaining to self, one's own, personal; ~ कल्याण one's own good; ~ कथा autobiography; ~ केंद्रित self-centered; ~ गत subjective; inner; ~ गौरव self-respect; ~ घात suicide; ~ चरित an autobiography; ~ ज/जात a son; ~ ज्ञान self-realisation, self-knowledge; ~ तत्त्व the true nature of soul or the Supreme Spirit; ~ तृप्ति self-satisfaction, self-fulfilment; ~ त्याग self-sacrifice; self-denial; ~ दाह self-immolation; ~ द्रोह revolt against self; ~ निंदा self-condemnation; – निरीक्षण introspection; – निर्णय self-determination; – निर्भर self-sufficient, self-reliant; ता self-reliance; self-sufficiency; ~ निष्ठ subjective; –प्रदर्शन self-display; –प्रशंसा self-praise; ~ बल spiritual force, psychic force;

–बलिदान self-sacrifice; ~ मोह narcissism; ~ रक्षा self-defence, self-preservation; ~ रति self-love, amour propre; ~ वंचना self-deception, self-deceit; ~ वाद spiritualism; ~ वादी spiritualist; spiritualistic; ~ विश्वास self-confidence; ~ स्तुति self-praise; –संतोष self-satisfaction; –समर्पण surrender [of oneself]; ~ सम्मान self-respect, self-regard; – साक्षात्कार self-realisation; ~ सात् assimilated; – साधना self-realisation; ~ सिद्धि self-realisation; – स्वीकृति confession; ~ हत्या/हनन/हिंसा suicide, self-killing.

आत्मा [*nf*, also used as *nm* by Sanskritists] soul, spirit.

आत्माभिमान [*nm*] self- respect.

आत्माभिव्यक्ति [*nf*] self-expression.

आत्मिक [*adj.*] spiritual; pertaining to self.

आत्मीय [*adj.*] pertaining to self, one's own, intimate; [nm] kith and kin; ~ ता cordiality; intimate relationship, close affinity.

आत्यंतिक [*adj.*] extremistic, excessive.

आदत [*nf*] a habit; ~ न by force of habit, as a matter of habit.

आदम [*nm*] Adam [the first man supposed to have been created on earth]; ~ कद of human-size; ~ ख़्ज़ोर man-eater, cannibal; ~ खोर human being, born of man.

आदमियत [*nf*] gentleman-liness; humanity, humanness.

आदमी [*nm*] man, human being.

आदर [*nm*] respect, deference, esteem; ~ णीय respectable, reverend.

आदर्श [*nm*] an ideal, a model, norm; pattern; [*adj.*] ideal, model; ~ वाद Idealism; ~ वादी idealist [ic].

आदर्शोक्ति [*nf*] a motto.

आदान [*nm*] receiving, taking; –प्रदान giving and taking, exchange.

आदाब [*nm*] manners; salutation.

आदि [*nm*] beginning; [ind] etcetera, [*adj.*] early, initial, primordial; ~ कालीन primitive; ~ रूप prototype.

आदितः [*adv.*] ab initio; de novo.

आदिम [*adj.*] primitive, early; first.

आदिवासी [*nm*] an aboriginal; [*adj.*] aboriginal; –जनजाति aboriginal tribe.

आदी [*adj.*] habitual; habituated, accustomed.

आदेश [*nm*] command; [in Grammar] substitution of one letter for another; precept.

आद्यंत [*adv.*] from beginning to end.

आद्य [*adj.*] first, initial; primitive; archaic.

आद्योपांत [*adv.*] from beginning to end.

आधा [*adj.*] half; moiety; –तीतर आधा बटेर intermingling of heterogeneous elements, discordant objects jumbled together; –साझा equal partnership; आधी छोड़ सारी को धावे, आधी रहे न सारी पावे he who grasps all, loses all.

आधार [*nm*] base; basis, foundation; data; receptacle; ~ भूत fundamental; –रेखा base; – वाक्य promise; ~ शिला foundation stone; – सामग्री data.

आधारित [*adj.*] based [on].

आधिकारिक [*adj.*] official, authoritative; [nm] the main plot.

आधिक्य [*nm*] abundance, plenty; excess.

आधिदैविक [*adj.*] proceeding from divine or supernatural agencies.

आधिपत्य [*adj.*] supremacy; power.

आधिभौतिक [*adj.*] material; derived or produced from the primitive elements.

आधीन [*adj.*] see अधीन.

आधीनता [*nf*] see अधीनता.

आधुनि/क [*adj.*] modern; ~ कीकरण modern-isation, adoption of modern techniques.

आधृत [*adj.*] based [on].

आध्यात्मिक [*adj.*] spiritual; pertaining to the soul or the Supreme Spirit.

आनंद [*nm*] bliss, happiness; joy, pleasure, delight.

आन [*nf*] honour, prestige; –की आन में instantaneously; –बान honour and dignity, pomp and show; grace; –तोड़ना to break one's pledge/honour; –रखना to keep one's pledge/honour.

आनन-फ़ानन (में) [*adv.*] instantaneously, at once.

आना [*v*] to come; [*nm*] an anna [coin]; आनी-जानी transitory, short-lived; आया-गया guest, visitor.

आना-कानी [*nf*] procrastination, evasion, prevarication.

आनुवंशिक [*adj.*] hereditary; ~ ता heredity.

आनुषंगिक [*adj.*] contingent; accidental.

आप [*pro.*] [deferential] you [second person]; – काज महाकाज achievement of one's own end is the greatest achievement; better do a thing than wish it to be done; ~ बीती the story of one's own suffering; self-experiences; –मरे जग परलै (परलो) the death's day is the doomsday; –भला तो जग भला good mind, good find.

आपातकाल [*nm*] emergency.

आपत्ति [*nf*] objection; predicament, trouble.

आपदा [*nf*] distress, adversity.

आपस [*pro*] each other, one another; [nm] fellowship, kindred.

आपसदारी [*nf*] reciprocity, mutual relationship.

आपसी [*adj.*] mutual; reciprocal.

आपा [*nm*] consciousness; one's own entity; ego, vanity; –खोना to forget or lose consciousness of real self; to become abnormal; आपे में न रहना, आपे से बाहर होना to be overwhelmed by emotion, to lose self-control.

आपात [*nm*] an emergency; catastrophe.

आपाधापी [*nf*] a mad race [for self-gratification].

आपेक्षिक [*adj.*] comparative, relative.

आप्लावन [*nm*] inundation; immersion, complete submergence.

आफ़त [*nf*] distress, trouble; –उठाना to create havoc; –का टुकड़ा/परकाला a dare devil, a sharp astute fellow; –का मारा distress-stricken; –ढाना to work havoc; –मचाना to make excessive haste; to create havoc; –मोल लेना, –सिर पर लेना to invite trouble, to own unnecessary botheration.

आब [*nf*] lustre, brilliance; water; ~ दार brilliant, lustrous.

आबकारी [*nf*] excise.

आबदस्त [*nm*] post-excrement wash.

आबपाशी [*nf*] irrigation.

आबरू [*nf*] honour, chastity.

आबहवा [*nf*] climate.

आबाद [*adj.*] inhabited; populated; prosperous.

आबादी [*nf*] population; habitation; [signs of] prosperity.

आभा [*nf*] lustre, splendour; tinge; ~ मंडल a halo.

आभार [*nm*] obligation; indebtedness.

आभारी [*adj.*] obliged; grateful; indebted.

आभास [*nm*] an inkling, a glimpse; semblance, fallacious appearance; phenomenon; effect.

आभासी [*adj.*] pseudo; unreal, apparent; visual.

आभिजात्य [*nm*] aristo-cracy; classicism.

आभूषण [*nm*] ornament; decoration; embellishment.

आभूषित [*adj.*] ornamented; decorated; embellished.

आभोग [*nm*] plenty, surfeit, fullness, abundance.

आभोग्य [*adj.*] unfit for use, not to be used.

आभ्यंतर [*adj.*] the interior, internal.

आमंत्रण [*nm*] an invitation, a call, solicitation.

आमंत्रित [*adj.*] invited.

आम [*nm*] a mango; [*adj.*] common; general; –आदमी the common man; –के आम गुठलियों के दाम earth's joys and heaven's combined.

आमद [*nm*] arrival, approach, coming; revenue; ~ रफ़्त traffic, coming and going.

आमदनी [*nf*] income, revenue.

आमना-सामना [*nm*] an encounter; confrontation; coming face to face.

आमने-सामने [*adv.*] face to face, opposite one another; head on; vis-a-vis.

आमरण [*adv.*] till death; till the end, throughout one's life.

आमादा [*adj.*] intent; bent upon, ready.

आमाशय [*nm*] stomach.

आमुख [*nm*] the preamble.

आमुष्मिक [*adj.*] transcendental, other-worldly.

आमूल [*adj.*] radical, fundamental.

आमोद [*nm*] pleasure, joy, delight; –प्रमोद merriment, regaling; orgy; –यात्रा a pleasure-trip, आमोद-आलाप, m. an entertaining conversation. आमोद-प्रमोद, [*nm*] diversion, pastime, joking, bantering.

आमोदित [*adj.*] delighted, full of joy.

आय [*nf*] income, revenue; receipt.

आयत [*nf*] a rectangle; sentence or verse of the Quran; [*adj.*] wide; long, stretched.

आयतन [*nm*] bulk, volume.

आयताकार [*adj.*] rectangular; mesomorph.

आया [*conj.*] ayah, a female attendant; [ind] whether, whether or not.

आयात [*nm*] import.

आयाम [*nm*] magnitude; dimension; amplitude; regulation.

आयु [*nf*] age, duration of life.

आयुर्विज्ञान [*nm*] Medical Science.

आयुर्वेद [*nm*] the Indian medicinal system; Medical Science [lit. the science of health and longevity].

आयुर्वेदिक [*adj.*] of or pertaining to आयुर्वेद–the Indian medicinal system.

आयुष्मान [*adj.*] having long life; blessed with longevity.

आयोग [*nm*] a commission [a body of persons having authority].

आयोजन [*nm*] convening, sponsoring; organising.

आरंभ [*nm*] start, beginning; outset; commencement; inception.

आरंभिक [*adj.*] initial, preliminary; pertaining to or related with the beginning.

आरज़ू [*nf*] keen desire; yearning; ~ मंद desirous; –मिन्नत supplication; request; beseeching.

आरती [*nf*] a ceremony performed in adoration of a deity or any outstanding personage or guest by circular movement of a lighted lamp before his person.

आर-पार [*adv.*] across; [*nm*] the two banks of a river; pond, etc; astride.

आराइश [*nf*] dressing; decoration, embellishment; ornamental trees, flowers, etc.

आराधक [*nm*] a worshipper, an adorer.

आराधना [*nf*] worship; adoration.

आराम [*nm*] rest; comfort; relief; ~ कुर्सी an easy chair.

आरामतलब [*adj.*] indolent; slothful, easy-going.

आरी [*nf*] a small saw, table saw.

आरोग्य [*nm*] freedom from disease, health; ~शाला a sanitorium; nursing home; ~ शास्त्र hygiene.

आरोप [*nm*] allegation, charge; imputation; projection, imposition, superimposition; transplantation.

आरोहण [*nm*] ascension; ascent; climb.

आर्त्त [*adj.*] aggrieved; persecuted; distressed; afflicted.

आर्थिक [*adj.*] economic.

आर्द्र [*adj.*] wet; damp; humid; moist; tender; full of feeling.

आर्य [*nm*] an Aryan; [*adj.*] noble, of noble stock.

आर्यपुत्र [*nm*] a classical form of address or reference to respectable personages, esp. from a wife to her husband.

आर्यसत्य [*nm*] the great truths [four such truths are enumerated in Buddhist Philosophy].

आर्यावर्त [*nm*] the land of Aryans [extending from the eastern to western sea and bounded on north and south by the Himalayas and Vindhya mountain ranges respectively].

आर्ष [*adj.*] relating or belonging to, or derived from the sages (ऋषि).

आलंकारिक [*a*] rhetorical, pertaining to rhetorics; ornamental; figurative.

आलंबन [*nm*] foundation; base; [in poetics] the object that arouses emotion; [in rhetorics] the natural and necessary connection of a sensation which excites it; reason; cause.

आलमारी [*nf*] see अलमारी.

आलस [*nm*] laziness, lethargy.

आलसी [*adj.*] lazy, lethargic.

आलस्य [*nm*] same as आलस [see].

आला [*nm*] a niche or recess; an instrument; [*adj.*] superior; excellent; wet, moist.

आलाप [*nm*] preliminary modulation of voice before singing; a prelude to singing; low elaboration of राग with or without rhythm.

आलारासी [*adj.*] slow and slothful, indolent.

आलिं/गन [*nm*] an embrace, embracing; clasp, clasping; hence ~ गित [adj.] clasped, enclasped, embraced.

आलिम [*adj.*] scholarly, learned.

आली [*nf*] [a woman's] female friend; a row; range; [a] grand; excellent; ~ जनाब/जाह your Exalted Highness!; one occupying a pre-eminent position.

आलीशान [*adj.*] grand, magnificent.

आलू [*nm*] potato.

आलो/क [*nm*] light, lustre; enlightenment.

आलोचक [*nm*] a critic.

आलोचना [*nf*] criticism.

आलोच्य [*adj.*] worth criticising; fit to be criticised; under review.

आल्हा [*nm*] a ballad, a chivalrous poem, a madrigal, the name of Hindu warrior of Mahoba and the contemporary of Prithviraj.

आवभगत [*nf*] hospitality.

आवरण [*nm*] a cover, covering; sheath; screen; lid, envelope; cladding; –पृष्ठ cover page.

आवर्त [*nm*] a whirlpool; densely populated place; recurrent.

आवर्ती [*adj.*] recurring.

आवश्यक [*adj.*] necessary; essential; binding, obligatory.

आवश्यकता [*adj.*] necessity, need, requirement.

आवाँ [*nm*] a potter's kiln; furnace; –का आवाँ बिगड़ना degeneration of the whole lot/clan.

आवागमन [*nm*] coming and going; transmigration.

आवाज़ [*nf*] sound, voice; report; –उठाना/ऊँची करना/बुलंद करना to raise the voice; –कसना to pass unwelcome remarks; –भर्राना, –भारी होना to have the voice rendered hoarse.

आवाज़ा [*nm*] **1** = आवाज़, **2** taunting, jeers. –आवाज़ा-तवाज़ा, innuendoes.

आवारगी [*nf*] loafing; vagary profligacy; reckless extravagance.

आवारा [*nm*] a vagabond, loafer; [*adj.*] vagrant, wandering, loitering, profligate.

आवारागर्दी [*nf*] loafing; loitering, vagrancy.

आवा/स [*nm*] residence, dwelling place; ~ सी resident.

आवासन [*nm*] immigration.

आवासिक [*adj.*] residing, in residence.

आवाहन [*nm*] invocation [of a deity, etc.]; a call, summoning.

आविर्भाव [*nm*] advent; emergence; manifestation, becoming visible.

आविर्भूत [*adj.*] emerged; manifested, become visible.

आविष्कर्ता [*nm*] an inventor, a discoverer.

आविष्कार [*nm*] an invention.

आविष्कारी [*adj.*] inventing, inventive.

आविष्कृत [*adj.*] **1** discovered; made known. **2** invented.

आवृत [*adj.*] covered; enveloped, surrounded.

आवृत्त [*adj.*] turned round, whirled; repeated; reverted.

आवृत्ति [*nf*] repetition; recurrence, reversion; turning round; edition; frequency.

आवेग [*nm*] impulse; wave; passion; emotion; paroxysm.

आवेदन [*nm*] an application, petition; –पत्र an application, petition.

आवेश [*nm*] charge; agitation, intense emotion; frenzy, wrath.

आशंका [*nf*] apprehension, scruple.

आशनाई [*nf*] intimacy; illicit love.

आशय [*nm*] intention, intent, design; purport, import, meaning; receptacle.

आशा [*nf*] hope; ~जनक hopeful; promising; –टूटना to lose hope; –बाँधना to have [one's] hope raised; ~ ओं पर पानी फिरना to have [one's] hopes shattered.

आशातीत [*adj.*] beyond hope, unexpected.

आशा/वाद [*nm*] optimism; ~वादी an optimist; optimistic.

आशिक [*nm*] a lover, an inamorato; [*adj.*] enamoured.

आशीष [*nf*] blessings, benediction.

आशीर्वाद [*nm*] blessings, benediction.

आशु [*adj.*] prompt; quick; speedy; swift; extempore, impromptu; –कवि an impromptu poet.

आश्चर्य [*nm*] wonder, surprise; astonishment.

आश्रम [*nm*] hermitage; abode; one of the four stages in the life of caste Hindus, [viz. Brahmacharya; Grihastha; Vanprastha Sannya:s].

आश्रय [*nm*] shelter, refuge; retreat; seat.

आश्रित [*adj.*] depending or relying on; enjoying the support of; [*nm*] a dependent, refugee; protege.

आश्व/स्त [*adj.*] assured; convinced; composed.

आश्वासन [*nm*] assurance; guarantee.

आश्विन [*nm*] the seventh month of the Hindu calendar, also called क्वार.

आषाढ़ [*nm*] the fourth month of the Hindu calendar.

आस [*nf*] hope, expectation; support; –टूटना to lose hope; to be disappointed; –बंधाना to extend assurances; to arouse hopes; –लगाना to look hopefully [to].

आस-औलाद [*nf*] progeny.

आसक्त [*adj.*] attached; fond, fascinated, charmed; addicted.

आसक्ति [*nf*] attachment; fondness, fascination; addiction.

आसन [*nm*] a posture; seat; saddle; stage; –जमाना to entrench; stick on; to be seated firmly; –डिगना/डोलना to be allured or tempted; to get panicky or nervous.

आसन्न [*adj.*] imminent, impending.

आस-पास [*adv.*] near about, in the vicinity.

आसमान [*nm*] the sky; –के तारे तोड़ना to realise an impossibility; –पर चढ़ना to exalt to the skies; to spoil [somebody] by extravagant praise/flattery; –पर थूकना lit. to spit at the sky –to puff against the wind; –पर दिमाग होना to be too conceited/vain; –सिर पर उठा लेना to create havoc, to make excessive noise or mischief; –से गिरकर खजूर पर अटकना to fall from the frying pan into the fire; –से बातें करना to vie with the sky, to rise sky-high.

आसमानी [*adj.*] azure, sky blue; pertain to the sky.

आसरा [*nm*] reliance; shelter.

आसव [*nm*] nourishing and intoxicating liquor prepared from yeast or ferment.

आसवन [*nm*] distillation.

आसान [*adj.*] easy; simple; convenient.

आसानी [*nf*] convenience; easiness.

आसन्न [*adj.*] **1** near, adjacent. **2** approaching; impending. – ~ काल] early morning; the hour of death. ~ कोण, math. an adjacent angle. ~ भूत-काल, gram. perfect tense.

आसमान [*nm*] the sky; the heavens. – ~ के तारे तोड़ना, to shatter the stars: to be very skilled in a difficult activity; to attempt, or to achieve, the impossible. ~ ज़मीन एक करना, to work very hard ~ ज़मीन के कुलाबे मिलना, to boast wildly; to make wildly ambitions plans. ~ झाँकना, or ताकना, to have a high opinion of oneself; to be in fine fettle (as a fighting cock.) ~ टूटना, the sky to fa in (on one): to be overtaken or overwhelmed (by misfortune). ~ दिखाना (को)] to throw (one) flat on one's back (as in wrestling; also fig). ~ पर उड़ना, to boast wildly; to behave haughtly. ~ पर क़दम रखना, to be of exuberant moral. ~ चढ़ाना, to extol; to flatter, to wheedle. ~ पर थूकना, to spit at the sky: to demean oneself by expostulation or criticism. ~ सिर पर उठाना, to cause a hullabaloo; to stir up a scandal; to make gigantic efforts. ~ के तारे तोड़ना. ~ से गिरना, to be obtained unexpectedly, or without effort; to be undervalued. ~ से टक्कर ख़ाना, or लेना, ~ से बातें करना, to reach to the sky, to be loftly. दिमाग़ ~ पर चढ़ना, or होना, (one's, का) mood, or morale, to be inflated; to give oneself airs. – आसमान खोंचा, somethingg. very high or tall (as a pole, a man). आसमान-ज़मीन का फ़रक़, a world of difference. आसमान-फाड़, ear-splitting (as laughter).

आसार [*nm*] symptom; sign; breadth of a wall.

आस्तिक [*nm*] a theist; [*adj.*] devout, having a religious disposition.

आस्तीन [nf] a sleeve; –का साँप a foe in the guise of a friend.

आस्था [*nf*] faith, belief.

आस्वाद [*nm*] flavour, relish.

आस्वादन [*nm*] relishing, tasting, gustation.

आह [*interj.*] indicating pain [*nf*] a sigh indicating deep agony; –पड़ना to be accursed, to be afflicted by curses; –भरना to heave a sigh.

आहट [*nf*] noise, sound [as of footsteps].

आहत [*adj.*] injured, wounded; offended.

आहार [*nm*] food, diet, victuals; –विहार routine; physical activities and dealings.

आहन [*nm*] iron.

आहनगर [*nm*] one who works in iron, a blacksmith.

आहिस्ता [*adv.*] slowly, gently, softly.

आहुति [*nf*] an oblation or offering [esp. to a deity]; a sacrifice.

आल्हाद [*nm*] delight, joy mirth.

आल्हादित [*adj.*] delighted pleased, mirthful.

आह्वान [*nm*] a call, summons; invocation; –करना to summon; to invoke.

इ

इ the third letter and the third vowel of the Devanagari: alphabet.

इ – देवनागरी वर्णमाला का तीसरा (स्वर) वर्ण है। इसका उच्चारण स्थान तालु है।

इंगलिस्ता/न [*nm*] England; ~ नी English.

इंगित [*nm*] an indication, hint, sign; gesture; [*adj.*] indicated.

इंच [*nm*] [an] inch.

इँचना [*v*] **1** to be pulled, drawn; to be tightened. **2** to be attracted. **3** to be extracted. **4** to be sucked up, or in. **5** to hold oneself aloof.

इंजन [*nm*] an engine.

इंजीनिय/र [*nm*] an engineer; ~ री engineering.

इंतक़ाल [*nm*] death, demise.

इंतज़ाम [*nm*] management, arrangement.

इंतख़ाब [*nm*] **1** selection, choice. **2** election.

इंतज़ार [*nm*] wait.

इंतहा [*nf*] limit; extremity.

इंद्र [nm] the king of the gods; the god of rains; ~ जाल magic; trickery; –का अखाड़ा the court of lord Indra; an assembly wherein beautiful damsels abound.

इंद्राणी [*nf*], 1 the wife of the god Indra; a title of the goddess. Durgā. 2 a kind of creeper (= इंद्रायन), 3 name of a medicine or plant, Vitex negundo.

इंद्रधनुष [*nm*] a rainbow.

इंद्रिय [*nf*] sense, an organ of sense or action; the generative organ; –निग्रह self-control, control over one's sensual pleasures or appetites; –सुख sensual pleasure; वाद sensualism.

इंद्री [*nf*] = इंद्रिय. – ~ जुलाब, a diuretic medicine.

इंद्रियातीत [*adj.*] transcending the senses, trans-sensual.

इंसा/न [*nm*] a human being, a man; ~ नी human, humane.

इंसानियत [*nf*] humanity.

इंसाफ़ [*nm*] justice, equity.

इंस्पेक्टर [*nm*] an inspector.

इक an allomorph of एक used as the first member in numerous compound words; ~ लौता only [son]; sole.

इकट्ठा [*adj.*] collected, gathered; [adv] together, in one lot.

इकतरफ़ा [*adj.*] unilateral.

इकतालीस [*adj.*] forty-one; [*nm*] the number forty-one.

इकत्तीस [*adj.*] thirty-one; [*nm*] the number thirty-one.

इकल्ला [*adj.*] alone.

इकसठ [*adj.*] sixty-one; [*nm*] the number sixty-one.

इकसार [*adj.*] uniform, even.

इकबाल [*nm*] **1** admission; confessioon, acknowledgement. **2** acceptance. **3** prestige; prosperity. – इक़बाल-दावा, admission of a claim. इक़बालमंद fortunate; prosperous.

इकहत्तर [*adj.*] seventy-one; [*nm*] the number seventy-one.

इकहरा [*adj.*] single, single-folded; lean and thin.

इकाई [*nf*] a unit; the unit's place in numeration.

इका/र [*nm*] the vowel i (इ) and its sound; ~ रांत [a word] ending in (इ).

इक्का [*nm*] a small one-horse carriage; an ace [in the game of cards].

इक्कीस [*adj.*] twenty-one; [*nm*] the number twenty-one.

इक्यानबे [*adj.*] ninety-one; [*nm*] the number ninety-one.

इक्यावन [*adj.*] fifty-one; [*nm*] the number fifty-one.

इक्यासी [*adj.*] eighty-one; [*nm*] the number eighty-one.

इच्छा [*nf*] a desire; wish; will; -शक्ति will power.

इच्छित [*adj.*] desired; willed.

इच्छुक [*adj.*] desirous; willing.

इजरा (य) [*nf*] issue [of a decree]; execution.

इजलास [*nm*] court; bench.

इजाज़त [*nf*] permission.

इज़ारबंद [*nm*] a lace used as belt.

इजा/रा [*nm*] monopoly; ~ रेदार a monopoly-holder, monopolist; ~ रेदारी monopoly, monopoly holding.

इज्ज़त [*nf*] prestige, honour; respect; –उतारना to insult, to put to disgrace; to humiliate; –खोना/गँवाना to be disgraced, to lose one's honour or dignity.

इज्ज़तदार [*adj.*] respectable; reputed as honest and decent.

इठलाना [*v*] to act affectedly, to assume swaggering airs.

इतना [*adj.*] this much, so much.

इत्मीनान [*nm*] conviction, assurance; trust, confidence.

इतराना [*v*] to assume an air of exaltation, to behave in a self-conceited manner.

इतवार [*nm*] Sunday.

इति [*nf*] end, conclusion; [ind] a word denoting conclusion.

इतिवृत्त [*nm*] a narrative; chronicle, an annal.

इतिहास [*nm*] history; ~ कार a historian.

इत्तफ़ाक [*nm*] coincidence; chance.

इत्तला [*nm*] information; notice.

इत्यादि, ~ क [*ind]* etcetera, so on and so forth.

इत्र [*nm*] perfume, scent; essence.

इधर [*adv.*] this side, this way; here; –उधर की हाँकना to gossip; –की उधर लगाना to indulge in back-biting; to create strife; –की दुनिया उधर हो जाना to have an impossibility materialised; –या उधर this way or that.

इनक़लाव [*nm*] revolution; –ज़िन्दाबाद long live revolution; इनक़लाबी revolutionary.

इनकार [*nm*] refusal; denial; disapproval.

इनाम [*nm*] prize, reward, award.

इनायत [*nf*] favour, obligation.

इने-गिने [*adj.*] very few, selected few.

इबार/त [*nf*] text; writing, word; ~ ती textual, pertaining to the text; written.

इमला [*nf*] dictation [matter written at somebody's instance].

इमारत [*nf*] building, structure; edifice.

इम्तहान [*nm*] examination, test.

इरादा [*nm*] intention, idea.

इर्द-गिर्द [*adv.*] around, about, nearby.

इल्ज़ाम [*nm*] allegation, accusation, charge.

इलाक़ा [*nm*] area; sphere; district, zone, region, territory; range; locality.

इलाज [*nm*] treatment; remedy, cure.

इल्म [*nm*] knowledge, learning.

इल्लंत [*nf*] botheration, malady; addiction to vice.

इशा/रा [*nm*] sign, signal; hint, indication; gesture; ~ रेबाजी gesticulation; winking [at].

इश्क़ [*nm*] love; amour.

इश्तहार [*nm*] advertisement; poster.

इष्ट [*adj.*] adored; favoured; favourite; ~ तम optimum.

इस [*pro.*] this, it; –हाथ दे उस हाथ ले early sow, early mow.

इस्पात [*nm*] steel.

इसलाम [*nm*] the religion of the Mohammedans.

इस्तरी [*nf*] a smoothing iron, press.

इस्तीफ़ा [*nm*] resignation.

इस्तेमाल [*nm*] use; application.

इहलीला [*nf*] life in this world; mundane life.

इह/लोक [*nm*] this world, the present world; ~ लौकिक world, mundane.

ई the fourth vowel and the fourth letter of the Devanagari: alphabet.

ई - देवनागरी वर्णमाला का चौथा (स्वर) वर्ण, 'इ' का दीर्घ रूप है। इसका उच्चारण स्थान तालु है। इसे प्रत्यय के समान कुछ शब्दों में लगाकर संज्ञा, विशेषण, स्त्रीलिंग आदि और भाववाचक संज्ञा आदि बनते हैं।

ईंगुर red lead, vermillion.

ईंट [*nf*] a brick–से ईंट बजाना to raze [a building], to bring to total ruination.

ईंधन [*nm*] fuel, firewood.

ईका/र [*nm*] the vowel (ई) and its sound; ~ रांत a word ending in (ई)।

ईख [*nf*] sugarcane.

ईजाद [*nf*] an invention.

ईमान [*nm*] faith, belief; –खोना to lose integrity; –डिगना to have one's integrity shaken;–बेचना to sell one's conscience.

ईमानदार [*adj.*] honest; faithful; having integrity.

ईमानदारी [*nf*] honesty; faithfulness; integrity.

ईर्ष्या [*nf*] jealousy.

ईश्वर [*nm*] God; –निंदा blasphemy; ~ वाद theism; ~वादी a theist; theistic; ईश्वरीय Godly, divine; –न करे! May God forbid! Heaven forbid!

ईस्वी [*adj.*] pertaining to Christ, Christian; –सन् Christian era.

ईसा [*nm*] Jesus Christ.

ईसाई [*nm*] a Christian, follower of the Christian faith.

उ the fifth letter and the fifth vowel of the Devanagari: alphabet.

उ - देवनागरी वर्णमाला का पाँचवाँ (स्वर) वर्ण इसका उच्चारण स्थान ओष्ठ है।

उँ exclamation expressing interrogation; or petulance, displeasure, &c. eh/ oh! ~ करना, to be petulant; to whimper.

उँगली [*nf*] a finger;–उठाना to reproach; to point a censuring finger at;–पर नचाना to make somebody dance to one's tune.

उँड़ेलना [*v*] to pour.

उऋण [*adj.*] debt-free;–होना to pay off a debt.

उकता/ना [*v*] to get bored or tired, to be sick [of]; ~ताहट boredom, weariness.

उकटना [*v*] to cut out: **1** to dig up, to root up; to unearth. **2** to unearth (a secret). **3** to return to, to hark back to (a matter). **4** to abuse, to revile. – ~उकट डालना, to tear up; to destroy utterly. – उकटा पुरान, an old matter brought into the open again.

उकसना [*v*] to rise, to come up, to emerge.

उकसाना [*v*] to raise, to incite, to provoke, to instigate.

उक्त [*adj.*] said, stated, mentioned.

उक्ति [*nf*] saying, statement; dictum.

उखड़ना [*v*] to be uprooted, to be struck off; to be dislodged; to be dislocated.

उखड़वाना to cause to be uprooted.

उखाड़-पछाड़ [*nf*] ado; indiscriminate wire-pulling, pulls and pushes, manoeuvring.

उगना [*v*] to grow; to germinate; to spring up; to rise.

उगलना [*v*] to spit out; to disgorge, to eject.

उग्र [*adj.*] violent, fierce; wrathful; radical; sharp.

उग्रता [*nf*] **1** fierceness, fury; cruelty. **2** direness. **3** over-intensity (as of conviction).

उघड़ना [*v*] **1** to be uncovered, exposed; to be laid bare; to be unsheathed (a weapon). **2** to be revealed.

उघाड़ना [*v*] to uncover, to expose; to bare.

उचंती [*adj.*] in suspense, not finally accounted for.

उचकना [*v*] to stand on tiptoe; to be extra-curious.

उचकाना [*v*] **1** to lift up. **2** to jerk up; to shrug (the shoulders).

उचक्का [*nm*] a swindler, a pilferer.

उचक्कापन [*nm*] **1** pilfering, thieving. **2** swindling, defrauding.

उचाट [*adj.*] affected by ennui; mentally wearied; [nm] ennui, mental weariness.

उचाटना [*v*] **1** to drive or to turn away (from, से); to scare away. **2** to cause to rebound, to deflect; to cause to splash. **3** to separate, to detach. **4** to alienate (the heart, जी, from); to dissuade (from). **5** to dishearten; to sadden, to make anxious.

उचित [*adj.*] proper; suitable; reasonable, fair; advisable; appropriate.

उच्च [*adj.*] high, tall; lofty; elevated; ~ता altitude, elevation, loftiness.

उच्चारण [*nm*] pronunciation; articulation, utterance.

उच्छिष्ट [*adj.*] leavings; remainder [esp. of food, etc.], residual; waste.

उच्छृंखल [*adj.*] licentious, unrestrained; impertinent; indisciplined, disorderly.

उच्छ्वास [*nm*] exhalation; sigh; aspiration; a chapter [of a book].

उछरना [*v*] to emerge [out of water or any other liquid].

उछल-कूद [*nf*] gambol, hopping and jumping, jumping about; frisk.

उछलना [*v*] to leap, to jump, to spring; to gambol; to rebound [as a ball].

उछालना [*v*] to toss, to throw up.

उजड्ड [*adj.* and *nm*] boorish, rude, uncivil; a ruffian; ~पन boorishness, rudeness, incivility.

उजला [*adj.*] clean; bright; white.

उजागर [*adj.*] brilliant; renowned; well-known; manifest.

उजाड़ [*adj.*] deserted, desolate, devastated; barren.

उजाड़ना [*v*] to ruin, to destroy or devastate, to render desolate.

उजाला [*nm*] light, brightness, splendour; [*adj.*] bright, shining, luminous.

उज्ज्वल [*adj.*] bright, splendid; clear; radiant.

उज्र [*nm*] an objection.

उठना [*v*] to rise, to get up; to be rented out; उठती जवानी blossoming youth; –बैठना close association; intimate relationship.

उठाईगी/र, ~रा [*nm*] a pilferer, a petty thief.

उड़द [*nf*] horse-bean, black gram.

उड़न [*nm*] act of flying ~छू होना to disappear all of a sudden, to vanish; ~ दस्ता a flying squad.

उड़/ना [*v*] to fly; to fade, to get dim; to vanish; to explode; ~ ती ख़बर an unconfirmed news; a rumour.

उड़ाऊ [*adj.*] extravagant, squandering; on the verge of a take off; –खाऊ a squanderer; squanderous.

उड़ाकू [*adj.*] flying, sky-going; capable of flying.

उड़ान [*nf*] a flight; sortie.

उड़ाना [*v*] to fly; to squander; to steal or kidnap; to explode, to blow away.

उतना [*adj.*] that much, to that extent.

उतरन [*nf*] second hand/old, worn-out clothes; cast-off clothing.

उतरना [*v*] to get down, to alight; to go down [as बुखार–]; to come off or decay; to be dislocated [as बाँह–]; to land, to disembark.

उतार [*nm*] descent; depreciation; fall; ebb-tide; down-gradient, falling gradient.

उतार-चढ़ाव [*nm*] rise and fall, fluctuation; vicissitude, variation.

उतारू [*adj.*] bent upon, intent; ready for.

उतावला [*adj.*] rash, impatient, harum scarum.

उतावलापन [*nm*] rashness, impatience; hastiness.

उतावली [*nf*] haste; impatience.

उत् a Sanskrit prefix denoting over, above, transgression, elevation, predominence, etc.

उत्कंठा [*nf*] curiosity; longing, craving; ardour.

उत्कट [*adj.*] excessive, keen, intense; richly endowed with.

उत्कर्ष [*nm*] exaltation, excellence; eminence; prosperity.

उत्कृष्ट [*adj.*] excellent; eminent, outstanding; superior.

उत्तम [*adj.*] the best; excellent, good; –पुरुष first person.

उत्तर [*nm*] an answer, a reply; north; –प्रत्युत्तर reply and counter-reply, argument.

उत्तरदायित्व [*nm*] responsibility; obligation; onus; accountability.

उत्तरदायी [*adj.*] responsible; answerable, accountable.

उत्तराधिका/र [*nm*] inheritance; succession, right of succession; ~ री inheritor; heir, successor.

उत्तरार्ध [*adj.*] the latter half.

उत्तरी [*adj.*] northern.

उत्तरोत्तर [*adj.* and *adv.*] progressive, successive; progressively, successively.

उत्तीर्ण [*adj.*] passed, got through [an examination].

उत्तेजक [*adj.*] provocative; exciting; stimulating.

उत्तेजना [*nf*] provocation; excitement; stimulation.

उत्थान [*nm*] rise [up], act of rising.

उत्पत्ति [*nf*] production, produce; birth; origin.

उत्पन्न [*adj.*] produced; born; originated.

उत्पात [*nf*] mischief, confusion, nuisance.

उत्पादक [*nm*] a producer; an originator.

उत्पादन [*nm*] production, product, produce; out-turn, output; reproduction.

उत्पीड़क [*nm*] an oppressor; [*adj.*] oppressive.

उत्पीड़न [*nm*] oppression, persecution; harassment.

उत्पीड़ित [*adj.*] oppressed; harassed; persecuted.

उत्फुल्ल [*adj.*] blossomed; delighted, in high spirits.

उत्सर्ग [*nm*] sacrifice; abandonment.

उत्सव [*nm*] festival, celebration; festivity.

उत्साह [*nm*] enthusiasm, zeal.

उत्साही [*adj.*] enthusiastic; [*nm*] an enthusiast.

उत्सुक [*adj.*] curious, eager, keen.

उथल-पुथल [*nf*] upheaval, turmoil.

उथला [*adj.*] shallow.

उदय [*nm*] rising; rise; accent, emergence; [fig.] prosperity.

उदर [*nm*] abdomen, stomach.

उदरीय abdominal.

उदात्त [*adj.*] sublime, lofty; acute [accent].

उदार [*adj.*] generous, liberal; magnificent; ~ ता magnanimity, generosity, liberality.

उदारता [*nf*] **1** nobleness. **2** generosity, liberality. – उदारतापूर्वक, nobly; generously. उदरतावाद, liberalism; ई, liberal; a liberal.

उदास [*adj.*] sad, dejected, gloomy.

उदासी [*nf*] sadness, dejection, melancholy.

उदासीन [*adj.*] indifferent, disinterested, nonchalant; ~ता indifference, disinterestedness non-chalance.

उदासीनता [*nf*] indifference, (see उदासीन)

उदाहरण [*nm*] an example, instance; illustration.

उदाहरणार्थ [*ind*] for instance, for example, e.g.

उदीयमान [*adj.*] rising, ascending.

उद्गम [*nm*] origin, fountain-head, source; rising, coming up.

उद्गार [*nm*] [expression of] inner feelings/sentiments.

उद्घाटन [*nm*] inauguration; uncovering.

उद्घोष [*nm*] proclamation.

उद्दंड [*adj.*] insolent, impertinent; rude; rebellious.

उद्दाम [*adj.*] unrestrained, unbound; violent, impetuous.

उद्दीपन [*nm*] stimulus, stimulation; provocation; incandescence.

उद्दीपक [*adj.*] **1** blazing, glowing, **2** stimulating, exiting; provoking.

उद्देश्य [*nm*] object; purpose; motive; subject [in Grammar]; end.

उद्धत [*adj.*] haughty; ill-behaved; boorish; impudent.

उद्धरण [*nm*] quotation; citation; extract, extraction.

उद्धार [*nm*] deliverance, salvation; redemption, riddance; restoration; uplift.

उद्धृत [a] quoted, cited.

उद्बोधक [*adj.*] **1** awakening, enlightenment. **2** arousing, inciting. – उद्बोधन- भाषण, keynote address.

उद्बोधन [*nm*] awakening.

उद्भव [*nm*] birth; origin; coming into existence.

उद्भावक [*nm*] an originator; one who conceives an idea; inventor.

उद्भावना [*nf*] idea, concept; imagination.

उद्यत [*adj.*] ready, prepared.

उद्यम [*nm*] enterprise; venture; exertion: diligence.

उद्यमी [*nm*] an entrepreneur; [*adj.*] enterprising; diligent.

उद्योग [*nm*] industry; labour, effort;–धंधा industry; ~ पति an industrialist.

उद्योगीकरण [*nm*] industrialisation.

उद्रेक [*nm*] overflow; abundance, preponderance, excess.

उद्विग्न [*adj.*] restless, troubled, unquiet.

उद्वेग [*nm*] restlessness, uneasiness, unquiet.

उधर [*adv.*] on that side, that way.

उधार [*nm*] borrowing; credit, loan; debt; –खाता credit account.

उधेड़ना [*v*] to unsew; to unravel; to open up; to unroll, to untwist; to excoriate.

उधेड़बुन [*nf*] lit. unpicking and weaving–hence a process of indecisive, uneasy and constant reflection.

उनचास [*adj.*] forty-nine; [*nm*] the number forty-nine.

उन [pro] those, the oblique plural form of वह.

उनताली(लि)स [*adj.*] thirty-nine; [*nm*] the number thirty-nine.

उनती (ति)स उनत्तीस [*adj.*] twenty-nine; [*nm*] the number twenty-nine.

उनसठ [*adj.*] fifty-nine; [*nm*] the number fifty-nine.

उनहत्तर [*adj.*] sixty-nine; [*nm*] the number sixty-nine.

उनींदा [*adj.*] sleepy, drowsy; dozing.

उन्नत [*adj.*] elevated, high, lofty; developed; improved.

उन्नति [*nf*] progress; rise, promotion; improvement, betterment, development.

उन्नयन [*nm*] progress; development; uplift; elevation.

उन्नायक [*nm*] champion [of a cause]; exponent; uplifter.

उन्निद्र [*adj.*] insomnolent; –रोग insomnia.

उन्नीस [*adj.*] nineteen; [*nm*] the number nineteen.

उन्मत्त [*adj.*] intoxicated; wild; crazy.

उन्माद [*nm*] insanity, lunacy, mania; intoxication; rabidity, frenzy, intense passion.

उन्मुक्त [*adj.*] liberated, free; unrestricted, unrestrained; open.

उन्मुख [*adj.*] inclined, disposed [towards]; intent.

उन्मूलन [*nm*] uprooting, rooting out; abolition; extermination, extirpation.

उन्मेष [*nm*] opening; blooming.

उन्यासी [*adj.*] seventy-nine; [*nm*] the number seventy-nine.

उप a Sanskrit prefix denoting proximity, commencement, dimunition, subordination, secondary character, etc. - अनुभाग sub-section.

उपकरण [*nm*] appliance; equipment, apparatus.

उपकार [*nm*] beneficence, benefaction; good.

उपकारी [*adj.*] beneficial; favourable; helping, obliging; [*nm*] a benefactor.

उपक्रम [*nm*] preparation; a beginning; prelude.

उपचार [*nm*] treatment, remedy; attending [upon]; formality; seasoning.

उपज [*nf*] produce, product; out-turn; crop, harvest, yield.

उपजना [*v*] to be produced; to be born; to grow; to spring up.

उपजाऊ [*adj.*] fertile, productive; ~ पन fertility, productivity.

उपदेश [*nm*] precept, sermon; preaching, teaching.

उपदेशक [*nm*] a preceptor, sermoniser.

उपद्र/व [*nm*] riot, disturbance; mischief; tumult; ~ वी riotous, rowdy; mischievous; naughty; a rioter, rowdy.

उपनगर [*nm*] a suburb.

उपनयन [*nm*] a ceremony marking the investiture of the sacred thread (यज्ञोपवीत).

उपनाम [*nm*] a pen-name; nickname.

उपनिवेश [*nm*] a colony; settlement; ~वाद colonialism.

उपन्या/स [*nm*] a novel; ~सकार a novelist.

उपपति [*nm*] a paramount.

उपबंध [*nm*] a provision, proviso.

उपभोक्ता [*nm*] a consumer; user.

उपभोग [*nm*] enjoyment; consuming, consumption; using.

उपमा [*nf*] a simile; comparison.

उपयुक्त [*adj.*] proper, suitable; appropriate; used.

उपयोग [*nm*] use, utilisation/utility; exploitation.

उपयोगिता [*nf*] usefulness, utility; use; ~वाद utilitarianism.

उपयोगी [*adj.*] useful; helpful, serviceable.

उपरांत [*adv.*] after, afterwards.

उपर्युक्त [*adj.*] aforesaid, above-mentioned.

उपलक्ष्य [*nm*], –में on account of.

उपलब्ध [*adj.*] available; acquired.

उपलब्धि [*nf*] achievement, accomplishment, attainment.

उपवास [*nm*] a fast.

उपसंहार [*nm*] an epilogue; conclusion, concluding chapter [of a book].

उपसर्ग [*nm*] a prefix.

उपस्थित [*adj.*] present.

उपस्थिति [*nf*] presence; attendance; roll-call.

उपहार [*nm*] a present, gift.

उपहास [*nm*] derision, ridicule, mockery.

उपहासास्पद [*adj.*] ridiculous, absurd, worth being laughed at.

उपाख्यान [*nm*] an episode, a subordinate tale or story; anecdote.

उपादान [*nm*] material [cause]; ingredient.

उपादेय [*adj.*] useful, of utility, beneficial.

उपाधि [*nf*] a degree; qualification; title; attribute; botheration.

उपाध्यक्ष [*nm*] Vice-President; Vice-Chairman; Deputy Speaker.

उपाय [*nm*] a way, measure; device; cure, remedy.

उपार्जन [*nm*] earning; acquisition, acquirement.

उपालंभ [*nm*] complaint; reproach.

उपासक [*nm*] a worshipper, an adorer.

उपासना [*nf*] worship, adoration.

उपास्य [*adj.*] adorable, worthy of worship, fit to be revered or honoured.

उपेक्षा [*nf*] negligence; neglect; disregard.

उपेक्षित [*adj.*] neglected; ignored, discarded, disregarded.

उफ़ [*interj.*] alas! oh! –न करना to endure quietly, not to utter a sigh or syllable [in face of unbearable agony].

उफनना [*v*] to boil over; to effervesce; to fume or froth.

उफान [*nm*] effervescence; ebullience, ebullition.

उबकाई [*nf*] nausea, a feeling of vomiting.

उबटन [*nm*] a cosmetic paste rubbed over the body for cleaning and softening of the skin.

उबरना [*v*] to be liberated; to get rid of, to be free; to be salvaged.

उबलना [*v*] to boil, to simmer.

उबारना [*v*] to liberate, to emancipate, to rid, to salvage.

उबाल [*nm*] boiling, seething, simmering.

उबालना [*v*] to boil, to cause to simmer; to heat till a liquid boils.

उबासी [*nf*] a yawn.

उभय [*adj.*] both; two.

उभरना [*adj.*] to emerge; to protrude or project; to bulge out.

उभार [*nm*] a bulge, bulging; bossing; projection or protrusion.

उमंग [*nf*] aspiration; gusto, zeal.

उमड़ना [*v*] to surge; to overflow, to flood, to burst with; to gust, to gather thick.

उमदा [*adj.*] nice, fine, excellent.

उमस [*nf*] sultriness, sultry weather.

उम्मीद [*nf*] hope, expectation.

उम्मीद/वार [*nm*] a candidate; ~ री candidature.

उम्र [*nf*] age, lifetime.

उरोज [*nm*] the female breast.

उर्फ़ [*nm*] alias.

उर्वर [*adj.*] fertile, productive; ~ ता fertility, productivity, fecundity.

उर्वरक [*nm*] fertiliser.

उलझन [*nf*] complication; entanglement; perplexity.

उलझना [*v*] to be entangled, to be involved or ravelled up; to become complicated; to be entwined [as रस्सी].

उलटना [*v*] to overturn or be overturned; to subvert; to turn over.

उलट-फेर [*nf*] shuffling, upsetting; changes; vicissitudes.

उलटा [*adj.*] reverse/reversed; topsy-turvy; opposite, contrary; overturned; inverted; –चोर कोतवाल को डाँटे the thief threatening the policeman; –पुलटा topsy-turvy deranged; confused, higgledy-piggledy; –सीधा absurd, irrelevant; hurriedly performed; उलटे बाँस बरेली को carrying coals to New-castle.

उलटी [*nf*] vomit, vomiting; [a] upside down; topsy-turvy; backwards; –पट्टी पढ़ाना to poison the mind of, to mislead;–समझ perverted/erroneous understanding, perversion.

उलाहना [*nm*] complaint; twitting, reproach.

उलीचना [*v*] to drain out, to empty [something full of water or other liquid] with the help of some device or one's palm.

उल्का [*nf*] a falling star, meteor; flame; firebrand.

उल्था [*nm*] rendering into another language, a free translation; interpretation.

उल्लंघन [*nm*] violation; contravention.

उल्लास [*nm*] joy, delight, merriment; revelry; elation; a chapter [of a book].

उल्लू [*nm*] an owl; an idiot, a fool.

उल्लेख [*nm*] mention, reference; citation, quotation.

उल्लेखनीय [*adj.*] remarkable; worthy of being mentioned.

उस [*pro.*] oblique singular form of वह.

उसाँस [*nf*] a sigh.

उसूल [*nm*] a principle.

उस्तरा [*nm*] a razor [blade].

उस्ताद [*nm*] a teacher; master; [*adj.*] cunning, tricky.

उस्तादी [*nf*] adtfull, teaching, tact, ingenuity.

उस्तुरा [*nm*] see, उस्तरा।

उहदा same as ओहदा a rank.

ऊ the sixth vowel and the sixth letter of the Devanagāri: alphabet.

ऊ - देवनागरी वर्णमाला का छठा (स्वर) वर्ण है। इसका उच्चारण स्थान ओष्ठ है। यह 'उ' का दीर्घ रूप है। कहीं-कहीं यह अव्यय के रूप में भी और सर्वनाम के रूप में, वह के अर्थ में प्रयुक्त होता है।

ऊँघ [*nf*] drowsiness; sleepiness. – ~ आना (को), to become drowsy.

ऊँघन [*nf*] dozing, drowsiness (= ऊँघ).

ऊँघना [*v*] to doze, to nap; to be sleepy/drowsy.

ऊँच-नीच [*nf*] pros and cons; good and evil; ups and downs; high and low; an untoward incident.

ऊँचा [*adj.*] high, lofty, elevated; –सुनना to be hard of hearing; ऊँची दुकान फीका पकवान great boast, little roast.

ऊँचाई [*nf*] height, altitude, elevation; loftiness.

ऊँछना v.t. to comb (the hair).

ऊँट [*nm*] a camel; (देखिए)–किस करवट बैठता है [let's] wait and watch/see how things turn out;–के मुँह में जीरा a drop in the ocean.

ऊँटनी [*nf*] a female camel.

ऊँहूँ [*interj.*] denoting refusal.

ऊटपटांग [*adj.*] slipslop; absurd, ridiculous, incoherent.

ऊद [*nm*] an otter, a beaver, a fool. – ऊद-बिलाब, an aquatic cat.

ऊदा [*adj.*] violet.

ऊत [*adj.*] idiotic, doltish.

ऊध/म [*nm*] hurly-burly, shindy; uproar; mischief; ~ मी mischievous, naughty.

ऊन [*nf*, also *nm*] wool; [a] less [than], small, trifling.

ऊनी [*adj.*] woollen, woolly.

ऊपर [*adv.*] on, upon; above; upward; over; –ऊपर (से) externally, superficially.

ऊपरी [*adj.*] upper; superficial, artificial, showy.

ऊब [*nf*] boredom, tedium, monotony; ennui.

ऊबड़-खाबड़ [*adj.*] ruffled, uneven.

ऊबना [*v*] to be bored, to feel irked.

ऊर्जस्वी [*adj.*] strong, glorious, powerful, potent.

ऊर्जा [*nf*] energy.

ऊर्ध्व [*adv.*] on high, above [*adj.*] erect, raised [*nm*] standing posture (of body).

ऊर्ध्वगति [*nf*] beatitude, salvation, final emancipation.

ऊर्ध्वगामी [*adj.*] attaining emancipation, rising above.

ऊर्ध्वलोक [*adj.*] heaven, the sky.

ऊर्मि [*nf*] a wave, affliction, motion, pain, agony.

ऊल-जलूल [*adj.*] slob, slipslop, irrelevant, absurd, ridiculous.

ऊषण [*nm*] black pepper. 2. dry ginger.

ऊष्म [*nm*] warmth.

ऊष्मा [*nf*] heat.

ऊसर [*nm*] barren or fallow [land].

ऊह [interj.] exclamation of pain, distress, or of astonishment, or of indifference.

ऊह [*ind.*] reasoning, deliberation; inference. – ऊहापोह, m. inferring and denying: uncertainty, indecision.

ऊहापोह [*nm*] reflection on pros and cons [of a problem]; indecisive reflection.

ऋ the seventh vowel and the seventh letter of the Devanagari: alphabet. In Hindi, however, ऋ is used in writing only तत्सम words, and is not accepted as a vowel within the Hindi phonetic set-up.

ऋ - देवनागरी वर्णमाला का सातवाँ (स्वर) वर्ण इसका उच्चारण स्थान मूर्द्धा है।

ऋक् [*nf*] a Vedic Mantra, [*nm*] the Rigveda.

ऋका/र [*nm*] the letter ऋ [ri] and its sound; ~ रांत [a word] ending in ऋ [ri].

ऋक्थ [*nm*] inheritance, legacy.

ऋचा [*nf*] a Vedic hymn.

ऋजु [*adj.*] straight; simple; not crooked.

ऋजुता [*nf*] **1** directness, simplicity of manner). **2** honesty, uprightness.

ऋण [*nm*] a debt; loan; minus.

ऋणी [*adj.* & *nm*] **1** adj. indebted (to, का) **2** under obligation (to). **3** m. a debtor.

ऋणात्मक [*adj.*] negative; pertaining to or concerning a debt.

ऋणी [*adj.*] indebted; [*nm*] a debtor.

ऋत [*nm*] a fixed order, cosmic order.

ऋतु [*nf*] season.

ऋद्धि [*nf*] prosperity, accomplishment; wealth and prosperity.

ऋषि [*nm*] a sage, seer; preceptor.

ए the Eights vowel and the eighth letter of the present day Devanagari: alphabet. [If ऋ [ri] and also ऌ [lri], are taken into account ए becomes the Eleventh.]

ए - देवनागरी वर्णमाला का 11वाँ, ऋ, ऌ, को छोड़ने पर 8वाँ (स्वर) वर्ण है। इसका उच्चारण स्थान कंठ व तालु है। 'ए' स्वर वर्ण अ और इ के योग से बनता है।

एक [*adj.*] one, a, single, alone; [*nm*] the number one; ~ छत्र having absolute authority, autocratic; ~ रस monotonous; constant; ता monotony; ~ रूप uniform; ता uniformity; –और एक ग्यारह होते हैं lit. 'one and one make eleven' -strength lies in union; –चना भाड़ नहीं फोड़ सकता a lone soldier cannot win a battle; –थैली के चट्टे-बट्टे birds of the same flock, cast in the same mould; –पंथ दो काज to kill two birds with one stone; –परहेज सौ इलाज diet cures more than doctors; –मछली पूरे/सारे तालाब को गंदा कर देती है one fish infects the whole mass of water; –म्यान में दो तलवारें two of a trade seldom agree; –लाठी से हाँकना to rule all men with the same rod; –हाथ से ताली नहीं बजती it takes two to make a quarrel.

एकक [*nm*] a unit.

एकठा [*nf*] a small boat rowed by sculling.

एकटक [*adv.*] without blinking, without a wink.

एकड़ [*nf*] an acre.

एकतंत्र [*nm*] autocracy.

एकतरफा [*adj.*] unilateral, one way; one-sided; ex-parte.

एकता [*nf*] oneness; unity, solidarity.

एकत्र [*adj.*] together, in one place, collected.

एकत्रित [*adj.*] collected, accumulated, gathered.

एकत्रीकरण [*nm*] embodiment.

एकदम [*ind*] suddenly, in one breath; completely; [*adj.*] perfect.

एकदा [*adv.*] **1** once, at one time. **2** on one occasion. **3** at once.

एकबारगी [*adv.*] all at once, all of a sudden.

एकमत [*adj.*] having complete accord, unanimous.

एकमात्र [*adj.*] sole, solitary, the only one.

एकमुश्त [*adj. & adv.*] lump [sum]; in a lump/lot.

एकरंगा [*adj.*] monochrome; not diverse.

एकवचन [*adj.*] singular [number].

एकसार [*adj.*] even, uniform, smooth.

एकांकी [*adj. & nm*] one act [play]; ~ कार a one-act playwright.

एकांगी [*adj.*] partial, biased; one-sided.

एकांत [*adj.*] exclusive; [*nm*] solitude; seclusion.

एकांतिक [*adj.*] **1** directed towards one object (as love, or zeal). **2** pertaining to one place or region.

एकांती [*nm*] **1** withdrawn, solitary (by temperament). **2** an ascetic (esp. one devoted to a particular view, see एकांतिक).

एकांतिक [*adj.*] **1** directed towards one object (as love,

एकांतता [*nf*] privacy; seclusion, secludedness.

एकांतर [*adj.*] alternate.

एका [*nm*] oneness; unity, solidarity.

एकाएक [*adv.*] suddenly, unexpectedly, all at once.

एकाकी [*adj.*] lonely, solitary; single; ~ पन [a feeling of] loneliness.

एकाग्र [*adj.*] concentrated on the same point, intent, resolute.

एकाग्रता [*nf*] concentration [of mind], resoluteness.

एकादशी [*nf*] the eleventh day of either fortnight of the lunar month.

एकाधिकार [*nm*] monopoly.

एकार [*nm*] the vowel e (ए) and its sound; ~ रांत [a word] ending in e (ए)

एकीकरण [*nm*] integration; amalgamation.

एकेश्वरवाद [*nm*] monotheism.

एड़ [*nf*] spur; stroke of the heel.

एड़ी [*nf*] heel; एड़ियाँ रगड़ना to run about under the stress of circumstances; –चोटी का पसीना एक करना to leave no stone unturned, to put in all possible efforts.

एतबार [*nm*] confidence, trust; belief.

एतराज़ [*nm*] objection, exception.

एलान [*nm*] an announcement.

एवज़ [*nm*] substitution.

एवज़ी [*nm*] substitute; [*adj.*] officiating, acting; relieving.

एहतियात [*nm*] precaution; ~ न by way of precaution; एहतियाती precautionary.

एहसान [*nf*] obligation; beneficence; ~ फ़रामोश ungrateful.

एहसानमंद [*adj.*] grateful, obliged.

एहसास [*nm*] feeling.

ऐ the ninth vowel and the ninth letter of modern Devanagari: alphabet. [If ऋ [ri] and ऌ [lri] are also taken into account, it becomes the twelth].

ऐ - देवनागरी वर्णमाला का 12वाँ, ऋ, ऌ, को छोड़कर 9वाँ (स्वर) वर्ण है। इसका उच्चारण स्थान कंठ व तालु है।

ऐंच [*nm*] **1** pulling, dragging. **2** stretching, tightening. **3** scarcity, dearth. **4** holding aloof. **5** delay. ऐंचातानी [*nf*] a pull from two sides, persistence to hold one's view, a tug of war.

ऐंचना [*v.t.*] **1** to pull, to drag; to draw (a sword). **2** to draw (a line); to write, to scribble; to sketch. **3** to hang, to execute. **4** to winnow (grain). **5** to take in, to absorb (e.g. as lime does moisture). **6** to inhale. **7** to extort, to exact (a levy, & c). 8 to take upon oneself (a duty, & c). 9. to draw back or away. – ऐंची आँखवाला, [*adj.*] squint-eyed. – ऐंच-तानकर, [*adv.*] with effort, by hook or by crook. – ऐंचा-ताना, [*adj.*] pulled askew. ऐंचा-तानी, [*nf.*] tugging and pulling, effort; tussle, struggle; entanglement, toils.

ऐंठ [*nf*] twist, twine, ply; torque; convolution; stiffness; conceit; perk.

ऐंठन [*nf*] twist (as of strands). **2** turn, coil (as of rupe). **3** tension (as of rope). **4** contortion; spasm; colic. – रस्सी जल गई - नहीं गई, the rope is burnt, but not its coils (said of one defeated who does not accept his defeat).

ऐंठना [*v*] to twist; to contort; to extort; to warp; to fleece; to cramp; to be conceited/perky; to stiffen.

ऐंठना **1** to be twisted. **2** to writhe, to wriggle. **3** to be cramped, or contorted. **4** to become rigid, stiff, **5** to struit, (= अकड़ना). **6** to twist; to wind; to spin (as wool). **7** to make crooked: to spin (as wool). **8** to make crooked: to distort. **9** to squeeze, to wring. **10** to extort. – कान ~ to twist the ear (of, का by way of punishment). – ऐंठकर, stiffly; affectedly.

ऐंठवाना [*vt.*] **1** to cause to be twisted, *c. (by, से). **2** = ऐंठाना

ऐंठा [*nm*] reg. **1** twist, turn (= ऐंठ, ऐंठन); hank, skein. **2** = ऐंठ, string of a spinning-writhe, &c. **4** to cause to strut, &c.

ऐंठू [*adj* & *nm*] **1** adj. proud, haughty. **2** affected. **3** m. an extortionist, blackmailer.

ऐंठूपन [*nm*] **1** pride, hauteur. **2** affectation.

ऐंठूपना [*nm*] = ऐंठूपन।

ऐका/र [*nm*] the vowel ai (ऐ) and its sound; ~ रांत [a word] ending in ai (ऐ).

ऐच्छिक [*adj.*] optional, voluntary.

ऐतिहासिक [*adj.*] historic, historical; ~ ता historicity, historical genuineness.

ऐन [*adj.*] exact, just.

ऐनक [*nf*] spectacles.

ऐब [*nm*] defect; vice; ~ दार defective, having lapses or demerits.

ऐबी [*adj.*] defective, faulty; having defective limbs; vicious.

ऐयार [*adj.*] shrewd, wily, sly; [*nm*] a shrewd person, a skilled manipulator having the requisites of a gifted detective.

ऐयारी [*nf*] wiliness, shrewdness.

ऐयारपन [*H.*] **1** cunning; villainy. **2** a wizrd's magical power.

ऐयाश [*adj.* and *nm*] [a] debauch, lewd, one addicted to luxurious life.

ऐयाशी [*nf*] debauchery, lewdness, lechery; luxurious living.

ऐरा-ग़ैरा [*adj.*] inferior, trifling, having no status; alien; –नत्थू खैरा,–पचकल्यानी Tom, Dick and Harry.

ऐरावत [*nm*] **1** mythollogical. the name of Indra's elephant. **2** a thunder-cloud.

ऐलान [*nm*] = एलान babble.

ऐवान [*nm*] **1** palace (esp. royal). **2** hall, chamber; gallery; portico.

ऐश [*nm*] enjoyment, luxury.

ऐश्वर्य [*nm*] opulence; prosperity, glory and grandeur. babble.

ऐश्वर्यीय [*nm*] **1** supremacy, dominion. **2** superhuman power or quality; divine majesty. **3** grandeur, pomp; majesty. **4** prosperous state. – ऐश्वर्य-प्रेम, love of grandeur, ostentation. ई, adj. ऐश्वर्यवान, adj. prosperous, affluent. ऐश्वर्यशाली.

ऐसा [*adj.*] such, of this type; –वैसा trifling, of no consequence.

ऐसे [*adv.*] in this way, thus; [*adj.*] such, of this type.

ऐहिक [*adj.*] mundane, worldly, secular.

ऐहलौकिक [*adj*] of this world (cf. ऐहिक).

ओ the tenth vowel and the tenth letter of modern Devanagari: alphabet. [If ऋ & ॡ are also taken into account, it becomes the thirteenth].

ओ - देवनागरी वर्णमाला का 13वाँ, ऋ, ॡ, को छोड़कर 10वाँ (स्वर) वर्ण है। इसका उच्चारण स्थान कंठ व तालु है। यह अ+उ के मेल से बना है।

ओक [*nm*] **1** the palm hollowed to drink from. **2** water, &c. drunk from the hollowed palm.

ओंकार [*nm*] the sacred and mystical syllable *om* ॐ.

ओकाना [*v*] to vomit.

ओका/र [*nm*] the vowel and the sound ~(ओ) ~रांत [a word] ending in ओ [o].

ओखली [*nf*] a small mortar.

ओग [*nm*] levy, tribute. – ओग-दुवास, m. a Hindu festival held on the twelfth day of the dark fortnight of the month Bhādon.

ओगरा [*nm*] a kind of gruel, pottage.

ओगार [*nm*] juice (as of pān), running from the mouth.

ओगारना [*vt.*] to drain, or to clean, a well.

ओघ [*nm*] **1** stream, torrent. **2** multitude; collection; heap.

ओघरा [*nm*] = ओगरा.

ओछा [*adj.*] petty, mean, low, trifling, small; shallow; ~ पन pettiness, meanness, smallness; shallowness.

ओछाई [*nf*] = ओछापन.

ओज [*nm*] vigour and virility; lustre, splendour; ~स्वी vigorous and virile, brilliant; hence ~स्विता.

ओज [*nm*] **1** light. **2** splendour, lustre. **3** brilliance, fervour. – ओजपूर्ण, adv. shining, resplendent; brilliant (esp. of poetic quality or style).

ओजस्विता [*nf*] **1** splendour. **2** brilliance (esp. of poetic quality or style).

ओजस्वी [*adj.*] = ओजपूर्ण

ओझ [*nm*] entrails; paunch.

ओझल [*adj.*] out of sight; evanescent.

ओझा [*nm*] **1** a country doctor; sorcerer, wizard. **2** name of a subcommunity of brahmin. **3** a member of the ojhā sub-community.

ओझाइन [*nf*] **1** the wife of an ojhā. **2** a sorceres. witch.

ओझाई [*nf*] the practice of sorcery. – ओझाईगीरी

ओट [*nm*] a cover, shelter.

ओटन [*nm*] an appliance for cleaning cotton.

ओटना [*v*] to remove cotton seed from cotton.

ओटनी = ओटन.

ओठ [*nm*] a lip.

ओढ़ना [*v*] to cover [the body] with.

ओढ़नी [*nf*] a woman's mantle.

ओत[1] [*nf*] **1** gain, advantage; benefit. **2** surplus. **3** recovery (from sickness). – ~ पढ़ना, a profit, to be made. – ओत-कसर, profit and loss.

ओत[2] **1** woven. **2** warp. – ओत-प्रोत, crosswise and and lengthwise, warp and woof; through and through.

ओत-प्रोत [*adj.*] full of, inspired/permeated by, well mixed.

ओद [*nm*] wetness, moistness.

ओद [*adj.*] wet, moist, damp.

ओदन [*nm*] boiled rice; food.

ओप [*nf*] lustre, polish.

ओपना [*v.i. & v.t.*] **1** v.i. to be polished; to be lustrous, or beautiful. **2** v.t. to polish, & c.

ओपनी [*nf*] the process of polishing sword, dagger etc.

ओफ़ [*interj.*] Oh!, Ah me!, an expression of pain, grief, wonder, etc.

ओभी [*nf*] a pit for catching wild animals.

ओम् [*nm*] the sacred word prefixed and suffixed to the Veda mantras symbolising God Almighty.

ओर [*nm*] side, direction; initial point.

ओरहन [*nm*] = उलहना.

ओरी [*nm*] protector; supporter.

ओरी [*nf*] **1** eaves (of house). **2** bank (of pond or stream).

ओर-छोर [*nm*] the beginning and the end; the two ends.

ओल [*adj.*] pungent, edible root.

ओलती [*nf*] eaves (of thatch).

ओला [*nm*] a hailstone, hail.

ओष्ठ [*nm*] the lip.

ओषधि [*nf*] a medicinal herb; medicine.

ओस [*nf*] dew.

ओसारा [*nm*] a verandah, a porchway.

ओह [*interj.*] oh! an exclamation of sorrow or wonder.

ओहदा [*nm*] post; rank; status; designation.

ओहार [*nm*] covering; curtain of a litter (for protection, or concealment).

ओहदेदार [*nm*] an officer; an office-bearer.

ओहो [*interj.*] alas! an expression of regret.

औ the Eleventh vowel and the eleventh letter of the Devanagari: alphabet [exclusive of ऋ and ऌ which are not accepted as Hindi vowels by modern phoneticians].

औ – देवनागरी वर्णमाला का 14वाँ, ऋ, ऌ, को छोड़कर 11वाँ (स्वर) वर्ण इसका उच्चारण स्थान कंठोष्ठ है। यह अ+ओ के मेल से बना है।

औंधना [*v*] to be overturned, to be emptied, Brbh. = औंधाना, to lower (the sky with clouds).

औंधा [*adj.*] upside down, inverted, overturned, with the face downwards.

औंधाना [*v*] **1** to overtun; to upset. **2** to empty (a vessel); to pour out (water). **3** Brbh. to hang down (the head).

औंस [*nm* & *an*] ounce.

औकार [*nm*] the letter au (औ) and its sound; ~ रांत [a word] ending in au (औ).

औकाल [*adj.*] untimely; premature.

औगी [*nf*] a whip made of twisted cord, ornamental edging (on shoes), reel or skein, stick, goad.

औगी [*nf*] pit for catching large animals.

औघट [*adj.*] rough, impassable (as a road), inaccessible; unfrequented.

औचित्य [*nm*] propriety, appropriateness; validity.

औज़ार [*nm*] an instrument.

औज़ारी [*adj*] having to do with equipment, &c.

औटना [*v*] to continue to boil [for a long time] on slow fire.

औटाना [*vt.*] to cause to boil (as milk), to boil down (as milk).

औटावनी [*nf*] reg. earthen vessel in which milk is boiled.

औढ़र [*nm* & *adj.*] nm consulting one's own inclination. compassion for the lowly. – औढ़र-दानी, [*adj.*] giving at (one's) will: a title of the Lord Shiva.

औदुंबर [*nf*] *adj.* made of fig wood. made of copper. [*nm*] fig wood, copper, a vessel of fig wood, or of copper.

औदार्य [*nm*] generosity (of spirit); nobility, liberality, munificence.

औद्योगिक [*adj.*] industrial.

औद्योगिकी [*nf*] technology.

औद्योगीकरण [*nm*] industrialisation.

औने-पौने [*adj.* and *adv.*] at a discount, below par, [at] a lesser price.

औपनिवेशिक [*adj.*] colonial.

औपचारिक [*adj.*] formal; ceremonial; ~ ता formality.

औपन्यासिक [*adj.*] pertaining to, or of the nature of, a novel; [nm] a novelist.

और [*conj.* & *adv.*] more; else; other.

औरत [*nf*] a woman; wife.

औरस [*adj.*] legitimate [child]; ~ता legitimacy.

औलाद [*nf*] a progeny, an off-spring.

औषध [*nm*] a medicine, drug.

औषधालय [*nm*] a dispensary.

औसत [*adj.*] average; [nm, also nf] the average; mean.

औसान [*nm*] wits, presence of mind; –खता होना to lose wits, to be demoralised.

क the first consonant and the first member of the first pentad [i.e., कवर्ग] of the Devanagari: alphabet.

क - देवनागरी वर्णमाला का पहला (व्यंजन) वर्ण है। इसका उच्चारण स्थान कंठ है।

कंक [*nm*] a partic. flesheating bird, the white kite (white vulture), a heron.

कंकड़ [*nm*] a gravel, pebble; small piece of stone.

कंकण [*nm*] a bracelet.

कंकरीट [*nm*] concrete–a mixture of gravel, lime, cement and sand.

कंकाल [*nm*] a skeleton, bare physical frame.

कँखवारी [*nf*] an armpit boil.

कंगन [nm] see कंकण a bracelet.

कंगारू [*nm*] a kangaroo.

कंगाल [*nm*] a pauper, poor man; [*adj.*] penniless, impecunious.

कंगाली [*nf*] penury, poverty; pauperism, pauperdom; –में आटा गीला yet another misery for an already miserable man.

कँगू/रा [*nm*] niched battlement [of a castle]; an ornamental cornice; turret; ~ रेदार having niched battlement, turreted.

कंघा [*nm*] a comb; comb-shaped appliance for weaving.

कंचन [*nm*] gold.

कंचुक [*nm*] braziers; armour.

कंजर [*nm*] a nomadic tribe; [*adj.*] low-born, shabby.

कंजा [*adj.*] having greyish blue eyes.

कंजू/स [*adj.*] miserly, miser, niggardly, parsimonious; ~सी miserliness, parsimony, niggardliness.

कँटीला [*adj.*] thorny, prickly.

कंठ [*nm*] the throat; neck; larynx, voice-box; –संगीत vocal music; ~स्थ memorised, committed to memory; ~हार a necklace; –बैठना to develop a sore throat; the voice to turn hoarse; –होना to be memorised, to be committed to memory.

कंठाग्र [*adj.*] committed to memory, on the tip of the tongue.

कंठी [*nf*] a string of small beads [of तुलसी, etc.] donned esp. by Vaishnavas as a matter of faith.

कंठ्य [*adj.*] guttural.

कंडी [*nf*] a basket.

कंडील [*nf*] a lamp [made of paper clay or mica].

कंद [*nm*] an esculent tuber-root; sugar candy; an edible root [radish, etc.].

कंदरा [*nf*] a cave, cavern.

कंधा [*nm*] a shoulder; –देना to lend a shoulder in carrying a dead body; कंधे से कंधा छिलना to be over-crowded [so as to have shoulders rubbing with one another]; कंधे से कंधा मिलाना to stand shoulder to shoulder with somebody, to lend full cooperation.

कंप [*nm*] trembling (= काँप). – कँपकँपी, = कँपकँपी.

कंपन [*nm*] a tremor, quivering; shivering; trembling; vibration.

कंपायमान [*adj.*] tremu-lous, trembling; quivering, shivering; wavering.

कंबल [*nm*] a blanket, rug.

ककहरा [*nm*] alphabet, a b c [of something].

ककड़ी [*nf*] a kind of cucumber.

कक्ष [*nm*] a room, chamber; armpit; side, flank.

कक्षा [*nf*] a class, classroom; orbit.

कगार [*nm*] a precipice, scarp.

कचकच [*nf*] an altercation; a chattering/clattering noise.

कचरा,~ ड़ा [*nm*] refuse, rubbish; sweepings; debris; breezing.

कचहरी [*nf*] a court of justice, court of law.

कचाई [*nf*] rawness; imperfection; inexperience.

कचूमर [*nm*] anything well-crushed.

कचोट [*nf*] a lingering agony; a smarting pain.

कच्चा [*adj.*] uncooked; unboiled; raw; unripe; green; crude; incomplete, unfinished; rough;

imperfect, immature; inauthentic; doubtful; vague; weak; built of mud-bricks; provisional; not fast [as sleep, colour]; –असामी a temporary cultivator; –चिट्ठा bonafide detailed account, inside story, real tale; –पक्का half-cooked; half-baked; –माल raw material; –रंग not fast colour, colour that will wash out; कच्ची उम्र immature age, impressionable age; कच्ची बात loose talk; unconfirmed report.

कछुआ [*nm*] a turtle, tortoise.

कज [*nf*] a defect, flaw.

क़ज़ा [*nf*] death; destiny.

कटकटाना [*v*] to gnash; to produce a snapping or cracking sound.

कटखना [*adj.*] snappish, prone to bite; of aggressive disposition.

कटना [*v*] to be cut, to be wounded [by a blade, etc.]; to die in battle; to be destroyed; to pass away time; to complete [a journey, etc.]; to be ashamed; to be disconnected; कटे पर नमक छिड़कना to add insult to injury.

कटपीस [*nm*] cutpiece [cloth].

कटरा [*nm*] an enclosed yard [for residential purposes or turned into a market place]; a buffalo-calf.

कटाई [*nf*] harvesting; cutting; cutting charges.

कटाकटी [*nf*] bloodshed, bloody encounter; hostilities.

कटाक्ष [*nf*] a side-glance, ogling, leer; a taunt, taunting remark.

कटार [*nf*] a dagger, poniard.

कटाव [*nm*] erosion; recess.

कटु [*adj.*] bitter; unpleasant.

कटोरदान [*nm*] a tiffin-carrier.

कटोरा [*nm*] a big bowl.

कटौती [*nf*] rebate, discount; deduction; reduction; cut.

कट्टर [*adj.*] strict; obdurate; dogmatic; fanatic; rabid; ~ पंथी a religioner, dogmatic; fanatic, bigot.

कठघरा [*nm*] a bar, dock; a wooden enclosure.

कठपुतली [*nf*] a puppet; an underling.

कठमुल्ला [*nm*] a bigot, fanatic; quack religious leader.

कठि/न [*adj.*] difficult, arduous; tough; stiff; hard; severe; ~नता/नाई difficulty.

कठोर [*adj.*] hard; severe, stern, stringent, rough, cruel; rigid, rigorous.

कड़कड़ाना [*v*] to crack/crackle [as oil, etc., on boiling]; to break with a crackling sound; decrepitate.

कड़वा [*adj.*] bitter; unpleasant.

कड़ा [*adj.*] hard; strict; stiff; harsh, cruel; arduous; sharp; rigid; strong; [nm] a bangle, metal ring.

कड़ा/का [*nm*] a loud crack; going without food, a rigid fast; ~ के का severe [as जाड़ा]; sharp.

कड़ा/ह [*nm*] a big boiling pan; frying pan; ~ ही [diminutive, nf].

कढ़ाई [*nf*] embroidery; the process or act of embroidering; a huge frying pan.

कण [*nm*] a particle; an iota, very small quantity; granule.

क़तई [*adv. & adj.*] wholly, entirely; finally; certainly; final; conclusive.

कतरना [*v*] to clip, to chip; to cut; to pare; to scrim.

कतर-ब्योंत [*nf*] contrivance, manipulation, adjustment and readjustment.

क़तरा [*nm*] a drop; fragment; cutting.

कतराना [*v*] to slink away [from]; to go out of the way [of], to avoid an encounter or coming face to face.

कताई [*nf*] [the act of or wages paid for] spinning.

क़तार [*nf*] a line, row; series.

कत्थई [*adj.*] catechu-coloured.

कत्था [*nm*] catechu.

क़त्ल [*nm*] murder; slaughter.

कथन [*nm*] saying, statement, utterance; speech.

कथनी [*nf*] anything said or uttered; speech; –और करनी profession and practice.

कथा [*nf*] a story, tale, fable; narrative; religious discourse; ~ सार a synopsis.

कथानक [*nm*] the plot.

कथोपकथन [*nm*] the dialogue.

कथ्य [*nm*] content, subject-matter; [*adj.*] worth saying.

क़द [*nm*] size; height; –काठी stature; figure and frame.

क़दम [*nm*] step, pace; foot-step; -ब-क़दम step by step; in the footsteps of; slowly; ~ बोसी kissing the feet [as a mark of deep respect or for flattering].

कदाचित् [*adv.*] perhaps, possibly, may be.

कदापि [*adv.*] ever; –नहीं never.

क़द्दावर [*adj.*] tall and towering, possessing an imposing stature.

कद्दू [*nm*] a pumpkin; gourd.

क़द्र [*nf*] worth, merit; estimation, appreciation; ~दाँ, ~दान a connoisseur, just appreciator; patron.

कनखी [*nf*] an ogle, a leer; side-glance; a sign with an eye.

कनस्तर [*nm*] a canister.

क़नात [*nf*] an awning, curtain; can screen.

कनी [*nf*] a particle; broken piece of rice; diamond dust; drop.

कन्नी [*nf*] border; the ends of a kite; edge; trowel; –काटना to slink away, to evade.

कन्या [*nf*] a virgin; daughter; girl; ~ दान giving away a daughter in marriage.

कप/ट [*nm*] fraud, ruse, guile; artifice; trickery; hypocrisy; dissimulation; ~टी dissimulator, crafty, fraudulent.

कपड़ा [*nm*] cloth; clothing; fabric; textile; –लत्ता clothings; articles of apparel; clothes.

कपाट [*nm*] [the leaves of] a door; shutter; sluice; valve.

कपाल [*nm*] the skull, head, cranium; destiny; a begging bowl; –क्रिया the ceremony of breaking the skull of a corpse.

कपास [*nf*] cotton; cotton-plant.

कपूत [*nm*] an unworthy or wicked son, an undutiful son; [*adj.*] degenerate, disobedient.

कपूर [*nm*] camphor.

कप्तान [*nm*] a captain.

कफ [*nm*] phlegm, mucus.

कफ़ [*nm*] a cuff.

कफ़न [*nm*] shroud; pall; –खसोट/चोर penny-pincher; penny pinching, stingy, cheese-paring; –सिर से बाँधना to be ready to risk life or court death; to engage in a perilous venture.

कब [*adv.*] when, at what time; –कब how often; rarely.

कबड्डी [*nf*] a typical outdoor Indian game.

कबाड़ [*nm*] junk, scrap; any disorderly stuff; ~खाना a junk-store, junk-house.

कबाड़िया, कबाड़ी [*nm*] a junk-dealer; one engaged in a low occupation.

कबीला [*nm*] a tribe.

कबूतर [*nm*] a pigeon; ~खाना a pigeon house, pigeon hole; dovecot.

क़बूल [*nm*] agreement, consent; admission; confession.

क़ब्ज़ [*nm*] constipation.

क़ब्ज़ा [*nm*] possession, occupation; a handle, grip; hinge.

क़ब्ज़ियत क़ब्ज़ी [*nf*] constipation.

क़ब्र [*nf*] a grave; –में पाँव लटकाये होना to be on the verge of death.

क़ब्रिस्तान [*nm*] a graveyard, cemetery.

कभी [*ind*] sometime; ever; –कभी sometimes, now and then, occasionally.

कमंडल [*nm*] the pot used by mendicants.

कम [*adj.*] little, few, scanty; less; short; small; deficient; [adv] rarely, seldom; ~ ख़्वाब brocade, silk wrought with gold and silver flowers; ~तर smaller; lesser; –ख़र्च वाला नशीन economical and yet of a superior quality; low cost, great show.

कमज़ो/र [*adj.*] weak, feeble; ineffectual; ~री weakness, feebleness; deficiency; debility.

कमब/ख़्त [*adj.*] unfortunate, ill-fated, unlucky; ~ख़्ती misfortune, bad luck, adversity; का मारा fallen in adversity, accursed, ill-fated.

कमनीय [*adj.*] lovely, beautiful; pretty.

कमर [*nf*] waist, loins, girdle; the middle part of something; ~ बंद a girdle; –कसना to gird up one's loins, to be all set for action; –टूटना to be rendered hopeless; to be demoralised, to lose all self-confidence; –बाँधना to get ready for, to resolve; –सीधी करना to relax for a while.

कमरा [*nm*] a room, chamber.

कमल [*nm*] a lotus flower and its plant.

कमाई [*nf*] earnings.

कमाऊ [*adj.*] earning.

कमान [*nm*] a bow; an arch; a curve; command.

क़माना [*v*] to earn; to merit; to process [leather, etc.]; to clean [w.c., etc.]

कमानी [*nf*] a spring; ~दार fitted with a spring.

कमाल [*nm*] a miracle, wonder; excellence, miraculous perfection.

कमी [*nf*] deficiency; shortage, paucity, lack, want, scarcity, scantiness; abatement; defect, failing; reduction.

कमीज़ [*nf*] a shirt.

कमीना [*adj.*] mean, wicked, vile; ~पन meanness, wickedness.

क़यामत [*nf*] the day of judg-ment, the day of resurrection; anni-hilation, destruction; –बरपा करना to raise a commotion, to create a stir; to bring about a devastating crisis.

कर [*nm*] a hand; ray; the trunk of an elephant; tax, duty, custom; tribute; as a suffix it imparts the sense of an agency or agent.

करतब [*nm*] a feat; performance; exploits; skill; acrobatics, jugglery.

करतार [*nm*] the Creator, the Master.

करतूत [*nf*] misdeed, evil deed; doing.

करना [*v*] to do; to perform; to complete; to act; to execute; to commit; to hire; to have as man or wife; to run or set up [as दुकान–]; to practise [as वकालत–]; to solve [as सवाल–]; to cohabit. मेरा जी बाहर जाने को कर उठा, I suddenly felt a longing to get away. **4** to put, to place (often कर देना); to arrange, dispose of: to apply; to set up, to establish; to convey. वापस ~, to return (sthg). उसने पानी घड़े में कर दिया, he poured the water into the pot. दीवार पर रंग करो! paint the wall! **5** to attend to. चौका (बरतन) ~, to do the dishes. **6** to make use of, to avail oneself of. रिक्शा ~, to go by rickshaw. दवा ~, to take medicine. धोती करना, to wear a dhotī **7** to make, to form, to produce; to devise, to contrive (usu. कर लेना); to work (an appliance). चोटी ~, to do one's hair (a woman). रोटी ~, to make the bread, to do the cooking. **8** to appoint (to a post). **9** to impart, to bestow. **10** to render, to cause to be or to become (often कर देना); to turn or to change (into).

करनी [*nf*] doing, deed; a mason's trowel.

करवट [*nf*] lying on one side, the position of lying or sleeping on one side; a bank.

करामत a miracle performed by a saint or a righteous man.

करामात [*nf*] a miracle; thaumaturgy; feat.

करामाती **1** miraculous, marvellous. **2** a person having supernatural power; magician.

करार [*nm*] an agreement, a contract; commitment, undertaking; ~नामा a written agreement.

करारा [*adj.*] crisp; strong; stout, sturdy; sharp.

कराहना [*v*] to groan, to moan, to cry in pain.

करिश्मा [*nm*] a miracle, miraculous feat, magic.

क़रीना [*nm*] orderliness; method; symmetrical techniques.

क़रीब [*adv.*] near, close by; about, approximately, almost.

करुण [*adj.*] touching; pathetic, tragic.

करुणा [*nf*] pity, compassion, pathos; benignity; tenderness of feelings.

करोड़ [*adj. & nm*] ten million; ~पति a multi-millionaire.

कर्कश [*adj.*] hard, harsh, screechy; hoarse.

कर्ज़ [*nm*] loan; debt; ~दार a debtor.

कर्ण [*nm*] an ear; helm; rudder [of a boat]; hypotenuse.

कर्तव्य [*nm*] duty; [*adj.*] proper/fit to be done, what ought to be done.

कर्ता [*nm*] doer; the Creator; subject [in Grammar]; head of a joint Hindu family; author; –धर्ता all in all; the active or the managing member of a social, political or any other unit.

कर्तृवाच्य [*nm*] the active voice.

कर्तृत्व [*nm*] the act or property of being; an agent, agency; doing; achievement.

कर्म [*nm*] deed; action; any religious action or rite; fate; object; ~ कांड the body of religious ceremonies commanded by Hindu law or convention; the cult of religious rituals; ~ कारक the objective case; ~ चारी an employee, an official, a worker, servant, member of the staff; a hand; ~ फल the outcome of one's deeds; ~ योग the philosophy of the discipline of detached action, unmindful of results; ~ वाच्य the passive voice; ~ वाद the theory that one has to face the consequences of one's action–good or bad; ~ शाला a workshop; ~ शील industrious; ~ हीन unlucky, unfortunate.

कर्मठ [*adj.*] diligent, assiduous, active and energetic [person]; ~ ता diligence, hard work, assiduousness.

कर्मणा [*adv.*] by deed, by action.

कर्मण्य [*adj.*] industrious, hard-working; active.

कर्मेन्द्रिय [*nf*] an organ of action [the hand, the foot, etc.]

कलंक [*nm*] blemish, stigma; slur, disgrace; –का टीका a blot, a mark of disgrace.

कलंकित [*adj.*] disgraced; blemished.

कल [*adj.*] sweet; soft and tender; gentle; low and weak [tone]; [*nf*] tomorrow; yesterday; peace, tranquillity, comfort; a machine or its parts; –बेकल होना to be ill at ease, to lose physical or mental normalcy, to be disturbed or disquieted; –हाथ में होना to exercise complete control, to have full sway [over].

कलई [*nf*] whitewash; tin; tin plating; stone lime, coating; show; external grandeur.

कलगी [*v*] a plume, crest; a gem studded ornament fixed in the turban; the comb [of a cock].

कलपना [*v*] to lament, to bemoan or bewail.

कलफ़ [*nm*] starch; ~ दार starched.

कलम, क़लम [*nf*] a pen; a painter's brush; a school or style of painting; graft; cutting, chopping; the growth of hair on man's temples; ~दान a pen and ink case; pen-tray, pen-stand; ~ बंद penned, put into black and white, reduced to writing, written; –करना to chop off, to cut; to prune; –तोड़ना to work wonders in one's writing, to write amazingly well.

कलमा [*nm*] the basic statement or confession of Mohammedan faith.

कलसा [*nm*] a metal picher.

कलह [*nm*] quarrel, scramble, strife, broil; dispute.

कलाँ [*adj.*] large, larger; big, bigger; elder.

कला [*nf*] art, craft, skill; a portion, division; a digit or one sixteenth of the moon's diameter; sport, play; degree; very minute division of time; ~ कार an artist; ~ कृति a work of art, an artistic creation; ~ बाज़ an acrobat; ~ बाज़ी acrobatics, acrobatic feat, taking a somersault; ~ वंत an artiste, possessed of artistic skill.

कलाई [*nm*] wrist.

कलि ~ युग ~ [*nm*] the kali age, the fourth and the last age of the universe according to the Hindu mythology; [fig.] the age of vice.

कली [*nf*] a bud; gusset; [fig.] a maiden who has yet to attain youth.

कलुष [*nm*] turbidity, impurity; sin; [*adj.*] turbid, impure; sinful, wicked.

कलूटा [*adj.*] blacky, dark-complexioned.

कलेंडर [*nm*] a calendar.

कलेजा [*nm*] liver; heart; courage; –छलनी होना to be afflicted by taunts and sarcastic remarks; –जलना to suffer extreme agony, to be heartsore; –टूटना to lose all hope, to be completely demoralised; –ठंडा/तर होना to be fulfilled or gratified, to be assuaged [on account of an adversary's distress]; –धकधक करना to have a violent heart-throb [on account of fear, apprehension, etc.]; –निकाल कर रख देना to surrender one's all; to give away what is best or dearest; –पत्थर का करना to become stone-hearted; to get ready to face the worst eventuality; –फटना to have the heart rent by deep sorrow; –मुंह को आना to be restless on account of grief; कलेजे का टुकड़ा core of one's heart, something or somebody dearest to one's heart; कलेजे पर साँप लोटना to be struck with jealousy, to be under a sense of deep grief [on recollection of some unwelcome event]; to repine; कलेजे में तीर लगना to be deeply wounded emotionally; कलेजे से लगाना to embrace fondly, to caress.

कल्पना [*nf*] imagination; fiction; supposition, assumption; –शक्ति imagination, imaginative faculty.

कल्पनातीत [*adj.*] unimaginable, beyond imagination; incomprehensible.

कल्याण [*nm*] welfare, benediction.

कल्ला [*nm*] a sprout; interior part of the cheek.

कल्लोल [*nm*] play, sport, frolic.

कवच [*nm*] an armour; amulet; shell.

कवयित्री [*nf*] a poetess.

कवर्ग [*nm*] the ka-pentad of five soft-palatal consonants in the Devanagari: script, viz., क, ख, ग, घ, ङ.

क़वायद [*nm*] exercise, drill.

कवि [*nm*] a poet; –समय age-old traditional description.

कविता [*nf*] poetry; a poem.

कवित्व [*nm*] poetic content or quality; –शक्ति poetic faculty/power.

क़व्वाली [*nf*] a form of group vocal music and song.

कश [*nm*] a whip, lash; drawing, pulling; whiff, puff, inhalation; a suffix used to denote one who pulls or lifts, e.g., मेहनतकश~मकश struggle, divergent pulling, wrangling. .

कशीदा [*nm*] ornamental needlework, embroidery.

कष्ट [*nm*] suffering, pain; hardship; distress; ~साध्य difficult; troublesome; onerous.

कस [*nm*] assay, test; strength, power; ~बल strength, power.

कसक [*nf*] smarting pain, aching sensation; internal pain; lingering agony.

कसकना [*v*] to have an aching sensation/lingering agony.

कसना [*v*] to tighten; to fasten; to bind; to gird up, to brace; to test [on a touchstone]; to assay; to reduce to thin shreds.

क़सबा [*nm*] a township, small town.

क़सम [*nf*] oath, swearing; –खाना to swear, to take an oath; –खाने को nominally; –तोड़ना to violate an oath;–दिलाना to administer an oath [to]; to make one swear; to put under an oath.

कसर [*nf*] deficiency; loss; drawback; lacuna; shortcoming; –खाना/उठाना to suffer loss or damage; –पूरी होना be compensated; to be avenged.

कसर/त [*nf*] physical excercise; abundance, plenty; ~ती athletic; built-up by physical exercise [as body].

क़साई [*nm*] a butcher; [*adj.*] cruel, pitiless; ~खाना/घर butchery, slaughter house.

कसा/ला [*nm*] toil, labour; –ले का toilsome [business].

कसाव [*nm*] tightness; the quality of being well-knit; terse [language style]; muscularity.

क़सूर [*nm*] fault; guilt; ~वार a guilty person.

कसैला [*adj.*] astringent.

कसौटी [*nf*] a touchstone; test, criterion.

क़हक़हा [*nm*] a burst of laughter.

क़हत [*nm*] famine; utter scarcity.

कहना [*v*] to say, to state, to tell, to utter; [nm] saying, utterance, order; advice; –सुनना persuation, inducement; wrangling; कह-बदकर with explicit resolution, challengingly; कहें खेत की, सुनें खलिहान की to talk of chalk and to hear of cheese.

कहाँ [*adv.*] where; –अमुक, कहाँ अमुक the one being no match to the other, a world of difference between the two.

कहा [*nm*] saying, advice, order; –सुनी altercation, verbal duel.

कहानी [*nf*] a story, tale.

कहावत [*nf*] a saying, proverb.

कहीं [*ind*] somewhere; anywhere; lest; –कहीं in some cases/ places; –की ईंट कहीं का रोड़ा, भानुमती ने कुनबा जोड़ा a queer combination of heterogeneous elements; –बूढ़े तोते भी पढ़ते हैं? Can you teach an old woman to dance?

काँच [*nm*] glass; intestinum rectum; the end of the lower garment [dhoti] which is tucked up to the waist at the back.

काँटा [*nm*] a thorn, spicule; fork; hook; fishing hook; prong; balance; the tongue of a balance; hands of a watch; the process of testing the correctness of a multiplication sum; bone of fish; obstacle; seeds of distress or misfortune; काँटों में घसीटना to embarrass [by undue exaltation].

काँटेदार [*adj.*] thorny; prickly, spiky.

कांड [*nm*] incident, event; sectional division; chapter; shaft.

कांत [*nm*] husband; [*adj.*] lovely, pleasant; pleasing.

कांति [*nf*] brightness, lustre, splendour, gloss; loveliness.

काँपना [*adj.*] to tremble; to quiver; to shiver.

काँव-काँव [*nf*] crowing; unpleasant sound/words.

काँसा [*nm*] bronze.

का a post-position expressive of genitive case–of, belonging to, pertaining to, related with.

काइयाँ [*adj.*] cunning, shrewd, crafty [man].

काई [*nf*] moss; –सी फटना to be scattered, to go helter-skelter.

काक [*nm*] a crow; cunning fellow.

काग [*nm*] a crow; cork.

काग़ज़ [*nm*] paper; ~ पत्र documents; papers.

काग़ज़ात [*nm*] papers, documents.

काग़ज़ी [*adj.*] made of paper; documentary, written; [e.g.–सबूत]; having a thin rind [e.g. –बादाम]; action limited merely to paper; delicate; [nm] a paper merchant; –सबूत documentary/ written evidence.

काजल [*nm*] collyrium; soot.

क़ाज़ी [*nm*] a Muslim judge or magistrate; one who performs the ceremony of *nikah* in a Muslim marriage.

काजू [*nm*] a cashew nut.

काट [*nm*] a cut; [act of] cutting; section; rebuttal; counter; erosion; incision; dissection.

काट/ना [*v*] to cut; to chip; to chop; to bite; to trim; to prune; to shear; to reap; to mow; to interrupt [e.g., बात ~ ना]; to fell [e.g., पेड़ ~ ना]; to pass/mark [e.g., वक्त ~ ना]; to while away; to fleece; to divide a number leaving no remainder.

काठ [*nm*] wood; timber; a block; [fig.] wooden, feelingless person; –कबाड़ lumber, useless or cumberous material; –का उल्लू an absolute blockhead; –की हाँड़ी a means for dupery.

काठी [*nf*] a saddle; frame; structure.

काढ़ना [*v*] to embroider; to extricate; to draw; to comb [hair].

काढ़ा [*nm*] a decoction.

कातना [*v*] to spin.

कातिक [*nm*] the eighth month of the Hindu calendar.

क़ातिल [*nm*] a murderer.

कान [*nm*] an ear; –का कच्चा easily misguided; too credulous; –खाना to pester, to dig into the ears [of]; –पर जूं न रेंगना to be utterly heedless; –फूटना to become deaf; to be deafened; –भरना to poison the ear [of], to excite dissension by tale-bearing; –में (कोई बात) डाल देना to apprise somebody [of something]; कानों-कान खबर न होना to have a veil of absolute secrecy; not to allow a secret to be divulged.

काना [*adj.*] one-eyed; [a fruit]/ partly eaten away by insects; having slight obliquity [as कपड़ा]; ~ फूसी whispering; tell-tale.

कानू/न [*nm*] law; ~न legally, lawfully; by law; ~ नी legal, lawful.

कापी, कॉपी [*nf*] an exercise book; a copy.

काफ़िर [*nm*] a disbeliever [in the tenets of Islam]; an atheist; [*adj.*] infidel; merciless.

क़ाफिला [*nm*] a caravan, convoy.

काफ़ी [*adj.*] enough, sufficient, adequate; [nf] coffee.

क़ाबिल [*adj.*] able; worthy; capable, competent.

क़ाबिलियत [*nf*] ability, capability, competence.

काबू [*nm*] control; hold.

काम [*nm*] work, task; job; employment; performance; function; passion, lust; desire; needlework; embroidery; –कला the art of love; ~देव Cupid, god of love; ~बाण the fire of passion, the flowery arrows of Cupid; –भावना amoristic sentiment; –वासना libido, sexual craving; ~ वृत्ति sexual instinct; –तमाम करना to put an end to; to destroy; to undo; to kill; –बनना to have a purpose served; –से काम रखना to mind one's own business; –होना to have one's purpose served; to have to do a job.

कामकाजी [*adj.*] busy; active; industrious.

कामगार [*nm*] a worker, labourer, labour.

कामचलाऊ [*adj.*] work-able, serviceable; caretaker [government]; answering as a makeshift.

कामचोर [*adj.*] malingerer, shirker.

काम/धंधा [nm] work; occupation, business; –धाम.

कामना [*nf*] desire; lust, passion.

कामया/ब [*adj.*] successful; ~ बी success.

कामिनी [*nf*] a [lustful] woman; a beautiful lady.

कामी [*adj.*] sexually crazy, libidinous, amorous.

कामुक [*adj.*] amorous; salacious, libidinous; sensual; hence ~ ता.

क़ायदा [*nm*] a rule, practice; primer; –कानून rules and regulations.

क़ायम [*adj.*] firm; established; located.

कायर [*adj.*] coward, timid; ~ ता cowardice, timidity.

क़ायल [*adj.*] acknowledging, extending recognition [to]; consenting; convinced; –होना to be convinced; to yield; to be silenced.

काया [*nf*] the body, person; soma; ~ कल्प, ~न्तरण metamorphosis, metamorphism; rejuvenation; ~ पलट metamorphosis.

कारक [*nm*] a case [in Grammar]; factor, a suffix denoting the factor responsible for a result, e.g., हानिकारक.

कारकुन [*nm*] an agent; employee.

कारख़ा/ना [*nm*] a factory, workshop; mill; ~ नेदार owner of a factory/workshop/mill.

कारगर [*adj.*] effective.

कारगुज़ारी [*nf*] an achievement, attainment.

कारण [*nm*] reason, cause; agency, instrument.

कारतूस [*nm*] a cartridge.

कारनामा [*nm*] a feat, laudable deed; deed, doing.

कारबार [*nm*] see कारोबार.

कारवाँ [*nm*] a caravan.

कारसाज़ [*adj.*] working wonders, dexterous, adroit, efficient; trickster.

कारा/गार ~ **गृह** [*nm*] a prison; jail.

कारावास [*nm*] imprisonment; captivity; a prison.

कारिंदा [*nm*] a work agent, an agent.

कारिस्तानी [*nf*] doing; trickery, craftiness; misdeed.

कारीग/र [*nm*] an artisan, craftsman; mechanic; tradesman, workman; ~ री craftsmanship; workmanship.

कारोबा/र [*nm*] business; occupation; ~ री busy; pertaining to business; owning or having a business.

कार्टून [*nm*] a cartoon; ~ कार a cartoonist.

कार्बन [*nm*] a carbon.

कार्य [*nm*] job, task, work; function; religious function; ceremony; role; transaction; denouement [in a drama]; effect.

कार्यकर्त्ता [*nm*] a worker; an employee.

कार्यकुशल [*adj.*] efficient; ~ ता efficiency.

कार्यक्रम [*nm*] programme; ~ ण programming.

कार्यक्षम [*adj.*] potential; competent; ~ ता potentiality; competence.

कार्यवाहक [*adj.*] acting; officiating.

कार्यवाही [*nf*] action; proceedings.

कार्यसूची [*nf*] the agenda [of a meeting].

कार्यान्वित [*adj.*] executed, implimented.

कार्यालय [*nm*] an office, bureau.

काल [*nm*] time; period; age, era; tense [in Grammar]; death; famine; calamity; season.

कालकोठरी [*nf*] a death cell, solitary cell, black hole.

कालक्रम [*nm*] chronology; passage of time; ~ विज्ञान chronology.

काला [*adj.*] black; dark; strained; –कलूटा jet black; –कानून black law; –नाग a cobra; a venomous/wicked person; –पानी life imprisonment; the Andamans where the Indians sentenced for life were deported during the British regime; –भुजंग pitch dark.

कालिख [*nf*] soot, blackness; stain, stigma; –पुतना/लगना to be stigmatised, to come to disgrace, to have one's reputation sullied.

कालिमा [*nf*] blackness; stigma; blemish.

कालीन [*nm*] a carpet.

कालेज, कॉलिज [*nm*] a college.

कालौंच [*nm*] blackness, sootiness.

काल्पनिक [*adj.*] imaginary, fictitious; utopian.

काव्य [*nm*] poetry; –कला the art of poetry; ~कार a poet; –कृति a poetic work; –पाठ recitation.

काश [*ind*] Had God willed thus!

काश्त [*nf*] cultivation, farming; holding; ~ कार cultivator, farmer; tenant; ~ कारी cultivation, farming.

काहि/ल [*adj.*] slothful, lazy, indolent; ~ ली laziness, lethargy, indolence.

किंकर्त्तव्य ~ **विमूढ़** caught in a dilemma, placed on the horns of a dilemma.

किंचित् [*adj.*] a little, somewhat, slight.

किंतु [*ind*] but.

किंवदंती [*nf*] rumour; hearsay; tradition.

कि [*ind*] that; for.

किचकिच [*nf*] altercation, quarrel; useless prattling.

कितना [*adj.*] how much.

कितने [*adj.*] how many.

किताब [*adj.*] a book.

किधर [*adv.*] where, whither.

किन [*pro.*] an oblique plural form of कौन [see].

किनारा [*nm*] bank; shore; edge, border, verge; ~ कशी the act of drawing away; –करना to draw afar.

किफ़ायत [*nf*] economy, thrift, frugality; ~ शार spendthrift; frugal, thrifty; ~ शारी thrift, frugality, economy; किफ़ायती economical; thrifty.

किरकिरी [*nf*] a particle of foreign matter fallen in the eye; humiliation, disgrace.

किरण [*nf*] a ray, beam.

किराना [*nm*] grocery.

किराया [*nm*] rent, hire; fare.

किरायेदार [*nm*] a tenant.

किलकना [*v*] to produce a joyful outcry.

किलकारी [*nf*] joyful shriek/outcry.

क़िला [*nm*] a fort, castle; ~ बंदी fortification.

किवाड़ [*nf*] door leaf; shutter.

किशमि/श [*nf*] raisin; ~ शी raisin-coloured; of raisin.

किशोर [*adj.*] adolescent; youthful; ~ ता adolescence; youthfulness.

किश्त [*nf*] a checkmate [in the game of chess].

किश्ती [*nf*] a boat, ferry.

किस [*pro*] oblique singular form of कौन [see].

किसान [*nm*] a farmer, peasant.

किसी [*pro*] oblique singular form of कोई [see].

क़िस्त [*nf*] an instalment.

क़िस्म [*nf*] type; kind; quality; variety.

क़िस्मत [*nf*] fate, fortune, lot, luck; –का चक्कर/फेर [a stroke of] bad luck; –का धनी lucky, fortunate; –का लिखा the decree of fate, the dictates of destiny; –का हेठा one who is humbled by fortune, not a favourite of Dame Luck; –खुलना/चमकना/जागना/फिरना to have a favourable turn of fortune, to have an advent of good luck; –फूटना to fall into adversity, to have a stroke of bad luck.

क़िस्सा [*nm*] a story, tale; quarrel, dispute; –कहानी fiction, tales.

कीचड़ [*nm*] mud, slime, sewage, sludge; mattery discharge that collects in the corner of the eye; –उछालना to throw mud on; to indulge in denunciatory remarks [about]; to cast aspersions on one's character; to indulge in character assassination.

कीटाणु [*nm*] a germ.

कीड़ा [*nm*] an insect, a worm.

क़ीम/त [nf] price; cost, value; ~ ती precious; costly, valuable.

कीमिया [*nf*] alchemy; ~ गर an alchemist.

कीर्तन [*nm*] devotional singing/song.

कीर्ति [*nf*] reputation, fame, renown, glory; ~ मान enjoying reputation, renowned; record.

कील [*nf*] a nail; pin; peg; wedge, spike, spline; core [of a boil]; a gold or silver pin worn by women on one side of the nose.

कुँआरा [*adj.*] bachelor, unmarried.

कुंकुम [*nf*] saffron; rouge.

कुंज [*nf*] a grove, bower, arbour.

कुँजड़ा [*nm*] a vegetable vendor, green grocer.

कुंजी [*nf*] a key.

कुंठा [*nf*] frustration.

कुंड [*nm*] a reservoir; pool; cistern.

कुंडल [*nm*] a large-sized ear-ring.

कुंडली [*nf*] a coil, horoscope.

कुंडी [*nf*] a hasp; an iron chain fixed in a door [for locking].

कुंद [*nm*] a kind of flower; [*adj.*] obtuse; blunt; slow.

कुंदा [*nm*] the butt [end of a gun]; log; block of wood; handle [of an instrument].

कुँवर [*nm*] a prince; son.

कु a Sanskrit prefix meaning deterioration, depreciation, deficiency, want, littleness, hindrance, reproach, contempt, guilt; ~ दृष्टि ominous glance, a glance resulting in bad luck.

कुआँ [*nm*] a well; कुएँ पर से प्यासा आना to be at the destination and yet return frustrated; कुएँ में बाँस डालना to make a frantic search.

कुकरे [*nm*] [used in pl.] trachoma.

कुक/र्म [*nm*] evil deed, misdeed, sin; ~ र्मी evil-doer, sinner.

कुख्या/त [*adj.*] notorious, infamous, of ill-repute; ~ ति notoriety, infamy.

कुच [*nm*] the female breast; ~ मंडल the female breasts.

कुच/क्र [*nm*] a conspiracy, plot; ~ क्री conspirator, plotter.

कुचलना [*v*] to crush, to trample [over].

कुछ [*pro. & adj.*] some, a few; something; –कुछ somewhat; to some degree; –का कुछ something altogether different, something just the contrary; –गुड़ ढीला कुछ बनिया, –सोना खोटा कुछ सुनार to have some deficiency at either end; –न चलना to have no say; –भी हो come what may; –समझना to assume airs.

कुटनी [*nf*] bawd, procuress.

कुटिल [*adj.*] crooked; curved, tortuous, perverse; ~ ता crookedness; curvature; perversity, tortuosity.

कुटी [*nf*] a cottage, hut, hermitage; cut grass and weeds [for cattle to eat].

कुटीर [*nm*] cottage; –उद्योग cottage industry.

कुटुंब [*nm*] a family, household.

कुढ़ना [*v*] to fret or grieve, to begrudge, to repine.

कुतरना [*v*] to nibble; to gnaw.

कुतुबनुमा [*nm*] a compass.

कुतूहल [*nm*] curiosity; inquisitiveness.

कुत्ता [*nm*] a dog, कुत्ते की दुम कभी सीधी नहीं होती, कुत्ते की पूँछ टेढ़ी की टेढ़ी natural characteristics persist forever, a leopard never changes its stripes; curst cows have short horns; कुत्ते की मौत मरना to die a miserable death; कुत्ते के भौंकने से हाथी नहीं डरता the dog barks while the elephant passes by.

कुत्सित [*adj.*] contemptible, despicable; vile.

कुदकना [*v*] to hop.

कुदरत [*nf*] the nature.

कुनबा [*nm*] family, kinsfolk; ~ परस्ती nepotism.

कुनैन [*nf*] quinine.

कुपथ्य [*nf*] unwholesome/unsalubrious food; consuming such food.

कुपित [*adj.*] enraged, angry, irate.

कुप्पा [*nm*] a big flask; –होना to be inflated [with joy]; to become plump.

कुप्पी [*nf*] a funnel; small flask; small metallic lamp.

कुप्रबन्ध [*nm*]mismanagement, maladministration.

कुफ्र [*nm*] blasphemy, heresy; a belief that defies Islam.

कुबड़ा [*adj.*] hunch-backed; bent.

कुमक [*nf*] reinforcement; relief.

कुमार [*adj.*] bachelor.

कुमुद, कुमुदिनी [*nm* & *nf*] a lily [flower].

कुम्हड़ा [*nm*] field pumpkin, ash gourd.

कुम्हलाना [*v*] to fade; to wither; to shrivel; to lose lustre.

कुम्हार [*nm*] a potter.

कुरकुरा [*adj.*] crisp.

कुरता [*nm*] a lose-fitting upper garment.

कुरती [*nf*] a blouse [for women]; jacket, jerkin.

कुरान [*nf*] the sacred book of the Mohammedans [said to be inspired by God].

कुरीति [*nf*] condemnable/evil practice or custom.

कुरूप [*adj.*] ugly, unsightly, hideous.

कुरेदना [*v*] to rake; to scoop.

कुर्क [*adj.*] attached.

कुर्की [*nf*] attachment.

कुरबानी [*nf*] sacrifice.

कुर्सी [*nf*] a chair; plinth [of a building].

कुल [*adj.*] total; aggregate; entire; [nm] lineage, pedigree; family; ~ नाम surname; ~ पति. Vice-chan-cellor [of a university]; head of a family; –मर्यादा the dignity of a family; ~ वधू woman of a dignified family.

कुलटा [*nf* and *adj.*] [an] unchaste [woman], [*adj.*] lewd [woman]; a trollop.

कुलफ़ी [*nf*] ice-cream frozen in a conical mould.

कुलबुलाना [*v*] to wriggle; to creep; to be restless.

कुलाँच [*nf*] a leap; bound; somersault.

कुलाधिपति [*nm*] Chancellor [of a university].

कुलाध्यक्ष [*nm*] Visitor [of a university].

कुला/बा [*nm*] a hinge; hook; ~ बे मिलाना, ज़मीन-आसमान के to try to bring heaven and earth together; to build castles in the air.

कुली [*nm*] a coolie; – कबाड़ी a rag-tag.

कुलीन [*adj.*] belonging to higher castes, aristocratic, noble, of noble descent.

कुल्ला [*nm*] gargle, rinsing the mouth.

कुल्हड़ [*nm*] a small earthen bowl.

कुल्हा/ड़ा [*nm*] a large axe; ~ ड़ी a small axe.

कुशल [*adj.*] skilful, skilled, deft, proficient, dexterous; [*nm*] well-being, happiness; –क्षेम well-being, happiness; –मंगल welfare, well-being.

कुशलता [*nf*] dexterity, skill, deftness; well-being.

कुशाग्र [*adj.*] sharp; pointed; ~ बुद्धि sharp, of keen intelligence, perspicacious.

कुशासन [*nm*] bad government, maladministration.

कुश्ती [*nf*] wrestling.

कुष्ठ [*nm*] leprosy.

कुसंग~ति [*nm*]~[*nf*] bad company, evil association.

कुसुम [*nm*] a flower.

कुसूर [*nm*] fault, omission; default; ~ मंद/वार defaulter; at fault.

कुहकना [*v*] to coo; to twitter, to warble.

कुहनी [*nf*] an elbow; a hanger.

कुहरा [*nm*] fog, mist.

कुहराम [*nm*] uproar, tumult; loud lamentation, bewailing.

कुहासा [*nm*] mist, fog.

कूँची [*nf*] a brush, a small broom.

कूँड़ा [*nm*] a large shallow earthen bowl; basin.

कूकना [*v*] to coo; to warble; to wind [a watch, etc.]

कूच [*nm*] march, departure; –का डंका बजाना to commence a march.

कूचा [*nm*] a lane, bylane.

कूट [*nm*] a hill-top; enigmatical verse; [a] counterfeit; forged; false; pseudo; ~ नीति diplomacy; underhand manoeuvring; ~ युद्ध, deceptive warfare; ~ लिपि code-script.

कूटना [*v*] to pound, to pestle; to crush; to beat; to thrash.

कूड़ा [*nm*] rubbish; sweepings, refuge; trash; –करकट waste materials, rubbish, midden.

कूढ़ [*adj.*] stupid, dull-headed; ~ मग्ज़ a dullard, nincompoop.

कूदना [*v*] to jump; to skip; to leap.

कूबड़ [*nm*] a hump, hunch.

कूल्हा [*nm*] haunch, hip.

कृतकार्य [*adj.*] successful; fulfilled; one who has accomplished his assignment.

कृतकृत्य [*adj.*] fulfilled, gratified.

कृतघ्न [*adj.*] ungrateful, thankless; hence ~ ता.

कृतज्ञ [*adj.*] grateful, indebted, obliged; hence ~ ता.

कृतार्थ [*adj.*] gratified; obliged.

कृति [*nf*] a work [esp. of art or literature], composition, performance; deed; ~ कार the author, the creator.

कृती [*adj.*] creative; one who has laudable achievements to his credit.

कृत्य [*nm*] performance; duty; function.

कृत्रिम [*adj.*] artificial; synthetical; pseudo; spurious; fictitious; sham; affected; laboured.

कृदंत [*nm*] participle.

कृपण [*adj.*] miser, stingy, parsimonious, niggardly; hence ~ ता.

कृपया [*ind*] kindly, please.

कृपा [*nf*] kindness; favour; grace; kindly disposition; favourable attitude; ~ कांक्षी seeking favour; –पात्र deserving favour; favourite.

कृपालु [*adj.*] kind, compassionate, benign; hence; ~ ता.

कृश [*adj.*] lean, thin; feeble, emaciated.

कृषक [*nm*] a farmer, peasant; cultivator.

कृषि [*nf*] farming; cultivation; ~ जीवी a professional farmer.

कृष्ण [*adj.*] black, dark; [*nm*] Lord Krishna; –पक्ष the dark half of the month, the fortnight of the waning moon.

केंचुआ [*nm*] an earthworm.

केंचुली [*nf*] the slough [of a snake].

केंद्र [*nm*] the centre.

केंद्र/क [*nm*] a nucleus; centroid; ~ कीय nuclear.

केंद्रित [*adj.*] concentrated; centered.

केंद्रीकरण [*nm*] centralisation.

केंद्रीय [*adj.*] central.

केतली [*nm*] a kettle.

केला [*nm*] a banana; a plantain tree.

केलि [*nf*] amorous sport, amorous dalliance; fun and frolic; sexual intercourse.

केवट [*nm*] a boatman.

केवड़ा [*nm*] pandanus, screwpine; fragrant pandanus water.

केवल [*adj*] only, mere; merely; simply.

केसर [*nf*] saffron.

केसरी [*nm*] a lion.

कैंची [*nf*] scissors; shears; a trick applied in wrestling.

कैडा [*nm*] established standard or size; norm; scale; trick.

कैंसर [*nm*] cancer.

कैंसिल [*adj.*] cancel.

कै [*nf*] vomit, vomiting.

कै/द [*nf*] imprisonment, confinement, incarceration; bondage; ~ दी a prisoner.

कैफ़ियत [*nf*] description; account; remarks.

कैमरा [*nm*] a camera.

कैवल्य [*nm*] the ultimate realisation.

कैसा [*adj.*] of what condition or kind; what sort of; [*adv.*] how.

कैसे [*adv.*] how, in what way; what type of.

कोंचना [*v*] to prod; to goad; to coax.

कोंपल [*nf*] a new and tender leaf [just sprouting].

को a post-position denoting accusative and dative case; to; for; on the point of; towards.

कोई [*pro*] any, anybody; a few; someone; –कोई some; –न कोई someone or the other.

कोकीन [*nf*] cocaine.

कोख [*nf*] womb.

कोट [*nm*] a coat; citadel, castle.

कोटा [*nm*] quota.

कोटि [*nf*] degree, rank; quality; category; ten million, the end of a bow.

कोठरी [*nf*] a cabin; closet; cell, small room.

कोठा [*nm*] a big room [esp. in the upper storey]; an extensive chamber; a warehouse; the stomach; square [of a chess-board, etc.]; a prostitute's habitat.

कोठी [*nf*] a bungalow, mansion; a banking firm.

कोड़ा [*nm*] a whip, lash, scourge.

को/ढ़ [*nm*] leprosy, leprosis; [fig.] heinous, evil; ~ ढ़ी a leper; thoroughly indolent man.

कोण [*nm*] an angle; a corner.

कोतवाल [*nm*] the police officer incharge of a कोतवाली.

कोतवाली [*nf*] city's main police station.

कोताही [*nf*] deficiency, dearth, want; decrease.

कोप [*nm*] fury, anger, wrath.

कोफ़्त [*nf*] ennui, tedium.

कोमल [*adj.*] soft; tender; delicate; slender; a flat note in music; hence ~ ता.

कोयल [*nf*] a cuckoo.

कोय/ला [*nm*] coal, charcoal; ~ ले की दलाली में हाथ काले evil association must leave its impress.

कौर [*nm*] morsel.

कौल [*nm*] a promise; agreement; contract; statement, dictum; –करार mutual promise; –का पक्का true to one's word; –हारना to pledge [one's] word [to].

कौशल [*nm*] skill, dexterity, adroitness.

क्या [*pro*] what; –कहने/खूब excellent! well done! Bravo!

क्यों [*ind*] why; ~ कर how; ~ कि because; since.

क्रम [*nm*] order; system; method; rank; sequence; ~ ब, orderly; systematic; –से in order; respectively; ~ हीन irregular; unsystematic; disorderly.

क्रमशः [*adv.*] respectively, in order.

क्रमांक [*nm*] roll number.

क्रमिक [*adj.*] serial, successive, turn by turn.

क्रांति [nf] a revolution; ~ कारी revolutionary.

क्रिकेट [*nf*] [the game of] cricket.

क्रिया [*nf*] action, act; function; a religious performance; verb; –अकर्मक intransitive verb; –कर्म last rites, funeral rites; ~ कलाप activity; ~ पद a verb; ~ विशेषण adverb.

क्रियात्मक [*adj.*] functional; active; verbal.

क्रियान्विति [*nf*] implementation.

क्रियाविधि [*nf*] procedure; methodology.

क्रियाशील [*adj.*] active, functional.

क्रिस्तान [*nm*] a Christian.

क्रीड़ा [*nf*] a play, game, sport, dalliance; fun; –कौतुक fun and frolic.

क्रुद्ध [*adj.*] angry, infuriated, enraged, wrathful.

क्रूर [*adj.*] cruel, unkind, merciless, ruthless; ~ ता cruelty, ruthlessness, mercilessness.

क्रोध [*nm*] anger, wrath, fury, rage; ~ वश out of anger.

क्रोधित [*adj.*] see क्रुद्ध

क्रोधी [*adj.*] short-tempered, hot-tempered; irascible.

क्ल/र्क [*nm*] a clerk; ~ र्की clerical job/profession.

क्लांति [*nf*] weariness, tiredness; exhaustion, languor.

क्लास [*nf*] a class [of students].

क्लिष्ट [*adj.*] difficult, incomprehensible; far-fetched.

क्लेश [*nm*] anguish; affliction; pain; misery.

क्वार [*nm*] the seventh month of the Hindu calendar.

क्वार्टर [*nm*] a quarter.

क्षण [*nm*] a moment, an instant.

क्षणिक [*adj.*] momentary, transient, fleeting, transitory.

क्षत [*adj.*] injured, wounded, hurt; –विक्षत wounded all over.

क्षति [*nf*] loss, harm; injury, detriment; wastage; damage.

क्षतिपूर्ति [*nf*] compensation; reparation; indemnity.

क्षमता [*nf*] efficiency, competence, capacity; power.

क्षमा [*nf*] condonation; remission; forgiveness, pardon.

क्षम्य [*adj.*] pardonable, forgivable.

क्षय [*nm*] decay, decadence, loss; waste; tuberculosis.

क्षार [*nm*] an alkali.

क्षितिज [*nm*] the horizon.

क्षीण [*adj.*] feeble, weak, slender; delicate; languid; impaired; emaciated.

क्षुद्र [*adj.*] small; mean, base, petty; wicked; contemptible; hence ~ ता .

क्षुब्ध [*adj.*] agitated; excited, unquiet.

क्षेत्र [*nm*] field, ground, range; region, area.

क्षेत्रफल [*nm*] area.

क्षेम [*nf*] welfare, well-being.

क्षोभ [*nm*] agitation; excitement, commotion; fret.

ख kha the second consonant and the second member of the first pentad [i.e., कवर्ग] of the Devanagari: alphabet.

ख – देवनागरी वर्णमाला का दूसरा (व्यंजन) वर्ण है। इसका उच्चारण स्थान कंठ है।

खँखारना [*v*] to expectorate, to hawk.

ख़ंजर [*nm*] a dagger, poniard.

खंड [*nm*] a portion, part, fragment, piece, bit, scrap; lump; chunk; section; clause; block; segment; canto; volume; factor; region, division; ~ वाक्य a clause.

खंडन [*nm*] refutation; repudiation; – मंडन repudiation and vindication.

खँडहर [*nm*] ruins; a dilapidated building.

खंडित [*adj.*] broken; fragmented; split; repudiated.

खंदक [*nm*] a moat, ditch, trench.

खंभा [*nm*] a pillar, column; post, pole.

खग्रास [*nm*] complete/whole eclipse.

खचाखच [*a* and *adv*] overcrowded, overpacked; absolutely [full].

खच्चर [*nm*] a mule.

ख़जांची [*nm*] a treasurer, cashier.

खज़ाना [*nm*] treasure; treasury; repository.

खटकना [*v*] to click; to pinch, to offend; to raise apprehensions or misgivings; to be an eye-sore [to]; to have a wrangling, to become estranged [with].

खटका [nm] an apprehension, doubt; click; catch.

खटखटाना [*v*] to tap; to keep on reminding.

खटना [*v*] to toil, to labour hard.

खटपट [*nf*] wrangling, squabbling, estrangement.

खटमल [*nm*] a bed-bug.

खटमिट्ठा, खटमीठा [*adj*] having a mixed taste of sour and sweet.

खटाई [*nf*] a powder prepared from dried up [raw] mango parings [used as spice]; sourness, tartness; – में पड़ना to be kept in abeyance; to keep on dragging [some job or assignment].

खटाखट [*nf*] rap, constant clicking; tapping noise; [*adv*] quickly, briskly.

खटास [*nf*] a touch of sourness/tartness, rancidity.

खट्टा [*adj*] sour, tart.

खड़खड़ाना [*v*] to rustle; to clatter, to rattle.

खड़ा [*adj*] standing, erect; upright, straight; vertical; steep, high; stationary; unreaped [as खड़ा खेत]; whole, entire.

खड्ड [*nm*] a deep pit.

ख़त [*nm*] a letter; line; hand-writing.

ख़तरनाक [*adj*] dangerous, hazardous, risky.

ख़तरा [*nm*] danger, hazrd, risk.

ख़ता [*nf*] fault, guilt; error; ~ वार guilty.

ख़त्म [*adj*] ended; completed; concluded.

खदेड़ना [*v*] to rout; to drive away, to chase out.

खद्दर [*nm*] hand-spun coarse cloth.

खनकना [*v*] to jingle/clink, to produce a jingling/clinking sound.

खनिक [*nm*] a miner.

खनिज [*a* and *nm*] mineral.

खपत [*nf*] consumption; sale.

खपना [*v*] to be consumed; to be sold; to be destroyed/ruined.

ख़फ़ा [*adj*] displeased, angry.

ख़बर [*nf*] news, information.

ख़बरदार [*a*] cautious, watchful.

ख़/ब्त [*nm*] craze, mania, fad, eccentricity; ~ ब्ती a maniac, an eccentric; crazy, faddish.

ख़म [*nm*] a kink; bend; curl; curve.

ख़ामियाज़ा [*nm*] retribution.

ख़रगोश [*nm*] a rabbit, hare.

ख़रबू/ज़ा [*nm*] a musk melon; ~ ज़े को देखकर खरबूज़ा रंग बदलता है association inevitably breeds affinity.

खरल [*nm*] a mortar.

खरा [*adj*] pure, genuine; straightforward; upright; honest; plain speaking; overhot; [e.g., खरा तवा, खरी आँच]; –आसामी a good paymaster, a straightforward person.

ख़रा/ब [*adj*] bad; spoiled; wicked; defective, faulty; depraved; miserable; ~ बी badness, wickedness; defect, fault, demerit.

खरी [*adj*] feminine form of खरा [see]; chalk; oil cake; –खरी सुनाना to speak out the unpalatable truth; –खोटी सुनाना to give a bit of one's mind, to take to task; –मजूरी, चोखा काम good servant, good wages.

ख़रीद [*nf*] purchase, buying.

ख़रीदना [*v*] to buy, to purchase.

ख़रीदा/र [*nm*] a buyer, vendee; ~ री buying, purchasing.

ख़रीफ़ [*nf*] the kharif crop.

खरोंचना [*v*] to scratch, to bruise.

ख़र्च [*nm*] expenditure, expense; cost.

ख़र्चा [*nm*] expenditure, expense; cost, outlay.

ख़र्चीला [*adj*] spendthrift; extravagant; expensive, costly; uneconomical.

खर्रा [*nm*] a long sheet, roll [of paper]; lengthy account.

खर्राटा [*nm*] snore.

खलबली [*nf*] agitation, commotion.

ख़लल [*nm*] interruption, disturbance; obstruction.

खलिहान [*nm*] a barn; threshing floor.

ख़सम [*nm*] husband, master; –करना to take a husband.

ख़सरा [*nm*] measles.

ख़सख़स [*nm*] poppy seed.

ख़सलत [*nf*] nature, disposition.

खसोटना [*v*] to snatch, to seize quickly or unexpectedly.

ख़स्ता [*adj*] crisp; brittle; ~ हाल afflicted, in distress, ragged; brittle, fragile, worn out.

खाँचा [*nm*] a groove, recess, slit, vallecula; a big basket; coop.

खाँड [*nf*] unrefined sugar.

खाँसना [*v*] to cough.

खाँसी [*nf*] cough.

खाई [*nf*] a ditch, trench, moat; entrenchment.

ख़ाक [*nf*] ashes, dirt and dust; anything trivial; precious little; nothing whatever; –उड़ना to be ruined; –छानना to beat the air; to wander all round; –में मिलना to be reduced to dust or ashes.

ख़ाका [*nm*] a sketch, outline; map, layout; –

खींचना [*v*] to make a fun [of], to pull one's leg.

ख़ाकी [*adj*] dull yellow-coloured, dust-coloured.

खाट [*nf*] a cot, bedstead.

खाड़ी [*nf*] a bay.

ख़ाता [*nm*] ledger; account.

ख़ातिर [*nf*] hospitality; [ind] for, for the sake of; ~ जमा assurance; ~ रखना to rest assured; ~ दारी hospitality, warm reception.

ख़ातिरी [*nf*] hospitality.

खाद [*nf*] manure, fertilizer.

खाद्य [*nm*] food; [*adj*] eatable.

खान [*nf*] mine, quarry; recepticle, storehouse; an abridged form of खाना used as the first member in compound words (खान-पान).

ख़ान/दान [*nm*] family, kinsfolk; ~ दानी familial; traditional; belonging to a high or noble family.

खाना [*v*] to eat; to live on; to corrode; to misappropriate; to sting; to destroy; to squander; to take a bribe; [*nm*] food, meal; खाता-पीता well-to-do, fairly prosperous.

ख़ाना [*nm*] a shelf; column; compartment; abode; chest or case; ~ खराबी ruination; state of being homeless; ~ तलाशी search, house-search; ~ बर्बादी ruination.

ख़ानाबदोश [*nm*] a nomad, an idle wanderer.

ख़ामी [*nf*] a defect, drawback, flaw.

ख़ामो/श [adj] silent; ~ शी silence.

ख़ार [*nm*] a thorn; animosity, rancour; –खाना to nurse a spirit of rancour [against].

खारा [*a*] brackish; saline, salty; ~ पन salinity; brackishness.

ख़ारिज [*a*] dismissed, rejected.

ख़ारिश [*nf*] scabies, itches.

खाल [*nf*] skin; hide; –उधेड़ना to beat black and blue; –खींचकर भूसा भर देना to inflict severe physical punishment.

ख़ालिस [*a*] pure; unmixed.

ख़ाली [*a*] empty, vacant; unoccupied; blank; unemployed; unaccented beat [in music]; ineffective [e.g., वार-जाना]; fallow; only; mere [e.g., –बात].

ख़ास [*adj*] special; particular; peculiar; proper; important; chief; own [e.g., मेरा खास आदमी]; ~ कर particularly.

ख़ासा [*adj*] fairly good, ample.

ख़ासियत [*nf*] characteristic; peculiarity; speciality; distinctive quality; natural disposition.

खिंचना [*v*] to be pulled; to be tightened; to be expanded; to be attracted towards [–, की ओर]; to be extracted, to be removed; to be drawn [apart]; to be repelled.

खिंचाव [*nm*] strain; stretch; draught.

खिचड़ी [*nf*] a preparation of rice and pulse boiled together; a mixture, medley; hotch-potch; the festival known as मकर संक्रांति; [*a*] mixed.

खिड़की [*nf*] a window.

ख़िताब [*nm*] a title.

ख़िदमत [*nf*] service; lackeying.

खिन्न [*a*] gloom, glum, depressed; sad.

खिलखिला/ना [*v*] to burst into laughter; to laugh heartily; hence ~ हट।

खिलना [*v*] to blossom, to bloom; to blow; to be delighted; to split up, to be rent asunder; to befit.

खिलवाड़ [*nf*] frolic, fun and frolic, pastime.

खिलाड़ी [*nm*] a player, sportsman; [a] playful, frolicsome.

ख़िलाफ़ [*a*] against, opposed; adversely disposed.

खिलौना [*nm*] a toy, plaything.

खिल्ली [*nf*] derision, making fun, ridiculing.

खिसकना [*v*] to move slowly; to move farther; to slip away.

खिसिया/ना [*v*] to feel piqued/disparaged/ embarrassed; to be in an impotent rage; hence ~ हट।

खींचना [*v*] to pull; to draw; to tighten; to expand; to extract; to attract; to drag; खींचा-तानी manipulation, tussle and tugging; twisting and distorting, far-fetching.

खीझ (खीज) [*nf*] vexation, fret; hence ~ ना।

खीर [*nf*] a sweetened preparation of rice and milk boiled together.

खीरा [*nm*] a cucumber.

खुजली [*nf*] itch, itchiness, itching sensation; scabies.

खुजाना [*v*] to itch; to scratch.

ख़ुद [*pro*] self; [adv.] of one's own accord, voluntarily; –ब-खुद on one's own, self, by itself.

ख़ुदग़रज़ [*a*] selfish, self-seeking.

खुदरा [*a*] retail [goods]; small coins.

ख़ुदा [nm] God; the Lord; ~ ई Providence; Godhood; Creation.

खुदाई [*nf*] engraving, carving; digging, excavation; charges in respect thereof.

ख़ुफ़िया [*a*] detective, secret; [*nm*] a detective; spy.

ख़ुमार [*nm*] hangover [of a drink]; slight intoxication; drowsiness [resulting from inadequate sleep, etc.]

खुरचना [*v*] to scrape, to erase.

खुरदरा [*a*] rough, coarse; scabrous.

ख़ुराक़ [*nf*] dose; diet; ration; nutritive diet.

ख़ुर्दबीन [*nf*] a microscope.

खुलना [*v*] to be opened; to be uncovered; to be exposed; to be unfolded [as भेद]; to be dispersed [as बादल]; to be laid aside [as पाबंदी, etc.]; to start [as गाड़ी, etc.] to be set up [as दुकान, etc.]; to be restored [as भूख खुलना]; to become favourable [as भाग्य खुलना]; to acquire fullness or depth [as रंग खुलना]; खुलकर openly, frankly; खुलकर खेलना to indulge in misdeeds openly.

ख़ुलासा [*nm*] summary, gist; abstract; essence; [a] clear, brief.

खुल्लम-खुल्ला [*a*] publicly, openly, unreservedly.

ख़ुश [*a*] happy, pleased; good; ~ खत good handwriting; one who possesses a good handwriting; ~ दिल jovial, merry, cheerful.

ख़ुशकिस्मत [*a*] fortunate; lucky.

ख़ुशख़बरी [*nf*] good news.

ख़ुशनसी/ब [*a*] fortunate, lucky; ~ बी good fortune, good luck.

ख़ुशबू [*nf*] fragrance, aroma; perfume; scent.

ख़ुशमिज़ाज [*a*] cheerful, gay, good-tempered.

ख़ुशहा/ल [*a*] prosperous, well-to-do, flourishing; ~ ली prosperity, well-being.

ख़ुशाम/द [*nf*] flattery; ~ दी flattering; [*nm*] a flatterer, sycophant.

ख़ुशी [*nf*] joy, delight, happiness; –से फूल उठना to exult, to be in exultation, to tread on air.

ख़ुश्क [*a*] dry; withered.

ख़ुश्की [*nf*] dryness; drought; [dry] land; dandruff.

ख़ूँख़ार [a] ferocious, murderous.

खूँटा [*nm*] a stake, peg; –गाड़ना to establish oneself; to fix one's tether.

खूँटी [*nf*] a small peg; spike; stump [of a tree, etc.], root of the hair; ear of a stringed musical instrument.

ख़ून [*nm*] blood; murder; –ख़राबी bloodshed; massacre; –उतरना, आँखों में to be filled with fury; –का प्यासा blood-thirsty; sworn enemy; –के घूँट पीना to suppress one's fury; –खौलना the blood to boil; to be in a bloody rage; –पसीना एक करना to toil in the sweat of one's brow; –बहाना to shed blood; to cause bloodshed; –सूखना to be mortally scared, to be unnerved.

ख़ूनी [*nm*] a murderer, an assassin; [a] blood-thirsty, ferocious; involving bloodshed.

ख़ूबसूर/त [*a*] beautiful, pretty; handsome; comely; hence ~ ती।

ख़ूबी [*nf*] merit; characteristic, quality; speciality.

खेत [*nm*] a field, farm; –रहना to be killed in action.

खेतिहर [*nm*] a farmer, cultivator.

खेती [*nf*] farming; cultivation; agriculture; –बारी (ड़ी) agriculture, agricultural undertaking.

खेद [*nm*] regret; sorrow.

खेप [*nf*] a trip; quantity or number transported in one lot.

ख़ेमा [*nm*] a tent, camp.

खेल [nm] play, game, sport; show; –कूद sports; fun and frolic; –बिगड़ना to have a game or business spoilt; –समझना to consider damn easy; to look through one's game.

खेलना [*v*] to play; to stage [e.g., नाटक); to eat, drink and be merry; खेला-खाया well-versed in the ways of life.

ख़ैर [*nf*] well-being, welfare; [ind] well, all-right; ~ ख़्वाह a well-wisher; well-wishing.

ख़ैरात [*nf*] charity, alms; ~ ती charitable.

ख़ैरियत [*nf*] welfare; safety.

खोखला [*a*] hollow.

खोज [*nf*] search, quest, investigation; discovery; exploration; –ख़बर लेना to enquire about one's welfare.

खोजना [*v*] to seek, to search; to explore; to investigate; to discover.

खोटा [*a*] defective, faulty; false, counterfeit; spurious; adulterated, malicious.

खोदना [*v*] to dig; to engrave; to excavate.

खोना [*v*] to lose; to squander.

खोपड़ी [*nf*] skull.

खोलना [*v*] to open; to unfold; to untie; to detach; to unravel; to unroll; to unfasten.

ख़ौफ़ [*nm*] fear, dread; ~ नाक dreadful, terrible.

खौलना [*v*] to boil; to effervesce.

ख्याति [*nf*] fame, reputation, renown.

ख़्याल [*nm*] an idea; thought; view; opinion; one of the principal forms of modern Hindustani classical vocal music; –से उतरना to slip out of memory/mind; to forget; to become indifferent [to].

ख़्याली [*a*] imaginary, fancied; assumed; –पुलाव पकाना to build castles in the air, to indulge in absurd fancies.

ख़्वाब [*nm*] a dream.

ख़्वाहमख़्वाह [*ind*] uselessly, for no rhyme or reason, without any purpose.

ख़्वाहिश [*nf*] wish, strong desire; ~ मंद desirous, solicitous.

ग the third consonant and the third member of the first pentad [i.e., कवर्ग] of the Devanagari alphabet.

ग - देवनागरी व्यंजन में कवर्ग का तीसरा वर्ण है। इसका उच्चारण स्थान कंठ है।

गंज [*nf*] baldness; [*nm*] a market place.

गंजा [*adj*] bald, bald-headed.

गंजीफ़ा [*nm*] a pack or game of cards.

गँठबंधन [*nm*] wedding; intimate relationship; alliance.

गंतव्य [*nm*] destination.

गंदगी [*nf*] dirtiness, filthiness, filth; morbidity.

गंदा [*a*] dirty, filthy; morbid.

गँदला [*a*] muddy [as water].

गंध [*nf*] smell, odour.

गंभीर [*a*] serious, grave; sober; grim; reserved; deep; profound; ~ ता seriousness; gravity; sobriety; reservedness; depth; profundity.

गँवाना [*v*] to lose; to waste; to squander.

गँवार [*a*] uncivilised; rustic, stupid; ~ पन uncivilised manners; rusticity; rudeness; stupidity; vulgarity.

गँवारू [*a*] rustic; rude; vulgar; slang [language, etc.]

गऊ [*nf*] a cow; [a] meek, gentle.

गच्चा [*nm*] a pitfall; –खाना to be hoodwinked/defrauded; to be subjected to a pitfall.

गज़ [*nm*] a yard; yardstick.

ग़ज़ब [*nf*] a calamity; fury, wrath; tyranny, outrage; –का extremely amazing, wonderful; –ढाना to commit an outrage/atrocity, to be outrageous/atrocious.

गटकना [*v*] to swallow, to gulp.

गट्टा [*nm*] plug; sprag; wrist- joint; ankle; a joint or knot.

गट्ठर [*nm*] a large bundle, bale; package.

गठन [*nf*] build, structure, construction; composition.

गठरी [*nf*] a bundle, package.

गठिया *nf*] gout, rheumatism.

गठीला [*a*] compact; well-built; muscular [body]; knotty; nodose.

गड़गड़ा/ना [*v*] to gurgle; to rumble, to produce a thundering sound; hence ~ हट।

गड़पना [*v*] to swallow; to usurp.

गड़बड़ [*nf*] muddle, mess; confusion, disorder, disquiet; ~ झाला a medley, confusion, disorder.

गड़बड़ी [*nf*] see गड़बड़।

गड्डी [*nf*] a pack, bundle.

गड्ढा [*nm*] a pit, ditch; hollow.

गढ़ [*nm*] a fort, castle, citadel; stronghold; –जीतना/तोड़ना to achieve a resounding victory, to accomplish a difficult job.

गढ़ंत [*a*] imaginary, fancied; [nf] forging.

गढ़ना [*v*] to forge; to fabricate; to mould, to form, to fashion; to carve [as a statue].

गण [*nm*] a community, union, group; a body [signifying collectivity]; an attendant, agent; totem.

गणतंत्र [*nm*] a republic; republican system of government.

गणतंत्रात्मक/गणतंत्रीय [*a*] republican.

गणना [*nf*] counting; calculation, reckoning.

गणराज्य [*nm*] a republic, republican state.

गणिका [nf] a prostitute, harlot.

गणित [*nm*] Mathematics; ~ ज्ञ a mathematician; गणितीय mathematical.

गतांक [*nm*] the last issue [of a paper, magazine, etc.]

गतानुगतिक [*a*] tradition bound, traditional; ~ता traditionality, unquestioning adherence to tradition.

गति [nf] motion, movement; speed; state, condition; plight; shape, appearance; access, approach, pass; destiny; salvation; ~ विधि

activity, goings; developments; ~ शील dynamic; ~ हीन inert, inactive, static.

गति/मान [*a*] active, dynamic, moving; ~ मत्ता dynamism; activity.

गत्ता [*nm*] strawboard; card-board.

ग़दर [*nm*] a rebellion, mutiny.

गदराना [*v*] to be half-ripe; to attain the state of youthful bloom.

गद्गद [*a*] overwhelmed [by ecstatic emotion], in ecstasy.

गद्दा [*nm*] a bed cushion; cushion; pack-saddle.

ग़द्दार [*nm* and *a*] [a] traitor; traitorous.

गद्दी [*nf*] a cushion; throne; seat; pack-saddle; pad; –पर बैठना to ascend the throne; to be enthroned.

गद्य [*nm*] prose; ~ काव्य prose-poetry; गद्यात्मक prosaic.

गधा [*nm*] an ass, a donkey; a damn fool, stupid fellow; ~ पन folly, stupidity; गधे को बाप बनाना to flatter a fool for expediency.

ग़नीमत [*nf*] a redeeming feature, consoling factor.

गन्ना [*nm*] a sugarcane.

गप [*nf*] a gossip, hearsay; ~ शप gossip, tittle-tattle; chit-chat; –मारना to [indulge in boastful] gossip; to brag and boast.

गपोड़ [*nm*] a gossiper; chatterer; ~ बाजी gossiping; chattering.

गप्पी [*nm*] a gossiper; chatterer; [*a*] boastful, indulging in gossips.

गफ़ [*a*] compact, dense, densely woven.

ग़फ़लत [*nf*] negligence, carelessness; swoon, unconscious state.

ग़बन [*nm*] embezzlement.

ग़म [*nm*] sorrow, grief, woe; ~ गीन gloomy, full of sorrow; –खाना to be tolerant, to endure; –ग़लत करना to comfort or solace oneself; to drown [one's] sorrows in an intoxicant.

गमला [*nm*] a flower-pot.

ग़मी [*nf*] death; mourning, the period of mourning.

ग़रज [*nf*] thunder; roar; fulmination.

ग़रज़ [*nf*] concern; interestedness, interested motive; need; [adv] in short, briefly speaking; ~ मंद needy; desirous [of]; having an interested motive [in]; –का बावला a slave to one's interests; –बावली होती है a self-seeker has no moral code; गरज़ी यार किसके दम लगाई खिसके the dinner over, away go the guests.

गरजना [*v*] to thunder, to roar, to fulminate.

गरदन [*nf*] the neck; –उड़ाना to behead, to chop off one's head; to decollate, to cut the throat; to put to tremendous harm; –पर सवार होना to have complete sway; to subjugate [somebody], to keep on pestering; –फँसना to be embroiled in a mess; to be involved in a difficulty; to be in somebody's grip; –मारना to behead.

गरम [*a*] hot; warm; burning; fiery; zealous; ardent; woollen [cloth]; –खबर hot news; ~ मिज़ाज hot-tempered, fiery; –होना to fly into a rage, to get infuriated.

गरमागरम [*a*] hot; heated; fresh [as news].

गरमागरमी [*nf*] excitement; heated exchange.

गरमाना [*v*] to warm up; to be excited; to fly into a rage.

गरमी [*nf*] heat, warmth; summer; passion; anger, violence; ardour; syphilis.

गरिमा [*nf*] dignity, grace; gravity.

गरिष्ठ [*a*] heavy [esp. food], indigestible.

ग़रीब [*a*] poor; meek, humble; ~ खाना humble dwelling [i.e., my humble home–said out of modesty]; ~ परवर sustaining the poor, merciful to the poor; Your Exalted Self.

ग़रूर [*nm*] vanity; pride; haughtiness.

गर्त [*nm*] a pit; recess.

गर्द [*nf*] dirt, dust; –गुबार dust and dirt.

गर्दन [*nf*] the neck.

गर्दिश [*nf*] distress, trouble; vicissitudes [of fortune]; circulation, revolution.

गर्भ [*nm*] the womb; pregnancy; foetus; the interior; ~ धारण conception; ~ पात miscarriage; ~ वती pregnant; ~ स्राव abortion.

गर्भाधान [*nm*] impregnation; insemination.

गर्भाशय [*nm*] the womb.

गर्भिणी [*a*] pregnant.

गर्व [*nm*] pride; elation.

गर्हित [*a*] wicked, vile, contemptible.

ग़लत [*a*] wrong, incorrect, untrue; erroneous; improper.

ग़लतफ़हमी [*nf*] misunderstanding, misgiving.

ग़लती [*nf*] a mistake, an error; a fault.

गलना [*v*] to melt; to decay, to rot; to be boiled or cooked till softened; to be frost-bitten.

गला [*nm*] neck; throat; gullet; voice; collar [of a garment]; neck of a pot; –कटना to be beheaded; to suffer a heavy loss; to be deprived of one's due;– घोटना to throttle, to strangle; –दबाना to throttle; to choke; to exercise undue pressure; –पकड़ना to catch hold by the neck; to harass; to produce irritation in the throat [by some eatable]; –पड़ना/बैठना to develop a sore throat/ hoarse voice; –फाड़ना to vociferate, to bellow; गले पड़ना to become an encumbrance, to be obliged to endure; गले मिलना to embrace, to hug.

गली [*nf*] a lane, alley, alley-ways.

ग़लीचा [*nm*] a carpet.

गल्प [*nf*] a tale, story.

ग़ल्ला [*nm*] grain, corn; a shopkeeper's sale proceeds for the day [also the cash box]; herd, flock.

गँवाना [*v*] to lose; to waste; to suffer detriment.

गवारा [*a*] –करना to tolerate, to stand.

गवाह [*nm*] a witness, deponent.

गवाही [*nf*] evidence, testimony.

गवैया [*nm*] a singer.

ग़श [*nm*] swoon, fainting, fit; –आना/खाना to faint, to swoon.

गश्त [*nf*] patrol, beat; –लगाना to patrol.

गहन [*a*] deep; intricate; impregnable; obscure; mysterious; dense; inaccesible.

गहना [*nm*] an ornament.

गहरा [*a*] deep; profound; intimate, close [as दोस्त]; bold [as रंग]; secretive; grave [as संकट]; sound [as नींद]; intricate, unintelligible [as चाल]; strong [as भाँग]; –हाथ मारना to reap a rich harvest; to inflict a severe stroke or blow.

गहराई [*nf*] depth; profundity.

गहराना [*v*] to deepen; to become more dense; to be overcast [with].

गाँठ [*nf*] a knot; tie; node; knob; bale; bundle; joint; hardened or enlarged gland; bulb; –कटना to have one's pocket picked; –करना to pocket, to misappropriate; –का पूरा आँख का अंधा having a full purse and an empty head; –पड़ना to harbour ill feeling towards; to have estranged relation; –बाँधना to make a note of, to keep in mind; –से जाना to be lost, to suffer loss or detriment.

गांभीर्य [*nm*] depth, profundity; gravity; solemnity, seriousness.

गाँव [*nm*] a village.

गाज [*nf*] a thunder-bolt, lightning; –गिरना/पड़ना to be thunder-struck, to be afflicted by a calamity.

गाजर [*nf*] carrot; –मूली petty things.

गाड़ना [v] to bury; to lay; to implant; to fix; to sink; to drive [as कील]; to pitch [as तंबू]; to cover [as आग].

गाड़ी [*nf*] a cart, coach, cab; vehicle, carriage; train; ~ वान a cart/coach-driver, cabman.

गा/ढ़ा [*a*] thick; dense; close [as दोस्ती]; deep; concentrated [as द्रव]; strong [as चाय]; [nm] a thick coarse cloth; ~ ढ़ी कमाई hard-earned money; ~ ढ़े दिन times of crisis, difficult days; ~ ढ़े पसीने की कमाई hard-earned money; – ढ़े में in a crisis.

गाना [*v*] to sing, to chant; [nm] a song.

गाफ़िल [*a*] negligent, unaware; unconscious.

गाय [*nf*] a cow; [*a*] meek and humble, harmless.

गायक [*nm*] a singer; musician; vocalist; –वृंद chorus.

गायन [*nm*] singing; vocal music.

ग़ायब [*a*] vanished, disappeared; lost.

गाल [*nm*] a cheek; –फुलाना to sulk; to get into a sulky mood.

गाली [*nf*] an abuse, invective; abusive songs sung by women as part of [marriage] celebrations; –गलौज/गुफ्ता (र) exchange of abuses.

गावदी [*a*] stupid, doltish, blockheaded; [*nm*] a nitwit, dolt.

ग्राहक [*nm*] a customer, purchaser.

गिचपिच [*a*] clumsy; crowded; crowding.

गिटपिट [*nf*] unintelligible chattering.

गिड़गिड़ाना [*v*] to entreat, to beseech, to implore humbly.

गिद्ध [*nm*] a vulture.

गिनती [*nf*] counting; calculation; reckoning; number; –के counted few.

गिनना [*v*] to count, to enumerate; गिने-गिनाये exact[ly]; in a limited number; गिने-चुने a few; selected few.

गिरगिट [*nm*] a chameleon; –की तरह रंग बदलना to change colours, to make frequent somersaults.

गिरजाघर [*nm*] a church, cathedral.

गिरना [*v*] to fall, to come down; to collapse; to drop; to stumble, to tumble; to decrease [e.g., भाव]; to be degraded; to be spilt.

गिरफ़्ता/र [*a*] arrested, captured, apprehended; ~री [*nf*] arrest, capture, apprehension.

गिरवी [*nf, a*] mortgage [d], pawn [ed]; pledge [d].

गिरह [*nf*] a knot; joint; fold in the loincloth used for safe keeping of money; somersault; a measure–one sixteenth part of a yard; ~ कट a pick-pocket.

गिरावट [*nf*] fall, downfall, degradation; slump; decrease.

गिरोह [*nm*] a gang, group, band.

गिला [*nm*] complaint; reproach.

गिलाफ़ [*nm*] a cover, pillow-cover; case.

गिलास [*nm*] a tumbler.

गिल्ली [*nf*] a toggle; – डंडा the game of tip-cat.

गीत [*nm*] a song, lyrical poem.

गीति [*nf*] a lyric.

गीदड़ [*nm*] a jackal; –भभकी a mere/false threat, blustering.

गीला [*a*] moist, wet.

गुंजन [*nm*] buzzing; humming [sound].

गुंजाइश [*nf*] scope; capacity; accommodation.

गुंजार [*nm*] humming, buzzing.

गुंडई [*nf*] scoundrelism; rascality, roguery, hooliganism.

गुंडा [*nm* and *a*] [a] rogue, scoundrel, hoodlum, hooligan; ~ गर्दी hooliganism, rowdyism.

गुंफन [*nm*] stringing.

गुंबद [*nm*] a dome, vault.

गु/च्छा [*nm*] a bunch, cluster; tuft; ~ च्छेदार tufty.

गुज़र [*nf*] maintenance; living; passing of time; –बसर maintenance; livelihood; –जाना to pass away; to cross.

गुज़रना [*v*] to pass; to cross- over; to pass away.

गुज़ारना [*v*] to pass time.

गुज़ारा [*nm*] subsistence; livelihood.

गुट [*nm*] a bloc, faction, clique; group: ~ बंदी/बाज़ी groupism, factionalism.

गुट्ठी [*nf*] the stone [of a fruit, etc.]

गुठली [*nf*] the stone [of a fruit, etc.]; ~ दार stony.

गुड़ [*nm*] jaggery; –खाना गुलगुले से परहेज करना to swallow a camel, to strain at a gnat; –गोबर करना to mar a happy occasion; –दिखाकर ढेला मारना to commence with a caress and conclude with a stab; –न दे गुड़ जैसी बात करे/कह दे a good word costs nothing; –से मरे तो जहर क्यों दे? why should administer quinine, if sweet stuff serves the purpose?

गुड़िया [*nf*] a doll.

गुड्डी [*nf*] a kite.

गुण [*nm*] quality; attribute; property; virtue; merit, ~ कारक/कारी effective [as औषधि]; beneficial; ~ गान a panegyric, encomium; ~ धर्म property; ~ वाचक/वाची attributive.

गुणन [*nm*] multiplication.

गुणा [*nm*] multiplication.

गुणानुवाद [*nm*] encomium, eulogy; singing praises [of].

गुणित [*nm*] multiple; [*a*] multiplied.

गुणी [*a*] meritorious, possessing merits; adept in [some] art.

गुत्थमगुत्था [*nm*] a scuffle, brawl, close combat.

गुत्थी [*nf*] a knot, entanglement; riddle, enigma.

गुदगुदा [*a*] soft; plump, fleshy.

गुदगुदा/ना [*v*] to tickle, to titillate; hence ~ हट.

गुदगुदी [*nf*] see गुदगुदाहट।

गुनगुना [*a*] lukewarm, tepid.

गुनगुनाना [*v*] to hum; to sing to oneself in subdued tones.

गुनहगार [*a*] guilty, sinful; [nm] sinner.

गुना a suffix denoting times or fold [as तिगुना– three times or threefold].

गुनाह [*nm*] sin; fault, guilt.

गुप्त [*a*] hidden, secret, latent; confidential.

गुप्त/चर [*nm*] detective, spy; ~ चर्या espionage.

गुफा [*nf*] a cave, cavern.

गुबार [*nm*] dirt, dust; affliction; spite.

गुब्बारा [*nm*] a balloon.

गुम [*a*] lost; missing; ~ नाम anonymous; ~ राह misled, [led] astray; ~ शुदा missing; ~ सुम quiet, taciturn.

गुमान [*nm*] pride, vanity; surmise; guess.

गुमाश्ता [*nm*] an agent, representative, manager.

गुर [*nm*] formula, device.

गुरदा [*nm*] kidney; courage.

गुरु [*nm*] a teacher; mentor, preceptor; spiritual guide, jupiter; [*a*] grave; heavy; difficult; long [syllable]; ~ कुल in olden times in India, a residential teaching institution run by an outstanding scholar; ~ भाई brother by virtue of preceptorial affinity, a fellow disciple; ~ मंत्र an initiatory mantra from a spiritual guide.

गुरुता [*nf*] the office or position of a guru; eminence; gravity; heaviness.

गुरुत्व [*nm*] see गुरुताख–केंद्र the centre of gravity.

गुरुत्वाकर्षण [*nm*] gravitation.

गुरुघंटाल [*a*] knave; astute, crafty [fellow].

गुर्गा [*nm*] a henchman, an agent.

गुर्ज़ [*nm*] a mace, club.

गुर्रा/ना [*v*] to growl, to snarl; to gnarl; hence ~ हट।

गुलगपाड़ा [*nm*] uproar, tumult, din.

गुलगुला [*a*] soft; [nm] a kind of sweet preparation.

गुलचा [*nm*] a light stroke of the fist on the cheek.

गुलछर्रे [*nm*] merry-making, revelry.

गुलाब [*nm*] rose; ~ जल rose water.

गुलाबी [*a*] rosy; mild [as जाड़ा].

गुला/म [*nm*] a slave; ~ मी slavery; servility; bondage.

ग़ुसल [*nm*] a bath.

ग़ुसलख़ाना [*nm*] a bathroom.

गुस्ता/ख [*a*] impertinent, impudent; hence ~ खी [*nf*].

गुस्सा [*nm*] anger, rage, fury; गुस्सेबाज irascible, choleric.

गुस्सैल [*a*] irascible, choleric, hot-headed.

गूँ/गा [*a*] dumb, mute; [*nm*] a dumb person; ~ गे का गुड़ an experience that defies expression.

गूँज [*nf*] an echo, a reverberation.

गूँजना [*v*] to echo, to resound.

गूँथना [*v*] to braid, to plait.

गूँधना [*v*] to knead.

गू [*nm*] faeces; –में घसीटना to subject [somebody] to grave humiliation and embarrassment.

गूढ़ [*a*] occult, mysterious; abstruse; obscure; hence ~ता।

गूदड़ [*nm*] rags, tattered clothes.

गूदा [*nm*] flesh [of fruits and vegetables, etc.]; pulp.

गृह [*nm*] a residence; –उद्योग cottage industry; –प्रवेश house- warming ceremony; ~ युद्ध civil war; ~ लक्ष्मी a deferential term for a housewife; ~ स्वामी the master of the household.

गृहस्थ [*nm*] a householder.

गृहस्थी [*nf*] household; family.

गृहिणी [*nf*] wife, housewife.

गेंद [*nf*] a ball.

गेरुआ [*a*] ochrous, of the colour of red ochre, russet.

गेरु [nm] red ochre, ochre, ruddle.

गेहुँआ [*a*] wheat-coloured, wheatish.

गेहूँ [*nm*] wheat; –के साथ घुन भी पिस जाता है when bulls fight, crops suffer.

गैंडा [*nm*] a rhinoceros.

ग़ैर [*a*] stranger, other; [prefix] non-, un-, in-; ~ कानूनी illegal, unlawful; ~ जरूरी unnecessary; unimportant; ~ जिम्मेदार irresponsible; ~ सरकारी non-governmental; unofficial; private; ~ हाज़िर absent; ~ हाज़िरी absence.

ग़ैरत [*nf*] sense of honour, self-respect; ~ मंद having a sense of honour; self-respecting.

गोंठना [*v*] to stitch in a rather crude manner; to skirt the edges; to encircle.

गोंद [*nm*] gum, wood-gum; ~ दानी a gum bottle.

गो [*nf*] a cow; sense [of perception, etc.]; ~ दान the gifting away of a cow; ~ धन cattle-wealth; ~ धूलि dusk, evening; ~ प a cowherd; ~ पालन tending the cows; ~ मांस beef; ~ रक्षा cow protection; ~ वध cow slaughter.

गो [*ind*] although, though; ~ कि though, although.

गोचर [*a*] perceptible, experienced through the senses.

गोटा [*nm*] gold or silver lace, edging.

ग़ोता [*nm*] dive; dip; ~ खोर a diver; ~ मार diver, submarine.

गोत्र [*nm*] lineage.

गोद [*nf*] the lap; –लेना to adopt [a child]; –सूनी होना to lose the only child.

गोदना [*v*] to tattoo; to pick; to prick; to puncture; to goad; [*nm*] a tattoo-mark.

गोदाम [*nm*] a godown, warehouse.

गोदी [*nf*] the lap; a dock, dockyard.

गोपी [*nf*] a cowherd's wife.

गोबर [*nm*] cow-dung; dung; ~ गणेश a plump fool, nitwit, an inert blockhead.

गोया [*ind*] as if; –कि as if.

गोरा [*a*] white, fair-skinned; [*nm*] a whiteman; an European.

गोरिल्ला [*nm*] a gorilla.

गोलंदाज़ [*nm*] a gunner, marksman.

गोल [*a*] round; circular; globular; [*nm*] a goal [in games]; misappropriation; mess, confusion; gang; ~ मटोल equivocal; vague; fat, corpulent; ~ माल mess, confusion; ~ मोल vague, ambiguous; hotch-potch.

गोला [*nm*] a ball; cannon-ball; a bomb; kernel of a coconut; sphere; globe; a large round beam [of wood]; colic; ~ ई roundness, rotundity; sphericity; curvature; ~ बारी shelling, bombardment; –बारूद ammunition.

गोलार्ध [*nm*] a hemisphere.

गोली [*nf*] a bullet; pill; tablet, ball; [nm] a goalkeeper.

गोशाला [*nf*] a cowshed, cow-tending centre.

गोश्त [*nm*] flesh, meat, ~ खोर a meat-eater.

गोष्ठी [*nf*] a seminar; discussion.

गौ [*nf*] see गो।

गौण [*a*] secondary, subsidiary, auxiliary; minor.

ग़ौर [*nm*]; –करना to take note of; to ponder, to deliberate, to think attentively.

गौरव [*nm*] pride, glory, honour; heaviness; ~ शाली glorious, dignified.

ग्यारह [*a*] eleven; [*nm*] the number eleven.

ग्रन्थ [*nm*] a book; voluminous book; ~ कार a writer, author [of a book]; ~ विज्ञान [the science of Bibliography]; ~ सूची a bibliography; a list of books.

ग्रीष्म [*nm*] the summer.

ग्लानि [*nf*] remorse, repentance.

ग्वाला [*nm*] a milkman, cowkeeper.

घ the fourth consonant and the fourth member of the first pentad [i.e., कवर्ग] of the Devanagari; alphabet.

घ - देवनागरी वर्णमाला के व्यंजनों में से कवर्ग का चौथा व्यंजन है। इसका उच्चारण स्थान कंठ या जिह्वा-मूल है।

घंटा [*nm*] a bell; gong; clock; an hour; ~ घर a clock tower.

घंटी [*nf*] a small bell, tintin-nabulum; the ringing of a bell; uvula.

घंटिका [*nf*] **1** a small bell. **2** a jar for water.

घटक [*nm*] a factor, component, constituent.

घटना [*v*] an incident, event; incidence, occurrence; phenomenon; [*v*] to happen; to be reduced, to decrease; to lessen; –बढ़ना to fluctuate, to vary; –स्थल the site/scene of an incident.

घटा [*nf*] a dark cloud; mass of dark clouds; –घिरना/छाना gathering of thick dark clouds.

घटाना [*v*] **1** to cause to be lessened: to be lessened: to lessen; to reduce (as prices); to alleviate. **2** to deduc; math. to subtract. **3** to cause to deteriorate; to impair. – घटाकर बोला जाना, to be quoted at a reduced price (a commodity).

घटिया [*adj*] inferior, of low quality or standard; cheap; shoddy.

घटिहा [*nm*] **1** a collector of ferry charges. **2** [*nf*] a boat.

घ/ड़ा [*nm*] a pitcher, pot; ~ डों पानी पड़ना to be flushed with shame, to suffer extreme humiliation.

घड़ी [*nf*] a watch; timepiece; moment; a time interval of 24 minutes; ~ साज a horologist, watch-maker; ~ साजी horology, watch-maker's profession; घड़ियाँ गिनना to count every passing moment restlessly; to await keenly.

घड़िया [*nf*] **1** a small earthen pot; crucible. **2** [*nm*] honeycomb.

घन [*nm*] a hammer, sledge- hammer; cube; cloud; [a] dense; solid; ~ घोर very dense; terrible, profound; ~ चक्कर a blockhead; dolt.

घनघ्रनाना [*v*] to produce a deep ringing sound [as of a gong].

घना [*a*] dense, thick; intensive [as cultivation]; compact.

घनिष्ठ [*a*] close; closest, most intimate.

घपला [*nm*] bungling; mess; confusion; disorder.

घबड़ा(रा)ना [*v*] to be nervous, to lose nerve; to be non-plussed; to get panicky; ~ हट nervousness; restlessness; panic.

घमं/ड [*nm*] conceit; vanity; ~ डी conceited**; vain.**

घमंडी **1** proud, arrogant, conceited. **2 vain. 3** such a person.

घमासान [*a*] fierce; –युद्ध/लड़ाई fierce fight or battle.

घर [*nm*] home; house, residence; apartment, room; compartment; native place, homeland; office [as तारघर, डाकघर], square or cell [in a chess-board]; –गृहस्थी household; family; ~ जँवाई one who lives with, and is subordinated to, one's in-laws; –द्वार household effects; home and hearth; ~ बार household; ~ वाला husband; the master of the household; ~ वाली wife; the mistress of the household; –उजड़ना ruination of a household/family; the demise of one's wife; –का घर the entire family;–का जोगी जोगना (ड़ा) आन गाँव का सिद्ध a prophet is not honoured in his own country; –का न घाट का belonging neither here nor there; –का नाम डुबोना to bring disgrace to the fair name of a family; –का भेदी लंका ढाये traitors prove to be the worst enemies; – का मर्द/शेर a hero within one's own four walls; household hero; –की मुर्गी दाल बराबर what is easy to procure, does not score; –चलाना to run a household; ~ फूँक तमाशा देखना to ruin one's household for the sake of an idle pleasure; –फोड़ना to spell internecine quarrel in a household; –बिगाड़ना to bring ruin to a household; –भरना to amass wealth; to achieve prosperity; –में गंगा आना to achieve one's purpose without a stroke of work; to gain divine visit without effort; –में डालना to take as a mistress; –में सूत न कपास जुलाहे से लट्ठम-लट्ठा count not your chickens till they are hatched.

घराना [*nm*] a family, clan.

घरेलू [*a*] domestic; private.

घरौंदा [*nm*] a toy- house.

घाई [*nf*] **1** a time; a turn. (= घात) **2** side. direction (= ओर).

घसीटना [*v*] to drag; to trail; to scribble; to scrawl.

घहराना [*v*] to thicken [as clouds]; to thunder; to gurgle.

घाघ [*nm* and *a*] cunning, shrewd [person].

घाट [*nm*] wharf, quay; berth; ferry, bank; –घाट का पानी पीना to wander from pillar to post, to gather varied experience.

घाटा [*nm*] loss; deficit.

घाटिया = घाटवाल, see घाट।

घात [*nf*] ambush, ambuscade; killing; slaughter; stroke; power; degree; –में फिरना/रहना to mark time for an ambuscade; –लगाना to lie in ambush.

घातक [*a*] lethal; fatal; ruinous; [*nm*] a killer, murderer.

घायल [*a*] wounded; injured; hurt.

घाव [*nm*] wound; injury; –पर नमक छिड़कना to add insult to injury; –पुरना/भरना a wound to heal up.

घास [*nf*] grass; –पात/फूस rubbish, weed and straw; worthless food; –खोदना/छीलना to undertake a petty/worthless job; to idle away one's time.

घासलेट [*nm*] vegetable oil; inferior stuff; [*a*] trash.

घिग्घी [*nf*]; faltering in speech; hiccup –बँधना to have the throat choked [out of fear or emotional upsurge]; to be so stunned as to become tongue-tied.

घिचपिच [*a*] crowded; clumsy; illegible; [*nf*] congestion; clumsiness.

घिन [*nf*] abhorrence; odiousness; nausea.

घिनौना [*a*] abominable; loathsome; odious; nauseation.

घिराव [*nm*] gherao–the act of surrounding a person or persons to press home certain demands.

घिसघिस [*nf*] higgling; drudgery; dull routine work.

घिसना [*v*] to rub; to be worn out/to wear out; to be impaired/to impair; घिसा-पिटा hackneyed; worn out.

घी [*nm*] ghee; –के चिराग़/दीये जलाना lit. to light up ghee lamps –to celebrate [the fulfilment of some cherished desire] by merrymaking/ festivity.

घुँघराले [*a*] curly.

घुग्घू [*nm*] an owl; a fool.

घुटना [*v*] to be suffocated; to experience suffocation; to be clean-shaven; [*nm*] a knee; घुटा हुआ cunning and clever; clean-shaven.

घुट्टी [*nf*] digestive medicine or tonic given to infants.

घुड़ an allomorph of घोड़ा used as the first member in compound words; ~ चढ़ी a ceremonial horse-riding of the bridegroom to the bride's house forming a part of the marriage celebration; ~ दौड़ horse-race; ~सवार a horse-rider; a cavalier; ~ साल a horse-stable.

घुड़की [*nf*] brow-beating; a sharp reprimand/ rebuff.

घुन [*nm*] a weevil, wood-worm; –लगना to be in the grip of canker; to suffer internal decay.

घुन्ना [*a*] perversely reticent; rancorously secretive.

घुप्प [*a*]; –अँधेरा pitch dark; total black-out.

घूमना **1** to revolve; to spin, to whirl. **2** to move in a circle; to go round or about; to travel; to wander; to travel; to wander. **3** to turn, to bend (as a road). **4** to turn round (a person). **5** to be or to become dizzy; to swim (the senses). – सिर ~, to be dizzy; to be drowsy; to be tipsy. – घूमना-घामना, colloq. to wander about.

घुमक्कड़ [*a*] fond of/in the habit of wandering about, roving; [*nm*] a rover, wanderer.

घुमड़ना [*v*] to gather up [as clouds or sentiments]; to converge and concentrate.

घुमाव [*nm*] a turning; curvature; twist; ~ दार winding; circuitous, curved.

घुलना [*v*] to be dissolved; to be liquefied; to be mixed; to languish; to suffer decadence or to waste away; to become lean and thin;

घुलकर काँटा होना to be reduced to a skeleton; घुल-घुलकर जान देना to waste oneself away to death; घुल-घुल कर बातें करना to have a tete-a-tete.

घुसना [*v*] to enter; to pierce; to penetrate; to thrust into; to intrude.

घुसाना to cause to enter or to penetrate; to thrust or to force (into, में); to cram (in).

घुसपैठ [*nf*] intrusion; infiltration; access; घुसपैठिया an intruder; infiltrator.

घुसेड़ना [*v*] to thrust into; to pierce; to penetrate.

घूँ/सा [*nm*] fist; fist-blow; ~ सेबाजी fisticuffs, boxing.

घूँघट [*nm*] face-veil; veil.

घूँघर [*nm*] curl [of hair]; ~ वाले curly.

घूँट [*nm*] a draught, gulp, sip.

घूमना [*v*] to [take a] walk, to stroll; to wander; to gyrate; to revolve; to whirl; to turn; to return; to roll; to spin; to waggle; to swim [as head].

घूरना [*v*] to stare [at]; to gloat; to frown [at].

घूस [*nf*] bribe, illegal gratification; a bandicoot rat; ~ खोर bribee; ~ खोरी bribery.

घृणा [*nf*] hatred, scorn, abhorrence; loathing.

घृणित [*a*] abominable; abhorred, heinous.

घेरना [*v*] to besiege; to encircle; to hem in; to blockade; to confine.

घेरा [*nm*] siege; an encirclement; enclosure; cordon; fence skirt; girth; circumference; rim –डालना to besiege, to surround, ~बंदी encirclement; siege; blockade.

घोंसला [*nm*] a nest.

घोटना [*v*] to cram up, to commit to memory; to levigate; to choke; to strangle [e.g., गला घोटना] to smoothen; to shave.

घोटाला [*nm*] bungling; confusion, mess; disorder.

घोड़ा [*nm*] a horse; hammer of a gun.

घोर [*a*] awful; formidable; terrible; dense, thick; deep; sharp.

घोल [*nm*] a solution; myrrh.

घोलना [*v*] to dissolve; to mix.

घोषणा [*nf*] a declaration, proclamation.

च the first letter of the second pentad [i.e., चवर्ग) of the Devanagari: alphabet.

च - देवनागरी वर्णमाला का छठा व्यंजन, चवर्ग का पहला वर्णं इसका उच्चारण स्थान तालु है।

चंग [*nf*] crooked or bent; musical instrument.

चंगा [*a*] healed, recovered; good; sound.

चंगुल [*nm*] claw; clutch; talon; grasp; –में फँसना to fall into the clutches [of]; to be in the cruel grasp [of].

चंचल [*a*] unsteady, transient; inconstant; fickle, flickering; quivering; shaking; fidgety; restless; skittish; playful; coquettish; nimble; hence~ ता [*nf*].

चंट [*a*] cunning, clever, wily.

चंडाल [*nm*] a caste amongst the shudras taken to be the lowest in the traditional Hindu caste hierarchy; [*a*] low-born; wretched, wicked, depraved; cruel.

चंडालिनी [*a*] the wife of a Chandal, a wicked woman, a sinful woman. चंडालीन।

चंद [*nm*] the moon; [*a*] a few, some.

चंदन [*nm*] sandalwood, sanders.

चंदा [*nm*] the moon; contribution; subscription; donation.

चंद्र [*nm*] the moon; crescent; ~**ग्रहण** lunar eclipse; ~बिंदु the nasal sign represented by a crescent with a dot over it [ँ], as distinct from अनुस्वार represented by a dot above the top [-]; ~बिंब the lunar disc; ~मंडल the halo of the moon; ~मुखी woman blessed with a moon-like face; ~लोक the sphere or heaven of the moon; ~वार Monday; ~हार a kind of broad necklace.

चंद्रमा [*nm*] the moon.

चंद्रिका [*nf*] moonlight, moonshine.

चंपक [*nm*] a garland of Champa flowers.

चंपत [*a*] vanished, disappeared; absconded; – बनना/होना to turn tails, to take to one's heels; to run away.

चक [*nm*] holding, a lot of land; discus; a kind of circular toy played with a string.

चकती [*nf*] a patch; soap-cake.

चकनाचूर [*a*] shattered [to pieces]; broken into fragments; wearied; de-spirited.

चकबंदी [*nf*] consolidation of holdings.

चकमक [*nm*] flint.

चकमा [*nm*] dodge; trick; trickery; –खाना to suffer a dodge; to be tricked; –देना to dodge, to play a trick.

चकरबा uproar, quarrel.

चकमेबाज़ [*nm*] a dodger; trickster, fraudulent person.

चकराना [*v*] to feel dizzy; to whirl; to revolve; to be confounded/astounded.

चकला [*nm*] a brothel; pastry-board; circular wooden or stony board for spreading dough into a bread.

चकल्लस [*nf*] fun, jocularity, drollery; ~बाजी drollery, fun, indulgence in fun.

चकाचौंध [*nf*] dazzle, dazzlement, dazzling effect; brilliance, brilliant display.

चकित [*a*] amazed, surprised; flabbergasted, wonder-struck.

चक्कर [*nm*] circle, ring; whirl; twirl; spin; rotation; round; revolution; circumambulation; vertigo, giddiness; confusion; trick; fraud; –आना to suffer from vertigo, to feel giddy; –में आना/पड़ना to be taken in [by]; to be in a mess; to suffer harassment; to be dodged.

चक्की [*nf*] quern; mill; grinding mill; knee-pan; cake [e.g., soap-cake].

चक्र [*nm*] a wheel; cycle; circle; disc, discus; discus-shaped missile; ~वर्ती universal; [an emperor] ruling over a vast empire; ~वात a whirl-wind, cyclone; ~वृद्धि compound [interest]; ~व्यूह a circular array of troops; impregnable battle-array [as practised in ancient Indian military strategy].

चक्षु [*nm*] an eye; ~ गोचर visible, tangible, perceptible.

चखना [*v*] to taste, to relish.

चचा [*nm*] paternal uncle; ~ज़ाद born of paternal uncle.

चचेरा [*a*] pertaining to or related with paternal uncle.

चट [*adv*] instantly, instantaneously, at once; [nf] snap; crack, snapping, breaking or cracking sound; ~पट very promptly, immediately, with utmost urgency; ~सार a nursery school; –से instantly, instantaneously; –कर जाना to polish off, to consume hurriedly and entirely; –मँगनी पट ब्याह to propose this moment, to marry the very next.

चटक [*nf*] glitter, splendour, brilliance; agility; crack; sprain; a sparrow; [a] bright, brilliant [colour]; ~दार brilliant, gaudy; –मटक gaud, gaudiness; coquetry; ornamentation, glitter.

चटकीला [*a*] brilliant, bright; gaudy, glittering.

चटखनी [*nf*] a latch, bolt, tower bolt.

चटखारा [*nm*] a clack of the tongue with the palate [expressive of relishing experience].

चटनी [*nf*] sauce, indigenous sauce.

चटपटा [*a*] pungent, spicy.

चटाई [*nf*] a mat; the act or process of licking; –नाप two-dimensional measurement.

चटाक [*nf*] a crackling sound; smack; –पटाक promptly, swiftly.

चटोर/चटोरा [*a*] gastronome, greedy of delicious dishes; ~पन gastronomy, greediness for delicious dishes.

चट्टान [*nf*] a rock, cliff.

चढ़ना [*v*] to go up; to ascend; to be ascendant; to climb; to rise; to mount; to ride; to be offered [to a deity, etc.]; to launch an attack; to charge; to be recorded; to take possession of [as by an evil spirit]; to be placed on fire for cooking; to be in a tide; to increase, to be on the increase; to be covered by something; चढ़ बनना to have a run of good luck, to enjoy a lucky spell; चढ़ बैठना to ride on; to overpower; to trample down.

चढ़ाई [*nf*] ascent, bank, climb; rise, invasion.

चढ़ावा [*nm*] oblation, offering [to a deity, etc.]; ornamental gift presented to the bride [from the bridegroom's side].

चतुर [*a*] clever, shrewd; wise; skilful, skilled; ~ता cleverness; shrewdness; wisdom; skill.

चतु/र used as the first member of Sanskrit compound words being an allomorph of चत: meaning four; ~रंग quadripartite, consisting of four members or parts; ~रंगिणी comprised of four members or parts; [used esp. to denote an army comprised of four departments, viz. elephants, cavalry, chariots and the infantry]; a complete army; ~र्दिक्/र्दिश all round, on all the four sides; ~र्भुज quadrangle, quadrilateral; an epithet of Lord Vishnu having four arms; ~र्विध of four types, fourfold.

चतुराई [*nf*] cleverness; wisdom; skill.

चना [*nm*] gram; –चबैना parched gram and allied grains; poor people's diet.

चपकन [*nm*] a kind of long tight coat.

चपटा [*a*] flat.

चपड़-चपड़ [*nf*] lap, offensive sound made during chewing; tattle, unavailing and unending prattle.

चपड़ा [*nm*] shellac.

चपत [*nm*] a slap; [*nf*] loss; damage.

चपरकनाती [*a*] stupid, foolish; of no consequence; [*nm*] a riff-raff.

चपरासी [*nm*] a peon; ~गीरी a peon's functions or office.

चपल [*a*] unsteady; wavering; flippant; tremulous; restless; quick; nimble; hoity-toity; hence ~ता.

चपाती [*nf*] a thin bread of the Indian style.

चपेट [*nf*] striking range; stroke [of misfortune, etc.]; involvement; a sudden involving blow or accident; –में आना to be embroiled in a blow or accident; to sustain injury/loss.

चप्पल [*nf*] a slipper [open at the front], sandal.]

चप्पा [*nm*] a hand-breadth, a measure of four fingers; a span, small piece of land; –चप्पा every span of land, every inch of ground.

चप्पू [*nm*] an oar.

चबाना [*v*] to chew; to munch; to masticate.

चबूतरा [*nm*] a raised platform.

चबे(बै)ना [*nm*] parched heterogeneous grains.

चमक [*nf*] flash; brilliance, lustre, shine; gloss; glare; radiance; a localised flash of pain; –

दमक glitter; brilliance; pomp and show; ~दार shining, brilliant, glittering, glossy.

चमकना [*v*] to shine, to glitter, to sparkle; to flash; to flare; to flare up, to get angry; to have a localised flash of pain.

चमकीला [*a*] see चमकदार.

चमगादड़ [*nm*] a bat; vampire.

चमचमाना [*v*] to shine, to glitter, to be glossy; to sparkle.

चमचा [*nm*] a large spoon; flunkey, flatterer.

चमड़ा [*nm*] leather, hide; skin.

चमड़ी [*nf*] skin; –उधेड़ना to beat bare; to flay; to skin; –जाये पर दमड़ी न जाये to suffer a flaying, to save a penny; to be excessively stingy.

चमत्का/र [*nm*] a marvel, miracle; wonder; thaumaturgy; spectacle; ~रिक thaumaturgic; marvellous, miraculous; spectacular; ~री miraculous; one who performs miracles, a thaumaturge.

चमाचम [*adv*] with a shine/gloss, brilliantly, brightly.

चमार [*nm*] a cobbler; shoe-maker; a scheduled caste amongst the Hindus traditionally living by shoe-making.

चम्मच [*nm*] a spoon.

चयन [*nm*] selection; picking up; compiling.

चयनिका [*nf*] an anthology, a selection/collection of choicest or representative writings.

चर [*nm*] a spy, secret messenger; emissary; a variable; [*a*] moving; unsteady; variable.

चरकटा [*nm*] a chaff-cutter; riff-raff, an insignificant person.

चरका [*nm*] fraud, swindle, rigging; –खाना to be swindled/defrauded.

चरखा [*nm*] a spinning wheel; hyena.

चरखी [*nf*] a reel, spool; pulley; sheaf; tourbillion, revolving firework; a catherine wheel.

चरण [*nm*] a foot of a verse; quarter; phase; step; –चिह्न footprint; ~तल sole of the foot.

चरना [*a*] to graze.

चरपरा [*a*] piquant, hot, of pungent taste; hence ~हट।

चरबी [*nf*] fat, grease; fats and oils; tallow; ~दार greasy; fatty.

चरम [*a*] absolute; ultimate; last, final, extreme.

चरवाहा [*nm*] a herdsman; grazier.

चरस [*nm*] an intoxicating drug prepared from the flowers of hemp; a huge leather bucket.

चरसा [*nm*] a large leather bag or bucket.

चरागाह [*nm, nf*] pasture, pasture land, meadow, graziery.

चराचर [*a*] movable and immovable, animate and inanimate; [*nm*] the entire creation.

चरित [*nm*] biography; doings, goings; ~कार/–लेखक a biographer.

चरितार्थ [*a*] validated; proven correct; gratified.

चरितार्थता [*nf*] significance, meaningfulness; fulfilment, success; validity.

चरित्र [*nm*] character; –चित्रण characterisation; ~वान [a man] of sound character; ~हीन profligate, depraved, characterless.

चरित्रांकन [*nm*] characterisation; portrayal, delineation.

चर्चा [*nf*] mention; discussion; rumour.

चर्चित [*a*] discussed; mentioned; smeared, anointed.

चर्म [*nm*] leather; skin; hide; ~कार a cobbler; shoemaker; tanner.

चलता [*nm*] mobility; unsteadiness; [*a*] mobile, moving; current; flourishing [as चलती दुकान) cursory [e.g., चलती निगाह) cunning, clever; workable; temporary; light; –पुरजा cunning; clever; –फिरता mobile;–फिरता नज़र आना to be making a move; –बनना to turn tails; to slip away.

चलन [*nm*] vogue; usage; custom; conduct.

चलना [*v*] to walk, to move, to proceed; to be in vogue/use/currency; to last; to flow; to be initiated/started [as बात]; to be pressed into use [as लाठी]; to blow [as हवा]; to be thrown [as तीर] to be effective; to go off [as बंदूक]; to be operated [as मशीन]; to be filed [as मुकदमा]; to pass [as सिक्का]; चल बसना to pass away; to expire.

चलवाना [*v*] to cause to go, to proceed.

चलनी [*nf*] a sieve.

चलाऊ [*a*] durable, lasting.

चलायमान [*a*] moving; fickle, wavering; unsteady.

चवन्नी [*nf*] a twenty five paisa [four anna] coin.

चवाई [*nm*] a slanderer.

चवर्ग [*nm*] the 'cha' pentad of five palatal consonants in the Devanagari: script viz. च, छ, ज, झ and ञ.

चवालीस [*a*] forty four; [*nm*] the number forty four.

चश्म [*nm*] an eye; ~दीद witnessed; seen; ~दीद गवाह an eye witness.

चश्मा [*nm*] spectacles, glasses; fountain; spring.

चसका [*nm*] proclivity, addiction; compelling habituation.

चस्पा [*a*] affixed, stuck; fitting; applicable.

चह/कना [*v*] to chip, to warble; to be merrily talkative; also ~ चहाना।

चहलक़दमी [*nf*] stroll, walk, ramble.

चहल-पहल [*nf*] hustle and bustle; commotion; gaiety merriment.

चहारदीवारी [*nf*] the four walls, boundary.

चहेता [*a*] beloved; favourite.

चाँटा [*nm*] a slap.

चांडाल [*nm an a*] see चंडाल।

चाँद [*nm*] the moon; the bull's eye; [nf] the crown [of]; the head; ~तारा a kind of fine muslin ~मारी shooting practice; range; –का टुकड़ा a beauty; –को गहन (ग्रहण) लगना to have a blot in a beauty; –सा मुखड़ा a face as lovely as the moon, lovely face.

चाँदना [*nm*] light.

चाँदनी [*nf*] moonlight; a large white sheet of cloth; bedsheet; canopy.

चाँदी [*nf*] silver; –काटना to be minting money; –का जूता monetary temptation; bribe; –होना to have fabulous earnings; to have all round gains.

चाकू [*nm*] a knife.

चाखना [*v*] to taste; to relish.

चा/चा [*nm*] paternal uncle; –ची paternal uncle's wife, aunt.

चाट [*nf*] a spicy preparation of cut fruits, vegetables, etc.; habit, compelling habituation, taste, irresistible proclivity.

चाटना [*v*] to lick; चाट जाना to consume the whole, to polish off.

चाटु [*nm*] flattery, adulation, false praise; ~ कार a flatterer; sycophant; adulator; ~ कारिता, ~ कारी flattery, sycophancy, adulation.

चादर [*nf*] sheet; plate; bedsheet, bedcover; coverlet; an upper cover garment used by women; ~बंदी sheeting; –देखकर पाँव फैलाना to cut one's coat according to the cloth.

चाप [*nf*] arc; pressure; a bow; [foot] sound/blow.

चापलूस [*a*] flattering, sycophantic, adulatoring.

चापलूसी [*nf*] flattery, sycophancy, adulation.

चापल्य [*nm*] चपलता।

चाबना [*v*] see चबाना।

चाबी [*nf*] a key; –देना to wind [a watch, etc.]

चाबुक [*nm*] a whip, flog, lash.

चाय [*nf*] tea; ~घर a tea house, canteen; ~दानी a tea-pot; पानी breakfast; tea and snacks, light refreshment; tea.

चार [*a*] four; several; a few; [nm] the number four; spying; ~खाना chequered cloth; ~दीवार fence walls, four walls; ~दीवारी boundary, four walls; –आँखें करना to exchange glances, to meet eye to eye; to come face to face; –के कान पड़ना to become public, to become known; –चाँद लगना to have a feather added to one's cap; to become more charming than ever; –दिन की चाँदनी a fleeting existence; a nine days' wonder, a limited period of merry-making; चारों खाने चित गिरना to fall at full stretch–to be beaten all ends up; to be thoroughly vanquished; to lose one's wits; चारों फूटना to suffer total blindness, to lose one's mental as well as physical vision.

चारण [*nm*] a wandering minstrel, bard; grazing; a sub-caste of Rajasthan Brahmans.

चारपाई [*nf*] a bedstead; bed, cot;–से लगना to be reduced to a skeleton.

चार सौ बी/स [*a*] fraudulent; deceitful; [*nm*] a fraud, forgerer; ~सी fraud, forgery; criminal deception.

चारा [*nm*] fodder, forage, feed; bait, lure; remedy; means; ~जोई proceedings; suit; –न होना, और कोई to have no other way out.

चाल [*nf*] gait; speed; march; motion; movement; move, trick, device; custom; a huge building inhabited by a large number of tenant families; –चलन conduct; –ढाल ways, bearing, demeanour; ~बाज़ crafty, cunning, trickster; ~बाज़ी craftiness; cunningness; trickery.

चालक [*a*] a driver; conductor.

चाला/क [*a*] cunning, clever, crafty; ~की cunningness, craftiness.

चालान [*nm*] a challan, invoice; prosecution.

चालीस [*a*] forty; [*nm*] the number forty.

चालू [*a*] current; prevalent; tenable; common place; moving, in motion; cunning, unscrupulous [e.g., –आदमी]

चाव [*nm*] fondness, eagerness.

चावल [*nm*] rice.

चाह [*nf*] liking, love, craving; desire; will; a well; –से राह बनती है where there is a will, there is a way.

चाहत [*nf*] liking, love, fondness.

चाहता [*nm*] owing, due.

चाहना [*v*] to wish, to want; to like; to love, to be fond of; to crave for, to desire; to require.

चाहे [*ind*] either...or; or ...or; even though/though ...yes/still; –कोई whichever; whoever; –जो हो come what may.

चिंतन [*nm*] thinking; reflection, contemplation; musing.

चिंता [*nf*] worry, concern; anxiety; care; ~जनक causing anxiety/concern.

चिंत्य [*a*] causing concern/anxiety; doubtful; questionable.

चिंदी [*nf*] shred, scrap.

चिक [*nf*] a screen of bamboo parings or reed, bamboo curtain.

चिकन [*nf*] embroidered fine muslin.

चिकना [*a*] smooth; glossy; oily or greasy; slippery; –चुपड़ा well made-up; looking smart and attractive; full of flattery, flattering [as चिकनी-चुपड़ी बातें)–घड़ा incorrigible, unabashing [person], shameless.

चिकनाई [*nf*] smoothness; greasiness; fat; lubricant.

चिकनापन [*nm*] smoothness; greasiness; glossiness.

चिकित्सक [*nm*] a physician, medical practitioner.

चिकित्सा [*nf*] treatment; remedy; medication, therapy; [a] medical, therapeutic; –शास्त्र medicine, medical science.

चिकित्सालय [*nm*] a hospital, dispensary.

चिकोटी [*nf*] pinch; tweak; twitch.

चिट्टा [*a*] white, fair.

चिट्ठा [*nm*] account book; day book; detailed list; muster roll.

चिट्ठी [*nf*] a letter; ~पत्री correspondence; letter, etc.; ~रसा a postman.

चिड़चिड़ा [*a*] irritable, irascible, petulant, peevish; hence ~पन।

चिड़िया [*nf*] a bird; shuttlecock [in the game of badminton]; the club [in a suite of cards]; ~खाना/घर a zoo; an aviary; –का दूध a non-existent commodity.

चिड़ी [*nf*] a hen or a bird.

चिढ़ [*nf*] irritation, huff, strong aversion; a teasing nickname.

चिढ़ना [*v*] to be irritated, to be teased; to [take] huff; to have a strong aversion.

चित [*a*] supine; [lying] flat on the back; [nm] mind; head [of a coin]; ~चोर alluring, appealing [person]; he who steals away one's heart; –पट करना to decide this way or that [by throw of a coin].

चितकबरा [*a*] variegated, spotted; piebald, mottled.

चितवन [*nf*] [compelling] glance, [fascinating] look.

चिता [*nf*] funeral pyre.

चितेरा [*nm*] a painter.

चित् [*nm*] consciousness; [*a*] conscious.

चित्त [*nm*] mind; [*a*] supine, flat on the back; –चढ़ना to take to heart; to develop a fondness [for]; –चुराना to steal [away] one's heart, to enchant; –देना to heed, to pay attention.

चित्ती [*nf*] a speck, spot; ~दार spotted, specked.

चित्र [nm] picture; painting; [still] film; ~कला [art of] painting; ~कार a painter; an artist; ~कारी [the profession or work of] painting; ~पट screen, cinema, film; –विचित्र mottled; variegated; picturesque; ~शाला a picture-gallery; ~सारी a picture-gallery.

चित्रण [*nm*] portrayal, delineation; painting, drawing.

चिथड़ा [*nm*] a rag, shred, tatter.

चिनगारी [*nf*] a spark.

चिनाई [*nf*] brick-laying, bilge and cantline.

चिपकना [*v*] to adhere; to stick, to cling; [*a*] adhesive; clinging/hanging [on].

चिपटना [*v*] to cling; to hang on; to embrace; to hold fast.

चिप्पी [*nf*] label, paster.

चिमटना [*v*] to cling to, to hang on; to embrace; to hold fast.

चिमटा [*nm*] tongs; pincers.

चिमनी [*nf*] a chimney; flue-pipe.

चिरंजीव [*a*] [one] blessed with longevity; a benedictory epithet prefixed with the names of youngers; [int] may you live long!; [*nm*] son.

चिरंतन [*a*] lasting, ever- lasting, perpetual.

चिर [*a*] long-lasting; lasting; perpetual; [ind] existing for a long time, ever; ~काल long time; ~जीवी blessed with long life, long-living; immortal; ~निद्रा sleep that knows no breaking, perpetual sleep; death; ~परिचित long known; ~प्रचलित long-current; long-prevalent; ~प्रतीक्षित long-awaited; ~स्थायी enduring; perpetual, permanent; ~स्मरणीय memorable; worth remembering [for long].

चिरना [*v*] to be torn; to be split; to be sawed; to be dissected; चिरा-फटा lacerated.

चिराग़ [*nm*] a lamp; light; –गुल करना to put out the lamp; –तले अँधेरा near the church, farther from heaven; –लेकर ढूँढ़ना to search every nook and corner; –से चिराग़ जलता है one lamp kindles another.

चिलचिलाना [*v*] shine scorchingly; चिलचिलाती धूप scorching sun/heat.

चिलम [*nf*] an earthen or metallic vessel on the top of a hubble-bubble for containing fire and tobacco; ~बरदारी flunkeyism; servitude.

चिलमची [*nf*] a [wash] basin.

चिलमन [*nf*] a bamboo-curtain.

चिल्लपों [*nf*] clamour, confused cries, hullabaloo.

चिल्लाना [*v*] to cry, to shout, to squeak.

चिह्न [*nm*] sign; mark, marking, brand; trait.

चीं [*nf*] warbling; chirp; –चपड़ jabber; protest explicitly; [expression of] resentment –बोलना to confess helplessness; to concede victory, to own defeat.

चींटी [*nf*] an ant; –की चाल very slow movement; –के पर निकलना to be heading for trouble/death; to outgrow oneself.

चीख़ [*nf*] a scream; shriek, screech, squeak; –पुकार shriek and scream, hubbub; loud supplication.

चीख़ना [*a*] to scream, to shriek; to squeak, to screech.

चीज़ [*nf*] a thing, an article; item, object; a commodity; an ornament; a wonderful or precious thing; –बस्त belongings, articles, goods and chattels.

चीता [*nm*] a leopard; panther.

चीत्कार [*nf*] a sudden scream/screech, loud shriek.

चीथड़ा [*nm*] rag, tatters.

चीनी [*nf*] sugar; a Chinese; [*a*] Chinese; pertaining or belonging to China; –मिट्टी clay.

चीरना [*v*] to saw; to rend; to cleave; to tear; to dissect, to cut open; to incise.

चीरा [*nm*] incision, a surgical operation.

चील [*nf*] a kite.

चुंगी [*nf*] octroi, terminal tax; ~घर octroi-post.

चुँधियाना [*v*] to be dazzled.

चुंबक [*nm*] a magnet.

चुंबन [*nm*] a kiss, kissing.

चुकाना [*v*] to settle; to pay off, to defray.

चुगल [*nm*] a back-biter; ~खोर a back-biter; ~खोरी back-biting.

चुगली [*nf*] back-biting, speaking ill of [somebody in his/her absence]; complaint.

चुटकी [*nf*] a pinch, snapping with the finger; –काटना to pinch; –बजाते (में) in a trice; in a moment; –बजाना to snap the fingers; चुटकियों में in a trice.

चुटकुला [*nm*] an anecdote; a joke, pleasantry.

चुटीला [*a*] wounded, hurt, incisive; penetrating, causing mental upheaval; three-stranded cotton or silken braid with tassels used for hairdo.

चुड़ैल [*nf*] a witch; shrew.

चुनना [*v*] to select, to choose; to pick; to elect.

चुनाँ (नां) चे [*ind*] thus, therefore.

चुनाव [*nm*] election; selection; –क्षेत्र constituency; –मंडल electorate.

चुनिंदा [*a*] selected; chosen; choicest.

चुनौती [*nf*] a challenge.

चुप [*v*] silent, quiet.

चुपचाप [*adv*] silently, quietly; stealthily; clandestinely.

चुपड़ना [*v*] to besmear, to anoint, to apply a greasy substance.

चुप्पा [*a*] taciturn; secretive.

चुप्पी [*nf*] silence.

चुभना [*v*] to be pricked/pinched/punctured; to feel bad, to have a pricking sensation within.

चुमकारना [*v*] to produce a kissing sound; to fondle, to caress.

चुम्मा [*nm*] a kiss.

चुरट [*nm*] a cheroot.

चुराना [*v*] to steal, to pinch.

चुलबुला [*a*] playful; fidgety, restless; frolicsome; hence ~पन।

चुल्लू [*nm*] the hollow cup formed by joining the fringes of the two palms together; the upturned hollow palm [of a single hand]; a handful/palmful [of liquid]; –भर a handful, meagre quantity; ~ पानी में डूब मरना lit. to be drowned in a palmful of water; to be ashamed beyond reprieve.

चुसकी [*nf*] a sip, suck.

चुस्त [*a*] active, smart, agile; tight; narrow; –चालाक sharp and smart; –दुरुस्त agile and active.

चुस्ती [*nf*] agility, alertness, smartness.

चुहल [*nf*] jollity, joviality, jocundity; ~बाज़ jolly; jovial, jocund.

चूँकि [*ind*] because, as.

चूकना [*v*] to miss, to fail; to err; to make a lapse, to default.

चूड़ी [*nf*] a bangle; ring; pucker; ~दार puckered.

चून [*nm*] flour, wheat-meal.

चूना [*v*] to leak; to drop; to ooze [as कोढ़]; [nm] lime; –लगाना (के) to dupe, to bamboozle.

चूमना [*v*] to kiss, to lip; –चाटना to kiss and caress.

चूर [*nm*] filings, powder; [*a*] pulverised; steeped in [as नशे में–]; exhausted, besotted.

चूरन [*nm*] powder, digestive powder.

चूर्ण [*nm*] powder, pulverised or powdered substance; digestive powder.

चूल्हा [*nm*] a fire place, hearth; चूल्हे में जाना/पड़ना to be damned, to go to hell; to go to pot; चूल्हे से निकलकर भट्ठी में (पड़ना) from the frying pan into the fire.

चूसना [*v*] to suck, to suck dry, to sip; to drink in; to exploit; to exhaust.

चूहा [*nm*] a rat; mouse; चूहे–दानी a rat-trap.

चेक [*nm*] a cheque; chequered cloth.

चेचक [*nf*] small-pox.

चेत [*nm*] consciousness, senses.

चेतन [*a*] animate; conscious; [*nm*] the conscious [mind]; the animate [world].

चेतना [*nf*] consciousness, awareness; animation; [*v*] to become conscious/animated; to become alert.

चेतावनी [*nf*] warning; alarm;–, अंतिम an ultimatum.

चे/ला [*nm*] a pupil, disciple; hence ~ली [*nf*].

चेष्टा [*nf*] effort, endeavour; movement; demeanour; gesture.

चेहरा [*nm*] face, countenance; mask; front; –मोहरा lineament; –पीला पड़/हो जाना to turn pale; to lose lustre; चेहरे पर हवाइयाँ उड़ना to be struck with panic; to lose colour, to be despirited.

चैत [*nm*] the opening month of the year according to the Hindu calendar.

चैतन्य [*a*] conscious, sensitive; alert and awake; [*nm*] consciousness, spirit.

चैत्य [*nm*] a monastery, [esp. Buddhist] shrine.

चैन [nm] relief; rest; tranquillity; calm and quiet; –की बंसी बजाना to enjoy oneself thoroughly; to have no worry whatever.

चोंगा [*nm*] a [telephone] receiver; cylindrical tinpot.

चोंच [*nf*] beak; bill, dolt.

चोखा [*a*] fine, good; genuine.

चोग़ा [*nm*] a gown, toga.

चोट [*nf*] injury; hurt; blow; stroke; –चपेट/फेंट wound, injury, bruise;–करना to strike a blow; to launch an attack; –खाना to receive a blow; to be wounded; –पर चोट पड़ना to suffer one blow after another.

चोटी [*nf*] an apex; crown; braid; a lock of hair on the top of the head [kept by traditionalist Hindus]; –का superb, of the highest order; –

दबना or हाथ में होना to be under one's thumb, to be in the clutches [of], to be under complete control [of].

चोर [*nm*] a thief; pilferer; burglar; –गली a secret lane; back lane; –चकार a thief or swindler; –दरवाज़ा/द्वार at rap-door; secret door- way; back door; –बाज़ार black market; –बाज़ारिया black marketeer, ~बाज़ारी black-marketing; –रास्ता a back stairs pathway; –सीढ़ी back stairs; –का साथी गिरहकट a thief will have another for company, birds of the same feather flock together; –चोरी से जाये पर हेरा-फेरी से न जाये a snake must still hiss, even if it does not bite.

चोरी [*nf*] theft, burglary, pilferage; –चोरी clandestinely, stealthily; –छिपे stealthily, surreptitiously; –से stealthily, clandestinely.

चोली [*nf*] brassiere; a pair of bodice; –दामन का साथ a perpetual association, an everlasting bond.

चौंकना [*v*] to be startled/startled; to be alarmed.

चौंतीस [*a*] thirty four; [nm] the number thirty four.

चौंधियाना [*v*] to be dazzled; to suffer a dazzling effect.

चौंसठ [*a*] sixty four; [*nm*] the number sixty four.

चौ chau an allomorph of चतु: (चार) used as the first member in compound Hindi words; ~कन्ना alert, vigilant; ~कस cautious, alert, watchful; in order, intact; ~कसी cautiousness, vigilance; ~कोर quadrilateral, quadrangular, four-sided; ~खट threshold; door-frame, door-sill; ~खटा frame; ~खना four-storeyed; ~खाना chequered cloth; ~गिर्द all round; ~ गुना fourfold, four times; ~तरफ़ा all round, from all the four quarters; ~पट razed; ruined, undone; ~पाया a quadruped; livestock; ~पाल a rural meeting place; a verandah used as drawing room in village houses; ~बारा an assembly room with a number of doors and windows; ~मासा the rainy season; four months comprising the rainy season extending from असाढ़ to क्वार ~मुहाँ/मुखा four-faced; all round; ~रस even, plane; ~रस्ता/राहा crossing; crossroads ~हद्दी boundary.

चौक [*nm*] a crossing; square; market place.

चौकी [*nf*] a post, check post; a low square or rectangular seat.

चौकीदा/र [*nm*] a watchman, guard; hence ~री।

चौड़ा [*a*] broad, wide; ~ई breadth, width; –चकला expansive; weighty and well-built.

चौथा [*a*] the fourth [in succession]; [*nm*] [the rituals observed on] the fourth day of somebody's death.

चौथाई [*a*] one-fourth.

चौदह [*a]* fourteen, [*nm*] the number fourteen.

चौधरी [*nm*] the headman of a clan or community; chief; chieftain.

चौबीस [*a*] twenty four; [*nm*] the number twenty four.

चौरानवे [*a*] ninety four; [*nm*] the number ninety four.

चौरासी [*a*] eighty four; [*nm*] the number eighty four.

चौवन [*a*] fifty four; [*nm*] the number fifty four.

चौवालीस see [*a, nm*] चवालीस।

चौहत्तर [*a*] seventy four; [*nm*] the number seventy four.

च्यु/त [*a*] fallen [from], deprived [of], banished; deviated [from]; strayed; ~ति lapse; default; eclipsis, banishment; fall.

च्युति [*nf*] a falling, a flowing out or down.

च्यूँटा [*nm*] चींटा. a large black ant.

छ the second letter of the second pentad [i.e., चवर्ग) of the Devanagari: alphabet.

छ – देवनागरी वर्णमाला में चवर्ग का दूसरा व्यंजन है। इसका उच्चारण स्थान तालु है।

छँटना [*v*] to be sorted; to be thinned [as भीड़) or diffused [as बादल) to be trimmed or reduced [as मोटापा, वादी) छँटा हुआ [it carries a derogatory sense] out and out, of the first order; a rascal, rogue.

छँटनी [*nf*] retrenchment; weeding out.

छंद[1] [*nm*] metre; measure; ~शास्त्र Prosody.

छंद[2] [*nf*] a wrist ornament.

छंदोब, [*a*] metrical, cast in a metrical form.

छकाना [*v*] to gratify, to cloy; to tease/harass; to outwit.

छक्का [*nm*] a set of six; sixer [in cricket]; the sixth in a pack of cards; the six [at dice, etc.]; छक्के छुड़ाना to out-manoeuvre, to demoralise, to put out of gear.

छछूँदर [*nf*] a mole, shrew.

छज्जा [*nm*] a balcony; terrace; drip stone; hood.

छटपटाना [*v*] to writhe in pain; to be restless, to toss and tumble about;. to long/yearn impatiently.

छटा [*nf*] refulgence; splendour, lustre; beauty.

छठ [*nf*] the sixth day of the lunar fortnight.

छठा [*a*] the sixth [in order].

छठी [*H.*] the sixth day after the birth of a child for giving the name to the child.

छड़ [*nf*] a rod, bar.

छड़ी [*nf*] a stick, cane.

छत [*nf*] the ceiling; roof.

छतरी [*nf*] an umbrella; a pigeon-umbrella; parachute; kiosk; pavilion; turret; a cenotaph in honour of a Hindu national or religious leader or a big feudal lord, etc.; ~धारी सैनिक a parachuter.

छत्ता [*nm*] a beehive, archway; corridor.

छत्तीस [*a*] thirty six; [*nm*] the number thirty six.

छत्र [***nm***] **an** umbrella; a cenotaph in honour of some outstanding personality; ~ छाया patronage, protection.

छन [*nm*] a moment, instant; [*nf*] the hissing sound produced when a drop of water falls on a hot plate; tinkling/jingling sound [as of a घुँघरू).

छनक [*nf*] a tinkling or jingling sound.

छप [*nf*] a splashing sound, splash; –छप splatter, a recurrent splashing sound.

छपना [*v*] to be printed or stamped.

छपाई [*nf*] printing; cost of printing.

छपाका [*nm*] a [violent] splash [produced by the impact of something on water].

छप्पन [*a*] fifty six; [*nm*] the number fifty six.

छप्पर [*nm*] a thatch, thatched roof; –फाड़कर देना to bestow an unexpectedly large fortune, to give as a windfall.

छबीला [*a*] spruce; foppish; dandy.

छब्बीस [*a*] twenty six; [*nm*] the number twenty six.

छरहरा [*a*] slim and smart; of spare frame.

छर्रा [*nm*] a buck shot.

छल [*nm*] guile, deception; trick, ruse; sham; –कपट dodge and duplicity; –छंद guile and wile; -छंदी fraudulent, deceitful; –छिद्र guile and wile.

छलकना [*v*] to overflow, to spill out from a full vessel [during movement].

छलछल the sound of splashing or overflowing.

छलनी [*nf*] a sieve; strainer.

छलाँग [*nf*] a leap, bound.

छलावा [*nm*] illusion; apparition; will-o-th' -wisp.

छलिया [*a* and *nm*] [a] cheat, fraudulent, deceitful [person].

छल्ला [*nm*] a ring, ringlet, stirrup; washer; eye curl.

छवि [*nf*] pretty features; features; splendour, beauty; winsomeness.

छ: [*a*] six; [nm] the number six.

छाँटना [*v*] to select, to sort out; to cut, to trim/prune; to cast out, to knock off; to reduce; to retrench, to chop [as कानून].

छाँव [*nf*] shade; shadow.

छाँह [*nf*] shade; shadow; shed; ~दार shady; shadowy; –से बचना to keep away from, to evade even the shadow of.

छाता [*nm*] an umbrella.

छाती [*nf*] breast, chest; bosom; spirit; –छलनी होना the heart to be battered; –जलना to have a heartsore, to be under the spell of grief; to be terribly jealous; –ठंडी करना to relieve oneself of one's heart-burning, to assuage one's feelings; –ठोक कर कहना to make an utterance with complete assurance; to take a pledge; –पत्थर की करना to mould one's heart to face the worst; –पर पत्थर रखना to endure patiently; to still the heaving of the heart; –पर मूँग दलना to indulge in an activity designed to inflict pain on somebody, to be calculatively pains giving; –पर साँप लोटना to burn with jealousy; to be tormented by envy; –फटना the heart to rend with grief; to be overwhelmed by grief; –से लगाना to embrace, to fondle.

छात्र [*nm*] a student; ~वृत्ति scholarship.

छात्रा [*nf*] a student; a pupil. – छात्रवृत्ति, a scholarship, grant for study. छात्रालय, next. छात्रावास student hostel.

छात्रावास [*nm*] a [student] hostel, boarding house.

छानना [*v*] to filter; to strain; to percolate; to sieve; to drink bhang; to screen.

छानबीन [*nf*] investigation, scrutiny, probe.

छाना [*v*] to cover, to thatch; to overwhelm, to shadow; to overspread.

छाप [*nf*] print, imprint; impression; stamp; mark; trademark; brand.

छापना [*v*] to print; to publish; to mark.

छापा [*nm*] imprint; stamp; raid; ~मार guerilla; a raider.

छापाख़ाना [*nm*] a printing press.

छाया [*nf*] shade; shadow; image; reflection; influence; resemblance; protection; phantom; –छूना to pursue the unreal; –से दूर रहना to keep away [from], to evade the shadow [of].

छाल [*nf*] bark.

छाला [*nm*] a blister; burn.

छावनी [*nf*] a cantonment, temporary or permanent troop lodging.

छिछला [*a*] shallow; ~पन shallowness.

छिछोरा [*v*] frivolous, trivial, petty; hence ~पन.

छिड़कना [*v*] to sprinkle or spray; to water [by sprinkling]; to asperse [with].

छिदरा [*a*] bored, perforated; thinned.

छिद्र [*nm*] pore; bore; slot, aperture; opening; defect, flaw.

छिनाल [*a* and *nf*] sluttish; dissolute; a woman of easy virtue.

छिन्न [a] incised; rent; cut-off; chopped off; -भिन्न cut; broken; scattered, shattered.

छिपकली [*nf*] a lizard.

छिपाना [*v*] to hide, to conceal; to cover/screen; to disguise.

छिपाव [*nm*] concealment; secrecy; hiding, reservation.

छियानबे [*a*] ninety six; [*nm*] the number ninety six.

छियालीस [*a*] forty six; [*nm*] the number forty six.

छियासी [*a*] eighty six; [*nm*] the number eighty six.

छिलका [*nm*] peel, skin; husk; bark; shell.

छिहत्तर [*a*] seventy six; [*nm*] the number seventy six.

छींक [*nf*] a sneeze, sternutation.

छींकना [*v*] to sneeze, to sternutate; छींकते नाक कटना to be over-penalised for a petty fault.

छींटा [*nm*] a sprinkle; splash; bespattering; slight shower [of rain]; aspersion; ironical remark; ~कशी [casting] aspersion, ironical utterance.

छीछालेदर [*nf*] muck; mess; humiliation; embarrassment; disgrace.

छीनना [*v*] to snatch, to grab, to seize.

छीलना [*v*] to scrap, to scratch; to shave; to chip; to peel; to take off the skin; to bruise.

छुआछूत [*nf*] untouchability; consideration of touchability and untouchability.

छुइमुई [*nf*] touch-me-not –Mimosa pudica; an oversensitive or overdelicate person.

छुटकारा [*nm*] riddance; acquittal; release; liberation.

छुट्टी [*nf*] leave; holiday; release; permission to leave.

छुतहा [*a*] contagious, carrying contagion.

छुरा [*nm*] a razor; dagger.

छुरी [nf] a knife; a small dagger.

छू [*nf*] sudden outblow of a gush of air from the mouth [as during incantation, conjuration, enchantment and magic, etc.]; ~मंतर an incantation; a charm; hey presto; ~मंतर होना [said of person or pain, etc.] to disappear forthwith, to vanish.

छूट [*nf*] rebate, discount; concession; riddance; release; remission; exemption; relaxation; liberty.

छूटना [*a*] to be left behind or out; to lag; to be dismissed/discharged or released; to get rid of; to be abandoned.

छूत [*nf*] contagion; contamination; –की बीमारी a contagious disease.

छूना [*v*] to touch; to feel.

छेड़खानी [*nf*] act of teasing or provoking; offensive activity; raillery; pranks.

छेड़छाड़ [*nf*] provocation; molestation; teasing; pricks and pranks.

छेड़ना [*v*] to tease, to irritate; to meddle; to disturb; to stir up; to commence [a work].

छेद [*nm*] a hole, bore; perforation; opening; incision, puncture.

छेदना [*v*] to bore, to make a hole; to perforate, to pierce; to incise.

छैला [*nm*] a dandy; a foppish person; [*a*] dandical; foppish.

छोकरा [*nm*] a lad, boy.

छोटा [*a*] small; little; short; young [er]; petty; subordinate; junior; insignificant; –मोटा petty, minor, insignificant, ordinary; –मुँह बड़ी बात proud words from a weak stomach.

छोटाई [*nf*] smallness; pettiness; shortness; juniority.

छोड़ना [*v*] to leave; to abandon; to omit; to release; to entrust to; to assign to [as किसी पर].

छोर [*nm*] the end, fag end; extremity; edge.

छौंकना [*v*] to season.

छौना [*nm*] a young one of swine.

ज ja the third letter of the second pentad [i.e., चवर्ग] of the Devanagari: alphabet; a suffix denoting the sense of born of [as जलज, अंडज, वातज, etc.]

ज - देवनागरी व्यंजन में चवर्ग का तीसरा अक्षर है। इसका उच्चारण शब्द तालु है।

जंग [*nf*] war; battle; fight. ~ करना, to make or to wage war. – जंगावर next. जंगजू seeking fight; warlike, aggressive. जंगबाज़ a warlike person. ई, war-mongering.

जंकशन [*nm*] a [railway] junction.

जंग [*nf*] war, battle, fight.

ज़ंग [*nm*] rust.

जंगम [*a*] moving; movable.

जंगल [*nm*] forest, wood; wilderness; –में मंगल a paradise in wilderness.

जंगली [*a*] savage; wild; beastly.

जंगलीपन [*nf*] **1** wildness, wild state. **2** uncouthness.

जंगी [*a*] martial, relating to war; huge, large; –बेड़ा a naval fleet.

जंजाल [*nm*] botheration; entanglement; embarrassment; cares, trouble; fuss; [*nf*] a small cannon.

ज़ंजीर [*nf*] a chain; shackle.

जंतरी [*nf*] an almanac.

जंतु [*nm*] a creature, an animal.

जँभाई [*nf*] yawning, a yawn.

जकड़ना [*v*] to grasp, to hold firmly; to tighten.

जकार [*nm*] the letter ज [ja] and its sound.

जकारांत [*a*] [a word] ending in ज.

ज़ख़ीरा [*nm*] stock, hoard, store.

ज़ख़्म [*nm*] a wound, cut, injury; ulcer; –पर नमक छिड़कना to afflict the afflicted, to add insult to injury.

ज़ख़्मी [*a*] wounded, hurt, injured.

जग [*nm*] the world, universe; people; ~हँसाई popular ridicule/mockery; open calumny.

जगत [*nf*] the world, universe.

जगत् [*nf*] the high platform surrounding a well.

जगना [*v*] to wake up, to be awake, to be aroused.

जगमगा/ना [v] to be refulgent, to glitter, to shine, to gleam; ~ हट refulgence, glitter, shine, gleam, glimmer.

जगह [*nf*] place; space, quarter; post; -जगह everywhere.

जगाना [*v*] to wake up, to awaken; to arouse.

जगार [*nf*] wake; state of being or keeping awake.

जघन्य [*a*] low; detestable, abominable; heinous.

जांघिया [*nf*] shorts.

ज़च्चा [*nf*] a woman in post-delivery confinement; ~खाना/घर maternity home; -बच्चा the new-born and the mother in confinement.

ज़ज्ब [*a*] absorbed; assimilated.

ज़ज्बा [*nm*] emotion, feeling; passion; [~ त plural]; ~ ती emotional.

जटा [*nm*] matted or tangled hair; fibrous root; -जूट matted hair rolled up over the head.

जटित [*a*] studded, embedded with.

जटिल [*a*] intricate, complicated; inaccessible; hence ~ ता.

जठ/र [*nm*] the stomach; ~राग्नि the digestive fire of the stomach.

जड़ [*nf*] root; [a] inanimate, immovable, inert; idiot; stupid; –जगत् the inanimate world; –पदार्थ matter; ~ बुद्धि/मति idiot; stupid; –उखाड़ना to root out, to strike at the root; to destroy completely; –जमना/पकड़ना to strike deep roots; to establish; to consolidate [oneself].

जड़ता [*nf*] inertia, torpor; insensibility; idiocy, stupidity; stupefaction.

जड़ना [*v*] to stud; to inlay; to fix, to set; to mount [as a तस्वीर]; to put in; to lay on [as तमाचा].

जड़ाऊ [*a*] studded or inset with jewels.

जड़ी [*nf*] a simple, medicinal root; -बूटी medicinal herbs, simples.

जताना [*v*] to apprise, to make known; to warn.

जत्था [*nm*] a band; gang; flock.

जन [*nm*] people; public; folk; ~गणना census; ~जीवन public life; public living; ~तंत्र democracy; ~पद rural region; ~पदीय regional; ~प्रिय popular; ~मत public opinion; ~संग्रह referendum; plebiscite; ~वासा a temporary dwelling for a marriage party; ~श्रुति tradition; rumour; ~संख्या population; ~समाज community at large; ~समुदाय crowd; community; ~समूह crowd; ~साधारण the common man; community at large; the masses; ~ हित public welfare/ interest.

ज़न [*nf*] a woman.

जनक [*nm*] father; procreator; originator.

जानकी [*s.*] mythol. daughter of Janak: title of Sitā.

ज़नख़ा [*nm*] a eunuch, womanly man.

जन/जाति [*nm*] a tribe; ~जातीय tribal.

जनता [*nm*] the public, people, masses.

जनना [*v*] to produce, to give birth, to bear.

जननी [*nf*] mother, progenitrix.

जनवरी [*nf*] [the month of] January.

जनाज़ा [*nm*] the corpse wrapped in a coffin-cloth; bier [with the corpse laid on it].

ज़नानख़ाना [*nm*] the harem, seraglio; female apartment.

ज़नाना [*a*] female, feminine; impotent; [*nm*] female apartment; a eunuch; ~पन effeminacy; impotence; hence जनानी.

जनाब [*a* and *nm*] mister; [int.] Sir!, your excellency; –आली Your Honour!, Your Excellency!

जन्म [*nm*] birth; origin; genesis; ~कुंडली a short horoscope; ~दाता progenitor; father; originator; ~दिन/दिवस birthday; ~पत्र/पत्रिका/पत्री a horoscope; ~भूमि motherland; ~स्थान birth place.

जन्मजात [*a*] congenital; inherent, innate.

जन्मांतर [*nm*] another birth; ~वाद doctrine of rebirth.

जन्मोत्तर [*a*] post-natal.

जन्मोत्सव [*nm*] birthday celebration.

जपना [*v*] to murmur or to utter quiet prayers; to repeat reverentially [God's name as a sacred formula].

जब [*adv*] when; ~कि when; whenever, at whatever time; ~तब sometime; at times; -उत्तर गयी लोई तो क्या करेगा कोई the shameless dreads no society; –तक साँस तब तक आस as long as there is life there is hope.

जबड़ा [*nm*] a jaw.

ज़बर [*a*] strong; huge.

जबरद/स्त [*a*] strong, powerful; vigorous, violent; high-handed; ~स्ती high handedness, injustice; by force, forcibly.

ज़बरन [*adv*] by force, forcibly.

ज़बह [*nm*] slaughtering, slaughter.

ज़बान [*nf*] tongue; language; ~दराज़ loquacious, sharp-tongued; कैंची-सी चलना the tongue to run on wheels; –को लगाम जरूरी है a bridle for the tongue is a necessary piece of furniture; –खुलना to find one's tongue; to talk with one's tongue in one's cheek; –चलाना to wag one's tongue, to be too talkative; –थामना to hold the tongue; –दबाकर कहना to utter in whispers; to say implicitly; –देना to pledge one's word [to], to make a commitment; –पकड़ना to cavil [at]; to hush up; –पर लाना to utter, to mention; –पलटना to go back on one's word; –पर ताला लगाना to be stricken dumb, to be rendered speechless; –बंद करना to silence, to render speechless; –में लगाम न होना to lose control on one's tongue; not to have a civil tongue in one's head; –सँभाल कर बोलना to keep a civil tongue in one's head; –हारना to be committed; to have pledged one's word; –हिलाना to speak out, to make an utterance.

ज़बानी [*a*] oral, verbal; unwritten; [*adv*] orally, verbally;–जमा ख़र्च sweet nothing, superficial utterances, tall talk.

ज़ब्त [*a*] forfeited, confiscated, impounded; [*nm*] forbearance.

जमघट [*nm*] crowded assembly, multitude.

जमा [*a*] collected, deposited; [*nm*] deposit; credit; accumulation; sum total; –ख़र्च debit and credit; receipts and disbursements; –जथा accumulation accumulated wealth; -पूँजी total accumulation.

जमाई [*nm*] a son-in-law.

जमात [*nm*] a class; assembly; group.

जमादार [*nm*] a jamadar, head of a group; sweeper.

ज़मानत [*nf*] surety; bail; security; guarantee.

ज़मानती [*a*] bailable, guaranteeing; [*nm*] a surety, guarantor.

ज़माना [*nm*] time [*a*] age, period; present day world; fortunate times; -पलटना/बदलना the tide to take a turn; ज़माने की गर्दिश temporal vicissitudes.

जमाव [*nm*] assembly, gathering; setting up, concentration; accumulation.

ज़मीं [*nf*] see जमीन.

ज़मीकंद [*nm*] a vegetable; the yam.

ज़मींदार [*nm*] a landlord; cultivator; ~री zamindari; landlordism; landed estate; cultivation.

ज़मीन [*nf*] the earth; land, ground; ground work; background; – आसमान एक करना to leave no stone unturned, to make all possible efforts; -आसमान के कुलाबे मिलाना to speak of heaven and earth in one breath, to speak in hyperboles; to try one's level best; –चटाना/दिखाना to fell/throw flat; –चूमना to lie prostrate; to be felled by face; –में गड़ जाना to be bashfully embarrassed, to be deeply ashamed/sheepish.

जम्हाई [*nf*] yawning; लेना to yawn.

जम्हाना [*v*] to yawn.

जयंती [*nf*] anniversary; jubilee.

जय [*nf*] conquest; victory; triumph; [*a*] used as a suffix in compound words meaning one who has achieved a victory or has triumphed over [e.g., मृत्युंजय धनंजय etc.]; [int] bravo! hurrah!.

जयकार [*nm*] applause, applausive shouts, cheers hailing victory.

जय-जयकार [*nf*] triumphal cheers, applausive shouts, applause hailing a victory.

ज़यी [*a*] winner, victorious; [*nm*] a conqueror.

ज़र [*nm*] wealth, riches; ~खरीद purchased, bought; ~ख़ेज fertile; ख़ेज़ी fertility.

ज़रदा [*nm*] scented and specially prepared tobacco, a special dish of rice treated with saffron.

जरनैल [*nm*] a general.

ज़रब [*nm*] trauma; blow, stroke; crack; multiplication; -तकसीम multiplication and division.

जरसी [*nf*] a jersey.

जरा [*nf*] old age, senility.

ज़रा [*a*] little, a bit, slight; [*adv*] for a while; slightly; just [as –ठहरो just wait]; please; kindly [as –मेरे साथ चलो]; -जरा in bits; petty, trivial; -सा some; small, a small quantity.

जरायु [*nm*] placenta; ~ज placenta.

ज़रिया [*nm*] means; medium, instrument.

ज़री [*nf*] gold brocade, gold lace.

जरीब [*nm*] a land-measuring chain.

ज़रूर [*adv*] certainly; undoubtedly, positively; without fail; -जरूर positively, without fail.

ज़रूरत [*nf*] necessity, importance; need, requirement.

ज़रूरी [*a*] important; necessary, needful; compulsory; indispensable.

जर्जर [*a*] decrepit, worn out; crushed, senescent; ~ता senescence, decrepitude.

ज़र्द [*a*] pale, yellow.

ज़र्दी [*nf*] paleness, yellowness; the yellow [part].

ज़र्रा [*nm*] an atom, a particle; –ज़र्रा each and every particle.

ज़र्रा/ह [*nm*] a [traditionally trained] surgeon, one who dresses wounds; ~ही surgery, dressing of wounds.

जल [nm] water, aqua; hydro– ~घड़ी a water-clock; -चर/चारी aquatic [animal, etc.]; -जंतु aquatic creatures; ~ज/जात aqueous; lotus; ~ डमरूमध्य a strait; ~द a cloud; ~ दस्यु a pirate; ~धर a cloud; ~धारा a water current; ~धि an ocean; ~प्रपात a waterfall, cataract; ~प्रलय cataclysm, deluge; ~प्रवाह a torrent/current of water; प्लावन inundation; ~भीति hydrophobia; ~मग्न submerged by or immersed in water; ~ मय submerged in water; watery, hydrous; ~मार्ग channel, waterways; watercourse; ~यात्रा a voyage; ~यान a ship, vessel; boat; ~युद्ध naval war; ~स्तर water level; ~स्थल land and water; ~स्रोत source of water; water current; ~हीन waterfree; without water.

ज़लज़ला [*nm*] an earthquake.

जलन [*nf*] a burning sensation; jealousy.

जल/ना [*v*] to burn, to be inflamed/kindled; to be scorched; to feel jealous, to envy; -भुन

कर कबाब/कोयला/राख होना to burn with rage or envy; ~ती आग में कूदना to knowingly burn one's fingers; ~ती आग में घी/तेल डालना to add fuel to the fire; जली कटी सुनाना to make caustic and stinging remarks; जले पर नमक छिड़कना to add insult to injury.

जलपान [*nm*] light refreshment; breakfast; at home.

जलवायु [*nf*] climate; ~विज्ञान climatology.

जलसा [*nm*] a meeting, function; festivity; social gathering.

जलाना [*v*] to light, to kindle; to burn, to scorch; to excite envy, to provoke jealousy.

ज़लालत [*nf*] meanness, wretchedness; disgrace.

जलावतन [*nm*] exile; [*a*] exiled.

जलावर्त [*nm*] a whirlpool.

ज़लील [*a*] mean, wretched, contemptible; disgraced, insulted.

जलूस [*nm*] a procession.

जलेबी [*nf*] a kind of sweetmeat; a kind of firework that shoots up like spiral.

जलोदर [*nm*] dropsy.

जलौका [*nf*] see जौंक.

जल्द [*adv*] quickly; swiftly; hurriedly; instantly.

जल्दी [*nf*] hurry, haste, [*adv*] quickly, urgently, immediately.

जल्लाद [*nm*] a slaughterer; butcher; [*a*] cruel or merciless [person].

जवान [*a*] young/youthful; [*nm*] a youth; soldier.

जवानी [*nf*] youth, young age, youthfulness;–का आलम the time of youthful frolic or adventure;–दीवानी है youth knows no bounds;–में माँझा ढीला young age, old ways.

जवाब [*nm*] reply, answer; response; counter-move; ~तलबी [seeking of] an explanation; ~देह responsible, answerable, accountable; ~देही responsibility, accountability; obligation.

जवाबी [*a*] counter; in the nature of or requiring a reply.

जवा/हर [*nm*] a jewel; ~हिरात jewellery.

जश्न [*nm*] festivity, merriment, festive celebration.

जहन्नुम [*nm*] hell, inferno.

ज़हर [*nm*] poison, venom; anything bitter or disagreeable; [*a*] disagreeable, unpalatable; ~वाद a carbuncle; septic; ~ उगलना to make venomous utterances; to speak spitefully; ~का घूँट a bitter/disagreeable phenomenon; mouthful of poison; ~ पीकर रह जाना to stand/suppress unbearable rage; to tolerate insult/humiliation.

ज़हरी/ला [*a*] full of venom; venomous, poisonous.

जहाँ [*adv*] where, wherever; -तक as far as;-तहाँ here, and there; everywhere, all round; –का तहाँ at the original place.

जहाज़ [*nm*] a vessel, ship; ~रानी shipping, navigation.

जहाज़ी [*a*] naval, nautical; [*nm*] a mariner, sailor.

जहान [*nm*] the world, the people.

जहालत [*nf*] illiteracy; incivility, boorishness.

जाँघ [*nf*] a thigh.

जाँघिया [*nf*] a lower underwear, short drawers.

जाँच [*nf*] investigation, examination; test; scanning; enquiry; -पड़ताल investigation, enquiry.

जाँचना [*v*] to investigate; to verify; to test; to evaluate.

जाकेट [*nf*] a jacket.

जागना [*v*] to rise, to wake up; to be alert; to be on the ascendance [as नसीब–]; to brighten up [as लौ–].

जागरण [*nm*] awakening, wakefulness; vigil; sitting through the night in religious or festive collective singing.

जागरूक [*a*] alert, vigilant, wakeful; hence ~ता.

जागीर [*nf*] property, landed property; land, etc. given by the government as a reward, jaghir; ~दार the holder of a जागीर, a fief, jaghirdar; ~दारी feudalism; jaghirdari.

जागीरी [*nf*] pertaining to or related to landed property.

जागृति [*nf*] awakening.

जाड़ा [*nf*] cold; winter.

जात [*a*] born; manifest; [*nf*] caste; -पाँत caste, caste and community.

ज़ात [*nf*] self; person; individual; individuality; breed; characteristic quality.

जाति [*nf*] caste; community; race, sect; genus; type; kind; breed; ~च्युत expelled from the community; -पाँति caste and community; -भ्रष्ट

fallen from one's caste/community; ~वाचक (संज्ञा) common [noun]; ~वाद casteism, racism, racialism; communalism.

जाती [*a*] personal, individual.

जातीय [*a*] racial; communal; generic.

जातीयता [*nf*] raciality; communalism.

जादू [*nm*] magic, juggling, charm; spell; -टोना sorcery; witchcraft; voodooism; –वह जो सिर पर चढ़ कर बोले magic manifests itself in procuring quiet obeisance; the means that achieve the end are the best means.

जादूगर [*nm*] a magician, juggler; sorcerer, conjurer.

जान [*nf*] life, animation; stamina, vitality, energy; essence; spirit; sweetheart; darling; ~बीमा life-insurance; ~व माल life and property/ belongings; ~का नुकसान loss of life; ~की ख़ैर मनाना to endeavour or pray for the safety of life;–के लाले पड़ना to be under the shadow of death, to be in an irretrievably risky position; –खाना to pester constantly;–छुड़ाना to get rid of, to skulk from;–देना to sacrifice; to be in passionate love [with]; –निकलना to become lifeless, to be in great agony; –पर आना, –पर आ बनना to be exposed to imminent danger, to be exposed to imminent risk of life; –पर खेलना to stake one's life, to put one's life in peril;– बची लाखों पाये security of life represents the greatest achievement; –में जान आना to feel relieved, to feel comforted; –लड़ाना to exert to the utmost, to strain every nerve;–लेना to kill, to inflict grave suffering; to put to arduous labour;–सूखना to be scared out of wits; to be stunned;–से मारना to kill;–से जाना to pass away; to give up life;–से मार डालना to deprive of life; –से हाथ धो बैठना to give up one's life, to have to abandon one's life;–है तो जहान है no life, no pleasure; the world lives as long as you live.

जानका/र [*a*] knowing; knowledgeable; conversant; [nm] one who knows; ~री knowledge, acquaintance.

जानना [*v*] to know, to become aware of; to perceive.

जान-पहचान [*nf*] acquaintance.

जानवर [*nm*] animal, beast.

जाना [*v*] to go, to depart; to lose [as मेरा क्या जाता है?]; to flow [as खून जा रहा है]; जा धमकना to appear on the scene all of a sudden.

जानिब [*nf*] side, direction. – की towards. – जानिबदार partial; a supporter; patron. (= जरुदार) support; partiality. जानिबदारी करना (की), to take the side or part (of); to be partial (to).

जापा [*nm*] delivery, childbirth; ~घर maternity home.

ज़ाब्ता [*nm*] rule, regulation; –दीवानी code of civil procedure; –फ़ौजदारी code of criminal procedure.

जाम [*a*] jammed; [*nm*] jam; a peg.

जा/मा [*nm*] attire, clothing; a long gown worn by the bride-groom; ~मे में फूले न समाना to be puffed up/swollen with joy; ~में से बाहर होना to be unable to contain oneself [out of joy or rage]; to transcend one's limits.

जामाता [*nm*] a son-in-law.

जामुन [*nf*] jambo, a black plum [the tree and its fruit].

ज़ाय/क़ा [*nm*] taste, relish; ~केदार delicious, tasty.

जायज़ [*a*] suitable; proper; befitting; legitimate.

जायज़ा [*nm*] scrutiny, survey.

जायदाद [*nf*] property.

जाया [*nf*] spouse, wife; [*a*] born [of].

ज़ाया [*a*] waste, ruined.

जार [*nm*] an adulterer, a paramour.

जारी [*a*] continued; current, running; issued; in force.

जाल [*nm*] a net, network; mesh; snare; plot; ~साज़ a conspirer; forgerer; deceitful; ~साज़ी plotting; conspiracy; forgery.

जाला [*nm*] a cobweb; net; flake; cataract.

ज़ालिम [*a*] cruel, atrocious, tyrannical; [*nm*] a tyrant.

जाली [*a*] forged, counterfeit; [*nm*] mesh; hammock; muzzle; grating.

जासू/स [*nm*] a spy, detective; ~सी espionage, spying, intelligence work; detective.

ज़ाहिर [*a*] apparent; obvious; evident.

जाहिल [*a*] illiterate; uncivil, boorish.

ज़िंदगी [*nf*] life; liveliness.

ज़िंदा [*a*] alive, living; not dead; ~दिल sprightly, lively, cheerful; ~ दिली sprightliness, liveliness, cheerfulness; ~बाद long live!

जिंस [*nf*] commodity; cereals.

जिक्र [*nm*] mention; reference.

जिगर [*nm*] the liver; heart; courage.

जिगरा [*nm*] courage.

जिगरी [*a*] pertaining to the liver, beloved, dear; very intimate; –दोस्त bosom friend, very intimate friend.

जिज्ञा/सा [*nf*] curiosity, inquisitiveness; learnership; ~सु curious, inquisitive; willing to learn; [*nm*] a learner.

जित/ना [*a*] as much as; ~ने as many [as].

ज़िद [*nf*] obstinacy, stubbornness; insistence.

ज़िद्दी [*a*] obstinate, stubborn, inflexible; insistent.

ज़िधर [*adv*] wherever, in whichever direction.

जिन [*nm*] Lord Buddha; the Jain tirthankars; [*pro*] the plural form of जिस.

ज़िना [*nm*] adultery.

जिन्न [*nm*] a jinnee.

ज़ि/म्मा [*nm*] responsibility, charge, obligation; ~म्मेदार, ~ म्मेवार responsible, answerable; ~म्मेदारी, ~म्मेवारी responsibility, obligation.

जिरह [*nf*] cross-examination, cross-questioning.

ज़िरहबख्तर [*nm*] armour.

ज़िला [*nm*] a district.

ज़िलाधीश [*nm*] district magistrate.

जिल्द [*nf*] binding [of a book]; cover; skin; ~बंद bound [book]; ~बंदी book binding work; ~साज़ a book binder, ~साज़ी book binding.

ज़िल्लत [*nf*] humiliation, insult.

जिस [*pro*] an oblique form of जो [see].

जिस्म [*nm*] body; physique.

जिहाद [*nm*] crusade.

जिह्वा [*nf*] the tongue, lingua.

जी [*nm*] mind; heart; [*ind*] an honorofic suffix, yes!, yes, sir !; –उचटना to be ennuied, get disinterested; not to be able to concentrate [on]; –करना to set heart on, to long [for]; –की जी में रहना [a wish or longing] not to have a chance for expression or materialisation; –खट्टा होना to be disenchanted/disgusted; –खोलकर freely, without any restraint or stint; to one's heart's content; –चाहना to desire, to long [for]; –चुराना to shirk [work]; to cast a spell [upon], to charm, to captivate; –छोटा करना to lose heart, to be discouraged; –जान से passionately; wholeheartedly; ~ कुर्बान devoted heart and soul; –दु:खाना to grieve, to cause grief [to]; –धकधक करना/धड़कना the heart to palpitate; to have the palpitation of heart enhanced; –बहलाना to recreate; to divert the mind, to amuse so as to dissipate reflection; –भर जाना lit. the heart to be full; to be touched with compassion or be deeply moved; –मितलाना/ मिचलाना to feel nausea, to feel like vomiting;–में आना to occur in one's mind; to have a fancy [for];–ललचाना to hanker after, to feel allured; –लुभाना to allure or entice, captivate the heart of; –से उतर जाना to lose the favour or regard of, to fall in the esteem of.

जीजा [*nf*] an elder sister's husband.

जीजी [*nf*] an elder sister.

ज़ीट [*nf*] boasting, bragging.

जीत [*nf*] victory; success.

जीतना [*v*] to win, to conquer, to prevail upon; to master.

जीता [*a*] living; won; -जागता living, lively; up and kicking; जीते रहो! may you live long!

ज़ीन [*nf*] a saddle; a kind of thick suiting [cloth].

जीना [*v*] to live, to be alive.

ज़ीना [*nm*] a staircase, ladder.

जीभ [*nf*] tongue, lingua; –का चटखारे लेना to have an inkling for dainties.

जीमना [*v*] to feast.

जीवंत [*a*] lively, living, life-like.

जीव [*nm*] a creature, living being; life; soul; -जंतु creatures; tiny creatures; ~धारी living being, organism; ~हत्या/हिंसा destruction of life; ~हीन lifeless.

जीवट [*nm*] courage; spirit; adventure; endurance.

जीवन [*nm*] life; animation; existence; ~चरित biography; ~चर्या living; routine of life; ~दान sacrifice of life; commitment to spare somebody's life; ~वृत्त/वृत्तांत biography, bio-data;

-संघर्ष struggle for life; struggle for existence; -स्तर standard of living; ~हीन lifeless; insipid.

जीवनी [*nf*] biography.

जीवाणु [*nm*] bacteria; microbe.

जीविका [*nf*] livelihood; subsistence.

जीवित [*a*] alive, living.

जुआ [*nm*] gambling; yoke; ~ खाना/घर a gambling den, gambling house.

जुआरी [*nm*] a gambler.

जुकाम [*nm*] cold, catarrh.

जुग [*nm*] see युग–जुग for ages, forever.

जुगत [*nf*] a skilful device, contrivance; tact.

जुटना [*v*] to be engaged [in a work] in full force; to unite; to assemble, to flock.

जुड़वाँ [*nm*] twins.

जुताई [*nf*] [the act or process of] ploughing; tillage.

जुदा [*a*] separate; disunited; ~ ई separation.

जुमला [*nm*] a sentence; [*a*] all, total.

जुमा [*nm*] Friday.

जुर्म [*nm*] crime; offence.

जुर्माना [*nm*] fine, penalty.

जुर्रत [*nf*] pluck, courage; effrontery; check.

जुर्राब [*nf*] socks, stocking.

जुलाई [*nf*] [the month of] July.

जुलाब [*nm*] a purgative.

जुलाहा [*nm*] a weaver.

जुलूस [*nm*] a procession.

जुल्फ़ [*nf*] [curled] lock of hair.

जुल्म [*nm*] oppression, tyranny, outrage.

जुल्मी [*a*] tyrant. tyrannical; oppressive.

जूँ [*nf*] a louse.

जूझना [*v*] to fight hard, to struggle; to combat.

जूट [*nm*] jute; matted hair.

जूठन [*nf*] leavings [of food, drink, etc.]

जूठा [*a*] defiled by eating, drinking or using otherwise.

जूड़ा [*nm*] a bun-shaped hair-do.

जूड़ी [*nf*] ague, malarial fever.

जूता [*nm*] a shoe, footwear; –चाटना to lick somebody's shoe, to be servilely flattering; जूतों से ख़बर लेना to apply the shoe, to inflict a shoe-beating; जूते से बात करना to straight-away resort to the application of shoe; जूते की नोक पर मारना to consider [somebody] as absolutely of no significance; to care a fig [for]; जूतमपैजार a shoe-fight, exchange of shoe-blows.

जूती [*nf*] a typical light shoe; ladies' footwear; –के बराबर समझना to treat with utter contempt, to consider as absolutely of no value; जूतियाँ सीधी करना to perform menial chores; to cringe to, to behave obsequiously.

जून [*nm*] [the month of] June; time; half-a-day.

जूरी [*nf*] the jury; –अदालत the court of the jury.

जेठ [*nm*] the third month of the Hindu lunar calendar; an elder brother of a woman's husband.

जेब [*nf*] a pocket; ~ कट/कतरा pick-pocket; ~ खर्च pocket expenses, pocket money.

जेल [*nf*] prison, jail/gaol; –काटना to suffer imprisonment, to be put behind the bars.

जेलख़ाना [*nm*] a prison- house, jail/gaol.

जेलर [*nm*] a jailor/gaoler.

जेवर [*nm*] an ornament; [*pl.*] jewellery.

जेहन [*nf*] intellect.

जैसा [*a*] similar to, like, resembling; [adv] as, like, such as; जैसे को तैसा tit for tat, measure for measure.

जैसे [*adv*] as, as if; according as; [ind] for example; for instance; –जैसे as; –तैसे somehow; somehow or the other; –ही as soon as, no sooner than.

जोंक [*nf*] a leech; [fig] a blood-sucker, parasite.

जो [*pro*] who; which; what; that; [ind] if; –भी हो however; at any rate; –हो, सो हो come what may.

जोखिम [*nm*] risk, danger; enterprise; –उठाना/लेना to take a risk, to run a hazard.

जोगिया [*a*] saffron, saffron-coloured.

जोगी [*nm*] an ascetic, a mendicant.

जोड़ [*nm*] sum, total; addition, union; joint; articulation; splice; seam; patch; match; –तोड़ manipulation, machination, contrivance; –का matching, equal to; –का तोड़ a match, counter; –बाकी debit and credit; addition and subtraction.

जोड़ना [*v*] to add, to sum up; to link; to unite; to connect; to attach; to collect, to accumulate; to weld; to bind; to cement; to set [as bone, etc.]; to assemble; to save up.

जोड़ा [*nm*] a pair, couple; suit.

जोड़ी [*nf*] a pair, couple; pair of clubs; –का matching; of equal status; ~ दार a match; comrade; matching.

जोत [*nf*] tillage, holding.

जोतना [*v*] to plough, to till; to yoke; to harness, to work.

जोबन [*nm*] blooming youth; youthful charm, full bloom; puberty; youthful breasts.

जोर [*nm*] strength; force, power; stress, strain; emphasis; support; influence; –आजमाइश trial of strength; –जबरदस्ती coercion, duress; force; –जुल्म oppression and injustice; ~ दार powerful; strong, forceful; influential; –शोर zest, enthusiasm; fast tempo; gusto; –का powerful, forceful, violent; vigorous; –डालना to put pressure [on], to influence, to insist; –पकड़ना to acquire momentum/strength; –पर होना to be in full swing, to be in speed.

जोरू [*nf*] wife; –न जाँता अल्ला मियाँ से नाता no household, no worldly cares.

जोश [*nm*] enthusiasm; excitement, fervour; passion; zeal.

जोशीला [*a*] spirited, enthusiastic, zealous; vigorous.

जौहर [*nm*] valour; skill or skilful manipulation, a mediaeval Rajput custom wherein the women performed self-immolation to save their honour.

जौहरी [*nm*] a jeweller; a connoisseur.

ज्ञा/त [*a*] known; comprehended; ~ ता one who knows, a scholar.

ज्ञान [*nm*] knowledge, learning; sense; –साधना pursuit of knowledge.

ज्ञानी [*a*] wise, learned; knowledgeable; well informed; one who has achieved self-realisation.

ज्ञानेंद्रिय [*nf*] the [five] senses of perception, viz. the eye, the ear, the nose, the tongue and the skin.

ज्ञापन [*nm*] memorandum; proclaiming; making known; hence ज्ञापित।

ज्यादती [*nf*] excess; high-handedness; injustice.

ज्यादा [*a*] more; many; much; plenty.

ज्यामि/ति [*nf*] Geometry; ~ तीय geometrical.

ज्येष्ठ [*a*] the eldest [brother, son, etc.], the senior-most; senior, elder.

ज्यों [*ind*] as, as if; –ज्यों as; –त्यों somehow, by manipulation; –ही as soon as; –का त्यों as it was before, intact.

ज्योति [*nf*] light; flame; lustre; vision.

ज्योतिष [*nf*] astronomy, astrology.

ज्योतिषी [*nm*] an astrologer.

ज्वर [*nm*] fever, pyrexia.

ज्वरित [*adj.*], suffering from fever; feverish.

ज्वार [*nm*] flood tide; [great] millet; –भाटा flood tide and ebb tide.

ज्वाला [*nf*] flame, blaze.

ज्वालामुखी [*nm*] a volcano; [*a*] volcanic; –पर्वत volcanic mountain, a volcano.

झ the fourth letter of the second pentad [i.e., चवर्ग] of the Devanagari: alphabet.

झ – देवनागरी व्यंजन वर्ण का नवाँ और चवर्ग का चौथा वर्ण है। इस वर्ण का उच्चारण स्थान तालु है।

झंकार [*nf*] tinkling, jingling; clinking sound; chirr.

झंकारना [*v*] **1** to ring; to clink, to jingle; to rattle; to clang; to resound (the string of a musical instrument). **2** to chirp (as a cricket). **3** to cause to ring or to resound; to pluck (a string).

झंझट [*nm*] botheration; mess; trouble; imbroglio.

झंडा [*nm*] a flag, banner, standard; ensign; –उठाना to hold a banner aloft; to take up a cause;– खड़ा करना to invoke people to fight for a cause; to establish a record; –गाड़ना to set up a flag, to plant a standard; to achieve a victory; –झुकना to lower a flag; to be in mourning.

झंडी [*nf*] a bunting, small flag.

झक [*nf*] whim; craze: [*a*] clean, tidy.

झकझोरनाद [*v*] to shake or jerk violently.

झकझोरा [*nm*] a violent jerk.

झकाझक [*a*] spotlessly clean, shiningly tidy, clean and -tidy.

झकार [*nm*] the letter झ [jha] and its sound; ~ रांत [word ending in झ [jha].

झकोरा [*nm*] **1** shaking (as of a tree by wind); a gust, blast (of wind); a heavy shower; squall; a large wave. **2** an impulse; blow, impact. – ~ खाना, to be buffeted, shaken or tossed. ~ देना, to shake, to buffer (as wind a tree).

झक्की [*a*] crazy, whimsical; whacky; given to prattling [out of indignation/discontentment].

झख [*nf*] a fish; craze, whim; –मारना to be engaged in a fruitless work, to idle away time.

झगड़ना [*v*] to quarrel; to altercate; to scramble.

झगड़ा [*nm*] quarrel, dispute, altercation, scramble, fray.

झगड़ालू [*a*] quarrelsome, disputatious, pugnacious.

झट [*adv*] instantly; at once.

झटकना [*a*] to jerk off, to twitch; to wrest, to snatch; to extort; to obtain by force or fraud.

झटका [*nm*] a jerk, jolt, shock; lurch; beheading [an animal] with one stroke; the meat of an animal so beheaded.

झटपट [*adv*] instantaneously; quickly, promptly.

झड़प [*nf*] a skirmish, snap; fight; altercation.

झड़ी [*nf*] incessant downpour; non-stop shower.

झनक [*nf*] tinkling, clinking, clink-clank.

झनझना/ना [*v*] to be benumbed or cramped; to be infused with a sharp benumbing sensation; to clang, to tinkle, to jingle; hence ~ हट।

झप –होना to be suddenly closed [eyes]; to be rendered visionless all of a sudden.

झपक **1** a closing or lowering of the eyelids; a nod (in drwowsiness). **2** a blink of the eye; a moment, twinkling of the eye. **3** swinging, swaying (as of a fan).

झपकना [*v*] to blink, to wink; to twinkle.

झपकी [*nf*] a nap, short sleep; blink.

झपटना [*v*] to make a sudden swoop, to pounce [upon], to dash; to snatch; to grab.

झपट्टा [*nm*] a swoop, pounce.

झमेला [*nm*] a mess; botheration; imbroglio.

झरना [*nm*] a spring; cascade, fall; [*v*] to flow forth, to spring; to fall; to trickle.

झरोखा [*nm*] an oriel, oriel window, network of airholes/apertures; mesh.

झलक [*nf*] a glimpse; semblance.

झलमलाना [*v*] to gleam, to glitter; to be aglow with a tremulous light.

झलाई [*nm*] welding; welding charges.

झल्लाना [*v*] to shout peevishly; to be irritated, to fret and fume; hence झल्लाहट।

झाँकना [*v*] to peep in or out, to peer.

झाँकी [*nf*] a glimpse; tableau; scene.

झाँसा [*nm*] wheedling, hood-winking.

झाग [*nm*] foam, lather; scum; froth; ~ दार foamy; frothy; lathery; scummy.

झाड़ [*nm*] a bush, shrub; small tree; chandelier; reprimand, scolding; –फानूस chandelier; –पिलाना to administer a reprimand.

झाड़न [*nf*] a duster; whisk; sweepings.

झाड़/ना [*v*] to sweep, to brush, to clean; to chide, to reprimand; to extort; to grab; to shake or knock off; to hocus-pocus; **–फूँक** hocus-pocus.

झाड़ी [*nf*] a bush, thicket.

झाड़ू [*nm*] a broom, besom.

झापड़ [*nm*] a full-blooded slap.

झाल [*nm*] solder, soldering.

झालना [*v*] to solder; to weld.

झालर [*nf*] festoon; frill, fringe.

झिझक [*nf*] hesitation, hitch.

झिझकना [*v*] to hesitate; to feel shy.

झिड़कना [*v*] to tick off, to snap, to snub.

झिड़की [*nf*] ticking off, snap, snub.

झिपना [*a*] to be shut/closed [as आँखें] per force.

झिलमिला/ना [*v*] to twinkle; to shimmer; to flicker; hence ~ हट.

झींकना [*v*] to repine; to fret; to grumble/grouse.

झीना [*a*] thinned, thin, threadbare.

झील [*nf*] a lake.

झुँझला/ना [*v*] to get irritated/petulant; to be peeved, to fret; hence ~ हट.

झुंड [*nm*] flock, herd; clump, cluster.

झुकना [*v*] to bow; to droop; to stoop; to bend; to yield; to lean [towards]; to be tilted.

झुकाव [*nm*] inclination, bent, bias; leaning; curvature; flexion; trend; tilt.

झुटपुटा [*nm*] twilight; morning or evening hour when the sunlight is very faint.

झुठलाना [*v*] to belie, to falsify; to give a lie to.

झुनझुना [*nm*] a child's rattle; rattling toy.

झुरमुट [*nm*] an abatis, a cluster of shrubs, grove.

झुर्री [*nf*] wrinkle, crinkle, fold.

झुलसना [*v*] to be scorched, to be singed; to be effected with a burning sensation; to be charred.

झूठ [*a*] false, untrue, incorrect; [*nm*] falsehood, lie, untruth; ~ मूठ falsely; without any rhyme or reason; just fun; ~ का sham, false.

झूठा [*a*] false; fictitious; untrue; sham; mock; feigned; [nm] a liar; झूठे का मुँह काला a liar is damned to ultimate exposure; झूठे पर खुदा की लानत the liar be damned.

झूमना [*v*] to swing in a gay mood or intoxication; sway to and fro.

झूलना [*v*] to swing; to oscillate; to dangle; to linger in suspense; [*nm*] see झूला।

झूला [*nm*] a swing; suspended scaffold; cradle.

झेंपना [*v*] to blush; to feel abashed/shy; to be put out of countenance; hence झेंपू।

झेलना [*v*] to bear; to endure, to suffer.

झोंकना [*v*] to throw in; to thrust in; to pour in.

झोंका [*nm*] a blast, puff, whiff, gust, jet.

झोंपड़ी [*nf*] a hut, small cottage.

झोल **1** bagginess, puckering; a rumple., pucker, tuck. **2** free or swinging end (as of a sari). **3** a screen, curtain. **4** sac, membrane; womb. – ~ खाना, to pucker; to hang, to sag. ~ डालना, to make baggy; to make a tuck. ~ निकालना, to remove bagginess, or a tuck, – ~ झोल-झाल, bagginess; loose. – झोलदार loose.

झोला [*nm*] a bag, kit, haversack, knapsack.

झोली [*nf*] a small bag; any cloth stretched out to collect something; begging bag; –फैलाना to beg; to seek a favour.

ट

ट the first letter of the third pentad [i.e., टवर्ग) of the Devanagari: alphabet.

ट - देवनागरी वर्णमाला में टवर्ग का पहला वर्ण व्यंजन है। इसका उच्चारण स्थान मूर्द्धा है।

टंकी [*nf*] a tank; cistern; reservoir.

टंकक [*nm*] a typist.

टँगड़ी [*nf*] a leg-trick [in wrestling].

टंटा [*nm*] wrangling; altercation; quarrel; encumbrance; botheration.

टकटकी [*nf*] gaze, stare, fixed look.

टकराना [*v*] to clash; to collide; to knock [against]; to dash [against]; to encounter.

टकसाल [*nf*] a mint.

टकसाली [*a*] genuine [coin, etc.]; standard [as speech]; [*nm*] mint-master.

टकसालीपन **1** genuineness, currency (as of language). **2** good quality (as of language). .

टका/र [*nm*] the letter ट and its sound; ~रांत [word] ending in ट

टक्कर [*nf*] a collision; clash; impact; –का matching, equivalent; -झेलना to suffer a loss; to endure a blow.

टखना [*nm*] an ankle; fetlock.

टटोलना [*v*] to feel; to sound; to grope; to probe; to reconnoitre.

टट्टी [*nf*] a screen [made of bamboo parings or reed, etc.]; latrine; stool, faeces.

टट्टू [*nm*] a pony.

टन [*nm*] a ton; [*nf*] a tinkling/twanging sound.

टपकना [*v*] to drip; to leak; to drop; to dribble.

टपाटप [*adv*] with successive tapping, producing successive tapping sound, patteringly.

टब [*nm*] a tub.

टमाटर [*nm*] a tomato.

टरकाना [*v*] to put off, to evade; to dispose of summarily.

टर्राना [*v*] to croak; to grumble haughtily.

टलना [*v*] to be averted; to be postponed; to slip or slink away; to make off; to get out of the way.

टवर्ग [*nm*] the third pentad of the Devanagari: alphabet incorporating the letters ट, ठ, ड, ढ and ण.

टस –से मस न होना not to budge an inch; to stay unimpressed/unmoved.

टहनी [nf] a twig, sprig.

टहल [*nm*] drudgery, menial service.

टहलना [*v*] to stroll, to ramble, to saunter; to slip off.

टहलुआ [*nm*] a drudge, menial servant.

टाँकना [*v*] to stud; to stitch; to cobble; to solder; to jot down.

टाँग [*nf*] a leg; –अड़ाना to intermeddle, to interfere.

टाँगना [*v*] to hang, to suspend, to beg.

टाइप [*nm*] type; typing; ~राइटर a typewriter.

टाइपिस्ट [*nm*] a typist.

टाइम [*nm*] time.

टाई [*nf*] a necktie.

टाट [*nm*] sack cloth; floor-mat; –उलटना to go bankrupt; –बाहर होना to be outcast; –में पाट की बखिया a silk patch on a rag.

टापना [*v*] to leap or spring over; to be left helpless; to be left in a lurch.

टापू [*nm*] an island.

टाल [*nf*] a stock, heap; a [fuel] shop; prevarication; postponement, deferment; evasion, avoidance; ~मटोल prevarication; putting off [on some pretext]; avoidance, evasion.

टालना [*a*] to postpone, to put off; to procrastinate; to avert, to avoid/evade.

टिकट [*nm*] a ticket; stamp; ~घर booking office.

टिकना [*v*] to last, to stay; to tarry.

टिकाऊ [*a*] durable, lasting, abiding.

टिकिया [*nf*] a small cake; tablet; pill.

टिड्डी [*nf*] a locust; –दल locust swarm.

टिप्पणी [*nf*] a note; annotation; comment, observation; critical remark.

टिप्पस [*nf*] manipulation, contrivance, manoeuvre, [for achieving an end.]

टिप्पा [*nm*] rebound, bounce.

टिमटिमाना [*v*] to twinkle; to glimmer; to flicker; to scintillate.

टिमटिमाहट twinkling, flickering.

टिमाक **1** finery. **2** airs, ostentation.

टीका [*nm*] vaccination; inoculation; commentary [on a book, etc.]; a small mark [of vermillion, sandalpaste, etc.] over the forehead; an ornament worn by a woman whose husband is alive; a pre-marriage ceremony.

टीकाकार [*nm*] a commentator.

टीन [*nm*] a can, tin; ~बंद canned, tinned.

टीपना [*v*] to enter; to record, to jot down; to point; to copy.

टीमटाम [*nm*] showing off; ostentation; finishing touches.

टीला [*nm*] a mount, mound, hillock.

टीस [*nf*] smarting pain.

टीसना [*v*] to smart, to suffer from a throbbing agony.

टुंडी [*nm*] the navel.

टुक/ड़ा [*nm*] a piece, fragment; part; splinter; [fig] leaving; ~ड़े तोड़ना to sponge on.

टुकड़ी [*nf*] a detachment [of troops]; group; stone slab.

टुच्चा [*a*] lowly, mean; petty; [*nm*] a skunk.

टुटपुँजिया [*a*] of meagre means/resources, bankrupt.

टूटना [*v*] to break, to be broken; to be fractured, to have twitching pain [as देह–]; to be dissolved [as साझेदारी]; to fail [as बैंक]; टूट–फूट wear and tear, breach; damage; टूटा–फूटा broken; damaged, decrepit, worn out; टूट पड़ना to attack; to pounce; टूटी–फूटी broken, imperfect [as o भाषा].

टेक [*nf*] a prop, stay, support; refrain, burden of a song; resolve; –पकड़ना to stick resolutely to one's resolve.

टेकना [*a*] to lean; to support; to rest, to prop, to set down.

टेढ़ा [*a*] curved; bent; oblique; skew; difficult; intricate; ~पन curvature; bend; obliquity; intricacy; skewness; –मेढ़ा crooked/zigzag, irregular; टेढ़ी खीर a hard nut to crack, difficult job.

टेव [*nf*] habit, wont, settled tendency.

टोंटी [*nf*] a tap; nozzle [water] faucet; spout; spigot.

टोकना [*v*] to interrupt; to question, to interrogate.

टोटा [*nm*] loss, damage; want, scarcity; butt-end [of a cigarette, etc.]; rench.

टोना [*nm*] magic, spell; totem; –टोटका witchcraft, black art, sorcery.

टोप [*nm*] a hat; helmet.

टोपी [*nf*] a cap; cover; cowl; percussion cap; –उछालना to expose publicly; to put to public disgrace; –उतारना to insult or humiliate.

टोल [*nm*] a band, batch.

टोली [*nf*] a team, batch, band, group, troop.

टोह **1** feeling (for); touching. **2** searching out, investigating. **3** information. **4** care (of or for), supervision. – ~ मिलना, information to come to light (about, की). ~ लगाना, or लेना (की) to search

टोहना [*v*] to sound, to reconnoitre, to take up the trace of.

टौरना [*v*] to investigate, to make a search, to essay.

ठ the second letter of the third pentad [i.e., टवर्ग) of the Devanagari: alphabet.

ठ - देवनागरी वर्णमाला (व्यंजन) में टवर्ग का दूसरा वर्ण है। इसका उच्चारण स्थान मूर्द्धा है।

ठंड [*nf*] cold; coldness, chilliness; ~क coolness.

ठंडा [*a*] cool; cold; bleak; dull; insipid, lifeless; unfeeling; –पड़ना to be pacified, to be subdued or tamed; to lose all passion or warmth; to be extinguished; –होना to be put out/extinguished; to pass away.

ठंडई [*nf*] a cold drink.

ठका/र [*nm*] the letter ठ [ṭha] and its sound; ~रांत [word] ending in ठ [ṭha].

ठग [*nm*] a thug, cheat; impostor; ~ई/पना/हाई [the practice or act of] cheating/thuggery/dupery.

ठगना [*v*] to cheat, to dupe, to defraud.

ठगनी [*nf*] **1** a woman who deceives, a seductive woman. **2** a seductive woman. **3** the wife of a robber.

ठगाना [*v*] **1** to be duped, deceived. **2** fig. to be charmed. **3** to dupe, **4** to cause to be duped. (= ठगवाना).

ठट्ठा [*nm*] fun, humour, joke, jest, wagging; ठट्ठेबाज a wag; given to joke and jest.

ठठरी [*nf*] a skeleton; a bier.

ठनाका [*nm*] a short sharp metallic ring, clink.

ठप [*a*] at a standstill; reduced to a state of inactivity; closed.

ठप्पा [*nm*] a stamp; mould; die; matrix, impression.

ठर्रा [*nm*] country liquor.

ठस [*a*] nitwit, dull; compact, dense; [a coin] of dull sound.

ठसक [*nf*] uppishness; perkiness; swagger, affectation.

ठसाठस [*a*] stuffed full; crowded, packed, cram-full; [*adv*] fully, crowdedly.

ठहरना [*v*] to stop, to halt, to pause; to stay; to wait; to stabilise.

ठहाका [*nm*] a peal/explosion of laughter.

ठाठ [*nm*] pomp, splendour, magnificence; a pattern of musical composition; concourse; -बाट pomp and show.

ठानना [*v*] to reslove, to determine; to launch.

ठिका/ना [*nm*] the destination; place, abode; station; trust; ~ने आना to veer round, to come to the proper course; ~ने का appropriate; trustworthy; reasonable; to the point; ~ने लगाना to put to proper use; to find an employment/a station; to put to death.

ठिंगना [*a*] short, short-statured, dwarfish.

ठिठकना [*v*] to hesitate; to wear; to pause and ponder.

ठिठुरना [*v*] to be chilled, to shiver with cold.

ठिठोली [*nf*] persiflage; banter; jesting, jocularity.

ठीक [*a*] right, correct, exact; proper; true; [*adv*] all right; precisely; accurately; -ठाक regularly, properly; shipshape; all right; regular; so-so.

ठुकराना [*v*] to kick off or knock away; to treat/reject contemptuously.

ठूँठ [*nm*] stump; stub; dead wood.

ठूँसना [*v*] to stuff full, to cram; to glut; to thrust forcibly.

ठेका [*nm*] a contract; halting place; rhythmic percussion or stress [in music]; ठेकेदार a contractor.

ठेठ [*a*] pure; genuine; unadulterated, unsophisticated; proper; typical.

ठेलना [*v*] to thrust, to shove, to propel, to thrust with force.

ठेलमठेल [*nf*] hustle and bustle; jostling.

ठेला [*nm*] a trolly; cart; truck; barrow; stroke, thrust, violent push.

ठेस [*nf*] a knock in the sole [causing lingering pain]; emotional shock.

ठोकना [*v*] to beat; to hammer; to drive into [as a nail]; to tamp.

ठोकर [*nf*] a kick, stroke; percussion; stumbling; toe; –मारना to kick off; to treat with contempt; –लगना to suffer a kick of adversity; to be knocked down.

ठोड़ी [*nf*] the chin.

ठोस [*a*] solid; sound.

ठोहना [*v*] to investigate, to search.

ठोहर [*nm*] scarcity.

ठौर [*nf*] place; –ठिकाना whereabouts, habitat.

ड

ड the third letter of the third pentad [i.e., टवर्ग) of the Devanagari: alphabet.

ड - देवनागरी वर्णमाला (व्यंजन) में टवर्ग का तीसरा वर्ण है। इस अक्षर का उच्चारण स्थान मूर्द्धा है। इसके दो रूप और दो उच्चारण है जैसे- ड - डब्बा और ड़ - लड़का।

डंक [*nm*] a sting; the tip of a nib or pen.

डंका [*nm*] a kettle-drum; –बजना to be renowned; to exercise sway over; to achieve fame all over; –बजना, लड़ाई का hostilities to commence to be launched; the battle to be initiated; –डंके की चोट (पर) कहना to proclaim aloud, to announce publicly without fear.

डंडा [*nm*] a staff, stick, wand.

डंडी [*nf*] beam of a scale; handle [as of an umbrella].

डँसना [*v*] to sting; to bite.

डकार [*nf*] a belch, eructation; [nm] the letter ड [ḍa] and its sound; –न लेना to appropriate another's due and not to let out any sign of it, to quietly assimilate another's due; –जाना/लेना to appropriate another's due; to swallow; डकारांत [word] ending in ḍa (ड)।

डकैत [*nm*] a dacoit, bandit; ~ती a dacoity, banditry.

डग [*nm*] a pace, step, stride; foot.

डगडगाना [*v*] to shake, to quiver, to stagger, to tremble.

डगमग [*adj.*] trembling, quivering.

डगमगाना [*v*] to falter, to stagger; to roll; to shimmy.

डटना [*v*] stay/stand firm; to take a stand; to be determined.

डपट [*nm*] **1** shouting, rebuking; a rebuke. **2** rushing forward; galloping.

डपटना [*v*] to administer a sharp rebuke, to reprimand.

डफ़ली [*nf*] a kind of small tambourine.

डबडबाना [*v*] to be tearful [said of eyes].

डबरा [*nm*] = a small pond, a puddle, a reservoir of water.

डब्बा [*nm*] a tiny box; chest; railway wagon; compartment.

डर [*nm*] fear, fright, dread.

डरना [*v*] to fear/dread, to be afraid/frightened.

डरपोक [*a*] coward [ly]; timid.

डरावना [*a*] fearful, dreadful; terrible, horrible.

डलिया [*nf*] a small open basket.

डाँट [*nf*] scolding, a sharp rebuke; –डपट rebuke and reproof; –फटकार rebuke and reprimand.

डाँटना [*v*] to scold, to rebuke sharply, to chide.

डाइन [*nf*] a witch; hag, sorceress; a scold.

डाक [*nf*] mail, post, dak; –खर्च postage; ~खाना a post office; –गाड़ी a mail train; ~घर a post office.

डाका [*nm*] a dacoity.

डाकिनी [*nf*] a lamia, hellcat.

डाकिया [*nm*] a postman.

डाकू [*nm*] a dacoit, bandit.

डाक्टर [*nm*] a doctor, medical practitioner.

डाक्टरी [*nf*] medical practice/profession.

डाची [*nf*] a young female camel that has calved once.

डाट [*nf*] a cork, spigot, plug, stopper; bung; archway; keystone.

डाढ़ [*nf*] a molar or grinding tooth.

डाढ़ा [*nf*] a fire, scrub fire.

डाढ़ी [*nf*] a beard, growth of hair on the face.

डामर [*nm*] tar, pitch, asphalt, bitumen.

डामाडोल = डाँवाडोल।

डायरी [*nf*] a diary.

डाल [*nf*] a branch.

डालना [*v*] to put in; to pour, to drop; to thrust.

डाली [*nf*] a branch; basket; basketful of fruits, sweets, etc. given as a present.

डावाँडोल [*a*] wavering; fluctuating; unsteady, fickle.

डाह [*nm*] jealousy, envy.

डिगना [*v*] to deviate; to swerve; to be shaken.

डिगरी [*nf*] a decree; degree.

डिबिया [*nf*] a tiny box, case or casket.

डींग [*nf*] bragging, braggadocio, boasting; –मारना/ हाँकना to brag, to boast.

डील [*nm*] stature, size, physique; –डौल physique; stature.

डुबकी [nf] a dip.

डूबना [v] to be drowned, to sink; to plunge, to be immersed/submerged; to set [as सूरज –]; to be sullied or disgraced; डूबते को तिनके का सहारा a drowning man catches at a straw; डूब मरना to drown out of disgrace.

डेढ़ [*a*] one and a half; –ईंट की मस्जिद चु (चि) नना, –चावल की खिचड़ी पकाना to blow one's lone trumpet.

डेरा [*nm*] a camp; encampment; billet, abode; temporary abode; [a] left [as हाथ).

डैना [*nm*] a wing [of a bird], pinion.

डोर [*nf*] string; thread.

डोरा [nm] thread, sewing or stitching thread; डोरे डालना to entice, to allure.

डोरी [*nf*] a string; lanyard.

डोल [*nm*] a round shallow pail [usually of iron]; skip.

डोलना [*v*] to swing, to oscillate; to rove about, to ramble, to wobble; to be titled sideways.

डौल [*nm*] the shape/form, appearance; method/ manner; device, opportunity.

ड्योढ़ा [*a*] one and a half times.

ड्योढ़ी [*nf*] the threshold; vestibule; ~वान a gate-keeper; watchman.

ढ

ढ the fourth letter of the third pentad [i.e., टवर्ग) of the Devanagari: alphabet.

ढ - देवनागरी वर्णमाला (व्यंजन) में टवर्ग का चौथा वर्ण है। इसका उच्चारण स्थान मूर्द्धा है। इसके दो रूप होते हैं- ढ-ढक्कन और ढ़ - चढ़ना।

ढंग [*nm*] manner, method, mode, way; demeanour; tact.

ढिंढोरा [*nm*] proclamation by beat of drum; proclamation; –पीटना to proclaim aloud.

ढकना [*v*] cover; to conceal; [*nm*] see ढक्कन।

ढका/र [*nm*] the letter ढ and its sound; ~रांत [word] ending in ढ

ढकोस/ला [*nm*] hypocrisy; humbug, sham; ~लेबाज़ a hypocrite, humbug.

ढक्कन [*nm*] a lid, cover, buckler.

ढचरा [*nm*] skeleton, worn out framework.

ढपोरसं(श)ख [*nm*] a talk-tall give-nothing person.

ढब [*nm*] manner, ways, conduct; fashion.

ढर्रा [*nm*] way[s]; path; method; style, fashion.

ढलाई [*nf*] moulding, casting; minting.

ढलान [*nm*] a slope, descent, ramp.

ढहना [*v*] to crash down, to fall or tumble down, to be razed or destroyed.

ढाँचा [*nm*] frame, framework; skeleton; carcass.

ढाई [*a*] two and a half.

ढाढ़स [*nm*] solace, consolation; –देना/बँधाना to console, to comfort.

ढाना [*v*] to demolish, to dismantle, to pull down, to raze to the ground.

ढाबा [*nm*] a small common-place hotel.

ढाल [*nf*] a shield; [*nm*] slope, declivity, falling gradient; pitch, ramp.

ढालना [*v*] to pour out [as liquor]; to mould or cast; to found.

ढालू [*a*] sloping, declivious, descending.

ढिठाई [*nf*] archness, pertness; impudence; audacity.

ढिलाई [*nf*] sluggishness, laxity; flexibility; softness; infirmity; leniency; flabbiness.

ढीठ [*a*] arch, pert; impudent, audacious.

ढील [*nf*] laxity; sluggishness; leniency; relaxation.

ढीलना [v] to let go; to free; to untie; to relax, to loosen.

ढीला [*a*] loose; slack, sluggish; soft; infirm; flabby; –ढाला loose; flabby; sluggish.

ढुलमुल [*a*] vacillating, wavering; fickle, unsteady.

ढूँढ़ना [*v*] to seek, to search; to trace.

ढेर [*nm*] a heap, pile, accumulation, bulk, lot; [a] plenty, abundant; –करना to kill; to strike down.

ढोंग [*nm*] hypocrisy; fraud; imposture.

ढोंगी [*a* and *nm*] impostorous, hypocritical, fraudulent; an impostor, hypocrite.

ढोना [*v*] to transport, to cart, to haul; to carry; to bear [on head or shoulder, etc.]

ढोल [*nm*] a tom-tom, large drum; barrel; –पीटना to publicise, to proclaim aloud.

ढोल/क [*nf*] a small drum played on both the ends; ~किया a drummer, one who plays on a ढोलक

त the first letter of the fourth pentad [i.e., तवर्ग] of Devanagari: alphabet.

त - देवनागरी वर्णमाला (व्यंजन) में तवर्ग का पहला वर्ण है। इस अक्षर का उच्चारण स्थान दन्त है।

तंग [*a*] narrow; scarce; troubled; harassed; girth, belt of a horse.

तंगी [*nf*] scarcity, poverty, tightness.

तंतु [*nm*] thread, fibre; filament; tendril; cord of string of a musical instrument.

तंत्र [*nm*] system; technique; a string gut; a body of mystical formulae for the attainment of superhuman powers; incantation; –मंत्र hocus-pocus, voodooism, spell and incantation.

तंत्रिका [*nf*] nerve.

तंत्री [*nf*] a practitioner of enchantments; a stringed musical instrument–a lyre.

तंदुरुस्त [*a*] healthy.

तंदुरुस्ती [*nf*] health.

तंदूर [*nm*] an oven.

तंद्रा [*nf*] drowse, drowsiness; somnolence.

तंद्रिल [*a*] drowsy.

तंबाकू [*nm*] tobacco.

तंबिया [*nm*] a dish made of copper, brass etc.

तंबू [*nm*] a tent, marquee.

तक [*adv. & prep.*] to, upto; till, until; by.

तक़दीर [*nf*] luck, lot, fate, fortune; –का खेल wonders wrought by luck; –का धनी/सिकंदर blessed with a lucky lot, favoured by Dame Luck; –का लिखा नहीं मिटता what is lotted cannot be blotted; –का हेठा having a wretched lot.

तकरार [*nf*] an altercation; wrangling, quarrel.

तक़रारी [*adj.*] disputant, disputing.

तक़रीबन [*adv.*] approximately, nearly.

तक़रीर [*nf*] a speech, lecture.

तकली [*nf*] a small spindle; bobbin of cotton.

तकलीफ़ [*nf*] trouble, distress; ailment.

तकल्लुफ़ [*nm*] formality; meticulous observance of propriety or etiquette.

तक़सीम [*nf*] division; distribution.

तक़ाज़ा [*nm*] dun; dunning; demand [of payment, one's due, etc.]

तका/र [*nm*] the letter ta (त) and its sound; ~रांत [word] ending in त

तक़ावी [*nf*] taccavi [loan].

तकिया [*nm*] a pillow, bolster.

तकियाकलाम [*nm*] a prop word, an expletive.

तख़्त [*nm*] a wooden structure of planks; throne.

तख़्ता [*nm*] a plank; board; –उलटना/पलटना to bring about a coup; to suffer a coup; to fall/throw into adversity.

तख़्ती [*nf*] a small wooden plate; small board to write on.

तख़्ता [*nm*] **1** a plank, board. **2** boarding, deck (of a ship). 3 a hoarding. **4** a blackboard. **5** a bench; berth, colloq. bed. **6** a sheet (of paper). – ~ हो जाना, to become wooden: to become hard, insensitive, inert. ~ उलटना, to overthrow (का: as a ruler, a government).

तगड़ा [*a*] strong, powerful, robust.

तगड़ी [*nf*] **1** thread or cord worn round the waist. **2** a chain, with bells attached, worn round the waist.

तजना [*v*] to abandon, to give up; to quit, to leave.

तजुरबा [*nm*] experience; experiment.

तट [*nm*] a bank; coast; shore.

तटस्थ [*a*] neutral; objective; indifferent; situated on a bank/coast; ~ता neutrality; objectivity; indifference, being situated on a bank/coast, etc.

तड़ [*nf*] a crack, cracking noise [as of a slap].

तड़क [*nf*] the act or process of crackling; a crack mark; snap; split; fissure; –भड़क tawdry, tawdriness, pompousness.

तड़का [*nm*] day-break, dawn; cracking noise; a snap; seasoning, heated oil or ghee in which spices and onion, etc. are well stirred and browned [to be administered as a relish to pulses, etc.]

तड़पना [*v*] to toss or roll about restlessly or uneasily; to writhe in pain; to yearn [for], to smart; to crack; to be restive/restless.

तड़ातड़ [*adv*] with successive reports; with promptitude, instantaneously; –जबाव देना to answer back in quick succession/unhesitatingly.

तड़ी [*nf*] braggadocio; ascendancy, overbearing conduct, overbearingness.

ततैया [*nf*] a wasp.

तत्ता [*adj.*] hot, heated.

तत्काल [*adv*] forthwith, immediately.

तत्त्व [nm] element; essence; principle; substance; factor; phenomenon; truth, reality; ~ज्ञान metaphysical knowledge, the realisation of the Supreme Truth; ~दर्शी one who realises the Supreme Truth, one who can perceive the Truth; ~दृष्टि vision, truth probing vision, insight; –मीमांसा metaphysics, elementism.

तत्त्वतः [*adv.*] essentially, in essence, in reality.

तत्त्वावधान [*nm*] auspices; –में, के under the auspices of.

तत्पर [*a*] ready; devoted; ~ ता readiness; devotedness.

तत्सम [*nm*] lit. same as that –a word of Sanskrit origin used as such in later languages.

तथा [*ind*] and; so.

तथाकथित [*a*] so-called.

तथापि [*ind*] even so; still, yet, in spite of that.

तथास्तु [*ind*] Be it so!

तथ्य [*nm*] reality; fact, factum.

तदनन्तर [*adv*] thereafter, thereupon, consequently.

तदनुसार [*ind*] accordingly, according to that, corresponding to.

तदबीर [*nf*] effort, means; device, contrivance.

तदर्थ [*a*] ad hoc.

तद्भव [*nm*] lit. evolved or born therefrom–words of Sanskrit origin which have assumed, and are used in, a modified form in later languages.

तन [*nm*] body.

तनख़्वाह [*nf*] pay, salary.

तनज़्ज़ुली [*nf*] demotion; decline, fall.

तनना [*v*] to be pulled tight; to be stretched full; to be pitched; to be upright; to run into a temper; to assume an air of affectation.

तनहाई [*nf*] loneliness, solitude.

तनाव [*nm*] tension, tenseness, strain; tautness.

तनिक [*a*] a little, slight.

तनिमन [*nm*] feebleness, leanness..

तनुज [*nm*] a son; hence तनुजा [*nf*].

तन्मय [*a*] identified [with]; fully engrossed/ absorbed [in]; ~ ता complete identification; trance.

तप [*nm*] devout austerity, asceticism, self-mortification, penance.

तपन [*nf*] heat; anguish; tingle, burning sensation [within or without].

तपना [*v*] to be heated; to burn with pain or grief; to practise self-mortification.

तपस्या [*nf*] penance, self-mortification; asceticism.

तपस्विता [*nf*] the state of self mortification.

तपस्वी [*a* and *nm*] [*an*] ascetic, devoutly austere [person], one who practises self-mortification; hence तपस्विनी [*nf*].

तपाक [*nf*] warmth; apparent cordiality; promptitude.

तपिश [*nf*] heat; mental anguish, affliction.

तपेदिक़ [*nf*] tuberculosis.

तपो an allomorph of तपस् [see तप] used in compounds; ~ बल the power acquired through penance; ~ वन an ascetic's grove, a grove where ascetics perform the religious activities.

तफ़तीश [*nf*] an investigation, probe.

तफ़रीह [*nf*] recreation, regalement, fun.

तफ़सील [*nf*] details, particulars.

तब [*adv*] then, at that time; afterwards, thereafter, thereupon; consequently.

तबक़ा [*nm*] a class; status.

तबदी/ल [*a*] changed, altered; exchanged; ~ ली change, alteration; transfer.

तबला [*nm*] a small tambourine. –a percussion musical instrument.

तबादला [*nm*] transfer.

तबा/ह [*a*] ruined, destroyed; ~ ही ruination, ruin, destruction.

तबीयत [*nf*] the state of [physical or mental] health; temperament, disposition; nature; –भर जाना to feel satiated, to be cloyed with; –लगना to feel at home.

तबेला [*nm*] a stable.

तभी [*adv*] at that moment, just at that time, just then; for this reason.

तमंचा [*nm*] a pistol, revolver.

तमग़ा [*nm*] a medal.

तमतमाना [*v*] the face to redden [with rage or heat].

तमन्ना [*nf*] an aspiration, longing.

तमस् [*nm*] darkness, gloom, anger, wrath.

तमाचा [*nm*] a slap.

तमाम [*a*] all; whole, entire.

तमाशबीन [*nm*] lit. a show-seer, an onlooker, a spectator; one having a superficial mentality.

तमाशा [*nm*] a show, spectacle; entertainment.

तमिल [*nf*] the oldest of the four major south Indian languages belonging to the Dravidian family.

तमीज़ [*nf*] etiquette, decorum; discrimination.

तमो [*S.*], darkness: – तमोगुण, m. = तमस्, **2** ई, adj. & m. dominated in temperament by the quality of *tamas*; an ignorant, morose, inert or malicious person.

तमोगु/ण [*nm*] one of the three qualities [viz. सतोगुण, रजोगुण, तमोगुण] incidental to creation or the state of humanity–the quality of darkness or ignorance; hence ~ णी

तमोली [*nm*] a betel-seller.

तय [*a*] decided, settled; fixed; covered.

तरंग [*nf*] a wave, ripple; whim, caprice.

तरंगी [*a*] whimsical, capricious; fanciful; unsteady.

तरंगिणी [*S.*], f. a river.

तर [*a*] wet, soaked; damp, fresh; a suffix used in comparative degree [as उच्चतर, महत्तर, बेहतर –ब-तर soaked, drenched; –ओ-ताज़ा fresh; refreshed.

तरकश [*nm*] a quiver.

तरकारी [*nf*] a vegetable [green or cooked].

तरकीब [*nf*] way, means; tact contrivance; device.

तरक़्क़ी [*nf*] progress; advancement, improvement; promotion, increment.

तरजीह [*nf*] preference; priority.

तरजुमा [*nm*] translation; ~ न a translator.

तरतीब [*nf*] order, arrangement.

तरफ़ [*nf*] side, direction; [*adv*] towards; ~ दार partisan; partial; supporter; ~ दारी the act of taking a side, partisanship; partiality; backing.

तरबूज [*nm*] a water-melon.

तरल [*a*] fluid; fickle, unsteady; [*nm*] a liquid; hence ~ ता.

तरस [*nm*] compassion, pity; –खाना to pity.

तरसना [*v*] to pine for, to crave or long for.

तरह [*nf*] kind, sort; method, way; likeness.

तराज़ू [*nf*] a balance, scales.

तराना [*nm*] a song, rhythmic musical composition using syllables.

तराबोर [*adj.*] soaked, drenched (= सराबोर)

तरावट [*nf*] coolness; dampness; freshness, verdure.

तराश [*nf*] trimming, paring, cutting.

तराशना [*v*] to cut; to trim; to chisel; to fashion.

तरी [*nf*] coolness; dampness; freshness, verdure; curry.

तरीक़ा [*nm*] method; mode, wāy, manner; technique; tact.

तरु/ण [*a*] young, youthful; [*nm*] a youth, youngman; hence तरुणी [nf]; hence ~ णाई [*nf*].

तर्क [*nm*] an argument, plea, contention; reason, reasoning; logic, abandonment, relinquishment; – वितर्क argumentation for and against, discussion.

तर्कशास्त्र [*nm*] [the science of] logic.

तर्ज़ [*nf*] tune [in music]; style, fashion; mode.

तर्जनी [*nf*] the forefinger, trigger-finger.

तर्पण [*nm*] gratification; libation of water to deceased ancestors or the manes.

तल [*nm*] the bottom; underpart; surface, floor.

तलक [*ind*] to, up to, till, until; even.

तल/ख़ [*a*] bitter; acrid; ~ खी bitterness; acridity.

तलना [*v*] to fry.

तलब [*nf*] an urge, craving; salary, wages.

तलबी [*nf*] summons, order to appear before.

तलमलाना [v.i.] **1** to be restless, uneasy; to be agitated; to be impatient, or tantalised. **2** to grieve. **3** to toss about.

तल/वा [*nf*] sole of the foot; ~ वे चाटना to lick the shoes of, to indulge in servile flattery.

तलवार [*nf*] a sword, sabre; – के घाट उतारना to put to the sword; to put to death.

तलहटी [*nf*] foothill; sub-mountain region.

तला [*nm*] the bottom; sole [of a shoe]; base; floor; keel [of a boat]; lower/under side.

तलाक़ [*nm*] divorce; ~ शुदा divorcee.

तलाश [*nf*] search, quest.

तलाशी [*nf*] search.

तले [*adv*] below; under; beneath.

तल्ला [*nm*] a storey; floor; sole [of a shoe, etc.].

तल्लीन [*a*] immersed [in]; deeply involved [in]; identified with; engrossed [in]; hence ~ ता

तवज्जो [*nf*] heed, attention.

तवा [*nm*] a griddle, an iron plate for baking bread; a gramophone record; small plate or shard in a चिलम on which tobacco is placed; a chest shield [used by warriors]; –सिर से बांधना to be ready to face blows/hardships.

तवायफ़ [*nf*] a prostitute, harlot, dancing girl.

तवारीख़ [nf] chronicle, history.

तवालत [*nf*] botheration, trouble.

तशरीफ़ [*nf*] a term signifying honour and respect, seldom used except with words like–रखना, लाना, ले जाना।

तश्तरी [*nf*] a plate; tray.

तसदीक़ [*nf*] verification; attestation; confirmation.

तसफ़िया [*nm*] a settlement, reconciliation.

तसमा [*nm*] a leather-strap.

तसला [*nm*] a shallow pan.

तसलीम [*nf*] admission, confession; salutation, greeting, responsive greeting.

तसल्ली [*nf*] satisfaction; patience; consolation; ~बख़्श satisfactory.

तस्वीर [*nm*] a picture, portrait; image.

तस्कर [*nf*] a smuggler, filibuster; तस्करी the act, process or practice of smuggling.

तह [*nf*] a layer; fold; bottom; ~ खाना a basement, subterranean/underground vault/cell/cellar.

तहक़ीक़ात [*nf*] an enquiry, investigation, probe.

तहज़ीब [*nf*] civilisation.

तहरी/र [*nf*] writing; anything written; ~री written.

तहलका [*nm*] turmoil, agitation, shemozzle.

तहस-नहस [*a*] ruined; devastated, destroyed.

तहाँ [*adv*] there, at that place.

ताँगा [*nm*] a tonga.

तांडव [*nm*] a violent manly dance-form; the mythological annihilatory dance of Lord Shiva.

ताँता [*nm*] a series, succession, train; influx; –बँधना/लगना to have an unbroken chain; a non-stop influx.

तांत्रिक [*nm*] a practitioner of तंत्र [*a*] pertaining to तंत्र

ताँबा [*nm*] copper.

ताईद [*nf*] support.

ताऊन [*nm*] plague; epidemic.

ताक़त [*nf*] power, force, strength, might; ~वर powerful.

ताकना [*v*] to state, to gaze, to watch intently; to view.

ताकि [*ind*] so that, in order that.

ताक़ीद [*nf*] an instruction; caution.

तागा [*nm*] thread.

ताज [*nm*] crown; diadem; the Taj.

ताज़गी [*nf*] freshness; newness.

ताज़ा [*a*] fresh; new; recent.

ताज्जुब [*nm*] wonder, astonishment.

ताड़ [*nm*] the palmyra tree, palm, toddy tree.

ताड़क [*adj*] one who punishes.

ताड़क [nm] an ornament worn on the ear.

ताड़ना [*nf*] admonition, rebuke; punishment; [*v*] to admonish; to guess, to smell, to perceive the reality in a flash.

ताड़नीय [*adj*] deserving punishment; punishable.

ताड़ी [*nf*] toddy, fermented juice of palm tree.

तात [*nm*] any venerable person; father; an address to anyone who is dear and younger.

तात्पर्य [*nm*] purport, meaning; design; spirit.

तादाद [*nf*] number, count.

तान [*nf*] a musical note; fast rhythmic movement; tone; stay.

तानना [*v*] to stretch, to spread; to tighten; to erect; to brandish [a sword, stick, etc.].

तानपूरा [*nm*] stringed instrument used to accompany singers.

ताना [*nm*] a taunt; sarcasm, gibe; the warp; –बाना warp and woof; the whole structure.

तानाशा/ह [*nm*] a dictator; ~ही dictatorship; dictatorial conduct; [a] dictatorial.

ताप [*nm*] heat; temperature; pyrexia, fever; affliction, mental agony; [*a*] thermal; ~मान temperature; ~मापी a thermometer.

तापना [*v*] to heat or to warm oneself or something.

ताबड़तोड़ [*adv*] in rapid succession, non-stop, incessantly; forthwith.

ताबे [*a*] subservient, subordinate; ~दार obedient, servile; attendant; ~दारी servility, servitude.

तामचीनी [*nf*] enam-elware, enamel.

तामझाम [*nm*] paraphernalia.

तामसिक [*a*] pertaining to, related with or inspired by तमोगुण

तामील [*nf*] carrying out, implementation [of an order]; service [of summons, etc.].

तार [*nm*] a wire; thread; fibre; chord; string; telegram; series, non-stop sequence; [*a*] high pitched.

तारक [*nm*] a star; asterisk.

तारकोल [*nm*] tar, coal tar, tarmac.

तारघर [*nm*] a telegraph office.

तारतम्य *nm*] harmony, harmonious relationship [of things]; sequence, ascending or descending order.

तारना [*v*] to cause to cross over; to deliver, to free from bondage.

तारपीन [*nm*] turpentine; –का तेल turpentine oil.

तारा [*nm*] a star; pupil [of the eye]; तारे तोड़ लाना to achieve the impossible, to perform a miracle; तारे दिखाई दे जाना lit. to see stars fleeting before the eyes –to come face-to-face with a hard realisation; to be overpowered by a hardship.

तारिका [*nf*] a small star; cine-actress.

तारीख़ [*nf*] a date; an appointed day; history; ~वार date- wise; तारीखी historical.

तारीफ़ [*nf*] praise; definition, description; introduction.

तारुण्य [*nm*] youth, youthfulness; young age, age of puberty.

ताल [*nm*] a pond, pool, tank; a musical measure; rhythm, rhythmic cycle; see ताड़; slapping with the palm, the inner side of the thigh as a gesture of challenge or defiance; ~पत्र palm leaf; palmyra leaf; ~ब, rhythmic [al].

तालमेल [*nm*] co-ordination; concordance, harmony, agreement.

तालव्य [*a*] palatal [sound, etc.].

ताला [*nm*] a lock; ~बन्दी a lockout.

तालाब [*nm*] a tank, pool.

तालिका [*nf*] a list; key; table, schedule.

तालिब [*nm*] a pupil; [a] desirous [of]; –इल्म a student, pupil, seeker after knowledge.

ताली [*nf*] a key; clapping [of hands]; –एक हाथ से नहीं बजती it takes two to make a quarrel.

तालीम [*nf*] education.

ता/लु, ~लू [*nm*] the palate.

ताल्लुक़ात [*nm*] pl. connections, concerns. dependencies.

ताव [*nm*] heat; rage, anger; overflow of passion; tempo; sheet of paper; –खाना to be infuriated; to be overheated, to have a stroke of heat; –पर होना to be in a state of readiness; to be ready for handling; to be in a temper.

तावीज़ [*nm*] an amulet, talisman.

ताश [*nm*] playing cards.

तासीर [*nf*] effect; property.

तिकड़/म [*nf*] manoeuvre, manipulation; expedient measures; unfair means; hence ~मी

तिकड़ी [*nf*] a trio.

तिकोन [*nm*] a triangle; [*a*] triangular, three-cornered.

तिकोना [*a*] triangular, three-cornered.

तिक्की [*nf*] a playing card having three pips.

तिक्त [*a*] acrid; pungent.

तिगुना [*a*] three times, threefold, triple.

तिजारत [*nf*] commerce, trade.

तिजारी [*nf*] tertian ague, intermittent fever occurring every third day.

तिजोरी [*nf*] an iron safe/chest.

तितर-बितर [*a*] scattered; dispersed; diffused.

तितली [*nf*] a butterfly; glamour girl.

तितिक्षा endurance, forbearance.

तिथि [*nf*] a date of a lunar or solar month. – तिथि-पत्र, m. an almanac (astrological).

तिथित [*adj*] dated.

तिनका [*nm*] a straw;–दाँतों में दबाना/पकड़ना to beg for mercy; तिनके का सहारा, डूबते को a drowning man catches at a straw; तिनके की ओट पहाड़ lit. a hill hidden behind a straw–a big secret hidden under an apparent trifle.

तिपाई [*nf*] a tripod.

तिमाही [*a*] quarterly.

तिमिर [*nm*] darkness.

तिरंगा [*a*] tri-coloured; [*nm*] the tri-colour flag.

तिरछा [*a*] slanting; oblique; skew.

तिरता [*a*] afloat.

तिरना [*v*] to float.

तिरपाल [*nf*] tarpaulin; dodger; awning.

तिरसठ [*a*] sixty three; [*nm*] the number sixty three.

तिर/स्कार [*nm*] contempt, slight, opprobrium; disregard, disrespect; hence ~स्कृत [*a*]

तिरानवे [*a*] ninety three; [*nm*] the number ninety-three.

तिरासी [*a*] eighty three; [*nm*] the number eighty three.

तिराहा [*nm*] a junction of three roads/paths.

तिरिया [*nf*] a woman; –चरित्तर a woman's wiles.

तिरोहित [*a*] disappeared, vanished.

तिल [*nm*] sesamum [plant and its seed]; a mole; small particle, the least bit;–का ताड़ करना to make a mountain out of a molehill;–की ओट पहाड़ a mountain hidden underneath a molehill; तिलों में तेल न होना to be dry and stingy; to yield nothing worthwhile.

तिलक [*nm*] an ornamental or religious mark over the forehead [signifying installation on the throne or engagement, etc.] a vermillion or sandal mark [over the forehead]; the most eminent member [of a clan or dynasty, etc.]; commentary [of a text].

तिलमि/लाना [*v*] to be in the grip of impotent anger; to writhe in agitation, to be painfully restless; to be dazzled; hence ~लाहट [*nf*].

तिलचट्टा [*nm*] a cockroach.

तिल/स्म [*nm*] magic, magical spell; talisman; hence ~स्मी.

तिलहन [*nm*] oilseed.

तिलांजलि [*nf*] originally–a handful of water mixed with sesamum seeds offered to the manes or deceased ancestors–now, bidding a final good-bye, giving up, abandonment.

तिल्ली [*nf*] spleen; niger; a fanlight.

तिहत्तर [*a*] seventy three; [*nm*] the number seventy three.

तिहाई [*a*] one-third.

तीक्ष्ण [*a*] sharp; keen; pungent; intelligent; penetrating; hence~ता.

तीखा [*a*] sharp, pungent; harsh.

तीतर [*nm*] a partridge.

तीतरी [*nf*] hen partridge.

तीन [*a*] three; [*nm*] the number three; –तेरह होना to dissipate, to go into disarray, to be scattered; –पाँच करना to squabble, to dilly-dally; to play tricks, to dodge.

तीमारदा/र [*nm*] an attendant; a person attending on a patient; hence ~री.

तीर [*nm*] an arrow; a shaft; bank, shore.

तीर्थ [*nm*] a place of pilgrimage; sacred place; ~यात्रा pilgrimage; ~यात्री a pilgrim.

तीव्र [a] fast; pungent; high, high-pitched; sharp; violent; intense, vehement; ardent, bright; strong; hence~ता.

तीस [*a*] thirty; [*nm*] the number thirty; ~मार खाँ a sham hero.

तीसरा [*a*] the third.

तुँदैला [*a*] paunchy, abdominous, having a big bulging belly.

तुक [*nf*] rhyme, sense; harmony; ~बंदी rhyming, improvising verses.

तुकांत [*a*] rhyming, having terminal alliteration.

तुक्कड़ [*nm*] a poetaster; mere versifier.

तुक्का [*nm*] a blunt arrow; unsure means, vain bid; –भिड़ाना/लगाना to make a conjecture; to make an unsure bid, to take a chance.

तुच्छ [*a*] petty, trivial, trifle, frivolous, contemptible; insignificant; ~ता pettiness, triviality; insignificance; frivolity.

तुझ [*pro*] oblique form of तू [see]; तुझे to/for thee, to/for you.

तुतला/ना [*v*] to lisp, to babble, to stutter; hence ~हट.

तुनकमिजा/ज [a] pettish, petulant; hence ~जी.

तुफ़ैल [*nm*] cause; means; intervention; –से through, by means of; through the grace of.

तुम [*pro*] you.

तुमुल [*a*] tumultuous, uproarious.

तुम्हारा [*pro*] your, yours.

तुम्हीं [*pro*] you alone, you and only you.

तुम्हें [*pro*] to you, unto you.

तुरंत [*adv*] at once, quickly, forthwith; immediately, instantly; soon.

तुरुप [*nf*] trump; –का पत्ता a trump card.

तुर्रा [*nm*] forelock, an ornamental tassel fitted on the turban; crest.

तु/र्श [*a*] sour; acidic; hence ~र्शी.

तुलना [*nf*] comparison; [v] to be weighed; ~त्मक comparative.

तुलनीय [*adj*] comparable.

तुलवाई [*nf*] 1 getting (sthg.) weighed. 2 price paid for having (sthg.) weighed.

तुला [*nf*] a balance, a pair of scales; the sign of Libra–seventh sign of the zodiac.

तुल्य [*a*] equivalent; like; hence ~ता.

तुष [*adj*] equality; similarity;. comparability.

तुषार [*nm*] frost.

तुष्टि [*nf*] satisfaction, gratification; contentment; hence तुष्ट [*a*].

तू [*pro*] thou; you; –तू मैं-मैं low-level altercation, squabbling.

तुष्टि [*nf*] 1 satisfaction. 2 pleasure.

तूतिया [*nm*] blue vitriol, sulphate of copper.

तूती [*nf*] a rosefinch; –बोलना to command overweening influence, to have unquestioned sway.

तूफ़ा/न [*nm*] a storm, tempest; hurricane; typhoon; hence ~नी.

तुमार [*nm*] fuss, magnifying a point beyond due limits; –बाँधना to create a fuss, to magnify a point beyond all reasonable limits.

तूर्य [*nm*] a trumpet.

तूल [*nm*] 1 cotton; cotton-like fibres (from semal and other pods). 2 bright red cotton cloth. 3 a red colour (bright, or dark).

तूली [*nf*] a painter's brush.

तूलिका [*nf*] a painter's brush.

तृतीय [*a*] the third; ~क tertiary.

तृ/प्त [*a*] contended; gratified; fulfilled; ~प्ति contentment; gratification; fulfilment.

तृ/षा [*nf*] thirst; ~षित thirsty.

तृष्णा [*nf*] thirst, longing, craving.

तेंदुआ [*nm*] a leopard.

तेईस [*a*] twenty three; [*nm*] the number twenty three.

तेग [*nf*] a sword; cutlass, scimitar.

तेज [*nm*] glow; splendour, brilliance, refulgence; awe.

तेज़ [*a*] sharp; sharp-pointed; dear, costly; acute; keen; penetrating [as नज़र]; acrid, pungent; corrosive, caustic; violent, fiery; swift, quick [as रफ़्तार], fleet; smart; intelligent, nimble-witted; –तर्रार fiery and fierce, caustic-tongued, sharp and smart.

तेजस्वी [*a*] brilliant, luminous, glowing; impressive, imposing.

तेज़ाब [*nm*] an acid.

तेज़ाबी [*adj*] see s.v. तेज़

तेज़ी [*nf*] sharpness; boom; dearness; keenness; acridity, pungency; quickness, swiftness; smartness; intelligence.

तैतालीस, तैंतालिस [*a*] forty three: [*nm*] the number forty three.

तैंतीस, तैंतिस [*a*] thirty three; [*nm*] the number thirty three.

तेरह [*a*] thirteen; [*nm*] the number thirteen.

तेरा [*pro*] thy, thine, your.

तेल [*nm*] oil; petrol; to perform the ceremony of pre-marital oil, an ointment.

तेली [*nm*] an oilman, a Hindu sub-caste which subsists on oil-extraction and sale.

तोतला [*adj*] 1 speaking indistinctly (as a child); lisping. 2 stammering, stuttering.

तेलहन [*nm*] = तिलहन seeds from which oil is extracted.

तेवर [*nm*] an eye-brow; a frown.

तैनात [*a*] deployed, posted; appointed.

तैया/र [*a*] ready, willing; ready-made; prepared; finished ripened, matured; in bloom, blooming; robust; fat; hence ~री.

तैरना [*v*] to swim; to float.

तैरा/क [*a*] an expert swimmer; ~की swimming.

तैश [*nm*] provocation; rage, wrath; –खाना,–में आना to be provoked; to fly into a rage.

तोंद [*nf*] paunch, potbelly.

तो [ind] then; therefore; more-over; an emphatic particle; at any rate, however; at least.

तोड़ [*nm*] antidote, counter, counter-measure; breach, break; whey; forceful current of water [in a river, etc.]: -फोड़ sabotage; breakage; destruction.

तोड़ना [*v*] to break; to violate; to fracture; to pluck; to disband; to twist; to demolish; to snap; to change [into coins or currency notes of smaller denomination].

तोड़ा [*nm*] scarcity; deficiency; name of an ornament worn round the wrist; rhythmic structure in instrumental music; a long narrow meshwork bag.

तोतला [*a*] lisping; [*nm*] [one] who lisps.

तोता [*nm*] a parrot.

तोप [*nf*] gun, cannon; ~खाना artillery; ~ची a gunner.

तोबा [*nf*] vowing to sin no more, vowing never to repeat [an act]; –करना to vow to do no more, to vow never to repeat.

तोल [*nf*] weight.

तोलना [*v*] to weigh; to balance.

तोहफ़ा [*nm*] a present, gift.

तोहमत [*nf*] slander; false accusation.

तौर [*nm*] mode, method, way; –तरीका ways, technique; -तरीके manners.

तौलिया [*nf*] a towel.

तौल [*nm*] a weight.

तौहीन [*nf*] insult; disrespect; humiliation.

त्याग [*nm*] abandonment; relinquishment, renunciation forsaking; sacrifice, abnegation; denial; ~पत्र [letter of] resignation; hence त्यागी, त्याज्य

त्यों [*ind*] thus; like that, so, in like manner; -त्यों so.

त्योहार [*nm*] a festival, gala, holiday, fete, a festal day, festivity

त्यौरस [*nm*] the year before last; the year after next.

त्यौरी [*nf*] wrinkles of the forehead, contracted eyebrows; –चढ़ाना to wrinkle up one's forehead, to scowl, to frown.

त्रपा [*nf*] shame, an unchaste woman, fame, renown [*adj*] ashamed.

त्रय [*adj*] third, three, trio, triad, threefold.

त्राण [*nm*] protection; means of protection, defence, shelter; salvation.

त्रास [*nm*] fear, fright, scare, terror, dread.

त्रास/द, ~दायी [*a*] frightening, terrifying, dreadful.

त्रासदी [*nf*] a [dramatic] tragedy; ~कार author of a tragedy; ~य tragic.

त्राहि, ~माम [*ind*] protect me!, save me!; deliver me!; -त्राहि मचाना to be resounded with calls of 'save me! deliver me!'; a disastrous chaos to be let loose.

त्रि [*a*] three; ~कालदर्शी a seer, sage, one gifted with a vision to see through the past, present and future alike; ~कोण a triangle; ~गुण the set of three गुण (सत्त्व, रज, तम); threefold, three times; possessing the three gunas; ~ फला a mixture of three myrobalans viz. myrobalan (हड़); belleric myrobalan (बहेड़ा) and emblic myrobalan (आँवला); ~भुज a triangle; ~वली three skin-folds above the navel –a source of feminine charm; ~शूल a trident.

त्रिया [*nf*] a woman; ~चरित्र wiles of a woman.

त्रुटि [*nf*] an error, mistake; defect, deficiency.

त्रैमासिक [*a*] quarterly, three monthly.

त्वचा [*nf*] the skin.

त्वरा [*nf*] haste; quickness; urgency.

थ the second letter of the fourth pentad [i.e. तवर्ग) of the Devanagari: alphabet.

थ - देवनागरी वर्णमाला (व्यंजन) में तवर्ग का दूसरा वर्ण है। इसका उच्चारण स्थान दन्त है।

थंभ [*nm*] a pillar, a support.

थकन [*nf*] growing tired थकान.

थकना [*v*] to be tired/wearied/fatigued; थका-मांदा worn and wearied, jaded.

थका/न [*nf*] weariness, fatigue, tiredness; exhaustion; also ~वट.

थक्का [*nm*] a clot; lump.

थन [*nm*] the udder.

थनी [*nf*] a pair of pauches hanging from the neck of some goats.

थनेला [*nm*] inflamed breast of a woman; inflamed udder. swelling or abscess in the breast.

थपकना [*v*] to pat, [as a child to sleep], to strike gently with the palm; to tap.

थपकी [*nm*] a pat.

थपड़ी [*nm*] clapping of hands.

थपथपा/ना [*v*] to pat, to strike gently with the palm; to tap; hence ~ हट.

थपना [*nm*] to be patted; to be patted into the shape of a cake.

थपेड़ा [*nm*] a blow, stroke; buffet; dash [as of violent waves].

थप्पड़ [*nm*] a slap; buffet; spank.

थमना [*v*] to stop; to come to a standstill; to wait, to be supported by or propped up.

थमाना [*nm*] to cause to be stopped. to stop. to hand.

थर-थर [*nm*] shaking, trembling. trembling tremble.

थरथरा/ना [*v*] to tremble, to shunder, to quiver; hence ~ हट.

थरथराहट [*nm*] trembling from fear.

थरथरी [*nf*] fit of shivering.

थर्मामीटर [*nm*] a thermometer.

थर्राना [*v*] to shudder, to tremble [with terror].

थल [*nm*] land; place.

थल/थल, ~ ला [*a*] flabby; flaccid.

थलकना [*v*] to hang loosely, to shake, to quiver tremble, to throb.

थलथलाना [*v*] to become loose or flabby. to shake, to quiver.

था [*v*] was.

थाती [*nf*] trust, anything entrusted to somebody's charge.

थान [*nm*] a long piece of cloth of standard size, a raised platform where a deity's image is installed, deity's abode; stall [of an animal].

थाना [*nm*] a police station.

थानी [*nm*] a householder.

थाने/दार [*nm*] a police sub-inspector; hence ~ री-.

थाप [*nm*] pat, slap, blow. sound of a drum struck with the palm of the hand.authority, power; prestige.

थापा [*nm*] mark, impression, stamp; distinguishing mark. mark made by the palm dyed with henna. on the wall of a house as on an auspicious occassion, or to mark the house out for robbery, a stamp instrument, a pug mark, देना, or लगाना to mark with the hand; to mark.

थाम [*nm*] a pillar.

थामना [*v*] to [cause to] stop; to hold, to grasp; to prop; to support; to restrain; to resist.

थाल [*nm*] a large flat metallic plate slightly edged up; basin.

थाला [*nm*] a basin; round a tree or plant.

थाली [*nf*] a smaller form of थाल [see].

थावर [*nm*] stationary, immovable; any inanimate object – थावर-जंगम, things inanimate and animate; all existent things.

थावस [*nf*] firmness, endurance, patience.

थाह [nf] depth; estimate of depth.

थाहना [*vt.*] to sound, to plumb, to fathom, to investigate.

थिर [*adj.*] fixed, firm, permanent, durable; settled, calm water, weather, temperament; equable.

थिरकना [*v*] to make the body parts vibrate rhythmically; to move the feet nimbly in a dance sequence.

थिरता [*nf*] स्थिरता.

थिरना [*v*] to grow calm or still as water; to clear liquid, to settle, to be precipitated from a liquid.

थिराना [*vt.*] to calm, to make calm or still as water; to cause to clear liquid, to precipitate from a liquid, to grow calm.

थुक्का-फ़जीहत [*nf*] reproach and reproof, censure and condemnation; altercation.

थू [*nf*] the sound made in spitting: [ind] an expression of indignation and contempt; for shame ! fie! pish!.

थूक [*nm*] spittle, sputum; saliva.

थूकना [*v*] to spit; to reproach and reprove.

थूथन [*nm*] muzzle, snout, ugly face, mug ~ फुलाना, to pout; to grimace.

थूथनी [nf] थूथन.

थून [*nm*] थूनी.

थूनी [*nf*] a post, pillar, prop, vertical support as for a roof, or the axle of a water-lever; upright at a well-mouth supporting the windlass.

थैला [*nf.*] a large bag, a sack.

थैली [*nf*] a money bag; small bag, pouch, pocket.

थोक [*nm*] whole lot, wholesale; bulk; a heap, mass; locality.

थोड़ा [*a*] little, some, meagre, scanty; short.

थोथ [*nm*] hollowness, emptiness.

थोथा [*a*] hollow; empty, worthless; unsubstantial.

थोथनी [*nf.*] थूथने.

थोपना [*v*] to impose, to thrust upon; to implant; to plaster.

थोबड़ा [*nm*] the snout of a beast.

थोरिक [*adj*] a bit, a little.

थ्यावस [*nm*] patience, stay, halt.

द

द the third letter of the fourth pentad [i.e. तवर्ग] of the Devanagari: alphabet.

द - देवनागरी वर्णमाला (व्यंजन) में तवर्ग का तीसरा वर्ण है। इसका उच्चारण स्थान दन्तमूल के जिह्वा के अग्रभाग के स्पर्श से होता है।

दंग [*a*] wonder-struck, astonished.

दंगई [*adj.*] दंगाबाज़

दंग/ल [*nm*] a wrestling tournament; wrestling arena; tumultuous assembly; hence ~ ली.

दंगली [*adj.*] having to do with a contest, quarrelsome, aggressive; victorious.

दंगा [*nm*] a riot; disturbance; tumultuous quarrel, fracas; दंगेबाज riotous, pugnacious; quarrelsome; lawless, rebellious.

दंगाई [*adj.*] quarrelsome, pugnacious. a quarrelsome or pugnacious person. a rioter.

दंड [*nm*] punishment; penalty, fine; a staff, rod; beam, shaft; stalk; a measure of time [about 24 minutes]; see डंड; ~ विधि criminal law; penal code; ~ शास्त्र penalogy.

दंडक [*s.*] दंड, a type of Hindi metre consisting of long lines. punishing — दंडक-वन, name of a forest in south India in which according to tradition Rām resided for some time, दंडकारण्य.

दंडवत [*nm*] prostration, prostrating oneself in reverence, deferential salutation [directed towards elders or holy persons].

दंत [*nm*] a tooth; ~ कथा a legend; traditions; ~ हीन edentate.

दंत्य [*a*] dental [sound]; pertaining to teeth.

दंदान [*nm*] a tooth; ~ साज a dentist.

दंपति [*nm*] a [married] couple, husband and wife.

दं/भ [*nm*] conceit, vainglory, vanity; ~ भी conceited, vain-glorious, vain.

दकियानू/स [*a*] conservative [person]; ~ सी conservative [person, idea, thinking].

दक्खि/न [*nm*] the south; ~ नी southern, pertaining to the south; South Indian form and style of Hindi.

दक्ष [*a*] efficient, expert; ~ ता efficiency; expertness.

दक्षता [*adj.*] dexterity, skill, see, दक्ष.

दक्षिण [*nm*] the south; right; favourably disposed; [in poetical jargon] attribute of a hero (नायक) who keeps all his heroines in good humour;— पंथ right; ~ पंथी rightist; hence दक्षिणी.

दक्षिणा [*nf*] honorarium [paid in olden days to a preceptor by his pupil at the successful conclusion of his student career; reward to priest, etc; remuneration.

दक्षिणावर्त्त [*a*] clockwise; — गति clockwise movement.

दख़ल [*nm*] interference; interruption; occupation; authority, go [in a subject].

दग़ा [*nm*] treachery; deception, perfidy; ~ बाज treacherous, deceitful, perfidious.

दढ़ियल [*a*] bearded.

दत्तक [*a*] adopted; [*nm*] an adopted son.

दत्तचित्त [*a*] fully attentive, concentrated, having concentration.

ददोरा [*nm*] a rash or swelling.

दनादन [*adv*] resoundingly; non-stop, incessantly.

दफ़नाना [*v*] to bury; to entomb.

दफ़ा [*nf*] time [as in counting the number of times, e.g. तीन दफ़ा three times, दस दफ़ा ten times]; section [in a code of law]; warding of; removing; —होना to move off; to get off.

दफ़्तर [*nm*] an office.

दफ़्तरी [*nm*] a daftry; a book-binder.

दबंग [*a*] overbearing, strong- headed; dauntless; of commanding presence; hence ~पन.

दबदबा [*nm*] awe; sway; overwhelming/ commanding influence.

दबना [*v*] to be pressed; to yield; to be subdued, to be repressed; to be tamed; to give way; to be covered; to be concealed; to be hushed up; to cool down; दबी जबान से कहना to speak in a subdued tone, to say in a hushed manner; दबे पाँव [walking] quietly/stealthily.

दबाऊ [*a*] weighty by the head.

दबाब [*nm*] pressure, duress; suppression, compression; compulsion, coercion; stress/strain.

दबोचना [*v*] to pounce; to swoop down upon, to seize suddenly.

दब्बू [*a*] tame; of meek or submissive nature.

दम [*nm*] breath; life; stamina; mettle; endurance; moment; trick; trickery; —खम stamina, vigour, strength; —दिलाना vain consolation;—घुटना to be suffocated; —टूटना to run short of breath, to be out of breath; to be exhausted;—देना to cheat, to hood-wink; to incite;—फूलना to breathe short, to become breathless; —भर a moment, an instant; —भरना to get out of breath, to be exhausted; to sing the praises [of]; to boast; to have faith [in]; —मारना to have an instant's rest, to rest a while; —में दम रहना/होना, जब तक as long as life exists; till one is alive; —लगाना to smoke, to take a puff at हुक्का or चिलम; –साधना to be still; to practise holding the breath, to try to gain control over the process of respiration; to keep mum.

दमक [*nf*] flash; brilliance; glimmer; glow; hence ~ना [*v*].

दमकल [*nf*] the fire-brigade, fire-engine.

दमन [*nm*] suppression; repression; subjugation; control.

दमा [*nm*] asthma.

दमित [*a*] suppressed; repressed; subjugated.

दयनीय [*a*] pitiable, inspiring pity.

दया [*nf*] pity; mercy, compassion; ~शील kindly, kind-hearted, merciful.

दयानत [nf] honesty; genuineness, truthfulness; ~दार honest; truthful, genuine; hence ~दारी.

दयालु [*a*] kind, kind-hearted, generous.

दर [*nf*] rate; [*nm*] door; pass; [*ind*] in, within; ~ असल (में) in reality, in fact, as a matter of fact; —दर की खाक छानना; —दर door to door, place to place;–दर मारे-मारे फिरना to be tossed about from one place to another; to knock at one door after another.

दरकार [*nf*] necessity, need; [*a*] necessary, needed.

दरख़्त [*nm*] a tree.

दरख़्वास्त [*nf*] application. petition; request.

दरगाह [*nf*] a shrine; holy place; tomb [of a saint which is a pilgrimage spot and a place of worship].

दरबान [*nm*] a doorkeeper, watchman.

दरबार [*nm*] a royal court; hall of audience.

दरमिया/न [*nm*] the middle; [*ind*] during, in between, within, among; ~ना middle; intermediary.

दरवाजा [*nm*] door; door leaves.

दरवेश [*nm*] a dervish.

दराज [*nf*] a drawer [of table etc.]; [*a*] long, prolonged.

दरार [*nf*] a crevice, slit, crack, fissure; breach, rift.

दरिंदा [*nm*] a beast, beast of prey; carnivorous beast.

दरिद्र [*a*] - poor, pauper; of low qualities; wretched; hence ~ता; ~नारायण the have-nots; the poor.

दरिया [*nm*] a river; ~ई riverine; ~ घोड़ा a river horse, hippopotamus; ~ दिल liberal, large-hearted.

दरियाफ़्त [*nm*] an enquiry.

दरी [*nf*] a cotton carpet; a cavern, cave, grotto.

दर्ज [*a*] recorded, entered.

दर्जन [*nm*] a dozen.

दर्जा [*nm*] a class; degree; rank, gradation, status, category, quality, order.

दर्ज़ी [*nm*] a tailor.

दर्द [*nm*] pain, ache; affliction; ~नाक painful, tragic, piteous; ~मंद compassionate; sympathetic.

दर्प [*nm*] arrogance, haughtiness.

दर्रा [*nm*] a [mountain] pass.

दर्शक [*nm*] an onlooker, a spectator; visitor.

दर्शन [*nm*] sight, view; appearance [a term used to express a sense of deference]; philosophy; —शास्त्र philosophy; hence दर्शनीय.

दल [*nm*] a party; group, team; troop, swarm, herd; petal, leaf; thickness of layers etc.; used in compound words as the second member to denote plurality; ~दार of thick layer, pulpy; —दल an army of followers and supporters.

दलदल [*nm*] marsh, mire, fen, swamp, bog.

दला/ल [*nm*] an agent; a broker, middleman; tout; hence ~ ली.

दलित [*a*] downtrodden; depressed.

दलील [*nf*] a plea, an argument.

दवा [*nf*] medicine, drug; cure; ~खाना a dispensary, clinic; —दारू medical treatment; medicine.

दवाई [nf] see दवा.

दवात [*nf*] an inkpot.

दशक [*nm*] a decade, decennium.

दशमलव [*nm*] decimal.

दशा [*nf*] condition, state; plight.

दस [*a*] ten.

दस्तंदा/ज़ [nm] an interferer, meddler; ~जी interference, meddling.

दस्त [*nm*] loose stool; hand.

दस्तक [*nf*] a knock or rap [with the palm, at the door].

दस्तका/र [*nm*] an artisan, craftman, tradesman; hence ~ री [*nf*].

दस्तख़त [*nm*] signature.

दस्ता [*nm*] a squad of troops, police, etc.]; handle; haft; sleeve hafting; quire [of loose sheets of paper]; bouquet [of flowers etc.]; pounder.

दस्ताना [*nm*] a hand-glove.

दस्तावर [*a*] laxative, purgative.

दस्तावेज़ [nm] a document; deed.

दस्तूर [*nm*] a custom, routine; practice; constitution.

दस्तूरी [*nf*] commission, customary discount.

दहकना [*v*] to blaze, to be very hot, to burn with a red hot flame.

दहन [*nm*] burning, combustion; ~ शील combustible.

दहलना [*v*] to be terrorised/terror stricken; to tremble [with fear], to be terribly alarmed.

दहलीज [*nf*] threshold; entrance.

दहशत [*nf*] terror; panic.

दहाई [*nf*] the figure ten; the place of tens [in numeration].

दहाड़ना [*v*] to roar; to cry or shout aloud.

दही [*nm*] curd, coagulated milk.

दहेज [*nm*] dowry.

दाँत [*nm*] a tooth; —काटी रोटी intimate friendship, close relationship; —तले उँगली दबाना lit. to bite the finger in astonishment etc. —to stand amazed; to be aghast; —निपोरना to whine, to crinch; —पीसना to gnash the teeth [in anger etc.]; दाँतों में तिनका दबाना to express complete submission, to yield unconditionally.

दांपत्य [*a*] conjugal, marital; [*nm*] conjugal relations; conjugal functions.

दाँव [*nm*] see दाव stake; opportunity, chance; sleight; a trick [in wrestling]; strategy: time [*s*]; turn [in games etc.]; —पेच tricks; strategical moves, manoeuvres.

दाईं [*a*] right, right hand.

दाई [*nf*] a midwife; nurse; ~ गीरी midwifery.

दाखिल [*a*] entered; admitted.

दाखि़ला [*nm*] admission; entry.

दाग [*nm*] cremation, setting on fire; —देना to cremate, to set on fire; to brand [a bull etc.].

दाग़ [*nm*] a speck; stain, scar, mark; stigma, blemish.

दागना [*v*] to burn, to ignite; to fire; to cauterise; to brand [a bull etc.].

दाढ़ [*nf*] a jaw tooth; grinder.

दाता [*nm*] a giver, donor, benefactor, a liberal or generous man; —से सूम भला फट से (ठावें) देय जवाब a point-blank refusal is better than an uneasy suspense.

दाद [*nf*] ring worm, shingles; vocal appreciation, praise.

दान [*nm*] donation; charity, alms; a religious gift [in cash or kind]; a suffix used to denote a stand, container or pot etc; the fluid that flows from the temples of an elephant while in rut; —दक्षिणा alms and donations; —धर्म religious practices, charity and munificence; —पत्र a gift-deed; ~ शील generous, bountiful, munificent.

दान/व [*nm*] a demon; giant; ~वीय demonic; giant-like.

दाना [*nm*] grain, parched grain corn; seed; food; a bead; pustule; pimple; piece; grainy diet of animals; a demon; [*a*] wise; —पानी livelihood; food and drink; ~ उठना to be uprooted; दाने-दाने

को तरसना to be in the clutches of starvation, to starve; दाने-दाने को मुहताज starving, poverty-stricken.

दानी [*a* and *nm*] generous/munificent [person].

दाब [*nf*] pressure; strain.

दाबना [*v*] to press; to press down.

दाम [*nm*] price; value; a rope; one of the four policies [as specified in ancient Indian diplomacy] for conquest over the enemy —the policy of monetary gratification.

दामन [*nm*] skirt of a garment; the extreme end of a सारी etc.

दामाद [*nm*] a son-in-law.

दाय [*nm*] heritage, inheritance.

दायजा [*nm*] dowry; presents.

दायरा [*nm*] a circle; ring; range.

दायाँ [*a*] right.

दायाधिकार [*nm*] inheritance; heritage.

दारुण [*a*] awful; horrible; severe; heart-rending.

दारू [*nf*] liquor.

दारोग़ा [*nm*] a sub-inspector [of police]; a superintending officer.

दारोमदार [*nm*] full capability to make or mar; main responsibility.

दार्शनिक [*nm*] a philosopher; [a] philosophical.

दाल [*nf*] pulse; —गलना a tricky measure to succeed; —में काला होना to have something fishy.

दालान [*nm*] a yard; verandah.

दावत [*nf*] feast, banquet; invitation.

दावा [*nm*] a claim; suit.

दावात [*nf*] an inkpot.

दावेदार [*nm*] a claimant.

दास [*nm*] a slave; servant, serf; thrall; hence ~ता; –प्रथा slavery, serfdom.

दास्ताँ, दास्तान [*nf*] a tale, narrative; account.

दाह [*nm*] burning, heat; inflammation; mental agony; cremation; scald; —कर्म/क्रिया cremation.

दाहिना [*a*] right.

दिक़ [*nf*] tuberculosis; [*a*] vexed, harassed; fed up.

दिक़्क़त [*nf*] difficulty; trouble; ~तलब troublesome; difficult.

दिक्सूचक [*nm*] a compass.

दिखना [*v*] to be visible/seen/sighted/viewed.

दिखाऊ [*a*] presentable; worth-seeing; ostensible, showy.

दिखावट [*nf*] show, display; ostentation; hence ~टी.

दिखावा [*nm*] show; ostentation; display.

दिग् an allomorph of दिक्; ~ विजय universal conquest, subjugation of many realms in all directions; ~विजयी a conqueror of many realms or the world; ~व्यापी/~व्याप्त permeating all space, spreading in all directions; gone far and wide.

दिग्दर्श/क [*nm*] a director [of a stage performance, film, etc.]; hence ~न.

दिन [*nm*] a day [comprised of twenty-four hours from sunrise to sunrise]; a day [extending from sunrise to sunset]; day time; time; -ब-दिन day by day, from day to day, daily, with the passage of time; —रात/रैन day and night, always, all the time; —काटना to drag out one's days, to survive in hardship; —को तारे दिखाना, –को तारे नज़र आना to have the stars dance before eyes [by a blow etc.] –को दिन, रात को रात न समझना to be completely lost in work; to take no notice of the passage of time; —चढ़ना the day to be far advanced, the sun to have gone up in the sky; to pass beyond the time [of menstruation]; —दहाड़े in broad day-light; —दूना रात चौगुना बढ़ना to grow by leaps and bounds; —पूरे होना to be gone full time; to have completed the period of gestation; —फिरना /बहुरना the times to take a favourable turn, prosperous phase of life to commence; —लगना to give oneself airs; to become vain.

दिनचर्या [*nf*] daily routine.

दिनांक [*nm*] date.

दिमाग़ [*nm*] brain, mind. intellect: conceit; —आसमान पर होना to think no end of oneself, to be very much conceited; — खाली करना to beat or rack the brain; —लड़ाना to exercise or tax one's brain; —सातवें आसमान पर होना see —आसमान पर होना.

दिमाग़ी [*a*] mental, pertaining to the brain or mind.

दिया [*nm*] a lamp, an earthen lamp; [v] past tense form of देना –gave; [*a*] given.

दियासलाई [*nf*] a matchstick; a matchbox, safety match.

दिल [*nm*] the heart; courage; spirit; will; ~कश attractive, alluring, charming; ~दार beloved; generous, bountiful; courageous; ~बर beloved; ~बस्तगी entertainment; —कड़ा करना to summon up courage; not to get unnerved; —का गुबार निकालना to let out one's wrath; to give free vent to one's grudge; —का बादशाह a king at heart; —की आग बुझाना to have one's passions fulfilled; —की कली खिलना to be in exultation, to be frisky; —की दिल में रहना to have a wish remain unfulfilled; an aspiration to wither away by non-fulfilment; —चुराना to lure one's heart away; —तोड़ना to break one's heart; —धड़कना heart to palpitate; to be unnerved; —फट जाना, —फटना to develop a sense of aversion; —बढ़ाना to encourage, to back up; —बैठा जाना the heart to be sinking; —में घर/जगह करना to be taken to heart: to find a place in one's inmost feelings; —में फफोले पड़ना to suffer intense mental torture; to be heart-rent; —में फ़र्क आना to have animus, to develop a mental reservation; —से उतरना to no longer occupy a venerable place in one's heart, to be out of favour; —से दूर करना to forget.

दिलच/स्प [*a*] interesting; ~स्पी interest.

दिलासा [*nm*] consolation, solace, assurance.

दिले/र [*a*] courageous, daring. brave; valorous; hence ~ री.

दिल्लगी [*nf*] jest, joke, fun; humour; ~बाज funny; humour-some, jocular; ~बाजी jocularity, funmaking.

दिवंगत [*a*] late, deceased.

दिवस [*nm*] a day.

दिवालियापन [*nm*] bankruptcy, insolvency.

दिवालिया [nm] a bankrupt; an insolvent.

दिव्य [*a*] divine, celestial; charming, beautiful, brilliant.

दिशा [*nf*] a direction, line.

दिसंबर [*nm*] [the month of] December.

दिसाव/र [*nm*] an other country/region; foreign market.

दीक्षांत [nm] the end of preceptorial period, the conclusion of a phase of education; —(अभि) भाषण a convocation address; —समारोह convocation.

दीक्षा [*nf*] initiation.

दीन [*a*] poor, miserable, humble; exciting a sense of compassion; [*nm*] religion; —दुनिया this world and the other world; ~ बंधु a helper of the poor, compassionate; an epithet of God.

दीपक [*nm*] a lamp.

दीप्त [*a*] radiant; luminous, brilliant, bright.

दीप्ति [*nf*] lustre, splendour, luminosity, brilliance; flash.

दीमक [*nf*] termite, white ant.

दीर्घ [*a*] long; large; wide; tall, huge; deep; ~सूत्री a slow-coach; dilatory; procrastinator.

दीर्घायु [*a*] long-lived, long-living, blessed with long life; [nf] longevity.

दीवान [*nm*] a Chief Minister [in a royal court]; a royal court; a collection of poems.

दीवा/ना [*a*] mad, crazy, insane; ~नापन madness, craziness, insanity; ~नगी craziness.

दीवानी [*nf*] a civil court; the office of a दीवान [see]; [a] civil [law etc., as opposed to criminal law]; feminine form of दीवाना.

दीवार [*nf*] a wall.

दु:ख [*nm*] sorrow; unhappiness; suffering; grief, distress;~ द/~दायक/ ~ दायी painful, grievous, sorrowful; dolorous; —द्वंद्व distress and affliction; ~प्रद see दु:खद; –बँटाना to share one's sorrow, to minimize sorrow through sympathy, —मानना to be sorry, to feel sorrowful, to be unhappy.

दु:खांत [*a*] tragic, culminating in a tragedy, resulting in grief; —नाटक a tragedy.

दु:खांतिका [*nf*] a tragedy, tragic play/drama.

दु:खी [*a*] sorrowful, sad, unhappy; grief-stricken, afflicted, woeful.

दु:साध्य [*a*] difficult, arduous, hard to accomplish.

दु:साह/स [*nm*] audacity effrontery, cheek; hence ~सी.

दु:स्वप्न [*nm*] a nightmare.

दु an allomorph of **दो** used as the first member in numerous compound words; ~गाना a duet;

~ गुना double; two-fold; ~तरफ़ा bilateral, two-sided; ~नाली double-barrelled; ~पट्टा a rochet, scarf, an overall cover cloth; ~पहर noon, mid-day; ~बारा a second time once again; ~विधा uncertainty, suspense; ~भाषिया an interpreter; ~मंजिला double-storeyed; ~मुँहा double-mouthed; having two mouths; ~रंगा two-coloured; duplex; treacherous, equivocal; ~लत्ती two-legged kick, kick with the two hind legs [as by a horse or an ass]; ~शाला a double shawl; shawl; ~हत्थी a double-handed stroke; ~हाजू married a second time.

दुआ [*nf*] prayer, blessings.

दुकान [*nf*] a shop; ~दार a shopkeeper; ~दारी shopkeeping.

दु:खड़ा [*nm*] the saga of sufferings, tale of woes; —रोना to narrate one's tale of woes, to describe the saga of one's sufferings.

दु:खाना [*v*] to inflict sorrow or suffering to cause pain, to torment.

दुखिया [*a*] suffering, in distress, afflicted with sorrow; also ~रा.

दुतकार [*nf*] a sharp indignant snub, snub, contemptuous reprimand; hence ~ ना [*v*].

दुधमुहाँ [*nm* and *a*] suckling, still feeding on mother's milk; an infant.

दुधा/र, ~रू [*a*] milch; yielding much milk.

दुनिया [*nf*] the world; people; ~दार worldly, worldly wise, absorbed in worldly affairs; ~दारी worldliness, worldly wisdom; worldly affairs; —के परदे पर on the face of the earth.

दुनियावी [*a*] worldly, mundane.

दुबला [*a*] lean, thin, weak; पतला lean and thin, scrawny.

दुम [*nf*] tail; hind-most part [of an animal]; one who is a constant close follower.

दूर [*ind*] stand off; be gone!

दुरभिसंधि [*nf*] a conspiracy, collusion, secret plot.

दुराग्र/ह [*nm*] pertinacity; importunity, obduracy, hence ~ही.

दुरा/चरण ~ चार [*nm*] misonduct, malfeasance, wickedness; immorality, depravity; hence ~चारी [*a*].

दुराव [*nm*] concealment; reservation.

दुरुपयोग [*nm*] misuse, misusage, misapplication.

दुरुस्त [*a*] proper, fit, correct, all right.

दुरूह [*a*] obscure, abstruse, unintelligible; hence ~ता.

दुर्गंध [*nf*] bad odour, disagreeable smell, stench. stink.

दुर्ग [*nm*] a fort, castle; citadel.

दुर्गति [*nf*] predicament; misery, miserable state; distress.

दुर्गम [*a*] difficult, difficult of access/approach, inaccessible.

दुर्गु/ण [*nm*] defect; fault, vice; hence ~ णी.

दुर्घटना [*nf*] an accident, mishap, tragic incident.

दुर्जन [*nm*] a wicked person, rascal, scoundrel.

दुर्जेय [*a*] inconquerable.

दुर्दम [*a*] indomitable, irrepressible; unyielding; difficult to subdue; also ~ मनीय.

दुर्दशा [*nf*] predicament, miserable plight, misery.

दुर्देव [*nm*] misfortune, ill-luck.

दुर्धर्ष [*a*] invincible, indomitable, difficult to subdue.

दुर्नि/वार, ~वार्य [*a*] unrestrainable, irrepressible; inevitable.

दुर्ब/ल [*a*] weak, feeble, powerless, emaciated; imbecile; ~लता weakness, emaciation, feebleness, debility; imbecility.

दुर्बुद्धि [*a*] evil-minded, perverse; foolish, stupid.

दुर्बोध [*a*] abstruse, obscure; unintelligible.

दुर्भाग्य [*nm*] misfortune, ill-luck; tragedy.

दुर्भाव [*nm*] malice, malevolence, ill-will; also~ना.

दुर्भिक्ष [*nm*] famine; scarcity, paucity.

दुर्लभ [*a*] rare; scarce; unattainable; unavailable; excellent; unique.

दुर्व्यवहार [*nm*] misbehaviour, misconduct, ill-treatment.

दुलकी [*nf*] trot, trotting.

दुलारा [*a*] beloved, darling [child], dear.

दुविधा [*nf*] dilemma, fix.

दुशवार [*a*] difficult.

दुश्चरित्र [*nm*] misconduct, malfeasance; depravity, profligacy; [*a*] depraved, degenerate; malfeasant; profligate.

दुश्म/न [*nm*] ememy, foe; ~ नी enmity, animus, hostility.

दुष्कर [*a*] difficult, hard, arduous.

दुष्कर्म [*nm*] a misdeed; sin vice, wrong.

दुष्ट [*a*] wicked, vile, knave, bad; malevolent; faulty; [*nm*] a scoundrel, rascal, scamp.

दुष्टता [*nf*] wickedness, viciousness, knavery; mischievousness; malevolence.

दुस्तर [*a*] difficult to cross, impassable; insurmountable, insuperable.

दुहना [*v*] to squeeze, to exploit.

दुहरा [*a*] two-fold, double-folded; double, dual.

दुहराना [*v*] to repeat, to say or do over again; to revise.

दुहाई [*nf*] an outcry or entreaty for help/mercy/ justice; plaint; oath; loud proclamation; process of or wages paid for milking [a cow etc.].

दूत [*nm*] a messenger, courier; legate; an emissary, envoy.

दूतावास [*nm*] an embassy; legation.

दूध [*nm*] milk; juicy substance of certain plants; —पूत men and money; —का दूध और पानी का पानी sifting of true from the false/just from unjust; —की मक्खी an-unwanted and inconsequential entity, an insignificant person; —के दाँत milk teeth; ~ न टूटना to be too young and raw; —छुड़ाना to wean; —फटना [milk] to decompose into its watery and substantial content; दूधों नहाना पूतों फलना to prosper in men and money.

दूधिया [*a*] milky; milk-white; with a substantial quantity of milk; juicy; tender, green; [nm] a milk-vendor; an opal.

दूना [*a*] double.

दूभर [*a*] difficult, onerous; arduous.

दूरंदे/श [*a*] far-sighted, prudent, sagacious; hence ~ शी.

दूर [*adv* and *a*] far off, far away, away; distant; remote; ~गामी far-reaching; ~~ दर्शक यंत्र a telescope; ~ दर्शिता far-sightedness, prudence, sagacity; ~दर्शी far-sighted, prudent, sagacious; ~बीन a telescope; ~संचार telecommunication; —की सोचना to visualise future course of events; to be sagacious, to be prescient.

दूरी [*nf*] distance, range.

दूल्हा [*nm*] a bridegroom; husband.

दूषण [*nm*] contamination, pollution, stigma; defect, flaw.

दूसरा [*a*] second; other, another; next.

दृढ़ [*a*] firm, resolute, strong-willed; tough; strong; hard; rigid, tenacious; hence ~ता.

दृश्य [*nm*] scene; sight, spectacle, view; [*a*] visible.

दृश्यमान [*a*] visible, perceptible, tangible; apparent, obvious.

दृष्टांत [*nm*] instance; illustration [a figure of speech]; precedent.

दृष्टि [*nf*] sight; view; vision; glance; ~कोण viewpoint, point of view; ~ गोचर visible; ~पात glance, glancing, viewing; ~हीन blind.

देखना [*v*] to see, to look; to view; to perceive; to observe; to read; to correct; to consider, to experience.

देख-भाल [*nf*] care; maintenance; supervision.

देख-रेख [*nf*] supervision; guidance, care.

देखा-देखी [*adv*] in emulation/imitation of, inspired by the example of.

देन [*nf*] contribution; gift; giving; ~दार, debtor; ~दारी payment, due; indebtedness.

देना [*v*] to give; to grant; to confer, to bestow; to entrust, to assign; to yield, to surrender; used freely and frequently as an auxiliary verb, as कर दिया, चल दिया, दे दिया etc.

देर [*nf*] delay, lag.

देरी [*nf*] delay, lag.

देव [*nm*] a god, deity; a respectable person; a giant, demon; ~दूत an angel; a prophet, divine messenger; ~स्थान a temple.

देव/ता [*nm*] a god, deity; divine being; ~त्व godhood, godliness.

देवनागरी [*nf*] the script which evolved in India during the post-Gupta era and ultimately developed into a systematic and scientific instrument of writing during the 10th and 11th centuries A.D.; —अक्षर a Devanagari letter; —वर्णमाला the Devanagari alphabet.

देव/र [*nm*] husband's younger brother; hence ~रानी [*nf*].

देवालय [*nm*] a temple, seat of a deity.

देश [*nm*] a country; land; native home; space; ~ज native; local; a word evolved indigenously, indigenous; ~भक्त a patriot; ~भक्ति patriotism.

देश/द्रोह [*nm*] treason, disloyalty to one's country; ~ द्रोही a traitor, one who is disloyal to one's country.

देशनिकाला [*nm*] expatriation; exile, banishment.

देशांतर [*nm*] terrestrial longitude, longitude; another/foreign country.

देशी [*a*] native, indigenous, local.

देसावर [*nm*] a foreign country; an export-centre, marketing centre.

देह [*nf*] body, person; physique; soma; ~ धारी possessing a physical form/body; corporeal; —छोड़ना to die; —धरना to be born.

देहरी [*nf*] the threshold, doorsill.

देहांत [*nm*] death, demise.

देहा/त [*nm*] countryside; village; ~ती a villager; rustic; rural.

देहावसान [*nm*] death, demise.

दैत्य [*nm*] a demon, giant, ogre.

दैनंदिन [*a* and *adv*] daily, diurnal, from day to day, day by day.

दैनिक [*a*] daily.

दैन्य [*nm*] meekness, humbleness; poverty, indigence.

दैव [*nm*] fate, fortune, destiny; ~योग chance, accident; ~वश by chance, accidentally.

दैवात [*adv*] by chance, accidentally.

दैहिक [*a*] physical, somatic, corporeal; material.

दो [*a*] two; [*nm*] the number two; ~गला a bastard, cross-bred; illegitimate; -टूक decisive, categorical, crystal clear [statement, talk, etc.]; ~पहर midday; noon; -दो हाथ करना to try out comparative strength; -नावों में पैर रखना to ride two horses at a time.

दोज़ख [*nm*] hell, inferno.

दोष [*nm*] a fault; flaw, guilt; culpa, defect, demerit; blame; disorder [of the humours of the body].

दोषी [*a* and *nm*] [the] guilty; culprit.

दोस्त [*nm*] a friend.

दोस्ताना [*nm*] friendship, friendliness; [*a*] friendly, worthy of a friend.

दोस्ती [*nf*] friendship.

दोहरा [*a*] double, two-folded, equivocal; stoutish [as बदन].

दोहराना [*v*] to revise, to recapitulate; to repeat, to reiterate; to make two-fold.

दौड़ [*nf*] a race; run, running; -धूप endeavour, running about; all-out effort.

दौड़ना [v] to run, to run about; to rush.

दौड़ाई [*nf*] running, scurrying, bustle दौड़-धूप.

दौड़ाक [*nm*] runner; athlete.

दौड़ाकी [*nf*] running; athletics.

दौड़ाना [*v.t.*] to cause to run; to urge on, to drive a horse, to despatch a person in haste, to impel; to move as pen over paper; to run the eyes in a given direction; to move quickly, to run sthg. into a new position, to extend as a canal, or electricity, to a new region, to give play to thought, imagination.

दौर [*nm*] a phase; stage; round; -दौरा sway, dominance.

दौरा [*nm*] a tour; fit.

दौरान [*nm*] इसी–in the mean-while; during this period; के–during.

दौरी [*nf*] reg. small flat basket of bamboo or grass without a lid, sling-basket used with rope in irrigation.

दौलत [*nf*] riches, wealth; ~खाना [euphemistically] residence; ~मंद rich, wealthy, opulent, moneyed.

द्युति [*nf*] radiance, lustre, brilliance, glow.

द्योत/क [*a*] illustrative [of], expressive [of], exemplifying/signifying; hence ~न.

द्योतन [*nm*] illumination.

द्रव [*nm*] a liquid, fluid.

द्रवक [*adj.*] running, flowing, fluid.

द्रवित [*a*] melted; moved [by emotion]

द्रवीभूत [*a*] melted; moved [by emotion].

द्रव्य [*nm*] substance, matter; money; [*a*] material, substantial.

द्रव्यत्व [*nm*] material nature of a thing.

द्रष्टा [*nm*] a seer, visionist, sage; spectator.

द्रष्टव्य [*adj.*] deserving inspection or scrutiny; notable, requiring attention, noteworthy.

द्रुत [*a*] fast, fast-moving, quick, swift; moved; melted.

द्रो/ह [*nm*] malice, rancour; rebellion, hostility; hence ~ही [*a*].

द्वंद्व [*nm*] conflict, quarrel; uproar; hubbub; duel, a pair; couple.

द्वादश [*adj.*] twelve, twelfth.

द्वादशी [*nf*] the twelfth day of a lunar fortnight.

द्वापर [*nm*] mythol. the third of the four ages of the world yugas which together make up one aeon kalpa.

द्वार [*nm*] a door; doorway; gate; exit; ~पाल/पालक a door-keeper, watchman; —खुला रखना to keep the door open [for negotiation etc.]; —बंद करना to shut the door [for negotiation etc.].

द्वारा [ind] by, through, through the agency of.

द्वितीय [*a*] the second; ~क second; secondary.

द्वितीयक [*adj.*] द्वितीय, duplicate.

द्विधा [*ind*] in two ways; in two parts.

द्वीप [*nm*] an island.

द्वीपी [*adj.*] having to do with an island; island-dwelling, an islander.

द्वेष [*nm*] malice; aversion, repugnance; ill-will; malevolence; dislike, disaffection; hence ~षी.

द्वेषी [*adj.*] hating; filled with aversion; hostile, one filled with ill will; an enemy.

ध

ध the fourth and penultimate letter of the fourth pentad [i.e. तवर्ग] of the Devanagair: alphabet.

ध - देवनागरी वर्णमाला (व्यंजन) में तवर्ग का चौथा वर्ण है। इसका उच्चारण स्थान दन्तमूल है।

धंधक [*nm*] धंधा, धंधक-धोरी, a toiler, drudge.

धंधा [*nm*] vocation, occupation; business; work.

धँधार [*adj.*] fire, tongue of flame.

धँसना [*v*] to sink; to penetrate into; to enter into; to get stuck into.

धँसान [*nf*] sinking as into soft ground: धँसन, a swamp, bog, hind, immersion of an idol in water, swampy.

धक [*nf*] palpitation; sudden suspension of normal heart-throb; –से रह जाना to be paralysed [through fear or astonishment], to be dumbfounded.

धक-धक [*nm*] beating, palpitation; tremor, perturbation, blaze of fire, a-tremble, करना, to beat fast the heart; to be perturbed; to blaze.

धकापेल [*nf*] indiscriminate shoving, shoving and pushing; jostling; [*adv*] vigorously, vehemently, non-stop.

धका/र [*nm*] the letter ध [*dha*] and its sound; ~रांत [word] ending in ध [dha].

धकेल [*nm*] a shove, push, — अकेल-गाड़ी, trolley, handcart.

धकेलना [*v*] to shove, to push.

धक्कमधक्का [*nm*] jostling, shoving and pushing; rush.

धक्का [*nm*] a push; shove; shock; setback; stroke, buffet; jostle, jolt, impact; ~मुक्की jostling, shoving; pushing; elbowing.

धज [*nf*] air, demeanour; mien, appearance, look; also धजा.

धज्जी [*nf*] a shred, strip, tatter; lath; धज्जियाँ उड़ाना to reduce to shreds, to tatter, to tear to pieces.

धड़क/न [*nf*] throbbing, palpitation, pulsation, hence ~ ना [*v*].

धड़धड़ाना [*v*] to make a rattling or banging sound; to rap-tap or knock [at a door]; to walk heavily and briskly.

धड़/ल्ला [*nm*]; ~ ल्ले का dauntless, fearless, overbearing; strong; ~ल्ले से dauntlessly, fearlessly.

धड़ाका [*nm*] an explosion, crash; a loud report.

धड़ाधड़ [*adv*] in a quick succession, one after the other; incessantly.

धड़ान [*nm*] thud, crash, loud report [of a falling body]; -से with a crash/loud report/thud; instantaneously.

धत् [*ind*] be off!, stand away!; you naughty!

धधकना [*v*] to blaze, to flare up, to burn intensely.

धन [*nm*] wealth, riches, money; plus; [a] positive [as an electric charge]; -दौलत wealth and affluence, riches; -धान्य all round prosperity, affluence; ~,मूल capital; ~दान wealthy, rich; ~हीन poor, moneyless, indigent; -सबको अंधा कर देय gold is the dust that blinds all eyes; —से धन आता है money begets money.

धनिक [*a*] opulent, wealthy, rich, moneyed; [nm] a wealthy person.

धनिया [*nm*] coriander.

धनी [*a*] rich, opulent, moneyed; effective; [nm] master, owner; —मानी eminent, affluent and effective; magnate.

धनुष [*nm*] a bow, an arch.

धन्य [*a*] blessed, worth felicitation, fortunate; [int] well done!, bravo!, blessings on you!, how fortunate!.

धन्यवाद [*nm*] thanks giving; an expression of gratitude; [*ind*] thanks!, thank you!

धब्बा [*nm*] blemish, blot, slur; stain, taint; speck.

धम [*nf*] thud, report resulting from the fall of a heavy object or its movement on the ground; -धम recurrence of the sound of धम.

धमक [*nf*] the vibrations caused by the impact or movement of a heavy object on a surface; thumping sound; the report of moving footsteps; stamping sound; throbbing sound; pulsation.

धमकाना [*v*] to threaten, to intimidate.

धमकी [*nf*] a threat; bluster.

धमनी [*nf*] an artery.

धमाका [*nm*] a loud report, explosion, burst.

धमाचौकड़ी [*nf*] a row; tumult. turmoil; gambol; frolic.

धरणि/णी [*nf*] the earth.

धरती [*nf*] the earth; world.

धरना [*v*] to hold; to place; to put; to arrest, to apprehend; to take as a husband/wife, to pawn, to pledge; [*nm*] picketing; sitting doggedly to enforce compliance of a demand.

धरातल [*nm*] surface; surface of the earth.

धराशायी [*a*] fallen, fallen aground, razed [to the ground].

धरोहर [*nf*] a trust [in cash or kind]; deposit.

धर्म [*nm*] religion; faith; justice; duty; property, attribute; ~ग्रंथ scripture; ~च्युत fallen or deviated from duty/religion: ~धुरीण staunchly devout, leading in piety; ~ध्वज/ध्वजी a religious hypocrite, pietist; pietical; -निरपेक्ष secular; ~ता secularism; ~पर/परायण religious, religious-minded, devout; ~परता/परायणता religiosity, devoutness; ~भीरु religionfearing; ~युद्ध crusade; righteous/principled fighting; ~रक्षक a protector of religion; ~रत devoted to religion; dutiful; ~शाला a hospice, a free-of-charge public lodging; ~शास्त्र theology; theological jurisprudence; ~संकट a dilemma: -सुधार reformation; —बिगाड़ना/लेना to cause religious dereliction; to violate the chastity of; —रखना to protect one's religion.

धर्मांध [*a*] frenzied [in religious matter], fanatic [al]; ~ता fanaticism, religious frenzy

धर्मात्मा [*a*] devout, religious.

धर्मादा [*nm*] endowment; charity.

धर्मार्थ [*a*] charitable.

धवल [*a*] white; clear; bright; beautiful.

धसकना [*v*] to be depressed, to sink; to lower, to move downwards.

धाँधली [*nf*] chaos, chaotic state; arbitrary conduct, arbitrariness; highhandedness, outrage.

धाक [*nf*] commanding/over-whelming influence, sway; awe.

धागा [*nm*] thread.

धाड़ —मारना–मारकर रोना to cry aloud/wildly, to lament loudly.

धातु [*nf*] metal; constituent elements [of the body]; semen; root.

धान [*nm*] paddy.

धानी [*a*] light green; [*nf*] a receptacle; stand; cupboard.

धान्य [*nm*] crop.

धाम [*nm*] residence, abode; seat of a diety.

धायँ [*nf*] [sound of] a gun-shot.

धार [*nf*] an edge; sharp edge; sharpness; current; flow; jet; an adjectival suffix meaning one who holds or supports [as कर्णधार].

धारण [*nm*] holding; wielding; supporting, maintenance, maintaining; wearing; assumption; retention.

धारणा [*nf*] impression; concept; notion, idea; [power of] retention [also -शक्ति].

धारा [*nf*] current; stream; flow [of water etc.], eddy; section [of law]; clause [of a bill]; ~प्रवाह fluent non-stop, incessant; ~वाहिक, वाही serial.

धारी [*nf*] a stripe; line; an adjectival suffix meaning one/who or that which holds/supports possesses/maintains/wears.

धार्मिक [*a*] religious, religious. minded.

धावा [*nm*] charge, raid, attack assault; –बोलना to launch an attack/expedition, to charge.

धिक्कार [*nm*] censure; curse; opprobrium, condemnation; hence ~ना [*v*].

धीमा [*a*] slow; dull; mild; low; gentle; hence ~पन.

धीर [*a*] patient; resolute, firm, steady; slow; [*nm*] consolation, solace; patience.

धीरज [*nm*] patience; fortitude; composure.

धीरे [*adv*] slowly; mildly. -धीरे by slow degrees, by and by.

धुंध [*nf, nm*] mist, fog; haze.

धुंधलका [*nm*] twilight, darkishness duskiness; haziness.

धुंधला [*a*] hazy, dim, misty, foggy; faded; blurred, vague; hence ~ पन.

धुआँ [*nm*] smoke; fume; ~धार fiery; violent; eloquent; torrential; धुएँ के बादल उड़ाना to indulge in tall talk, to talk through one's hat.

धुकधुकी [*nf*] throbbing [of the heart]; suspense.

धुत्त [*a*] stupefied [by liquor]; besotted [with]; steeped [in].

धुन [*nf*] assiduity, perseverence; mania, fad; ardour; tune, key-note; —का पक्का persevering; assiduous; resolute.

धुनना [*v*] to card or comb as [cotton]; to beat thoroughly; to go on repeating.

धुनी [*a*] perserving; assiduous; resolute.

धुप्पल [*nf*] bluff, bluffing.

धुरंधर [*a*] pre-eminent [as scholar]; leading, par-excellence; pastmaster.

धुर [*a*] extreme, remotest; [*nm*] extremity.

धुरी [*nf*] axis, pivot.

धुर्रा [*nm*] powder, dust; rustic, incivil; axle, axis.

धुलाई [*nf*] the act or process of washing, a wash; washing charges.

धूप [*nf*] the sun; sunshinase; incense, gum benzoin; ~ घड़ी a sun-dial; ~दार sunny; ~बत्ती an incense-stick; —में बाल सफ़ेद होना to be aged without experience; to be old and yet devoid of wisdom.

धूम [*nm*] smoke; fume; [*nf*] fanfare, tumult, bustle, pomp; ado; eclat; boom; -धड़क्का/धाम hustle and bustle, fanfare, tumult, eclat; pomp.

धूमिल [*a*] vague; blurred; fumigated.

धूम [*nm*] smoke; fume; [*a*] smoke-coloured; ~पान smoking.

धूर्त [*a*] knave, cunning, crooked; rascal; hence -ता.

धूल [*nf*] dust; dirt; –चटाना to humble to the dust, to knock down; —झाड़ना, —झाड़कर खड़े हो जाना lit. to dust off—to dust off the humiliation of defeat; —झोंकना, आँखों में to throw dust in somebody's eyes, to pull wool over somebody's eyes; —में मिलना to be ruined, to be devastated.

धूलि [*nf*] dust; dirt; —धूसरित steeped in dust, dusty.

धूलिया [*adj.*] of dust, made of dust, धूल, पीर की क़सम खाना, to swear an oath understood to have no significance.

धूसना [*v.t.*] to cram, ठूँसना to butt; to gore.

धूसर [*adj.*] dust-coloured; grey, khaki, dusty, grey or grey-brown colour.

धूसरित [*a*] filled or strewn with dust; turned dirty.

धृष्ट [*a*] impudent, insolent; obtrusive; impertinent; hence ~ता.

धृष्टता [*nf*] brashness; shamelessness, insolence, daring,

धैर्य [*nm*] patience, fortitude, endurance.

धोखा [*nm*] deception, deceit; fraud, cheating, guile; subterfuge; a scarecrow; -धड़ी beguilement; cheating, deceit; humbuggery; धोखेबाज a cheat, swindler; deceitful, guileful; fraudulent, shyster; धोखे की टट्टी a camouflage, false screen, a fraudulent device.

धोती [*nf*] loin cloth worn by Indians.

धोना [*v*] to wash, to launder; to cleanse.

धोबिन [*nf.*] a washerman's wife, a washerwoman, a wagtail.

धोबी [*nf*] a washerman, launderer; —का कुत्ता, न घर का न घाट का neither fish not fowl, a rolling stone gathers no moss; one who rides two boats is sure to be overthrown.

धौंकना [*v*] to blow with bellows etc,; to fan a fire.

धौंकनी [*nf*] bellows, blower; blow-pipe.

धौंका [*nf*] heat of the sun.

धौंकिया [*nm*] one who works on bellows; solderer, tinsmith; blacksmith.

धौंस [*nf*] bluster, awesome demeanour.

ध्यान [*nm*] attention, heed; meditation, contemplation; concentration of mind;—देना to heed; to contemplate or mediate;—धरना to mediate or contemplate; —में न लाना to ignore, not to mind;—लगाना to concentrate [upon], to meditate,—से उतरना to forget, to lose the memory of.

ध्यानी [*a*] meditative; given to meditation/ contemplation.

ध्येय [*nm*] aim, end.

ध्रुव [*nm*] a pole; the polar star; [*a*] fixed, firm; permanent; —तारा the polar star.

ध्रुवता [*nf*] fixity; stability, constancy, permanence.

ध्वंस [*nm*] ruination; destruction, devastation.

ध्वंसक [*adj.*] destructive; dangerous, naut, destroyer.

ध्वज [*nm*] a flag, banner, ensign, colours.

ध्वजा [*nf*] colours, flag, ensign, banner.

ध्वजी [*nm*] carrying a banner, bearing a symbol or emblem, standard-bearer.

ध्वन्य [*adj*] sarcastic.

ध्वस्त [*adj*] fallen, destroyer, ruined, broken.

ध्वांत [*nm*] gloom, darkness ~ चर a demon.

ध्वनि [*nf*] sound; [in poetics] suggestion, suggested meaning; ~विज्ञान phonetics; phonology.

ध्वनिक [*adj.*] phonetic.

न the last letter of the fourth pentad [i.e. तवर्ग] of the Devanagari: alphabet; [ind] no, not; a typical conversational particle used for laying; emphasis or ascertaining the other party's reaction [as चलो –, पत्र लिखोगे–]; isn't it; —तो न –neither ....nor; —करना to say 'no', to refuse; to decline; to deny, —घर का, न घाट का neither fish nor fowl, neither here nor there; —नौ मन तेल होगा, न राधा नाचेगी if the sky falls, we shall gather larks.

न – देवनागरी वर्णमाला (व्यंजन) में तवर्ग का पाँचवाँ वर्ण है। इसका उच्चारण स्थान दाँत और नासिका है।

नंग [*adj.*] नंगा, stark naked, नंक-पैरा, barefoot.

नंग-धड़ंग [*a*] stark naked, completely nude.

नंगा [*a*] naked, nude; bare, uncovered; exposed; leafless; shameless, wicked; ~पन nakedness, nudeness; shamelessness; wickedness.

नंगाई [*adj.*] nakedness; bareness.

नंगापन [*nm*] nakedness.

नंबर [*nm*] number; marks; counting.

नंबरी [*a*] notorious; the mark of authority; of one hundred [as—नोट]; bearing a number, numbered.

नकटा [*a* and *nm*] nose-clipt, noseless; hence नकटी.

नकड़ा [*nm*] inflammation of the nose in cattle.

नक़द [*a*] cash, hard cash; [*nm*] cash, ready money; money in [the form of] coins; [*adv*] in cash.

नक़ल [*nf*] a copy, duplicate; imitation; mimicking, mimicry.

नक़ली [*a*] counterfeit, false; artificial; fabricated, fictitious; sham; spurious; impostorous.

नक़्शा [*nm*] a map, chart, plan; pomp and show.

नक़ाब [*nf*] a mask; veil; visor, vizard; ~पोश [*a*] masked [man], wearing a mask.

नका/र [*nm*] the letter न [na] and its sound; [*nm*] decline; refusal; negation; denial; [a word] ending in न [na].

नकारना [*v*] to refuse; to decline; to negate; to deny; to dishonour [as चेक—].

नक़्क़ारख़ा/ना [*nm*] the kettle-drum chamber; ~ने में तूती की आवाज (कौन सुनता है) [who would listen to] a cry in wilderness.

नक़्क़ा/रा [nm] a huge kettle-drum.

नक्क़ाशी [*nf*] engraving, carving; etching; designing; ~दार engraved; carved; etched; carrying designs.

नक्कू [*a*] long-nosed [person]; [a person] who thinks too much of himself; non-conforming, a butt for accusing fingers; notorious for non-conformist initiatives; fastidious.

नक़्श [*a*] engraved; imprinted; [*nm*] features.

नक्षत्र [*nm*] a star; constellation, an asterism in the moon's path comprised of 27 or 28 stars.

नख़रा [*nm*] coquetry; flirtatious airs and graces.

नग [*nm*] a gem, jewel, precious stone; a piece, number; an item; a mountain.

नगण्य [*a*] trifle, trifling, trite; insignificant; worthless; inappreciable.

नगदी [*nf*] hard cash.

नग़मा [*nm*] a song; melody.

नगर [*nm*] a city, town.

नगरी [*nf*] a big city.

नगाड़ा [*nm*] a big kettle-drum, timbal, tomtom.

नगीना [*nm*] a gem, jewel.

नग्न [*a*] nude, naked; hence ~ता.

नज़दीक [*adv*] near, close, in the vicinity.

नज़र [*nf*] sight; eyesight, vision; look, glance; attention; gift, present offering; influence cast by an evil eye; ~बंद in detention, under watch; an internee, detenu; ~बंदी detention, internment; ~अंदाज करना to take no notice of, to overlook, to ignore, to disregard; —बदलना one's favours to be withdrawn; one's attitude to undergo a change; to assume a different posture;—लगना to be afflicted by an evil eye, to be struck by an ominous glance.

नज़राना [*nm*] a present, gift.

नज़ला [*nm*] catarrh, cold.

नज़ाकत [*nf*] delicacy, tenderness, grace.

नज़ारा [*nm*] a scene, view; spectable.

नज़्म [*nf*] a poem.

नट [*nm*] an acrobat; a rope-dancer, funambulist; tumbler; an actor.

नटख/ट [*a*] naughty, mischievous; hence ~पन.

नत [*a*] bent; tilted, curved; bowed; humble [d]; ~मस्तक having the head bowed down [through modesty, shame, etc.]; respectful.

नतीजा [*nm*] result; consequence; conclusion.

नत्थी [*a*] attached; annexed; appended, tagged.

नदारद [*a*] mising, not present; disappeared, vanished; absent.

नदी [*nf*] a river.

ननिहाल [*nf*] mother's paternal home.

नन्हा [*a*] tiny; small, wee; too young.

नपाई [*nf*] measurement; the process of and charges paid for measuring.

नपुंसक [*nm*] a eunuch; an impotent person; a coward; [*a*] impotent; cowardly, unmanly; hence ~ता/त्व.

नफ़रत [*nf*] hatred, dislike; contempt, abomination.

नफ़ा [*nm*] profit, gain, advantage.

नफ़ासत [*nf*] nicety, fineness; ~पसन्द dainty; one who has a liking for exquisiteness and excellence, cox-comb.

नफ़ीस [*a*] nice, fine, excellent, exquisite, dainty.

नब्ज़ [*nf*] pulse [of the hand].

नब्बे [*a*] ninety; [nm] the number ninety.

नम [*a*] moist; humid, damp.

नमक [*nm*] salt; table salt; [touch of] prettiness; ~हराम ungrateful, disloyal; faithless, unfaithful —खाना, किसी का to have subsisted on somebody's patronage [and, therefore, to be under a debt of gratitude]; —छिड़कना, कटे पर/घाव पर/जले पर to add insult to injury, to inflict one affliction upon another; -मिर्च लगाना to exaggerate [things]; to put forth a hyperbolic description.

नमकीन [*a*] salty, salted, saltish, saline; pretty, beautiful; [*nm*] a salty dish of snacks.

नमस्कार [*nm*] salutation, a term of greeting; adieu, so long.

नमस्ते [*nf*] lit. salutation to you; see नमस्कार.

नमा/ज [*nf*] a formal prayer [by the Muslims]; hence ~जी meticulously regular in नमाज, a devout Muslim.

नमी [*nf*] humidity; dampness; moisture.

नमूना [*nm*] a sample; specimen, model; design; type; pattern.

नम्र [*a*] modest, humble; polite; meek, submissive; hence ~ ता.

नयन [*nm*] an eye.

नयनाभिराम [*a*] charming, beautiful, attractive.

नया [*a*] new, novel; fresh; unused; green; recent; modern; raw; inexperienced; young; unacquainted; not known; hence ~पन; नए सिरे से ab initio, afresh.

नर [*nm*] a man; male; [*a*] male; ~बलि human sacrifice; ~भक्षी a man-eater; cannibal.

नरक [*nm*] the hell, inferno; a place of great torture or agony; a place unfit for human habitation; –दास living in hell, infernal stay, a stay involving great torture and agony.

नरम [*a*] soft, gentle; delicate; pliant, flexible; kind merciful; moderate; ~पंथी moderate.

नरमी [*nf*] softness; gentleness; delicacy; kindness; moderateness.

नराधिपति [*nm*] a king.

नरेश [*nm*] a king.

नर्त/क [*nm*] a dancer; ~ की a male dancer.

नर्स [*nf*] a nurse.

नल [*nm*] a pipe; tap. ~कूप a tube-well; ~का a pipe, hydrant.

नलिका [*nf*] a tubule; tube, pipe.

नली [*nf*] tube; tubule; pipe; spout; barrel [of a gun].

नवंबर [*nm*] [the month of] November.

नव [*a*] new, novel, neo-; young; fresh; recent; modern; nine; [*nm*] the number nine; ~युवक a young man; youth; ~युवती a young woman.

नवल [*a*] new, novel, neo—; fresh; young; recent.

नवाँ [*a*] the ninth [in order].

नवा/सा [*nm*] a daughter's son; hence ~सी; [*a* and *nm*] eighty nine.

नवीन [*a*] new, novel, neo-; modern; recent; fresh; youthful; young; ~सा novelty, newness; freshness.

नव्य [*a*] new, novel, neo; modern; recent.

नशा [*nm*] intoxication; inebriation; –पानी some intoxicating drink, specially भंग [see]; ~बंदी prohibition.

नशी/ला [*a*] intoxicating; inebrient; hence ~ली.

नशेबा/ज [*nm* and *a*] [an] addict, habitual drunkard, [one] addicted to an intoxicant; inebriate; hence जी.

नश्तर [*nm*] a lancet; surgical knife; —लगाना to operate upon; to lance.

नश्वर [*a*] perishable, destructible; transient.

नष्ट [*a*] destroyed, perished, annihilated; destructed, ruined; —भ्रष्ट destroyed; ruined, destructed.

नस [*nf*] a vein, sinew; nerve; ~बंदी vasectomy; -नस फड़क उठना the whole being to thrill in excitement; to be thrilled; -नस में all over the body, in one's whole being.

नस्ल [*nf*] breed, pedigree, genealogy.

नसीब [*nm*] fate, luck, fortune; destiny; —आजमाना to try one's luck; —का लिखा lot; dictates of destiny; —खुल जाना/चमकना/जागना/सीधा होना to be in luck, fortune to smile on someone, to be favoured by Dame Luck; —फूटना/सो जाना to be struck by ill-luck, to be under a spell of misfotutne.

नसीहत [*nf*] teaching, precept; counselling; preaching.

नसे (सै) नी [*nf*] a ladder; staircase, stairway.

नहर [*nf*] a canal, channel; waterway.

नहाना [*v*] to bathe, to take a bath; to perform ablution.

नहीं [*ind*] not, not; —तो otherwise, or else; if not; lest; but for; no, certainly not.

नाँवाँ [*nm*] money; cash.

ना [*ind*] a word denoting negation, no; ~ इंसाफ़ी injustice; ~उम्मीद hopeless; disappointed, despaired; ~उम्मीदी disappointment, despair; ~ क़ाबिल unworthy; unqualified; incapable; undeserving, not fit for; not worth; ~काम fruitless, ineffective; disabled; unsuccessful; ~कारा useless, worthless; unserviceable, good for nothing; idle; ~खुश unhappy; displeased; annoyed; ~खुशी unhappiness, displeasure, annoyance; ~गवार intolerate, unbearable; ~चाकी discord, estrangement, estranged feelings; ~ चीज़ worthless; insignificant; petty, trifling; ~ जायज improper; undue; illegitimate; ~दान ignorant, stupid, nincompoop; ~ की दोस्ती जी का जंजाल befriend a fool and suffer a thousand falls; ~दानी ignorance; stupidity; ~देहंद a habitual defaulter in due payment; ~पसंद not likeable, not to one's liking, repulsive; ~पैद rare, scarce; ~फ़रमानी disobedience, defiance; ~ बालिग़ minor, underage; ~मंज़ूर rejected disapproved; ~मर्द impotent, emasculate; coward; ~मर्दी impotence, emasculation; cowardice; ~माकूल unworthy, undeserving; unfit; improper, ~मुमकिन impossible; ~मुराद frustrated, ill-fated; ~याब unique, rare; precious; ~वाकिफ़ not knowing, not apprised [of]; ignorant; a stranger; ~साज indisposed.

नाईं [*ind*] like, in the manner of

नाई [*nm*] a barber.

नाक [*nf*] the nose; [a symbol of] prestige honour; pre-eminent person [in a class or group]; [*nm*] the heaven; a kind of crocodile; —कटना to have one's fair name tarnished; to be faced with humiliation; one's honour to be sullied; —की सीध में just in front; —चढ़ाना lit. to stretch the nostrils upwards –to express indignation/contempt; —पर गुस्सा होना to be very petulant, to be very short-tempered; —पर मारना to pay off readily [so as to keep one's image unsullied]; —फटना lit. the nose to be split up—foul smell to be unbearable; —बहना the nose to be running; –भौं चढ़ाना/सिकोड़ना lit. to turn up the nose and knit the brows—to frown, to express indignation; —में दम करना to pester, to plague, to harass; –रगड़ना to beseech very humbly; —सिनकना to blow the nose; नाकों चने चबवाना to torment, to cause excessive harassment.

नाक-नक़्शा [*nm*] features, facial cut.

नाका (के) बंदी [*nf*] a blockade, barring of entry and exit.

नाखून [*nm*] a nail.

नाग [*nm*] a cobra, snake; an elephant; [*a*] treacherous, venomous.

नागर [*a*] urban;civil, civic; civilian; wise [*nm*] a civilian.

नागराक्षर [*nm*] a Devanagari: character/letter.

नागरिक [*a*] civil; civilian, urbane; [*nm*] a citizen; civilian; ~ता citizenship; civility.

नागा [*nf*] absence [from work].

नाच [*nf*] dance; -गाना dance and music; ~ घर a dancing hall; -रंग merry-making, entertainment; – न जाने आँगन टेढ़ा a bad workman quarrels with his tools.

नाचना [*v*] to dance; to run about.

नाज़ [*nm*] coquetry, airs; feigned air; pride, vanity; -नखरा coquettishness, alluring gestures ; ~नी/नीन delicate beauty.

नाजुक [*a*] delicate, frail, tender; critical; ~बदन of a delicate frame, of a frail constitution.

नाटक [*nm*] a drama; play, ~कार a dramatist, playwright.

नाटकीय [*a*] dramatic; histrionic; ~ता dramatic element/character.

नाटना [*v*] to decline; to refuse; to deny.

नाटा [*a*] short, short-statured, dwarfish.

नाट्य [*a*] dramatic; histrionic; -कला dramatic art, histrionics; ~कार a dramatist, playwright; an actor; a performer [of a play]; ~शाला a theatre; ~शास्त्र dramaturgy.

नाड़ी [*nf*] pulse; vein; artery.

नाता [*nm*] relation; connection.

नाते [*nm*] relations, connections; [*adv*] by virtue of, for; the sake of, for; because of.

नातेदा/र [*nm*] a relative, kinsfolk; ~री relationship.

नाद [*nm*] a sound, musical sound; noise; [nf] a manger.

नाना [*nm*] maternal grandfather; [*a*] varied, diverse, manifold; miscellaneous.

नाप [*nm*] measure, measurement; —जोख/तोल measure and weight, measurement; assessment.

नापना [*v*] to measure.

नाबदान [*nm*] a drain, gutter.

ना/भि [*nf*] the navel; umbilicus, hub.

नाभि/क [*nm*] nucleus; ~कीय nuclear.

नाम [*nm*] name; title; appellation; renown, fame; ~करण naming; baptism: nomenclature; ~जद nominated; ~जदगी nomination; -धाम name and address, whereabouts; ~ धारी named, known by the name of; -निशान trace; vestige; ~पट्ट a name-plate; signboard; -पद्धति [system of] nomenclature; –मात्र को only in name, nominal; ~रासी name-sake; ~लेवा a survivor, one who remembers [a deceased]; ~वर renowned, famous; ~वरी renown, fame; —उछालना to bandy one's name about; to bring disgrace upon; —कमाना to earn a name; to acquire renown; —का only in name, nominal; —, डुबाना to tarnish the fair name [of]; to lose one's reputation/honour, to bring disgrace or infamy; —निकलना to become a byword; to become notorious; to become celebrated; —पर, (किसी के) in the name of; for the sake of; –पैदा करना to earn name and fame; —रखना to save or protect the honour/prestige of; —लगना to be branded [an accused]; –निशान बाकी न रहना to have no trace left; to be completely devastated, to be erased out of existence/memory.

नामक [*a*] named, bearing the name [of].

नामत: [*ind*] by name.

नामां/कन [*nm*] nomination; inscription of name.

नामी [*a*] famous, reputed, renowned, eminent; named, bearing the name [of]; -गिरामी famous, reputed, eminent.

नायक [*nm*] a hero; leader; chief; a military official of a low rank.

नायब [*a*] deputy; [nm] a deputy, an assistant.

नारंगी [*nf*] an orange.

नारा [*nm*] a slogan; नारेबाज a slogan-monger.

नाराज [*a*] angry, enraged; displeased.

नारियल [*nm*] the coconut tree and its fruit.

नाल [*nm*] a shaft; peduncle, stalk [as of a lotus]; barrel; tube; woodpipe, blowpipe; the navel string; the gullet; a weaver's spindle; a horse shoe; heavy stonering used in weight-lifting exercise; commission realised by a gambling den-owner from the gambling party.

नाला [*nm*] a rivulet; water-course, culvert; big drain, gutter.

नालाय/क़ [*a*] unworthy, worthless; unfit; incompetent; hence ~की.

नालिश [*nf*] a law-suit; suit; plaint.

नाली [nf] a drain, drain-pipe; sewer; scupper.

नाव [*nf*] a boat, ferry.

नाविक [*nm*] a sailor, seaman, boatman.

नाश [*nm*] destruction, ruination, devastation; waste.

नाश्ता [*nm*] breakfast.

नासम/झ [*a*] unintelligent, dull of understanding, stupid; hence ~झी.

नासिका [*nf*] the nose.

नासूर [*nm*] sinus.

नास्तिक [*nm*] an atheist, an unbeliever; hence ~ता.

नाहक़ [*adv*] in vain, for nothing, to no purpose, without rhyme or reason.

निं/दा [*nf*] ill-speaking, censure; condemnation; hence ~दक, ~ दनीय.

निःश्रेयस [*nm*] the summun bonum, highest good.

निःस्पृह [*a*] selfless, having no selfish motives; content [ed].

निःस्वार्थ [*a*] unselfish, selfless; hence ~ता.

निकट [*adj*] near, close, proximate; ~वर्ती/स्थ adjacent; near, close, proximal.

निकटता [*nf*] proximity, closeness, nearness.

निकम्मा [*a*] inert, idle, indolent; without employment; worthless, useless, good for-nothing.

निकलना [*v*] to get out; to emerge; to rise [as सूरज); to come out; to proceed; to emanate; to appear; to be extracted [as अर्क); to be deduced [as निष्कर्ष]; to be solved [as सवाल]; to issue; or be issued [as हुक्म); to be published [as पत्रिका, किताब]; to slink away; निकल जाना to go away; to be lost, to be wasted; to elope [with].

निकाह [*nm*] marriage, marriage ceremony.

निकृष्ट [*a*] inferior, inferiormost; low, base, vile.

निखट्टू [*a* and *nm*] indolent, idle; without employment; worthless; unearning; an idler, a drone.

नि/खार [*nm*] brightness; lustre; elegance; hence~खरना [*v*].

निगरानी [*nf*] supervision; guard, watch.

निगलना [*v*] to swallow; to gulp.

निगाह [*nf*] look, glance; sight, vision.

निगोड़ा [*a*] worthless; indolent, idle; an abusive term used by women for persons who are idle and indolent; [*nm*] an idler.

निग्रह [*nm*] restraint, self-repression, subdual.

निचला [*a*] lower; situated below, low lying.

निचोड़ [*nm*] essence; gist, substance; sum and substance; hence ~ना [*v*].

निज [*a*] own, one's own.

निजी [*a*] one's own, personal, individual; private; unofficial.

निठल्ला [*a*] idle, indolent, lazy; lolling; without any employment; [*nm*] an idler; hence ~पन.

निडर [*a*] fearless, daring, dauntless; intrepid.

निढाल [*a*] languid, wearied; spiritless.

नित [*adv*] every day, daily.

नितांत [*a*] excessive; absolute; complete.

नित्य [*a*] excessive; eternal; essential; invariable; [*adv*] constantly; always; daily ~ प्रति every day; daily.

निदान [*nm*] diagnosis; [*adv*] at last: consequently.

निदेश [*nm*] direction; directive; ~क director.

निदेशालय [*nm*] a directorate.

निद्रा [*nm*] sleep; slumber; —रोग narcolepsy.

निद्रालु [*a*] slumberous, somnolent; hence ~ ता.

निधन [*nm*] death; passing away.

निधि [*nf*] treasure; fund.

निन्यानवे [*a*] ninety-nine; [*nm*] the number ninety-nine.

निपट [*adv*] absolutely, exceedingly.

निपटना [*v*] to be settled; to be decided; to be finished; to be disposed of; to be relieved; to settle score with; to face.

निपटारा [*nm*] disposal; settlement; reconciliation; conclusion, termination.

निपुण [*a*] skilful, expert; dexterous; efficient; hence ~ ता.

निबंध [*nm*] an essay.

निब [*nf*] a nib.

निबटना [*v*] see निपटना.

निबल [*a*] weak, feeble; invalid,

निबाह [*nm*] subsistence, sustenance; maintenance, accommodation, carrying on, pulling on; fulfilment [as of ज़िम्मेदारी]; hence ~ना [*v*].

नि/भना [*v*] to be carried on; to be pulled on; to be accommodated; to be accomplished; to pass; to subsist, to sustain; hence ~भाना.

निमंत्रण [*nm*] an invitation; -पत्र [a letter of] invitation; invitation card.

निमित्त [*nm*] cause, reason; factor; purpose, motive; [ind] for the sake of; on account of.

निमि(मे)ष [*nm*] twinkling of an eye, blink, nictitation; time taken in the twinkling of an eye.

निम्न [*a*] low; mean; depressed; sunken; following, given below; ~लिखित undermentioned, the following, mentioned below.

नियंता [*nm*] a controller; ruler.

नियंत्रक [*nm*] a controller.

नियं/त्रण [*nm*] control; restraint; hence ~त्रित.

नियत [*a*] fixed; given, prescribed; decided; allotted; constant, invariable, unchanging.

नियति [*nf*] destiny, fate; luck.

नियम [*nm*] a rule, canon; law; principle.

नियमन [*nm*] regulation.

नियमावली [*nf*] rules, rules and regulations.

नियमित [*a*] regular; regulated; regularised; ~ता regularity.

नियामत [nf] a rare gift, divine blessing.

नियुक्त [*a*] appointed, employed.

नियुक्ति [*nf*] appointment, employment; posting.

निरंकुश [*a*] despotic; uncontrolled, unrestrained; absolute; unrule; ~ता despotism; absolutism.

निरंतर [*a*] continuous; uninterrupted, incessant, non-stop; perpetual; [adv] continuously; uninterruptedly, incessantly.

निरत [*a*] engaged; absorbed, engrossed.

निरपरा/ध, ~ धी [*a*] innocent; guiltless, faultless.

निरपेक्ष [*a*] absolute; indifferent; without expectation, unconcerned; —सत्य the absolute truth.

निरभिमा/न, ~ नी [*a*] prideless, not proud; humble.

निरर्थक [a] meaningless; vain; useless, fruitless, pointless; insignificant, worthless; empty; futile.

निरस्त्र [*a*] unarmed; disarmed.

निरस्त्रीकरण [nm] disarmament.

निरा [*a*] pure; absolute, entire; complete; mere; [*adv*] entirely, completely; merely; very much.

निराकरण [*nm*] abrogation, annulment, removal, act or process of dispelling [as of भ्रम/भय].

निराकार [*a*] shapeless, formless; incorporeal; [*nm*] the Formless [God].

निरादर [*nm*] disrespect, disgrace, dishonour.

निराधार [*a*] baseless; groundless, unfounded; without prop or support; false; hollow.

निरापद [*a*] secure, safe; protected; without trouble.

निरामिष [*a*] vegetarian.

निराला [*a*] unique, peculiar; uncommon; strange.

निराश [*a*] frustrated; disappointed, desperate, disheartened, despaired, hopeless.

निराशा [*nf*] frustration; despair, disappointment, pessimism, dejection, despondency; hopelessness; ~वाद pessimism.

निराश्रय [*a*] destitute, shelterless; forlorn, helpless.

निराहार [*a* and *adv*] without food; fasting.

निरीक्षक [*nm*] an inspector; invigilator.

निरीक्षण [*nm*] inspection; invigilation.

निरीह [*a*] innocent; harmless; simple; desiring nothing; hence ~ता.

निरुत्तर [*a*] silenced, rendered wordless; unable to answer back.

निरुत्साह [*a*] spiritless; devoid of enthusiasm.

निरुद्देश्य [*a* and *adv*] aimless[ly], without purpose.

निरू/पण [*nm*] representation; portrayal characterisation; exposition; demonstration; hence ~पित्त.

निरोगी [*a*] free from disease, healthy; in sound health.

निरोध [*nm*] restraint, control; obstruction; restriction; detention; hence ~क.

निर्ख़ [*nm*] rate; quotation.

निर्गुण [*a*] without attributes or qualities, without सत, रज and तम गुण an epithet of God who is beyond the three gunas; —ब्रह्म the Supreme Soul unlimited by the three गुण.

निर्जन [*a*] lonely, solitary; desolate, deserted; uninhabited; hence ~ ता.

निर्जल [*a*] anhydrous; without water; dry.

निर्जीव [a] lifeless, inanimate; dead; spiritless; insipid; inorganic.

निर्णय [*nm*] judgment, decision, conclusion.

निर्णायक [*nm*] a judge, referee, umpire; [*a*] decisive/deciding; concluding.

निर्दय [*a*] ruthless, merciless, cruel, heartless [person or act]; hence ~ता.

निर्दयी [*a* and *nm*] ruthless, cruel, heartless [person].

निर्दलीय [a] non-party; independent.

निर्दिष्ट [*a*] specified, explicit, expressed; directed; referred [to], pointed out; mentioned, alluded.

निर्देश [*nm*] specification; mention; reference; direction: ~क director, directing; ~न direction, guidance.

निर्दोष [*a*] faultless, flawless; guiltless; inculpable; innocent.

निर्द्वंद्व [*a*] carefree, without any inner conflict.

निर्धन [*a*] poor; moneyless, indigent, impoverished; destitute; hence ~ ता.

निर्धारण [*nm*] fixation; determining; laying down, prescribing; assessment.

निर्निमेष [*a* and *adv*] unwinking; with fixed look.

निर्बल [*a*] weak, feeble; powerless; frail, fragile; hence ~ता.

निर्भय [*a*] fearless, dauntless, undaunted; daring.

निर्भर [*a*] dependent; based [on]; subject or subordinate [to], depending [on], relying [on].

निर्भीक [*a*] fearless, dauntless, undaunted; hence ~ता.

निर्मम [*a*] cruel, heartless, ruthless; dry; unfeeling; hence ~ता.

निर्मल [*a*] clean; clear; pure; unsullied, spotless, stainless; hence ~ता.

निर्माण [*nm*] construction; creation; manufacture.

निर्माता [*nm*] a constructor, producer [as of a film etc.]; builder; creator.

निर्मित [*a*] constructed, built; produced; created.

निर्मूल [*a*] baseless, groundless, unfounded, rootless; perfectly uprooted/destroyed/ruined.

निर्मोही [*a*] unattached; cruel, stone-hearted.

निर्यात [*nm*] export.

निर्लज्ज [*a*] shameless, lost to shame, brazen-faced; impudent, immodest.

निर्लिप्त [*a*] detached; uninvolved; indifferent.

निर्वा/चन [*nm*] election; ~ चक an elector; ~ चन ~क्षेत्र constituency.

निर्वाण [*nm*] salvation, liberation [from existence; used in Buddhist Philosophy as a technical term]; extinction.

निर्वासित [*a*] expelled; exiled, expatriated, banished.

निर्वाह [*nm*] maintenance, subsistence; accomplishment; sustenance, adjustment.

निर्विकार [*a*] immutable, invariable; passionless.

निर्विघ्न [*a*] uninterrupted, unobstructed; smooth; [*adv*] freely, unobstructedly; smoothly.

निर्विरोध [*a* and *adv*] unanimous [ly]; unopposed; uncontested.

निर्विवाद [*a*] incontrovertible; indisputable.

निर्वेद [*nm*] disregard of worldly objects; resignation.

निवारण [*nm*] prevention, preclusion; redress; deterrence, determent.

निवास [*nm*] residence, abode, habitation, lodging, dwelling..

निवासी [*a*] inhabitant, resident; native; inmate.

निवृत्ति [*nf*] disencumbrance; retirement; resignation [from mundane activity]; freedom, liberation; absence of occupation; completion, finishing, termination.

निवेदन [*nm*] supplication, request; submission; application.

निशा [nf] night; ~ चर a demont; evil spirit.

निशाखातिर [*nf*] assurance, conviction.

निशान [*nm*] a sign, mark, landmark; marking scar; an impression; standard, flag; an emblem; a clue, trace.

निशा/ना [*nm*] a target; butt; mark, aim; ~ नेबाज a marksman, an expert shot; ~ नेबाजी marksmanship.

निशानी [*nf*] a memento, keepsake; token; mark, mark of identification; sign; trace.

निश्चय [*nm*] determination, resolution; settlement; decision; certainty; [*adv*] definitely, certainly; positively.

निश्चिंत [*a*] carefree; [self] assured; convinced; unconcerned; hence ~ ता [*nf*].

निश्चित [*a*] definite, certain, sure; ascertained; positive; hence ~ ता [*nf*].

निश्चेष्ट [*a*] still, motionless; inert; quiet; unconscious; hence ~ ता [*nf*].

निश्छल [*a*] straight-forward; honest; uncanny, without wiles, guileless; hence ~ ता [*nf*].

निशंक [*a*] unhesitating; unapprehensive; dauntless, intrepid, fearless.

निषिद्ध [*a*] tabooed; prohibited, forbidden, banned.

निषेध [*nm*] a taboo; prohibition, ban; negation.

निष्कर्ष [*nm*] conclusion, inference; extract, epitome.

निष्काम [*a*] disinterested; free from desires/ wishes, desireless, unselfish.

निष्का/सन [*nm*] expulsion; ejectment; ~ सित expelled; ejected.

निष्क्रिय [*a*] inactive, inert; idle, non-working; passive; ~ ता inactivity, inaction, inertia; idleness; passivity.

निष्ठा [*nf*] allegiance; loyalty, faith; fidelity; devotion.

निष्ठुर [*a*] ruthless, merciless, brutal; cruel, harsh; hence ~ ता.

निष्णात [*a*] adept, expert; skilled.

निष्पक्ष [*a*] objective; neutral, unbiassed; hence ~ ता.

निष्पाप [*a*] sinless, immaculate; innocent.

निष्फल [*a*] unavailing; ineffective, infructuous, inefficacious; vain; hence ~ ता.

निसबत [*nf*] connection; attachment; relationship; comparison; [*adv*] about; —, की as compared with.

निसार [*a*] sacrificed.

निस्तब्ध [*a*] still, without motion or noise; quiet; hence ~ ता.

निस्तार [*nm*] quittance, riddance, redemption; emancipation.

निस्तेज [*a*] lustreless, pallid; lifeless; spiritless; insipid.

निस्संकोच [*a*] unhesitating; inhesitant; [*adv*] unhesitatingly, without hesitation.

निस्सहाय [*a*] helpless; ~ ता helplessness.

निस्सार [*a*] unsubstantial, illusory; worthless; hence ~ ता.

निस्स्वार्थ [*a*] selfless, unselfish; ~ ता.

निहत्था [*a*] unarmed.

निहायत [*adv*] extremely, excessively, very much.

निहाल [*adv*] fulfilled, gratified; delighted.

निहित [*a*] inherent, implied; vested.

नींद [*nf*] sleep, slumber.

नींबू [*nm*] see नींबू.

नींव [*nf*] foundation; base; ground.

नीच [*a*] mean, base, vile; inferior; low, lowly; ~ ता meanness, baseness, vileness; inferiority; lowliness.

नीचा [*a*] mean, base, vile; low; deep; नीची निगाह से देखना to treat as low or inferior; to think as of no significance.

नीति [*nf*] policy; expediency; morality, ethics; ~ ज्ञ sagacious; politic; hence ~ ज्ञता; ~ मान.

नीबू [*nm*] a lemon.

नीम [*nm*] the margosa tree; [*a*] half, semi; ~ हकीम a quack; ~ खतरा ए-जान a little knowledge is a dangerous thing.

नीयत [*nf*] motive; intention.

नीरव [*a*] quiet, calm; still; hence ~ ता.

नीरस [*a*] sapless juiceless; dry flat; insipid; prosaic; uninteresting; hence ~ ता [*nf*].

नीरोग [*a*] free from disease; hale, healthy.

नील [*nm*] indigo; [a] blue.

नीलम [*nm*] a sapphire.

नीला [*a*] blue, azure.

नीलाम [*nm*] auction, public sale.

नुक़ता [*nm*] a point, dot; blot, patch.

नुक़सान [*nm*] loss, damage; harm; disadvantage.

नुकीला [*a*] pointed, sharp.

नुक्कड़ [*nm*] corner, bulging or protruding corner; end; turning point [of a road etc.]

नुक़्स [*nm*] defect; fault, flaw; deficiency.

नुमाइंदा [*nm*] a representative; delegate; hence ~ दगी.

नुमाइ/श [*nf*] an exhibition, show; display; ~ शी showy, ostentatious; meant for display.

नुसखा [*nm*] a prescription, recipe.

नूर [*nm*] light; lustre; resplendence.

नृत्य [*nm*] dance; dancing; ~ शाला a dancing hall.

नृप [*nm*] a king, monarch; also ~ ति.

नृशंस [*a*] atrocious; savage, cruel; hence ~ ता.

नेक [*a*] good, virtuous; ~ चलन of good conduct; ~ दिल virtuous, gentle; ~ नाम reputed, well-known, having a good, name; hence ~ नामी; ~ नीयत well intentioned, genuine; honest; hence ~ नीयती.

नेकी [*nf*] goodness; virtue; piety; ~ कर और कुएं में डाल do a good turn and forget it.

नेता [*nm*] a leader; pioneer; ~ गीरी leadership.

नेतृत्व [*nm*] leadership.

नेपथ्य [*nm*] the back of the stage, greenroom.

नेम [*nm*] routine; rule [of religious conduct]; religious practice; custom.

नेवला [*nm*] a mongoose.

नेस्ती [*a*] ominous; lazy; hence ~ पन.

नैतिक [*a*] moral, ethical; ~ ता morality.

नैमित्तिक [*a*] casual; occasional, accidental.

नैराश्य [*nm*] frustration; disappointment, despair.

नैवेद्य [*nm*] oblation, offerings made to a deity.

नैसर्गिक [*a*] natural; spontaneous.

नैहर [*nm*] a woman's paternal home.

नोक [*nf*] point; tip; end; forepart; ~ झोंक mutual repartee, pleasantry, mock altercation.

नोचना [*v*] to pinch; to scratch; to pluck.

नोट [*nm*] a note; currency note.

नोटिस [*nm*] a notice.

नोन [*nm*] salt, — घाव पर छिड़कना, घाव पर नमक छिड़कना, नोनचय, see, नोन-छार, brine; a kind of salt, नोन-तेल, salt and oil: household essentials, नोन-राई उतारना, राई-नोन उतारना.

नोनी [*nf*] butter.

नौ [*a*] nine; new, fresh; [nm] the number nine; a boat; ship; ~ जवान a youngman, in the prime of youth; ~ निहाल the growing/rising generation, youth; child; ~ परिवहन navigation, shipping; ~ शा the bridegroom; ~ सिखिया a novice, learner, fresher, not well-trained; ~ सेना navy, naval force; — दो ग्यारह होना to turn tails, to make good one's escape.

नौकर [*nm*] a servant; an employee; ~ चाकर [the whole] retinue of servants/attendants/employees; domestics; ~ शाही bureaucracy; bureaucratic.

नौकरनी same as नौकरानी.

नौकरी [*nf*] a service, job; an employment.

नौका [*nf*] a boat, ferry.

नौबत [*nf*] state of affairs; condition; turn; a kettledrum.

नौबती [*adj.*] occurring at, or having to do with, an occasion: periodical; intermittent as a fever, one who beats a kettledrum, door-keeper; watchman, guard, a tent.

न्याय [*nm*] justice; fairness; ~ पर/परायण just, fair, equitable; ~ परता/परायणता justness, fairness, equitability; ~ संगत just, fair, equitable.

न्यायाधीश [*nm*] a judge; justice.

न्यायालय [*nm*] a court of law; judicature.

न्यायी [*a*] just, justly, equitable.

न्यायोचित [*a*] just, equitable, fair.

न्याय्य [*a*] see न्यायोचित.

न्यारा [*a*] separate [*d*]; staying away [from a joint family]; unique, novel; distinct.

न्यास [*nm*] a trust; deposit; arrangement; ~ धारी a trustee.

न्यासी [*nm*] a trustee.

न्यून [*a*] a less; lacking, deficient; low, inferior; small.

न्यूनतम [*adj.*] minimal.

न्योता [*nm*] an invitation.

न्यूनता [*nf*] small amount or flaw; small size, deficiency, lack, inferiority — न्यूनता-बोधक, gram. diminutive.

प the first letter of the fifth and ultimate pentad i.e. पवर्ग of the Devanagari: alphabet.

प - देवनागरी वर्णमाला (व्यंजन) में पवर्ग का प्रथम वर्ण है। इसका उच्चारण स्थान ओष्ठ है।

पंक [*nm*] mud, slush; mire, bog, quagmire; ~ ज a lotus [flower].

पंक्ति [*nf*] a line, row; file, rank; queue.

पंख [*nm*] wing; pinion, feather; blade.

पंखड़ी [*nf*] a petal, blade.

पंखिया [*nm*] impure; wicked, an immoral or wicked man.

पंखा [*nm*] a fan.

पंग/त, ~ **ति** [*nf*] a row; a row of invitees taking meals en masse, community feast.

पंच [*a*] five; [*nm*] the number five; an arbitrator or a body of arbiters or jury; the headman of a caste or village; ~ नामा mutual written agreement between contending parties; ~ फैसला arbitration; the award of a Court of arbitration; ~ भूत the five elements viz. earth, fire, water, air and ether.

पंचक [*nm*] consisting of five parts, an aggregate of five; quintet, pentad, a payment, or charge, of five per cent.

पंचांग [*a*] having five members/parts/subdivisions; [nm] a calendar, an almanac, ephemeris.

पंचाय/त [*nf*] a village assembly; arbitration or a body of arbitrators; an assembly of elected representatives; [a gathering for] gossip-mongering; ~ ती pertaining or belonging to the community as a whole; common; public; run by elected representatives.

पंचम [*nm*] fifth, melodious see the fifth or the seventh note of the musical scale, name of a gram, a nasal consonant, पंचमांग fifth column, fifth columnist.

पंचमी [*adj.*] the fifth day of a lunar half month.

पंछी [*nm*] a bird.

पंजर [*nm*] a skeleton, frame; cage.

पंजा [*nm*] a claw, paw, forefoot; five fingers or toes; an aggregate of five; playing card having five pips.

पंजी [*nf*] a register; ~ करण/ ~ यन registration.

पंडाल [*nm*] a huge pavilion, marquee.

पंडि/त [*nm*] a [by caste]; a scholar; learned person; one well-versed in scriptures and performance of religious rites; ~ ताई scholarship; erudition; the function or profession of a pandit; ~ ताऊ pedantic, bookish, academic; befitting a pandit.

पंथ [*nm*] a path, road, creed, sect, cult; religious order [as कबीर पंथ, दादू पंथ], the sikh panth.

पंद्रह [*a*] fifteen; [*nm*] the number fifteen.

पंप [*nm*] a pump; a kind of shoe.

पंसारी [nm] a grocer.

पकड़ [*nf*] hold; grip; seizure; grasp; understanding; a hug; ~ धकड़ apprehensions, seizures, arrests.

पकड़ना [*v*] to catch [hold of]; to hold; to grasp, to seize/apprehend.

पकना [*v*] to ripen, to be cooked; to mature; to suppurate [as फोड़ा–]; to turn grey [as बाल—].

पकवान [*nm*] dressed foods; fried delicacies.

पकाना [*v*] to ripen; to cook; to bake; to season; to cure.

पकौ/ड़ा [*nm*] a fried saltish vegetable-stuffed gram-flour preparation; hence ~ ड़ी diminutive [*nf*].

पक्का [*a*] ripe; strong; lasting, permanent; firm; net; expert; confirmed; fried in ghee [as—खाना]; boiled.

पक्व [*a*] ripe; boiled; mature; strong.

पक्ष [*nm*] side; flank; aspect; party; a fortnight; wing.

पक्ष/पात [*nm*] partiality; favouritism; ~ पाती partial, partisan.

पक्षाघात [*nm*] hemiparesis, paralysis.

पक्षी [*nm*] a bird.

पख़ [*nf*] an obstacle, hindrance; condition; defect, flaw.

पखवाड़ा(रा) [*nm*] a fortnight.

पखारना [*v*] to cleanse, to wash clean.

पखेरू [*nm*] a bird.

पग [*nm*] a foot; step; pace.

पगडंडी [*nf*] a footway; track.

पगड़ी [*nf*] a turban.

पगार [*nm*] wages, salary.

पचड़ा [*nm*] mess, muddle; trouble.

पचना [*v*] to be digested; to be assimilated.

पचपन [*a*] fifty-five; [*nm*] the number fifty-five.

पचहत्तर [*a*] seventy-five; [*nm*] the number seventy-five.

पचास [*a*] fifty; [*nm*] the number fifty.

पचासी [*a*] eighty-five; [*nm*] the number twenty-five.

पचीस [*a*] twenty-five; [*nm*] the number twenty-five.

पच्ची/कार [*nm*] mosaic work expert, inlay work specialist; ~ कारी mosaic work; inlay work.

पच्चीस [*a* and *nm*] see पचीस.

पछताना [*v*] to repent; to be full of remorse, to be penitent.

पछताना [*nm*] repentance, penitence, remorse.

पछाड़ [*nf*] a dashdown, violent fall by or of a person falling back in a swoon.

पछाड़ना [*v*] to dash/knock down, to cause a fall, to throw down; to overcome, to overpower.

पजामा [*nm*] pyjamas, trouser.

पट [*nm*] a garment, piece of cloth; covering; screen; an allomorph of पट्ट meaning favourite, principal [as पटरानी]; a door leaf; tail [of a coin]; sound of falling or breaking or beating; septa; groomed lock of hair; [*a*] lying flat, upside down; ineffective waste [land]; effaced, wiped out; ~रानी the queen consort; the principal wife of a king.

पटकना [*v*] to dash down, to throw down, to enforce a violent fall.

पटकनी [*nf*] a knock/dash down, a fall.

पटना [*v*] to be covered; to be filled [with]; to be quit; to be repaid in full [as कर्ज]; to be taken in; to be veered round, to yield to persuasion.

पटरा [*nm*] a plank; harrow; —कर देना to devastate, to spell ruination; to demolish: to raze to the ground.

पटरी [*nf*] rail, trackway; pavement; a ruler, wooden strip; —बैठना to have harmonious relation, to have a rapport; to have an identity of purpose.

पटसन [*nm*] jute.

पटाका [*nm*] a cracker; an explosive stuff; the report of a cracker; explosion; the sound of 'पट'.

पटाक्षेप [*nm*] ringing down of the curtain, curtain fall; closing of an affair.

पटाखा [*nm*] see पटाका.

पटाना [*v*] to settle, to conclude; to persuade; to cause to veer round, to bring round; to repay in full.

पटाव [*nm*] the work of covering; covered place; covering, roofing.

पटु [*a*] ingenious, skilled, dexterous; efficient; clever.

पट्टा [*nm*] title deed, lease, lease deed, tenure; dog-collar; a plank.

पट्टी [*nf*] a band age; band, batten; strap; strip; fillet; shelf; plate, wooden plate [for beginners to write on]; misguidance; co-share [in landed property]; ~दार co-sharer, partner; banded; —पढ़ाना to tutor; to misguide; to persuade for selfish motives; to give a lesson so as to veer round to one's own line.

पट्ठा [*nm*] a robust young man; young one, offspring; nerve, sinew; wrestling apprentice/pupil.

पठनीय [*a*] readable, worth reading; intelligible.

पठार [*nm*] a plateau.

पड़ताल [*nf*] checking up, testing, investigation; survey; collation; re-measurement [of a field etc.]; vetting.

पड़ना [*nf*] fall, to fall down; to drop; to lie [down]; to occur; to befall; to be involved.

पड़वा [*nf*] the first day of each lunar fortnight.

पाड़ा [*nm*] he-calf of a buffalo.

पड़ाव [*nm*] a halt; halting place; bivouac; encampment.

पड़ोस [*nm*] neighbourhood; vicinity, proximity; ~सी a neighbour.

पढ़त [*nf*] reading.

पढ़ना [*v*] to read, to study; to recite.

पढ़ाई [*nf*] study; education, learning.

पतंग [*nf*] a paper kite; [*nm*] the sun.

पतंगा [*nm*] a moth, an insect.

पतझर [*nm*] the fall, autumn; defoliation.

पतन [*nm*] fall, downfall; decline; degeneration.

पतनोन्मुख [*a*] falling, tending to fall, degenerating.

पतला [*a*] thin, slender, tenuous; fine; flimsy, dilute[d]; narrow; hence ~पन.

पतलून [*nf*] a pantaloon; trousers.

पतवार [*nf*] rudder, helm; a large oar used for a rudder.

पता [*nm*] address; whereabout, information, knowledge.

पताका [*nf*] a flag, banner; pennant.

पति [*nm*] husband, master; ~ व्रता a faithful wife, virtuous wife.

पतित [*a*] fallen, depraved.

पतीली [*nf*] a typical cooking brass-kettle.

पत्तल [*nf*] a circular plate made up by tagging broad tree leaves together [for serving food]; food served on a pattal; (जिस) —में खाना, उसी में छेद करना to blow off the roof that provides shelter, to cut off the hand that feeds.

पत्ता [*nm*] a leaf; playing card; —न हिलना everything around to be still.

पत्ती [*nf*] a small leaf; foliage; share; flats; a narrow metal-sheet paring; lamination.

पत्थर [nm] stone; [fig.] hard-hearted; heartless, unfeeling;—का कलेजा/दिल/हृदय stony heart, unfeeling heart; —की छाती unmoving heart; unwavering will; —की लकीर indelible mark; undfaing/invariable truth; —पसीजना/पिघलना a stony heart to be moved.

पत्नी [*nf*] wife, a man's spouse.

पत्र [*nm*] a letter; paper; note; leaf; -पुष्प token payment; token of hospitality; -व्यवहार correspondence.

पदार्थ [*nm*] meaning of a term; matter, substance; an object; article.

पदार्पण [*nm*] arrival, stepping in; advent.

पदेन [*a*] ex-officio.

पदोन्नति [*nf*] promotion, rise in rank or status.

पद्धति [*nf*] method, system; process; custom.

पद्य [*nm*] verse, poetry.

पद्यकार [*nm*] a versifier, poetaster.

पद्यात्मक [*a*] versified, poetic.

पधारना [*a*] to grace [a place or occasion] by coming, to arrive [at]; to depart [said out of deference].

पन a suffix added to common and attributive nouns to form abstract nouns [e.g. लड़कपन]; a variant of पानी, पान, पण्य and पाँच in compound formations; ~ घट the periphery of a well etc. where water is drawn; ~ डुब्बी a submarine; ~ वाड़ी a betel-seller.

पनपना [*v*] to be revived/recovered; to flourish, to thrive, to prosper.

पनाला [*nm*] a gutter, drain.

पनाह [*nf*] shelter, refuge.

पनिया [*a*] aquatic, hydrous; [*nm*] water; ~ ना to run with water; to get wet; to be softened; priming.

पनीर [*nm*] cheese.

पनीला [*a*] watery; sodden.

पन्ना [*nm*] an emerald; leaf of a book; page; folio.

पपड़ी [*nf*] a thin crust, incrustation, encrustation; scurf; scale, scab; flake, thin cakes of wheat, gram, etc.

पपीता [*nm*] papaya.

परंतु [ind] but; however; ~ क a proviso.

परंपरा [*nf*] tradition; ~ गत traditional; orthodox; hence ~निष्ठ; ~ निष्ठता; ~ वाद traditionalism, orthodoxy; hence ~ वादिता; ~ वादी a traditionalist; traditional, orthodox.

पर [*ind*] but; yet; even so, even then; on; at after; [*a*] opposite, inimical; other, alien; higher; [*nm*] a wing; feather; plume; ~पुरुष other person, a man other than a woman's husband; stranger; ~बश dependent on others, under other's control/sway; ~ रति alloeroticism; —कट जाना to be rendered ineffective/inefficacious, to be incapacitated; —काट देना to render ineffective/ inefficacious; to incapacitate.

परकार [*nf*] callipers; a compass.

परकोटा [*nm*] a rampart; precints, boundary.

परख [*nf*] test, examination; distinguishing faculty.

परखना [*v*] to test, to examine.

परचना [*v*] to get thick, to establish a rapport; to get habituated.

परचा [*nm*] a piece of paper; question paper, a chit; introduction; proof.

परचून [*nm*] provisions, grocery; [*a*] retail.

परछाई [*nf*] a shadow, reflection.

परजीवी [*nm*] a parasite; [*a*] parasitic; heterotrophic.

परतंत्र [*a*] dependent; slave; subordinate [*d*], subjugated; heteronomous; hence, ~ ता.

परत [*nf*] a layer; fold; tuck.

परती [*nf*] fallow land; uncultivated/waste land; [a] uncultivated, fallow.

परदा [nm] a curtain; screen; veil; privacy; [ear] drum; surface [as दुनिया का परदा]; ~ नशीन veiled maintaining a veil; —डालना to conceal, to veil; to ring down a curtain; ~ फ़ाश करना to expose, to lay bare, to unearth, to tear the veil of secrecy; परदे के पीछे clandestine [ly], stealthily.

पर/देश [*nm*] foreign country, another country, a country other than one's native land; ~देशी an alien, foreigner, stranger.

परनाला [*nm*] a gutter, kennel, drain pipe.

परमाणु [*nm*] an atom; -बम an atom bomb; -युद्ध atomic warfare.

परमात्मा [*nm*] God; the Supreme Self/Being/Spirit.

परमानंद [*nm*] beatitude, the Ultimate Pleasure; God.

परमार्थ [*nm*] the ultimate end, the highest good, summum bonum; spiritual knowledge, salvation.

परमेश्वर [*nm*] God, the Almighty.

परराष्ट्र [*nm*] another country, foreign land.

परला [*a*] of the other side, of that side; —सिरा the other end; परले सिरे का of the first order [often in derogatory contexts [as परले सिरे का बेईमान/बेवकूफ etc.].

परलोक [*nm*] the other world, next world, heavenly paradise; —बनना/सुधारना the way to the next world to be paved [by good deeds]; —बिगाड़ना to spoil one's other-worldly prospects.

परवरदिगार [*nm*] the Almighty; He Who nurtures/fosters/protects the world.

परवरिश [*nf*] bringing up, fostering; nurture; patronising.

परवर्ती [*a*] later, subsequent.

परवश [*a*] dependent; subservient, under another's control; hence ~ ता.

परवाना [*nf*] a warrant; an order; a moth.

परवाह [*nf*] concern; care, heed.

परशु [*nm*] a battle axe.

परसना [*v*] to serve food; to touch, to feel [by touch].

परसर्ग [*nm*] a postposition [i.e. ने, को, से, में, पर].

परसों [*ind*] the day after tomorrow; the day before yesterday.

परस्पर [*ind*] mutual; reciprocal; hence ~ ता.

परहित [*nm*] benefaction, beneficence, benevolence.

परहेज [*nm*] abstinence; avoidance; regimen; keeping aloof.

पराँ(व)ठा [*nm*] a typical Indian pancake-like preparation from kneaded flour fried in ghee.

पराकाष्ठा [*nf*] climax; culminating point, extremity; extreme.

पराक्रम [*nm*] heroism, gallantry, valiance, bravery; ~मी heroic, gallant, brave; [*nm*] a hero, gallant/valiant/brave person.

पराग [*nm*] the pollen [of a flower].

पराजय [*nf*] defeat.

पराजित [*a*] defeated, vanquished; overthrown.

पराधीन [*a*] dependent, subjected; hence; ~ ता.

पराभव [*nm*] defeat, overthrow; ruin; humiliation; ~ भूत defeated, overthrown; ruined, humiliated.

परामर्श [*nm*] counsel, advice; consultation; ~ दाता an adviser, a counsel.

पराया [*a*] pertaining or belonging to another, not one's own; alien, foreign.

परार्थ [*nf*] altruism, benevolence, beneficence, [*a*] benevolent, beneficent; altruistic.

परास [*nf*] range.

परास्त [a] defeated, vanquished; overthrown.

परिंदा [*nm*] a bird.

परिक्रमा [*nf*] revolution; going round.

परिचय [*nm*] introduction; acquaintance, familiarity; -पत्र a letter of introduction.

परिचर्या [*nf*] attendance, attending on a patient; nursing.

परिचायक [*a*] introductory, illustrative [of]; [*nm*] one who or that which introduces/familiarizes.

परिचारक [*nm*] an attendant, a male nurse; hence ~ रिका.

परिचित [*a*] introduced; acquainted, familiar; [*nm*] an acquaintance.

परिच्छेद [*nm*] a chapter; section.

परिणति [*nf*] [ultimate] form; transformation, culmination.

परिणय [*nm*] wedding, marriage.

परिणाम [*nm*] result, outcome; consequence; conclusion; effect; magnitude; ~ स्वरूप as a result of, with the result; consequently.

परिताप [nm] heat; affliction; anguish.

परि/तुष्ट [*a*] gratified, fulfilled; fully satisfied; hence ~ तुष्टि.

परि/तृप्त [a] satiated; thoroughly satisfied; fulfilled, gratified; hence; ~ तृप्ति.

परितोष [*nm*] satisfaction; fulfilment, gratification.

परित्याग [*nm*] abandonment, abandon, giving up; sacrifice, renunciation.

परित्राण [*nm*] protection; deliverance, salvation.

परिदृश्य [*nm*] a landscape, panorama.

परिधान [*nm*] clothes; clothing, cladding.

परिधि [*nf*] circumference; periphery; boundary.

परिनिष्ठित [*a*] standard; —भाषा standard language.

परिपक्व [*a*] ripe; mature; fully developed; hence; ~ता.

परिपाटी [*nf*] a convention; ~ गत conventional.

परिपार्श्व [*nm*] perspective; flank.

परिपालन [*nm*] execution, implementation; maintenance.

परिपूर्ण [*a*] perfect; complete; self-contained; full [of]; infused by or imbued with.

परि/भाषा [nf] definition ~ भावागत/ ~ भाषापरक definitional; ~ भाषित defined.

परिमल [*nm*] fragrance, aroma.

परिमाण [*nm*] quantity; volume.

परिमा/र्जन [*nm*] cleansing, purging; refinement; ~र्जित cleansed; purged, refined.

परि/मित [*a*] finite, measured; limited; ~ मेय measurable, fit to be or worth being limited; rational.

परि/वर्तन [*nm*] change, alteration, variation; interchange; ~ वर्तित changed, altered, undergone variation; interchanged.

परिवर्धन [*nm*] development, growth; enlargement.

परिवहन [*nm*] transportation.

परिवार [*nm*] a family; household.

परिवेश [*nm*] environment; enclosure; precincts.

परिव्राजक [*nm*] a wandering religious mendicant, an ascetic.

परिशिष्ट [*nm*] an appendix; supplement; [*a*] remaining, left-over.

परिशीलन [*nm*] a study, critical study.

परि/शुद्ध [*a*] accurate, precise; absolute; pure; hence ~ शुद्धता/ ~ शुद्धि; ~ शोधन revision; purification; rectification; rectifying.

परि/श्रम [*nm*] labour, industry, hard work, exertion, diligence; ~श्रमी laborious, industrious, painstaking, hard working, diligent.

परि/श्रांत [*a*] wearied, tired, fatigued; worn out; exhausted; hence ~ श्रांति.

परिषद् [*nf*] a council; an association.

परि/ष्कार [*nm*] refinement; purification; ~ष्कृत refined; purified.

परिसंपत्ति [*nf*] assets.

परिसंवाद [*nm*] a symposium.

परिसर [*nm*] premises; enclave.

परिस्थिति [*nf*] circumstance [s]; hence ~ गत.

परिस्फुट [*a*] manifest; defined, evident.

परिहार [*nm*] avoidance; abstention, refraining [from]; forestalling; rectifying [a flaw, error].

परिहार्य [*a*] avoidable, that can be abstained/ refrained [from]; capable of being forestalled/ rectified.

परिहास [*nm*] joke; humour; ~ प्रिय humour-loving, humorous.

परी [*nf*] a fairy, nymph; dream girl, beautiful damsel; ~ खाना an abode of fairies; ~ लोक a fairyland; an abode of pretty women.

परीक्षक [*nm*] an examiner.

परीक्षण [*nm*] act or process of examination, examining, testing; trial.

परीक्षा [*nf*] an examination, test; -पद्धति examination system.

परीक्षार्थी [*nm*] an examinee.

परुष [*a*] hard, harsh, severe; unpleasant; rough; unkind, cruel, pitiless; hard-hearted, hence ~ता.

परे [*ind*] beyond; across; above; on the other side; a far; afterwards; outside; —बिठाना to outwit; to outmanoeuvre, to defeat/vanquish.

परेड [*nf*] parade.

परेशा/न [*a*] bothered, worried, troubled, harassed; ~नी botheration, worry, trouble, harassment.

परोक्ष [*a*] indirect; implicit; invisible, imperceptible, latent; secret; hence ~ता.

परोप/कार [*nm*] beneficence, benevolence; charity; altruism; ~ कारी beneficent, benevolent; charitable, altruistic, an altruist.

परोपजीवी [*a*] parasitic; [*nm*] a parasite.

परोसना [*v*] to serve food.

पर्चा [*nm*] a question paper; [news] paper; slip of paper.

पर्ची [*nf*] a slip of paper.

पर्ण [*nm*] a leaf.

पर्यंक [*nm*] a bed, bedstead.

पर्यंत [*ind*] till; up to; until; unto.

पर्यटक [*nm*] a tourist.

पर्यटन [*nm*] touring; tourism.

पर्यव/सान [*nm*] culmination, conclusion, termination, ~सित culminated. concluded, terminated.

पर्याप्त [*a*] enough, sufficient; ample; adequate.

पर्याय [*nm*] a synonym, synonymous/equivalent word; ~वाची synonymous.

पर्या/लोचन, ~ लोचना [*nm*], ~ [*nf*] thorough review; critical study; investigation.

पर्व [*nm*] festival, festial day, a day or occasion for performance of religious rites etc; a chapter.

पर्वत [*nm*] a mountain, hill; high heap or dump.

पर्वतारोही [*nm*] a mountaineer.

पर्वतीय [*a*] hilly, mountainous; pertaining or belonging to the hills/mountain.

पलंग [*nm*] a bed, bedstead; ~पोश a bed-sheet.

पल [*nm*] a measure of time equivalent to twenty-four seconds.

पलक [*nf*] an eye lid; -पाँवड़े बिछाना to extend a red carpet welcome, to give a deferential welcome; —मारना to wink [at]; to have a wink.

पलटन [*nf*] a platoon; a force.

पलटना [*v*] to turn back, to return; to alter; to overturn; to overthrow; to convert; to upset; to reverse.

पलटा [*nm*] a turn; change; return; relapse [as after illness].

पलड़ा [*nm*] a balance-pan; —भारी होना to have a stronger case, to be in a stronger position; to have an advantage over, to gain an upper hand.

पलना [*nm*] a cradle; [*v*] to be brought up, to be reared/fostered; to be nourished.

पलस्तर [*nm*] plaster.

पलायन [*nm*] escape, fleeing; ~ वाद escapism; ~ वादी [*an*] escapist.

पलीता [*nm*] a wick; an ignitor; guncotton.

पलीद [*a*] [rendered] impure, contaminated, unclean; vitiated, polluted; —करना to pollute; —करना, मिट्टी to cause disgrace to be heaped on, to occasion disgraceful embarrassment.

पल्लव [*nm*] a new tender leaf; — ग्राही a smatterer; smattering, superficial.

पल्लवित [*a*] having/growing new leaves; flourishing, thriving; expanded; prospered.

पल्ला [*nm*] the hem/border/extreme end of a cover garment, side; leaf; scale/pan of a balance;—पकड़ना to seek the support of; to be under the benevolent protection of; —भारी होना to have an upper hand; to be in a position of strength, to be stronger; —पल्ले से बाँधना to entrust to; marry off [to].

पल्लू [*nm*] extremity of a female garment [sa:ri:] used as a head-cover.

पवन [*nm*] air, breeze; wind.

पवर्ग [*nm*] the fifth pentad of the Devanagari: script beginning with the letter प and ending in म.

पवित्र [*a*] holy, sacred; pure; ~ ता holiness, sanctity; purity.

पशमीना [*nm*] very fine soft wool; superfine woollen cloth made of this wool.

पशु [*nm*] an animal; beast; cattle; a savage brute; ~ पालन cattle-breeding.

पशु/ता, ~ त्व [*nf*];[*nm*] beastliness; savagery brutality, savage conduct.

पश्चात् [*ind*] after, afterwards; behind.

पश्चाताप [*nm*] remorse, repentance, compunction.

पश्चि/म [*nm*] west; [a] western; ~ मी western.

पसं/द [*nf*] liking, choice, taste; ~ दीदा liked, chosen.

पसरना [*v*] to stretch full; to be dishevelled stretched; to be inert.

पसली [*nm*] a rib.

पसारना [*v*] to spread; to expand; to stretch; to diffuse all round.

पसावन [*nm*] the watery content of boiled rice.

पसीजना [*v*] to perspire; to ooze; to be moved by pity/compassion.

पसीना [*nm*] sweat, perspiration; पसीने की कमाई hard-earned money; पसीने-पसीने होना to perspire profusely.

पसोपेश [*nm*] dilemma, fix, hesitation.

पस्त [*adj*] wearied, weary; worn out; ~ हिम्मत demoralised; —होना to be vanquished, to be wearied out; to be demoralised.

पहचान [*nf*] acquaintance; familiarity; recognition, identification; identification mark.

पहचानना [*v*] to recognize; to distinguish, to discriminate, to identify.

पहनना [*v*] to wear [as clothes], to put on [as clothes; watch, ornaments, etc].

पहनावा [*nm*] dress; clothing; mode of dressing up.

पहर [*nm*] a measure of time equal to three hours;—, आठों throughout the day, day in and day out.

पहरा [*nm*] a guard; watch; पहरेदार guard, sentry, watchman; पहरेदारी watchmanship, act or process of guarding.

पहल [*nf*] initiative; ~कदमी initiative.

पहल/वान [*nm*] a wrestler; a muscle man; ~ वानी wrestling, the job or profession of wrestling; wrestling acumen.

पहला [*a*] first; foremost, most important; primary.

पहलू [*nm*] side; aspect; flank, facet; —में बैठना to sit in close proximity, to be seated in a compromising pose.

पहले [*nm*] first [of all]; in the beginning; in olden times, originally; before; beforehand; -पहल first of all; for the first time.

पहाड़ [*nm*] a mountain, hill; a huge heap; —से टक्कर लेना to cross swords with a giant; to defy a colossus; to stake against a rock.

पहाड़ी [*a*] mountainous, hilly; pertaining or belonging to the hills/mountain; [*nf*] a hillock; mount; ridge; [*nm*] a highlander.

पहिया [*nm*] a wheel.

पहुँच [*nf*] reach; access; arrival, intimation of arrival; receipt.

पहुँचना [*v*] to reach, to arrive.

पहुँचा [*nm*] the wrist.

पहेली [*nf*] the riddle, puzzle; —बुझाना to talk in riddles, to make an enigmatical utterance.

पाँच [*a*] five; [nm] the number five; पाँचों उंगलियाँ घी में होना to thrive on all fronts; to have one's bread buttered on both sides.

पाँचवाँ [*a*] fifth.

पांडित्य [*nm*] scholarship, learning; erudition.

पांडु [*a*] yellow; yellowish white; pallid; [*nm*] jaundice [a disease].

पांडु/लिपि [*nf*] a manuscript; also ~लेख.

पाँत, पाँति [*nf*] a row; a row of invitees in a feast; line.

पाँयचा [*nm*] a foot-rest.

पाँव [*nm*] foot; leg; –जमना to be well entrenched, to have one's position consolidated, to be firmly lodged; —तले की धरती खिसकना to develop cold feet, to be funky; to be dumb founded/flabbergasted; —पकड़ना to yield, to surrender oneself to somebody's mercy; to touch one's feet humbly; –पड़ना to make humble entreaties, to request humbly; —फटना to suffer from chilblains; —फूँक-फूँककर रखना to advance every step with utmost care; —फैलाकर सोना to enjoy a carefree sleep; —भारी होना to be in the family way.

पाँवड़ा [*nm*] a foot-rug; carpet.

पाँसा [*nm*] a dile, dice; —पलटना a scheme to misfire, a chance/order or situation to be topsyturvied.

पाक [*a*] holy, sacred, pure; clean; [*nm*] cooking; -ग्राफ clean; pure; upright; with no selfish motive.

पाकदाम/न [*a*] chaste, morally unassailable, virtuous; hence~नी [*nf*].

पॉकिट, पाकेट [*nf*] pocket; ~ मार a pick-pocket; ~मारी pick-pocketing.

पाक्षिक [*a*] fortnightly, biweekly.

पाखंड [*nm*] hypocrisy; pretence, pretension, sham, dissimulation.

पाखंडी [*a*] hypocritical, pretentious, sham, dissimulating; [*nm*] a hypocrite, dissimulator.

पाखाना [*nm*] privy, latrine; faeces, human excrement, stool.

पागल [*a*] mad, insane, lunatic, deranged, crazy; bedlamite, rabid; [*nm*] a lunatic, maniac, mad person; ~खाना bedlam, lunatic asylum; ~पन lunacy, insanity, madness, craziness.

पाचक [*a*] digestive; [*nm*] a digestive powder or medicine etc.

पा/चन [*nm*] digestion, hence ~ च्य.

पाजी [*a*] wicked, vile, depraved; mean; base; [*nm*]: a rascal, scoundrel; hence ~पन.

पाटना [*v*] to roof; to cover with earth etc.; to dump, to heap, to pile up.

पाठ [*nm*] lesson; text; recitation; reading, study; —पढ़ाना to teach a lesson, to initiate; to instigate someone into vile ways.

पाठक [*nm*] a reader.

पाठशाला [*nf*] a school.

पाठांतर [*nm*] version, variant text, variation of text.

पाठ्य [*a*] readable, worth reading; pertaining to a text/lesson: legible; ~क्रम curriculum, course, syllabus.

पाणि [*nm*] a hand; ~ग्रहण marriage, wedding.

पातक [*nm*] a sin, misdeed.

पाताल [*nm*] the nether-most world.

पातिव्रत [*nm*] chastity [of a woman], [woman's] loyalty/fidelity [to the husband].

पात्र [*nm*] a utensil, pot, vessel; container; character [in a play etc.]; a deserving person.

पाद [*nm*] a foot; leg; foot of a meter; quadrant; one-fourth part; ~तल sole of a foot; foot; ~प a plant; tree.

पादना [*v*] to break wind, to discharge foul wind [through the posterior opening].

पादरी [*nm*] a clergy, clergyman, Christian priest:a missionary.

पान [*nm*] betel, betel-leaf; [the act or process of] drinking [water or any other liquid]; ~दान a metallic box in which betel-leaves, lime and catechu etc. are kept, betel-leaf receptacle; -पत्ता insignificant/meagre offering or presents.

पाना [*v*] to get, to obtain; to acquire, to attain, to achieve; to be able to reach; to regain; to eat; [*nm*] a spanner.

पानी [*nm*] water, aqua; rain; essence; liquid substance; valour; lustre, brightness; climate; breed; honour; sense of self respect; thin coating/plating; —आना, मुँह में the mouth to water; —उतारना to disgrace, to dishonour, to humiliate; —कर देना to appease to the fullest satisfaction; —का बुलबुला as uncertain as a water bubble, transitory, having a momentary existence; —जाना, आँखों का to become shameless, to be lost to shame; —पड़ना to rain; -पानी होना to be put out of countenance; —पी-पीकर कोसना to heap curses upon; to lash out with a torrent of curses; -फेरना to undo, to dissipate, to destroy, to ruin; —बचाना/रखना to safeguard the honour of; —भर आना, मुँह में watering of the mouth, mouth to be salivated; —मरना water to go on being absorbed [by a wall etc, causing it to be weakened]; to be lost to shame; —में रह कर मगर से बैर to live in Rome and strife with the Pope; —लगना to be affected adversely; to assume pretentious ways.

पाप [*nm*] a sin, vice; evil; evil deed; -कर्म sin sinful deed; -कटना to get rid of sins, evil or unwarranted man or job etc; a botheration to come to an end; —मोल लेना to knowingly own a botheration or commit sinful acts.

पापात्मा [*a*] sinful, unholy; [nm] a sinner, an evil doer. पापी [*a*] sinning, sinful; immoral; [*nm*] a sinner.

पाबंद [*a*] bound, obliged; restricted; under control; ~*nm* binding, obligation; restriction, control, ban.

पायँ [*nm*] see पाँव.

पायंदाज़ [*nm*] a foot-rug, a thick mat for dusting the feet.

पायजामा [*nm*] pyjamas, trousers.

पायजेब [*nm*] an ornament for ankles, an anklet.

पायताबा [*nm*] a thin leather cut-piece inserted into the shoe etc. for the foot to comfortably rest on; stocking.

पायदान [*nm*] a foot-rest, foot-board.

पायदार [a] lasting; durable; firm, strong.

पाय(इ)रिया [*nm*] pyorrhoea, a do mouth diseased.

पायल [*nf*] an anklet.

पाया [*nm*] a leg [of a furniture etc]; post, pillar; prop, support.

पारंगत [*a*] adept, expert, well-versed, well-conversant; learned [in a subject].

पारंपरिक [*a*] traditional; hereditary; hence ~ता.

पार [*nm*] the other coast/bank/ side; [*adv*] across, on the other side/bank/coast; ~गम्य pervious; ~गम्यता perviousness; —पाना to be able to measure the depth or expanse of; to reach the end [of]; to equal [in struggle, etc.] or to defeat.

पारखी [*nm*] a connoisseur, one who can well appreciate merits [of].

पारदर्शक [*a*] transparent.

पारलौकिक [*a*] ultramundane, transcendental, relating to the other/next world; hence ~ता.

पारस [*nm*] the mythical [philosopher's] stone which is said to convert iron into gold by mere touch; an object of unusual merits.

पारस्परिक [*a*] reciprocal, mutual; hence ~ ता.

पारा [*nm*] mercury; —चढ़ना to get infuriated, to fly into a rage.

पारायण [*nm*] thorough reading, reading a book from beginning to end.

पारावार [*nm*] an ocean, a sea; limit; [both] shores.

पारितोषिक [*nm*] a reward, prize.

पारिभाषिक [*a*] technical; definitional, pertaining to definition; —शब्द a technical term; —शब्दावली technical terminology.

पारिवारिक [*a*] familial, pertaining to a family.

पारिश्रमिक [*nm*] remuneration.

पारी [*nf*] shift; turn; -पारी by turns; —का बुख़ार alternating fever, fever attacking every alternate day.

पार्थि/व [*a*] terrestrial, earthly; material, worldly, mundane.

पार्श्व [*nm*] side; flank, facet; armpit; vicinity, proximity, neighbourhood.

पार्सल [*nm*] a parcel.

पाल [*nf*] the sail; the process of ripening fruits by keeping them under the layers of straw, leaves, etc; a suffix denoting protector, maintainer, manager, administrator.

पालक [*nm*] a protector; one who or that which keeps/maintains/sustains/nourishes; spinach, spinage.

पालकी [*nf*] a palanquin; sedan chair.

पालतू [*a*] tame/tamed; domestic/domesticated.

पालथी [*nf*] a cross-legged sitting posture.

पालन [*nm*] abiding by, observance; upbringing; nourishing, fostering; tending, maintenance; -पोषण upbringing; nourishing, providing nourishment, fostering; nurture, nurturing, mothering, bringing up; cherishing.

पालना [*v*] to bring up, to rear; to nurture; to foster, to feed, to mother; to tame, to domesticate; [*nm*] a [swinging] cradle/crib; पाला-पोसा brought up, nourished, reared.

पाला [nm] frost; side; concern; —मारना to be frost-hit; to be frostbitten.

पाली [*nf*] turn; shift; side.

पाव [*nm*] one fourth of a seer; [*a*] one fourth; quarter; foot; —दान a pedal; footstep; treadle of a machine.

पावन [*a*] holy, sacred; pure; immaculate; a suffix denoting one who or that which purifies [as पतितपावन.

पाश [*nm*] a bond, tie; noose snare, trap; fetter, chain; mass; lock [as केश~].

पाशविक [a] brutal, beastly, beast-like, savage; hence ~ता.

पाश्चात्य [*a*] western, belonging to the west.

पाषाण [*nm*] stone.

पास [*nm*] a pass; [*adv*] near, [by], in the neighbourhood of, [a] passed, not failed; -जाना to go near, to be intimate; to cohabit with; —तक न फटकना to keep absolutely aloof, to keep at an arm's length [from].

पासा [*nm*] a dice; die; —पलटना the tide to be turned.

पाहुना [*nm*] a guest.

पिंगल [*nm*] prosody; [*a*] yellow, tawny.

पिंज/ड़ा, ~रा [*nm*] a cage, trap.

पिंजर [*nm*] a cage; skeleton, physical frame.

पिंड [*nm*] a body; the body; lump [of anything]; a ball, round mass; chunk; ~ज viviparous.

पिंडली [*nf*] the calf [of a leg]; back of the shank.

पिघलना [*v*] to melt, to be liquefied; to thaw; to fuse; to flow; to be moved by emotion, to become compassionate [towards somebody]; to be softened.

पिचकना [*v*] to be dented; to be contracted/deflated.

पिचकारी [*nf*] a syringe; flit gun.

पिछलगा [*nm*] a hanger on, lackey; satellite.

पिछड़ना [*v*] to lag, to lag behind, to be left behind; to be defeated, to be vanquished.

पिछला [*a*] hind, rear, hinder; back, back portion/part; latter; past; last.

पिटना [*v*] to be beaten, to be thrashed, to be belaboured; to be defeated; to flop [as a फ़िल्म].

पिटाई [*nf*] beating; thrashing; defeat; work or wages for beating/thrashing.

पिटारा [*nm*] a large basket; wickerwork pannier; big box/chest.

पिट्ठू [*a* and *nm*] a lackey, toady, sycophant; a playmate; a turn played in lieu of an imaginary playmate in games.

पिता [*nm*] father; procreator, progenitor; ~मह grandfather.

पितृ [*nm*] father; paternal ancestor; ~कुल paternal family; ~गण manes, deceased forefathers; ~भक्त devoted to one's father, loyal to one's father; ~भक्ति filial devotion; ~भूमि fatherland.

पित्त [*nm*] bile, gall; bilious humour; ~उबलना/खौलना to be bilious/fretful.

पित्ता [*nm*] gall bladder.

पिपा/सा [*nf*] thirst; yearning, craving; ~सु thirsty; possessed of a yearning/craving.

पियक्कड़ [*nm* and *a*] a drunkard, inebriate, boozy.

पिरोना [*v*] to thread, to string, to needle.

पिलपिला [*a*] flaccidly soft; dehardened; flabby, flaccid; hence ~ना; ~हट.

पिल्ला [*nm*] a pup, puppy.

पिशाच [*nm*] a devil, hellhound, demon, evil spirit.

पिस्ता [*nm*] pistachio-nut.

पिस्तौल [*nf*] a pistol, revolver.

पिस्सू [*nm*] a flea.

पीक [*nf*] spittle of chewed betel leaf, salivary secretion mixed with chewed betel; ~दान a spittoon, cuspidor.

पीछा [*nm*] the back, hinder part, rear; pursuit, chase; —करना to chase; to track, to hunt; to follow; to run after; —छुड़ाना to get rid of.

पीछे [*adv*] behind, on the back side of; after; afterwards; backwards; in the absence of; —चलना to imitate/emulate; to follow in the footprints of, to accept the lead of; —पड़ना to dog, to chase, to pursue; to tease, to harass continuously.

पीटना [*v*] to beat, to thrash; to strike; to punish; to defeat; to knock, to dash, to bang; to thump; to finish, to complete somehow; to earn somehow.

पीठ [*nf*] the back; [*nm*] a seat; an institute; —ठोकना to pat appreciatively; to praise; to give encouragement; —दिखाना to turn tails, to flee from the battlefield.

पीठिका [*nf*] background [as पूर्व~]; stroma; seat, base.

पी/ड़ा [*nf*] pain, ache, aching; anguish; agony, suffering.

पीढ़ी [*nf*] a generation.

पीतम [*nm*] the most beloved, [darling] husband.

पीतल [*nf*] brass.

पीना [*v*] to drink; to swill; to sip; to smoke [as सिगरेट—]; to conceal a secret [बात—]; to absorb; to suppress [as गुस्सा—].

पीप [*nm*] pus.

पीपल [*nm*] the pipal tree.

पीपा [*nm*] a cask, barrel; float; drum, ponton; buoy, keg, can, canister, tin.

पीर [*nf*] pain, ache; affliction; compassion; [*nm*] a Muslim saint, Muslim religious preceptor.

पीला [*a*] yellow, pale, pallid; anaemic; ~पन yellowness, pallor; etiolation.

पीलिया [*nm*] jaundice, chlorosis, icterus.

पीसना [*v*] to grind, to pound, to powder; to mill; to gnash [the teeth]; to cause to labour hard; to exploit.

पीहर [*nm*] a woman's parental house/family/kinsfolk.

पुं/ज [*nm*] a heap, mass; cluster; collection, multitude; ~जीभूत heaped together, massed together; accumulated, clustered collected.

पुकार [*nf*] call; roll-call

पुकारना [*v*] to call; to cry out; to call for help; to exclaim, to proclaim.

पु/ख़्ता [a] strong; lasting, durable; firm; mature; hence ~ख़्तगी.

पुचकारना [*v*] to fondle, to caress; to make love.

पुछल्ला [*nm*] a long tail, tail piece; any tail-like structure; tag; one who always tails after; a stooge, hanger-on, sycophant.

पुजारी [*nm*] a worshipper, adorer; a Hindu priest.

पुट [*nm*] seasoning; slight admixture, light touch, a little mixing; a hollow space [as अंजलिपुट], concavity; fold, cavity [as कर्णपुट].

पुट्ठा [*nm*] haunch, hip; spine [of a book].

पुड़िया [*nf*] a small paper-packet.

पुण्य [*nm*] good; virtue; right; good, deed righteous action; [a] sacred; holy [as-भूमि]; virtuous, righteous [as-कार्य]; -प्रताप celebrity acquired through good deeds, the bounty of good deed, the efficacy of virtue or religious merit; ~श्लोक saintly, pious; celebrated, of good fame or reputation.

पुण्यात्मा [*a*] good, virtuous, righteous, saintly, holy, of noble soul.

पुतला [*nm*] an effigy, a dummy; an image; mannequin, a toy; scare-crow.

पुतली [*nf*] a puppet, doll, marionettes; pupil of the eye.

पुत्र [*nm*] a son; ~वती a woman blessed with a son or sons; ~वत् like a son; ~वधू son's wife; daughter-in-law; ~हीन sonless, without a son.

पुनः [*adv*] again once more, anew, re—; ~स्थापन reinstatement, restoration, re-installation, rehabilitation.

पुनरागमन [*nm*] return, coming again; recurrence.

पुनरा/वृत्ति [*nf*] repetition; recurrence; ~वृत्त repeated; recurred.

पुनरीक्षण [*nm*] vetting; revision, reconsideration.

पुनरुक्ति [*nf*] repetition, tautology; reiteration.

पुनरुत्थान [*nm*] resurrection, resuscitation.

पुनर्गठन [*nm*] reorganisation recasting.

पुनर्जन्म [*nm*] rebirth, palingenesis, metempsychosis; ~वाद transmigrationism, the doctrine of rebirth.

पुनर्जागरण [*nm*] renaissance, restoration.

पुनर्निर्माण [*nm*] reconstruction, recreation, reproduction.

पुन/र्मुद्रण [*nm*] reprinting/reprint; ~मुर्द्रित reprinted.

पुनर्वास [*nm*] rehabilitation.

पुनर्विचार [*nm*] revision; re-deliberation, reconsideration.

पुनर्विवाह [*nm*] remarriage.

पुनीत [*a*] holy, pious; sacred; having a sanctity.

पुर [*nm*] a town, city; large leather pot for drawing huge quantities of water out of a well; chamber, room [as अंतःपुर]; [*a*] filled with, full of.

पुरअमन [*a*] peaceful, quiet.

पुरखा [*nm*] an ancestor; forefather.

पुरज़ा [*nm*] a chit; piece of paper, bill; slip; part of a machine; —, चलता a cunning/guileful man. पुरजे-पुरजे होना/उड़ना to be shattered to pieces.

पुरजोर [*a*] vigorous; powerful, forceful; hearty, warm, cordial.

पुरजोश [*a*] full of enthusiasm/zeal, zealous, enthusiastic.

पुरवाई [*nf*] east winds, easterly [wind]; originating/emanating from the east.

पुरसाँहाल [*nm*] one who is solicitous [of], enquirer after somebody's well-being; one who cares [for] and is concerned [about].

पुर/स्कार [*nm*] reward, prize; hence ~स्कृत.

पुरा [*adv*] in the past, in olden times; [nm] a small village, hamlet.

पुरातत्त्व [*nm*] archaeology, antiquity; ~विद्/वेत्ता an archaeologist.

पुरातन [*a*] ancient; old, of antiquity, archaic; hence ~ता; ~वाद; ~वादी.

पुराना [*a*] old, olden, ancient of the past, of bygone ages; old-fashioned; out-dated; chronic; stale;

primitive; antiquated, obsolete; seasoned, experienced; [as —डाक्टर]; dilapidated, decrepit; expert, masterly [as —हाथ]; —खुर्राट/घाघ very cunning/shrewd [person]; hence ~पन.

पुरालिपि [*nf*] palaeography; also ~ विज्ञान/शास्त्र.

पुरालेख [*nm*] epigraph; –विज्ञान/शास्त्र epigraphy.

पुरी [*nf*] a big city; the city of the deity Jagannāth [in Orissa].

पुरुष [*nm*] a man; virile man; person [in grammar]; ~ त्व manhood, virility, masculinity, potency, manliness.

पुरुषा/र्थ [*nm*] an object of human pursuit, the four basic aims of human existence, human effort or exertion; valour; industry; hence ~ र्थी.

पुरोहि/त [*nm*] a Hindu priest; priest, patrico; ~ ताई/ती priesthood, priestdom; office and function of a priest.

पुल [*nm*] a bridge; ~ बाँधना, किसी की तारीफ़ के to eulogize no end, to pay tributes in superlatives.

पुल/क [*nm*] thrill; erection or bristling of the hair of the body [through delight or rapture]; ~ कना to be thrilled; to have the hair of the body erected or bristling [through delight or rapture].

पुलाव [*nm*] a preparation of boiled rice mixed with vegetables [or meat] and seasoned with spices.

पुलिंदा [*nm*] a bundle; sheaf.

पुलिया [*nf*] a culvert.

पुलिस [*nf*] the police [force].

पुश्त [*nf*] the back; back portion; generation, ancestry.

पुश्तैनी [*a*] hereditary, ancestral.

पुष्ट [*a*] strong, robust, sturdy, stiff; well-built; shapely, nourished; mature; confirmed [as —समाचार]; seasoned [with].

पुष्टि [*nf*] confirmation; nourishment; strengthening.

पुष्प [*nm*] a flower; menses; ~ राग pollen; ~ रेणु pollen [of flowers]; ~ वती a woman in menses; — वृष्टि a shower of flowers or flower petals.

पुष्पित [*a*] blossomed; flowering; thriving, prospering.

पुस्त/क [*nf*] a book; ~ ककार writer/author of a book; ~ काकार in the form of a book, in book form; ~ कागार a library, collection of books; a book-depot ~ काध्यक्ष a librarian; hence ~ कीय bookish; of books.

पुस्तकाल/य [*nm*] a library; ~ याध्यक्ष a librarian.

पुस्तिका [*nf*] a booklet, pamphlet.

पूंछ [*nf*] the tail [of a beast]; rear part [of an object]; a hanger-on.

पूंजी [*nf*] capital; investment; ~ दार having capital or wealth; a capitalist; ~ निवेश investment; ~ पति a capitalist; ~ वाद capitalism; ~ वादी capitalistic; a capitalist.

पूछ [*nf*] [commanding of] respect; enquiry; ~ गछ, ~ ताछ ~ पाछ enquiry; investigation.

पूछना [*v*] to enquire, to ask; to investigate; to interrogate, to question.

पूज/न [*nm*] worship, adoring; hence ~ नीय [*a*].

पूजना [*v*] to worship; to adore, to revere, to respect; [a wish etc.] to be fulfilled / gratified.

पूजा [*nf*] worship, adoration; veneration; —करना to worship, to adore; to respect; to punish.

पूज्य [*a*] adorable, reverent, venerable.

पूत [*nm*] a son; [*a*] pious, holy, sacred; cleaned, purified.

पूरक [*nm*] a supplement; [*a*] supplementary; reinforcing.

पूरना [*v*] to fill; to complete, to supplement; to work a design on the floor with coloured chalk, flour or rice, etc.

पूर/ब [*nm*] the east; ~ बी eastern [language, land or people].

पूरा [*a*] complete; all, whole, entire, full; gross; total; thorough; पूरे होना, दिन death to be imminent, to have consumed one's allotted time [of life].

पूर्ण [*a*] complete, whole, entire; full; perfect; absolute; sufficient; finished, accomplished; plenary; ~ कालिक whole-time; —विराम full stop; —संख्या integral number.

पूर्ण/तः [*adv*] completely; fully, wholly, entirely.

पूर्ण/ता, ~ त्व [*nf*] [*nm*] perfection; completeness; wholeness, totality; ~ तावाद perfectionism.

पूर्णमासी [*nf*] see पूर्णिमा.

पूर्णांक [*nm*] an integer; non-fractional number, maximum marks.

पूर्णिमा [*nf*] the last day of the bright fortnight of a lunar month, the full-moon day.

पूर्ति [*nf*] fulfilment, completion, filling up:satisfaction; supply.

पूर्व [*nm*] the east; [*a*] former; previous, preceding, prior; anterior; ex—, fore—; ~ कालीन past, of the past, of previous time/ days / age; ~ कृत done or committed previously; ~ गामी preceding, prior, former; ~ ग्रह bias, prejudice; ~ ज ancestor [s], forefather [s]; ~ जन्म previous birth; ~ ता precedence; priority; ~ पीठिका background; introduction; prolegomenon; ~ पुरुष progenitor; ancestor [s], forefather[s]; ~ भूत existing previously; former; late; ~ राग incipient affection; courtship; ~ रूप previous form; prognosis; ~ लेख a protocol; ~ वत् as before; in tact; ~ वर्ती previous, prior, preceding precedent, happening before; a predecessor; ~ वृत्त antecedents; anteposition; ~ सूचक premonitory.

पूर्वानुमान [*nm*] forecast; estimate.

पूर्वापर [*ind*] the previous and the next, the preceding and the following; ~ क्रम sequence, succession.

पूर्वार्द्ध [*a*] the first/former half.

पूर्वावस्था [*nf*] pre-phase, pre-stage, earlier stage; initial stage.

पूर्वी [*a*] eastern.

पूर्वोक्त [*a*] aforesaid, mentioned before/above.

पृथक् [*a*] separate, isolated; peculiar; different, distinct; [adv] aloof, apart; ~ करण separation.

पृथ्वी [*nf*] the earth, ground, terrestrial globe.

पृष्ठ [*nm*] page; the back; rear, hind part of anything; ~ तः from behind, quietly; dorsally; ~ पोषक one who backs, helper, supporter.

पेंग [*nf*] a swing, oscillation of a swing.

पेंट [*nm*] paint; ~ र a painter.

पेंडल [*nm*] a pendant.

पेंदा [*nm*] the bottom; base; buttocks; बिना पेंदे का लोटा, an unprincipled man, a rolling stone.

पेंशन [*nf*] pension; ~ याफ़्ता a pensioner.

पेंसिल [*nf*] a pencil.

पेच [*nm*] a screw; complication, intricacy; part of a machine; the entwining of the threads of two flying [paper] kites for a mutual trial of skill, trick, a trick in wrestling; artifice; a kind of ornament for the head; ~ कश/कस a screwdriver; cork-screw; ~ दार intricate; complex, tricky; twisted.

पेचिश [*nf*] dysentery.

पेचीदगी [*nf*] intricacy, complication, complexity.

पेची/दा ~ ला [*a*] intricate, complicated, complex; ~ पन see पेचीदगी.

पेट [*nm*] the belly, abdomen, stomach; womb; mind; the front side of a thing as opposed to the back [as रोटी का पेट]; —का गहरा one who does not talk out secrets; who can contain secrets; —काटना to save money by imposing self-restraint; —का हलका one who cannot keep / contain secrets; — की थाह लेना to have an idea of one's inmost feelings, to fathom the depth of one's mind; —की आग बुझाना to satisfy one's hunger, to fill the stomach; —खोलना to talk out one's mind; to reveal one's secrets; to give vent to one's grouses/resentments feelings; —गिरना to abort, to commit abortion; —पालना to earn one's living somehow, to subsist by effort; —में दाढ़ी होना to be very shrewd and cunning, to be seemingly simple but actually shrewd; —रहना to become pregnant; —से होना to be in the family way, to be pregnant.

पेटी [*nf*] a casket, chest, small box; belt; girdle.

पेटीकोट [*nm*] a petticoat.

पेटू [*a*] gluttonous, voracious; [*nm*] a glutton; gourmand; hence ~ पन/पना.

पेटेंट [*a*] patent.

पेट्रोल [*nm*] petrol.

पेड़ [*nm*] a tree; —पौधे vegetation; trees and plants.

पेडल [*nm*] a pedal [in bicycle etc.].

पेय [*nm*] a beverage; [*a*] drinkable, potable.

पेरना [*v*] to crush [as sugarcane, linseed etc.]; to press hard; to torment; to cause to labour hard, to exploit [a person].

पेलना [*v*] to thrust in; to penetrate; to crush; to press; to perform hurriedly.

पेश [*adv*] in front of, before; —आना to treat, to happen; to be confronted with; —करना to present, to put forth; to introduce; ~ कश

an offer, a present; keepsake, memento; presenting; offering; putting forth; introducing ~ बंदी hedging operation; forestalling.

पेशगी [*nf*] an advance, advance money.

पेश्तर [*ind*] before, prior to.

पेशा [*nm*] a profession, an occupation.

पेशानी [*nf*] the forehead; lot, fate.

पेशाब [*nf*] urine; ~ खाना/घर urinal; ~ करना (किसी चीज पर) to treat with utter disdain, to damn care.

पेशी [*nf*] a muscle; presentation, to be presented; hearing of a law-suit.

पेशीनगोई [*nf*] forecast.

पेंग [*nf*] oscillation of a swing.

पेंग मारना [*v*] to be tossed from one side to another; to swing.

पैंठ [*nf*] a temporarily improvised market place.

पैंतालीस [*a*] forty-five, [*nm*] the number forty-five.

पैंतीस [*a*] thirty-five; [*nm*] the number thirty-five.

पैंसठ [*a*] sixty-five; [*nm*] the number sixty-five.

पैके(कि)ट [*nm*] a packet.

पैग़म्बर [*nm*] a prophet, divine messenger.

पैग़ाम [*nm*] a message.

पैठ [*nf*] access [to]; reach; admission; ingress, penetration; ~ ना to have access; to enter, to go into; to delve deep; to ingress, to penetrate.

पैडल [*nm*] a pedal [of a bicycle etc.]

पैड़ी [*nf*] a step, stair; staircase.

पैंत/रा [*nm*] an offensive or defensive move in a wrestling bout; stratagem; strategic move; countermove; ~ रेबाज a strategist, dodger; ~ रेबाजी strategy, dodging.

पैंताना [*nm*] the lower end of a cot/bedstead.

पैतृक [*a*] paternal, patronymic; hereditary, ancestral; —संपत्ति paternal/ancestral hereditary property.

पैदल [*a*] pedestrian, walking on foot [as सिपाही]; [nm] a footman, an infantryman; a pedestrian; a piece in chess; [adv] on foot.

पैदा [a] born; created; begotten; produced; earned; [*nf*] income; gain.

पैदाइ/श [*nf*] birth coming into existence; creation; hence ~ शी.

पैदावार [*nf*] produce, product, production; harvest; yield.

पैना [*a*] harp; acute; pointed; [*nm*] the goad of a ploughman; hence ~ पन.

पैबंद [*nm*] a patch.

पैमाइश [*nf*] measurement; surveying [of land].

पैमाना [*nm*] a scale, meter; any measuring device; a peg [for drinking liquor].

पैर [*nm*] a foot; leg; footing, footprint; ~ उखड़ना to be swept off one's feet, to be routed; —जमना to find one's feet, to be well-entrenched, to consolidate one's position; —न रखना, धरती पर to assume airs, to think no end of oneself; —पकड़ना to implore humbly, to beseech; — भारी होना [said of a woman] to be pregnant, to be in the family way.

पैरवी [*nf*] advocacy, pleading, championing; ~ कार an advocate, pleader; champion.

पैरा [*nm*] a paragraph, para.

पैरोकार [*nm*] a pleader, an advocate; a champion.

पैरोल [*nm*] parole; —पर छूटना to be released on parole.

पैशाचिक [*a*] satanic, demonical, in the fashion of or pertaining to a hell-hound, inhuman; horrible.

पैसा [*nm*] a pice; wealth, money; पैसे वाला a wealthy/moneyed person.

पोंगा [*a*] nincompoop, stupid; [*nm*] a simpleton; metallic or bamboo pipe.

पोंछना [*v*] to wipe; to clean/cleanse; to rub, to efface; [*nm*] a cloth used for wiping/cleaning etc.

पोटली [*nf*] a small bundle.

पोत [*nm*] a ship; tiny artificial pearl; [*nf*] time[s], number of times; rent of land paid by a tenant; young one of an animal.

पोतना [*v*] to besmear; to whitewash.

पोता [*nm*] a grandson; a son's son; the testicles; a cleansing cloth.

पोथा [*nm*] a voluminous book, big volume.

पोथी [nf] a book.

पोपला [*a*] toothless; hence ~ ना.

पोर [*nm*] a knuckle; the space between any two joints of a finger; finger tip.

पोल [*nf*] empty/hollow space, hollowness; [*nm*] a gate, an entrance [of a palace etc.]; —खुलना to be exposed; adverse fact [about somebody] to be revealed.

पोला [*a*] hollow, empty.

पोशाक [*nf*] clothes, dress, attire, raiment; accoutrements.

पोशी/दा [*a*] privy; secret; concealed, hidden; hence ~ दगी.

पोष/ण [*nm*] fostering, rearing, bringing up; nourishment; nutrition; protection; support; hence ~ क [a and nm].

पोसना [*v*] to rear, to bring up, to foster, to nourish; to pet; to domesticate.

पोस्ट [*nm*] post; —आफिस a post-office; —कार्ड a post-card; —बॉक्स a post-box; ~ मास्टर a post-master; ~ मैन a postman.

पोस्टमार्टम [*nm*] postmortem, autopsy.

पोस्टर [*nm*] a poster.

पो/स्त [*nm*] a poppy plant; poppy seed; ~स्ती an opium-addict; a slothful drowsy person.

पोहना [*v*] to string, to thread together.

पौ [*nf*] a ray of light; early dawn; one pip [in a dice].

पौद, ~ ध [*nf*] a seedling, sapling; young plant; [fig.] generation.

पौ/दा, ~ धा [*nm*] a plant, young plant; sapling.

पौन [*nm*] three-fourth, three quarter.

पौना [*nm*] a ladle with a long handle; [*a*] three quarters; three-fourth.

पौर [*a*] urban, municipal, civic, pertaining to the city; outer verandah in a house; [*nm*] a municipal councillor; ~, महा mayor.

पौराणिक [a] mythological; pertaining/belonging to the Puranas.

पौरुष [*nm*] manhood, manliness, masculinity; virility.

पौली [*nf*] a door, threshold.

पौष्टिक [*a*] nutritive, nutritious; -पदार्थ a tonic.

प्याऊ [*nf*] a water-booth, free water-kiosk.

प्या/ज़ [*nm*] union; ~ज़ी onion-coloured, light pink.

प्यादा [*nm*] a footman, an infantryman; pedestrian; a pawn [in chess].

प्या/र [*nm*] love; affection; amour, amorous relationship; ~रा [*a*] dear, beloved, loved; pleasing, lovely; pretty; [*nm*] a dear one, beloved.

प्याला [*nm*] a cup.

प्यास [*nf*] thirst; longing, lust.

प्यासा [*a*] thirsty.

प्रकट [*a*] manifest; apparent; obvious, evident, ostensible; overt; ~तः manifestly, apparently; obviously, evidently.

प्रकरण [*nm*] context; a division of a book—section, topic, chapter.

प्रकर्ष [*nm*] [rising to] eminence/excellence; exaltation, elevation.

प्रकाण्ड [*a*] outstanding, eminent; foremost, leading.

प्रकार [*nm*] kind; quality; mode, manner; way, method; type; pattern.

प्रकारांतर [*nm*] different/another method or manner.

प्रकाश [*nm*] light; sunshine; lustre; chapter of a book.

प्रकाशक [*nm*] a publisher; one who or that which illuminates, an illuminator.

प्रका/शन [*nm*] a publication; publishing; [the act or process of] bringing to light; ~शित published; brought to light, manifest, obvious; resplendent.

प्रकाशमान [a] glowing, shining; lustrous, resplendent, radiant.

प्रकृत [*a*] natural; spontaneous; unsophisticated; habitual; genuine; normal; ~वाद naturalism; ~वादी a naturalist; naturalistic.

प्रकृति [*nf*] the nature; temperament, disposition; habit; ~वाद naturalism; naturism; ~वादी a natur[al]ist; natur[al]istic; ~स्थ composed, cool and composed; poised, sane; ~स्थता composure; sanity.

प्रकोप [*nm*] wrath, rage, fury.

प्रक्रम [*nm*] a process; sequence, series.

प्रक्रिया [*nf*] a process; procedure, technique, method.

प्रक्षिप्त [*a*] projected; thrown; cast forth; interpolation.

प्रक्षेप [*nm*] projection; throw; casting forth; interpolation.

प्रखर [*a*] sharp; keen, acute; radical; fierce; hence ~ ता.

प्रख्यात [*a*] well-known, renowned, reputed.

प्रगट [*a*] see प्रकट.

प्रगति [*nf*] progress; development; ~वाद, ~वादिता progressivism; ~वादी progressive; a progressivist; ~शील progressive; ~शीलता progressivism; progress.

प्रगल्भ [*a*] mature; insolent, impertinent, cheeky; outspoken; venturesome; hence ~ता.

प्रगाढ़ [*a*] profound, deep; dense; exceeding, abundant.

प्रगी/त [*nm*] a song; lyric; ~ति a lyric; lyrical.

प्रचण्ड [*a*] excessively violent; impetuous, furious, fierce; passionate; virulent; terrible, direful; mighty, powerful; hence ~ता.

प्रच/लन [*nm*] currency, prevalence; custom; usage; movement; ~लित current, prevalent, in vogue, in usage; common; customary.

प्रचार [*nm*] propaganda, publicity; currency; prevalence; ~क a propagator; propagandist; publicist; hence प्रचारित.

प्रचुर [*a*] plentiful, copious, abundant; ample; hence ~ ता.

प्रच्छन्न [*a*] covered; concealed, hidden, latent, stealthy; secret; ~ ता concealment; latency; stealthiness, secrecy.

प्रजनन [*nm*] reproduction, (multiplying by) generation, breeding.

प्रजा [*nf*] subjects; public; ~तंत्र democracy; ~तंत्रात्मक democratic; ~तांत्रिक democratic.

प्रज्ञा [*nf*] prudence, intellect; ~चक्षु blind.

प्रज्व/लन [*nm*] ignition, burning, setting on fire; setting aglow; hence ~लित

प्रण [*nm*] vow, pledge.

प्रण/य [*nm*] love; affection, attachment; ~यी [*nm*] a lover; [*a*] having affection; amatorial.

प्रणयन [*nm*] writing, composition.

प्रणव [*nm*] the sacred and mystical syllable Om, God Almighty.

प्रणाम [*nm*] reverential salutation; bowing with respect; a term used in greeting elders.

प्रणाली [*nf*] a system, method, technique.

प्रणेता [*nm*] a writer; author; composer.

प्रता/प [*nm*] glorious grace, glory, dignity; glorious renown; overwhelming, influence; ~पी [*a*] glorious, dignified, possessing glory and renown/overwhelming influence.

प्रति [*nf*] a copy; a Sanskrit prefix imparting the meanings of towards, near to; against, in opposition to; back, again, in return; down upon; as also of likeness or comparison; anti; per.

प्रतिकार [*nm*] revenge, retaliation; return.

प्रतिकूल [*a*] adverse, unfavourable; contrary; opposite; hostile, hence ~ता.

प्रतिकृति [*nf*] a prototype, replica; an image.

प्रति/क्रिया [*nf*] reaction; ~क्रियात्मक reactionary; ~क्रियावाद reaction [ism]; क्रियावादी reactionary; a reactionist.

प्रतिक्षेप [*nm*] recoil, rebound; regurgitation.

प्रतिघात [*nm*] counter-attack, counter-offensive, counter-stroke.

प्रतिच्छाया [*nf*] a shadow; image; copy, facsimile; replica.

प्रतिज्ञा [*nf*] a pledge, vow; promise; enunciation; -पत्र a covenant, written pledge; bond.

प्रतिदिन [*ind*] every day, daily.

प्रतिद्वं/द्व [*nm*] conflict, mutual struggle, clash, contest; ~द्विता rivalry, mutual conflict, contest; ~द्वी rival, contestant; an antagonist.

प्रतिध्वनि [*nf*] echo, re-echo, reverberation: resonance; hence ~त.

प्रतिनिधि [*nm*] a delegate; representative; deputy; ~त्व representation; deputation, delegacy; ~मंडल a delegation, body of representatives, deputation.

प्रतिप/क्ष [*nm*] opposition, rival side, hostile camp, contesting party; hence ~क्षता; ~क्षी an opponent, rival, contestant; contralateral.

प्रतिपादन [*nm*] exposition; treatment; enunciation.

प्रतिपाद्य [*a* and *nm*] treated of, enunciated; the theme, the subject matter; to be enunciated.

प्रतिपालन [*nm*] protection; maintenance; observance; implementation; giving sustenance, providing subsistence.

प्रति/पूरक [*a*] complementary; ~पूर्ति compensation, recompense; reimbursement.

प्रतिफल [*nm*] requital, consideration; return; ~न culmination, conclusion; reflection.

प्रति/बंध [*nm*] restriction; ban; proviso; condition; hence ~वंचित; ~बद्ध, ~बद्धता.

प्रतिबिंब [*nm*] reflection, image, shadow.

प्रतिभा [*nf*] genius; brilliance; ~वान a genius; brilliant; ~शाली genius; brilliant.

प्रतिमा [*nf*] an image; icon, a statue; effigy.

प्रतिमान [*nm*] a pattern, specimen; prototype; standard.

प्रतियो/गिता [*nf*] competition, rivalry; match; tournament; contest, ~गी, a competitor, contestant; rival; matching.

प्रति/रक्षा [*nf*] defence; ~ रक्षात्मक defensive.

प्रति/रूप [*nm*] a pattern; prototype; specimen; counterpart; [*a*] enantiomorphic; type; ~रूपी typical; counterpart; prototype; specimen; enantiomorphic.

प्रतिरोध [*nm*] resistance; contest; obstruction; counter-action.

प्रति/लिपि [*nf*] a copy; duplicate copy; facsimile; ~क/कार copyist.

प्रतिलोम [*a*] inverse; reverse; resupinate; unwarranted; adverse, vile.

प्रतिवा/द [*nm*] a controversy; refutation, counter-statement; responsive argument; ~दी a defendant; respondent.

प्रतिवेदन [*nm*] report; representation.

प्रतिशत [*ind*] per cent.

प्रतिशोध [*nm*] revenge; vendetta, vengeance; reprisal.

प्रतिषेध [*nm*] prohibition; forbiddance; taboo.

प्रतिष्ठा [*nf*] prestige, dignity; status; establishment; installation, consecration of an idol in a temple.

प्रतिष्ठित [*a*] honourable, respectable; established; installed; consecrated; dignified; enjoying a prestige/status.

प्रति/स्पर्धा [*nf*] rivalry; contest; competition; hence ~स्पर्धी.

प्रतिहत [*a*] restrained, obstructed, hampered; defeated.

प्रतिहा/र [*nm*] a gate-keeper; watchman; also ~री.

प्रति/हिंसा [*nf*] vengeance, revenge; retaliation, counter-violence; ~हिंसात्मक revengeful, retaliatory; inspired by counter violence/ vengeance.

प्रतीक [*nm*] a symbol; fetish; ~वाद symbolism; ~वादी a symbolist; symbolical.

प्रती/क्षा [*nf*] waiting [for], wait; expectation; ~क्षालय a waiting room.

प्रतीत [*a*] appeared, seemed; known.

प्रतीति [*nf*] conviction, assurance, confidence; appearance.

प्रतीयमान [*a*] virtual; apparent.

प्रत्यंचा [*nf*] a bow string.

प्रत्यक्ष [*a*] visible, tangible, evident; apparent, obvious; disect; ~ दर्शी an eye-witness; ~ वाद positivism; ~ वादी a positivist; positivisitic.

प्रत्यक्षीकरण [*nm*] [the act or process] of coming face to face, seeing through one's own eyes; direct perception.

प्रत्यय [*nm*] an idea, concept; credit; assurance, conviction; suffix; –पत्र credentials, letter of credence; ~ वाद Idealism.

प्रत्याख्यान [*nm*] repudiation, refutation, rebuttal.

प्रत्याव/र्तन [*nm*] return; reversion; recurrence; restoration; hence ~ र्तित; ~ र्ती a reversioner.

प्रत्या/शा [*nf*] expectation, anticipation; hence ~ शित.

प्रत्या/शी [*nm*] a candidate.

प्रत्याह्वान [*nm*] recall, calling back.

प्रत्युत [*ind*] on the other hand, contrary to, but.

प्रत्युत्तर [*nm*] reply, replication.

प्रत्युत्पन्न [*a*] ready; prompt; born/emerged there and then; ~ मति witty, quick-witted person; [blessed with] ready wit.

प्रत्येक [*a*] each, every one, each and every one.

प्रथम [*a*] thc first, foremost; prima; ~ त: firstly, first of all, in the first place.

प्रथमा [*nf*] the nominative case [in gram]; ~ (the first half.

प्रथा [*nf*] custom; practice, usage.

प्रदक्षिणा [*nf*] circumambulation, to go round [a deity's idol] so as to always keep it to the right.

प्रदत्त [*a*] given, gifted, granted [by], bestowed.

प्रदर [*nm*] menorrhagia [a disease of women].

प्रदर्शन [*nm*] show; exhibition, display; performance; demonstration.

प्रदर्शनी [*nf*] an exhibition.

प्रदर्शित [*a*] showed; exhibited, displayed; performed; demonstrated.

प्रदान [*nm*] giving, delivery; donating; bestowing, granting.

प्रदी/प्त [*a*] illuminated, lit/lighted, glowing; awakened; roused; ~ प्ति light, glow; illumination.

प्रदेश [*nm*] a region, territory, zone, district.

प्रदेशीय [*a*] regional; belonging or pertaining to a region.

प्रधान [*nm*] the president, chairman; [a] chief, head, principal, main; ~ ता/त्व presidentship, chairmanship; dominance, supremacy; pre-eminence; ~ त: mainly, chiefly; primarily, first of all.

प्रपंच [*nm*] illusory creation, manifestation, delusion; mundane affairs; artifice, manipulation; hence ~ ची.

प्रपात [*nm*] a fall, water-fall, cataract.

प्रफुल्ल [*a*] blooming, blossomed; cheerful, gay, delighted; ~ मुख/बदन gay-looking; cheerful/ beaming face; hence प्रफुल्लित.

प्रबंध [*nm*] management, arrangement, administration; a dissertation; comprehensive connected narrative; ~ क, ~ कर्ता a manager; organiser; –काव्य an epic, epic poem.

प्रबल [*a*] strong; mighty, forceful, powerful, violent, vigorous; predominant, dominant; hence ~ ता.

प्रबुद्ध [*a*] awakened, aroused [from slumber]; conscious, enlightened; hence ~ ता.

प्रभंजन [*nm*] a hurricane.

प्रभविष्णु [*a*] influential; efficacious, effective; impressive; hence ~ ता.

प्रभा [*nf*] lustre, radiance, refulgence; ~ मंडल a halo.

प्रभात [*nm*] the morning dawn; –फेरी singing or slogan-raising groups going round in the morning [to celebrate an important event or for propaganda purposes].

प्रभाव [*nm*] influence; effect, impact; impression; ~ शाली influential; impressive; effective [person] etc.; ~ हीन unimpressive, devoid of any influence, causing no impact; void; hence ~ हीनता.

प्रभावित [*a*] influenced; impressed; receiving an impact.

प्रभु [*a*] sovereign, hegemonic; [*nm*] a sovereign; God, Master; —राज्य a sovereign state; —शक्ति a sovereign power; sovereignty.

प्रभु/ता, ~ त्व [*nf*]~[*nm*] sovereignty, hegemony; predominance, dominance; Mastery.

प्रभूत [*a*] plenty, abundant; ample.

प्रभेद [*nm*] variety; types, kinds.

प्रमाण [*nm*] evidence, proof; testimony; authority; –पत्र a certificate.

प्रमाणत: [*adv*] according to or by way of evidence/ proof.

प्रमाणित [*adv*] proved; testified; certified, authenticated.

प्रमाता [*nm*] one who can appreciate, one who understands a subject, one who has correct notion or idea [of something].

प्रमाद [*nm*] negligence, carelessness; ~ पूर्ण negligent, careless.

प्रमादी [*a*] negligent careless [person].

प्रमुख [*a*] chief; foremost, leading, outstanding, principal.

प्रमेय [*nm*] a theorem.

प्र/मोद [*nm*] entertainment; mirth; joy, delight; hence ~ मुदित.

प्रयत्न [*nm*] effort, endeavour; attempt.

प्रयाण [*nm*] departure, setting out; march; death.

प्रयास [*nm*] an effort, endeavour; attempt.

प्र/युक्त [*a*] used, employed; applied; practical; ~ योक्ता user, one who employs/applies; an experimenter.

प्रयोग [*nm*] an experiment; use, employment; application; exercise; ~ वाद experimentalism; ~ वादी n experimentalist; experimentalistic.

प्रयोगत: [*adv*] through experimentation; practically.

प्रयोजन [*nm*] purpose; motive, intention; cause; use.

प्रलंब [*a*] pendulous; suspended; prolonged, lengthened.

प्रलयंकर [*a*] catastrophic; devastating, causing destruction or ruin, spelling disaster.

प्रलय [*nf*] universal destruction; annihilation, destruction of the whole world; ~ कर/कारी see प्रलयंकर.

प्रलाप [*nm*] logorrhoea; prate, prattle, babble, disjointed/meaningless utterance.

प्रलेप [*nm*] an unguent, ointment, a salve.

प्रलोभन [*nm*] allurement, temptation, inducement.

प्रवं/चना [*nf*] circumvention; deceit, deprivation; ~ चित circumvented; deceived, deprived.

प्रवक्ता [*nm*] a spokesman.

प्रवचन [*nm*] a [religious] discourse, sermon.

प्रवर [*a*] senior; superior; select [ed]; eminent; as a suffix it means the best, most excellent [as पंडितप्रवर]; ~ ता seniority, superiority; selectness, eminence.

प्रवर्त/न [*nm*] pioneering, introducing something new; operation; persuasion; hence ~ क.

प्रवाहमान [*a*] flowing; fluent.

प्रवाद [*nm*] a rumour; slander, calumny.

प्रवास [*nm*] dwelling abroad, foreign residence; migration.

प्रवासी [*nm*] a migrant, one who stays abroad; [*a*] migratory.

प्रवाह [*nm*] flow; fluency; an unbroken sequence.

प्रविधि [*nf*] technique.

प्रवीण [*a*] proficient, adept, expert; hence ~ ता.

प्रवृत्ति [*nf*] mentality; trend, tendency; [mental] inclination/disposition; instinct; activity.

प्रवेश [*nm*] entry, admission; access; inlet; gate; entrance; –पत्र a ticket, an admission ticket; visa; –शुल्क admission fee.

प्रशं/सा [*nf*] praise, admiration; eulogy; ~ सक an admirer, eulogist, one who praises; a fan; ~ सनीय praise-worthy, admirable; laudable, commendable.

प्रशस्त [*a*] vast; wide, broad [as—ललाट]; extensive expansive.

प्रशस्ति [*nf*] praise, admiration; eulogy.

प्रशांत [*a*] pacific, pacified; tranquil, quiet, calm.

प्रशास/न [*nm*] administration; rule; ~ क an administrator; ruler.

प्रशि/क्षण [*nm*] training; hence ~ क्षक.

प्रश्न [*nm*] a question, query; interpellation; interrogation; problem; ~ पत्र a question paper; ~ माला questionnaire; interrogatives; ~ वाचक interrogative.

प्रश्नोत्त/र [*nm*] question and answer; ~ री catechism; interrogatories; quiz.

प्रश्रय [*nm*] patronage; protection, shelter; support, backing; hence ~ दाता.

प्रसंग [*nm*] context; occasion; sexual intercourse, coition.

प्रसन्न [*a*] pleased, happy, cheerful, delighted, glad; ~ ता pleasure, happiness, cheerfulness, delight.

प्रस/व [*nm*] delivery, childbirth, labour; [*a*] natal; ~ विनी a progenitress, woman who gives birth to a child, [a woman] begetting a child.

प्रसाद [*nm*] blessing, boon; grace; offerings made to an idol [and later distributed amongst the devotees]; leaving of food of a pre-eminent religious person; lucidity [of the style of writing etc.]—गुण lucidity [lucidity [of style] ~ त्व lucidity [of style of writing].

प्रसाधन [*nm*] make-up; make-up aids, beauty aids; cosmetics.

प्रसार [*nm*] expansion, dispersion; scattering, extensity; spread propagation.

प्रसा/रण [*nm*] broadcasting; [the act or process of] expanding/dispersing/scattering/extending/spreading/propagating; hence ~ रित.

प्रसि/द्ध [*a*] famous, reputed, well-known, renowned; ~ द्धि fame, repute, renown.

प्रसुप्त [*a*] dormant, asleep; in abeyance.

प्रसू/त [*a*] born; brought forth, delivered; ~ ता a woman after child-birth/in confinement.

प्रसूति [*nf*] child-birth, delivery; maternity; labour; offspring; —गृह maternity home.

प्रस्ताव [*nm*] resolution, motion; proposal.

प्रस्तावना [*nf*] a preamble, prologue, preface.

प्रस्तावित [*a*] proposed, projected.

प्रस्तुत [*a*] present [ed.]; submitted; produced; ready; [subject etc.] under study or discussion; at hand; [*nm*] anything that is in sight or of immediate concern.

प्रस्थान [*nm*] departure, setting out [on a journey]; march; articles placed in advance at the auspicious moment in the direction in which one is to journey [in case one's departure is delayed due to some reason].

प्रस्फुटन [*nm*] efflorescence; manifestation; opening up, blooming; becoming distinct.

प्रहर [*nm*] a measure of time equivalent to three hours, period of three hours.

प्रहरी [*nm*] a watchman, guard, sentinel.

प्रहसन [*nm*] a comedy; farce.

प्रहार [*nm*] an assault; a blow stroke.

प्रहेलिका [*nf*] a riddle; an enigma.

प्रांगण [*nm*] a courtyard; an enclave.

प्रांजल [*a*] lucid, clear; refined; ~ ता lucidity, clarity; refinement.

प्रां/त [*nm*] a province, territory, country, district; ~ तीय provincial, territorial; ~ तीयता provinciality, provincialism.

प्रांतर [*nm*] a territory, district.

प्राइमरी [*a*] primary [only in the context of a school].

प्राइवेट [*a*] private, personal; secret.

प्राकार [*nm*] a parapet, rampart.

प्राकृत [*a*] natural; unsophisticated, unprocessed; inherent, innate; common.

प्राकृतिक [*a*] natural, nature-made; physical; unsophisticated; unrefined.

प्राक्कथन [*nm*] a foreword.

प्राक्कलन [*nm*] estimate.

प्रागैतिहासिक [*a*] prehistoric [al].

प्राची [*nf*] the east, the eastern quarter, the orient.

प्राचीन [a] ancient, old; outdated; antique; ~ तर older, more ancient; earlier; ~ तम oldest, most ancient; earliest; ~ ता antiquity, ancientness.

प्राचीर [*nf*] a parapet, rampart, surrounding wall [of a city, fort, etc.].

प्राचुर्य [*nm*] abundance, plenty.

प्राच्य [*a*] east, eastern; oriental; belonging or pertaining to the east.

प्राज्ञ [*a*] prudent, intelligent, sharp, brilliant.

प्राण [*nm*] life; vital breath, vital air; vitality; soul, spirit; sweetheart; [in gram] aspiration in the articulation of letters; —का ग्राहक a seeker after one's life; –दंड capital punishment, punishment of death; ~ दाता lifegiver; one who saves somebody's life; ~ दान a gift of life, saving/sparing somebody's life; ~ धन as dear as life, beloved; ~ धारी a living being/ organism, a creature; ~ नाथ lord/master of life; husband; ~ प्रद life-giving, infusing or imparting life; ~ वायु vital breadth; ~ शक्ति vitality; ~ हानि loss of life; ~हीन lifeless, inanimate; —छूटना/जाना/निकलना the breath to leave the system, to expire, to die, life to come to an end; —डालना to infuse/inject life, to animate; —देना to die, to give up life; to love more dearly than life; —मुँह को आना to suffer mortal agony, to be in a fightful suspense; —मुट्ठी में /हथेली पर लिए फिरना to be ever-ready to court death; to face all sorts of risk; प्राणों से हाथ धोना to lose life, to be pushed out of existence; प्राणों पर खेलना/खेल जाना to stake one's life.

प्राण/वान् [*a*] full of vitality, spirited, animated; strong, powerful, vigorous; hence ~वत्ता.

प्राणांत [*nm*] the end of life, expiry, death.

प्राणायाम [*nm*] exercising control over the process of breathing, restraining or suspending the breath during the mental recitation of the name of a deity or as a religious or yogic exercise.

प्राणी [*nm*] a living being, living organism, a creature; an animal.

प्राणे/श~श्वर [*nm*] lord/master of life; beloved, darling.

प्राणोत्सर्ग [*nm*] sacrifice of life; martyrdom.

प्रात: [*nm* and *ind*] early [in the] morning, [at] dawn, ~काल early [in the] morning.

प्राथमिक [*a*] primary; elementary; having precedence; —उपचार first aid; —शिक्षा primary education.

प्राथमिकता [*nf*] priority; precedence.

प्रादु/र्भाव [*nm*] coming into existence; appearance, manifestation, becoming visible; hence ~भूत.

प्रादेशिक [*a*] regional territorial; ~ता regionalism.

प्राधान्य [*nm*] predominance, dominance, superiority; supremacy, hegemony.

प्राधि/कार [nm] authority; ~कारी [person in] authority; one who wields authority.

प्राध्यापक [*nm*] a lecturer, professor.

प्रा/प्त [*a*] got, obtained; procured, acquired; ~प्ति receipt; procuration, acquisition;

income; profit; ~प्य due; available; attainable, acquirable, procurable.

प्राप्तव्य [*nm*] due; to be got/obtained/procured/ acquired.

प्रामाणिक [*a*] authentic, genuine; authoritative; ~ता authenticity, genuineness; authoritativeness.

प्रायः [*adv*] often; usually, generally; almost, more or less; approximately, nearly

प्राय/द्वीप [*nm*] peninsula; ~द्वीपीय peninsular.

प्रायश्चित्त [*nm*] atonement, penance, expiation.

प्रायोगिक [*a*] experimental; practical; pilot [scheme etc.]; hence ~ता.

प्रारं/भ [*nm*] beginning, commencement; inception; the starting point; ~भिक starting; preliminary; elementary; nisi; original; initial.

प्रारब्ध [nm] destiny, fate, lot.

प्रारूप [*nm*] a draft.

प्रार्थना [*nf*] a prayer: request, solicitation; petition; -पत्र an application; a petition.

प्रार्थी [*nm*] an applicant; a petitioner; one who submits a request; one who prays.

प्रासंगिक [*a*] relevant; contingent; incidental; contextual; ~ता relevance; contingency; incidental nature or character; contextuality.

प्रासाद [*nm*] a palace, palatial mansion.

प्रिंट [*nm*] a print; printed design.

प्रिंटिंग [*nf*] printing; — प्रेस a printing press.

प्रिंसिपल [*nm*] a principal [of a school or college].

प्रिय [*a*] dear, darling, beloved; pleasing; pleasant; favourite, lilked; [*nm*] a lover; husband; ~जन a beloved one dear one; near and dear ones; ~तम dearest; most beloved; husband; ~दर्शी affectionate to all, looking towards all with compassion and kindness.

प्रिया [*a* and *nf*] beloved, darling; sweetheart; wife.

प्रीतम [*nm*] a lover; beloved.

प्रीति [*nf*] love; affection; -भोज a love-feast, banquet.

प्रेक्ष/क [*nm*] an observer; viewer, spectator, one who has seen; ~ण observing, viewing, seeing; witnessing.

प्रेक्षा/गार, ~गृह [*nm*] an auditorium; a theatre.

प्रेत [*nm*] a ghost, goblin, lemures, an evil spirit; a frightful person; ~लोक the world of the dead; -विद्या, –सिद्धि necromancy.

प्रेतनी [*nf*] a female spirit see प्रेत demoness.

प्रेम [*nm*] love; affection; -कथा/-कहानी a love-story, tale of love; -गीत a love-song; -पत्र a love-letter; -पात्र dear, beloved; -पाश bond of love; -भाव love, emotion of love; ~मय loving, affectionate; -विह्वल love-sick; -व्यापार love affair.

प्रेमालिंगन [*nm*] a loving embrace, an affectionate hug.

प्रेमिका [*nf*] a beloved.

प्रेमी [nm] a lover.

प्रेय [*nm*] mundane achievement, worldly pleasure/acquirement.

प्रेयसी [*nf*] a beloved, darling wife.

प्रेरक [*a*] inductive, that which inspires/prompts/ motivates; [*nm*] an inspirer, promptor; a motive.

प्रेरणा [*nf*] inspiration; urge, drive; motive; induction; -शक्ति motive force, inspiration, urge; -हेतु motive, inspiration.

प्रेरणार्थक [*a*];—क्रिया a casual verb.

प्रेष/क [*nm*] a despatcher; consigner; ~ण a despatch; consignment; transmission.

प्रेषण [*nm*] sending, despatch; delivery, a consignment, item of mail, remittance.

प्रेषणीयता [*nf*] communicability, effectiveness as of a work of art.

प्रेषित्र [*nm*] a transmitter, transmission instrument.

प्रेस [*nm*] a printing press.

प्रेसिडेंट [*nm*] a president.

प्रैक्टिस [*nf*] practice.

प्रोग्राम [nm] programme.

प्रोत्साहन [*nm*] encouragement, boosting up; incentive.

प्रोत्साहक [*nm*] one who exhorts, encourages.

प्रोफ़ेसर [*nm*] a professor.

प्रौढ़ [*a*] mature; full-grown, adult; ~ता/त्व maturity; full growth, adulthood; —शिक्षा adult education.

प्लवन [*nm*] inundation, flood, bathing, floating, swimming.

प्लावन [*nm*] inundation, flood, deluge; plunging.

प्लीहा; [*nf*] the spleen; enlargement of the spleen.

प्लेग [*nf*] plague name of a disease.

प्लैटफ़ार्म [*nm*] a platform; ~ टिकट a platform ticket.

फ the second letter of the fifth pentad [i.e. पवर्ग) of the Devanagari: alphabet.

फ - देवनागरी वर्णमाला (व्यंजन) में पवर्ग का दूसरा वर्ण है। इसका उच्चारण स्थान ओष्ठ है। इसे स्पर्श वर्ण कहते हैं।

फंका [*nm*] the quantity [of a powder etc.] chucked into the mouth in one lot.

फंकी [*nf*] diminutive of फंका [see]; the quantity [of medicinal or digestive powder etc.] chucked into the mouth.

फंदा [*nm*] a trap; noose, gin, snare; loop; trick; फंदेदार loopy, having a knot/loop/snare; — डालना to ensnare, to form a noose; to knot; फंदे में पड़ना to fall into a trap, to be ensnared; to be caught in a trick.

फँसना [*v*] to be entrapped/ensnared/baited, to be embroiled, to be caught in a trick; —बुरी तरह to be inextricably caught [in a mess]; hence फँसाव.

फँसाना [*v*] to trap/entrap, to snare/ensnare, to entangle, to trammel; to involve; to complicate, to ravel; to noose, to bait; to coil.

फँसवाना [*v.t*] to cause to be snared, by, से.

फक [*a*] pale, anaemic; clean, spotlessly clean; -पड़ना to turn pale, to lose lustre; to be scared out of wits.

फकड़ी [*nf*] फक्कड़, disgrace, dishonour; disparagement, lampoon.

फ़क़त [*a*] only, alone; [*adv*] simply, merely solely.

फ़की/र [*nm*] a Muslim mendicant/ saint, hermit, recluse; beggar, pauper; hence ~राना; ~री poverty, indigence; the manner or life of a फ़कीर; mendicity; [a] pertaining or belonging to a फ़कीर; फ़कीर -like.

फ़क्कड़ [*a*] carefree; indigent; ~पन carefreeness, carefree manner; indigence.

फ़क्कड़पन [*nm*] फक्कड़ी

फ़ख्र [*nm*] pride; egotism.

फ़जर [*nf*] day-break, dawn.

फ़ज़ल [*nm*] bounty, grace, favour, — ~ करना, to show grace, or favour to, पर है, all is well by God's grace, खुदा का ~ रहे! God's grace be with you!.

फ़जीता [*nm*] see फ़जीहत.

फ़जीहत [*nf*] insult, disgrace; embarrassment, discomfiture.

फ़ज़ीहती [*adj*] shameful a matter, shamed; infamous a person, फ़ज़ीहत.

फ़जूल [*a*] useless worthless; futile; ~खर्च extravagant; dissipating; ~खर्ची extravagance; dissipation.

फ़ज़्ल [*nm*] grace, favour, kindness.

फटकना [*v*] to winnow; to dust; to sift; to shake off, to knock off; to reach, to go near [as किसी के पास न फटकना); to be separated.

फटकार [*nf*] a reprimand, scolding, rebuke, chiding.

फटकारना [*v*] to rebuke, to scold, to chide, to reprimand; to give a violent jerk to a cloth [in order to undo its wrinkles].

फटकी [*nf*] a fowler's cage; net; bag, फटका.

फटना [*v*] to be torn, to be split; to burst, to explode, to crack; to tatter; [milk] to become sour; to be put off, to develop a sense of aversion, to be repulsed.

फटा [*a*] torn; rent; -पुराना shabby, old and shattered/ tattered; -फटाया torn and tattered; shabby; फटे हाल in a ragged condition, in tatters/rags.

फटीचर [*a*] shabby, shabbily dressed; putting on tattered/shattered clothes.

फ/ट्टा, ~ट्ठा [*nm*] a plank, long and wide piece of split plank.

फड़ [*nm*] a gambling party/spot; a shopkeeper's seat [for transacting business].

फड़कना [*v*] to be thrilled, to throb, to palpitate, to pulsate; to flutter; फड़क उठना to be thrilled, to be in extreme exaltation.

फड़फड़ा/ना [*v*] to flutter; to flap; to throb; hence ~हट.

फ/ण [*nm*] the hood of a snake; ~णी a snake, serpent.

फ़तवा [*nm*] a judgment/decree; a decree by a [Muslim] religious judge in accordance with the canons of Islam.

फ़तह [*nf*] victory, triumph, conquest; —का डंका/नक्कारा proclamation of victory; drumbeat marking a triumphal expedition.

फतिंगा [*nm*] an insect, a moth.

फन [*nm*] see फण.

फ़न [*nm*] an art, craft; skill, artifice; ~कार an artist; हर–मौला a master of all trades, a versatile person.

फ़ना [*a*] died, expired; ruined, destructed, devastated, [*nm*] death, expiry; ruin, destruction, devastation.

फप्फस [a] flabby, flaccid.

फफूँ/द ~दी [*nf*] fungus.

फफोला [*nm*] blister, eruption.

फबती [*nf*] a banter, sarcastic remark; befitting remark.

फबना [*v*] to befit, to become to suit, to beseem.

फ़रज़ी [*nm*] the queen in the game of chess; [a] see फ़र्ज़ी;–बनना, प्यादे से to rise to power from the position of a non-entity; to rise from the ranks to the seat of power.

फ़रमा [*nm*] a format, form, [in printing]; a [shoe-makers] frame.

फ़रमाइ/श [*nf*] an imperative request, an order; ~शी made to order; requested; [performed/presented] on specific request.

फ़रमान [*nm*] a royal edict/command/decree.

फ़रमाना [*v*] [a deferential usage] to [be so graceful as to] speak out; to [come out with an] order/command; to make an utterance.

फ़रवरी [*nf*] [the month of] February.

फ़रशी [*nf*] a hubble-bubble; [a] pertaining to the फ़र्श [see]; —सलाम see फ़र्शी सलाम [under फ़र्शी).

फरसा [*nm*] see परशु

फ़रग़त [*nf*] riddance; carefreeness; discharge of faeces.

फ़रार [*a*] at large, absconding; [*nm*] an outlaw, absconder, fugitive.

फ़रियाद [*nf*] a petition, complaint, supplication for help or justice; ~दी a petitioner, suppliant, one who makes an invocation for help or justice.

फ़रिश्ता [*nm*] an angel, a divine messenger.

फ़रीक़ [*nm*] a party [in a lawsuit], contender.

फ़रे/ब [*nm*] fraud, duplicity; wiliness, deception; double-dealing; ~ बी fraudulent, wily, deceptive [person]; a double-dealer. फ़रोश [*a*] Persian suffi used to impart to a word the sense of seller/dealer in,vendor [as दवा-फ़रोश, वतनफ़रोश, etc.]

फ़र्क़ [*nm*] difference, distinction; distance.

फ़र्ज [*nm*] duty; obligation; –करना to imagine, to asume, to suppose.

फ़र्ज़ी [a] imaginary; supposed, assumed; hypothetical; fictitious; see फ़रजी.

फ़र्द [*nf*] a list, catalogue; the upper fold of a quilt.

फ़र्म [*nf*] a firm/business concern.

फर्रा/टा [*nm*] fluency; promptitude, fastness; ~ टे से non-stop, fluently, promptly, hastily, unhesitatingly.

फ़र्राश [*nm*] a sweeper, menial worker.

फ़र्लांग [*nm*] a furlong.

फ़र्श [*nm*] floor [of a room etc.], flooring; carpet, mat; pavement.

फ़र्शी [*a*] pertaining to the फ़र्श [see]; –सलाम an extra-deferential salutation [by bending the head so low as almost to touch the ground].

फल [*nm*] a fruit; reward, return; effect, outcome, result, consequence; product; the point of a cutting or piercing instrument; a ploughshare; ~ त: consequently; therefore, accordingly; thus; ~ द/दायक/दायी/प्रद fruitful, fructuous; profitable; advantageous; productive; fruit-yielding, efficacious; effective; ~ दान the first present made from the bride's side to the bridegroom as a confirmation of the agreement for marriage; बती fruitful, fructuous; ~स्वरूप as a result of; —देना to yield fruit/result; to fructify; —पाना to be rewarded; to face the result of; to suffer for one's evil deeds;—भोगना to suffer the consequences [of].

फलक [*nm*] a face; blade; board, plank; palm, [of the hand], a sheet [of paper]; slab.

फ़लक [*nm*] the sky; heaven.

फलना [*v*] to bear fruit; to be fruitful/useful; to thrive, to prosper; —फूलना to be prosperous, to thrive.

फ़लाँ [*a*] so and so, such and such: also-फ़लां.

फ़लालैन [*nf*] flannel.

फला/हार [*nm*] fruitarian diet; subsisting on a diet of fruits alone; ~री fruitarian; pertaining to fruitarian diet; [nm] a fruitarian, one who subsists on fruits alone.

फलित [*a*] fructified, resulted, fulfilled; fruit-bearing; prospered, thrived; —ज्योतिष astrology.

फली [*nf*] a bean, pod of a leguminous plant.

फलीभूत [*a*] fructified, [that has] borne fruits, resulted in success.

फ़व्वारा [*nm*] a fountain.

फ़सल [*nf*] crop, harvest; season time.

फ़सली [*a*] seasonal; relating to the harvest/ crop;—बुखार seasonal fever.

फ़सा/द [*nm*] an altercation, row, quarrel, disturbance; ~दी [*a*] rowdy, one who initiates an altercation/row/quarrel.

फ़साना [*nm*] a story, a long narrative; see अफ़साना.

फ़सील [*nf*] a boundary wall; battlement, parapet.

फहराना [*v*] ro hoist; to wave; to flutter in the air to flap.

फाँक [*nf*] a cut slice [of fruit etc.] fillet, fragment/ paring; clove [of a garlic], cleft, slit.

फाँकना [*v*] to chuk some powdery thing into the mouth [esp. from the palm of the hand]; धूल ~ to knock about, to be tossed about, to run from pole to post.

फाँट [*nm*] the width, the distance between the two banks of river etc.

फाँदना [*v*] to jump across, to leap over; to skip; to spring; to cross.

फाँस [*nf*] a noose, snare; knot; trap; tiny thorn-like splinter [of a bamboo etc.].

फाँसना [*v*] see फँसना.

फाँसी [*nf*] [death by] hanging, execution; noose.

फ़ाइल [nm, also nf] file.

फ़ाउंटेन पेन [*nm*] a fountain pen.

फ़ाक़ा [*nm*] starvation, fast; ~कशी starvation, starving.

फ़ाक़ा (के)/मस्त [*a*] who is cheerful even in extreme poverty/starvation, one whose spirit is not damped even though starved, carefree; ~मस्ती carefreeness even though starved, maintenance of undamped spirit even in affliction.

फ़ाख़ता [*nf*] a dove.

फाग [*nf*] a typical song sung collectively or individually] during the Holi festival. Holi festival and its merrymaking.

फागुन [*nm*] the twelfth and last month of the year according to the Hindu calendar.

फ़ाज़िल [*a*] extra; additional; surplus; learned, scholarly.

फाटक [*nm*] a gate, main gate; entrance.

फाट/का [*nm*] speculation; ~केबाज a speculationist; ~केवाजी speculation.

फाड़ना [*v*] to tear off; to rend, to split; to [cause to] crack; to burst open, to lacerate; to cleave, to rip open, to pull apart.

फ़ातिहा [*nf*] oblation offered to the manes by Mohammedans, reading the first chapter of the —कुरान [see]; —पढ़ना to be frustrated/dejected, to be hopeless.

फ़ानूस [*nm*] a chandelier [for burning candles].

फ़ाय/दा [*nm*] gain, profit; advantage, benefit; utility, use; good result; ~देमंद profiable; advantageous, beneficial; useful, efficacious; giving good result.

फ़ारख़ती [*nf*] a deed of separation/riddance/ dissolution; quittance.

फ़ारसी [*a*] Persian; [*nf*] the Persian language; [*nm*] an inhabitant of Persia; ~दाँ one who knows the Persian language, a Persian scholar;—बघारना to show off one's pedantry.

फ़ारिग़ [*a*] freed, free [from work]; [one who has] fulfilled his obligation.

फ़ाल [*nm*] a blade, ploughshare; a stride/pace, measure of one pace; betelnut-paring.

फ़ॉल [*nm*] a fall [in sa:ri: etc.]

फ़ालतू [*a*] spare; extra, surplus; superfluous [as बात]; useless, worthless; [as—आदमी].

फ़ालसई [*a*] brownish red [coloured].

फ़ालसा [*nm*] a tree and its round tiny fruit — Grewia asiatica.

फालिज [*nm*] paralysis, palsy.

फ़ावड़ा [*nm*] a spade, mattock.

फ़ाश [*a*] exposed, uncovered, open [ed], disclosed, manifest; —करना to expose; to disclose a secret that undermines somebody's prestige.

फ़ासला [*nm*] a distance; gap; space, spacing; difference.

फ़ाहा [*nm*] a flock of cotton [used as a lint for dressing a wound]; flock of cotton impregnated with perfume.

फ़िकरा [*nm*] a sentence; sarcasm; taunt; —कसना to make a sarcastic remark, to taunt.

फ़िक्र [*nf*] worry, anxiety; care, concern; ~मंद worried, concerned.

फिटक (कि) री [*nf*] alum.

फ़ितना [*a*] crooked, shrewd, full of wiles, wily.

फ़ितर/त [*nf*] disposition, nature; wiliness, cunningness; mischievousness; ~ती natural; cunning, mischievous, wily.

फ़ितूर [*nm*] unsoundness; infirmity; craze.

फ़िदा [*a*] infatuated, charmed, attracted; devoted [to].

फ़िनाय(इ)ल [*nm*] naphthaline [liquid].

फ़िरंगी [*a* and *nm*] European; English.

फिर [*adv*] then; again; afterwards; thereafter; in future; a second time; —जाना to return, to go back; —से anew, afresh.

फ़िरक़ा [*nm*] a religious sect, sect; community; ~परस्त a communalist; sectarian; ~परस्ती communalism; sectarianism.

फ़िरकी [*nf*] a spool; reel [of thread]; whirligig.

फिरना [*s*] to turn; to return; to revolve; to wander; to ramble; to walk-about; to go round; to be proclaimed/circulated; to undergo a change [as दिन–फिरना); to go back [as—बात से).

फिराक [*nm*] expectancy [for], looking for, waiting for keeping a watch for; worry, anxiety; search.

फ़िलहाल [*adv*] at present, for the present, for the time being.

फ़िल्म [*nm* and *nf*] a film, movie; ~ल्मना to film, to filmise.

फ़िल्मी [*a*] pertaining to the films, cinematographic.

फिसड्डी [*a*] tailing behind [in a race], always lagging behind; sluggish, slothful; backward.

फिसल/न [*nf*] slipperiness; skid; ~ना to slip; to slide; to skid.

फ़ी [*ind*] each; every;—सदी percent, per hundred.

फीका [*a*] tasteless, insipid; unsweetened, unsweet; faded; dull-coloured; dim, dovoid of radiance; hence; ~पन.

फ़ीता [*nm*] a lace, ribbon; tape; strap; shoelace; fillet.

फ़ीरोज़ी [*a*] violet blue.

फ़ील [*nm*] an elephant; a piece in the game of chess; ~खाना a stable for elephants; ~पाँव/पा elephantiasis; ~दान an elephant-driver.

फ़ीस [*nf*] fee; tuition fee.

फुंकार [*nf*] hiss [of a snake], hissing.

फुंसी [*nf*] a small boil; pimple, whelk.

फुट [*nm*] a foot.

फुटक/र, ~ल [*a*] miscellaneous, retail; ~र चीजें odds and ends, miscellaneous articles, sundries.

फुटबाल [*nm*] football, the game of football.

फुनगी [*nf*] the top, tip, upper extremity, summit; cockade; sprout.

फुप्फुस [*nm*] a lung.

फुफकार [*nf*] hiss, hissing [of a snake etc.]; hence ~ना करना.

फु/रती, ~र्ती [*nf*] smartness, agility; promptness; ~रतीला, ~र्तीला smart, agile; prompt.

फुर्सत [*nf*] leisure; spare time; respite.

फुलका [nm] a [thin] bread.

फुलझड़ी [*nf*] a kind of fire-work which emits flower-like sparks; a provoking remark uttered in a lighter vein; —छोड़ना to utter a provoking remark non-seriously, to make a provocative remark in a lighter vein.

फुलवा/ड़ी, ~री [*nf*] a small flower-garden.

फुलस्केप [*a* and *nm*] foolscap [paper].

फुलाना [*v*] to puff up; to cause to become proud; to inflate; to pump in air; to [cause to] swell; to cause to blossom;—, मुँह to be sulky, to get angry.

फुलेल [*nm*] scented [hair] oil.

फुव्वारा [*nm*] a fountain.

फुसफुसा [*a*] hollow, fragile, not sturdy.

फुसफुसा/ना [*v*] to whisper, to speak in a hushed up voice or low tone; hence ~हट.

फुसला/ना [*v*] to allure, to entice, to wheedle; to seduce; to coax, to cajole; hence ~हट.

फुहार [*nf*] drizzle, fine dense drops of rain; spray.

फुहारा [*nm*] a fountain, shower.

फूंक [*nf*] puff; whiff, blow [ing].

फूंकना [*v*] to blow; to puff, to whiff; to burn, to ignite, to set on fire; to waste, to squander away; फूँक-फूँक कर क़दम/पाँव/पैर रखना to take every step with utmost caution; to be extra-cautious in one's movement.

फूट [*nf*] disunion/disunity, discord, rift, chasm; a species of large cucumber resembling a muskmelon in appearance that splits up on ripening.

फूटना [*v*] to break; to be broken; to crack; to split; to burst; to erupt, to explode; to sprout, to shoot; [a secret] to be revealed, to defect; [eyes] to become blind; फूट-फूट कर रोना to weep bitterly.

फूल [*nm*] a flower; flower in embroidery; post-cremation ashes; the burnt part of a wick etc; a very light thing; bronze; ~कारी embroidery; embroidering of flowers; ~दान a flower-vase/ flower-pot; ~दार flowery; embroidered; ~माला a flower-garland; wreath.

फूलना [*v*] to flower; to bloom, to blossom; to swell; to inflate; to be puffed up; to assume airs; to feel proud; -फलना to prosper; to flourish, to thrive; फूला न समाना to be too happy to contain oneself.

फूली [*nf*] a hard whitish out-growth in the pupil of the eye.

फूस [*nm*] straw, hay.

फूहड़ [*a*] sloven [ly]; unmannerly; devoid of a sense of proportion; [*nm*] a slattern; hence ~पन/पना.

फेंकना [*v*] to throw, to cast; to hurl; to fling; to toss; to waste; to emit.

फेंटना [*v*] to batter, to beat up into froth, to mix by trituration; to shuffle [as a pack of cards].

फेंटा [*nm*] the part of the धोती rolled and tucked up round the waist.

फेन [*nm*] foam, froth, lather, scum; फेनिल foamy, frothful, full of lather/scum.

फेफड़ा [*nm*] a lung.

फेर [*nm*] a detour, circuitous route; turn/turning; curvature; ambiguity; complication; -में पड़ना, निन्यान्वे के to be unseemly crazy to amass wealth; to get embroiled in an unseemly activity for material gains; to be involved in a predicament of one's own making.

फेरा [*nm*] going round; round, coming and going back; circumambulation; circuit; a matrimonial rite wherein the bride aud bridegroom move together round the sacred fire; फेरे पड़ना the matrimonial rites of going around the sacred fire to be performed, to be bound in wedlock.

फेरी [*nf*] going round; round; circumambulation; hawking.

फ़ेल [*a*] failed, unsuccessful, plucked; [nm] deed, going; action.

फ़ेहरिस्त [*nf*] a list, an inventory.

फ़ैक्टरी [*nf*] a factory.

फैलना [*v*] to spread; to be diffused; to expand; to extend, to be stretched; to be radiated [as किरणें—] to be scattered; to spill; to become public [as बात]; to be inflated; to be on the increase [as कारबार—].

फैलाव [*nm*] expanse, expansion; span; spread; stretch; scattering, radiation, space spacearea; roominess.

फ़ैशन [*nm*] fashion; ~परस्त fashionable; ~परस्ती fashionableness.

फ़ैशनेबल [*a*] fashionable.

फ़ैसला [*nm*] judgment; decision, settlement, resolution.

फोकट [*a*] free, free of charge; gratis; —में without payment, gratis.

फ़ोटो [*nm*] a photograph; ~ग्राफर a photographer.

फोड़ना [*v*] to break; to burst; to split; to successfully induce somebody to defect [as गवाह–]; to break into] [as दीवाल—].

फोड़ा [*nm*] a boil; ulcer, tumour.

फ़ोता [*nm*] a testicle; rent [of land]; फ़ोतेदार a treasurer; burser.

फ़ोरमैन [*nm*] a foreman.

फ़ौज [*nf*] an army; a multitude; ~दारी criminal breach of peace; a penal offence; criminal; ~ कानून criminal law; ~दारी, जाब्ता code of criminal procedure, the penal code.

फ़ौजी [*a*] pertaining to the army, military; martial; [*nm*] a soldier; —अदालत a military court.

फ़ौरन [*adv*] immediately, instantly, at once, there and then, in an instant.

फ़ौला/द [*nm*] steel; ~दी made of or pertaining to steel; strong, stout, sturdy; —आदमी an ironman.

फ़ौलादी [*adj*] made of steel, having to do with steel, steely; strong, unyielding.

फ्रांसीसी [*a*] French; [*nm*] a French, an inhabitant of France; [nf] the French language.

फ्रेम [*nm*] a frame.

ब the third letter of the fifth pentad [i.e. पवर्ग] of the Devanagari: alphabet; a prefix that imparts the meaning of along with, with, for, by, etc., e.g. बखूबी, बखैरियत.

ब - देवनागरी वर्णमाला (व्यंजन) में पवर्ग का तीसरा वर्ण है। यह दोनों होठों को मिलाने पर उच्चारित होता है।

बंक [*nm*] bent, curved, inaccessible; difficult of access, gallant, courtly, a lover, bend, curve as in a river.

बंकि/म [*a*] bent, curved; oblique; crooked; hence ~मा bend, flexure, curvature, obliquity; crookedness.

बंगला [*nm*] a bungalow; [*nf*] the Bengali lauguage; [*a*] belonging to Bengal [as —पान].

बंगाल [*nm*] an Eastern state of India, renamed पश्चिम बंगाल after division of the country.

बँचना [*v.i.*] to be read, read through.

बँचवाना [*v.t.*] to cause to be read by से; to make or hear one read.

बँचाना [*v.t.*] बँचवाना.

बंजर [*a*] barren, unproductive, fallow; [*nf*] fallow/ barren land.

बंजारा [*nm*] a gypsy, nomad; a nomadic tribe.

बँटना [*v.i.*] to be divided, बाँटना.

बँटवाना [*v.t.*] to cause to be divided by, से; to distribute among, में.

बँटवारा [*nm*] partition, distribution, division; separation.

बँटाई [*nf*] dividing, division.

बंटाधार [*nm*] complete ruination, devastation undoing.

बंडल [*nm*] a bundle.

बंडी [*nf*] a jacket, waistcoat.

बंद [*a*] closed, shut; locked [up]; stopped, discontinued; [nm] a bund, bank; knot; a string or strap; bodily joint; a stanza, verse; as a suffix it means that which ties or binds; —गली a blind alley; ~गोभी cabbage.

बंदगी [*nf*] salutation, prayer, worship.

बंदनवार [*nf*] festoon of flowers and green leaves [hung on festive occasions].

बंदर [*nm*] a monkey; harbour; —घुड़की/भभकी a hollow threat; mere browbeating/bluffing.

बंदरगाह [*nf*] a harbour, port.

बंदा [*nm*] a servant, slave; an individual; humble self [used by a speaker for himself out of modesty]; —, खुदा का a man of God, a creation of God; ~परवर [a deferential form of address] protector of one's own men.

बंदिश [*nf*] a restriction; forestalling; musical pattern.

बंदी [*nm*] captive, prisoner; a bard; ~गृह/घर a prison.

बंदूक [*nf*] a gun; ~ची a gunner, gunman.

बंदोबस्त [*nm*] [land] settlement; management.

बंध [*nm*] a bond; tie, fetters, string; a bund; ligature; -पत्र a bond.

बंधक [*nm*] pawn, mortgage; surety; mordant; -रखना to pawn, to mortgage to pledge.

बंधन [*nm*] a bond, tie; the act or process of binding/tying; bondage; restriction; a fetter.

बंधु [*nm*] a brother; relative, kinsman; -बांधव kinsfolk, relatives; ~ता/त्व fraternity, fraternalism; relationship, kinship, affinity; cognation.

बंधेज [*nm*] restriction; proviso; stipulation.

बंध्या [*nf* and *a*] [*a*] barren [woman]; sterile; issueless/childless; hence ~त्व/पन; -पुत्र an impossible phenomenon.

बंबा [*nm*] a hydrant; water-pipe.

बंसी [*nf*] a flute; fish gorge, fishing hook.

बक [*nm*] a heron; hypocrite, simulator; [*nf*] gabble, jabbering; -खुलना to go on talking idly; to be long-tongued.

बकझक [*nf*] babbling; gabble, garrulity; -करना to gab, to gabble, to jabber.

बख्तर [*nm*] an armour; ~बंद armoured

बकना [*v*] to babble, to gab, to gabble/jabber, to chatter, to make disjoined utterances; to admonish; to rave.

बकबक [*nf*] raving, gabble/jabble; twaddle.

बकरम [*nf*] buckram, a typical stiffened cloth used for stuffing coat-collars and sleeves etc.

बकरा [nm] a he-goat; बकरे की माँ कब तक खैर मनायेगी? how long shall the mother's prayers secure the ill-fated kid?

बक/वाद [*nf*] twaddle, palaver, tattle, gabble/jabbering; lalorrhea; ~वादी a twaddler, gabbler/jabber, tattler.

बक/वास [*nf*] see बकवाद, ~वासी see बकवादी [under बकवाद).

बकसुआ [*nm*] a buckle, fibula.

बक़ाया [*nm*] arrears, balance; [*a*] remaining, outstanding; payable.

बक़ौल [*ind*] according to, as said/stated by.

बखान [*nm*] description; exposition; eulogy; praise; ~ना to describe at length, to dwell in details; to eulogize, to sing the praises [of].

बखार [*nf*] a grain-store, granary, barn.

बख़िया [*nf*] back-stitching, basting; —उधेड़ना to deseam; to expose thoroughly; to analyse in wearying details.

बखुद [*ind*] by oneself, through self, by self.

बखूबी [*ind*] very well, thoroughly; amply.

बखेड़ा [*nm*] a row, broil; mess; complication; difficulty.

बखेरना [*v*] to spread, to scatter; to diffuse; to dishevel [as बाल–].

ब/खैर [*ind*] well, safely, safe and sound; also ~खैरियत.

बख़्त [*nm*] fate, fortune; lot; ~, कम ill-fated, unfortune; ~, नेक fortunate, lucky.

बख़्शना [*v*] to bestow, to grant; to give; to pardon; to forgive.

बख़्शीश [*nf*] a gift, grant; tip.

बग़ल [*nf*] a side; flank; an arm-pit; [adv] on one side, by the side [of], close by; —में on the flank; close by; in the armpit; —में छुरी मुँह में राम-राम a wolf in lamb's skin; बगलें झांकना to be completely cornered; to know no way to get out of a predicament; to be rendered witless; बगलें बजाना to be exceptionally happy, to be in manifest exaltation/delight.

बगला [*nm*] a heron; —भगत a hypocrite.

बगली [*a*] pertaining to the side/flank/armpit; [*nf*] a tailor's small bag for keeping his needle, thread etc; a wrestler's trick to dash the opponent down through one's side.

बग़ावत [*nf*] rebellion, revolt; —का झंडा उठाना, –की आवाज बुलंद करना to rise in revolt.

बग़ी/चा [*nm*] a small park, garden ~ची diminutive for बग़ीचा.

बगूला [*nm*] a whirlwind.

बग़ैर [*ind*] without, excluding, to the exclusion of.

बग्घी [*nf*] a typical horse carriage.

बघारना [*v*] to show off to boast, to talk tall [e.g. शेखी बघारना, पंडिताई बघारना etc.]

बचकाना [*a*] puerile, childish; hence बचकानी [feminine form].

बचत [*nf*] saving;/saving grace; profit, gain.

बचना [*v*] to be saved; to remain [unused or unspent]; to avoid, to keep away or aloof; to escape; -,बाल-बाल to have a narrow/hair-breadth escape.

बच/पन [*nm*] childhood; ~पना childhood; childishness; puerility.

बचाना [*v*] to save; to defend; to protect; to retain [unused or unspent]; to [cause to] avoid; to [cause to] keep away or aloof; to cause to escape; to spare.

बचाव [*nm*] safety, protection; defence.

बच्चा [*nm*] a child; kid; baby; infant; hence बच्ची [*nf*]; [a] inexperienced; raw, of unripe age; बच्चों का खेल an easy job.

बच्छा, बछड़ा [*nm*] a he-calf.

बछेड़ा [*nm*] a colt.

बजरबट्टू [*a* and *nm*] [*a*] fool, stupid [person]; nitwit, block-head.

बजा [*a*] proper, right, suitable.

बज़ाज़ [*nm*] a cloth merchant/dealer, clothier, draper.

बज़ाज़ा [*nm*] a cloth market.

बजाना [*a*] to play on a musical instrument, to ring, to produce a sound; to examine [as a coin]; to strike [against]; to execute [as हुकुम].

बजाय [*ind*] instead of, in place of, in lieu of.

बटन [*nf*] a button; switch; twist.

बटना [*v*] to twist [as thread, rope etc.]; to twine; see बँटना.

बंटवारा [*nm*] partition; distribution; division; apportionment.

बटाई [*nf*] crop sharing, share of [agricultural] yield.

बटाऊ [*nm*] a wayfarer, traveller.

बटालियन [*nf*] a battalion [in the army].

बटुआ [*nm*] a purse, money-bag.

बटेर [*nf*] a quail.

बटोरना [*v*] to collect; to accumulate; to gather [together], to amass.

बटोही [*nm*] a wayfarer, traveller.

बट्टा [*nm*] a discount; brokerage; deficit; loss; stone-pestle, round smooth mass of stone; blemish; looking glass; —खाता a bad-debt account; bad-debt, irrecoverable arrear.

बट्टी [*nf*] a cake, small pestle.

बड़ —an allomorph of 'बड़ा' used as the first member in several compound words [e.g. बड़प्पन, बड़बोला, बड़भागी]; [*nm*] a banyan tree.

बड़प्पन [*nm*] greatness, dignity.

बड़बड़ [*nf*] see बड़बड़ाना.

बड़ब/ड़ाना [*v*] to grumble; to mutter/murmur; to gabble/jabber; hence ~ड़िया.

बड़ा [*a*] big; large; great; huge; important; noble; reputed; commodious; expansive; elder [ly], senior; grown up; rich; [*adv*] very, exceedingly; [*nm*] small fried cakes of ground pulse; —दिन the Christmas day; —बाबू head clerk; -बूढ़ा elderly; बोल tall talk, boastful statement/utterance; —साहब the chief [of an office etc.]; बड़ी-बड़ी बातें करना to brag, to boast, to talk tall; बड़ी माता small pox; बड़े-बड़े the big guns; high ups, powerful people; men of reputation; बड़े बरतन की खुरचन leavings of a rich man's dishes; बड़े बोल का सिर नीचा pride goeth before a fall.

बड़ाई [*nf*] praise, eulogy; greatness.

बढ़ई [*nm*] a carpenter; a low caste in the Hindu caste hierarchy; ~गिरी the profession or work of a carpenter, carpentry.

बढ़ती [*nf*] increase, rise; growth; progress, prosperity.

बढ़ना [*v*] to inerease, to multiply; to rise; grow; to progress, to advance, to prosper, to excel/surpass/exceed/outdo; बढ़-बढ़ कर बोलना to brag, to boast, to talk too tall.

बढ़ाना [*v*] to increase, to multiply; to extend, to raise; to cause to progress/grow/prosper; to advance; to magnify, to exaggerate; to push ahead; to extinguish [as a दिया—]; to close [as दुकान–].

बढ़ावा [*nm*] encouragement, boosting, incentive, instigation.

बढ़िया [*a*] fine, excellent, of good quality, choice.

बढ़ोतरी [*nf*] increase; increment, addition; progress.

बतख [*nf*] a duck.

बताना [*v*] to say/speak, to tell to inform, to point out; to express; to teach a lesson; to instruct.

बतासा (**शा**) [*nm*] a semi-spherical crisp and spongy sugar cake; a typical firework.

बतौर [*ind*] as; like, just like; in the nature of; on the pattern of.

बत्ती [*nf*] a wick; lamp; taper; light.

बत्ती/स [*a*] thirty-two; [*nm*] the number thirty-two; ~सी the denture, the whole set of thirty-two teeth; ~ मिलना to laugh heartily, to be very happy.

बथुआ [*nm*] the pot herb—Chenopodium album.

बद [*a*] bad; wicked, vile; depraved; ~अमनी disturbance, breach of peace; ~इंतज़ाम maladroit; one who mismanages, bungling; hence ~इंतज़ामी; ~ कार depraved, debauch; vile, wicked; hence ~कारी; ~ क़िस्मत unfortunate, ill-fated; having a bad lot; hence ~क़िस्मती; ~गुमान suspicions, apprehensive; conceited; hence ~गुमानी; ~ चलन depraved, of immoral conduct; hence ~चलनी; ~ ज़बान foul-mouthed, ill-tongued; indecent of speech; hence ~ज़बानी; ~ ज़ात wicked, base, vile; ~ज़ायका distasteful, tasteless; insipid; ~तमीज़ unmannerly; uncivilised, rude, of intemperate conduct; hence ~तमीज़ी; ~तर worse [than]; ~दिमाग arrogant, conceited; hence ~दिमाग़ी; ~दुआ curse, malediction; ~नसीब unfortunate, ill-fated, luckless; hence ~नसीबी; ~नाम disreputed, infamous, of ill fame, notorious; hence ~नामी; ~नामी का टीका a stigma, a stain on one's name; ~नीयत [of] bad faith/intention, ill-intentioned malevolent; avaricious; hence ~नीयती; ~नुमा ugly; unpleasant; ~परहेज one who exercises no restraint in diet; one who takes insalubrious food; intemperate in habits [esp. eating habits]; hence ~परहेजी; ~बू foul smell, bad odour, stink; hence ~ दार; ~मिजाज़ tetchy, ill-tempered, short-tempered; petulant; hence ~मिजाज़ी; ~रंग of a bad colour; discoloured, tarnished; forced out of countenance; grown pallid; of a different colour than the trump [in playing cards]; ~शक्ल ugly, grotesque; unpleasant; ~सूरत ugly; grotesque; hence ~सूरती; ~हजमी indigestion; ~हवास stunned [out of wits], stupefied, bewildered; hence ~हवासी; —अच्छा बदनाम बुरा a bad man is better than a bad name..

बदन [*nm*] the body, physical frame; bet, betting;—टूटना the joints of the body to be aching/strained; —में आग लगना to be infuriated, to fret and fume.

बदना [*v*] to bet, to wager; to settle.

बदमा/श [a] wicked; lewd; rowdy; [*nm*] a hooligan, bad character, hoodlum; hence ~शी.

बदर [*nm*] the jejube tree and its fruit; [ind] out, out of gate.

बदल [*nf*] change, alteration [used as the second member of the compound फेर-बदल]; replacement.

बदलना [*v*] to change, to alter; to convert, to be converted; to replace; to go back [on one's word].

बदला [*nm*] revenge, vengeance; retaliation; recompense; exchange; return; lieu.

बदली [*nf*] cloudiness; a stray cloud; transfer; substitution.

बदस्तूर [*adv*] as usual; according to convention, in the customary manner.

बदाबदी [*nf*] competition, spirit of competition.

बदी [*nf*] the dark half of a lunar month; evil, wickedness.

बदौलत [*ind*] through the grace of; by means of; by virtue of; for, due to.

बधाई [*nf*] congratulations, felicitations.

बधावा [*nm*] festive and auspicious ceremonies [esp. on the birth of a male child].

बधिक [*nm*] a slaughterer; an executioner, a hunter.

बधिया [*nf*] a castrated bull/bullock; -करना to castrate; -बैठना a business, project, etc. to crash; to suffer an irreparable loss.

बनना [*v*] to be made/constructed/built/prepared; to be ready [for use]; to be obtained; to become; to feign; to assume airs; to be fooled; -ठनना/सँवरना to prank; to adorn oneself; to make [oneself] up.

बनाना [*v*] to make/construct/build/prepare, to make ready; to form; to befool; -बिगाड़ना to make or mar, to do or undo.

बनाम [*ind*] versus, as against.

बनाव [*nm*] composition; make-up, ornamentation; -सिंगार make up, prank.

बना/वट [*nf*] composition; structure, construction; make-up; show, get-up; sham; ~वटी artificial, sham; spurious; fictitious; showy.

बनिया [*nm*] a subdivision of the Hindu community, the third in the traditional hierarchical set-up — vaishya; a trader, grocer.

बनिस्बत [*ind*] as compared with, concerning; in regard to.

बनैला [*a*] wild; of the forest; savage.

बन्ना [*nm*] a bridegroom; hence बन्नी [*nf*].

बपतिस्मा [*nm*] baptism, christening.

बपौती [*nf*] heritage, inheritance.

बबर [*nm*] a lion; —शेर a lion.

बबुआ [*nm*] a [plastic] toy; a male child; a word of endearment.

बबूल [*nm*] the acacia tree.

बबूला [nm] a bubble; whirl-wind.

बम [*nm*] a bomb, shell; an interjection (बमबम or बमबम भोला) meant to propitiate Lord Shiv; the two projecting bamboos in a tonga or ekka between which a horse is harnessed.

बमचख़ [*nf*] an altercation, wordy duel, loud exchanges, brawl.

बम/बार, ~ मार [*a* and *nm*] a bomber: bomber aircraft; hence ~ बारी/मारी.

बय [*nf*] sale; ~ नामा a saledeed.

बया [*nm*] weaver-bird.

बयान [*nm*] a statement; deposition; an account.

बयाना [*nm*] an advance, earnest money.

बयालीस [*a*] forty-two; [*nm*] the number forty-two.

बयासी [*a*] eighty-two; [*nm*] the number eighty-two.

बर [*nm*] a bridegroom; [*a*] best, foremost; [*ind*] on the other hand; on, upon; beyond; ~क़रार intact, effective [as before]; maintained [in good form]; ~ ख़्वास्त dismissed, dissolved, discharged; ~ ख़्वास्तगी dismissal, dissolution; discharge; —आना to achieve fulfilment, to culminate in success.

बरकत [*nf*] prosperity, plenty and prosperity, abundance; auspiciousness.

बरगद [*nm*] a banyan tree.

बर/छा [*nm*] a lance, spear; hence ~ छी.

बरतन [*nm*] a utensil, a vessel.

बरतना [*v*] to use, to deal with.

बरदाश्त [*nf*] tolerance, endurance; forbearance; patience.

बरबस [*ind*] forcibly, willy-nilly; without any reasons; all of a sudden; unexpectedly.

बर/बाद [*a*] ruined, destroyed, wasted; hence ~ बादी.

बरमा [*nm*] a drill, auger.

बरस [*nm*] an year; ~गाँठ birth-day.

बरसना [*v*] to rain, to shower.

बर/सात [*nf*] the rainy season; rain; ~ साती a rain-coat; portico; an attic; rainy, pertaining to the rains or the rainy season.

बरसी [*nf*] the first death anniversary; the rites performed on the first death anniversary.

बरा/त [*nf*] a marriage party; ~ ती member of a marriage party.

बराबर [*a*] equal; even, level; adjoining; matching; [adv] abreast; constantly; continuously, ever, always; —करना to make even, to level, to smoothen; to ruin; to squander away; to leave nothing.

बराबरी [*nf*] equality, parity; vying, rivalry.

बरामद [*a*] recovered, seized, exposed.

बरामदा [*nm*] a verandah.

बरी [*a*] set free, acquitted; absolved.

बरौनी [*nf*] the eyelashes.

बर्ताव [*nm*] behaviour, treatment.

ब/र्फ [*nf*] ice; snow; ~ र्फ़ानी icy, snowy, snow clad; ~ र्फ़ीला snowy, icy; glacial.

बर्फ़ी [*nf*] a kind of rectangular sweetmeat prepared from खोया.

बर्बर [*a*] barbarian, savage; ~ ता barbarism, savagery.

बल [*nm*] strength power; force; potency; vigour, vitality; emphasis; stress; kink, twist, contortion; –बूता strength and vigour, strength; ~ वान powerful, strong, possessing vigour and vitality; ~ शाली. powerful, strong, possessing vigour and vitality; ~ हीन weak, powerless, having no strength; impotent; —पर कूदना, किसी के to draw one's strength from some extraneous source.

बलगम [*nm*] phlegm.

बलवा [*nm*] rebellion; riot, disturbance; ~ ई a rebel, rioter; riotous.

बला [*nf*] a calamity, an affliction; misfortune; an evil spirit; -करे/करने जाये, मेरी my foot!, why on earth shall I do that!; -का of the highest order, of miraculous proportions; extremely; —टलना to get rid of an affliction, —मोल लेना to deliberately subject oneself to an affliction, to own up a trouble.

बलात् [*ind*] forcibly; all of a sudden.

बलात्कार [*nm*] rape, ravishment, commitment of rape, criminal assault; violences; oppression.

बलि [*nf*] a sacrifice; an oblation; —चढ़ाना to sacrifice; to sacrifice oneself on another.

बलि/दान [*nm*] a sacrifice; offering; ~नी. one who has made sacrifices.

बलिष्ठ [*a*] strongest; very strong, powerful, having tremendous force/vigour/vitality.

बलिहारी [*nf*] sacrifice; —जाना to be ready to sacrifice oneself [for].

बली [*a*] strong, powerful.

बल्कि [*ind*] on the contrary, nay, but, rather.

बल्लम [*nf*] a lance, spear.

बल्ला [*nm*] a bat; racket; hence बल्लेबाज.

बल्ली [*nf*] a pole, long wooden staff.

बवंडर [*nm*] a typhoon, cyclone.

बवासीर [*nf*] piles, haemorrhoids.

बशर्ते [*ind*], —कि provided that, with the provision that, only if.

बस [*nm*] control; power; a bus; [*ind*] that's all, that'll do; enough.

बसना [*v*] to settle [down]; to inhabit; to stay; to live; to be situated/located [as a town, village, etc.]. to be imbued with [a scent etc].

बसर [*nf*] maintenance, subsistence.

बसाना [*v*] to colonize; to inhabit; to rehabilitate; to build [a city, town. etc].

बसेरा [*nm*] an abode, a dwelling; nocturnal stay; short stay.

बस्ता [*nm*] a bag, school bag, portfolio; a bundle.

बस्ती [*nf*] a settlement, satellite down, colony, inhabitation; population.

बहक [*nf*] rave, raving, incoherent talking [due to intoxication]; going astray, aberration.

बहकना [*v*] to rave; to talk incoherently; to be intoxicated; to go astray, to be aberrant; to be misled; to be enticed; to rave, to talk in an incoherent fashion.

बहकावा [*nm*] enticement, allurement; instigation.

बहत्तर [*a*] seventy-two; [*nm*] the number seventy-two.

बह/न [*nf*] a sister; ~ नापा sisterly relation [between women].

बहना [*v*] to flow, to float; to blow; to drift; to be swept away; to run; बहती गंगा में हाथ धोना to make hay while the sun shines.

बहरहाल [*ind*] at any rate, however, nevertheless, but for all that.

बहरा [*a*] deaf, hard of hearing; [fig.] heedless; hence ~पन.

बहलाना [*v*] to divert one's mind; to amuse, to recreate, to entertain; to allure, to entice.

बहलाव [*nm*] diversion; amusement; recreation; entertainment.

बहलावा [*nm*] allurement, enticement; false hope.

बहस [*nf*] a discussion, argumentation, debate; -मुबाहिसा discussion, debate.

बहादु/र [*a*] bold, brave gallant, valiant; hence ~ राना, ~ री.

बहाना [*nm*] a pretext, pretence, an excuse; make believe; [v] to cause to flow/blow; to set afloat; to squander [as पैसा बहाना]; to ruin, to destroy; बहानेबाज sham, make-believe; a pretender, given to putting forth excuses; hence बहानेबाजी.

बहार [*nf*] the spring [season], bloom; merriment; joviality.

बहा/ल [*ind*] reinstated, restored [to the original status/position]; hence ~ ली.

बहाव [*nm*] flow; flush, flux; outflow.

बही [*nf*] an account book; a register; ~खाता a ledger, an account book.

बहु [*a*] many; several; plural; ~ ज्ञ well-versed in many things, master of many trades; hence ~ ज्ञता; ~ धंधी multipurpose; variously occupied, occupied/ busy in multifarious activities; ~ पत्नी-प्रथा polygamy, polygamous system; ~ मुख/मुखी multifarious; ~ मुखता multifariousness; ~ मूल्य precious, invaluable; very costly; ~ रूपिया an expert in disguising oneself through a variety of make-up; one who assumes various forms; multimorphic; ~ विध multifarious, varied; hence ~ विधता; ~ विवाह polygamy/ployandry; ~ श्रुत well-informed; ~संख्या majority; ~ संख्यक majority.

बहुत [*a*] much; many; abundant; good deal, lots of, plenteous, plentiful; too; very much.

बहुतायत [*nf*] plenty, abundance.

बहुतेरा [*a*] much, abundant; [*adv*] in various ways, variously, fully, very much.

बहुतेरे [*a*] many, numerous.

बहुधा [*ind*] usually; in various ways; mostly, generally.

बहू [*nf*] wife; daughter-in-law; a newly-wed woman.

बहेड़ा [*nm*] the medicinal fruit of the tree Belleric myrobalan.

बहेलिया [*nm*] a hunter; fowler.

बाँक [*nf*] curvature; crookedness; a bend.

बाँ/का [a] dandy; foppish, showy, prankish; chivalrous; gallant [person]; hence ~ कपन, ~ कपना.

बाँग [*nf*] a prayer call by the Muazzin; crowing of a cock; loud shout.

बाँचना [*v*] to read, read aloud.

बाँझ [*a*] barren [woman]; unfertile, sterile [soil]; hence ~पन.

बाँट [*nm*] division, partition; distribution; [*nf*] share; deal [in the game of cards].

बाँटना [*v*] to distribute, to allocate; to apportion, to deal [in the game of cards]; to grind [with a pestle].

बाँदी [*nf*] a slave girl, bondmaid, female serf.

बाँध [*nm*] a dam; bund; dike; barrage, an embankment.

बाँधन [*v*] to tie, to fasten; to bind; to pack; to wrap around [as पगड़ी–, पट्टी].

बांधव [*nm*] brethren, kith and kin, fraternal relation.

बांबी [*nf*] an ant hill; a snake-hole.

बाँस [*nm*] a bamboo; pole; बाँसों उछलना to be in a state of rapture, to be immensely happy.

बाँसुरी [*nf*] a flute.

बाँह [*nf*] an arm; a sleeve.

बा a prefix to nouns meaning-having, containing, possessing, along with; ~अदब respectfully; respectful; humble; ~क़ायदा regular [ly], formal[ly], orderly, systematic[ally]; duly; according to rules, regular.

बाइबिल [*nf*] the Bible [Christian scripture].

बाई [*nf*] one of the three humours of the body [see बात]; gout, rheumatism; delirium; a girl/lady; a prostitute.

बाई/स [*a*] twenty-two; [*nm*] the number twenty-two; ~ सी a collection of twenty-two [verses, couplets etc].

बाएँ [*ind*] to the left, on the left-hand side.

बाकी [*ind*] but if..., but, nevertheless; [a and nf] see बाकी.

बाक़ी [*a*] remaining, left over; [*nf*] remainder; balance, arrears; subtraction.

बाग [*nf*] the reins; ~डोर the reins, halter; [*nm*] see बाग़.

बाग़ [*nm*] a garden; park; —बाग extremely delighted, very happy; ~ बान a gardener; horticulturist; hence ~ बानी.

बागान [*nm*] plantation, gardens.

बाग़ी [*a* and *nm*] [*a*] rebel; rebellious; revolting, mutineer.

बाग़ीचा [*nm*] a small garden.

बाछ [*nf*] the extremities of the lips; बाछें खिलना to be very happy, to be manifestly delighted.

बाज़ [*nm*] a hawk, falcon; a suffix appended to nouns to impart the meaning of one who does/indulges/plays with, or a performer or monger [e.g. पतंगबाज, जंगबाज]; [a] desisted; some.

बाजरा [nm] millet; pearl millet.

बाजा [*nm*] a musical instrument; band; -गाजा band; fanfare.

बाज़ार [nm] a market, market-place; -भाव market-rate; किसी चीज का–गरम होना to be rampant, to be very prevalent, to be the order of the day.

बाजा/री, ~ रू [*a*] belonging to the market place, common place, vulgar [as language]; cheap; of easy virtue.

बाज़ी [*nf*] a stake; wager, bet; play; performance; turn [as खेलने की बाज़ी किसकी है]; ~ गर an acrobat; juggler, magician; ~गरी acrobatics; jugglery, magical performance.

बाजू [*nm*] an arm; side; overside; flank; wing ~ बंद an armlet; —दायाँ lit. the right arm—the most vital/staunchest supporter.

बाट [*nf*] path, way, course; [*nm*] a weight; —जोहना/देखना to wait for, to await anxiously.

बाड़ [*nf*] a fence; hedge.

बाड़ी [*nf*] a small orchard; an enclosure; house.

बाढ़ [*nf*] a flood, freshet, spate, inundation; salvo, volley.

बाण [*nm*] an arrow.

बात [*nf*] a thing; matter, fact; point; counsel; talk; discussion; negotiation; saying; utterance, statement; commitment; word; context; credit; —काटना to cut one short, to intervence, to interrupt one in one's speech; -का धनी/पक्का/सच्चा true to one's word, faithful to one's promise; -का बतंगड़ much ado about nothing; making a mountain out of a mole-hill, to exaggerate beyond all limits; —की बात just a technicality; just a question of prestige; just to preserve one's honour; —की बात में in an instant, instantaneously, suddenly; —न करना, सीधे मुँह to be too arrogant to talk, to give no life;—न पूछना to evince no care/concern/feeling for; to care nothing for; - पकड़ना to seize censoriously on what is said, to carp or cavil at;

to take a statement rather too literally; —पचना a secret to be contained, a secret to be kept within; —पर अड़ना to be firm on one's stand, to stick unmovably to one's statement; — पूछना to pose a question; to enquire after, to evince care/concern/feeling for; —बढ़ाना to aggravate a dispute, to spin out an altercation, to make a serious affair of; —बनना to successfully attain one's aim, to answer well, things to mould as wished; to gain credit; —बनाना to talk much, to make up stories; to talk grandly. to boast; —मुँह से ले जाना to take words out of one's mouth. to anticipate and reproduce somebody's intended utterance; —में बात मिलाना to chime in, to concur; —लगना to feel hurt or offended by one's words; बातें, चिकनी-चुपड़ी oily words, flattering utterances; बातें मिलाना/लगाना to tell tales, to backbite, to calumniate; बातों में आना to be taken in; to be cajoled into accepting one's words at their face value.

बातूनी [*a* and *nm*] talkative; loquacious, garrulous; a chatter-box great talker.

बाद [*ind*] after, later, subsequently; [*adj*] subtracted, deducted; —करना/देना to deduct, to subtract; —का later; subsequent; —में later, subsequently.

बादबान [*nm*] a sail [of a boat etc.].

बादल [*nm*] a cloud; —छँटना/फटना the clouds to be diffused/scattered; —छाना the sky to be overcast with clouds; बादलों से बातें करना to be very high up in the skies.

बादशाह [*nm*] a king, ruler; a piece [the king] in chess; ~ ज़ादा a prince; ~ज़ादी a princess.

बादशाहत [*nf*] rule, government; rulership, sovereignty; kingdom.

बादशाही [*a*] kingly, royal, imperial; [*nf*] rulership.

बादा/म [*nm*] almond; ~ मी almond-coloured; light yellow; prepared from almonds.

वादी [*nf*] fat, flatulence; wind; [*a*] flatulent; windy.

बाधक [*a*] causing hindrance/obstruction/ impediment; obstructive, impedimental, troublesome.

बाधा [*nf*] a hindrance, an obstacle/obstruction, impediment; bar handicap; interference, interruption; trouble; disturbance; obsession [of an evil spirit etc.].

बाध्य [*a*] obliged, compelled, forced.

बान [*nm*] an arrow; cord of twisted grass etc. used for bottom of beds [and other purposes]; [*nf*] habit, wont, custom; a suffix that signifies a keeper, man [as दरबान].

बानगी [*nf*] a specimen, sample; foretaste.

बानबे [*a*] ninety-two; [*nm*] the number ninety-two.

बाप [*nm*] father; -दादा fore-fathers, ancestors; —रे बाप an exclamation signifying wonder, fear or agony; gosh! goodness!

बाबत [*ind*] about, pertaining to, in respect of, concerning.

बाबा [*nm*] grandfather; an old man; ascetic; —बादाम the most primitive/earliest man.

बाबुल [*nm*] father [in the context of a girl].

बाबू [*nm*] an educated man, gentleman; middle class man; a clerk.

बायस्कोप [*nm*] a biscope, movie film.

बायाँ [*a*] left, sinistral; adverse; बायें हाथ का काम/खेल a very easy job, too easy to worry about.

बायें [*ind*] to the left, in the opposite camp; adversely disposed.

बारंबार [*ind*] again and again, time and again; repeatedly.

बार [*nf*] time [*s*]; turn; [*nm*] door [in the compound घर ~]; burden, weight.

बारजा [*nm*] a balcony.

बारदाना [*nm*] the fare.

बारह [*a*] twelve; [*nm*] the number twelve; ~खड़ी the aggregate of forms a consonant in the Devanagari: alphabet assumes in combination with the vowels [e.g. क, का, कि, की, कु, के, कै, को, कौ, कं, कः); ~ मासी perennial, all weather, functioning or flowering round the year; ~ सिंगा a stag; बारहों महीने throughout the year, the whole twelve months; ~ बाट करना to scatter all round; to cast to winds: to spell ruination.

बारहवाँ [*a*] the twelfth; [nm] the twelfth day of post-death rites.

बारहा [*ind*] a number of times, time and again, repeatedly.

बारा/त [*nf*] a wedding party; ~ ती member of a wedding party.

बारादरी [*nf*] lit. having twelve doors—a house or a well-knit locality having twelve indoors/ entrances.

बारिश [*nf*] the rain, shower; the rainy season.

बारी [*nf*] a turn; millet; [*nm*] a low Hindu caste in the traditional caste set-up.

बारी/क [*a*] fine, thin; slender; subtle; ~ की fineness; subtlety.

बारूद [*nf*] gunpowder; ~खाना a magazine; ~घर a magazine.

बारे [*ind*], —में about, pertaining/relating to, in respect of.

बाल [*nm*] a hair; young one. a child; boy; a crack [in glass etc.]; [*nf*] an ear of corn; ~कमानी a spring [in a watch]; ~गोपाल the children; ~चर a boy scout; ~ संघ a boy scouts' association; -बच्चे children; family -बुद्धि puerility; childishness; boyishness; puerile, childish; boyish; -ब्रह्मचारी a life-log celebate; -रोग infantile/children's disease; -विधवा childhood widow, child widow, -विवाह early marriage, boyhood marriage; ~सफ़ा hair-removing; ~ हठ childish insistence; —की खाल खींचना/निकालना to indulge in hair-splitting; to be too carping; धूप में —पकाना to age without experience; —बराबर hair-breadth, very narrow; -बाँका न होना to remain unscathed; to emerge from an ordeal without so much as a scratch; -बाल the whole being from head to foot; hair-breadth, very narrow; -बाल बँधा होना the whole being to be under a debt; to be thoroughly bound by obligation; -बाल बचना to have a hair-breadth escape, to have a very narrow escape.

बालक [*nm*] a boy, child, minor; an ignorant person; ~पन childishness, boyishness; puerility.

बालम [*nm*] a lover, beloved; husband.

बाला [*nm*] an ear-ornament; [*nf*] an adolescent girl; young woman; [*a*] puerile; childly; high, aloft.

बालिग [*a*] adult, major; -मताधिकार adult franchise, adult suffrage.

बालिश्त [*nm*] a hand-span; —भर का too tiny.

बाली [*nf*] an ear-ring; ear of corn.

बालूका [*nf*] sand.

बालू [*nf*] sand; ~दानी a sand-box.

बालटी [*nf*] a bucket, pail.

बाल्य [*a*] of childhood; belonging to a child; —काल childhood.

बावजूद [*ind*] in spite of, despite.

बावड़ी [*nf*] a deep well with a flight of stairs down to the surface of water.

बावन [*a*] fifty-two; [*nm*] the number fifty-two; तोले पाव रत्ती proper and precise, precisely correct, balanced and correct.

बावरची [*nm*] a cook; ~ खाना the kitchen.

बावला [*a*] mad, crazy; insane; hence ~पन.

बावेला [nm] uproar, tumult, shemozzle.

बाशिंदा [*nm*] a resident, an inhabitant.

बाष्प [*nm*] steam, vapour.

बास [*nf*] foul smell, bad/disagreeable odour.

बासठ [*a*] sixty-two; [*nm*] the number sixty-two.

बासन [*nm*] household utensil.

बासा [*nm*] a habitat, dwelling place.

बासी [*a*] stale, kept overnight; -कढ़ी में उबाल old age, young ways a Lilliputian posing as a giant; -बचे न कुत्ता खाये to polish off all and leave nothing to Paul.

बाहर [*ind*] out, outside, exterior, without; beyond; away; [*nm*] a foreign land.

बाहरी [*a*] outward, external, exterior; superficial; alien.

बाहु [*nf*] an arm; ~ पाश an arm-embrace; arm-girdle; ~बल strength of one's arms, valour.

बाहुल्य [*nm*] abundance, plenty.

बाह्य [*ind*] out, outside; beyond; [*a*] external, outward, exterior; superficial; ostentatious.

बिंदी [*nf*] a point, dot; zero, cipher; a small round mark [of vermilion, sandal, etc.] on the forehead.

बिंदु [*nm*] a point, dot; zero, cipher, spot; [in Indian dramaturgy] a point in drama where a minor episode begins to take shape; **see** अनुस्वार; a drop; bull's eye [in **shooting**].

बिंब [*nm*] an image; shadow, **reflection**; the disc of sun or moon; the plant **Memordica** mondelyha.

बिकना [*v*] to be sold.

बिकाऊ [*a*] for sale, saleable.

बिक्री [*nf*] sale, marketing; disposal.

बिखरना [*v*] to be scattered/strewn; to be dispersed; to be diffused; to be dishevelled.

बिखेरना [*v*] to scatter to strew, to diffuse; to dishevel.

बिगड़ना [*v*] to be angry/enraged, to lose temper; to be spoilt/damaged; to be deteriorated; to be wasted; to follow a wrong path, to go astray, to develop bad habits/character; to be spoilt due to extravagance; to be on bad terms [as उन दोनों में बिगड़ गई है]; to go out of order [as मशीन-].

बिगाड़ [*nm*] discord, rift, friction; rancour, unhappy relations.

बिगाड़ना [*v*] to spoil; to destroy, to ruin; to damage; to put out of order; to foil; to cause to go astray.

बिगुल [*nm*] bugle.

बिचकाना [*v*] to startle; to make wry [face]; —मुँह to make a wry face.

बिचला [*a*] [belonging to the] middle, mid; central.

बिचारा [*a*] poor, helpless; ~पन helplessness.

बिच्छू [*nm*] a scorpion; nettle, prickly plant.

बिछाना [*v*] to spread out [esp. a bed or mat etc.]

बिछावन [*nm*] bedding, anything spread out.

बिछुड़ना [*v*] to part company, to get separated.

बिछोह [*nm*] separation [from the beloved].

बिजली [*nf*] electricity; lightning; thunderbolt; an ear-ornament, tops; ~घर a power house, power station.

बिटिया [*nf*] a daughter.

बिताना [*v*] to spend, to pass [time].

बित्ता [*nm*] a hand span.

बिदकना [*v*] to be alarmed/startled; to be provoked.

बिदा [*nf*] departure; farewell, adieu.

बिदाई [*nf*] a send-off, farewell, an adieu.

बिनती [*nf*] an entreaty, a request, supplication.

बिनना [*v*] to knit, to weave; to be picked up.

बिना [*ind*] without, in the absence of, minus;— बुलाये मेहमान, कोई न करता मान uninvited guests sit on thorns.

बिनाई [*nf*] the work/method/process of knitting/weaving/picking up [unwanted stuff to clean grains etc.] or the wages paid there for.

बिनौला [*nm*] cotton seed.

बियाबान [*nm*] a desert, wilderness; [*a*] uninhabited; deserted.

बिरता [*nm*] power, strength, capacity; capability.

बिरला [*a*] rare, scarce.

बिरही [*a* and *nm*] [one who is] suffering the pangs of separation.

बिराजना [*v*] to be seated, to grace [by sitting]; to grace [an occasion] by one's presence.

बिरादरी [*nf*] fraternity, brotherhood; community.

बिराना [*a*] alien, not one's own; [*v*] to offend by making wry faces, to jeer, to make mouths at.

बिरोजा [*nm*] turpentine; resin.

बिल [*nm*] burrow; hole; cavity; bill.

बिलकुल [*a* and *adv*] quite, all, complete; wholly, absolutely, completely; utter; sheer.

बिलखना [*v*] to wail, to weep bitterly, to lament.

बिलगा/ना [v] to separate/isolate, to keep aloof; to disjoin, to detach; hence ~व.

बिलटी [*nf*] a railway receipt; —काटना to despatch.

बिलबिलाना [*v*] to wriggle; to whine; to be restless with pain, to toss about in torment.

बिलाना [*v*] to disappear, to vanish.

बिलार [*nm*] a he-cat.

बिलाव [*nm*] a tom-cat, big cat.

बिलोना [*v*] to churn; to stir.

बिलौटा [*nm*] a kitten.

बिल्ला [*nm*] a tom-cat.

बिल्ली [*nf*] a cat; —का रास्ता काटना, —का रास्ता काट जाना a cat to cross one's way [taken to be an ill omen], to have an ill foreboding; —ने शेर पढ़ाया, बिल्ली को खाने आया my foot, my tutor.

बिल्लौ/र [*nm*] crystal, quartz; ~री crystalline, quartziferous.

बिवाई [*nf*] chilblain [s]; —फटना to have chilblain [s].

बिसात [*nf*] a chess-board; capacity, capability, power; —के बाहर beyond [one's] capacity.

बिसातख़ाना [*nm*] haberdashery, a general merchandise shop.

बिसाती [*nm*] a haberdasher, a general merchant.

बिसूरना [*v*] to wail, to lament; to sob.

बिस्कुट [*nf*] a biscuit.

बिस्त/र, ~रा [*nm*] a bedding, bed: ~रबंद a hold-all.

बिस्मिल्ला, ~ह [*nf*] beginning, commencement; [ind] with the name of God, a word used by Muslims at the commencement of a work; —करना to commence [an act], to make a beginning; —ही ग़लत होना to misfire at the very outset, to have a wrong beginning.

बिहा/र [*nm*] an eastern state of the Indian Union; a Buddhist monastery; ~री belonging or pertaining to बिहार; [*nm*] an inhabitant of बिहार.

बिहिश्त [*nm*] the paradise; —को ठोकर/लात मारना to kick off the greatest attraction, to reject the most attractive thing.

बींधना [*v*] to pierce, to bore a hole into.

बीघा [*nm*] a measure of land—five-eighth of an acre.

बीच [*nm*] the middle [part], centre; —का intermediary, intermediate; central, middle; -बिचाव mediātion; —में पड़ना to mediate, to act as a mediator; to interfere to cause obstruction.

बीचों (चो) बीच [*adv*] just/exactly in the middle or centre, midway.

बीज [*nm*] seed; pip; origin; beginning; germ; semen; cause; nucleus.

बीजक [*nm*] an invoice; a bill [of purchase].

बीजगणित [*nm*] Algebra.

बीट [*nf*] dung of a bird.

बीड़ा [*nf*] seasoned and folded betel-leaf; —उठाना to undertake an assignment; to accept a challenge.

बीड़ी [*nf*] bidi [crude form of cigarette rolled within a leaf].

बीतना [*v*] to pass; to be spent [as time]; to elapse; to expire; to befall/happen/occur.

बीन [*nf*] a [snake charmer's] flute; a classical Indian stringed instrument generally called वीणा.

बीनना [*v*] to pick up; to pluck [as flowers]; to choose.

बीबी [*nf*] a respected lady; a respectful word used by a woman for a younger sister of her husband.

बीभत्स [*a*] abhorrent, disgusting, loathsome; [nm] one of the nine rasas in poetry-the sentiment of abhorrence or disgust.

बीमा [*nm*] insurance.

बीमा/र [*a*] sick, ill; diseased; indisposed, unwell; [nm] a patient, valetudinarian; ~री illness, sickness, ailment; disease.

बीर [*a*] brave; intrepid; [*nm*] brother; ~न a brother [often used by a sister].

बीवी [*nf*] wife.

बीस [*a*] twenty; [nm]the number twenty.

बीहड़ [*a*] dense, thick [as जंगल]; rough and rugged; [nm] a dense forest.

बुँदकी [*nf*] a small round spot/dot; ~दार spotted, dotted.

बुंदा [*nm*] an ear-top [an ornament; a dot; point.

बुआ [*nf*] father's sister.

बुखार [*nm*] fever.

बुज़दि/ल [*a*] coward, timid; ~ली cowardice, timidness.

बुजुर्ग [*a*] elderly, old; venerable, respected; [*nm*] forefathers; elderly people; ~ वार elderly, used deferentially for old and respected people.

बुजुर्गाना [*a*] elderly; befitting elders/elderly people.

बुझाना [v] to extinguish [as आग—]; to put out [as दिया]; to quench [as प्यास]; to slake [as चूना–]; to temper by dipping into a solution of poison [as जहर में–]; to solve;—, पहेली to talk in riddles, to speak enigmatically.

बुड्ढा [*a*] old, aged, senile.

बुढ़ापा [*nm*] old age, senility.

बुढ़िया [*nf*] an old woman.

बुत [*nm*] an idol, a statue, image; [*a*] dumb and lifeless, motionless [like an image]; ~परस्त an idolater; idol-worshipper; ~परस्ती idolatry, idol-worship, iconolatry.

बुदबुदाना [*v*] to mutter; to jabber; to effervesce.

बुद्ध [*nm*] Lord Buddha.

बुद्धि [*nf*] intellect intelligence, wisdom; mind; sense; ~जीवी an intellectual; वर्ग the intellectuals.

बुद्धिमत्ता [*nf*] intelligence, wisdom, prudence.

बुद्धिमा/न [*a*] intelligent; wise, prudent; sensible, sagacious, brilliant; hence ~नी.

बुद्धू [*a*] stupid, foolish, dullard, block-headed, nincompoop; hence ~पन/पना.

बुध [*nm*] Wednesday; Mercury; [*a*] wise, intelligent, learned; ~वार Wednesday.

बुनकर [*nm*] a weaver.

बुनना [*v*] to weave, to knit, to intertwine.

बुनवाई [*nf*] the act or charges for weaving/knitting.

बुनाई [*nf*] the act, process or the wages paid for weaving/knitting; texture [of a cloth etc.].

बुनावट [*nf*] texture of a knitted/woven thing.

बुनिया/द [*nf*] foundation, base; basis; ~दी basic; fundamental; शिक्षा basic education.

बुभु/क्षा [*nf*] appetite, hunger; ~क्षित, ~क्षु hungry.

बुरक़ा [*nm*] a veil, mantle.

बुरा [*a*] bad; wicked; evil; ill [as —व्यवहार ill-treatment]; mis- [as mismanagement]; faulty; defective; —भला bad and good, loss and gain; abuse; —मानना to take ill, to resent, to feel bad; —लगना to feel bad, to be to somebody's disliking.

बुराई [*nf*] evil, vice; flaw, fault; defect; badness, wickedness.

बुरादा [*nm*] saw-dust.

बुरी [*a*] feminine form of बुरा; —संगत से अकेला भला better alone than in a bad company.

बु/र्ज [*nm*] a tower; turret, pinnacle; also ~र्जी [*nf*].

बुर्जुआ [*a* and *nm*] bourgeois; borgeoisie.

बुलं/द [*a*] high, lofty; ~दी height, loftiness.

बुलबुल [*nf*] a nightingale.

बुलबुला [*nm*] a bubble; [a] transitory, transient.

बुला/ना [*v*] to call, to summon, to send for; to invite; ~वा call, summons, invitation; also ~हट.

बुवाई [*nf*] sowing.

बुहारना [*v*] to sweep, to broom, to sweep clean.

बुहारी [*nf*] a broom.

बूंद [*nf*] a drop.

बूंदाबांदी [*nf*] a drizzle, light shower.

बू [*nf*] a disagreeable smell/odour; foul smell.

बूचड़ [*nm*] a butcher; ~खाना a slaughter-house, butchery.

बूझना [*v*] to understand, to make out; to solve; to enquire, to ask.

बूट [*nm*] a boot; gram pod, green pod of gram.

बूटा [*nf*] a large sized embroidered or printed flower design [on cloth; sa:ri: etc.]

बूटी [*nf*] a herb, medicinal plant; small flower or round design embroidered on cloth; a pip [on a playing card]; see भांग.

बूढ़ा [*a*] old, aged senile; -तोता राम-राम नहीं सीखता it is difficult to teach an old man.

बूता [*nm*] capacity; capability; power.

बूरा [*nm*] unrefined powdered sugar.

बृक [*nm*] a wolf.

वृह/त् [*a*] large; big, huge; ~त्तर larger, bigger.

वृहस्पति [*nm*] the name of the preceptor of gods according to Hindu mythology; Jupiter, the largest planet of the solar system; Thursday.

बेंच [*nf*] a bench.

बेंड़ा [*a*] oblique, crooked; difficult, unmanageable [as a man]; a draw-bar, log for fastening a door.

बेंत [*nm*] a cane, stick.

बे —a Persian prefix which imparts the meaning of without or devoid of; an interjectional particle signifying indignation and disrespect (क्यों बे?); ~अदब; ill-mannered, impolite, rude; impudent; hence ~अदबी; ~आबरू insulted, disgraced, humiliated, dishonoured; ~इज्जत disgraced humiliated. insulted; hence ~ इज्जती; ~ ईमान dishonest, unscrupulous, having no integrity; hence ~ईमानी; ~क़द्री non-appreciation; disgrace, dishonour, disrespect; ~क़रार restless, uneasy; hence ~क़रारी; ~ कली perturbed state of mind, restlessness, uneasiness; ~ कस helpless; humble; hence ~ कसी; ~ क़सूर innocent, faultless, not guilty; ~क़ाबू uncontrolled, unrestrained; beyond control; ~क़ायदा irregular; illegal; contrary to rule/law; ~कार unemployed; idle; useless; good-for-nothing; ~कारी unemployment; idleness, uselessness; ~खटके without hitch/apprehension/reserve; unhesitatingly; ~ खबर unaware, uninformed; oblivious; senseless; unconscious; hence ~ खबरी; ~ गाना alien, stranger; ~गुनाह not guilty, guiltless, innocent; hence ~गुनाही; ~ घर homeless, having no home and hearth; ~ चारा

poor, helpless; ~ चैन restless, uneasy, restive; hence ~चैनी; ~ जा improper, unfair, undue; ~ जान lifeless, dead; feeble, colourless; ~ ज़ार fed up, tired, feeling miserable, afflicted, troubled; hence ~ ज़ारी; ~ जोड़ matchless, unparalleled, unprecedented; inharmonious, incongruous; ~ टिकट without ticket, ticketless; ~डौल unsymmetrical, disproportionate; ugly; ~ ढंगा unsystematic, disorderly; unsymmetrical, silly; slovenly; ~ ढब unmanageable; crooked, outlandish; unsystematic; excessively, thoroughly; ~तकल्लुफ़ informal, observing no formality, unsophisticated; unostentatious; hence ~ तकल्लुफ़ी; ~ तरतीब unsystematic, disorderly; hence ~ तरतीबी; ~ तरह improperly; unsuitably; thoroughly, excessively, very much; ~ तहाशा at top speed, very swiftly; wildly; recklessly, indiscreetly; ~ ताव see ~ चैन; ~ ताबी see ~ चैनी; ~ तार wireless; ~ तुका absurd; irrelevant, ridiculous; silly; incongruous, inharmonious; unsymmetrical, grotesque; hence ~ पन; ~ दखल ejected, evicted, ousted, forced out; hence ~दखली; ~ दर्द cruel, heartless, hard-hearted, unsympathetic; hence दर्दी; ~ धड़क unhesitating [ly], dauntless [ly], bold [ly], intrepid [ly], fearless[ly]; ~नज़ीर unprecedented; unparalleled, peerless, matchless; ~ पनाह shelterless; helpless,very much, excessive; ~ पर की उड़ाना to talk tall, to indulge in baseless gossip, to brag; ~परदगी see ~ परदा; ~ परदा naked, unveiled, having no privacy, exposed; ~ फिक्र carefree, careless; unworried, unmindful; hence ~ फ़िक्री; ~ बस helpless; ~ बसी helplessness; ~ बाक forthright, intrepid, dauntless; ~ बाकी dauntlessness; intrepidness, forthrightness; ~ भाव unaccounted for, unlimited, boundless; ~ मन reluctant [ly], unspirited, without any enthusiasm; ~ मानी useless, meaningless, irrelevant, ridiculous; ~ मेल incoherent, inharmonious, mismatched; ~ रहम cruel, merciless; hence ~ रहमी; ~ रुखी inconsiderateness, indifference, disregard; ~ रोक टोक unobstructed, unhampered; smoothly, unhesitatingly, without any hitch; ~ रोज़गार unemployed; ~ रोजगारी unemployment; ~ लाग frank, forthright, straightforward; without any circumlocution; ~ लौस frank, forthright, indulging in no pleasantries; ~ वफ़ा infidel, faithless, disloyal; ~ वफ़ाई infidelity, faithlessness; ~ शऊर mannerless, silly, slovenly, slipshod; knowing no etiquette; hence ~ शऊरी; ~ शक of course; certainly, undoubtedly; ~शरम/शर्म shameless; ~ शरमी/शर्मी shameless; ~ शुमार innumerable countless, numberless; ~ सब्र impatient; restive; fidgety; hence ~सब्री; ~ सुध. senseless; unconscious; careless, carefree; ~ सुर/सुरा out of tune, inharmonious; inopportune; ~ हया shameless; ~ हयाई shamelessness; ~ हाल miserable, in a sad plight, distressed, afflicted; ~ हिसाब unlimited, infinite; too much, very much; ~ होश unconscious, senseless; fainted; in a swoon; hence ~ होशी.

बेग [*nm*] a word deferentially appended to the name of Mohammedans of Moghut lineage; a bag.

बेगम [*nf*] a [Muslim] lady; Mrs. बेगमात plural of बेगम; बेगमी pertaining to or belonging to a बेगम.

बेगा/र [*nf*] forced labour, unremunerative work; drudgery; one who is made to work without remuneration/wages; ~ री forced labour; the act of forcing some one to do unremunerative work.

बेचना [*v*] to sell, to vend; to dispose of.

बे/टा [*nm*] a son; hence ~ टी [*nf*].

बेड़ा [*nm*] a fleet; raft; —पार करना/लगाना to cause to reach one's destination, to salvage, to help achieve one's end, to help one cross over; —पार होना to reach one's destination, to achieve the end, to cross over.

बेड़ी [*nf*] fetters, shackles.

बेध [*nm*] bore; astronomical observation; ~ शाला an observatory.

बेधना [*v*] to pierce; to puncture; to bore.

बेर [*nm*] a plum, jujube.

बेल [*nm*] wood-apple—Angle mamelos; [*nf*] a creeper, flowery decoration-lace.

बेलदा/र [*nm*] a labourer; ~ री labourer's job.

बेलन [*nm*] a roller, cylinder.

बेलना [*nm*] a roller [for rolling kneaded flour into flat round breads/cakes]; [*v*] to roll kneaded flour into flat cake/bread.

बेला [*nm*] a variety of jasmine; a kind of violin; a household utensil; [*nf*] time; sea-shore.

बेवा [*nf*] a widow.

बेशक़ीम/त, ~ती [*a*] costly, precious; invaluable.

बेशी [*nf*] excess.

बेसन [*nm*] gram flour.

बेहत/र [*a*] bank; ~ री betterment; well-being.

बैंक [*nm*] a bank; ~ र a banker.

बैंग/न [*nm*] brinjal; ~ नी violet; violet-coloured.

बैजनी [*a*] see बैगनी.

बैंड [*nm*] a band.

बै [*nf*] sale [of a farm or plot of land, etc.]; ~ नामा the sale deed [of a plot of land farm, etc.].

बैंकुठ [*nm*] the paradise; ~ धाम the paradise; ~ वासी, ~ वासी deceased, late.

बैटरी [*nf*] a battery; torch.

बैठक [*nf*] sitting, meeting; drawing room; a kind of exercise performed by repeated alternation of sitting and standing postures; a seat; base; a pedestal [of an idol]; ~खाना a drawing room; ~ बाज habituated to prolonged sittings [devoted to gossiping, idle talk, etc.]; hence ~ बाजी.

बैठना [*v*] to sit; to squat; to occupy a seat; to cling; to settle down; to sink; to be adjusted; to be satisfied [as a condition, provision etc.]; to withdraw [as from a contest]; to be without occupation/work; to appear [in some examination]; to cave in; to crash down; to ride on; to fit in; to live as wife; to become adept [as हाथ].

बैत [*nm*] couplet; verse; ~बाजी a verse-reciting competition.

बैताल [nm] a bard, minstrel; ghost.

बैरंग [*a*] bearing [letter]; —लौटना to return empty-handed, to fail in the one's mission.

बैर [*nm*] enmity, animosity, hostility; —मोल लेना to knowingly create bad blood, to antagonize somebody deliberately.

बैरा [*nm*] a bearer [in a hotel etc.].

बैरागी [*nm*] a recluse; a sect of वैष्णव saints.

बैरिस्ट/र [*nm*] a barrister-at-law; hence ~ री.

बैरी [*nm* and *a*] an enemy, [a foe: hostile; hence बैरिन [*nf*].

बैरोमीटर [*nm*] a barometer.

बैल [*nm*] an ox, a bullock; गाड़ी a bullock-cart.

बैलून [*nm*] a balloon.

बैशाख [*nm*] the second month of the year according to the Hindu calendar.

बैशाखी [*nf*] a Hindu festival celebrated on the full moon; day of the month of बैशाखी; a crutch [used by a lame person while walking].

बोआई [*nf*] [the act, process of or wages paid for] sowing:

बोझ [*nm*] a burden; load; -उतरना to be relieved of a burden; to be relieved of a responsibility.

बोझिल [*a*] heavy, weighty; burdensome.

बोटी [*nf*] a chop, piece or slice of flesh; —बोटी करना/काटना to mince; to cut into small pieces; —बोटी फड़कना to be very fidgety. to be restive; the whole being to be filled with a thrill.

बोतल [*nf*] a bottle.

बोदा [*a*] timid, meek, lazy; hence ~पन.

बोध [*nm*] perception, sense, knowledge; understanding; ~गम्य intelligible, understandable.

बोधिसत्व [*nm*] lit. one whose essence is perfect knowledge, one who is on the way to attainment of perfect knowledge or Enlightenment [i.e. a Buddhist saint when he has only one birth to undergo before attaining the state of a Supreme Buddha and then Nirva:n].

बोनस [*nm*] bonus.

बोना [*v*] to sow, to plant.

बोरा [*nm*] a bag, sack, gunnybag.

बोरिया [*nf*] a small sack or gunny-bag;-बँधना/बिस्तर one's belongings, household effects/goods; ~उठाना/समेटना/सँभालना to make preparations for departure, to leave.

बोरी [*nf*] a small sack or gunny bag.

बोर्ड [*nm*] a board.

बोर्डिंग हाउस [*nm*] a boarding house, hostel.

बोल [*nm*] speech; utterance; opening words of a song taunt; -चाल conversation, talk; speaking terms; ~का colloquial;–पट the talkie.

बोलना [*v*] to speak, to utter; to pronounce; to bid [as बोली-].

बोलबाला [*nm*] overbearing influence, away.

बोलाचाली [*nf*] speaking terms.

बोली [*nf*] a dialect; mode of speaking; bid [in auction]; taunt. sarcastic remraks; —कसना/बोलना/मारना to taunt; to make slighting remarks;—देना/बोलना/लगाना to bid [in auction]; बोली बोलने/लगाने वाला a bidder.

बोहनी [*nf*] the first sale of the day, commencement of sale.

बौखला/ना [*v*] to be furious, to fret and fume, to be terribly enraged; ~हट fury, rage.

बौछार [*nf*] a shower, drift of rain, splash.

बौड़म [*a* and *nm*] stupid, silly, nincompoop; hence ~पन.

बौद्ध [*a*] pertaining or belonging to Lord Buddha or the religion propounded by him; ~धर्म/मत Buddhism, Buddhist faith.

बौद्धिक [*a*] intellectual; hence ~ता.

बौना [*nm* and *a*] a dwarf, pigmy; dwarfish.

ब्याज [*nm*] interest [on money]; ~खोर a usurer; ~खोरी usury; -दर-ब्याज compound interest.

ब्याना [*v*] to foal, to reproduce, to give birth to [used only in the context of animals].

ब्याह [*nm*] marriage, wedding.

ब्याहता [*a*] married [woman]; [*nf*] wife, lawfully married woman.

ब्याहना [*v*] to marry [off], to wed; to get somebody married.

ब्यूरो [*nm*] a bureau.

ब्योंत [*nm*] measurements, cutting of a cloth for tailoring. used as the second member in the compound कतर-ब्योंत meaning contriving and manipulating.

ब्योंतना [*v*] to cut the cloth according to measurements; to take the measurement [of a person's garment].

ब्यो/रा [*nm*] details, particulars; ~रेवार detailed systematic.

ब्रज [*nm*] see ब्रजभाषा; the tract of land around and near Mathura: where Lord Krishnā is supposed to have grown into an adolescent youth amongst all the fun and frolics of his cowherd mates which have found expression in various Indian languages; also ~भूमि/मंडल.

ब्रजभाषा [*nf*] a dialect of Hindi spoken in the ब्रज area.

ब्रह्म [*nm*], God, the Eternal spirit; a knowledge; ~ ज्ञ/ज्ञानी one who has realized God/the Supreme Spirit; one who has acquired Eternal knowledge; ~ ज्ञान divine knowledge; realisation of the Supreme Spirit; ~ भोज collective feeding of the Bra:hmāns; ~ विद्या theology; ~हत्या murder/assassination of a bra:hmān.

ब्रह्मचर्य [*nm*] the first of the four stages (आश्रम) in a man's life as prescribed by the Hindu scriptures extending till the twenty-fifth year during which one is expected to live strictly as a celebate dedicated to the consummation of his educational efforts under his preceptor's direction and guidance.

ब्रह्मचारी [*nm*] a celebate; one who is in the ब्रह्मचर्य आश्रम.

ब्रह्मांड [*nm*] the universe, cosmos; - विद्या cosmology.

ब्रह्मा [*nm*] one of the trinity of mythological Hindu deities, the Creator.

ब्राह्म [*a*] pertaining or belonging to ब्रह्म/ब्रह्मा/ब्राह्मण, —मुहूर्त the small hours of the morning; —विवाह. marriage solemnized according to the prescribed Hindu traditions wherein the daughter is given away in marriage to a suitable match.

ब्राह्मण [*nm*] the first of the four castes in traditional Hindu Social hierarchy whose main duty, as prescribed, was to study, to teach, to perform यज्ञ and to subsist through alms; the theological portion of the Vedas; ~त्व brahmanhood; the quality, duty, privilege or dignity of a brahmāñ.

ब्राह्मी [*nf*] a medicinal plant; a widely used ancient Indian script which was the source of evolution of the Devanagari: and other indigenous Indian scripts.

ब्राह्मणी [*nf*] brāhmaṇ woman, wife of a brāhman

ब्रिगे/ड [*nm*] a brigade [in an army]; ~ डियर a brigadier.

ब्रिटिश [*a*] the British, English; —राज the British rule.

ब्रेक [*nm*] a brake.

ब्रैकेट [*nm*] a bracket.

ब्याज [*nm*] pretext, pretence; see ब्याज [and entries thereunder].

ब्लेड [*nm*] a blade.

ब्लैक [*nm*] black market, में बेचना, to sell on the black market.

भ the fourth letter of the fifth and ultimate pentad [i.e. पवर्ग] of the Devanagari: alphabet.

भ - देवनागरी वर्णमाला (व्यंजन) में पवर्ग का चौथा वर्ण है। इसका उच्चारण स्थान ओष्ठ है।

भंग [*nm*] dissolution, breach, split; disbandment, destruction; fracture; [nf] an intoxicating drug made from the leaves of Cannabis saliva, hemp; ~ ड़/ ~ ड़ी [one who is] addicted to the consumption of भंग in a large quantity.

भंगड़ [*nm*] a drinker of भाँग.

भँगड़ा [*nm*] a Punjabi folk-dance.

भँगरा [*nm*] a medicinal plant.

भंगराज [*nm*] the racket-tailed drongo.

भंगिमा [*nf*] pose, posture; curvature; obliquity.

भंगी [*nm*] a sweeper, scavenger; a low caste in the traditional Hindu caste set-up; see भंगिमा.

भँगेड़ा [*adj*] addicted to bhang.

भंगुर [*a*] brittle, fragile; transient; perishable; hence ~ता.

भजन [*nm*] [the act of] breaking, breach; fracture; destruction, ruination: demolition.

भँजना [*v.t.*] changing money, a sum of money to be changed, folding, twisting.

भंडा [*nm*] a secret; —फूटना a secret to be exposed/ revealed/leaked.

भंडाफोड़ [*nm*] exposure/revelation [of a secret].

भंडा/र [*nm*] a store, storehouse, storage, depository; emporium; hence ~ री.

भंडारा [*nm*] a feast for all, esp. the mendicants.

भँवर [*nm*] a whirlpool, swirl; eddy; ~ जाल the whirlpool of mundane bonds, the net of worldly affairs.

भँवरा [*nm*] a black bee.

भक्त [*nm*] devotee.

भक्ता [*nf*] devotedness, faith.

भक्ति [*nf*] devotion; ~पूर्वक devotedly; in a devoted manner.

भक्षक [*a* and *nm*] [one] that eats/devours; eater; destroyer.

भक्षण [*nm*] eating, feeding [on], devouring.

भक्षणीय [*adj*] proper to be eaten, fit to eat, edible.

भक्ष्य [*a*] eatable, edible; [nm] diet, food, feed.

भगंदर [*nm*] fistula in the anus.

भग [*nf*] the female genital, vulva.

भगत [*nm* and *a*] [a] devotee, one having a religious bent of mind; hence भगतिन [feminine].

भगदड़ [*nf*] rout, stampede, running helter-skelter; panic.

भगवा [*a*] saffron [coloured].

भगवान् [*nm*] God, Lord Almighty.

भगाना [*v*] to drive off; to scare away; to cause to run away; to kidnap; to abduct.

भगिनी [*nf*] a sister.

भगोड़ा [*nm* and *a*] [a] fugitive, truant; runaway.

भग्न [*a*] broken, shattered; demoralised.

भग्नावशेष [*nm*] wreckage, ruins.

भजन [*nm*] a devotional song, hymn; repetition of the name of God; -पूजन devotion and adoration.

भजना [*v*] to repeat the name of God, to remember God; to be engaged in devotional practices; ~ नंदी concentrated in and enjoying devotional chores.

भजनीक [*nm*] one who sings devotional songs while delivering religious discourses.

भट [*nm*] a soldier, a warrior.

भटकना [*v*] to lose one's way; to go astray; to gad, to meander, to wander about.

भटियारखाना [*nm*] an inn-keeper's abode; a noisecentre, dwelling of lowly vulgar people.

भटिया/रा [*nm*] an innkeeper; hence ~ रिन, ~ री [*nf*].

भट्ट [nm] a bard; scholarly brahmān.

भट्/टा, ~ ठा [*nm*] a kiln, furnace.

भट्/टी, ~ ठी [*nf*] a fireplace; an oven; a distillery.

भड़क [*nf*] gaud; show, pomp, ostentation, tawdry [generally used in this sense as the second member in the compound तड़क-भड़क]; flare; blaze.

भड़कना [*v*] to flare up; to be provoked/excited/enraged; to burst forth; to go ablaze, to blow up into flame; to be startled.

भड़कीला [*a*] gaudy, showy; tawdry; provocative; hence ~ पन.

भड़भड़ [*nf*] impetuosity; rashness, thoughless haste, hastiness; thump.

भड़भड़ाना [*v*] to be impetuous, to be rash, to be thoughtlessly hasty; to thump.

भड़भूँजा [*nm*] one whose profession is to patch grain [cereals] and sell the same; a subcaste amongst the Hindus who subsist by the said profession.

भड़ास [*nf*] stored up spite, accumulated grudge.

भड़ुआ [*nm*] professional procurer; tout; parasite on the earnings of a prostitute.

भती/जा [*nm*] a nephew; ~ जी a niece.

भत्ता [*nm*] an allowance.

भदंत [*a*] honourable, reverend; adored.

भदेस [*a*] rustic, unsophisticated; disproportionate, clumsy; hence ~ पन.

भद्दा [*a*] ugly, clumsy, ungainly, unseemly, gawky; unsymmetrical; obscene, vulgar, dirty; untoward; hence ~पन.

भद्र [a] gentle, good, boble; auspicious; an ancient courteous form of address.

भनक [*nf*] a ring, low/inarticulate sound; clue.

भनभनाना [*v*] to hum, to buzz; to be infuriated, to go on venting one's anger in low tones.

भनभनाहट [*nf*] hum [ming], buzz [ing].

भबका [*nm*] a still retort, an alembic, blast of a furnace; sudden emission of stench.

भबकी [*nf*] a bluff, hollow threat.

भभक [*nf*] flaring, sudden burst into flame, sudden blaze; sudden emission of stench.

भभकना [*v*] to flare up; to burst suddenly into flame, to blaze; to be provoked, to burst into a fit of fury.

भभूत [*nf*] sacred sacrificial ashes applied to the forehead or other parts of the body by devotees; —रमाना to renounce the world, to turn an ascetic.

भयंकर [*a*] fearful, frightful, dreadful, terrible, horrible, dangerous; hence ~ ता.

भय [*nm*] fear, fright, dread, horror, scare, danger.

भयभीत [*a*] afraid, frightened, terrified, horrified, fear-stricken.

भयानक [*a*] dreadful, terrible, horrible frightened, fearful, dangerous.

भयावना [*a*] terrifying/terrible, horrifying/horrible, frightening; awful.

भयावह [*a*] causing fear/terror/horror, frightening, horrible, terrible; awful.

भर [*nm*] a sub-caste amongst the Hindus traditionally deemed as untouchable; [*a*] all, whole, entire, full, complete; [*adv*] through, by means of; used as a suffix to denote that which or one who contains or carries, ~ पाई quittance, payment in full; receipt acknowledging payment in full; ~पूर full, full to the brim; thorough; fully, complete [ly], thoroughly; plentiful, forceful; ~सक as far as possible, to the best of one's ability, with all one's might; utmost.

भरण [*nm*] alimentation, nourishing; feeding; bearing; ~ पोषण alimentation, maintenance, maintaining, subsistence.

भरत/खंड [*nm*] Bha:rat [varsha] — i.e. India; ~ भूमि India; ~वाक्य the concluding benedictory verse in traditional Sanskrit drama.

भरती [*nf*] recruitment; enrolment; admission; packing, filling or helping to fill a void.

भरना [*v*] to fill, to refil; to impregnate; to stuff, to heal [as a घाव]; to load [as बंदूक]; to become fleshy; to match in; भरा हुआ full of rage, having long accumulated grudge.

भरम [*nm*] illusion; secret; credit.

भरमाना [*v*] to create an illusion; to mislead, to cause to go astray; to delude, to hoodwink.

भरमार [*nf*] super-abundance, abundance, plenty.

भराव [*nm*] filling; fleshiness; stuffing; packing piece; embankment.

भरोसा [*nm*] trust, faith, confidence, reliance.

भर्त्ता [*nm*] one who provides maintenance/sustenance; lord; husband.

भर्त्तार [*nm*] husband; Master.

भर्त्सना [*nf*] admonition, reproach.

भर्राना [*v*] to whizz; [throat] to be choked; [voice] to turn hoarse.

भलमनसाहत [*nf*] gentlemanliness, nobility.

भलमनसी [*nf*] see भलमनसाहत.

भला [*a*] gentle, noble, good; [*nm*] well-being; good; ~ ई gentleness; goodness; well-being, welfare; good; -चंगा hale and hearty, healthy, in good health; sound; reasonably good; -बुरा good and evil; good and bad; virtue and vice; one's own interest; reproach, admonition; ~ मानस a gentleman, good/noble person.

भले [*ind*] well! good!; -ही even if, even though.

भव [*ind*] the world; mundane existence; birth; Lord Shiv; -चक्र the perpetual wheel of birth and death; -बंधन the mundane bond, the bond of existence, the inevitability of recurrent births and deaths; -भय the fear of recurrent births and deaths; -मोचन God —who liberates the soul from worldly bonds; -समुद्र/सागर/सिंधु the ocean of mundane existence.

भव/दीय [*ind*] yours; yours sincerely; yours faithfully; -दीया feminine form of भवदीय.

भवन [*nm*] a house; building, mansion; an edifice.

भवानी [*nf*] goddess Durga: —the spouse of Lord Shiv (भव.)

भवितव्य ~ ता, ~ [*a*] fated; inevitable.

भविष्य [*nm*] the future; ~ दर्शी a seer, one who can see through into the future; ~ वक्ता a prophet; an astrologer; ~ वाणी an oracle,prediction, prophecy.

भविष्यत् [*a*] future, that is yet to come; [*nm*] the future tense;—काल the future tense.

भव्य [*a*] grand; divine; pretty; hence ~ ता.

भस्म [*nf*] ash, cinders calx; ~ सात् reduced to ashes, burnt to ashes.

भस्मावशेष [*a*] reduced to ashes, surviving only in the form of ashes.

भस्मीभूत [*a*] burnt to ashes, completely burnt; ruined.

भहराना [*v*] to crash down; to give way all of a sudden.

भाँग [*nf*] the intoxicating hemp-Cannabis sativa.

भाँजी [*nf*] back-biting, censure; —मारना to create obstacles [in the way of], to hamper accomplishment of.

भाँड़ [*nm*] a clown, buffoon, jester.

भाँड़ा [*nm*] a utensil; —फूटना to be exposed, a secret to become public.

भांडा/र [*nm*] a store, store-house; ~ रिक, ~ री a store-keeper; custodian of a store-house.

भाँति [*nf*] kind, type; manner, mode, method; -भाँति varied; variegated; of different types/kinds.

भाँपना [*v*] to guess the [undisclosed] truth, to look through the reality; to make out, to divine.

भाँपू [*a*] adept in guessing/looking through the truth; [nm] [one] who reaches the essence of a secret.

भाँवर [*nf*] circumambulation of the sacrificial fire made by both the bride and the bridegroom at the wedding time, going round; भाँवरें पड़ना the wedding to be solemnized, to be married.

भाई [*nm*] a brother; ~ चारा fraternity, brotherhood, fraternisation, fraternal understanding; -बंद kith and kin, relation, brethren.

भाग [*nm*] portion, part, fragment, fraction, share, luck, division; ~फल the quotient; ~वंत/वान fortunate, lucky; —खुलना/जागना to have an advent of good luck, to have a run of good luck; to be graced by the smile of Dame Luck; —फूटना to have a stroke of misfortune, to have a run of ill-luck, adverse times to commence.

भाग-दौड़ [*nf*] running about; strenuous effort.

भागना [*v*] to run, to run away, to escape; to flee; to take to heels; to abscond, to give the slip; to make off; to elope [with].

भागी [*a* and *nm*] a co-sharer, partner; participant.

भाग्य [*nm*] fortune, fate, luck; destiny; ~परायण a fatalist; ~परायणता fatalism; -बल the force of luck/fortune; -लिपि/लेख the writ of destiny; ~वश luckily, fortunately; ~वाद fatalism; ~वादी a fatalist; ~वान lucky fortunate; -विधाता fortune-maker, controller of destiny, providence; -विधान providence; ~हीन unlucky, unfortunate, ill-fated.

भाजक [*nm*] divisor; [a] dividing.

भाजन [*nm*] utensil, vessel, container; one who deserves; used as a suffix with nouns to mean one who enjoys/suffers/deserves.

भाजी [*nf*] a vegetable [cooked or otherwise].

भाज्य [*nm*] a divided; [*a*] divisible; -फल the quotient.

भाट [*nm*] a bard, minstrel: sycophant.

भाटा [*nm*] the ebb [tide], low tide, falling tide.

भाड़ [*nm*] a parcher's oven.

भाड़ा [*nm*] fare, rent, freight.

भात [*nm*] boiled rice.

भादों [nm] the sixth month of the year according to the Hindu calendar.

भाद्रपद [*nm*] see भादों.

भान [*nm*] change [of small denomination] ; awareness; inkling.

भानजा [*nm*] a sister's son; hence भानजी [*nf*].

भाना [*v*] to be liked, to be agreeable, to be pleasing/appealing.

भाप [nf] steam, vapour.

भाभी [nf] a sister-in-law, brother's wife.

भार [*nm*] load; weight, burden; encumbrance; onus, obligation; responsibility; ~वाह/वाहक /वाही a carrier; porter; —उठाना, किसी का to bear the responsibility of, to undertake the responsibility of.

भारत [*nm*] India; ~माता mother India; ~वर्ष India, the Indian subcontinent; ~वासी an Indian, a native of India.

भारती [*nf*] speech, Saraswati: —the goddess of speech; letters: mother India.

भारतीय [*a* and *nm*] [*an*] Indian—a native of India; pertaining to India; ~करण Indianisation; ~कृत Indianised; ~ता Indianness.

भारी [*a*] heavy; difficult to digest; weighty, massive; grave; burdensome; hence ~पन. -भरकम voluminous, heavy, large-sized; of massive structure; profound.

भार्या [*nf*] wife, better half.

भाला [*nm*] a spear, lance, javelin.

भालू [*nm*] a bear.

भाव [*nm*] emotion, sentiment, feeling; idea; rate, quotation; existence, existing state; being; sense, purport, gist; nature, temperament, disposition; -प्रकाश (न) expression of one's sentiment; -प्रधान primarily emotional; dominated by emotion, emotional; -प्रवण sentimental, emotional; -प्रवणता sentimentality, emotional disposition; -बोध the comprehension of a sentiment; emotive content; ~बोधक expressive; -रूप abstract, intangible, existing only on a mental plane; existent; ~वाचक ~ वाची abstract; ~वाच्य neutral voice; denoting the abstract notion of verb; ~व्यंजक expressive: ~शून्य devoid of emotion; unattached; insensitive; hence ~शून्यता; ~ हीन cold, devoid of emotion, unemotional, unfeeling.

भावक [*a*] appreciative; [*nm*] one who is gifted with the faculty of appreciation.

भावज [*nf*] sister-in-law; brother's wife.

भावन [*nm*] conception; comprehension; thinking; hence भावित.

भावना [*nf*] sentiment, feeling, emotion; ~त्मक emotional, emotive; sentimental.

भावानुवाद [*nm*] free translation.

भावार्थ [*nm*] sense; purport, substance.

भावी [*a*] future, coming.

भावुक [*a*] sentimental; emotional; hence ~ता.

भावोत्कर्ष [*nm*] emotional excellence/elevation.

भावोन्मत [*a*] overwhelmed by emotion, emotion-crazy.

भावोन्मेष [*nm*] advent/emergence of an emotion or sentiment.

भाषण [nm] speech; address; -कला elocution; ~कार a speaker.

भाषांतर [*nm*] translation, rendering into another language; interpretation; ~कार a translator; interpreter.

भाषा [*nf*] language; speech; -विज्ञान/शास्त्र linguistics; philology; ~बिंदु a linguist; -वैज्ञानिक/ शास्त्री linguistician; philologist; linguistic; philological; -वैज्ञानिक/~शास्त्रीय linguistic; philological.

भाषाई [*a*] linguistic.

भाषिक [*a*] linguistic.

भाष्य [nm] commentary, annotation; ~कार commentator.

भास [*nm*] brilliance, brightness; appearance; ~मंत brilliant, bright, flashing; ~मान appearing; apparent.

भिंडी [*nf*] [the vegetable called] lady's finger.

भिक्षा [*nf*] alms, charity; begging; -वृत्ति a beggar's occupation, beggary.

भिक्षु [*nm*] a beggar; Buddhist mendicant; hence ~णी [nf].

भिक्षुक [*nm*] a beggar.

भिखारिणी [*nf*] a begging woman, a female beggar.

भिखारी [*nm*] a beggar; pauper.

भिगोना [*v*] to wet; to drench; to soak; to moisten.

भिड़ंत [*nf*] clash, skirmish; encounter, confrontation; fighting hand to hand.

भिड़ [*nf*] a wasp; —का छत्ता a cluster of wasps; an irritable lot.

भिड़ना [*v*] to collide; to clash; to quarrel.

भितल्ला [*nm*] the inner side [of a cloth]; the lining.

भिदना [*v*] to penetrate; to be pierced; to be absorbed; to be assimilated.

भिनकना [*v*] to hum/buzz; to swarm; to be extremely shabby/dirty [so as to invite humming bees/flies].

भिनभिनाना [*v*] to go on buzzing/humming.

भिन्न [*a*] separate, different, distinct; diverse, dissimilar, [*nf*] a fraction; ~ता difference, distinction, dissimilarity.

भिन्नाना [*v*] to feel indignation [e.g. तबीयत—]; to feel giddy [e.g. सिर—].

भिश्ती [*nm*] a water-carrier.

भींचना [*v*] to grasp tightly; to tighten, to hold close together [as ओठ भींचना]; to bring heavy weight to bear [on]; to squeeze.

भी [*ind*] also; too; even.

भीख [*nf*] alms; begging.

भीगना [*v*] to get wet, to be soaked; to be drenched; to moisten; भीगी बिल्ली बनना to be very meek and quite, to behave in too submissive manner.

भीड़ [*nf*] a crowd; mob, multitude; crisis [e.g. भीड़ पड़ना]; -भड़क्का/भीड़ hustle, a jostling crowd, rush.

भीत [*a*] afraid; terrified, horrified, scared, fear-stricken; [nf] a wall.

भीतर [*ind*] in, inside, within; –ही भीतर within oneself, in the heart of hearts; in a clandestine fashion, on the quiet.

भीतरी [*a*] internal; interior, inner, inward; secret; unexpressed.

भीति [*nf*] fear, fright, scare, terror; awe; phobia.

भीनी [*a*] pleasant, sweet [smell]; used as a suffix with nouns to mean impregnated/filled/saturated with etc. [as भावभीनी, रसभीनी].

भीम [*a*] terrible, awful; gigantic, tremendous.

भीरु [*a*] timid, coward; fearing; shy; hence ~ता.

भील [*nm*] a tribe inhabiting the Indian states of Madhya Pradesh, Rajastha:n etc.

भीषण [*a*] fearful, frightening, scaring; awful; tremendous; hence ~ ता.

भीष्म [a] terrible, awful, horrible.

भुक्क(क्ख)ड़ [*a*] starving/starved, hungry; voracious, gluttonous.

भुक्त [*a*] enjoyed; used; consumed; ~भोगी experienced; one who has enjoyed or suffered [certain experiences].

भुक्ति [*nf*] enjoyment; use, possession.

भुख/मरा [*a*] starving/starved, hungry; voracious, gluttonous; ~मरी starvation; famine; hunger.

भुगतना [*v*] to suffer, to bear; to undergo; to be accomplished/concluded.

भुगतान [*nm*] payment; delivery; settlement.

भुगताना [*v*] to pay; to deliver; to settle; to conclude, to accomplish.

भुजंग [*nm*] a snake, serpent; hence भुजंगी [*nf*]; also ~म.

भुजा [*nf*] an arm; side of a geometrical figure.

भुट्टा [*nm*] maize-corn.

भुतनी [*nf*] a female ghost; a woman having utterly dishevelled looks.

भुनगा [*nm*] an insect; a maggot; an inconsequential creature.

भुनभुनाना [*v*] gabbering; inarticulate non-stop expression of indignation/petulance/rage.

भुनाना [*v*] to get parched; to encash, to cash; to change [into smaller denomination currency].

भुरभुरा [*a*] crisp; friable; dry and powdery; hence ~पन.

भुलक्कड़ [*a*] forgetful temperamentally prone to forget.

भुलावा [*nm*] an illusion, feint, dodge.

भुवन [*nm*] the world; earth.

भुस [*nm*] straw, chaff.

भूंकना [*v*] to bark; to gabble [said indignantly in respect of a human being].

भूंजना [*v*] to parch; to blast.

भू [*nf*] the earth; the world; ground; soil; land; a suffix denoting born of [as स्वयंभू, मनोभू]; ~धर a mountain; ~मंडल the earth, the globe; ~लोक the earth; the present world; ~विद् a geologist; ~विद्या geology; ~वैज्ञानिक a geologist.

भूकंप [*nm*] an earthquake; seism; ~ विज्ञान/शास्त्र seismology.

भूख [*nf*] hunger, appetite; desire; -हड़ताल hunger strike.

भूखा [*a*] hungry; esurient; craving.

भूगर्भ [*nm*] underground; the interior of the earth; ~विज्ञान/विद्या/शास्त्र geology; ~वैज्ञानिक/शास्त्री a geologist; ~वैज्ञानिक/शास्त्रीय geological.

भूगोल [*nm*] geography, ~वेत्ता a geographer.

भूचाल [*nm*] see भूकंप.

भूटानी [*a*] pertaining or belonging to Bhu:ṭa:n situated in north of असम; [*nf*] Bhu:ṭa:nī: language; [*nm*] a native of Bhu:ṭa:n.

भूत [*a*] past, bygone; [*nm*] a ghost, an evil spirit; matter; one of the five elements (पृथ्वी, जल, वायु, अग्नि) and आकाश — the ether]; any animate or inanimate object of creation; the past tense [also ~काल); a suffix which means 'become' 'turned' or 'rendered' [as घनीभूत, पूंजीभूत]; ~ काल the past [tense]; ~ कालिक pertaining to the past or past tense; ~नाथ an epithet of Lord Shiv; ~पूर्व ex, former, past, previous; -प्रेत evil spirits; ~विद्या ghostology.

भूतत्त्व/विज्ञान [*nf*] geology; ~विज्ञ/विद् a geologist; ~वैज्ञानिक a geologist; geological scientist.

भूतल [*nm*] the surface of the earth; the world.

भूदान [*nm*] gift of land; a movement launched by Acha:rya Vinoba Bhave [in India] for the gifting away of land by big land-owners for the betterment of the landless.

भूनना [*v*] to parch; to fry; to broil; to roast; to blast; to smash; to reduce to ashes.

भूप, ~ ति [*nm*] a king, an emperor.

भूपाल, भूपेंद्र [*nm*] a king, an emperor.

भूमध्य [*nm*] the middle of the earth; ~रेखा the equator; —सागर the mediterranean sea.

भूमि [*nf*] the earth; land; soil; zone; ~गत underground; sub-terranean; ~धारी a land holder or owner; -लोक the earth; -विज्ञान pedology.

भूमिका [*nf*] introduction, preface; background; role; —बाँधना to prepare the background.

भूरा [*a*] brown, grey.

भूरि [*a*] much, very much; -भूरि very much.

भूल [*nf*] a slip, error; lapse, omission, mistake; fault; over-sight; -चूक a lapse, error; -भुलैया a labyrinth, maze; -सुधार correction, rectification; errata.

भूलना [*v*] to forget; भूला-भटका strayed, one who has lost his way.

भूषण [*nm*] an ornament; decoration, anything decorative, embellishment.

भूसा [*nm*] cut-straw; chaff; —भरना lit. to beat hollow and fill with straw; to beat blue and black.

भूसी [*nf*] husk, bran.

भृकुटि [*nf*] eyebrow; frown; —चढ़ना to frown; to scowl, to get into a temper.

भेंट [*nf*] present, gift. offering; meeting, interview.

भेंटना [*v*] to embrace; to meet.

भेजना [*v*] to send [forth], to cause to go; to transmit; to remit; to consign.

भेजा [*nm*] the brain; [*a*] sent; —खाना to pester [with persistent queries, doubts, clarifications, etc.]

भेड़ [*nf*] a sheep; timid person; —चाल the tendency of following blindly in others' footsteps; mobmentality.

भेड़ा [*nm*] a ram.

भेड़िया [*nm*] a wolf.

भेड़ियाधसान [*nm*] see भेड़चाल [under भेड़].

भेद [*nm*] a secret; difference, distinction; discrimination; divergence; division, schism, split; variety; kind/type; -भाव discrimination; differentiation; —की बात a secret.

भेदन [*nm*] the act of piercing/boring/disuniting; cleavage.

भेदिया [*nm*] a spy, intelligence agent.

भेदी [*nm*] a secret sharer, a confidant.

भेली [*nf*] a lump of गुड़ —esp. of specified weight [as two and a half seers, five seers, etc.].

भेष [*nm*] see भेस; —बदलना to [be] disguise[d].

भेषज [*nm*] a drug, medicine; remedy.

भेस [*nm*] appearance; dress, garb; get-up; guise; —बदलना to [be] disguise [d]; -बनाना to assume the guise [of]; to be peculiarly dressed up.

भैंगा [*a*] squint-eyed, cross-eyed [person].

भैं/स [*nf*] a she-buffalo; an extra-fat woman; ~सा a he-buffalo; stout and sturdy man.

भैया [*nm*] a brother; a vocative word for an elder brother as also for youngers or those of equal age.

भैरवी [*nf*] a kind of song sung in small hours of the morning.

भोंकना [*v*] to poke, to pierce through; to stab [as चाकू-]; see भूंकना.

भों/डा, ~ ड़ा [*a*] illshaped; unsymmetrical; ugly; grotesque; uncouth; indecent; crude; hence ~ पन.

भोंदू [*a*] dullard; booby, simpleton, stupid, silly; hence ~ पन/पना.

भोंपा, भोंपू [*nm*] a siren; horn.

भोक्ता [*nm* and *a*] [one] who enjoys/eats/uses.

भोग [*nm*] enjoyment; suffering sexual pleasure; result of good or evil deeds; experience of pleasure or pain; food offered to an idol; usufruct; ~वाद epicureanism; hedonism; hence ~वादी; -विलास sexual pleasure; enjoyment; luxury; debauchery.

भोगना [*v*] to enjoy; to suffer; to undergo; to derive sexual pleasure; to experience [pleasure or pain].

भोग्य [*a*] enjoyable, sexually enjoyable; to be used/consumed/enjoyed; hence भोग्या.

भोज [*nm*] a banquet; feast.

भोजन [*nm*] food, meals; diet; victuals; -भट्ट a glutton.

भोजनीय [*adj*] भोज्य.

भोजपुरी [*adj*] having to do with the region of Bhojpur Shahabad, the speech of the Bhojpur area.

भोजनालय [*nm*] a mess; restaurant, eating-house.

भोजपत्र [*nm*] the bark of the birch tree [which was used to write on in olden times].

भोज/पुरिया, ~ पुरी [*nf*] a dialect of Hindi spoken in eastern parts of Uttar Pradesh and western parts of Biha:r; [*nm*] a Bhojpuri speaker; [*a*] pertaining to भोजपुरी dialect or its speakers.

भोथ/र, ~ रा [*a*] blunt, blunt-edged.

भोर [*nm*] dawn, day-break.

भोला [*a*] innocent; unsophisticated; simple - hearted; hence ~ पन: -भाला innocent, ingenuous, honest and simple.

भौं [*nf*] an eyebrow; -चढ़ाना/तानना/सिकोड़ना lit. to twist the eyebrows—to frown, to scowl.

भोलापन [*nm*] simplicity, innocence.

भोलेपन [*nm*] भोलापन.

भौंकना [*v*] to bark; to jabber [said while indignantly referring to a man]; to penetrate, thrust into [as a sword etc.].

भौंरा [*nm*] a black-bee, beetle; a top [kind of toy].

भौंह [*nm*] see भौं.

भौगोलिक [*a*] geographical; ~ता geographicality.

भौच/क, ~क्का [*a*] aghast; non-plussed, dumb-founded, flabbergasted.

भौतिक [*a*] material; physical, mundane; corporeal; elemental; ~वाद materialism; ~वादी a materialist; materialistic; -विज्ञान physics.

भौतिकी [*nf*] physics; ~य physical.

भौम [*a*] pertaining to, born of or concerning the earth; [*nm*] the Mars; ~वार/वासर Tuesday.

भौमिक [*nm*] having to do with the earth, name of a north Indian and Bengal community.

भौमिकी [*nf*] geology.

भ्रंश [*nm*] breach, breakdown; fall [ing]; ruin, destruction.

भ्रम [*nm*] misunderstanding, illusion, misconception; confusion; -जाल illusion.

भ्रमण [*nm*] walk; going round; excursion; travel, roaming.

भ्रमर [*nm*] large blackbee; beetle.

भ्रमरी [*nf*] black bee, a plant of the genus Ferula.

भ्रमित [*adj*] set turning, revolving. erring, misled.

भ्रमता [*nf*] state of error.

भ्रष्ट [*a*] corrupt [ed]; spoilt; fallen, depraved; ruined; wanton; hence ~ता.

भ्रष्टाचार [*nm*] corruption; depravity; wantonness.

भ्रष्टाचारी [*a* and *nm*] [one who is] corrupt/depraved/wanton.

भ्रष्टपन [*nm*] fallen or degraded state.

भ्रांत [*a*] misled, mistaken; aberrated, strayed [as —व्यक्ति]; wrong, incorrect [as —धारणा].

भ्रांति [*nf*] error, mistake; illusion.

भ्राता [*nm*] a brother.

भ्रातृ [*nm*] a brother; ~त्व brotherhood; fraternity.

भ्रात्रीय [*adj*] fraternal.

भ्रामक [*a*] illusory, confusing.

भ्रू [*nm*] an eyebrow; ~भंग/भंगिमा attractive movement or contraction of eyebrows, a twist of the eyebrows; frown; ~विक्षेप frowning; scowling; ~विलास amorous movement of the eye-brows.

भ्रूण [*nm*] foetus, embryo; -विज्ञान embryology; -हत्या foeticide.

म the fifth and final letter of the fifth pentad [i.e. पवर्ग] of the Devanagari: alphabet.

म – देवनागरी वर्णमाला (व्यंजन) में पवर्ग का अंतिम व्यंजन है। इसका उच्चारण ओष्ठ और नासिका के द्वारा होता है। जिह्वा के अग्रभाग का दोनों होठों से स्पर्श होने से इस शब्द का उच्चारण होता है। यह स्पर्श और अनुनाशिक वर्ण है।

मंग [*nm*] the head of a boat.

मँगता [*nm*] a beggar.

मँगती [*nf*] reg. asking; request, begging, importuning.

मँगनी [*nf*] betrothal, engagement; loan, a borrowed thing.

मंगल [*nm*] [the planet] Mars; auspiciousness; well-being, welfare; Tuesday; [a] auspicious; ~कामना good, wishes; benediction; ~कारक/कारी good, auspicious; benedictory; ~कार्य a festive occasion, an auspicious ceremony/function; -गान/गीत auspicious song/singing; -ध्वनि the tumultuous sound of auspicious songs etc.; marriage-music or singing; ~मय good, happy, auspicious; ~वार/वासर Tuesday; ~सूचक auguring good luck, auspicious; ~सूत्र lit. the lucky thread—the sacred marriage thread worn by a woman as long as her husband lives; the thread wrapped round the wrist on auspicious occasions.

मंगला [*nf*] a title of the goddess Pārvatī.

मंगली [*adj*] born under the influence of the planet Mars.

मँगवाना [*v.t.*] to cause to be sent for or asked for by, to obtain, to order through.

मंगलाचरण [*nm*] benediction, benedictory verse [s] recited on an auspicious occasion; pronouncing a blessing; the initial verse in a book meant to invoke divine blessing.

मंगलाचार [*nm*] initial benedictory recitations or songs etc. marking the commencement of a ceremony/festive occasion.

मँगाना [*v*] to cause to bring to order.

मँगेतर [*nm* and *nf*] fiance or fiancee; [*a*] betrothed.

मंच [*nm*] a dais, stage, platform; forum.

मंचन [*nm*] staging of a play.

मंचित [*adj*] staged a drama.

मंजन [*nm*] tooth powder, dentifrice.

मंजर [*nm*] मंजरी.

मंज़र [*nm*] a sight, view, a landscape.

मंजरी [*nf*] a sprout, new shoot/cluster of flowers; an ear of corn.

मँजाई [*nf*] [process or act of] cleansing/polishing or the remuneration paid therefor; refinement, polishing.

मंज़िल [*nf*] a destination, stage; storey.

मँजीरा [*nm*] cymbal [s].

मंजु [*a*] beautiful, pretty, comely, lovely.

मंजुल [*a*] see मंजु.

मंजूर [*a*] approved; sanctioned; granted; accepted; ~शुदा approved; sanctioned; okayed.

मंजूरी [*nf*] approval; sanction; acceptance.

मंजूषा [*nf*] a casket, box, chest.

मँझधार [nf] see मझधार.

मँझला [*a*] see मझला.

मंझा [*nm*] the kite-flying thread made sharper and stiffer by being treated with powdered glass.

मँझोला [*a*] see मझोला.

मंडन [*nm*] corroboration; support through argumentation; decoration, ornamentation, embellishment.

मंडप [*nm*] a pavilion.

मँडराना [*v*] to hover, to hang around; to gather thick.

मंडल [*nm*] a circle; ring; zone, territory; board; orbit; the path or orbit of a heavenly body; halo; multitude, collection; each of the ten divisions (मंडल) of the Rigved.

मंडली [*nf*] a party; team; ring, gang; band; circle.

मंडी [*nf*] a wholesale market, market, market place.

मंतर [*nm*] spell; incantation.

मंतव्य [*nm*] intention; design; opinion, view.

मंत्र [*nm*] an incantation; charm, spell; a Vedic hymn; -पाठ recitation of a मंत्र in the traditional way; ~मुग्ध spellbound, charmed; ~सिद्धि successful culmination of the endeavour to wield a मंत्र effectively.

मंत्रणा [*nf*] advice, counsel.

मंत्रालय [*nm*] ministry, the offices headed by a minister.

मंत्रिमंडल [*nm*] cabinet, ministry.

मं/त्री [*nm*] a minister, secretary [of an organisation etc.]; hence ~त्रित्व.

मंथन [*nm*] churning; stirring, agitating; deep pondering over something [for acquisition of knowledge etc.].

मंथर [*a*] slow, slow-moving; sluggish, tardy.

मंद [*a*] slow, tardy; mild; dull [as बुद्धि]; inert; low [as स्वर]; faint, weak, feeble; ~भाग/भागी unlucky, ill-fated, unfortunate.

मंदा [*a*] slow; tardy, slack; cheap; [*nm*] depression.

मंदाग्नि [*nf*] indigestion, dyspepsia.

मंदिर [*nm*] a temple.

मंदी [*nf*] depression in price, slump [in the market]; [*a*] feminine form of मंदा.

मंशा [*nm, nf*] intention, purpose, motive.

मंसूख़ [*a*] cancelled, rescinded.

मई [*nf*] the month of May.

मकई [*nf*] maize.

मकड़ी [*nf*] a spider.

मक़बरा [*nm*] a tomb, mausoleum.

मकरंद [*nm*] the juice of a flower.

मकर [*nm*] the Capricornus—tenth sign of the zodiac; a crocodile; one of the nine nidhis of Kuber—the god of wealth; hence मकरी [*nf*].

मकान [*nm*] n a house, residence; abode; ~दार a house-owner landlord: -मालिक house-owner, landlord.

मक्का [*nm*] maize, corn.

मक्का/र [*a*] cunning, deceitful, crafty, hypocrite; hence ~री.

मक्की [*nf*] maize, corn.

मक्खन [*nm*] butter; ~बाज a flatterer, sycophant; ~बाजी flattery, sycophancy.

मक्खी [*nf*] a fly; ~मार a fly-killer; flykilling, idle, slothful; —निगलना, जीती to connive at a wrong, to deliberately perpetuate a wrong.

मक्खीचूस [*a*] terribly parsimonious, niggardly person.

मख़मल [*nm*] velvet, plush.

मख़मली [*a*] velvety, velutinous, plushy; pertaining to मख़मल; soft and tender/delicate.

मखाना [*nm*] a kind of dry fruit [prepared by parching lotus seeds].

मख़ौल [*nm*] joke, jest; mikery, derision.

मगज़ [*nm*] brain; kernel: pith, marrow; ~पच्ची too much of brain-taxing, mental over-exertion; assiduous concentration on or constant pondering over something.

मगज़ी [*nf*] edging, border; hem.

मगर [*nm*] crocodile; [conj.] but; ~मच्छ a crocodile.

मग़रूर [*a*] proud; arrogant.

मगसर [*nm*] see अगहन.

मगही [*nf*] a dialect of Hindi spoken in parts of Bihar province; [*a*] belonging to or produced in मगध [southern part of Bihar].

मगन [*a*] absorbed, engrossed; engaged, busy; immersed, drowned; glad, happy, delighted.

मचकना [*v*] to tramp; to creak or to be bent under pressure as a bedsteād].

मचना [*v*] to be occasioned, to happen, to be caused, to be raised up, to be committed, to be perpetrated.

मचलना [*v*] to be wayward/perverse/obstinate, to go on insisting [upon]; to be cross; to sulk; to pant [as a wayward child].

मचली [*nf*] nausea; —आना to nauseate, to feel like vomiting.

मचान [*nm*] a raised platform [for shooting wild animals from or for scaring beats away from farms].

मच्छ/ड़, ~र, [*nm*] a mosquito, gnat; ~ड़दानी/रदानी a mosquito curtain/net; ~ड़/र पर तोप लगाना small kill, big bill.

मछली [*nf*] fish; pisces; —खाने वाला piscivorous; —सारे/पूरे तालाब को गंदा करती है, एक one dirty fish infects the whole water.

मछुवा, ~ छुआ [*nm*] a fisherman.

मजदूर [*nm*] a labourer, worker; -वर्ग the working class; the labour class; -संघ labour union.

मज़दूरी [*nf*] wage [s] ; labour charges.

मजनूं [*nm*] the celebrated lover of Laila:; a mad or insane man, a love-lorn person; an emaciated man.

मजबू/त [*a*] strong, sturdy; lasting, durable; firm; ~ती strengh durability; firmness.

मजबू/र [*a*] helpless; obliged, compelled; forced, constrained; hence ~री.

मजबूरन [*ind*] under pressure, being compelled/forced/obliged; having no alternative.

मजमुआ [*nm*] a collection; gathering; crowd; hotch-potch assembly.

मज़मून [*nm*] a topic, subject; text; essay.

मजलिस [*nf*] an assembly, meeting; congregation.

मज़ह/ब [*nm*] a religion; creed; ~ बी religious.

मज़ा [*nm*] pleasure, relish; savour; taste, flavour; fun, jollity.

मज़ाक [*nm*] a joke, jest; prank, waggery, humour, fun, buffoonery; ridicule.

मज़ाकिया [*a*] witty, humorous, waggish, pranky, funloving; [*nm*] a wag, jester, witty or humorous man.

मजाल [*nf*] ability, audacity; strength, power

मज़ेदार [*a*] delicious, savoury, tasty, full of relish, enjoyable; packed with fun and frolic; humoursome.

मजीरा [*nm*] small cymbals.

मज्जा [*nf*] marrow, bonemarrow; pith.

मझधार [*nf*] mid stream, mid-current.

मझला [*a*] middle; mid; medium.

मझोला [*a*] medium-sized, neither big nor small, of average size.

मटकना [*v*] to affect coquettish gestures, to strut, to swagger; to show off with affected gracefulness; hence मटकाना.

मटका [*nm*] a large earthen pitcher/pot.

मटमैला [*a*] dusty, dust-coloured.

मटर [*nf*] pea.

मटरग/श्त [*a*] vagrant; roving, wandering, rambling; hence ~श्ती.

मटियामेट [*a*] undone, ruined, destroyed; razed [to the ground].

मटियाला [*a*] dust-coloured, dusty.

मट्ठा [*nm*] butter-milk.

मठ [*nm*] monastery; ~ धारी an abbot, chief of a monastery.

मढ़ना [*v*] to frame, to mount; to gild, to cover [with]; to impose, to impute.

मणि [*nf*] a jewel. gem.

मतंग [*nm*] an elephant.

मत [*nm*] an opinion, view, belief, tenet, doctrine; sect, creed, faith; vote; ~दान poll, polling, casting of votes; -केन्द्र polling station/booth; ~दाता a voter, an elector.

मतभेद [*nm*] disagreement, difference of opinion; dissension.

मत/वाद [*nm*] dogma; doctrine; ~वादी dogmatic; doctrinaire.

मतल/ब [*nm*] meaning, purpose; aim, motive; concern; self-interest; ~बी selfish, self-concerned.

मतलाना [*v*] to nauseate, to feel like vomiting, to feel sick; —, जी to nauseate, to feel like vomiting, to feel sick.

मतली [*nf*] nausea, a feeling like vomiting.

मतवाला [*a*] intoxicated, drunken; wayward; tipsy; [*nm*] a kind of toy; hence ~पन.

मताधिकार [*nm*] franchise, suffrage; eligibility to vote; —, बालिग/वयस्क adult franchise.

मताधिकारी [*nm*] an eligible voter, one who is authorised to vote.

मतानुयायी [*a and nm*] following; [a] follower.

मतावलंबी [*a* and *nm*] see मतानुयायी.

मति [*nf*] intellect; understanding; opinion; view; ~भ्रष्ट deranged, mentally derailed; ~हीन stupid, foolish.

मतैक्य [*nm*] unanimity, agreement, unison, unity of view.

मत्त [*a*] drunken, intoxicated.

मत्था [*nm*] the forehead; head.

मत्स्य [*nm*] a fish.

मत्स्यावतार [*nm*] the first of the ten incarnations of Lord Vishnū [in the form of a big fish].

मथना [*v*] to churn; to stir deeply; to batter; to agitate; to probe profoundly.

मद [*nm*] intoxication; passion; arrogance, pride; a fluid substance which oozes out from the temple of a passionate male elephant; [nf]

item; head, category; ~मत्त intoxicated; full of passion, passionate.

मदद [*nf*] help, assistance, aid; support; relief; reinforcement; ~ गार helper; supporter; assistant.

मदन [*nm*] see कामदेव.

मदरसा [*nm*] a school.

मदरासी [*nm*] a native of Madras [capital of the South Indian State of Tamilnadu]; a [] belonging or pertaining to Madras.

मद/होश [*a*] dead drunk, intoxicated out of senses; rendered senseless; ~शी drunkenness, intoxicatedness.

मदारी [*nm*] a juggler, conjurer, trickster; hence ~पन.

मदिर [*a*] intoxicating, intoxicative.

मदिरा [*nf*] liquor, wine, spirit; ~गृह/लय a bar.

मदोन्मत्त [*a*] arrogant; intoxicated.

मद्ध(द्धि)म [*a*] slow; dim; moderate.

मद्धे [*adv*] in the account of; about; concerning; with regard to; regarding.

मद्य [*nm*] wine, liquor, spirit; -निर्माणशाला a distillery; -पान drinking, consuming liquor.

मधु [*nm*] honey, wine, liquor; juice of flowers; the spring; ~करी female black bee; cooked food gathered in alms from different sources; ~प large black bee; ~मक्खी/मक्षिका honey-bee, bee; ~मेह diabetes; ~मेही a diabetic; a patient of diabetes; ~शाला a bar.

मधुर [*a*] sweet; melodious, pleasant; mellifluous; ~ता/त्व sweetness; melodiousness, mellifluence; softness.

मधुरिमा [*nf*] sweetness, harmoniousness, melodiousness, mellifluousness.

मध्य [*a*] middle, central, mid—; [nm] middle; centre; the middle part or region; ~पद the term situated in between; ~पूर्व middle east; pre-middle; ~मान mean; ~मार्ग middle course, moderate course; ~युग the middle ages; ~वर्ती central; intermediary, medial, intermediate.

मध्यम [*a*] medium; middle, intermediate; fourth note, of the Indian gamut; slow; dim; -पुरुष second person [in grammar]

मध्यमा [*nf*] the middle finger; [*a*] lying in the middle; medial, intermediary.

मध्यस्थ [*a*] intermediate; situated in the middle, intermediary, medical; [*nm*] a mediator; middleman; ~ ता mediation.

मध्यांतर [*nm*] an interval.

मध्याह्न [*nm*] noon, midday.

मनःकल्पित [*a*] imaginary/imagined, fancied, fabricated.

मन [*nm*] mind; heart; desire, wish; disposition; maund-a weight equal to forty seers, ~ गढ़त/गढ़ंत fabricated; concocted; imaginary/imagined; ~चला fidgety; frivolous, easy prey to female brandishments; ~ चाहा/चीता favourite, desired, wished or longed for; ever thought of; ~ बहलाव amusement, entertainment, recreation; ~ भावन favourite, liked, beloved; charming, attractive; ~ माना arbitrary; licentious self-willed; high-handedness; ~मुटाव estrangement, rift; antagonism; ~ मौजी whimsical, self-willed; capricious; — फटना to be disillusioned; to be estranged; —बहलाना to amuse, to recreate; —भरना to be fed up, to be satiated/satisfied; —मारना to suppress one's feelings; —में मैल आना ill will to be aroused within; a sense of dishonesty to prevail within; —हरा होना to feel happy, to be delighted.

मनका [*nm*] a bead.

मनन [*nm*] meditation, contemplation; brooding, pondering/thinking deeply over something; ~ शील meditative/contemplative; thoughtful.

मनचिकि/त्सा [*nf*] psychotherapy, psychological treatment; ~त्सक an alienist, a psychotherapist.

मनसब [*nm*] an office; status in official hierarchy; ~दार an officer.

मनसा [*a*] desire, wish, the mind; -वाचा कर्मणा through the mind, speech and deed.

मनसू/ख [*a*] cancelled; ~ खी cancellation.

मनसूबा [*nm*] intention; plan, design.

मनस् [*nm*] the psyche, psychic element, mind.

मनस्वी [*a*] wise; strong-minded single-minded; thoughtful, contemplative.

मनहू/स [*a*] ominous, inauspicious; ill-fated; gloomy, sombre; hence ~ सियत.

मनहूसी [*nf*] gloominess, sombreness.

मना [a] forbidden, prohibited; ~ ई see मनाही.

मनाना [*v*] to persuadc; to appease, to bring round by persuasion [to one's point of view]; the act or process of bringing round by persuasion; appeasement.

मनाही [*nf*] forbiddance; prohibition.

मनिहार [*nm*] a bangle-dealer.

मनीआर्डर [*nm*] a money order.

मनीषी [*a* and *nm*] [the] wise; thinker/thoughtful.

मनु [*nm*] the primogenitor of human race; ~ ज/जात the offspring of मनु, man.

मनुष्य [*nm*] a man, human being.

मनुष्य/ता, ~ त्व [*nf*], ~ ttv [nm] humanity; humaneness, the aggregate of human qualities.

मनुहार [*nf*] persuasion; entreaty; appeasement; persuasive effort to restore [somebody] to normal mental disposition.

मनोकामना [*nf*] a desire, wish.

मनोज [*nm*] Cupid—the god of love.

मनोनीत [*a*] nominated; designated/designate.

मनोबल [*nm*] morale, moral strength.

मनोयोग [*nm*] concentration, single-mindedness.

मनो/रंजक [*a*] interesting; amusing, entertaining, recreative; hence ~ रंजकता [*nf*] ; ~रंजन amusement, entertainment, recreation.

मनोरथ [*nm*] desire, wish; longing.

मनोरम [*a*] lovely, pretty, charming, attractive.

मनोविकार [*nm*] emotion, feeling, passion; mental derangement.

मनोविज्ञान [*nm*] psychology.

मनोविनोद [*nm*] amusement, pastime, hobby.

मनो/विलास [*nm*] reverie, musing, fancy; hence ~विलासी.

मनोविश्लेषण [*nm*] psycho-analysis.

मनोवृत्ति [*nf*] mentality; mental disposition/ attitude.

मनोवेग [*nm*] a passion; impulse.

मनोवैज्ञानिक [*a* and *nm*] psychological; a psychologist.

मनोव्यथा [*nf*] affliction, mental agony.

मनो/हर [*a*] lovely, comely, charming, alluring, captivating; also ~ हारी.

मनौती [*nf*] offerings pledged to a deity on fulfilment of some desire, a vow of offering.

मन्नत [*nf*] see मनौती; –मानना to vow to make an offering to a deity [on fulfilment of a wish].

मन्मथ [*nm*] Cupid—the god of love.

मम/ता, ~ त्व [*nf*] ~ [*nm*]affection, attachment, the sense of owning or being one with something or somebody.

मय —a Sanskrit suffix imparting the meanings of abounding in, full of, comprised/composed of, etc. to the nouns they are appended to; along with; [*nf*] wine, liquor.

मयस्सर [*a*] available.

मयूर [*nm*] a peacock.

मरकत [*nm*] an emerald.

मरघट [*nm*] a cremation ground.

मरण [*nm*] death, demise, expiration; mortality.

मरणांतक [*a*] fatal, killing, culminating in death.

मरणासन्न [*a*] on the verge of death, facing imminent death.

मरणोन्मुख [*a*] dying, decaying, heading towards the end, facing imminent death.

मरतबा [*nm*] rank, order; turn, time.

मरता [*a*] dying, on the verge of death; —क्या न करता a desperate man leaves nothing to chance.

मरना [*v*] to die, to pass away; to wither away; to become ineffective; to vanish, to disappear; to continue to be absorbed [as पानी–]; to be out [as in a game]; to fall for [somebody]; [nm] death; post death rites.

मरभुक्खा [*a*] famished; voracious, ravenous; greedy.

मरम्मत [*nf*] repair, mending.

मरहम [*nf*] an ointment; -पट्टी dressing/bandage.

मराठा [*nm*] an inhabitant of Maha:ra:shṭra.

मराठी [*nf*] the language spoken in Maha:ra:shtra.

मराल [*nm*] a goose, swan.

मरियल [*a*] sickly, feeble, rickety.

मरीचिका [*nf*] a mirage, illusion.

मरीज़ [*a* and *nm*] a patient, diseased.

मरु [*nm*] a desert; ~ देश/भूमि/स्थल deserted land.

मरुत [*nm*] the air; the air god.

मरोड़ [*nf*] twist; torsion, contortion, spasm; wrench.

मरोड़ना [*v*] to twist; to contort; to wring.

मर्ज़ [*nm*] a disease, malady, ailment.

मर्ज़ी [*nf*] desire, will; inclination; pleasure.

मर्त्य [*a*] mortal; ~ लोक the mortal world, the earth.

मर्द [*nm*] a man; potent male; brave/fearless person; husband; [a] manly, dauntless.

मर्दन [*nm*] massage; rubbing; crushing down, trampling.

मर्दानगी [*nf*] bravery, valour; masculinity.

मर्दाना [*a*] male; masculine; potent; valorous.

मर्म [*nm*] vulnerable/vital part [of the body]; core; secret; real meaning; ~ ज्ञ one who knows the inner meaning; having deep penetration into the secret; ~ पीड़ा/व्यथा intense mental agony; ~ भेदी moving, touching; poignant; heart-rending; —वचन touching words; subtle words; ~ स्थल vulnerable point; vital spot; ~ स्पर्शी touching, moving, poignant, heart-rending.

मर्मर [*nm*] marble; rustling; —ध्वनि rustling noise.

मर्मांतक [*a*] heart-rending, fatal; poignant.

मर्यादा [*nf*] dignity, decorum, propriety of conduct; ethical self-restriction; rank, ambit; limit, moderation.

मल [*nm*] faeces, excrement; sewage; rubbish, filth, dirt; -मूत्र urine and faeces, excrement.

मलना [*v*] to rub; to press hard; to anoint, to smear; to massage.

मलबा [*nm*] debris, wreckage.

मलमल [*nf*] muslin.

मलय [*nm*] a south Indian mountain abounding in sandal trees wherefrom cool and fragrant air currents are said to emanate; the part of Western Ghats lying South of Mysore and east of Travancore; ~ गिरि the Malay mountain; —समीर air current emanating from the Malay-mountain.

मलयाचल [*nm*] see मलयगिरि [under मलय].

मलयानिल [*nm*] see मलयसमीर under मलय.

मलयालम [*nf*] one of the four major Dravidian languages—spoken in the extreme south Indian state of Kerala.

मलयाली [*a*] of or pertaining to Malayalam.

मलाई [*nf*] cream.

मलाल [*nm*] remorse, compunction; regret.

मलिन [*a*] dirty, filthy, tarnished, shabby; gloomy.

मलेरिया [*nm*] malaria.

मल्ल [*nm*] a wrestler; —युद्ध wrestling, hand to hand fight.

मल्ला/ह [*nm*] a sailor, boatman, mariner; hence ~ ही.

मल्हार [*nm*] a राग [musical mode] in Indian music sung esp. in the rainy season.

मवाद [*nm*] pus, purulent matter.

मवाली [*nm*] a barbaric south-Indian tribe; [*a*] boorish, barbaric; uncouth.

मवेशी [*nm*] cattle; ~ खाना a cattle pond.

मशक [*nm*] a mosquito; [nf] a large leathern water-bag [used for sprinkling water on the roads etc.].

मशक़्क़/त [*nf*] toil, hard labour; hence ~ ती.

मशविरा [*nm*] advice, counsel.

मशहूर [*a*] famous, well-known, reputed.

मशाल [*nf*] a torch; ~ ची a torch-bearer.

मशीन [*nf*] a machine: ~ गन a machine gun.

मश्क़ [*nf*] practice, exercise.

मस [*nf*] soft hair appearing above the upper lip of a lad heralding the imminent advent of youth; [*nm*] a mosquito; ~ हरी a mosquito net/curtain; मसें भींजना/भीगना to be on the threshold of youth.

मसकना [*v*] to press, to press hard; to spilt, to burst, to tear asunder.

मसख़रा [*a*] funny, humoursome, waggish; [nm] a jester, funny man; wag; buffoon; hence ~पन.

मसख़री [*nf*] waggery/ wagging; fun, buffoonery, jesting.

मसजिद [*nf*] a mosque.

मसनद [*nf*] a bolster, large round pillow [to recline on].

मसल [*nf*] a saying, proverb; illustration.

मसलन [*nf*] rubbing, pressing, pressing hard, crushing; [ind] for example, for instance, to cite an example.

मसलना [*v*] to rub; to press, to press hard; to crush.

मसलहत [*nf*] expediency; suitability.

मसला [*nm*] an issue, question, problem.

मसविदा [*nm*] a draft.

मसा [nm] see मस्सा.

मसान [nm] a cremation ground.

मसाला [*nf*] spices, condiments; material; मसालेदार spiced, pungent, treated with condiments.

मसी/ह [*nm*] Jesus Christ—the founder of Christianity; ~ही [*a*] Christian; ~ धर्म Christianity.

मसीहा [*nm*] a messiah, one endowed with powers to revive the dead; ~ ई messianic.

मसू/ड़ा ~ **ढ़ा** [*nm*] the gums.

मसूर [*nf*] lentil, a kind of pulses.

मसृण [*a*] soft, smooth, soft and smooth.

मसोसना [*v*] to press, to repress; to restrain, to subdue; to grieve within.

मसौदा [*nm*] a draft.

मस्त [*a*] intoxicated; intoxicated by passion; carefree wanton; sexually excited; radiant with joy, in a lively frolic.

मस्तक [*nm*] head; forehead.

मस्ताना [*v*] to be in an intoxicated state; to get intoxicated with passion; to be sexually excited; to be in a wanton mood, to be radiant with joy, to be in a lively frolic; [a] intoxicated; wanton; sexually excited; frolicsome, carefree.

मस्तिष्क [*nm*] the brain, cerebrum, mind.

मस्ती [*nf*] [state of] intoxication, joi de vivre; passionateness, sexual excitement; carefreeness, wantonness, joyous radiance, frolicsomeness.

मस्तूल [*nm*] the mast [of a boat].

मस्सा [*nm*] a wart.

महँगा [*a*] dear, expensive, costly; ~ ई dearness; expensiveness, costliness.

महँगी [*nf*] high cost, costliness, expensiveness, scarcity; [a] feminine form of महँगा.

महंत [*nm*] head priest of a temple, a monk; self-willed leader.

महक [*nf*] fragrance, aroma, perfume, scent; hence ~दार.

महकना [*v*] to emit fragrance/perfume.

महकमा [*nm*] a department.

महज़ [*a*] merely, only; absolutely; simply.

महताब [*nm*] the moon.

महतारी [nf] mother.

महत् [*a*] great; big; excellent,

महत्तम [*a*] greatest, biggest; best, most excellent; —समापवर्त्तक G.C.M. [greatest common measure].

महत्तर [*a*] greater, bigger; better.

महत्ता [*nf*] importance, significance; greatness; magnitude.

महत्त्व [*nm*] see महत्ता; ~ पूर्ण important, urgent, significant, superb.

महत्त्वाकां/क्षा [*nf*] ambition; ~ क्षी ambitious.

महफ़िल [*nf*] a private assembly/congregation, recreational assembly.

महबूब [*a*] beloved, dear.

महर्षि [*nm*] a great sage [seer].

महल [*nm*] a palace, palatial mansion.

महसूल [*nm*] duty, custom, levy.

महसूस [*a*] experienced; felt; perceived.

महा allomorph of महत् as it appears in numerous compounds; ~ कवि a great poet; an epic poet; ~ काल the Annihilator; the Time Infinite; ~ काव्य an epic; ~देव an epithet of Lord Shiv; ~ देवी an epithet of goddess Parvati: —Shiv's spouse; the queeen consort; ~ नगर/नगरी a metropolis; cosmopolitan city; ~ पातक a great sin [five such sins have been enumerated by the Hindu scriptures]; ~पातकी a great sinner; ~ पाप see ~पातक; ~ पापी see ~ पातकी; ~पुरुष a great man; ~ प्रयाण see ~ प्रस्थान; ~ प्रलय the great deluge; ~ प्रस्थान death; the final journey; ~प्राण an aspirate; possessing tremendous vitality; ~ ब्राह्मण a bra:hmān who performs cremation rituals and accepts payment therefor in cash or kind; ~ मना noble; liberal; ~ महिम Your/His Majesty; ~ रथी a great warrior; a leading luminary in any field of activity; ~ समुद्र/सागर an ocean.

महाज/न [*nm*] a private banker, money-lender; ~ नी banking money-lending [business].

महात्मा [*a* and *nm*] a saint, sage, saintly [person], noble/enlightened soul.

महान [*a*] great; big; eminent; ~ ता greatness: eminence, nobility.

महानुभाव [*nm*] a great noble/liberal-minded person; also used as a respectable form of address.

महामारी [*nf*] an epidemic; plague.

महायुद्ध [*nm*] a war, world war.

महारत [*nm*] practice expertise; skill.

महा/राज [*nm*] a king; a term of respect; a cook; ~ राजा a king, ruler; ~ राजाधिराज a king of kings, an emperor; ~ राज्ञी the queen consort; ~ राणा a title held by some rulers of former Indian princely states; ~ रानी a queen.

महा/राष्ट्र [*nm*] the south-western Indian state comprising the Marathi-speaking areas of the country; ~ राष्ट्रीय belonging, pertaining or relating to Maharashtra.

महावत [*nm*] a mahaut, elephant-driver.

महावर [*nm*] the red lac-solution used by women to adorn their feet.

महाविद्यालय [*nm*] a college.

महावीर [*a*] having tremendous valour, extremely valorous/gallant.

महाशय [*a* and *nm*] noble/liberal [person]; a form of address meaning—Mr.

महा/सभा [*nf*] a congress; ~ सभाई member of a महासभा.

महि [*nf*] the earth.

महिमा [*nf*] exaltation, greatness, dignity; majesty; importance.

महिला [*nf*] a lady.

महि/ष [*nm*] a he-buffalo; -षी a she-buffalo; queen consort.

महीन [*a*] thin; soft.

महीना [*nm*] a month; menses; महीने से in menses.

महोत्सव [*nm*] a big celebration, great festival.

महोदय [*a*] Sir; an honorofic used as a form of address or otherwise; hence महोदया madam.

माँ [*nf*] mother.

माँग [*nf*] demand; requirement; requisition, indent; the line of demarcation in parting and setting the locks of hair on the head; —उजड़ना/लुटना to be widowed, to be deprived of the protection of the husband.

माँगना [*v*] to demand; to ask/call for; to claim; to invite [as tender]; to solicit.

मांगलिक [*a*] auspicious, propitious; benedictory.

माँजना [*v*] to cleanse, to scour; to polish; to refine; to practise.

माँझी [*nm*] a boatman; steersman, sailor.

माँड़ [*nm*] rice-starch, boiled rice-water.

माँड़ना [*v*] to knead [flour]; to separate grain from the ears of corn; to wage [as रार—].

माँद [*nf*] a lair, den [of a beast etc.].

माँदा [*a*] fatigued, tired; ill, sick, diseased.

मांस [*nm*] meat; flesh; ~ पेशी a muscle; ~ ल fleshy, corpulent, plump; carnal; tangible, concrete; hence ~ लता.

मांसाहा/र [*nm*] non-vegetarianism; meat-eating; ~ री non vegetarian; meat-eating; carnivorous.

माई [*nf*] mother; a maid-servant; an old woman.

माघ [*nm*] the eleventh month of the year according to the Hindu calendar.

माचिस [*nf*] safety matches, a match-box; match stick.

माजरा [*nm*] matter, affair; incident, occurrence.

मात [*a*] defeated, vanquished; outdone; outwitted; [*nf*] defeat.

मातबर [*a*] trustworthy, reliable, credible.

मातम [*nm*] mourning, bereavement; grief; ~पुरसी expression of condolence [s].

मात/हत [*a*] subordinate, subservient, under; hence ~ती.

माता [*nf*] mother; small pox; [*a*] intoxicated; pride-ridden.

मातामह [*nm*] maternal grandfather, mother's father.

मातृ [*nf*] mother [used in this form only in compound words]; ~ त्व maternity, motherhood; ~ भाषा mother-tongue; ~ भूमि motherland.

मात्र [*ind*] only; merely, barely; mere, bare, sheer.

मात्रक [*nm*] a unit.

मात्रा [*nf*] quantity; scale; a dose; degree; a vowel-mark in the Devanagari: and other allied scripts; length of time taken in pronouncing a vowel or consonant; ~त्मक/मूलक quantitative; based on मात्रा.

माथा [*nm*] the forehead; forepart; ~ पच्ची करना to tax one's brain; to take pains in elucidating something; to over-exert mentally [to bring home a point to somebody].

मादक [*a*] intoxicating; bewitching, fascinating; hence ~ता.

मादा [*a*] female, of female sex [used only with animals as—चीता].

माद्दा [*nm*] ingredient; element; essence; pith; capability.

माधुर्य [*nm*] sweetness; pleasantness; one of the poetic qualities which is marked by the exclusive usage of soft or liquid sounds and sound-combinations.

माध्यमिक [*a*] secondary; middle, intermediary.

मान [*nm*] esteem, respect; prestige, dignity; value; measure, scale; conceit, arrogance; amorous sulking; ~ चित्र a map; ~ दंड a standard; criterion; ~ पत्र an address [of welcome].

मान/क [*a* and *nm*] standard, norm; ~ कीकरण standardization.

मानता [*nf*] importance; recognition, reckoning [as great, powerful, etc.]; see मनौती.

मानना [*v*] to agree; to accept; to admit, to confess; to regard, to respect; to presume, to suppose; to assume, to imagine; to take for granted; to accede to; to yield.

माननीय [*a*] honourable; revered, respectable; [int] your honour !

मानव [*nm*] a man, human being, mankind.

मानवता [*nf*] humanity; mankind; ~ वाद humanism; ~ वादी a humanist; humanistic.

मानवीय [*a*] human/humane, pertaining to man/human beings.

मानवोचित [*a*] humane, befitting a man/mankind.

मानस [*nm*] the psyche, mind; heart; a famous lake मानसरोवर [in the Himalayas]; [*a*] mental, psychical.

मानसरोवर [*nm*] a famous lake in the Himalayas.

मानसिक [*a*] psychic, mental.

मानसून [*nm*] the monsoon.

मानहानि [*nf*] defamation.

मानिंद [*a*] like, similar; resembling.

मानिनी [*a*] arrogant; amorously sulking [woman]; [*nf*] a woman who sulks on account of her lover's lapse.

मानी [*nm*] meaning, purport, import; [*a*] proud; haughty.

मानीटर [*nm*] a monitor.

माने [*nm*] meaning, purport, import.

मानो [*ind*] as if, as though; supposing.

मान्य [*a*] respectable, honourable; respected; having a privileged position in relationship -e.g. sister's son, son-in-law, etc.; valid, tenable; recognised; ~ ता recognition; validity.

माप [*nm*] measurement, measure; size; dimension; ~ दंड touchstone; standard.

मापना [*v*] to measure, to scale; to assess.

मापनी [*nf*] a scale, ruler.

माफ़ [*a*] excused, pardoned, forgiven.

माफ़िक़ [*a*] agreeable, suitable, favourable; fit, befitting.

माफ़ी [*nf*] forgiveness, pardon; condonation; remission; exemption; rent free grant, freehold/rent-free land.

मामला [*nm*] a case; an affair; matter; business; cause.

मामा [*nm*] a maternal uncle.

मामूली [*a*] ordinary, so-so; common; commonplace, usual; moderate.

मायका [*nm*] mother's home maternal house/village/city/place [of a married woman].

माया [*nf*] illusion, delusion; unreality; riches; earthly ignorance; phāntasm, phantam; -मोह illusion and attachment.

मायाबी [*a*] illusive, delusive; phantasmal; deceitful.

मायू/स [*a*] frustrated, dejected, disappointed; hence ~ सी.

मार [*nm*] beating, thrashing, belabouring; see कामदेव; -काट bloody encounter, mutual killing/fight; -धाड़ fighting and killing; noisy encounter; -पीट scuffle, exchange of blows; beating; battery.

मारका [*nm*] mark, sign, trade-mark.

मारना [*v*] to kill; to beat, to belabour; to hit, to strike; to punish; to subdue [as गुस्सा—]; to misappropriate; not to repay [as पैसा—]; to chop off [as गर्दन—]; to win [as मैदान—]; to turn ineffective [as जहर—]; to reduce to ashes [as धातु—]; —मन to exercise self-restraint, to subdue one's desires.

मारफ़त [*ind*] through, through the agency of, through the medium of; by; care of [c/o].

मार्ग [*nm*] way, path, route, course; road; track; passage, outlet; ~ (प्र)दर्शक a guide; pioneer; -प्रदर्शन guidance.

मार्च [*nm*] the month of March; [*nf*] march/ marching pacing ahead [as of troops].

मार्दव [*nm*] softness; gentleness; compassionateness; leniency; mildness.

मार्फ़त [*ind*] see मारफ़त.

मार्मिक [*a*] poignant; touching, moving; vital, affecting the vital parts; hence ~ ता.

माल [*nm*] goods, commodity; stuff; merchandise; cargo; produce; stock; riches; public revenue; dainties; [nf]. a wide highway; garland; series; ~खाना warehouse, storehouse; ~गाड़ी a goods train; ~ गुज़ारी land revenue, rent; ~ गोदाम a godown, warehouse; storehouse; -टाल wealth, riches, money; assets; ~ दार wealthy, rich; opulent; –मत्ता assets, riches, wealth; effects; –महकमा the department of revenue; —मारना to embezzle, to misappropriate, to usurp somebody's money.

माला [nf] a garland, wreath; rosary, string of beads; series, chain; row, line.

मालामाल [a] opulent, very prosperous, immensely rich.

मालिक [*nm*] a master, employer; owner, lord [as landlord]; proprietor; husband.

मालिकाना [*nm*] proprietorship, ownership; [*a*] proprietory; masterly, in the fashion or style of an emplayer/landlord/proprietor/ master.

मालिकी [*nf*] ownership, proprietorship.

मालियत [*nf*] value, worth; wealth.

मालिश [*nf*] massage.

माली [*nm*] a gardener; garlander; [*a*] economic.

मालुम [*a*] known.

मालूम [*a*] see मालुम.

माश [*nm*] black gram.

माशा [*nm*] a weight equivalent to eight rattis or one-twelfth of a tola:.

माशू/क़ [*nm*] a beloved; hence ~ काना, ~ क़ी.

मास [*nm*] a month.

मासिक [*a*] monthly; per mensem; [nm] menstruation; a monthly magazine; —धर्म menstruation, monthly course.

मासू/म [*a*] innocent; harmless, guiless; hence ~ मियत.

मास्ट/र [*nm*] a teacher, master; ~ री teaching [profession/job].

माह [*nm*] a month, ~ वार monthly, per mensem; ~ वारी monthly; menstruation.

माहात्म्य [*nm*] greatness; glory; efficacy of a deity of god.

माहिर [*a* and *nm*] [an] expert; a specialist; adept.

मिकदार [*nf*] quantity; measure.

मिचकाना [*v*] to wink, to blink [as आँखें].

मिचना [*v*] to be shut, to be closed [per force].

मिचलाना [*v*]; —, जी to nauseate, to feel like vomiting, to feel sick.

मिचली [*nf*] feeling like vomiting, nausea.

मिजाज [*nm*] temperament; nature disposition; temper, mood; conceit; fastidiousness; ~ पुरसी enquiring after one's well-being; —मुबारक, –शरीफ़ how do you do?; —सातवें आसमान पर होना to be too hot-headed, to be too conceited ; to think no end of oneself.

मिज़ाजी [*a*] conceited, arrogant; fastidious.

मिटना [*v*] to be effaced, to be erased; to be ruined, to be undone, to be destructed.

मिट्टी [*nf*] earth, soil; clay; dust; —का तेल kerosene oil; —के मोल damn cheap; —ठिकाने लगाना to duly perform the last rites; —पलीद होना to be in a miserable plight; to be humiliated/ insulted/embarrassed; the last rites not to be duly performed; —में मिलाना to be razed to the ground; to be ruined/wasted.

मिट्ठी [*nf*] a kiss [esp. when planted on a child's cheek].

मिट्ठू [*nm*] a parrot.

मिठबोला [*a*] sweet-spoken.

मिठाई [*nf*] sweetmeat; confectionery.

मिठास [*nf*] sweetness.

मिडिल [*a*] middle; ~ ची [said indignantly] one who has studied only upto the middle standard.

मितव्यय [*nm*] thrift, frugality; hence ~ यिता, ~ यी.

मिती [*nf*] a date according to the lunar month; ~ काटा discount.

मित्र [*nm*] a friend; an ally; ~ ता/त्व friendship, intimacy; alliance.

मिथ्या [*a*] untrue, false, pseudo; sham, spurious; delusory; [nm] untruth, falsehood; illusion.

मिनट [*nm*] a minute.

मिनमिनाना [*v*] to speak in an inarticulate fashion; to speak through the nose.

मिन्नत [*nf*] entreaty, request; supplication.

मियाँ [*nm*] a respectful address for a Mohammedan; husband; -बीबी husband and wife; ~ मिट्ठू a sweet-spoken person; a parrot; —की जूती मियाँ की चाँद, – की जूती मियाँ के सिर to beat somebody with his own stick; —मिट्ठू बनना, अपने मुँह to indulge in self-praise, self-praise is no recommendation.

मिया/द [*nf*] duration; time limit, term, tenure; period; hence ~ दी, ~ दी बुखार typhoid.

मियान [*nf*] a sheath, scabbard.

मिरगी [*nf*] epilepsy.

मिर्च [*nf*] chillies, pepper.

मिल [*nf*] a mill; -मजदूर a mill-worker; -मालिक a mill-owner.

मिलता-जुलता [*a*] resembling, having resemblance, like, almost identical.

मिलन [*nm*] a meeting; union; contact; ~ सार sociable; affable; hence ~ सारी.

मिलना [*v*] to meet; to encounter; to be mixed, to be mingled; to unite; to merge; to tally; to conform, to obtain, to get; to acquire/to be acquired, to beget; to embrace.

मिलान [*nm*] comparison; reconciliation; collation; tallying; [of accounts etc.].

मिलाना [*v*] to unite; to compare; to reconcile; to mix, to mingle, to blend; to join, to connect; to harmonize; to tune; to cause to meet, to bring together.

मिलाप [*nm*] meeting; reconciliation; union, unity.

मिलावट [*nf*] adulteration/adulterant; blend, mixing; alloy.

मिल्कियत [*nf*] property; estate, landed property.

मिश्र [*a*] mixed; blended, combined; ~ ण a mixture, blend; combination.

मिष्टान्न [*nm*] sweetmeat, confectionery.

मिसरा [*nm*] one-half of a couplet.

मिसरी [*nf*] sugarcandy.

मिसाल [*nf*] precedent; example.

मिसिल [*nf*] a case-file; file.

मिस्त्री [*nm*] a mechanic, mistry, technician; artisan, craftsman.

मींचना [*v*] to shut, to close [as eyes etc.].

मीज़ान [*nm*] sum, total.

मीटर [*nm*] a metre, meter.

मीटिंग [*nf*] a meeting.

मीठा [*a*] sweet; pleasant; [*nm*] sweetmeat; —पानी fresh water; —मुँह कराना to offer sweetmeat [to celebrate a good news or a happy occasion].

मीना [nm] a false gem of blue colour; enamel; blue colour, ~ कार an enameller; hence ~ कारी.

मीनार [*nf*] a minaret, tower.

मीमां/सा [*nf*] one of the six systems of Indian Philosophy; profound thought or reflection, deep deliberation, thorough investigation; hence ~ सक.

मीर [*nm*] —a nobleman; chieftain; leader; winner in a competition.

मीरी [*nm*] the winner in competitions, one who stands first; leadership.

मील [*nf*] a mile.

मुंडन [*nm*] shaving of the head, the tonsure ceremony, a Hindu ritual involving the first-ever shaving of the hair on a child's head.

मुँड़ना [*v*] to have the head, shaven; to be fleeced, to be relieved of one's money or belongings.

मुँडे(ड़)/र [*nf*] a demarcation wall; parapet; battlement; also ~ री a small ~ र.

मुंतजिम [*nm*] a manager; organiser; one entrusted with arrangements; [*a*] entrusted with arrangements; [a] having organising capability, good at making arrangements.

मुँदना [*v*] to be closed/shut; to be covered/hidden.

मुंशी [*nm*] a scribe, clerk [esp of a pleader or an advocate], munshi; a [urdu or Persian] teacher; ~ गीरी the work or profession of a scribe/clerk.

मुंसिफ़ [*nm*] a munsif—judge of a subordinate civil court; मुंसिफ़ी the work, post, profession or court of a मुंसिफ.

मुँह [*nm*] mouth; face; forepart [of anything]; an opening,orifice, hole, aperture; inlet; outlet; source; courage, strength; fitness; countenance; ~ जबानी verbal, oral; ~ ज़ोर

insolent impertinent, impudent; high-spirited, hard-mouthed [as a घोड़ा]; hence ~ जोरी; ~ तोड़ apt, befitting; crushing, incontro-vertible, retaliatory [as मुँहतोड़ जवाब]; -दर-मुँह face-to-face; ~ देखी superficial; involving sham regard; just for appeasement; ~ फट loose-tongued, outspoken, intemperate in speech; ~ बोला adopted; ~ माँगा as explicitly demanded or asked for; fully answering one's wish; ~ लगा insolent, impudent, given too much/ allowed too much liberty; —उतरना the face to grow lustreless; to be dismal-looking; to have the face withered due to shame/disease/ exhaustion/tiredness; the face to become shrunken/reduced/drawn; —का कौर/निवाला to be damn easy, as easy as the swallowing of a morsel; —काला करना lit. to blacken one's face, to be disgraced; to disgrace; to go about wenching; to get out of sight; to damn [it]; ~ की खाना to suffer a humiliating defeat; to receive a blow on the face, to be brow-beaten; —की बात छीनना – से बात छीनना to snatch words out of somebody's mouth; —खुलना to speak out; to speak out unrestrictedly;—खोलना to speak out; to ask for something; to be vituperatively outspoken; —चिढ़ाना to make faces at, to mock, to ridicule; छिपाना/छुपाना to evade [somebody], to skulk, to be bashful, to hide one's face; —देखते रह जाना to be lost in astonishment; to look aghast, to be taken aback; —पर on one's face, in the presence of; —पर ताला लग जाना to be tongue tied; to be rendered mute; not to utter a word; —पीला पड़ना to turn pale or pallid [from fear etc], to lose lustre; —फक हो जाना to turn pale; —फुलाना/सुजाना to sulk, to be sulkily reticent, to be displeased, to make a wry face, to distend the cheeks; —फेरना to abstain [from]; to avoid, to shun; to be averse to; to turn the face away from; —बंद करना to hold one's tongue; to bribe, to give hush money [to]; —बनाना to make a wry face; to look displeased/sour; to frown or scowl; to mock; —मीठा करना to give one a treat; to offer sweets to celebrate a happy occasion or a good news; —में कालिख पुतना/लगाना to be disgraced, to face ignominy;—में जबान न रखना to be tongue-tied; not to speak at all; to be very meek; -में दाँत न पेट में आँत to be very old; —में लगाम न होना to be absolutely intemperate in speech; to have no restraint whatever over one's utterance, to be in the habit of saying any and everything; —लगना to suit the palate of; to be agreeable to the taste of; to become used to; to bandy words [with]; —लेकर रह जाना, अपना-सा to face severe discomfiture; to be thoroughly chagrined; —से फूल झड़ना soft words to flow out, to be very gentle in speech; [ironical] to condemn in round terms, to reproach or abuse; —ही मुँह में in an inarticulate fashion, within oneself, to oneself.

मुँहासा [*nm*] [*a*] pimple [on the face supposedly signifying the advent of youth].

मुअत्त(त्ति)/ल [*a*] suspended; ~ ली suspension.

मुआ [*a*] dead; good for-nothing [an abuse often used by womenfolk].

मुआइ(य)ना [nm] inspection; visit.

मुआवज़ा [*nm*] compensation, recompense; indemnity; remuneration.

मुक़दमा [*nm*] a case; suit, law-suit.

मुक़दमेबा/ज [*a* and *nm*] [*a*] litigant; ~जी litigation.

मुक़द्दर [*nm*] fate, luck, destiny.

मुकरना [*v*] to deny, to refuse; to go back upon one's word; to belie.

मुक़र्/र [*a*] fixed, appointed; posted; employed, deployed.

मुक़ाब(बि)ला [*nm*] encounter; opposition; comparison, competition; equality.

मुक़ाम [*nm*] a place, site; quarter, halting place, halt.

मुक़ामी [*a*] local, colloquial.

मुकुट [*nm*] a crown; diadem, crest.

मु/क्का [*nm*] a fist-blow, punch; ~ क्केबाज a boxer, pugilist; ~क्केबाजी boxing, fist-fight, pugilism.

मुक्त [*a*] free/freed, independent, released; unfettered; liberated, delivered, emancipated; ~ कंठ से freely, without any reserve/ reservation; enjoying liberty of speech; ~हस्त liberal, bounteous, मुक्तक muktak [a and nm] stray, independent, not forming a connected whole; independent poems or couplets; —काव्य independent poetic verses, poetry that is not epical in character.

मुक्ता [*nf*] a pearl.

मुक्ति mukti: [nf] salvation; emancipation, deliverance; release, freedom; exemption, riddance; ~दाता who brings salvation/ emancipation, rescuer; -लाभ [achievement of] salvation, deliverance, emancipation.

मुख [*nm*] the mouth; face; forepart, front; brim; opening; exit or entrance; principal; -चित्र the fronticepiece; cover-design; -पत्र an organ; ~ पृष्ठ the cover-page; ~मंडल the face, countenance; -सुख economy of effort [in pronunciation], ease of pronunciation.

मुखड़ा [*nm*] face, pretty face.

मुख़तार [nm] an agent, attorney; ~ नामा power of attorney; मुखतारी attorneyship.

मुख़बिर [*nm*] an approver, informer: ~बिरी the act of an approver/informer.

मुख/र [*a*] explicit; out-spoken, loud; talkative, garrulous; ~ रित explicit; outspoken, loud; voiced.

मुख़ातिब [*a*]; —होना, किसी की ओर to address [somebody], to talk to, to turn towards [for speaking to].

मुख़ाल(लि)फ़त [*nf*] opposition; antagonism.

मुख़ालिफ़ [*a*] an opponent, adversary; antagonist.

मुखिया [*nm*] a chief, head, leader; the headman [of a village or clan etc.]

मुखौटा [*nm*] a mask.

मुख्य [*a*] principal, chief; main; salient; staple; leading; capital, cardinal; pre-eminent; predominant; ~तः primarily; chiefly, mainly.

मुख्यार्थ [*nm*] main/principal meaning.

मुख्यालय [*nm*] head-quarters.

मुगदर [*nm*] a mace/club [used in physical exercise].

मुग़ालता [*nm*] illusion, mistake, misconception.

मुग्ध [*a*] infatuated; charmed, under a spell, attracted [towards].

मुचलका [*nm*] a personal bond; recognizance.

मुजरा [*nm*] deduction; salutation; a singing session [by a prostitute].

मुजरिम [*nm*] a criminal.

मुज़ायका [*nm*] obstruction; worry, anxiety.

मुजाहिद [*nm*] a crusader.

मुझ [*pro*] oblique form of मैं.

मुझे [*pro*] to me.

मुटाई [*nf*] thickness; sturdiness.

मुटापा [*nm*] fattiness, fleshiness, plumpness.

मुट्ठी [*nf*] fist; grip; clutch[es]; the breadth of a closed palm; handful;—गरम करना to bribe; to accept bribe;—भर handful; —में होना to be under one's control, to be under the sway of.

मुठभेड़ [*nf*] an encounter, a confrontation, clash.

मुड़ना [*v*] to turn; to be twisted; to bend/to be bent; to return.

मुड्ढा [*nm*] the shoulders; the joints of the shoulders and arms.

मुतअल्लिक मुतल्लिक़ [*a*] concerning; —, के about, concerning, regarding, as regards.

मुताबिक़ [*ind*] in accordance with, according to.

मुदर्रि/स [*nm*] a teacher; ~सी the teaching profession, teachership; a teaching job.

मुदित [*a*] pleased, happy, delighted.

मुद्दई [*nm*] a plaintiff, complainant.

मुद्द/त [*nf*] period, length of time, limit; duration; a long time; ~ती old, antiquated, time-worn; of fixed duration.

मुद्दा [*nm*] theme, intention, purport.

मुद्दालेह [*nm*] defendant; respondent.

मुद्रक [*nm*] a printer.

मुद्र/ण [*nm*] printing; ~ णालय a printing press.

मुद्रा [*nm*] a seal; stamp; money, coin; countenance, demeanour; mien, pose, posture.

मुनक्का [*nm*] a large-size dried grape, big currant.

मुनहस(सि)र [*a*] depended, based.

मुनादी [*nf*] proclamation [esp. by beat of drum].

मुनाफ़ा [*nm*] profit, gain; ~ ख़ोर a profiteer; ~ ख़ोरी profiteering.

मुनासिब [*a*] reasonable, appropriate, proper, fit.

मुनि [*nm*] an ascetic, a hermit.

मुनीम [*nm*] an indigenous, system accountant.

मुन्ना [*nm*] a term of endearment for a child, small one, a dear child.

मुफ़लि/स [*a*] poor, indigent; pauper; ~ सी poverty, indigence; pauperdom.

मुफ़स्स(स्सि)ल [*a*] mofussil; detailed; [*nm*] a suburb of a town/city/centre.

मुफ़ीद [*a*] useful, beneficial.

मुफ़्त [*a*] free of charge, without price, gratis; ~ ख़ोर/खोरा a social parasite, one who lives on others' earnings; hence ~ख़ोरी.

मुवलि(ल)ग़ [*a*] in all, numbering, totalling; [nm] the amount.

मुबारक [*a*] auspicious; blessed, fortunate; ~वाद congratulations, felicitations.

मुब्तला [*a*] involved [in], occupied [with].

मुमकिन [*a*] possible, feasible.

मुमानि/अत, ~ यत [*nf*] prohibition, forbiddance.

मुरझाना [*v*] to wither, to fade; to lose lustre; to become dejected/gloomy.

मुरदा [*nm*] a corpse, dead body; [a] dead, lifeless; devoid of verve; ~दिल lifeless, devoid of verve, melancholy; hence ~ दिली; मुरदे की नींद सोना या मुरदे से शर्त बाँध/लगा कर सोना to go into a sleep as if never to awake, to go into a deep carefree sleep.

मुरब्बा [*nm*] jam, conserve; [a] square.

मुरली [*nf*] a flute, pipe.

मुरब्ब/त [*nf*] considerateness, gentility, obligingness, benevolent politeness, affability; hence ~ ती.

मुराद [*nf*] desire, wish; longing, craving.

मुरीद [*nm*] a follower, disciple.

मुर्ग़ा [*nm*] a cock, fowl.

मुर्ग़ाबी [*nf*] a guinea-hen.

मुर्चा [*nm*] rust.

मुर्दनी [*nf*] deathly stillness, mournfulness; melancholy; —छाना a melancholy heaviness to dawn upon [the atmosphere, face, etc.], to be overwhelmed by melancholia.

मुर्दा [*nm*] a corpse, dead body; ~ घर mortuary.

मुलज़िम [*nm*] an accused.

मुलम्मा [*nm*] gilding, plating, coating; external show, ostentation; ~गर/साज a gilder, plater.

मुलाक़ा/त [*nf*] meeting, visit; interview; acquaintance; hence ~ ती.

मुलाजमत [*nf*] employment, service.

मुलाजिम [*nm*] an employee, servant.

मुलाय/म [*a*] soft, tender; gentle; ~ मियत softness, tenderness; gentleness.

मुलाह(हि)जा [*nm*] seeing, having a look; regard, consideration.

मुल्क [*nm*] a country.

मुल्तबी [*a*] postponed; adjourned.

मुल्ला [*nm*] a Muslim priest; a Muslim teacher of the Quran; —की दौड़ मस्जिद तक a priest goes no further than the Church.

मुवक्क(क्कि)ल [*nm*] a client [of a pleader].

मुशायरा [*nm*] a poetic symposium.

मुश्किल [*a*] difficult, hard; intricate; [nf] difficulty, hardship.

मुसक(कु)रा/ना [*v*] to smile; ~ हट a smile.

मुसकान [*nf*] a smile.

मुसन्निफ़ [*nm*] a writer [of a book].

मुसम्मात [*nf*] a woman; an honorofic affixed to the name of a woman; [*a*] named [used for women only].

मुसलमान [*nm* and *a*] a Mohammedan; Muslim.

मुसलिम [*nm* and *a*] see मुसलमान.

मुसाफ़िर [*nm*] a traveller, wayfarer; passenger; ~ खाना a waiting room [at a railway station or bus-station].

मुसाहि/ब [*nm*] one meant chiefly to provide a company, flunkey, sycophant, ~ वियत, ~ वी flunkeyism, sycophancy.

मुसीबत [*nf*] difficulty, disaster, affliction; misfortune, calamity; ~ जदा, —का मारा afflicted, struck by misfortune/calamity.

मुस्टंडा [*a*] stout-bodied, robust; rough and robust.

मुस्तक़िल [*a*] permanent, confirmed; fixed, settled.

मुस्तै/द [*a*] agile, vigilant; ready, active; hence ~ दी.

मुहताज [*a*] dependent on, needy, necessitous, poor.

मुहब्बत [*nf*] love, affection, fondness.

मुहर [*nf*] seal; stamp; a gold coin; ~ बंद sealed.

मुहरा [*nm*] the front-part, face, countenance; a pawn or piece of chess; vanguard.

मुहर्र/म [*nm*] the day of Imam Hussain's martyrdom which is held sacred by Mohammedans and celebrated as a day of mourning; ~मी melancholy, gloomy, dismal.

मुहर्रि/र [*nm*] a scribe, clerk; hence ~ री.

मुहलत [*nf*] [period of] grace; [span of] extra time [to do a thing or to get ready].

मुहल्ला [*nm*] a locality/ward [in a city or town].

मुहाना [*nm*] estuary, source or mouth of a river.

मुहाल [*a*] difficult; impossible; [*nf*] facade.

मुहावरा [*nm*] idiom; practice, habit.

मुहिम [*nf*] an expedition, campaign; an arduous task.

मुहूर्त्त [*nm*] auspicious moment [to commence or undertake a work]; a moment of future possibilities.

मुहैया [*a*] available, procured.

मूँग [*nf*] green lentil.

मूंगफली [*hf*] ground-nut.

मूंगा [*nm*] coral.

मूंगिया [*a*] of dark-green colour.

मूँछ [*nf*] moustaches, whiskers:; —नीची होना to suffer humiliation, to be disgraced; —पर ताव देना to be on the top of the world; to twist one's moustaches out of haughtiness/pride; to be safe and secure; to care for nothing in the world; —मुंडाना to concede victory, to concede superiority to the other party; to get the moustaches shaven as an admission of defeat.

मूंड(ड़)ना [*v*] to shave, to shave the hair of the head; to fleece; to cheat; to initiate somebody into an ascetic's life.

मूंदना [*v*] to close, to shut; to cover; to hide.

मूक [*a*] dumb; mute, speechless; hence ~ ता.

मूज़ी [*a*] crudely stingy, niggardly close-fisted.

मूठ [*nf*] a hilt; handle, haft; grip; knob; an application of a sorcerer's spell.

मूढ़ [*a*] stupid, foolish, imbecile, silly; infatuated; ~ता stupidity, foolishness; silliness, imbecility; infatuation.

मूत [*nm*] urine, piss.

मूतना [*v*] to piss, to make water, to pass urine.

मूत्र [*nm*] urine, piss.

मूत्राशय [*nm*] urinary bladder, vesica.

मूर्ख [*a*] foolish, stupid, idiot, dullard, silly, dolt, booby; ~ मंडली an assembly of fools; a group of idiots.

मूर्खता [*nf*], मूर्खत्य [*nm*] folly, foolishness, stupidity, idiocity, silliness.

मूर्च्छना [*nf*] cadence, modulation [in music]; the scale obtained by a moule shift within a gamut.

मूर्च्छा [*nf*] fainting, swoon, fit; state of unconsciousness, syncope.

मूर्च्छित [*a*] fainted, swooned; unconscious.

मूर्त [a] concrete; corporeal, tangible; solid; formal; -अमूर्त concrete and abstract.

मूर्ति [*nf*] an idol, statue; image; —कला sculpture; statuary; ~कार sculptor, statuary.

मूर्तिमान [*a*] personified, incarnate.

मूर्द्धन्य [*a*] top-ranking, leading, pre-eminent [as विद्वान]; cerebral.

मूल [*nm*] root; an edible tuber/root; principal [sum]; origin, source; the nineteenth नक्षत्र; the original text [of a book etc.]; [*a*] radical; original; essential; fundamental, basic; principal, chief; parent; ~ त: basically, fundamentally, primarily; essentially; —तत्त्व the essential/basic/main element; —धन the principal; —पाठ text, original text; ~ भूत fundamental, essential, basic; original; —मंत्र the key-note, essence, essential element; —स्रोत main source, original source.

मूलाधार [*nm*] one of the six ganglions in the human body [according to हठयोग].

मूली [*nf*] radish.

मूल्य [*nm*] cost, price; value; worth; ~वान valuable, costly, precious.

मूल्यांकन [*nm*] assessment, evaluation/valuation.

मूस/ल [*nm*] a spigot; pounder; pestle; ~ लचंद stout, sturdy [person]; ~ लचंद, दाल भात में a wrong man in a wrong place, an intruder.

मूसलाधार [*a*] heavy [rain], torrential.

मृग [*nm*] a deer; ~ चर्म/छाला deer-skin; ~ जल/तृष्णा/मरीचिका mirage.

मृगया [*nm*] hunting.

मृणा/ल [*nf*] the root of a lotus plant; lotus-stalk; ~लिनी a lotus-plant; lotus.

मृत [*a*] dead; extinct.

मृतक [*nm*] a dead body, corpse; the dead.

मृत्युंजय [*nm*] one who has conquered death; [*a*] immortal, deathless; an epithet of Lord Shiv.

मृत्यु [*nf*] death, demise; mortality/fatality, the end; -लोक the mortal world, the earth, this world; ~शय्या death-bed; ~शोक bereavement, mourning.

मृदंग [*nf*] a drum-like Indian musical percussion instrument.

मृदु [*a*] soft; sweet; tender, gentle, mellow, mild; slow [as —गति]; ~ ता softness; sweetness; mildness, gentleness, tenderness; mellowness; slowness; ~ भाषी soft-spoken.

मृदुल [*a*] soft; sweet; tender; gentle, mild; ~ ता softness; sweetness; mildness.

मृषा [*a*] false, untrue; [*adv*] falsely; uselessly; in vain.

में [*ind*] in; into; among; between; at; on; of;—से out, of; from.

मेंढक [*nm*] a frog, toad.

मेंब/र [*nm*] a member; ~ री membership.

मेंह [*nm*] rain.

मेंहदी [*nf*] myrtle [the leaves of this shrub are powdered and the powder when soaked in water over a period leaves red stain on application on the palms, feet etc. and it used as such by Indian women].

मेख [*nf*] a nail; peg; [*nm*] a ram; the first sign of the Zodiac —Aries.

मेखला [*nf*] a girdle; zone, range.

मेघ [*nm*] a cloud; typical musical mode associated with rains.

मेज़ [*nf*] a table; ~ पोश a table cloth; table cover.

मेज़बान [*nm*] a host.

मेट [*nm*] a foreman [of labourers].

मेढ़ा [*nm*] a ram, tup.

मेदा [*nm*] stomach.

मेदिनी [*nf*] the earth.

मेधा [*nf*] intellect, brilliance, mental sharpness; ~ दान/ ~ वी intelligent, brilliant, sharp-witted.

मेम [*nf*] madam; European lady; —साहिबा lady, madam.

मेमना [*nm*] a lamb, lambkin.

मे/रा [*pro*] my, mine; hence ~ री [femine form].

मेरु [*nm*] a mythological mountain supposed to be of gold; also called सुमेरु.

मेरुदंड [*nm*] spine, backbone; spinal cord.

मेल [*nm*] concord; consonance, agreement; match; mixture, combination; unity; conciliation; connection; mail; hence -जोल/मिलाप intimacy; reconciliation, rapproachement; union; -मुलाकात approach; association, friendly relationship.

मेला [*nm*] a fair; festival crowd.

मेवा [nm] dry fruit.

मेष [*nm*] Aries—the first sign of the Zodiac; a ram.

मेह [*nm*] rain, rainfall; diabetes.

मेहत/र [*nm*] a sweeper, scavanger; hence ~रानी.

मेहनत [*nf*] labour, industry, hard work, toil; exercise; ~ कश a labourer.

मेहनताना [*nm*] remuneration [as to a lawyer]; wages.

मेहनती [*a*] laborious, industrious, hard working, diligent.

मेहमान [*nm*] a guest; ~ खाना a guest house; ~दार host; ~दारी playing as the host; hospitality.

मेहमानी [*nf*] staying as a guest, enjoying the hospitality [of].

मेहर/बान [*a*] kind, compassionate; ~बानी [act of] kindness; favour.

मेहराब [*nm*] an arch; vault; ~दार arched; vaulted.

मेहरी [*nf*] a woman who works as household utensil-cleaner.

मैं [*pro*] I.

मैच [*nm*] a match.

मैत्री [*nf*] friendship, cordiality.

मैथुन [*nm*] coition, cohabitation, sexual/carnal intercourse, copulation; [*a*] pertaining to a couple.

मैदा [*nm*] very fine wheat- flour.

मैदान [*nm*] a field; plains; battlefield;—में आना/उतरना to enter into the battlefield/arena; to be ready for a fight;—साफ़ कर देना to clear all obstacles; to kill or rout all the adversaries.

मैदानी [*a*] pertaining to plains; even.

मैना [*nf*] a black Indian bird famous for its melodious notes.

मैनेजर [*nm*] a manager.

मैल [*nf*] dirt, filth; scum; ~ खोर/खोरा dust-absorbing.

मैला [*a*] dirty, filthy; unclean; foul; [*nm*] excrement, faeces; hence -कुचैला [a].

मोढ़ा [*nm*] a stool made of reeds.

मोक्ष [*nm*] salvation, deliverance, final liberation.

मोच [*nf*] sprain, twist.

मोची [*nm*] a shoe-maker, cobbler.

मोज़ा [*nm*] socks; stocking.

मोटर [*nf*] a motor-car;motor; ~कार a motor-car; -साइकिल a motor-bicycle.

मोटा [*a*] fat, plump; corpulent; thick; coarse, rough; gross; -आसामी a moneyed man; ~ ई fatness, plumpness, corpulence; thickness; coarseness, roughness; grossness; -ताजा chubby, fleshy; robust; मोटे तौर पर roughly speaking.

मोटापा [*nm*] fatness, plumpness, fleshiness, corpulence.

मोड़ [*nm*] a turn; turning point; bend; twist.

मोड़ना [*v*] to turn; to turn back or in another direction.

मोतदिल [*a*] moderate, temperate [as आबहवा].

मोतिया [*nm*] a kind of jasmine flower; [a] pearl-coloured.

मोतियाबिंद [*nm*] cataract [formed in the eye].

मोती [*nm*] a pearl; ~झरा typhoid.

मोदी [*nm*] a grocer; ~ ख़ाना a provision store.

मोम [*nf*] wax; ~जामा oil-cloth, oil-skins; tarpaulin; ~ बत्ती a candle-stick.

मोमी [*a*] made of wax; wax.

मोर [*nm*] a peacock; ~ नी a peahen; ~ पंख a peacock-feather; ~ पंखी of the colour of peacock-feather.

मोरचा [*nm*] a battle-front, front; rust [also मुर्चा]; ~बंदी stratagem, battle-array, taking up strategic positions; —मारना/लेना to achieve victory on a front.

मोरी [*nf*] a culvert; drain, sewer, conduit; drain hole.

मोल [*nm*] cost, price.

मोह [*nm*] illusion; ignorance; affection; infatuation, fascination; spell; ~ पाश the snare of worldly illusion; ~ भंग disillusionment; -ममता affection and attachment.

मोहक [*a*] charming, fascinating, casting a spell; causing illusion.

मोहन [*a*] charming, attractive; tempting; [*nm*] enchantment; charm, mantra employed for purposes of sorcery; an epithet of Lord Krishnā.

मोहना [*v*] to cast a spell, to charm, to attract; to tempt; to infatuate.

मोहनी [*nf*] a spell; enchantment, delusion.

मोहब्बत [*nf*] see मुहब्बत.

मोहर [*nf*] a stamp; seal; a guinea, gold coin.

मोहरा [*nm*] the mouth [of a pot etc.]. opening, facing; fore-end, stock; a pawn in chess, chessman.

मोहरी [*nf*] the circumference of each of the lower openings of trousers or pants.

मोहल्ला [*nm*] a locality, ward, street.

मोहित [*a*] charmed, attracted, enchanted, spell-bound; fallen in love.

मोहिनी [*a*] who tempts/charms/attracts/casts a spell [feminine adjectival form]; [nf] see मोहनी.

मौक़ा [*nm*] chance; occasion; location; situation; site, work-site, site of occurrence; मौक़े पर at the appropriate time; on the spot; मौक़े से duly, just in time.

मौखिक [*a*] verbal, oral; —परीक्षा viva-voce [test].

मौख्य [*nm*] मुख्यता.

मौज [*nf*] a whim, caprice; delight; luxury; a wave.

मौज़ा [*nm*] a village.

मौजी [*a*] capricious, whimsical, merry, mirthful.

मौज़ूं [*a*] reasonable, befitting, suitable.

मौजूद [*a*] present; existing, ~ गी presence; existence.

मौजूदा [*a*] current, present.

मौजूदगी [*nf*] presence, existence, — में, in the presence of; during the existence.

मौत [*nf*] death, demise; mortality; —का सिर पर खेलना death to hover around the corner; —के घाट –उतारना to put to death; —के मुँह में जाना to risk one's life; to be in the cruel clutches of death.

मौद्रिक [*adj.*] monetary, fiscal, financial.

मौन [*a*] mum, quiet, silent, speechless, mute; tacit; [nm] silence, quiescence; -व्रत a vow to keep quiet, to adopt silence.

मौना [*nm*] a beehive: a large jar, or basket, reg. a bee.

मौनी [*nm*] a basket of wicker-work, an ascetic who observes a vow of permanent or perpetual silence.

मौर [*nm*] a pyramid-like wickerwork crown worn by the bridegroom in traditioanl Indian marriage ceremonies, a crown; diadem; as an adjectival suffix it imparts the meaning of one that stands out as pre-eminent [as सिरमौर].

मौराना [*v.i.*] to blossom; to flourish.

मौरूसी [*a*] hereditary, patrimonial.

मौलवी [nm] a scholar of Islamic law, Arabic and Persian; an Arabic/Persian teacher.

मौला [*nm*] the Master; a typical carefree man with no encumbrances whatever.

मौलाना [*nm*] a title given to a great Muslim scholar; a scholar of Arabic.

मौलिक [*a*] original; primordial; fundamental; essential; radical; ~ ता originality.

मौसम [*nm*] season; weather; opportune time; ~ विज्ञान/शास्त्र meteorology.

मौ/सा [nm] the husband of mother's sister; hence ~सी, ~सेरे.

म्याऊँ [*nf*] mewing [of a cat]; —का मुँह पकड़ना to bell the cat, to face the real hazard.

म्यान [*nf*] sheath.

म्लान [*a*] wilt, withered, faded; languid; hence~ता.

म्लानी [*nf*] withering, fading, weariness, dejection, dirt, filth, dark areas of the moon's surface.

म्लेच्छ [*nm*] an alien [invader]; a non-Aryan; [a] lowly; unclean, shabby; un-Indian [in a contemptuous sense].

य the first of the य, र, ल, व series of the Devanagari: alphabet, traditionally called अंत:स्थ [semi-vowels]. Modern Phoneticians, however, regard only य and व as semi-vowels.

य - देवनागरी वर्णमाला का छब्बीसवाँ व्यंजन वर्ण है। इसके उच्चारण में कुछ आंतरिक प्रयत्न तथा कुछ बाह्य प्रयत्न होते हैं।

यंत्र [*nm*] a machine; an instrument; amulet, talisman; mystical diagram; ~चालित mechanized, machine operated; ~ वत् like a machine; -विधान mechanism; -सज्जित mechanized.

यंत्रणा [*nf*] torture; torment.

यंत्रिका [*nf*] a small of delicate instrument; gadget.

यंत्रीकरण [*nm*] mechanization.

यक [*a*] one; alone; used in compound words as यक-व-यक, यकबारगी etc. in place of एक.

यका/र [*nm*] the letter य and its sound; ~ रांत [word] ending in य [ya].

यक़ीन [*nm*] trust, faith, confidence; certainty; assurance.

यक़ीनन [*adv.*] certainly, assuredly.

यकृत [*nm*] the liver.

यक्ष [*nm*] a class of mythological demi-gods.

यक्ष्मा [*nm*] tuberculosis.

यजन [*nm*] the act of sacrificing.

यजमान [nm] one who performs a यज्ञ; client of a priest or of attendants [who do household chores on auspicious occasions or rituals].

यजमानी [*nf*] the work, function or position of a यजमान.

यजुर्वेद [*nm*] the third of the four Vedas a holy book of hindu.

यज्ञ [*nm*] sacrifice, an ancient Hindu institution of religious sacrifice and oblation.

यज्ञीय [*adj*] fit for sacrifice, sacrificial.

यज्ञोपवीत [*nm*] the sacred thread traditionally worn by caste Hindus; one of the sixteen major Sanskaras [also called यज्ञोपवीत संस्कार] wherein a young lad is given a sacred thread to wear for the first time.

यत [*adj*] to be striven for.

यति [*nf*] a pause, check, caesura [in meter]; [*nm*] an ascetic, anchorite [who has subdued his passions].

यतीम [*nm* and *a*] [an] orphan; ~ खाना an orphanage.

यतिनी [*nf*] female ascetic, a widow.

यतनीय [*adj*] to be striven for.

यत्किंचित [*adv*] somewhat, a little, to a slight degree.

यत्न [*nm*] effort, endeavour; attempt; care.

यत्र [*adv*] where; -तत्र here and there, hither and thither; ~ सर्वत्र here, there and everywhere.

यथा [*adv*] as per; thus; for example, for instance; in whatever manner; ~क्रम in order, systematically; successively, respectively; methodical, systematic, regular; ~ तथ्य as it is, intact; exact, accurate; ~ नियम as per rule; ~ निर्दिष्ट as mentioned; as directed; ~ पूर्व as before, status quo; ~ मूल्य ad valorem; ~ योग्य suitably, properly; according as one deserves; ~ वत् in situ, intact, as before; ~ वसर according to opportunity/time, as the occasion demands; ~शक्ति/शक्य as far as possible, according to one's power/capacity; ~ शीघ्र as early/promptly as possible; ~संभव as far as possible; ~समय in due course, at the proper time, when an opportunity comes; ~स्थान at the proper place.

यथार्थ [*a*] real, actual; accurate; ~ त: de facto; really, actually; factually; ~ ता reality; accuracy; ~ वाद realism; ~वादिता realism; reality; ~वादी a realist; realistic.

यथार्थता [*nf*] accordance with reality: real or factual nature; genuineness; truth; fact, reality objectivity; dispassionateness.

यथेच्छ [*a* and *adv*] as one likes, according to one's wish/desire; arbitrary.

यथेष्ट [*a*] sufficient, enough; adequate.

यथोचित [*a*] due; proper, appropriate, reasonable; rightful; [*adv*] duly; properly; reasonably; rightfully.

यदि [*ind*] if, in case, provided that.

यदृ/च्छ [*a*] arbitrary; random; ~च्छा arbitrariness; randomness.

यद्यपि [*ind*] though; although, even though.

यम [*nm*] the god of death; restraint of passions; two; ~दूत a messenger of the god of death; ~पुर/पुरी/लोक the world of the god of death; the infernal world, the world where sinners are supposed to be lodged after death; ~ पहुँचाना to put to death.

यमक [*nm*] a particular wordbased figure of speech.

यमुना [*nf*] one of the most important Indian rivers [considered to be sacred by the Hindus].

यवन [*nm*] a Greek; a Mohammedan; hence यवनी [*nf*].

यवनिका [*nf*] a curtain; drop scene.

यश [*nm*] fame, reputation, renown, glory; ~स्वी celebrated; reputed, renowned; glorious.

यशोगान [*nm*] encomium, eulogy, singing the praises [of].

यष्टि [*nf*] a stick; rod.

यह [*pro*] this; it; —मुँह और मसूर की दाल like lip, like lettuce.

यहाँ [*adv*] here, hither, in/at this place.

यहीं [*adv*] at this veryplace here itself.

यही [*a*] this very.

यहूदी [*nm*] a Jew.

यांत्रि/क [*a*] mechanical; [*nm*] a mechanist; mechanic.

या [*conj*] or, either; —इलाही/खुदा Oh God!, My God!

याचक [*nm*] a beggar; suppliant; hence ~ ता.

याचना [*nf*] begging, entreaty; asking for something.

याचिका [*nf*] a petition.

यातना [*nf*] torture, torment.

यातायात [*nm*] traffic, coming and going.

यात्रा [*nf*] a journey, travel; wayfaring; trip, tour; pilgrimage; march; a kind of popular play prevalent in Bengal.

यात्रिक [*nm*] a traveller, wayfarer, passenger; pilgrim.

यात्री [*nm*] a traveller, wayfarer, passenger; pilgrim.

याद [*nf*] memory, recollection, remembrance.

यादगा/र [*nf*] a monument; memorial; memento; also ~ री.

याददाश्त [*nf*] memory.

यादृच्छि/क [*a*] random; arbitrary, ~कता arbitrariness; randomness.

यान [*nm*] a van; vehicle.

या/नी ~ **ने** [*ind*] that is, that is to say.

याफ़्ता —a suffix used to denote one who has been awarded/given [as सजायाफ़्ता, सनदयाफ़्ता].

यामिनी [*nf*] the night.

याम्योत्तर [*a*] meridian.

यायावर [*nm*] a nomad; wanderer.

यार [*nm*] a friend, companion; paramour, lover, ~बाश a friend of friends, good companion.

याराना [*a*] friendly; [*nm*] friendship; illicit relationship/intimacy.

यारी [*nf*] friendship; romantic intimacy; illicit love.

यीशु [*nm*] Jesus Christ; ~मसीह Jesus Christ.

युक्त [*a*] united, combined; joined with; fitted with; befitting, suitable; proper, right.

युक्ति [*nf*] device; means; tactics, artifice, manoeuvre; skill; argument, plea; ~ युक्त befitting; logical, rational, reasonable; proper, suitable; ~संगत reasonable, logical, rational.

युग [*nm*] an age; epoch; era; period; times; one of the four ages—viz, सतयुग, त्रेता, द्वापर, कलियुग-of the world according to Indian tradition; a pair, couple; -चेतना age-consciousness; ~धर्म contemporaneity, conformation to the times; ~पत् simultaneously; simultaneous.

युगांत [*nm*] the end of an age, cosmic destruction.

युगांतर [nm] another/new era, advent of a new epoch; ~कारी revolutionary, epoch-making.

युग्म [*nm*] pair; couple; [a] two.

युद्ध [*nm*] war/warfare; battle; fight/fighting; combat, hostilities; -क्षेत्र battle-field, theatre of war; -नीति strategy; -पोत warship, man of war; -बंदी a prisoner of war; cessation of hostilities; ~विराम cease-fire.

युयु/त्सा [*nf*] pugnacity, bellicosity, belligerence; ~त्सु pugnacious, bellicose, belligerent.

युवक [*nm*] a youth; youngman.

युवती [*nf*] a young woman, youthful woman.

युवराज [*nm*] a prince.

युवराज्ञी [*nf*] a princess.

युवा [*a*] youthful; [nm] youth.

यूं [*adv*] in this way, in this manner; like this, thus.

यूनिवर्सिटी [*nf*] a university.

यूरो/प [*nm*] Europe; ~ पीयन European; ~पीय European.

ये [*pro*] these.

येन-केन-प्रकारेण [*adv*] somehow, somehow or the other, by fair or foul means; by hook or by crook.

यों [*adv*] like this, in this way/manner.

योग [*nm*] total, sum total; recipe; combination; addition; joining together; conjugation; mixture; contribution; a system of concentration and meditation, concentrational exercise; means of salvation, union with the Universal Soul by means of contemplation; one of the six schools of Indian philosophy; an auspicious or opportune moment; opportunity; device; -क्षेम welfare, well-being; ~दान contribution; ~ फल total, the sum total, sum; ~ भ्रष्ट one who has aberrated/astrayed/deviated from योग: ~ रूढ़ि a compound word used in a much more restricted sense as compared with the direct meaning of its components.

योगिनी [*nf*] female ascetic.

योगिनिद्रा [*nf*] योग-निद्रा.

योगाभ्यास [*nm*] the practice of योग.

योगी [*nm*] one who practises योग, ascetic; hence योगिनी [feminine form].

योग्य [*a*] qualified; able, deserving, capable, competent; worthy; eligible, suitable, meritorious; hence ~ ता.

योजक [*a*] uniting, joining; [nm] one who or that which unites/ joins; -चिह्न a hyphen.

योजन [*nm*] joining, uniting; union; junction; a measure of distance [roughly equal to eight miles].

योजना [*nf*] a plan/planning, scheme; disposition; arrangememt [as शब्द-योजना]; -आयोग Planning Commission.

योजित [*adj*] joined, formed, established, planned.

योजनीय [*adj*] योज्य.

योद्धा [*nm*] a warrior, fighter, combatant.

योद्धापन [*nm*] soldiering, bravery, valour.

योनि [*nf*] vagina, female organ of generation; the form of existence or station fixed by birth [according to Hindu traditional belief these forms number eighty four lac].

यौगिक [*a*] pertaining to योग; compound; conjunctive, derivative.

यौन [a] sexual; vaginal; -तृप्ति sexual gratification; —सम्बन्ध sexual relations.

यौवन [*nm*] youth, youthfulness.

र —the second amongst the series य,र,ल,व of the Devanagari: alphabet, traditionally designated as semi-vowels —अंतःस्थ; see य.

र - हिन्दी वर्णमाला का सत्ताइसवाँ व्यंजन वर्ण और दूसरा अंतस्थ वर्ण है। इसका उच्चारण जीभ के अग्रभाग को मूर्द्धा के साथ स्पर्श करने से होता है।

रंक [*a*] poor, indigent, pauper; [*nm*] a beggar, penniless person.

रंकता [*nf*] poverty.

रंकिणी [*nf*] a poor, or deprived, woman.

रंग [*nm*] colour; dye; complexion; paint; a suit, trump [in playing cards]; grandeur; beauty; ways; influence; whim; kind, category; gaiety; stage; -ढंग ways, manners, demeanour, conduct; ~ पीठ a theatre; -बिरंगा variegated, multi-coloured; ~ भूमि theatre, stage; arena; ~मंच stage; ~ मंडप theatre, theatrical pavilion; ~महल the apartment meant for amorous sport, private apartment; -रंगीला variegated; colourful; -रूप physical appearance, looks; ~शाला theatrum, theatre; ~साज a painter; ~ साज़ी painting, —आना to assume fullness; to assume true colours; to become colourful; to achieve youthful grace and grandeur; —उड़ना/उतरना to fade; to lose facial lustre; to lose wits; to turn pallid; —चढ़ना to be in high spirits; to be coloured; to be influenced; to be colourfully youthful; to be in full bloom; —जमना to have attained influential position; to establish supremacy; to be held in esteem; to be in full swing [as महफ़िल में रंग जमना]; to be enjoying thoroughly; —फीका पड़ना/होना to fade out; to lose brightness/lustre; one's influence to be on the wane; —भरना to fill in colours; to impart fullness/completeness [to a picture]; —में ढलना to be moulded according to some influence, to be under somebody's sway; -में भंग करना to mar a happy occasion, a melancholic to appear in a gay gathering; —में रँगना to mould after one's image; to exercise overwhelming influence.

रंगत [*nf*] colour; complexion; plight, condition; relish; delight.

रंगना [*v*] to colour; to dye; to paint; रँगा सियार a wolf in lamb's guise, a hoax, sham gentleman.

रंगरूट [*nm*] a recruit; novice.

रंगवाना [*v.t.*] to cause to be coloured, dyed, painted by, से.

रंगरेज़ [*nm*] a dyer.

रंगरे/ली [*nf*] usually used plural form; ~लियाँ rejoicing merry-making/merriment.

रंगाई [*nf*] dyeing; dyeing charges.

रंगावट [*nf*] dyeing [pattern].

रंगीन [*a*] coloured; colourful, gay, luxury-loving; jovial; ~मिज़ाज gay, colourful, sportive; mirthful luxury-loving.

रंगीनी [*nf*] colourfulness gaiety, sportiveness, mirthfulness.

रंगीला [*a*] colourful, gay sportive, mirthful; hence ~पन.

रंच, ~क [*a*] slight; somewhat, a little.

रंचक [*adj*] a little.

रंज [*nm*] sorrow, grief; sadness gloominess.

रंजक [*nm*] colouring, dyeing, रंजक, moving, exciting emotion, or the heart: e.g. मनोरंजक, entertaining, a dyer, a dye as henna, red sandalwood or vermillion.

रंजित [*a*] coloured, dye delighted.

रंजिश [*nf*] animus, animosity; rancour, ill-feeling.

रंजी/दा [*a*] grieved, sad, gloomy; ~दगी state of be grieved/sorry, sadness, gloominess.

रँडा(ड़ा)पा [*nm*] widow-hood.

रंडी [*nf*] a prostitute, harlot woman of easy virtue; ~ बाज one who wenches with prostitutes ~बाजी wenching with prostitutes.

रंडुआ [*nm*] widower.

रंदा [*nm*] a carpenter's plane.

रंध्र [*nm*] a hole, orifice, aperture; stomata.

रका/र [nm] the letter **'र'** [and its sound; ~ रांत [word ending in र.

रईस [*nm*] a nobleman; rich man, grandee; [*a*] rich, wealthy; her ~ज़ादा.

रईसी [*nf*] nobility; grandiosity; wealthiness, richness.

रक़म [*nf*] a sum, an amount; cunning, crafty [person].

रकाब [*nf*] a stirrup.

रक़ाबत [*nf*] rivalry [in love].

रकाबी [*nf*] a plate, dish.

रक़ीब [*nm*] a rival [in love].

रक्त [*nm*] blood; [*a*] red, saffron; attached; ~क्षीणता anaemia: ~पात bloodshed; shedding of blood; -पिपासा blood-thirst; -पिपासु blood-thirsty, sanguinary; ~रंजित bloody; sanguinary; causing bloodshed.

रक्तिम [*a*] red-tinged, sanguine, ruddy.

रक्षक [*a* and *nm*] protectant/protector; saviour, defender; guard; keeper; custodian.

रक्षण [*nm*] protection, guarding; reservation, custody; maintaining/safe-keeping.

रक्षा [*nf*] defence; protection, guarding; safe-keeping; custody; —सेना defence force.

रक्षात्मक [*a*] defensive; safeguarding; protective, ensuring custody.

रखना [*v*] to put; to place; to keep; to possess; to have; to employ, to appoint; to keep as wife/husband; रख-रखाव maintenance; safe-keeping.

रखवाला [*nm*] a guard, watchman.

रखवाली [*nf*] guarding, watch/watchmanship, safe-keeping, safeguarding, care.

रखाना [*v*] to guard, to watch; to care; to maintain.

रग [*nf*] a vein; fibre; -पट्ठा veins and muscles; —दबना to be under somebody's sway; to be under overbearing influence [of] to be under subjugation; —पहचानना to know thoroughly well; to know the inner secret; —में दौड़ जाना to have a profound effect, to infuse each and every nerve; -रग में all over, in each and every nerve; -रग से वाकिफ़ होना to know through and through; रगों में खून दौड़ना to be in high spirits; to be excited.

रगड़ [*nf*] run, friction; bruise; abrasion.

रगड़ना [*v*] to rub, to scrub; to grate; to bruise; to cause harassment; to toil without progress.

रगड़ा [*nm*] a rub, rubbing; friction; bruise; toil.

र/चना [*nf*] composition, artistic creation structure; [v] to create; to compose; to make; to form, to construct; hence ~चित.

रचयिता [nm] creator, composer; author.

रजत [*nm*] silver; [*a*] silvery; white; bright; —जयंती silver jubilee.

रजनी [*nf*] night.

रजवाड़ा [*nm*] native state, a former princely state of India.

रज(स्) [*nm*] menstruation; the second of the three गुण characterising human nature [see रजोगुण]; ~कण dust particle.

रजस्वला [*a*] menstruous, [woman] in menstruation.

रज़ा [*nf*] will, wish; consent, permission; ~मंद willing; consenting, agreeing; ~मंदी will; consent, agreement.

रज़ाई [*nf*] a Quilt.

रजिस्ट्री [*nf*] registration; registered post; ~शुदा registered.

रजोगुण [*nm*] one of the three attributes of nature which manifests itself in luxuriousness, merry-making, exhibitionism and such other trends.

रजो/दर्शन, ~धर्म [*nm*] monthly course, menstruation.

रटंत [*nf*] cramming, memorizing, commission to memory.

रट [*nf*] constant repetition/reiteration.

र/टना [*v*] to repeat/reiterate constantly; to cram, to commit to memory, to memorize; ~ट्टू a crammer; ~ पीर an adept in cramming, a crammer.

रण [*nm*] war, battle, fighting, combat; ~क्षेत्र the battle-field, theatre of war; -नीति strategy; ~बाँकुरा valorous; a great fighter.

रत [*a*] attached, loving; [used as a suffix to mean] engaged in, occupied with [as कार्यरत]; —an allomorph of 'रात' used as the first member in certain compound words; ~जगा keeping awake the whole night [to celebrate a happy occasion through singing devotional songs or otherwise].

रति [*nf*] love, enjoyment of love, sexual passion, oestrus; copulation; name of the wife of काम

देव [Cupid] —hence, a very pretty woman; ~क्रिया copulation, sexual intercourse; ~जन्य venereal, born of sexual intercourse; ~दान sexual intercourse, copulation.

रतौंधी [*nf*] nyctalopia, night-blindness.

रत्न [*nm*] a gem, precious stone; the most outstanding individual of a class.

रत्नाकार [*nm*] the sea, ocean.

रथ [*nm*] a chariot.

रथी [*a*] riding a chariot; [*nm*] a fighter, warrior.

रद्द [*a*] rejected; cancelled; annulled.

रद्दी [*a*] worthless; inferior, of inferior quality; rough; [nf] waste paper; spoilage.

रद्दोबदल [*nf*] change, alteration; spoilage.

रन [*nm*] a run [in cricket]; a reclaimed part of the sea [e.g. कच्छ का रन].

रनिवास [*nm*] the seraglio, female apartment [in a palace].

रपट [*nf*] a report; slipping, sliding/slipperiness.

रपटना [*v*] to slip; to slide; to skid; [*a*] slippery.

रफल [*nf*] a woollen wrapper, shawl.

रफ़ा [*a*] settled, finished;—दफ़ा settled, finished.

रफ़ू [*nm*] darning; ~ गर a darner; ~गरी darning.

रफ़ूचक्कर —होना to show a clean pair of heels, to turn tails, to make good one's escape.

रफ़्तार [*nf*] speed, pace.

रफ़्ता-रफ़्ता [*adv*] slowly, gradually, by degrees.

रबड़ [*nf*] rubber; an eraser.

रबड़ी [*nf*] a typical sweetmeat prepared from boiled milk and sugar.

रबर [*nf*] see रबड़.

रबी [*nm*] spring; crop reaped in the spring season.

रब्त [*nm*] practice; association, intercourse, mixing;-जब्त association, social intercourse; relations.

रमणी [*nf*] a pretty woman, young woman.

रमणीक [*a*] beautiful, pretty charming, winsome, attractive; hence ~ ता.

रमणीय [*a*] beautiful, pretty, charming, winsome, attractive; enjoyable; hence ~ता.

रमना [*v*] to enjoy, to make merry; to roam/rove, to wander about.

रम्य [*a*] beautiful, pretty, winsome; charming, attractive; hence ~ ता [nf].

रर(ड़)क [*nf*] smarting, painful sensation [as when an alien matter falls into the eye].

रर(ड़)कना [*v*] to smart, to produce a painful sensation [as by a coal particle falling into the eye].

रव [*nm*] noise, tumult.

रवाँ [*a*] trained, practised, well-versed.

रवा [*nm*] a particle, grain; crystal; filings; ~दार granular; crystaline.

रवानगी [nf] depature, setting out.

रवाना [*a*] departed, set out; despatched; —होना to depart, to set out.

रवानी [*a*] flow; fluency.

रविश [*nf*] walking passage between flower beds; movement, speed.

रवैया [*nm*] attitude, behaviour; practice.

रश्क [*nm*] jealousy, envy.

रश्मि [*nf*] a ray.

रस [*nm*] juice; [aesthetic] relish; sentiment; pleasure, enjoyment; taste, flavour; ~दार juicy, luscious; tasty, relishing; ~भरी raspberry; ~भीना full of flavour, well-steeped in sentiment; ~राज the king of all sentiments—the erotic sentiment; ~वाद pleasant/erotic talk, wrangle; taking interest in erotic talks; talkativeness; ~वादी one who takes interest in erotic talks/quarrels; talkative.

रसद [*nf*] supply/supplies, provision [s].

रसवं/त [*a*] full of relish; juicy; having aesthetic sense; [nm] one who has enjoyed love-making/aesthetic relish; hence ~ती.

रसवती [a] full of juice–aesthetic relish/enjoyment; juicy.

रसा [*nf*] the earth; soup, broth; juice.

रसाई [*nf*] approach; association, contacts.

रसातल [*nm*] the netherworld, hell.

रसात्मक [*a*] full of juice; juicy; aesthetic, beautiful.

रसायन [*nm*] Chemistry; [*a*] chemical; ~ज्ञ well-versed in Chemistry; -विज्ञान/शास्त्र Chemistry.

रसास्वाद [*nm*] aeshetic relish, emotive relish; hence ~न.

रसिक [*a* and *nm*] a man of taste, one having aesthetic sense, one who appreciates beauty or excellence; an amorist; dilettante; hence ~ता [*nf*].

रसिया [*nm*] having aesthetic relish; liking juicy talks; frivolous; a class of typical folk songs sung during the month of फागुन in parts of U.P.

रसीद [*nf*] a receipt.

रसीदी [*a*] regarding or pertaining to a receipt; fixed on a receipt.

रसीला [*a*] juicy; tasteful, delicious; loving juicy talks; amorous; frivolous.

रसूल [*nm*] prophet, divine messenger.

रसोइया [*nm*] a cook. One who is cooking food.

रसोई [*nf*] cooked food; kitchen; ~खाना/घर a kitchen.

रसौली [*nf*] a tumour; a disease attended with tumour formation over the eyebrows.

र/स्म [*nf*] a ceremony, ritual; formality; custom; practice; ~स्मी formal, ceremonial; related to or conforming to a ritual.

रस्सा [*nm*] a stout thick rope; ~कशी a tug-of-war.

रस्सी [*nf*] a rope, cord.

रहट [*nf*] a Persian wheel [for drawing water out of a well].

रहन [*nm*] a pawn pledge, mortgage; [mode of] living; -सहन living; ways.

रहना [*v*] to live; to stay; to reside; to remain; to continue.

रहम [*nm*] pity, mercy, compassion; hence ~दिल, ~दिली.

रहस्य [nm] a secret; secrecy, mystery.

रहस्योद्‌घाटन [*nm*] revelation, disclosure of mystery.

रहित [*a*] without, devoid of, bereft of.

राँ/ग, ~गा [*nm*] tin; solder.

राँड़ [*nf*] a widow; a term of abuse.

राइफ़ल [*nf*] a rifle.

राई [*nf*] mustard, black mustard; —का पर्वत/पहाड़ करना/बनाना to make a mountain of a mole hill; -रत्ती करके in the minutest details.

राक्षस [*nm*] a demon, monster.

राक्षसी [*nf*] an ogress, monstress; [*a*] monstrous, demonic.

राख [*nf*] ash[es].

राखी [*nf*] a sacred thread tied by a sister on the wrist of her brother[s] as a mark of affection [that binds the brother to protect her in times of crisis].

राग [*nm*] a melodic mode or structure with a fixed sequence of notes, melody; tune; attraction, attachment; emotion; passion, love; -द्वेष attachment and malevolence; love and hatred/rancour.

रागिनी [*nf*] a musical mode or a variation/modification thereof.

राज [*nm*] a kingdom, realm; state; reign; an allomorph of 'राजा' which when prefixed or suffixed to numerous other words denotes excellence, supremacy etc; a builder, mason; ~काज public affairs, affairs of the state; governance; ~कुमार a prince; —कुमारी a princess; ~कोष fisc, public/state exchequer; treasury; ~गद्दी royal throne; ~तंत्र monarchy, monarchical system of government; तंत्रवादी royalist[ic], monarchist[ic]; ~तंत्रीय monarchical; ~तिलक coronation, anointing at the time of coronation; ~दूत an ambassador; ~दूतावास an embassy; ~द्रोह lese majesty, sedition, treason; ~द्रोहपूर्ण, ~ द्रोहात्मक seditious; ~द्रोही a seditionist; ~धर्म state religion; royal duty; ~पथ a highway; ~पाट region, royal throne; ~पूत a class of kshatriyas known for their valour and bravery; ~प्रासाद a palace; ~भक्त a loyalist; one loyal to the ruler/state; ~भक्ति loyalism, loyalty or allegiance to the ruler/state; ~मर्मज्ञ a statesman; ~मर्मज्ञता statesmanship; ~मुद्रा signet, royal seal; ~यक्ष्मा tuberculosis; ~योग an auspicious combination of planets [in one's horoscope] that forebodes elevation to royalty; ~रोग an incurable or long-lasting disease; tuberculosis —लक्ष्मी regal majesty, royal grandeur, kingly prosperity and splendour; state goddess of prosperity; ~वंश a dynasty; ~वैद्य royal physician; an eminent physician; -व्यवस्था polity; ~श्री royal grandeur/majesty, regal splendour and prosperity; ~सत्ता royal authority; monarchy; ~सत्तात्मक monarchical, pertaining to a system of government where authority is wielded by a ruler; ~सभा a royal court; ~समाज an assembly of princes, princely assembly; royal court; ~सिंहासन the royal throne.

राज़ [*nm*] a secret; ~दाँ one who knows the secret, one who shares [somebody's] secret, confidant.

राजकीय [*a*] royal; public, official; pertaining to the state.

राजधानी [*nf*] a capital, metropolis.

राजन/य [*nm*] diplomacy; ~यज्ञ a diplomatist; ~यिक a diplomat; diplomatic.

राजनीति [*nf*] politics; ~क political; ~ सत्ता political authority/power; ~ज्ञ a politician; -शास्त्र politics, political science.

राजप/त्र [*nm*] a gazette; ~त्रित gazetted.

राजभवन [*nm*] governor's house; palace.

राजभाषा [*nf*] the official language.

राजर्षि [*nm*] a princely sage, seer born in a kshatriya family.

राजवित्तीय [*a*] fiscal.

राजस [*a*] born of रजोगुण; [nm] excitement; arrogance; rage.

राजसिक [*a*] born of रजोगुण.

राजसी [*a*] royal, regal, kingly, princely, befitting or becoming a king or prince; —ठाठ-वाट royal prank, regal grandeur and splendour.

राजस्था/न [*nm*] one of the several Hindi-speaking states of the Indian Union, traditionally known for its chivalry and valour; ~नी a sub-language of Hindi comprised of many dialects spoken in Rajastha:n; pertaining or belonging to Rajastha:n.

राजस्व [*nm*] revenue.

राजा [*nm*] a king, monarch, prince; darling; —बेटा good boy.

राजाधिराज [*nm*] a king of kings, an emperor.

राजित [*a*] to be resplendent, to shine, to be illuminated.

राज़ी [*a*] willing, agreeable; [*nf*] willingness; well-being; -खुशी welfare, well-being; ~नामा an agreement; compromise.

राजीव [*nm*] a lotus flower.

राजेश्वर [*nm*] a monarch, an emperor.

राज्य [*nm*] a state; the state; kingdom; polity; ~च्युत dethroned, deposed; -तंत्र polity; -त्याग abdication; ~त्व statehood; -द्रोह sedition; ~द्रोही a seditionist; ~पाल a governor; -प्रमुख head of a state; -विप्लव coup d' etat; -व्यवस्था polity, state system; -सभा the Upper House of the Indian Parliament.

राज्याध्यक्ष [*nm*] head of a state.

राज्याभि/षेक [*nm*] coronation, installation or accession to the throne; ~षिक्त installed on/ acceded to the throne.

राज्यारोहण [*nm*] accession to the throne.

राणा [*nm*] a title of Rajput kings of certain Rajputana states and Nepal.

रात [*nf*] the night; -का राजा an owl; -दिन day and night; ever, always, at all times; ~रानी a typical fragrant flower that blooms during the night, also called rajanigandha:.

रातिब [*nm*] food for cattle, concentrates.

रात्रि [*nf*] the night.

रानी [*nf*] a queen; beloved.

राम [*nm*] Ramchandra—the greatest of the ancient Indian kings of the Solar dynasty and the hero of the great Indian epic—Ramayan; God, an incarnation of Vishnū; ~ कहानी a tale of woe; narration of events of one's own life; ~बाण a panacea, an unfailing remedy, sure cure; ~रज yellow ochre; ~रस salt; ~राज्य the rule of Ra:m—golden rule, just, equitable and ideal rule; Utopia: -राम a form of mutual salutation; Good God!, an interjectional utterance expressive of hate, surprise, indignation, etc.; -राम जपना पराया माल अपना a robber in the garb of a saint; ~लीला a celebration involving enactment of the deeds and adventures of Lord Ram.

राय [*nf*] opinion, view, advice; [nm] a king.

रायता [*nm*] a dish prepared by mixing minced vegetables etc. in salted curd.

रार [*nf*] a quarrel, wrangling, dispute, altercation.

राल [*nf*] resin; ~दार resinous.

राव [*nm*] a prince, title of the princes of certain former states of India.

रावण [*nm*] the king of ancient Ceylon who kidnapped Lord Ram's queen Sita: and later fought him and was killed, villain of the great epic Ramayan.

राशन [*nm*] ration/rationing.

राशि [*nf*] a sum, amount; quantity; heap; sign of the zodiac; ~चक्र Zodiac;—मिलना to be agreeably inclined to each other by temperament; to be born in mutually concordant sign of the zodiac.

राष्ट्र [*nm*] a nation; -गान/गीत the national anthem; -चिह्न the national emblem; ~त्व nationhood; -ध्वज the national flag; -नीति national policy; -पताका see -ध्वज; ~ पति President [of a country/ Nation]; ~भाषा the national language; ~वाद nationalism; ~वादी a nationalist; nationalistic; -संघ the League of Nations; -समाज comity of Nations; ~हीन stateless.

राष्ट्रिक [*a* and *nm*] [*a*] national; ~ ता nationality.

राष्ट्रीय [*a*] national; ~करण nationalisation; ~कृत nationalised; -ता nationality; nationalism.

रास [*nm*] a circular dance performance associated with the legend of Krishnā and the gopi:s: [also ~लीला]; reins [of a horse etc.]; [a] favourable, befitting; —आना ro prove favourable/good/ beneficial; —लेना to adopt [a child].

रासायनिक [*a*] chemical.

रास्ता [*nm*] way, path, route, course; passage; an approach; —देखना to wait [for]; —पकड़ना to take to one's course, to go one's way; —बताना to evade; to get rid; रास्ते पर लाना to bring round; to lead on to the proper course.

राह [*nf*] a way, path, route, course; passage; and approach; ~गीर a traveller; wayfarer; pedestrian; -चलता wayfaring; a stranger; ~ज़न a highwayman; brigand; ~ज़नी waylaying; brigandage.

राहत [*nf*] comfort; relief; -कार्य relief operations;—देना to give comfort, to relieve;—मिलना to get comfort, to get relief.

राही [nm] a traveller, wayfarer, pedestrian.

रिआय/त [*nf*] concession; favour; ~ती on concession, concessional; ~ दर concessional rate.

रिकार्ड [nm] a record; gramophone record;—तोड़ना to break a record.

रिक्त [*a*] empty, void; evacuated; ~ता vacancy; vacuum, void.

रिक्थ [*nm*] legacy.

रिक्शा [*nm*] a rickshaw.

रिझाना [*v*] to captivate, to fascinate, to charm.

रिटायर [*a*] retired; —होना to be retired.

रिपोर्ट [*nf*] a report; ~र a reporter.

रिमझिम [*nf*] drizzling [of rain].

रियाज़ [*nm*] practice, exercise.

रिया/सत [*nf*] a state; a former princely state of India; hence ~ती.

रिरियाना [*v*] to beslaver; to supplicate meekly, to talk in a very submissive manner.

रिवाज [*nm*] custom; vogue, practice.

रिवाल्वर [*nm*] a revolver.

रिश्ता [*nm*] relation, relationship; affinity; connection.

रिश्ते/दार [*nm*] a relative, relation; kinsman; kith and kin; -नाते relations and connections; ~दारी relationship, kinsmanship.

रिश्वत [*nf*] a bribe, illegal gratification; ~खोर a bribee, one who takes bribe; ~खोरी bribery.

रिसना [*v*] to leak; to ooze; to percolate.

रिसालदार [*nm*] a Risaldar—a non-commissioned officer of the cavalry.

रिसाला [*nm*] cavalry; a journal, magazine.

रिहर्सल [*nf*] rehearsal.

रिहा [*a*] released, set free; discharged; ~ई release, setting free; discharge.

रिहाइ(य)श [*nf*] lodging; residence; ~शी residential.

री [*ind*] a non-honorofic vocative particle used in addressing a female [as क्यों री].

रीछ [*nm*] a bear.

रीझना [*v*] to be fascinated/charmed/infatuated/ attracted.

रीढ़ [*nf*] back-bone, spine.

रीति [*nf*] method, manner, mode; custom, way, practice, vogue; style; -रिवाज customs; traditions.

रीम [*nm*] ream [of paper]; rim [as of a wheel].

रील [*nf*] a reel [of thread or film etc.].

रुँधना [*v*] to be choked; to be obstructed.

रुआँ [*nm*] fuzz; wool.

रुई [*nf*] cotton.

रुकना [*v*] to stop; to halt; to stay; to stagnate; to stand.

रुकावट [*nf*] hurdle, obstacle, hindrance; barricade; blockade; bar; resistance.

रुक्का [*nm*] a chit, slip; note; promissory note; a briefly scribbled letter.

रुख़ [*nm*] attitude; direction; trend; aspect; the rook in chess; forepart, face; favourable eye; [*a*] in the direction.

रुख़स/त [*nf*] permission; departure; leave; leisure; ~ती farewell, departure [esp. of bride]; [a] concerning leave/departure.

रुखाई [*nf*] curtness; harshness, roughness; bluntness.

रुग्ण [*a*] ill, sick; unwell, indisposed; diseased, morbid; hence ~ता.

रुचना [*a*] to be agreeable; to be of interest, to be interesting; to be to one's liking, to be liked.

रुचि [*nf*] interest; liking; taste, relish; fancy; ~कर, ~कारक, ~कारी interesting, to one's liking/taste/relish, tasteful.

रुचिर [*a*] winsome; pleasing, agreeable, beautiful, sweet.

रुझान [*nm*] inclination; aptitude, proclivity, propensity; trend, tendency; bias.

रुतबा [*nm*] status; rank; position; ~दार of high rank, occupying high position.

रुद्ध [*a*] hindered, obstructed, stopped, choked.

रुधिर [*nm*] blood.

रुनझुन [*nf*] tinkling [of small bells].

रुपया [*nm*] a rupee; money, wealth; -पैसा money; wealth, रुपये वाला opulent, rich, wealthy, moneyed.

रुपहला [*a*] silvery.

रुलाई [*nf*] a feeling like crying; weeping, crying, wailing.

रुलाना [*v*] to cause to weep/cry/lament; to harass, to trouble.

रुष्ट [*a*] displeased, angry.

रू [*nm*] face, countenance; frontage; -ब-रू face to face, in the presence of; -रियायत consideration; leniency.

रूखा [*a*] dry; rough; harsh, curt, blunt, unsympathetic, inconsiderate; to which ghee has not been added [as रूखा खाना]; hence ~पन; -सूखा plain and simple [esp. used for food]; without ghee; dry.

रूठना [*v*] to sulk/to be sulky, to be displeased.

रूढ़ [*a*] established; current, popular; traditional, conventional; stereotyped; indivisible [as a number].

रूढ़ि [*nf*] convention/conventionalism; usage; ~बद्ध conventionalised; ~वाद conventionalism; ~वादिता conventionality; ~वादी a conventionalist; conventionalistic.

रूप [*nm*] form, shape, appearance; beauty; aspect; image; mould; type; ~गत formal; ~विज्ञान morphology; ~वैज्ञानिक a morphologist; morphological; ~शाली beautiful, handsome, good looking.

रूपक [*nm*] a metaphor; a play, feature.

रूपरेखा [*nm*] an outline, a synopsis.

रूपवंत [*a*] beautiful, handsome, good-looking.

रूप/वान [*a*] handsome, goodlooking. hence ~वती.

रूपसी [*nf*] a beautiful/handsome damsel, a beauty.

रूपांतर [*nm*] metamorphosis, transformation; variation; adaptation; modification.

रूपी [*a*] a suffix used in the sense of having the form of; or of the shape of; similar to.

रूमानी [*a*] romantic.

रूमाल [*nm*] handkerchief.

रू/ह [*nf*] soul; spirit; essence; ~ हानी spiritual.

रेंकना [*v*] to bray; to sing/shout hoarsely.

रेंगना [*v*] to creep; to crawl.

रें/डी, ~ड़ी [*nf*] the castor seed; —का तेल castor oil.

रे [*ind*] a vocative particle used out of indifference, contempt or disrespect (क्यों रे!) ; [*nm*] the second note in the Indian musical scale.

रेख [*nf*] a line; mark; the just-grown whiskers in early youth.

रेखां/कन [*nm*] lining, lineation, underlining; demarcation; ~कित lined, underlined; straited; demarcated.

रेखांश [*nm*] terrestrial longitude.

रेखा [*nf*] a line, lineament; mark; furrow; [pl.] lines on the palm of the hand—fate; destiny; ~गणित geometry; ~चित्र a sketch; figure; line-drawing.

रेगमाल [*nm*] sand-paper, emery paper.

रेगिस्ता/न [*nm*] a desert; ~नी sandy; pertaining to a desert.

रेचक [*a*] purgative; [*nm*] a purgative, jalap; a stage in प्राणायाम when deeply inhaled air is expelled through the nose.

रेज/गारी, ~कारी [*nf*] change [of currency], smaller coins.

रेडार [*nm*] a radar.

रेडियम [*nm*] radium.

रेडियो [*nm*] radio.

रे/ढ़ [*nf*] ruination, destruction; ~ढ़ी one who ruins/destructs.

रेत [*nf*] sand.

रेतन [*nf*] filings.

रेतना [*v*] to file, to rasp; to polish by filing/rasping.

रेता [*nm*] sand.

रेताई [*nf*] work/process of filing or the remuneration paid therefor.

रेती [*nf*] a file; sand.

रेतीला [*a*] sandy; gritty.

रेफ [*nm*] the letter र or its allographs—(प्र), (ट्र) or (र्म).

रेल [*nf*] rail, railway; railway line; railway train; a flow; current; abundance.

रेल, ~पेल [*nf*] abundance; plenty, overcrowding; immense influx; rush, throng; jostle.

रेलवे [*nf*] railway.

रेला [*nm*] a rush, push; huge wave, influx, flood.

रेश/म [*nm*] silk; ~मी silken, silk.

रेशा [*nm*] a fibre, crude fibre; grain; staple.

रेहन [*nm*] mortgage, pawn; ~दार mortgage; ~ नामा mortgage deed.

रैड़ी [*nf*] a handcart.

रैन [*nf*] the night.

रैयत [*nf*] subject; tenant; ~दारी tenancy.

रोंगटा [*nm*] small and soft hairs on human body.

रोआँ [*nm*] small and soft hair on the body.

रोएँदार [*a*] hairy, woolly.

रोक [*nf*] a ban, restriction, check; prevention; scotch, hedge; hindrance; barrier; -टोक restriction, obstruction; opposition; –थाम prevention; check, temporary remedy.

रोकड़ [*nf*] cash, ready money; cash book; —जमा opening balance; —बाकी cash balance in hand; रोकड़िया a cashier, treasurer.

रोकना [*v*] to stop; to detain; to prevent, to check; to ban; to withhold; to cease; to stay; to discontinue; to forbid; to impede; to suppress, to repress, to curb.

रोग [*nm*] disease; illness, ailment, sickness; ~ग्रस्त ailing; diseased, ill, sick; ~नाशक/हर/हारी curative; cure.

रोगन [*nm*] varnish, paint; polish; grease.

रोगी [*nm*] a patient, diseased; valetudinarian; [*a*] ailing.

रोचक [*a*] interesting, pleasing, entertaining.

रोज़ [*nm*] day; [*adv*] everyday, daily;-ब-रोज everyday; daily; day-by-day; ~मर्रा everyday, daily.

रोज़गार [*nm*] a business, trade; employment; profession, occupation.

रोजनामचा [*nm*] a diary; daily account book; daily report book.

रोज़ा [*nm*] a fast [observed by Muslims during the month of Ramjan].

रोज़ाना [*adv*] daily, everyday.

रोज़ी [*nf*] livelihood; living, means of subsistence; -रोटी livelihood, means of subsistence.

रोटी [*nf*] bread; meals, food; —दाल lit. bread and pulse-plain and simple food, the barest minimum in respect of diet.

रोडवेज [*nm*] roadways.

रोड़ा [*nm*] pebbles, fragments of stones or bricks, obstruction, impediment; रोड़े अटकाना/डालना to obstruct, to create an obstacle/impediment; to pave the way with obstructions.

रोना [*v*] to weep, to cry; to bewail, to lament; [nm] weeping, crying; bewailing, lamenting; -धोना/पीटना to weep and wail; weeping and wailing, to lament/lamenting.

रोपना [*v*] to plant, to implant, to transplant; to sow.

रोब [*nm*] overbearing influence, sway; commanding/imposing quality; -दाब awe, overbearing influence, sway; ~दार commanding, awe-inspiring, imposing.

रोबीला [*a*] see रोबदार.

रोम [*nm*] [small and soft] hair [on the body]; ~कूप the pores on the surface of the skin; -रोम में in the whole being, throughout the body.

रोमांच [*nm*] horripilation, titillation, standing of the hairs on end; ~चित thrilled, in rapture, horripilated/horripilant, titillated.

रोमानी [*a*] romantic.

रोमा/ली [*nf*] the line of hairs over the body [esp. extending above the navel].

रोयाँ [*nm*] see रोम; ~ रोयेंदार hairy, woolly; रोयें खड़े होना ro horripilate: to be thrilled.

रोली [*nf*] a mixture of turmeric and lime powder [used for applying तिलक on the forehead on auspicious occasions].

रोशन [*a*] lighted, lit; shining, bright; famous; manifest; ~दान a ventilator.

रोशनाई [*nf*] ink.

रोशनी [*nf*] light, illumination; eye-sight.

रोष [*nm*] anger, rage, wrath; resentment; —में आना to fly into a rage, to be in a temper.

रोषी [*adj*] angry see, रोष

रोषण [*adj*] angry.

रोषित [*adj*] angered, see रोष.

रोहे [*nm*] trachoma.

रौंद [*nm*] trampling [over], crushing under the feet; round.

रौंदना [*v*] to trample down, to tread over, to crush down.

रौ [*nf*] motion, flow; inpulsive mood; strong trend.

रोज़ा [*nm*] a tomb.

रौद्र [*a*] terrible, fearful, furious; —रस the sentiment of wrath or furiousness in Indian poetics.

रौद्रता [*nf*] fearsomeness, see रौद्र

रौनक़ [*nf*] gaiety, splendour, brightness and brilliance; ~दार gay, splendid, bright and brilliant.

रौख [*v.i.*] formidable, dreadful, savage [*nm*] the name of hell.

रौला [*nm*] a clamour, a tumult, an alarm, an uproar.

ल traditionally, the third of the semi-vowel series य,र,ल,व, of the Devanagari: alphabet. Modern phoneticians do not, however, recognise this letter as a semi-vowel [in Hindi] but as a consonant.

ल – देवनागरी वर्णमाला का अट्ठाईसवाँ व्यंजन और तीसरा अंतस्थ वर्ण है। इसका उच्चारण स्थान दंत है।

लंक [*nf*] the waist, lower back.

लंका [*nf*] Ceylon—the island in the Indian Ocean where Ravān, the demon king and villain of the ancient epic Ramayan, ruled.

लंकाई [*adj*] Singhalese.

लंकायिका [*nf*] a pot-herb resembling spinach, Trigonella corniculata.

लंगड़ा [*a*] lame, limp; [nm] a lame person; ~ना to limp; -लूला cripple/crippled.

लंगर [*nm*] an anchor; a public kitchen, an alms-house; a heavy wooden piece/block tied to a cattle's neck [to check it from running about]; a privy cover worn by wrestlers; a piece of stone tied at the end of a long thread; [*a*] mischievous, naughty; vile.

लंगूर; लँगूर [*nm*] a kind of black-faced monkey with a stiff long tail, an ape.

लँगो/ट, ~टा [*nm*] a strip of cloth tucked round the waist to cover privities; ~टिया यार a chum, bosom friend.

लंघन [*nm*] going without meals, forcible or imposed fast/fasting; transgressing, crossing.

लँघनी [*nf*] fasting, fast.

लाँघना [*v.t.*] to cause to jump over.

लंठ [*a*] stupid; boorish, uncivil.

लंपट [*a*] lewd, wanton; lascivious [person]; unchaste; hence ~ता.

लंब [*nm*] a perpendicular; [*a*] long; an allomorph of लंबा; -तड़ंग strapping, tall and tough.

लंबाई [*nf*] length, tallness, लंबाई-चौड़ाई, length and breadth, extent, area: capacity; size as of clothes, fit.

लंबर/दार [*nm*] a headman [of a community, village, etc.]; ~दारी headmanship.

लंबा [*a*] long, lengthy; tall; -चौड़ा vast, spacious, extensive; tall and well-built. -तड़ंगा strapping, tall and tough.

लंबाई [*nf*] length; height.

लंबायमान [*a*] lengthened, lying flat; prolonged, pendent.

लंबित [*a*] penduline; prolonged; lengthened; pending.

लंबी [*a*] long; tall; -चौड़ी हाँकना to boast/brag, to talk tall; —तानकर सोना to enjoy a carefree sleep;—तानना to sleep carefreely.

लकड़बग्गा [*nm*] a hyena.

लकड़हारा [*nm*] a woodcutter, woodman.

लकड़ [*nm*] a stockade, barricade, लकड़तोड़, as hard on the feet, as wood: stiff of shoes, लकड़दादा, colloq, any distant ancestor, लकड़फोड़, woodpecker, लकड़बग्घा, hyena, लकड़हारा, wood-cutter; wood-seller, हारिन.

लकड़ा [*nm*] a beam, a log.

लकड़ी [*nf*] wood; fuel, firewood; timber; a stick.

लक़दक़ [*a*] shining, brilliant; spotlessly white, neat and clean.

लक़वा [*nm*] paralysis, palsy.

लकीर [*nf*] a line; trail, streak; stripe; —का फ़कीर a conventionalist/traditionalist, one wedded irrevocably to convention/tradition; —पीटना to follow the traditions; to repent, to be remorseful.

लक्ष [*a* and *nm*] a lac; the number one hundred thousand; a mark, target.

लक्षण [*nm*] a symptom; indication; trait, characteristic feature; characteristic mark.

लक्षणा [*nf*] indirect, implied or figurative sense of a word; -शक्ति the word-power of indirect or implied/figurative expression.

लक्षि/त [*a*] implied, hinted, indicated; marked; observed; reflected; hence ~तार्थ.

लक्ष्मी [*nf*] the goddess of wealth and spouse of Lord Vishnū; prosperity, fortune; used deferentially for a woman as symbolising prosperity.

लक्ष्य [*nm*] aim, object/objective, target, goal; [a] indicated, implied; लक्ष्णार्थ indicated, implied or figurative meaning of a word].

लखपति [*a* and *nm*] a millionaire, very wealthy person.

लगन [*nf*] devotion; perseverence; inclination; attachment; an auspicious moment [for performing a ceremony].

लगना [*v*] to seem, to appear; to be engaged [in]; to be employed; to be united/attached/connected; to strike roots [as पौधा—]; to be grafted; to be related [as वह मेरा साला लगता है]; to be applied [as मलहम–]; to have a painful sensation, to cause pain [as आँखों में दवा लग रही है]; to be affixed to; to be struck, to be hit [as डंडा—]; to be burnt [as दूध–,दाल]; to cost [as इस पर चार रुपये लगे]; to devote oneself to (कल से उस काम में लगूँगा]; to continue, to be wounded by [as गोली—]; to follow [as पीछे—]; to be levied [as टैक्स–]; to feel bad, to pinch [as बात—]; to smart; to be rubbed; to scratch; to pierce [as काँटा—]; to have an affect [as पानी—]; to be caused [as भीड़—]; to have a quarrel (उनकी आपस में लगती है); to fall in love with (दोनों ओर लगी हुई है]; to bear [as फल —]; to have sexual intercourse; लगती बात an utterance that pinches; लगी लगाई fixed; settled.

लगभग [*ind*] approximately, almost, about; roughly, nearly.

लगातार [*adv*] continuously, incessantly, constantly; [*a*] continuous, continual, sustained.

लगान [*nm*] land revenue.

लगाना [*v*] to engage; employ; to attach, to join, to connect; to plant [as पौधा—]; to apply [as मलहम—]; to affix [as टिकट—]; to make someone hang around [as पीछे—]; to levy [as टैक्स—]; to touch [as हाथ—]; to invest [as पैसा —]; to paste, to stick [as इश्तहार–]; to set, to fix; to shut, to close [as दरवाजा—]; to keep; to backbite, to inflame; to add; -बुझाना to backbite, to distort facts so as to instigate, to indulge in instigatory talks.

लगाम [*nf*] reins, bridle, hackmore.

लगाव [*nm*] attachment, love, affection.

लग्गू [*a* and *nm*] who sticks to a man/work; who dogs/follow; a hanger-on; a paramour.

लग्न [*nf*] an auspicious moment for performance of a ceremony or commencement of a work, an appointed day of marriage etc.; [a] attached, connected; -पत्र/पत्रिका a formal letter or document in which the date and time etc. of the marriage ceremony are intimated.

लघु [*a*] tiny, small, little, short; light; acute [as कोण]; insignificant; low; mean; reduced; ~तम minimum, lowest; smallest; ~ समापवर्त्य least common multiple [l.c.m.]; ~तर smaller; lower; ~ता/त्व insignificance; smallness; meanness; humiliation; ~शंका urine; making water, urinating.

लचक [*nf*] elasticity, flexibility, resilience; springiness; ~दार flexible, elastic, resilient/resiling; ~ना to resile, to spring; to bend

लचर [*a*] untenable, weak; ineffective; unstable.

लचीला [*a*] flexible, elastic, resilient, pliable; springy, willowy; ~पन flexibility, resilience, elasticity, pliability.

लच्छा [*nm*] skein [of thread/yarn etc.], hank; a circular silver ornament for the feet; a kind of sweetmeat.

लच्छी [*nf*] skein [of thread/yarn], hank.

लच्छेदार [*a*] having fine shreds; interesting, fascinating [as—बातें].

लजाना [*v*] to blush, to feel shy; to be ashamed.

लज़ीज़ [*a*] tasteful, tasty, delicious.

लजीला [*a*] shy, bashful.

लज़्ज़त [*nf*] taste, relish; deliciousness; tastefulness; ~दार tasty, delicious, tasteful.

लज्जा [*nf*] shame; modesty; shyness, bashfulness.

लज्जित [*a*] ashamed; blushed.

लट [*nf*] a tress, lock of hair, tangled hair; ringlet.

लटकना [*v*] to hang, to overhang; to swing; to lop; to suspend, to be in a suspense, to keep in a state of indecision; to be delayed.

लट/का [*nm*] a formula, tip; nostrum; device, trick; affected movement; ways; mannerism; ~केबाज one who shows off typical mannerism, one who tries to impress through typical devices; hence ~केबाजी.

लटकाना [*v*] to hang, to overhang; to suspend; to keep waiting, to keep in suspense; to delay.

लट्टू [*nm*] a [spinning] top; bulb; knob.

लट्ठ [*nm*] a cudgel; long heavy staff, [*a*] blockhead, stupid; ~ बंद equipped with a लट्ठ; a cudgel-wielder; one who is equipped with a लट्ठ; skilled in wielding or brandishing a लट्ठ: ~ बाजी cudgel fighting; skill in wielding a लट्ठ; ~ मार uncivil, harshly forthright.

लट्ठा [*nm*] a log, raft; a five and half hand-span long bamboo used for land-measurement; long cloth, a kind of white cloth.

लठैत [*a* and *nm*] skilled in wielding/brandishing a लाठी, an expert in brandishing a cudgel.

लड़ [*nf*] a string; row.

लड़क/पन, ~पना [*nm*] childhood; boyhood; childishness, puerility.

लड़का [*nm*] a boy, lad; male child; son; an inexperienced person; लड़केवाला the bridegroom's father/guardian; लड़के-वाले progeny; members of bridegroom's party/side.

लड़की [nf] a girl, daughter; hence ~वाला, ~ वाले.

लड़खड़ा/ना [*v*] to stagger, to stumble; to falter, to totter, to wobble, to titubate; hence ~हट.

लड़ना [*v*] to quarrel; to fight; to struggle; to collide, to clash; to contend; to wrestle, to combat; -भिड़ना to pick up quarrels; to have altercations quarrelling/altercation.

लड़ाई [*nf*] fight; war, battle; quarrel; encounter, clash; enmity; -झगड़ा broil, altercation, quarrel.

लड़ा/का, ~का, ~ कू [*a*] quarrelsome; pugnacious; warlike, militant, bellicose, hence ~कापन.

लड़ी [*nf*] a string; chain; row.

लड्डू [*nm*] a typical ball-like Indian sweetmeat.

लत [*nf*] an addiction, a bad habit; an allomorph of लात used as the first member in some compound words.

लता [*nf*] a creeper; vine.

लताड़ [*nf*] scolding, rebuke; ~ना to scold roundly, to rebuke.

लती/फ़ा [*nm*] an anecdote, a witticism; hence ~फ़ेबाज, ~फ़ेबाजी.

लत्ता [*nm*] a rag, tatter, a tattered piece of cloth.

लथपथ [*a*] soaked, drenched [in], besmeared [with].

लदना [*v*] to be loaded/laden/burdened; to be apprehended.

लद्धड़ [*a*] lethargic, slothful, slow [moving]; hence ~पन.

लपक [*nf*] addiction [to grab advantage]; flash, flame; gusto, swiftness.

लपकना [*v*] to catch, [as गेंद—]; to rush forth; to pounce upon, to go out with a gusto.

लपट [*nf*] flame; blaze; heat wave; a blast of fragrance.

लपलपा/ना [*v*] to be resiliently flexible [as a cane]; to be bent repeatedly; to brandish [as a sword]; to show out the tongue [as a quick breathing]; hence ~हट [nf].

लपेट [*nf*] a fold, twist; winding, turn; ambiguity; involvement, embroilment; striking range.

लपेट/ना [*v*] to roll up, to fold; to reel; to wind; to cover, to furl; to involve; to entangle/implicate/embroil; ~वाँ folding; wrapping.

लपेटा [*nm*] fold, twist; winding, turn.

लप्पड़ [*nm*] a slap, blow of the palm.

लफ़ं/गा [*nm* and *a*] a loafer/rouge; roguish, of loose character; ~गेबाजी roguery, swindling.

लफ़्/ज [*nm*] a word; ~फ़्जी wordy, of words; ~ मानी word-meaning, direct meaning.

लफ़्फ़ा/ज [*a*] verbose; using high-sounding phraseology; talkative; ~जी verbosity, talkativeness; use of high-sounding phraseology.

लब [*nm*] lip; brim; edge, rim; bank [of a river etc]; ~रेज full to the brim.

लबादा [*nm*] a cloak, gown; a heavy overall.

लबालब [*adv* and *a*] full to the brim; brimful.

लब्ध [*a*] obtained, got, acquired; [*nm*] a quotient; ~कीर्ति/नाम/प्रतिष्ठ renowned, who has acquired fame.

लब्धि [*nf*] acquirement, achievement; quotient.

लभ्य [*a*] available, attainable, accessible, within reach.

लमहा [*nm*] a moment.

लय [*nf*] rhythm; concord; cadence, melody, tune; fusion; merging; destruction, annihilation of the world; ~बद्ध rhythmic, attuned.

ललक [*nf*] craving, yearning, longing.

ललकना [*v*] to crave, to have a longing.

ललकार [*nf*] a challenge, gage.

ललकारना [*v*] to [hold out] a challenge, to halloo.

ललचना [*v*] to be tempted, to be allured, to feel greedy.

ललचाना [*v*] to tempt, to allure, to wheedle, to entice, to covet; —जी to feel tempted, to be allured; to covet.

ललना [*nf*] a woman.

ललाई [*nf*] redness, ruddiness.

ललाट [*nm*] forehead; destiny, fortune; -रेखा, —का लिखा writ of [individual] destiny.

ललित [*a*] pretty, comely, sweet; elegant, graceful; -कला fine arts; —साहित्य belles lettres.

लल्ला [*nm*] an affectionate term of address for a child/boy.

लल्ली-चप्पी, लल्ली-पत्ती [*nf*] huggery, wheedling adulation.

लव [*nm*] a very small division of time; whit, particle, see लौ; ~लीन absorbed, engrossed [as in thought]; ~लेश a whit; very small quantity.

लवण [*nm*] salt.

लश(श)क/र [*nm*] a cantonment, encampment [of army]; host, irregular army; ~री pertaining to army.

लसलसा [*a*] glutinous, sticky, adhesive; hence ~हट.

लसीला [*a*] glutinous, sticky, adhesive; hence ~पन.

लस्टम-लस्टम [*ind*] somehow or the other; slowly and slothfully, in a disorderly or ill-arranged manner.

लस्त [*a*] exhausted, weary, worn out; -पस्त wearied; exhausted.

लस्सी [*nf*] a cold beverage.

लहँगा [*nm*] a long loose skirt worn round the loins flowing down to the ankles.

लहकना [*v*] to rise up into flames, to blaze; to glitter, to glare; hence लहक.

लहजा [*nm*] tone, accent, into nation; manner of speech.

लहमा [nm] a moment.

लहर [*nf*] a wave, ripple; surge; undulation; caprice, whim; a wavy pattern; vertigo caused by the poisonous effect of snake-bite; impulse; ~दार wavy; undulatory, sinuous/sinuate.

लहराना [*v*] to undulate, to wave; to shimmy; to fluctuate; to waver.

लहरिया [*nm*] the total effect to wavy lines, wavy design or pattern of lines; hence ~दार.

लहलहाना [*v*] to flourish, to bloom; to be green; to be verdant; to wave; hence लहलहा.

लहसुन [*nm*] garlic.

लहसुनिया [*nm*] cat's eye, a precious gray-coloured stone.

लहालोट [*a*] bursting with laughter, extremely delighted, enamoured.

लहू [*nm*] blood, ~लु (लो) हान blood-smeared, drenched in blood, blood-stained; —उबलना blood to boil through rage; to simmer; to be red-hot in rage;—का घूँट पीकर रह जाना to suppress one's rage; to endure somebody's excesses; —का प्यासा blood-thirsty, after one's blood; —पीना to harass/pester no end, to trouble constantly; —सफेद हो जाना to be lost to human emotion, to become inhuman.

लाँघना [*v*] to cross, to jump over; to transgress.

लांछन [*nm*] a stigma, blemish; slander.

लांछित [*a*] stigmatised, blamed; slandered.

लाइन [*nf*] a line.

लाइब्रेरी [*nf*] a library.

लाइलाज [*a*] incurable, irremediable.

लाइसेंस [*nm*] a licence; ~दार licensed; a licencee.

लाक्षणिक [*a*] metaphorical; symbolic; allegorical; pertaining or belonging to the meaning conveyed through लक्षणा.

लाख [*nf*] lac; sealing lac; shellac; [*nm*] the number one lac; [*a*] a hundred thousand, lac; a large number.

लाग [*nf*] hostility, rancour; competition; skill in performing a job; -डाट rancour, rivalry; competition.

लागत [*nf*] cost, cost price, expenditure; outlay.

लागू [*a*] applicable; enforceable.

लाघव [*nm*] skill, dexterity, smartness; littleness; minuteness.

लाचा/र [*a*] helpless; compelled; obliged, constrained; [*adv*] being helpless/constrained; ~री helplessness; compulsion.

लाज [*nf*] shame; shyness, bashfulness; modesty; honour; ~वंत shamefaced; modest; shy, bashful; ~वंती/वती a very sensitive plant called touch me-not; feminine form of ~वंत -के मारे due to shame/shyness; out of modesty.

लाजवाब [*a*] unique, matchless, peerless; speechless, unable to reply back.

लाज़िमी [*a*] essential, inevitable, obligatory, compulsory; incumbent [on].

लाट [*nm*] a lord, governor; pillar, lofty pillar.

लाटरी [*nf*] lottery.

लाठी [*nf*] a big staff, cudgel, lathi.

लाड़ [*nm*] affection, fondness, endearment; caressing; -चाव/प्यार see लाड़;—करना/लड़ाना to fondle, to caress; -लड़ैता fonded, dear/darling.

लाड़ला [*a*] dear, darling [child, baby, son etc.].

लात [*nf*] a leg; kick; —के देवता बात से नहीं मानते rod is the logic of fools; —मारना to kick; to spurn, to abandon with contempt.

लादना [*v*] to load, to burden; to cumber; to heap one upon the other.

लादी [*nf*] the load placed on the back of a beast of burden; a bundle of dirty clothes meant for washing.

लानत [*nf*] condemnation, reproach, reproof; rebuke, censure; मलामत reproach, reproof; curse.

लाना [*v*] to bring, to bring along, to fetch; to introduce.

लापता [*a*] missing; disappeared, gone underground.

लापरवा/ह [*a*] careless, negligent; heedless, inattentive; ~ही carelessness, negligence; heedlessness, inattention.

लाभ [nm] profit, gain, advantage, benefit; dividend; ~कर/ कारक/कारी/दायक/दायी profitable; gainful; advantageous; beneficial.

लाभांश [*nm*] dividend; bonus.

लाम [*nm*] war-front; army; ~बंदी mobilisation.

लामा [*nm*] a Buddhist monk.

लामुहाला [*ind*] being constrained/forced/obliged, having no other way out.

लाय/क [*a*] able, capable, competent; worthy, fit; proper; ~कियत ~की ability, capability; competence; worthiness.

लार [*nf*] drivel; saliva; —आना, मुँह में to drivel; the mouth to water; to have eager desire to eat/obtain a thing.

लारी [*nf*] a lorry.

लाल [*a*] red, ruddy; angry, infuriated; communist [as —चीन]; [*nm*] beloved/dear child/boy/son; beloved person; a kind of small bird; ruby; -बुझक्कड़ village wiseacre, an ignorant fool who thinks very highly of himself and feels competent to answer any question; -पीला होना to be infuriated, to be red hot with rage.

लाल/च [*nm*] greed, greediness, covetousness; avarice; allurement; temptation; ~ची greedy; covetous; avaricious.

लालटेन [nf] a lantern.

लालन [*nm*] caressing, fondling; -पालन rearing; nurturing.

लालसा [*nf*] craving, longing, yearning.

लाला [nm] a word of respect prefixed to the names of certain Hindu castes like बनिया and कायस्थ etc. [as—लाजपतराय]; a term of address used for both elders and youngers; a kind of flower or its plant.

लालायित [*a*] eager; tempted, enamoured.

लालित्य [*nm*] grace, gracefulness delicacy.

लालिमा [*nf*] redness; reddishness, ruddiness.

लाली [nf] redness, ruddiness; lipstick; rouge.

लाले —पड़ना to become rare/inaccessible/beyond reach.

लाव [*nm*]; -लश्कर an array of followers/ companions, large paraphernalia, goods and chattels.

लावण्य [*nm*] charm, beauty, loveliness, comeliness.

लावा [*nm*] lava; puffed paddy, parched rice.

लावारि/स [*a*] [used both for men and things] unclaimed, unowned; heirless.

लाश [*nf*] corpse, dead body; carcass; ~घर mortuary.

लासा [*nm*] a glutinous/adhesive substance; bird-line; a bait, lure.

लिंग [*nm*] male genital organ, penis, phallus; the phallus deity representing Lord Shiv; gender [in grammar]; sex.

लिए [*ind*] for, with a view to, for the sake of, on account of; [a] taking, carrying, bearing.

लिक्खाड़ [*nm*] a prolific writer [used sarcastically].

लिखत [*nf*] writing; document; -पढ़त document, documentation; written deed.

लिखना [*v*] to write, to note down, to record, to inscribe; to enter [in a book]; पढ़ना to study; writing and reading, studying.

लिखाई [*nf*] writing, the act/process of writing or the remuneration paid therefor; -पढ़ाई study, education.

लिखापढ़ी [*nf*] written agreement; correspondence; documentation [of conditions etc.].

लिखावट [*nf*] hand, handwriting; writing.

लिखित [*a*] written, recorded, reduced to black and white.

लिपटना [*v*] to embrace; to cling, to coil around; to be smeared; to concentrate on a work.

लिपाई [*nf*] the process of or wages paid for pargetting/plastering; -पुताई plastering and white-washing; cleaning and tidying; giving a face-lift; hence लिपा-पुता.

लिपि [*nf*] a script; writing; ~बद्ध recorded, written, reduced to black and white.

लिपिक [nm] a clerk, scribe.

लिप्त [*a*] engrossed, absorbed; deeply attached, involved.

लिप्यंतरण [*nm*] transcription; transliteration.

लिप्सा [*nf*] lure, greed, ardent desire.

लिफ़ाफ़ा [*nm*] an envelope wrapper, cover.

लिफ़ाफ़िया [*a*] showy; delicate, weak, feeble; not durable.

लिबलिबी [*nf*] trigger.

लिबास [*nm*] dress, attire.

लियाक़त [*nf*] ability, merit; qualification.

लिहाज [*nm*] considerateness, deference; respect, point of view.

लिहाज़ा [*ind*] thus, therefore, on this account; accordingly.

लिहाफ़ [*nm*] a quilt.

लीक [*nf*] track, trackway; rut; trace; —पीटना to follow the tradition, to blindly follow the beaten path; to stick to worn-out tradition; -लीक चलना to follow an established course, to follow the tradition.

लीचं/ड़, ~र [*a*] lethargic, sluggish, slow; stingy; clumsy in one's dealings; hence ~पन.

लीड/र [*nm*] a leader; लीडराना befitting a leader, leader-like; in the nature of a leader.

लीन [*a*] absorbed, engrossed; merged; vanished, disappeared.

लीपना [*v*] to plaster; to coat; to smear; -पोतना to clean and tidy up; to whitewash and plaster.

लीलना [*v*] to swallow, to gulp.

लीला [*nf*] sport, play; amorous sport; fun and frolic; stage representation [of the deeds of divine incarnations, e.g. रामलीला, रामलीला].

लुंगी [*nf*] a sarong, a strip of cloth tucked round the waist:

लुं/ज, ~जा [*a*] crippled; fieshy and flaccid; -पुंज flaccid and feeble/flashy, having no muscles.

लुआब [*nm*] slime, pith; essence, gist; ~दार slimy, sticky.

लुकना [*v*] to hide, to be concealed; to go underground.

लुकाछिपी [*nf*] hide and seek; clandestine existence/goings.

लुगदी [*nf*] pulp.

लुगाई [*nf*] a woman; wife.

लुच्चा [*a* and *nm*] vile; wanton [person], abject, depraved; a scoundrel, black sheep; hence ~पन.

लुटना [*v*] to be robbed/plundered/marauded.

लुटेरा [*nm*] a robber, plunderer, marauder, bandit; hence ~पन.

लुढ़कना [*v*] to roll down; to be toppled, to tumble down.

लुत्फ़ [*nm*] fun, pleasure, enjoyment.

लुनाई [*nf*] the process or act of reaping a harvest or the wages paid for it; prettiness; beauty.

लुप्त [*a*] disappeared, vanished; hidden; extinct; obsolete, missing, omitted.

लुभाना [*v*] to lure; to charm, to attract to tantalise; to entice; to captivate; to be lured/charmed/attracted/tantalised/captivated/enticed.

लुहार [*nm*] a blacksmith; ~री the profession or work of a blacksmith.

लू [*nf*] warm air; heat wave; sunstroke; —लगना to have a sunstroke.

लूट [*nf*] plunder; booty; spoil; -खसोट plunder, pillage, maraudery;-पाट/मार plundering and killing, pillage, marauding.

लूटना [*v*] to plunder, to maraud; to pillage, to loot.

लूला [a] handless, with a dismembered hand; maimed; -लँगड़ा crippled, disabled.

लेंस [*nm*] a lens.

लेई [*nf*] [adhesive] paste [prepared from floor or arrowroot etc.]; due.

लेकिन [*ind*] but, on the other hand, however.

लेख [*nm*] an article, paper; writing, handwriting; writ.

लेखक [*nm*] a writer, an author.

लेखन [*nm*] writing, writing work; -कला art of writing; calligraphy; chirography; -शैली handwriting; style of writing; -सामग्री stationery, writing material.

लेखनी [*nf*] a pen.

लेखा [*nm*] account [s], record; -जोखा calculation; estimate; account.

लेटना [*v*] to lie, to lie down; to repose, to recline.

लेन [*nm*] taking, receiving; ~दार a creditor; -देन transaction, exchange; dealings.

लेना [*v*] to take; to accept; to borrow; to buy; to hold; to receive; —, आड़े हाथों to put to shame by sarcastic remarks, to rebuke and reprove; ले-देकर on the whole, somehow; with great difficulty; —एक न देना दो to have no concern whatsoever; for nothing, for no purpose at all; लेने के देने पड़ना to have the table turned upon oneself; to sustain a blow while trying to hit; to lose while expecting to profit.

लेप [*nm*] ointment; smearing.

लेपना [*v*] to anoint; to coat; to smear.

लेवा [*nm*] a thin mattress of [shattered] cloth; one who takes [e.g. नामलेवा].

लेश [*a*] very little; [*nm*] modicum, iota, trace; whit.

लैंगिक [*a*] sexual; phallic.

लैंप [*nm*] a lamp.

लैला [*nf*] the heroine of the celebrated love-tale of लैला-मंजनूँ; —मजनूँ crazy lovers.

लैस [*a*] equipped/fitted [with]; ready.

लोंदा [*nm*] a ball of any wet powder [as मिट्टी का—]; —, मिट्टी का absolutely inert [person], inactive and slothful.

लोक [*nm*] the world; one of the three worlds—स्वर्ग, पृथ्वी, पाताल; one of the fourteen worlds [of which seven are above and seven below]; people, folk; public; [a] popular, public; -कथा a folk tale, folk love; -कल्याण public welfare; ~ गीत a folk song; ~तंत्र democracy; ~तंत्रीय democratic; ~तांत्रिक democratic; a democrat; -निंदा public slander; -नृत्य folk dance; ~प्रिय popular, ~ ता popularity; ~मत public opinion/view; -मर्यादा popular observance; bounds of democracy/established usage or custom;-मानस the popular mind; ~रंजन popular entertainment/satisfaction/welfare; serving popular interest; -लीक popular course, popular tradition; ~सभा House of the People [the lower house of the Indian Parliament]; ~सम्मत enjoying popular support, having the backing of the people; -सेवा public service; -हित public welfare; philanthropy; -हितैषी a philanthropist.

लोकाचा/र [*nm*] ethos, mores; convention, popular custom/tradition; ~री worldlywise; practical.

लोकोक्ति [*nf*] a proverb; popular saying.

लोकोत्तर [*a*] supernatural, transcendental; extra-worldly; extraordinary.

लोकोपका/र [*nm*] philanthropy; ~रक a philanthropist/philanthrope; ~री philanthropic.

लोग [*nm*] a man; people, public; -बाग people; men in general.

लोच [*nf*] flexibility, elasticity; tenderness; hence ~दार.

लोचन [*nm*] eye [s].

लोट [*nf*] rolling, lying; [*nm*] a [currency] note; -पोट rolling; resting; bursting with laughter, roling around in laughter.

लोटना [*v*] to roll, to wallow, to welter, to toss.

लोटा [*nm*] a small round metal utensil for the household.

लोथ [*nf*] corpse; carcass; —गिरना to fall dead, to be killed.

लोथड़ा [*nm*] a lump of flesh.

लोनी [*nf*] a kind of green vegetable; unprocessed butter.

लोप [*nm*] disappearance; elimination; elision; obsolescence.

लोबान [*nm*] [gum] benzoin, oil creosote.

लोभ [*nm*] greed; avarice; covetousness; temptation, lure.

लोभी [*a*] greedy, avaricious, covetous.

लोम [*nm*] soft hair on the body, wool.

लोमड़ी [*nf*] a fox.

लोरी [*nf*] a lullaby.

लोलुप [a] see लोभी.

लोहा [*nm*] iron; [a] very hard, very strong; -बजना battle/war to be waged, fighting with swords to ensue;—मानना, किसी का to acknowledge/ confess supremacy, to concede somebody's superiority/superior skill;—लेना, किसी से to cross swords, to wage war; लोहे के चने चबाना to undertake an assiduous task.

लोहार [*nm*] a blacksmith; forgeman.

लोहित [*a*] red, reddened.

लोहिया [*nm*] an iron-dealer; a Hindu sub-caste [amongst Vaishyas] whose original profession was iron-mongering.

लोहू [*nm*] blood.

लौंग [*nf*] a clove; nose-stud.

लौंडपन [*nm*] boyishness, brattishness.

लौंडिया [*nf*] [derogatory usage] a lass, girl.

लौंडी [*nf*] a servant girl, slave girl, bond-maid.

लौंद [*nm*] an intercalary month मलमास, का महीना.

लौंदरा [*nm*] a shower towards the end of the hot weather.

लौंदा [*nm*] a lump as of earth, or of butter; clod.

लौ [*nf*] flame, glow; unwavering deep concentration; attachment; -लगाना to concentrate on; to be deeply attached to.

लौका [*nm*] pumpkin gourd.

लौकिक [*a*] secular; earthly, worldly, mundane; hence ~ता.

लौकिकता [*nf*] worldliness, worldly currency or custom.

लौकी [*nf*] bottle gourd.

लौट [*nf*] returning; -पौट topsy turvy/topsyturvied; -फेर substantial change [of order etc.]; modification.

लौटना [*v*] to return, to come back; to retreat; to withdraw; to topsyturvy/to be topsyturvied; to be upturned.

लौटाना [*v*] to return, to give back; to send back; to refund; to topsyturvy; to upturn.

लौटानी [*ind*] while returning or coming back, in return trip.

लौह [*nm*] iron; [*a*] made of iron; ferrous; ~पात्र ironware; -पुरुष an iron man; –युग iron age.

व—the last of the traditional semi-vowel set य,र,ल,व. Modern phoneticians, however, regard only य and व as semi-vowels and not र and ल which, according to them, are pure consonants.

व - देवनागरी वर्णमाला का उन्तीसवाँ व्यंजन वर्ण है। इसका उच्चारण शब्द दाँत और होंठ की सहायता से किया जाता है। अतः इसे दंत्यौष्ठ कहते हैं।

वंक [*nf*] curved: the pommed of a saddle.

वंकिम [*a*] slightly curved/bent.

वंग [*nm*] the eastern Indian state of Bengal; tin or tin ash.

वंगीय [*adj*] having to do with Bengal a society.

वंचित [*a*] deprived; cheated, deceived, tricked.

वंदन [*nm*] adoration, obeisance; vermilion; ~वार bunting of green leaves [that are hung up on auspicious occasions].

वंदना [*nf*] deferential salutation; obeisance, worship, hence वंदनीय.

वंदित [*adj*] praised; adored, renowned honour.

वंदी [*nm*] a panegyrist; bard.

वंध्या [*a*] barren, unfertile, unproductive; ~त्व barrenness, unfertility, unrpoductivity.

वंश [*nm*] lineage; family; stock; dynasty; a bamboo; ~गत pertaining to a family/lineage; ~ज a descendant, progeny; -परंपरा lineage; family tradition; ~वृक्ष a genealogical tree; bamboo tree.

वंशी [*nf*] a pipe, flute; flfe; fishing hook.

वंशिक [*adj*] pertaining to a family, lineal; genealogical.

वक़त [*nf*] value, worth.

वकालत [*nf*] advocacy, pleadership/pleading; practising law; ~नामा power of attorney.

वकील [*nm*] a lawyer, pleader, an advocate.

वक़्त [*nm*] time; opportunity; —का पाबंद punctual; —आ जाना the destined time to arrive; the hour of death to come; —गुज़ारना to lead a tight life, to mark time; to be in straits; बेवक्त at all times; in times of difficulty/crisis.

वक्तव्य [*nm*] a statement; [*a*] worth stating.

वक्ता [*nm*] a talker; spokesman; speaker.

वक्तृ/ता ~त्व [*nf*], [*nm*] eloquence, art of speaking, oratory; speech.

वक्र [*a*] curved; oblique; cunning; -गति zigzag motion; -दृष्टि oblique glance; an angry look, frown, scowl.

वक्रता [*nf*] curvature/curvedness; crookedness; obliquity.

वक्रोक्ति [nf] innuendo; an oblique utterance.

वक्ष [*nm*] chest, thorax; ~स्थल chest, chest region.

वगै/रह, ~रा [*ind*] etcetera [etc].

वचन [*nm*] utterance, speech; talk; a quotation of a treatise or scripture; number [in grammar]; commitment, promise, pledge; —तोड़ना to break a promise; —देना to make a promise, to commit, to vow; ~बद्ध committed; -पालना to adhere to one's word, to implement one's promise; —भंग करना to break a promise; —हारना to be pledged, to be committed.

वज़न [*nm*] weight; importance, value; the measure of an alphabet or metre in Urdu or Persian language; ~दार weighty, heavy; important.

वज़नी [*a*] heavy, weighty; important.

वजह [*nf*] cause, reason.

वज़ीफ़ा [*nm*] a scholarship, stipend.

वज़ीर [*nm*] a minister; the queen [in chess].

वज़ू [*nm*] washing of hands and feet [by a Mohammedan] before prayers.

वजूद [*nm*] existence; presence.

वज्र [*nm*] thunderbolt, lightning; a fatal weapon; [*a*] very hard, impenetrable.

वज्रपात [*nm*] the stroke of lightning/thunderbolt.

वज्राघात [*nm*] a thunder stroke, stroke of lightning.

वट [*nm*] a banyan tree; also ~वृक्ष.

वणिक [*nm*] a trader, businessman, merchant; a member of the Vaishya community.

वतन [*nm*] homeland, native country.

वतनी [*nm*] a compatriot; [*a*] pertaining or belonging to a certain country, native.

वत्स [*nm*] offspring. progeny; used as a vocative word for son, nephew and younger relatives or near ones in general.

वत्सर [*nm*] an year.

वत्सल [*a*] affectionate, tender; ~ता affection, fondness, tenderness.

वदन [*nm*] the face, features.

वध [*nm*] killing, murder.

वधिक [*nm*] a murderer, an executioner; a hunter, fowler.

वधू [*nf*] a bride, wife.

वन [*nm*] wood, forest, jungle; water; ~चर a forester, woodman. forest-farer; ~देवता a satyr, sylvanus; ~देवी a dryad; -महोत्सव an Indian movement for augmentation of the forest wealth; ~राज a lion; ~रोपण afforestation; ~लक्ष्मी a forest-beauty; forest-goddess; ~वास dwelling in a forest; hence ~वासी.

वनस्पति [*nf*] vegetation; vegetable; hydrogenated oil of groundnut etc; —विज्ञान/शास्त्र Botany; hence -वैज्ञानिक, ~शास्त्री, ~ शास्त्रीय.

वन्य [*a*] wild, born in a forest; savage.

वफ़ा [*nf*] fidelity, loyalty; ~दार faithful, loyal; ~दारी loyalty fidelity, faithfulness.

वबाल [*nm*] a curse, calamity, affliction.

वमन [*nm*] vomiting, puke.

वय [*nf*] age.

वयस्क [*a*] adult; major.

वयस्कता [*nf*] adulthood; majority.

वयोवृद्ध [*a*] aged, old.

वर [*nm*] bridegroom; a boon; [*a*] good, excellent, beautiful.

वरक़ [*nm*] thin and fine leaves of silver or gold; page of a book; the petals of a flower.

वर/ण [*nm*] selection, choice; marriage by choice; hence ~णीय.

वरदान [*nm*] a boon.

वरदी [*nf*] uniform.

वरन [*ind*] but, on the other hand.

वराह [*nm*] a boar, pig.

वरिष्ठ [*a*] senior; best, most prefereble.

वरीय [*a*] senior, having precedence; ~ता seniority, precedence.

वरुण [*nm*] the presiding deity of waters according to the Hindu mythology; waters.

वर्ग [*nm*] a class, category, group; a group of letters pronounced from the same part of the vocal organ [as कवर्ग, चवर्ग etc.]; a square; square number; ~गत pertaining to a class, characteristic of a class; —, निम्न the lower class;—, निम्न मध्य lower middle class; ~फल square; -भेद class distinction/discrimination; ~मुक्त classless; ~मूल square root; ~वार classwise; -संघर्ष class struggle, class conflict; -समाज class society; -स्वार्थ class interest; -हित class interest; ~हीन classless; ~ समाज classless society.

वर्गीकरण [*nm*] classification, categorisation; taxonomy.

वर्गीकृत [*a*] classified, categorised.

व/र्जन [*nm*] inhibition, taboo, prohibition; ~र्जनीय worth being or to be inhibited/tabooed/prohibited; ~र्जित inhibited, tabooed, prohibited; ~र्ज्य see वर्जनीय.

वर्जना [*nf*] an inhibition, a taboo; prohibition; [*v*] to inhibit, to taboo, to prohibit.

वर्ण [*nm*] a caste; colour; dye [used for colouring or writing]; a letter of the alphabet; -क्रम colour scheme, spectrum; classification; alphabetical order; ~क्रमानुसार in alphabetical order; -धर्म the duty or the profession of a particular caste; -भेद colour discrimination/distinction; ~माला the alphabet; -विन्यास spelling; -विपर्यय metathesis, transposition of letters; -व्यवस्था the caste system; ~संकर cross-breed, hybrid;hence ~संकरता; ~हीन casteless; colourless; etiolated; hence ~हीनता.

वर्णन [*nm*] description, narration; hence वर्णना [nf].

वर्णनातीत [*a*] indescribable, defying description.

वर्णनीय [*a*] describable, fit to be described or narrated.

वर्णाश्रम [*nm*] the caste and the stage of life i.e. आश्रम; -धर्म duties related to the caste and the stage of life (आश्रय).

वर्ण्य [*a*] fit to be described/narrated; —विषय the theme; topic of description/treatment.

वर्तनी [*nf*] spelling.

वर्तमान [*a*] present, existing; current.

वर्धमान [*a*] developing, growing, increasing.

वर्ष [*nm*] a year; vast tract of land [as भारतवर्ष]; ~गाँठ birthday, birth anniversary; ~फल astrological predictions for a [particular] year.

वर्षा [*nf*] rain, rainfall.

वलय [*nm*] a ring, circle; fold.

वली [*nm*] guardian, master; -वासि guardian or heir; near relative; kith and kin.

वल्कल [*nm*] the bark of a tree.

वल्गा [*nf*] rein, bridle.

वल्द [*ind*] son of.

वल्लरी [*nf*] a creeper, creeping plant.

वल्लाह [*ind*] Good God! oh! oh God!

वश [*nm*] power; control; subjugation; subjection; —में करना to tame, to bring under control/ subjugation.

वशीकरण [*nm*] fascinating or enchanting into submission/control.

वशीभूत [*a*] overpowered, tamed, brought under control; fascinated.

वसंत [*nm*] the spring [season]; a kind of ra:g in Indian classical music sung during the spring.

वसंती [*a*] pertaining to 'वसंत' [spring]; light yellow; [nm] light yellow colour.

वसीक़ा [*nm*] a document, deed; a stipend.

वसीय/त [*nf*] a will, testament, legacy; also ~तनामा.

वसुंधरा [*nf*] the earth.

वसूल [*a*] realised, collected; —करना to realise, to collect.

वसूली [*nf*] realisation [of dues etc.], recovery.

वस्तु [*nf*] an article, thing; object; substance, material; action/plot of a drama: -जगत substantial world; phenomenal world; ~निष्ठ objective; ~निष्ठता objectivity; ~निष्ठतावाद, ~निष्ठावाद objectivism; positivism; -रचना plot structure; ~वाद objectivism; objectivity; ~ वादी an objectivist; objectivistic; ~स्थिति reality, real position, actual circumstances.

वस्तुतः [*ind*] de facto; actually, in reality.

वस्त्र [*nm*] cloth[es], textile, fibre, raiment.

वस्ल [*nm*] lovers' union, cohabitation.

वह [*pron*] he; she; it; that; as a suffix it imparts the sense of one who or that which bears or carries [e.g. गंधवह, भारवह].

वह/न [*nm*] conveying, carrying, bearing; transportation; hence ~नीय.

वहम [*nm*] doubt, suspicion, false notion; superstition.

वहमी [*a*] suspicious; superstitious.

वहशत [*nf*] savagery; embarrassment.

वहशियाना [*a*] wild, fierce, [like or resembling a] savage.

वहशी [*a*] savage, barbarous; ~पन savagery, barbarousness.

वहाँ [*adv*] there

वहीं [*ind*] there itself; at that very place/point, on the spot; ibid.

वही [*pron*] the same.

वह्नि [*nf*] fire.

वांछनीय [*a*] desirable, worth wishing for; hence ~ता.

वांछित [*a*] desired, wished for.

वा [*ind*] or, or else; either—or, whether—or; [int] oh! ah! alas!

वावै(वे)ला [*nm*] weeping and wailing; outcry; row, havoc; —करना/मचाना to kick up a row, to raise an outcry, to create a havoc.

वाइसराय [*nm*] a viceroy.

वाक़ई [*ind*] in fact, actually, really.

वाक़िफ [*a*] acquainted; conversant; [*nm*] acquaintance.

वाक़िफियत [*nf*] acquaintance; conversance.

वाक़िया [*nm*] incident, event, happening.

वाक् [*nf*] speech, voice; utterance; goddess of speech; ~पटु eloquent, skilled in speech; ~पटुता/पाटव eloquence, skill in speech.

वाक्य [*nm*] a sentence; -रचना syntax, construction of a sentence; -विन्यास amphibology, the order of a sentence.

वाग्जाल [*nm*] confused mass or multitude of words, grandiloquence; prevarication.

वाग्दान [*nm*] betrothal, engagement.

वाग्देवी [*nf*] Saraswati: —the goddess of speech.

वा/ग्मिता [*nf*] eloquence, apt and forceful use of words; hence ~ग्मी.

वाग्युद्ध [*nm*] an altercation, wordy quarrel.

वाग्वैदग्ध्य [*nm*] eloquence, skill in speech; wittiness.

वाङ्मय [*nm*] literature [in general].

वाचक [*nm*] a narrator; reader; [*a*] denoting; signifying.

वाचन [*nm*] reading; narration, citation.

वाचनालय [*nm*] a reading room.

वाचस्पति [*nm*] master of speech—Brihaspati, mythologically, the preceptor of gods.

वाचाल [*a* and *nm*] outspoken, talkative; chattering, gabby; hence ~ता.

वाचिक [*a*] vocal, verbal, oral; [*nm*] acting through speech.

वाच्य [*a*] predicable, expressible through words; [nm] denoted/literal meaning; voice [as कर्तृवाच्य —active voice, कर्मवाच्य—passive voice, भाववाच्य—neutral voice].

वाच्यार्थ [*nm*] literal/primary meaning [of a word].

वाजि/ब [*a*] reasonable, proper, incumbent; ~बी reasonable, proper, incumbent.

वाटिका [*nf*] a small garden.

वाणिज्य [*nm*] commerce; trade.

वाणी [*nf*] speech, voice; Saraswati:—the goddess of speech.

वात [*nm*] air; wind—one of the three humours of the body [the other two being पित्त and कफ]; gout, rheumatism.

वातानुकू/लन [*nm*] airconditioning; ~लित airconditioned.

वातायन [*nm*] a ventilator.

वातावरण [*nm*] atmosphere.

वात्या [*nf*] a whirwind; ~चक्र a whirlwind.

वात्सल्य [*nm*] affection, affectionate love, fond/tender feeling [esp. towards the offspring]; —रस manifestation or relish of the sentiment of affection.

वाद [*nm*] a suit, law-suit, cause; discussion; dispute, controversy; theory;-ism; -प्रतिवाद discussion, disputation; controversy; -विवाद dispute, discussion; controversy.

वादक [*nm*] an instrumentalist, one who plays on a musical instrument.

वादन [*nm*] playing on an instrument; hence वादित [*a*].

वादी [*nm*] a suitor, plaintiff; complainant; the dominant or the most important note in a ra:g; [*nf*] a valley; -प्रतिवादी the plaintiff and the defendant.

वाद्य [*nm*] a musical instrument; [*a*] [musical instrument] that can be played upon; [fit] to be played upon; ~वृंद the orchestra.

वानप्रस्थ [*nm*] the third of the four stages (आश्रम) of life prescribed by tradition for caste Hindus—the stage of abandoning worldly things; hence—आश्रम; वानप्रस्थी [*nm* and *a*].

वानर [*nm*] a monkey, an ape.

वापस [*a*] returned, given back; come back; reverted; refunded, reimbursed; hence वापसी.

वाम [*a*] left, sinistral; reverse, contrary, adverse, perverse; vile, base;—मार्ग the Ta:ntrik cult [which prescribes wine, woman etc. as essentials]; ~मार्गी a follower of —मार्ग; pertaining to the —मार्ग.

वामन [*nm*]a dwarf, dwarfish/short-statured person; a pigmy; the name of the fifth incarnation of Vishnū wherein he assumed the form of a dwarf; [a] dwarfish, short statured.

वायदा [*nm*] a promise; commitment; ~खिलाफी breach of a promise incarnation of a commitment.

वायवीय [*a*] aerial; windy, airy; ethereal, impalpable.

वायु [*nf*] air, wind; windy humour; wind formation within the system; ~मंडल atmosphere; -मार्ग airways; -वेग having the velocity of wind; -सेना air force.

वायुयान [*nm*] an aeroplane, aircraft.

वारंट [*nm*] a warrant.

वारंवार [*ind*] again and again; frequently.

वार [*nm*] an assault; a stroke, blow; a day of the week; the nearer side [as against पार—the farther side]; -पार full expanse; this side and the other; across, from this side to the other; -पार होना to be run through; to traverse the whole expanse.

वारदात [*nf*] a mishap, unfortunate/untoward event; an affray.

वारना [*v*] to sacrifice [on someone]; to dedicate; to make an offering of.

वारनिश [*nf*] varnish.

वारांगना [*nf*] a prostitute.

वाराणसी [*nf*] the holy city of Benares.

वारा-न्यारा [*nm*] settlement, decisive culmination; outcome.

वारि [*nm*] water.

वारिस [*nm*] an heir, successor.

वारुणी [*nf*] wine, liquor.

वार्डन [*nm*] a warden.

वार्ता [*nf*] a talk; talks, negotiation; ~कार a talker; negotiator.

वार्तालाप [*nm*] conversation, talks; negotiation.

वार्तिक [*nm*] a gloss; commentary.

वार्द्धक्य [*nm*] senility, old age.

वार्षि/क [a] annual, yearly; per annum; ~की annuity.

वालंटियर [nm] a volunteer.

वाला —a suffix denoting an agent, doer, owner, possessor, keeper or inhabitant; hence वाली feminine form.

वालिद [*nm*] father.

वालिदैन [*nm*] parents.

वावैला [*nm*] uproar, tumult, turmoil, row; outcry.

वाष्प [*nm*] vapour.

वास [*nm*] habitation, dwelling, residence; fragrance, aroma; ~भूमि homestead.

वासना [*nf*] passion, intense desire.

वासर [*nm*] a day.

वासी [*nm*] a dweller, inhabitant.

वास्तव [*a*] real, acutal, factual; genuine; substantial.

वास्तविक [*a*] real, actual, factual; genuine, bonafide; substantial, true; ~ता reality, truth.

वास्ता [*nm*] concern; connection; relation; —देना to invoke the name of;—पड़ना to be concerned with; to have to deal with; —होना to be concerned with, to be related with, to have dealings with.

वास्तु [*nm*] buildings; -कर्म building work; –कला/विद्या/शिल्प architecture.

वास्ते [*ind*] for, for the sake of; in the name of.

वाह [*ind*] an exclamatory word denoting admiration appreciation, contempt, opposition; surprise, etc; well done! bravo! excellent! how can that be! that can't be so!; a suffix denoting one who or that which carries or bears; -वाह hurrah, very good! excellent!; ~वाही applause; cheer.

वाहक [*nm*] a carrier, bearer, porter.

वाहन [*nm*] a vehicle, conveyance; an animal used to ride upon.

वाहिनी [*nf*] an army.

वाहियात [*a*] nonsense; useless; ridiculous.

वाही —a suffix meaning he who or that which carries, bears, causes to flow; -तबाही irrelevant nonsense.

विंदु [*nm*] a dot; drop; point; speck.

विंध्याचल [*nm*] the mountain range in Central India dividing north India from the South and extending to the northern end of पश्चिमी घाट and पूर्वीघाट.

वि—a prefix [generally to verbs and nouns and other parts of speech derived from verbs] to express division, distinction, distribution, arrangement, opposition or deliberation as also the sense of through, between; sometimes it gives a meaning opposite to the idea contained in the simple root or also intensifies the idea.

विकच [*a*] blooming; opened up.

विकट [*a*] horrible, dreadful, frightful, monstrous, formidable.

विकराल [*a*] horrible, dreadful, frightful, hideous; monstrous, formidable.

विकर्ण [*nm*] a diagonal.

विकर्षण [*nm*] repulsion; aversion, distaste.

विक/ल [*a*] restless, agitated, dismembered, mutilated, crippled; ~लांग crippled, disabled; ~लित restless; agitated.

विकल्प [*nm*] an option, alternative, uncertainty.

विकसित [*a*] bloomed; opened; grown, developed.

विकार [*nm*] deformation, defilement; change or variation [for the worse]; deviation from a natural state; perversion; disorder; hence विकारी.

विकास [*nm*] evolution; development, growth; bloom; ~वाद theory of evolution; evolutionism; ~शील developing; evolving.

विकृत [*a*] deformed, defiled, mutilated; changed [to the worse]; deviated from the natural course, perverted; distorted, disordered; strained; oblique; hence विकृति.

विक्रम [*nm*] heroism, valiance, valour; name of an ancient great king of Ujjain, founder of an era which commenced earlier than the Christian era [also known as विक्रमादित्य].

विक्रमी [*a*] heroic, valiant, valorous; pertaining to विक्रम or his era.

विक्रय [*nm*] sale, selling; hence विक्रेय.

विक्रेता [*nm*] a seller, vendor; salesman.

विक्षत [*a*] wounded, injured.

विक्षिप्त [*a*] mad, crazy; bewildered; perplexed; hence ~ता.

विक्षुब्ध [*a*] see विक्षोभ.

वि/क्षोभ [*nm*] agitation, perturbation, disturbance; turbulence; hence ~क्षुब्ध.

विख्यात [a] renowned, well-known, famous, reputed, celebrated.

विगठन [*nm*] disorganisation, disintegration.

विगत [*a* and *nm*] [the] past;used as a suffix it means deprived/divested of minus, one who or that which has lost.

विगलन [*nm*] fusion, melting away; moving.

विग्र/ह [*nm*] strife, quarrel; form, idol [e.g. देवविग्रह]; [in grammar] resolution [of a compound word] into constituent parts, separation or analysis of a compound word.

विघटन [*nm*] disintegration, disorganisation; disruption; decomposition; disbandment; dismemberment [e.g. of a state]; dismantlement; hence विघटित.

विघ्न [*nm*] an interruption; interference, meddling, obstacle, disturbance; -विनाशक one who removes/counters all obstructions; an epithet of the deity Ganesh [whose worship is supposed to counter all obstacles].

विचक्षण [*a*] extremely sagacious, far-sighted.

विचर [*a*] strayed, wandered or swerved from; [*nm*] a variable; ~ण wandering, strolling; movement; variation.

विचलन [*nm*] departure; deviation; moving about; yaw; unsteadiness; hence विचलित.

विचार [*nm*] thought, thinking; idea; view, observation [s]; pondering, deliberation; reflection; contemplation, reasoning; consideration, trial; ~क a thinker; one who deliberates/contemplates; -गोष्ठी a seminar; -विमर्श discussion, exchange of views; ~धारा ideology; ~शील thoughtful, reflective, contemplative/reasoning; hence ~ शीलता, -स्वातंत्र्य freedom of thought; hence ~ण, ~ णा.

विचारणीय [*a*] to be deliberated upon, worth/needing consideration, fit to be given thought to; dubious, questionable.

विचारना [*v*] to think, to deliberate on, to consider.

विचाराधीन [*a*] under consideration; under trial, subjudice.

विचित्र [*a*] strange; surprising, amazing, wonderful; queer, curious; peculiar; hence ~ता.

विच्छिन्न [*a*] isolated, cut off; discontinued; disjoined, disconnected; hence ~ता.

विच्छेद [*nm*] dissection; division; difference; disintegration, separation; discontinuance; breach; breaking up.

विछोह [*nm*] separation [from the beloved].

विजन [*a*] solitary, lonely; [nm] a lonely place, solitude.

विजय [*nf*] victory, conquest, triumph; -देवी the goddess of victory; -ध्वज/पताका the banner of victory, triumphal flag; ~लक्ष्मी/श्री the goddess of victory; —सिद्धि accomplishment of victory/conquest.

विजया [*nf*] Durga ~दशमी Dussehra.

विजयोत्सव [*nm*] a festival to celebrate victory.

विजा/ति [*nf*] another/different caste, class or genre; ~तीय of different caste, class or genre; heterogeneous.

विजेता [*nm*] a conqueror, victor, one who has achieved victory.

विज्ञ [*a* and *nm*] knowledgeable, learned, wise [person].

विज्ञप्ति [*nf*] a communique; -, प्रेस a press communique.

विज्ञान [*nm*] science; ~वेत्ता a scientist, man of science; ~वाद Idealism—the doctrine that only intelligence has reality [and not the objects exterior to us]; ~वादी an idealist. a believer in the doctrine of विज्ञानवाद; idealistic.

विज्ञानी [*nm*] a scientist.

विज्ञापन [*nm*] an advertisement; announcement; a poster.

विटप [*nm*] a tree.

विडंबन [*nm*] mimicry; -काव्य a parody.

विडंबना [*nf*] anomaly; mockery.

वितंडा [*nm*] perverse argumentation, ungainly controversy; ~वाद arguing for the sake of argument; perverse argumentation; ungainly controversy.

वितरण [*nm*] distribution; disbursement; delivery, service.

वितर्क [*nm*] discussion reasoning.

वितृष्णा [*nf*] repulsion, repugnance.

वित्त [*nm*] finance, wealth.

वित्तीय [*a*] financial.

विदग्ध [*a*] witty; ingenious; skilful; hence ~ता.

विदा [*nf*] taking leave; farewell, adieu; a woman's departure from her mother's or from her in-law's house either way.

विदाई [*nf*] farewell, sending off; departure; present made at the time of departure.

विदित [*a*] known.

विदीर्ण [*a*] lacerate, rent asunder, torn, ripped open, split up.

विदुषी [*nf*] a learned/wise woman.

विदूषक [*nm*] a jester, buffoon; the jocose companion and confidential friend of the hero in traditional Sanskrit drama.

विदेश [*nm*] a foreign land/country.

विदेशी [*a*] foreign, alien, exotic; [*nm*] a foreigner, foreign national.

विदेशीय [*a*] foreign; alien; exotic.

विदेह [*a*] incorporeal; beyond physical bonds.

विद्यमान [*a*] present, existent; extant.

विद्या [*nf*] learning, knowledge, education; science, discipline; skill; -दान teaching, imparting knowledge; -देवी Saraswati: —the goddess of learning; ~पीठ a school, seat/centre of learning; -मंदिर temple of learning; ~विहीन illiterate; stupid;—झूठी पड़ना learning/skill to prove of no avail; —फलना learning/skill to bear fruit.

विद्याभ्या/स [*nm*] pursuit of learning, study; ~सी studious.

विद्यार्थी [*nm*] a student; scholar.

विद्यालय [*nm*] a school, educational institution.

विद्युत् [*nm*] electricity, power; lightning.

विद्योपार्जन [*nm*] acquisition of education study.

विद्रुम [*nm*] coral; the coral tree.

विद्रूप [*a*] distorted, ugly, hideous; monstrous; [*nm*] ludicrousness; monstrosity; irony; a parody; —काव्य a parody.

विद्रो/ह [*nm*] uprising, revolt, rebellion, mutiny, insurrection; ~ही revolting, a rebel/rebellious; mutineering.

विद्वत्ता [*nf*] learning; scholarship.

विद्वान् [*a* and *nm*] learned [man]; a scholar.

विद्वे/ष [*nm*] rancour, malice, spitefulness; hence ~षी.

विध/र्म [*nm*] heresy, a religion other than one's own, nonconformist religion; [*a*] unjust, inequitable; hence ~मी.

विधवा [*nf*] a widow.

विधा [*nf*] genre, form, type; device.

विधाता [*nm*] the Creator—Brahmā: Destiny personified; a legislator, law -maker.

विधान [nm] legislation rule, regulation; manner/method; -परिषद् legislative council; ~पालिका legislature; -मंडल legislature; -सभा legislative assembly.

विधायक [*a* and *nm*] legislative, creative; a legislator; creator.

विधायी [*a*] legislative; creative.

विधि [*nf*] law; method, manner, system; direction; rule; a prescribed act or rite or ceremony, prescription; imperative; destiny, providence; [*nm*] the Creator—Lord Brahmā:—और व्यवस्था law and order; ~तः ipso jure, de jure; -निषेध dos and don'ts, prescription and negation; ~पूर्वक duly; methodically, systematically; ~लिंग the potential mood [in grammar]; ~वत् duly, methodically, systematically; in conformity with rules, as prescribed by law; ~वश/वशात् by providence; -विधान method and manner; writ of providence; ~ पूर्वक/से methodically, following elaborate prescription; ~विहित prescribed by law, ordained by law; ~वेत्ता a juris consultant; -शास्त्र jurisprudence; ~शास्त्री a jurisprudent, jurist.

विधु [*nm*] the moon.

विधुर [*nm*] a widower; [*a*] widowed.

विधेय [*a*] that can be legislated; to be performed or practised; to be enjoined [as a rule etc.]; [*nm*] the predicate; hence ~तः [adv]: ~ता [*nf*]; ~ त्व [nm]; -विशेषण predicative adjective.

विधेयक [*nm*] a bill [in a legislature].

विध्यात्मक [*a*] positive.

विध्वंस [*nm*] destruction, devastation; subversion; demolition.

विध्वंसी [*nm*] a destroyer; one who or that which destroys.

विनत [*a*] bowing/bowed; modest, humble.

विनती [*nf*] prayer; request, entreaty.

विनम्र [*a*] humble, meek, submissive; respectful; courteous; hence ~ ता.

विनय [*nf*] modesty, politeness, humbleness, humility; hence ~शील, ~ शीलता.

विनयी [*a*] modest, polite, humble.

विनश्वर [a] perishable, transient, transitory; hence ~ तै.

विनष्ट [*a*] perished, destroyed, devastated; wrecked; ruined.

विनायक [*nm*] the gourl Ganesh.

विनाश [*nm*] destruction, devastation; disaster, ruin, wreck; hence विनाशी.

विनि/मय [*nm*] exchange; ~मेय exchangeable.

विनियम [*nm*] a regulation.

विनिर्माण [*nm*] manufacture/manufacturing; hence विनिर्मित.

विनीत [*a*] humble, modest; submissive, meek; hence ~ता.

विनोद [*nm*] wit, humour, amusement, recreation; skit; hence ~शील, ~ शीलता.

विनोदी [*a*] witty, humorous, jolly, jovial.

विन्यास [*nm*] structure, disposition, arrangement; setting, plan, lay-out; marshalling.

विपक्ष [*nm*] the opposition [party/side]; adversary.

विपक्षी [*a*] opposition, rival, hostile: [*nm*] an opponent, a rival; an enemy.

विपणन [*nm*] marketing.

विपत्ति [*nf*] distress, affliction; calamity; hardship; ~ग्रस्त afflicted, distressed, fallen into calamity; ~वाद catastrophism; —भोगना to suffer hardships, to endure a calamity; —मोल लेना, —सिर पर लेना to own up avoidable distress/calamity, to get oneself [foolishly] embroiled in a calamitous/troublous affair, to ask for it.

विपद् [*nf*] distress, affliction, hardship, calamity, crisis; ~ग्रस्त in a crisis, in distress, afflicted; struck by a calamity.

विपन्न [*a*] distressed, afflicted; fallen into a calamity, in a critical state.

विपरीत [*a*] opposite/opposed; contrary; reverse.

विपर्यय [*nm*] metathesis, transposition; reversal.

विपर्याय [*nm*] an antonym, antonymous word; ~वाचक/वाची antonymous.

विपर्यास [*nm*] upsetting, disarray; controriety; interchange; peripeteia/reversal [of the situation].

विपिन [*nm*] a forest, jungle.

विपुल [*a*] large, big; abundant, copious; extensive; mammoth, colossal; hence ~ता.

विप्र [*nm*] a Brahman.

विप्रलंभ [*nm*] separation [of lovers]; —श्रृंगार according to Indian poetics one of the two types of श्रृंगार wherein the lovers suffer separation from each other; hence विप्रलब्ध.

विप्लव [*nm*] insurrection, insurgency, revolt.

विफल [*a*] failed, unsuccessful; vain, inefficacious; fruitless, futile; hence ~ता.

विभक्त [*a*] divided; partitioned; separated.

विभक्ति [*nf*] a case ending/termination, inflection, case; division; -प्रधान inflectional; -रूप declension [s].

विभव [*a*] potential; [*nm*] omnipresence; wealth, riches, affluence, prosperity; luxury.

विभा [*nf*] shine, glow, brilliance, lustre.

विभाग [*nm*] a department; division; portion, part.

विभागीय [*a*] departmental.

विभाजक [*a*] dividing, parting; [*nm*] a divisor.

विभा/जन [*nm*] division, partition; hence ~जित, ~ज्य, ~ज्यता.

विभाव [*nm*] any condition which excites or develops a particular state of mind or body, any cause that rouses an emotion [as आलंबन, उद्दीपन—].

विभाषा [*nf*] a sub-language, dialect.

विभिन्न [*a*] different, various, diverse; ~ता variety, diversity.

विभीषण [*nm*] the youngest brother of रावण and a devotee of राम in the epic story of Ramayan; a traitor, renegade.

विभीषिका [*nf*] horror, terror; of act or means of terrifying.

विभु [*nm*] God—the all-pervading, omnipresent; mighty; powerful, omnipotent; hence ~ता.

विभूति [*nf*] ash; majesty/magnificence; an outstanding personality, personage.

विभूषित [*a*] adorned, ornamented, decorated, embellished.

विभेद [*nm*] variety, kind; subdivision, distinction. difference, discrimination; hence ~क/कारी; ~न.

विभेद्य [*a*] differentiable, distinguishable; separable; pierceable, penetrable.

विभो [*int*] vocative form of विभु—O, God Almighty!

विभोर [*a*] fully overwhelmed/engrossed/absorbed.

विभ्रम [*nm*] delusion, confusion, flurry; restlessness, unsteadiness; amorous gestures or action of any kind.

विभ्रांति [*nf*] confusion, perturbation; mistake, error.

विम/त [*nm*] contrary/dissenting opinion; counter principle; [*a*] having contrary opinion/principle; dissenting; ~ति dissent, disagreement, discord.

विमर्श [*nm*] consultation; consideration, examination; reflection, deliberation.

विमल [*a*] clear, clean; dirtless, spotless, flawless; pure.

विमा [*nf*] dimension.

विमाता [*nf*] step-mother.

विमान [*nm*] an aeroplane, aircraft, airliner; -चालक a pilot; ~न aviation; -पत्तन airport; -परिचारिका air-hostess.

विमु/क्त [*a*] acquitted, released, exempted; emancipated, delivered, liberated; hence ~क्ति.

विमुख [*a*] indifferent, indifferently disposed, disinclined, having a sense of aversion; hence ~ता.

विमुग्ध [*a*] imfatuated; fascinated, attracted, charmed; ~कारी infatuating, fascinating; attractive, charming.

विमूढ़ [*a*] see मूढ़.

विमोचन [*nm*] acquittal, liberation, release.

वियु/क्त [*a*] separated; deserted, abandoned; isolated; ~क्ति separation; isolation.

वियोग [*nm*] separation, disunion; bereavement.

वियो/गी [*a* and *nm*] a lover/husband separated from his beloved/wife; hence ~गिनी.

वियोजन [*nm*] separation; disintegration; disjoining; abscission; hence ~जक; ~ जित separated; disunited, disintegrated; disjoined.

विरं/च, ~ **चि** [*nm*] Brahmā: —the Creator of the universe.

विर/क्त [*a*] detached [from the world]; disaffected, averse; indifferent; [*nm*] a recluse; hence ~क्तता/क्ति.

विरचित [*a*] composed, written.

विर/त [*a*] detached, disaffected; desisted disengaged; indifferent; hence ~ति.

विरल [*a*] thin; sparse; rare, scarce; hence ~ता; ~न rarefaction; thinning, becoming sparse; hence विरलित.

विरह [*nm*] separation, parting.

विरहाग्नि [*nf*] the anguish/agony of separation.

विरहिणी [*a* and *nf*] [one] separated from her lover/husband.

विरही [*a* and *nm*] [one] separated from his beloved/wife.

विरा/ग [*nm*] renunciation, detachment; aversion, dislike, indifference; hence ~गी.

विराजना [*v*] to grace [an occasion, place, etc.]; to take seat, to be seated [used in a deferential context]; to look splendid/glorious; hence विराजित [*a*].

विराजमान [*a*] [graciously] seated; sitting [used deferentially], gracing; an occasion] by one's presence; looking splendid/glorious.

विराट [*a*] colossal, gigantic, emormous, huge; hence ~ ता.

विराम [*nm*] pause; pause in or at the end of a sentence; [full] stop; stoppage; repose, rest; halt; respite; interval/intermission; -चिह्न full-stop; punctuation mark.

विरामावस्था [*nf*] interkinesis, position of rest.

विरासत [*nf*] legacy, inheritance.

विरुद [*nm*] laudatory attributes [of an eminent personage]; a laudatory poem, panegyric.

विरुदावली [*nf*] [totality of] laudatory attributes; a panegyric.

विरुद्ध [*a*] against, opposed; opposite; contrary, adverse, hostile.

विरेचक [*a*] cathartic, purgative; [*nm*] a purgative.

विरेचन [*nm*] catharsis, purgation; -सिद्धांत the theory of catharsis [in Poetics]; hence विरेचित, विरेच्य.

विरोध [*nm*] opposition, antagonism; hostility; resistance, objection; antimony, contrariety; protest; contradiction.

विरोधाभास [*nm*] a paradox.

विरोधी [*nm* and *a*] an adversary, rival; opponent; objector; hostile, opposing; antagonistic; contradictory; contrary.

विलं/ब [*nm*] delay, procrastination; lag, tardiness; ~बित delayed, late, tardy, procrastinated; slow tempo [in music].

विलक्षण [*a*] queer, strange, peculiar, wonderful; remarkable, exceptional, extra-ordinary; fantastic; prodigious; precocious; hence ~ता.

विलय [*nm*] annihilation/destruction [of the world], dissolution/dissolving; merger/merging.

विलाप [*nm*] lamentation, crying, weeping, wailing.

विलाय/त [*nf*] a foreign land/country; Europe; England; ~ती foreign: English; European; ~ पन foreignism; Englishism; Europeanism.

विलास [*nm*] enjoyment; luxury; amorous playfulness; wantonness; lust.

विला/सी [*a* and *nm*] lustful, debauch, pleasure-seeking, wanton; luxury-loving; ~सिता debauchery, wantonness; ~सिनी [a and nf].

विलीन [*a*] vanished, disappeared; merged; absorbed, engrossed.

विलुप्त [*a*] extinct; obsolete; vanished, disappeared.

विलोकित [*a*] seen beholden, viewed.

विलो/ड़न [*nm*] thorough investigation/study; stirring up, churning; whirling; hence ~ड़ित.

विलो/प [*nm*] extinction; disappearance; obsolescence; hence ~पन; ~पित.

विलोम [*a* and *nm*] reverse; converse; contrary; antonym; -शब्द an antonym; a word having opposite meaning.

विव/क्षा [*nf*] implication; meaning, purport; desire; ~क्षित implied; intended; desired; ~ अर्थ implied/intended meaning.

विवर/ण [*nm*] an account, description; commentary; particulars, details; minutes; briefing; report, statement; ~णिका a brochure.

विवर्ण [*a*] faded, dimmed; [rendered] colourless; pallid; of a low caste [as opposed to सवर्ण].

विवर्त [*nm*] a whirpool; illusion, falsity.

विवश [*a*] helpless; compelled, under compulsion; forced, obliged; disabled; hence ~ता.

विवा/द [*nm*] a dispute; altercation, quarrel; discussion; contention, controversy; ~ दास्पद controversial.

विवाह [*nm*] marriage; wedding, matrimony; -सम्बन्ध matrimonial relation; विवाहित married [man]; विवाहिता married [woman]; विवाहोत्सव nuptials, marriage celebrations.

विवि/क्त [*a*] isolated, separated, aloof; ~क्ति isolation, separation, aloofness.

विविध [*a*] different; diverse, various, miscellaneous; ~ता diversity, variety, variation.

विवृ/त [*a*] open, exposed, uncovered; unravelled; expanded; hence ~ति.

विवृ/त्त [*a*] going/whirling round; opened, uncovered; hence ~त्ति.

विवे/क [*nm*] reason, discretion; wisdom; ~की prudent, wise, discreet.

विवेच/न [*nf*] critical appreciation; evaluation, investigation; argument, discussion, discrimination; hence ~क.

विवेचित [*a*] critically appreciated, discussed, evaluated, investigated.

विशद [*a*] elaborate, detailed; clear-cut; hence ~ ता.

विशारद [*a*] expert, learned.

विशाल [*a*] huge, large, big, spacious; grand, extensive, vast; great, gigantic, colossal; hence ~ता.

विशिष्ट [*a*] special, specialised, specific; particular; prominent; characteristic, typical; ~ष्टता speciality specificity; singularity; characteristic.

विशिष्टाद्वैत [*nm*] qualified non-quality.

विशुद्ध [a] pure/purified/chaste, virtuous; genuine; unmixed/unadulterated; ~ता genuineness; purity; chastity.

विशुद्धि [*nf*] purity, chastity, virtuosity.

विश्रृंखल [*a*] disintegrated, disorderly, disarrayed; hence ~ ता [*nf*].

विशेष [*a*] special, specific; particular; distinctive, characteristic; typical; ~ज्ञ an expert, a specialist; ~ज्ञता specialisation; ~ता speciality; peculiarity; singularity; quality; attribute; ~ताएँ characteristics.

विशेषण [*nm*] an adjective; attribute, epithet; —पद attributive.

विशेषांक [*nm*] a special issue/number [of a newspaper, journal or magazine etc.].

विशेषाधिका/र [*nm*] privilege; ~ कारी a special officer; privileged person.

विशेषित [*a*] specialised; qualified.

विशेषी/करण [*nm*] specialisation; ~कृत specialised.

विशेष्य [*nm*] that which is qualified; a noun with an adjective qualifying it, substantive.

विश्रां/त [*a*] reposed, one who has taken rest, calm at ease; ~ति rest, repose; ease; interval/intermission.

विश्राम [*nm*] rest, repose, relaxation.

विश्रुत [*a*] renowned, reputed, famous, well-known.

विश्लेषण [*nm*] analysis.

विश्लेषित [*a*] analysed.

विश्व [*nm*] the world, universe; ~कोश an encyclopaedia; भ्रातृत्व world fraternity; -राज्य world-state; -विख्यात world known, renowned throughout the world; ~विजयी a world-conqueror, conqueror of the world; ~विद्यालय a university; ~ विश्रुत see ~विख्यात; ~व्यापक/व्यापी all pervading, omnipresent, pervading the whole universe/world; -शांति world peace; -संगठन/संस्था world organisation.

विश्वसनीय [*a*] reliable, dependable, trustworthy; believable credible; hence ~ता.

विश्वस्त [*a*] see विश्वसनीय; confidential; confident.

विश्वास [*nm*] belief, trust, faith; reliance, confidence; assurance; ~घात betrayal, treachery, violation of trust; infidelity; ~घाती treacherous, one who betrays, a traitor; ~पात्र/भाजन a reliable trustworthy/dependable [person], confidant.

विश्वासी [*a* and *nm*] one who believes/trusts, trustful; a believer.

विष [*nm*] poison, venom; ~धर a snake, poisonous snake; ~वमन vituperative/virulent utterance; -वृक्ष a poison-tree—a beginning that causes ever greater harm.

विषण्ण [*a*] melancholic, gloomy, sombre; downcast; hence ~ता.

विषम [*a*] odd; heterogeneous, incongruous; uneven, rough; adverse, dissimilar; difficult [to traverse]; disagreeable; —कोण an oblique angle; ~ ता contrast; dissimilarity; inequality, oddity; difficult; disproportion, incongruity. heterogeneousness; ruggedness.

विषय [*nm*] a subject; topic; matter; content; sexual pleasure/enjoyment; an affair; object; ~रत sexy, engrossed in sexual pleasure; ~लोलुप voluptuous, lustful, sexy, sensual; -वासना sexuality and lust; sensuality, sensualism; ~वस्तु theme; -सुख sensual pleasure, sexual pleasure; -सूची a list of contents, table of contents.

विषयक [*ind*] concerning/pertaining to or related with.

विषयांतर [*nm*] digression; another topic.

विषयानुक्रम/णिका, ~ णी [*nf*] subject index; list of contents.

विषयास/क्त [*a*] sensual, lustful, given to sexual indulgence; debauch, lewd; [*nm*] debauchee; hence ~ क्ति.

विषयी [*a*] voluptuous, lustful; sensual; a subject [as opposed to object—विषय]; [*nm*] a sensualist.

विषाक्त [*a*] toxic, poisonous, venomous; vituperative; hence ~ ता.

विषाद [*nm*] gloom, sombreness, melancholy, despondency.

विषुवत् [*a*] equatorial.

विषूचिका [*nf*] cholera.

विषैला [*a*] poisonous; venomous, toxic, vituperative, virose; hence ~पन.

विष्कंभक [*nm*] an interlude [in a drama].

विष्ठा [*nf*] faeces, excrement, night soil.

विष्णु [*nm*] one of the Hindu mythological divine trinity-ब्रह्मा, विष्णु and महेश, the preserver of the world; God Almighty.

विसंग/त [*a*] irrelevant, illogical; incoherent; ~ति irrelevance/irrelevancy, illogicality; incoherence.

विसं/पर्क [*nm*] isolation; segregation; hence ~पृक्त.

विसम्म/त [*a*] dissenting, disagreeing; ~ति disagreement, dissent.

विसर्ग [*nm*] a colon like sign [:] used in the Devanagari: script, characteristic of Sanskrit word formations and resembling 'h' in pronunciation.

विस/र्जन [*nm*] dispersal; abandonment; ~ र्जित dispersed; abandoned.

विस्तार [*nm*] expanse, span, spread; extent; extension, elaboration; enlargement; details; volume; ~पूर्वक extensively; in details, elaborately.

विस्तीर्ण [*a*] expanded, spread out; spacious; elaborate, copious.

विस्तृ/त [*a*] expanded; commodious; voluminous; elaborate, detailed; lengthy; hence ~ति.

विस्था/पन [*nm*] displacement; ~पित displaced.

विस्फारित [*a*] opened wide; spread.

विस्फोट [*nm*] explosion, blast; burst; crack[ing]; ~क explosive; a cracker.

विस्मय [*nm*] wonder, surprise, astonishment, amazement.

विस्मरण [*nm*] forgetting, oblivion; ~शील forgetful, oblivious; ~शीलता forgetfulness, obliviousness.

विस्मित [*a*] wonderstruck, amazed, surprised, astonished.

विस्मृ/त [*a*] forgotten, gone into oblivion; ~ति forgetfulness, oblivion.

विहंग [*nm*] a bird; ~म a bird.

विहंगावलोकन [*nm*] a bird's eye-view.

विहग [*nm*] a bird.

विहान [*nm*] day-break.

विहार [*nm*] merry-making, having good time, pastime; wandering, roaming; sexual enjoyment; a [Buddhistic] monastery.

विहिप [*a*] prescribed, ordained, enjoined [by]; in order, valid.

विहीन—a suffix used to impart a negative sense—without/deprived of/divested of.

विह्वल [*a*] overwhelmed; perturbed, agitated; hence ~ता; ~ हृदय

वी/चि, ~ ची [*nf*] a ripple, wave.

वीणा [*nf*] a typical Indian lute [with a large gourd at either end]; ~पाणि/वादिनी an epithet of goddess सरस्वती; ~ वादक a lute player, one who plays on a वीणा; ~ वादन playing on a वीणा.

वीत—an adjectival prefix used to impart the sense of past/finished/left off/beyond/ended/freed from/without, etc.; ~राग free from passions or affections; dispassionate; ~शोक free from sorrow/gloom.

वी/थि, ~ थिका, ~ थी [*nf*] an alley, avenue; gallery.

वीर [*a*] heroic; brave, valiant, valorous, gallant; [nm] a hero; brother; -काव्य heroic poetry, poetry eulogizing heroic deeds; ~गति heroic end, the attainment of heaven which is supposed to be the happy lot of a warrior killed in action; ~ को प्राप्त होना/करना to achieve a heroic end, to be killed in action, to attain access to heaven through martyrdom;—रस the sentiment of heroism [in Indian Poetics].

वीरता [*nf*] heroism; bravery, valour, daring, gallantry.

वीरा/न [*a* and *nm*] deserted, devastated, desolate; uninhabited [place]; hence ~ना; ~ नी desolateness, desertedness.

वीरासन [*nm*] a heroic posture, particular sitting posture.

वीरोचित [*a*] heroic, befitting a hero, gallant, valorous, valiant.

वीर्य [*nm*] semen; potency; manly vigour, valour; virility; heroism; ~हीन impotent.

बुजूद [*nm*] existence, being.

वृंत [*nm*] a stalk, stem or main axis [of a plant etc].

वृंद [*nm*] multitude, assembly; ~गान chorus; ~गायक the chorus, collective singers; ~गायन collective/choral singing.

वृक्ष [*nm*] a tree.

वृत्त [*nm*] circle, ring; account, record; news; verse, meter; -चित्र a documentary [film].

वृत्तांत [*nm*] news; a report, narrative, account.

वृत्ताकार [*a*] circular, round.

वृत्ति [*nf*] instinct; mentality; profession, vocation; [conventional] function; stipend [as छात्रवृत्ति]; commentary [esp. oa a su:tra]; ~कार a commentator.

वृथा [*a*] useless; fruitless; ineffective; [*adv*] in vain, vainly, to no effect.

वृद्ध [*a*] old, elderly, aged; [*nm*] an aged man, old man; hence ~द्धा [*a* and *nf*].

वृद्धावस्था [*nf*] old age, senility.

वृद्धि [*nf*] increase/increment; rise, growth; progress; enlargement, augmentation; enhancement; magnification.

वृश्चिक [*nm*] a scorpion; —राशि Scorpio—the eighth sign of the zodiac.

वृष [*nm*] a bull, bullock; -राशि the zodiacal sign—Taurus.

वृषभ [*nm*] a bull, bullock; -राशि the zodiacal sign, Taurus.

वृष्टि [*nf*] rain.

वृह/त् [*a*] large, big; great; also ~द् an allomorph of वृहत्.

वे [*pro*] they, those.

वेग [*nm*] speed, velocity; momentum.

वेणी [*nf*] a braid of hair or braided hair.

वेणु [*nf*] a flute; bamboo.

वेतन [*nm*] pay, salary; wages; ~भोगी salaried, receiving wages; stipendiary; -वृद्धि increment.

वेताल [*nm*] a goblin, evil spirit, ghost.

वेत्ता [*nm*] one who knows; a Sanskrit word used as a suffix to impart the sense of one who knows or who is an expert in, as तत्त्ववेत्ता, विधिवेत्ता, etc.

वेद [*nm*] the most ancient and sacred scriptures of the Hindus, four in number, viz. ऋग्वेद, यजुर्वेद, सामवेद, अथर्ववेद; knowledge, divine knowledge; ~ज्ञ conversant with the Vedas, Vedic scholar; ~त्रय/त्रयी the three comparatively earliet Vedas, viz the ऋग्वेद, यजुर्वेद and सामवेद; -पाठ recitation of the Vedas;~पाठी reciter of the Vedas; -मंत्र a Vedic verse/hymn;-वचन Vedic text or statement; -वाक्य a Vedic quotation; an irrefutable statement/truth; ~विद see ~ज्ञ; ~ विहित prescribed by or enjoined in the Vedas.

वेदना [*nf*] ache, pain, agony.

वेदांग [*nm*] the six subordinate branches of the Vedas, viz. शिक्षा, कल्प, निरुक्त, छंद, ज्योतिष, and व्याकरण.

वेदांत [*nm*] one of the six systems of Hindus philosophy [so called either as teaching the ultimate scope of the Veda or simply as explained in the Upanishads, which come at the end of the Vedas].

वेदांती [*a* and *nm*] [one] conversant with or adhering to the Vedant system of philosophy.

वेदिका [*nf*] see वेदी.

वेदी [*nf*] an altar, a platform; terrace; a suffix used in the sense of a knower or scholar of the Vedas.

वेध [*nm*] perforation; penetrating/piercing; [planetary] observation; ~शाला an observatory [of stars and planets etc.].

वेला [*nf*] time; an hour; coast, shore.

वेश [*nm*] guise, external appearance; dress, costume; -भूषा apparel; get-up, appearance.

वेश्या [*nf*] a prostitute; ~गामी one who indulges in prostitution; -वृत्ति [profession or institution of] prostitution.

वेश्यालय [*nm*] a brothel.

वैकल्पिक [*a*] optional, alternative.

वैकुंठ [*nm*] the heaven, paradise; also ~पुरी/लोक.

वैचित्र्य [*nm*] peculiarity, typicalness; characteristic quality; strangeness.

वैजयंती [*nf*] a shield; banner; mythological garland of Lord Vishnū.

वैज्ञानिक [*nm*] a Scientist; [*a*] scientific.

वैतनिक [*a*] salaried, on payment or salary basis.

वैतालिक [*nm*] a minstrel, bard.

वैदग्ध्य [*nm*] wits, intelligence; sharpness, acuteness.

वैदिक [*a*] pertaining or belonging to or related with the Vedas; of the Vedas, Vedic.

वैदुष्य [*nm*] scholarship, learning.

वैदेशिक [*a*] foreign, external; pertaining to a foreign country.

वैदेही [*nf*] daughter of विदेह —an epithet of सीता.

वैद्य [*nm*] an Ayurvedic physician.

वैद्यक [*nf*] the Indian medicinal system, the science or practice of medicine.

वैध [*a*] valid, legal, legitimate; tenable; hence ~ता.

वैधर्म्य [*nm*] heresy; heterogeneity [as साधर्म्य -वैधर्म्य].

वैधव्य [*nm*] widowhood.

वैभव [*nm*] grandeur, glory, magnificence; wealth, prosperity, riches; hence ~शाली.

वैमनस्य [*nm*] rancour, malice, hostility, enmity.

वैमानि/क [*a*] aeronautical, pertaining or related with aviation/aircraft; ~की aeronautics; ~कीय aeronautical, aviational.

वैयक्तिक [*a*] individual, personal; private; subjective; ~ता individuality; subjectivity.

वैयाकरण [*nm*] a grammarian.

वैर [*nm*] enmity, animosity, hostility.

वैरागी [a and nm] detached; a recluse, one who is not attached to worldly affairs.

वैराग्य [*nm*] [attitude of] renunciation, detachment [from worldly affairs].

वैरी [*nm*] an enemy, a foe, hostile person.

वैवाहिक [*a*] matrimonial, nuptial, married.

वैशाख [*nm*] the second month of the Hindu calendar.

वैशिष्ट्य [*nm*] speciality; characteristic [quality]; peculiarity.

वैशेषिक [*nm*] one of the six major systems of Indian Philosophy.

वैश्य [*nm*] the third वर्ण [caste] in the traditional Hindu hierarchical caste set-up with trade as its main profession, a trader.

वैषम्य [*nm*] see विषमता.

वैषयिक [*a*] subjective, pertaining to the subject; pertaining to sex or sexual enjoyment, sensual.

वैष्णव [*nm*] a devotee of विष्णु; [a] pertaining to or belonging to विष्णु; hence वैष्णवी [nf].

वैसा [*a*] of that kind/nature, like that, such as that.

वैसे [*ind*] that way, in that manner, in the same manner.

व्यंग्य [*nm*] suggestion; irony, sarcasm, innuendo; caricature; -चित्र a cartoon; ~ कार a cartoonist; —रूपक a skit.

व्यंग्यार्थ [*nm*] suggested meaning; suggestion.

व्यंग्योक्ति [*nf*] a sarcastic/ironical utterance or remark, sarcasm.

व्यंजक [*a*] expressive, suggestive.

व्यंजन [*nm*] a consonant; rich [cooked] food, dainties.

व्यंजन [*nf*] suggestion, suggested meaning.

व्यंजित [*a*] suggested, conveyed through suggestion.

व्यक्त [*a*] expressed, manifest[ed]; articulate.

व्यक्ति [*nm*] an individual, a person; subject; ~गत subjective; individual, personal; ~त्व personality; individuality; ~निष्ठ subjective; ~वाचक proper; ~ संज्ञा proper noun; ~वाद individualism; ~वादिता individualism; individualistic outlook; ~वादी an individualist; individualistic.

व्यग्र [*a*] restless, perturbed, concerned; impatient; hence ~ ता.

व्यतिक्रम [*nm*] metathesis, violation of established order; default, infraction; hence~ण.

व्यतिरे/क [*nm*] difference; contrast; discontinuance.

व्यतीत [*a*] passed, past.

व्यथा [*nf*] pain, agony, anguish.

व्यथित [*a*] in agony/anguish, pained, afflicted.

व्यभिचा/र [*nm*] fornication, wenching; lewdness, debauchery; adultery; hence ~रिणी; ~ री a debauchee; an adulterer; lewd, libertine; ~ भाव [in poetics] a transitory mental [or physical] state [such states number thirty-four according to Indian poeticians].

व्यय [*nm*] expense, expenditure; cost, outlay; consumption.

व्यर्थ [*a*] useless, fruitless; futile; ineffective; unprofitable; hence ~ता.

व्यवधान [*nm*] hindrance; intervention, interruption.

व्यवसा/य [*nm*] profession, vocation; calling, occupation; practice; ~यिक professional, vocational, occupational; ~यिक रंगमंच professional stage; ~यी professional; a practitioner.

व्यवस्था [*nf*] order, system; management, arrangement; organisation; provision; ruling.

व्यवस्थाप/क [*nm*] an organiser, a manager, one who directs/systematizes; hence ~न.

व्यवस्थित [*a*] systematic, in order, methodical; settled; provided [for].

व्यवहर्ता [*nm*] a practitioner.

व्यवहार [*nm*] behaviour; dealings, treatment; transaction; practice; usage, use; application; -कुशल tactful in one's dealings, worldly wise; knowing the ways of the world; hence -कुशलता.

व्यवहार्य [*a*] practicable, feasible; ~ ता practicability, feasibility.

व्यवहृत [*a*] used; applied; practised.

व्यष्टि [nm] an individual; ~वाद individualism; ~वादी individualistic; an individualist; ~सुखवाद individualistic hedonism.

व्यसन [*nm*] addiction [esp. to a vice].

व्यसनी [*a* and *nm*] addicted [esp. to a vice]; an addict.

व्यस्त [*a*] busy, occupied engaged.

व्याकरण [*nm*] grammar.

व्याकरणिक [*a*] grammatical.

व्याकुल [*a*] perturbed, [mentally] upset, restless, impatient; hence ~ता.

व्याख्या [*nf*] interpretation; explanation, elaboration; commentary, annotation; exposition; ~कार a commentator; an annotator; ~ता a commentator; an interpreter; lecturer; ~त्मक explanatory; interpretative.

व्याख्यान [*nm*] speech, lecture, oration; exposition, interpretation, elaboration.

व्याघात [*nm*] interruption; hindrance, obstruction; contradiction.

व्याघ्र [*nm*] a tiger.

व्याध [*nm*] a hunter, fowler.

व्याधि [*nf*] a malady, disease, an ailment.

व्यापक [*a*] comprehensive; extensive, widespread; pervasive; hence ~ता/त्व.

व्यापार [*nm*] trade, business; traffic; function; phenomenon.

व्यापारिक [*a*] pertaining or related with a trade/business, mercantile, commercial.

व्यापारी [*nm*] a businessman, trader, merchant; [*a*] engaged in trade/business.

व्यापी—a suffix used to give the sense of pervasive/permeating/comprehensive/spread or spreading [as सर्वव्यापी विश्वव्यापी दूरव्यापी].

व्या/प्त [*a*] pervaded, permeated, spread, extended; ~ प्ति permeability/permeation, pervasiveness, extensity/extensiveness.

व्यामोह [*nm*] illusion, mental confusion; bewilderment.

व्यायाम [*nm*] physical exercise, exercise; gymnastics; ~शाला a gymnasium.

व्यायामी [*a* and *nm*] [an] athlete; [*a*] gymnast; pertaining to athletics/gymnastics.

व्याल [*nm*] a snake, serpent.

व्यावर्तक [*a*] differentiating, distinctive, distinguishing.

व्यावसायिक [*a*] professional, vocational; —रंगमंच professional stage.

व्यावहारिक [*a*] practical; customary; hence ~ ता.

व्यास [*nm*] diameter, calibre; diffusion; a celebrated ancient Indian sage and savant; -शैली diffused style.

व्युत्क्रम [*nm*] anastrophe; reversal, cross order; reciprocal.

व्युत्पत्ति [*nf*] etymology [of a word], derivation; origin; -विज्ञान/शास्त्र [science of] etymology.

व्युत्पन्न [*a*] derived, originated; learned; accomplished; ~गति witty; accomplished.

व्यूह [*nm*] a military array; strategic disposition/placement.

व्योम [*nm*] the sky.

व्रज [*nm*] ब्रज.

व्रज्या [*nf*] poet, travelled on a path.

व्रण [*nm*] a boil; ulcer, wound.

व्रत [*nm*] a fast; vow, pledge.

व्रती [*a* and *nm*] [one who is] observing a fast/vow, one who takes a pledge; engaged in a religious observance.

व्रतति [*nf*] a creeper.

व्रात [*nm*] a multitude, group, troupe.

व्रात्य [*nm*] an outcaste from the first three caste groups, a person having parents of mixed low caste.

व्री/डा, ~ ड़ा [*nf*] bashfulness; modesty.

व्रीड़ित [*adj*] ashamed, abashed; modest, bashful.

श—the first of the conventional sibilant-trio (श, ष, स) of the Devanagari: alphabet. In current Hindi sound-pattern, however, the cerebal (ष) has merged its identity into the palatal sibilant (श).

श - देवनागरी वर्णमाला में व्यंजन का तीसवाँ वर्ण है। इसका उच्चारण स्थान तालु है।

शंकर [*nm*] causing happiness: a title of Siva, name of a Vedānta monist philosopher, mus. name of a rāg.

शंका [*nf*] doubt; suspicion; mistrust; ~शील suspicious [by nature], of suspicious disposition; hence ~शीलता; -समाधान setting a doubt at rest, allaying suspicion/mistrust; ~स्पद doubtful, questionable, fit to be doubted/suspected/distrusted.

शंकालु [*a*] [of] suspicious [nature], mistrustful; hence ~ ता.

शंकित [*a*] alarmed; filled with mistrust/doubt/suspicion.

शंकु [*nm*] a cone.

शंख [*nm*] a conchshell; a number equal to a thousand billion or 10,00,000 crore; ~ध्वनि/नाद blowing of a conch-shell signifying commencement of battle; —बजाना to rejoice; to go about announcing one's achievements; —फूँकना to make a declaration of war; to arouse/awaken.

शंखिनी [*nf*] one of the four major categories of women according to ancient Indian sexologists.

शंभु [*nm*] Lord Shiv.

शऊर [*nm*] mannerliness, decency; discretion; sense; ~दार mannerly; sensible; discreet.

शक [*nm*] doubt, suspicion; —संवत् an era introduced by emperor Shalivahan of India [in 78 A.D.] and revived by the post Independence government of the country.

शका/र [*nm*] the consonant श and its sound; ~रांत [word] ending in 'श' [sha].

शकरी [*adj*] sugary; white: मुनिया, the white-backed munia.

शकुन [*nm*] an omen, augury; -आना/जाना receiving/sending of auspicious articles on happy occasions [like marriage etc.]; –देखता/निकालना/विचारना to look for a good omen, to look for an auspicious conjunction of planets; to practise augury.

शक्कर [*nf*] sugar.

शक्की [*a*] suspicious [by] [nature], sceptic.

शक्ति [*nf*] power, strength, potency, energy; name of the goddess personifying divine power; ~मान strong, powerful/forceful, potent.

शक्तिमत्ता [*nf*] powerfulness/forcefulness, potentiality.

शक्तिमान [*a*] powerful/forceful, having potential.

शक्ल [*nf*] shape, form; looks, appearance, countenance; -सूरत looks, appearance; —तो देखीं [ironically] look at the cheek!, what a man and what a mind!; —न दिखाना not to turn up/show up, to shun a meeting; —बनाना to wear a strange look; to be out of countenance.

शख़्स [*nm*] a human being; person, an individual.

शख़्सियत [*nf*] personality; individuality.

शख़्सी [*a*] individual, personal.

शग़ल [*nm*] a pastime, recreation; hobby.

शगुन [*nm*] see शकुन.

शठ [*a*] wicked, knave, crafty, cunning; hence ~ता.

शत [*nm*] one hundred; -प्रतिशत cent per cent.

शतक [*nm*] a century, one hundred.

शतरंज [*nf*] the game of chess; a chess board.

शतशः [*ind*] in a hundred ways.

शता/ब्द, ~ ब्दी [*nf*] a century, span of hundred years.

शती [*nf*] a collection of hundred; century.

शत्रु [*nm*] an enemy, a foe; ~ता enmity, animosity, hostility.

शनाख़्त [*nf*] identification.

शनि [*nf*] Saturn—the seventh of the nine planets; Saturday; ~वार Saturday.

शनिश्चर, शनीचर [*nm*] see शनि.

शनैः [*ind*] gradually, slowly; -शनैः by degrees, little by little, gradually.

शपथ [*nf*] an oath, swearing; —दिलाना to administer an oath; -पत्र an affidavit.

शफ़ा [*nf*] [restoration to] health; curative power; ~खाना a clinic, dispensary.

शब [*nf*] night.

शबनम [*nf*] dew; a fine quality of Muslim.

शब्द [*nm*] a word, term; sound; ~कोश a dictionary; -रचना word-construction, word-formation; -रूप the [grammatical] form of a word; ~वेधी hitting at the sound [as an arrow], hitting at an object perceived only through the ear; -शक्ति the force or signification of a word; -शास्त्र lexicography; grammar; -संग्रह a glossary; -सौष्ठव elegance of words; grace of style; ~हीन speechless, mute.

शब्दशः [*ind*] verbatim, word by word; -अनुवाद word by word translation.

शब्दाडंबर [*nm*] bombast, verbiage/verbosity.

शब्दानुवाद [*nm*] a literal translation.

शब्दार्थ [*nm*] the literal meaning; -विज्ञान/शास्त्र semasiology, semantics.

शब्दालंकार [*nm*] a word-based figure of speech.

शब्दावली [*nf*] vocabulary; terminology.

शमन [*nm*] the act or process of pacification, allaying; quenching; suppression.

शमा [*nf*] a candle, lamp.

शयन [*nm*] sleep, [the act of] sleeping, lying down; -कक्ष/गृह/शाला a bed chamber, bedroom.

शयनागर [*nm*] a bed-chamber, bed-room.

शय्या [*nf*] a bed, bedstead.

शर [*nm*] an arrow.

शरअ [*nf*] custom, convention.

शरण [*nf*] shelter, refuge; recourse; protection; —देना to afford refuge, to grant shelter, to harbour.

शरणा/गत [*a* and *nm*] [one who has] come for shelter/protection; a refugee; hence ~गति.

शरणार्थी [*nm*] a refugee, shelter-seeker.

शर/त् [*nf*] the autumn; also ~द्.

शरब/त [*nm*] sweet beverage [of different kinds]; syrup; ~ती of the colour of ~त; sweet; syrupy.

शरह [*nf*] rate; detailed account.

शराफ़त [*nf*] gentlemanliness, civility, nobility.

शराब [*nf*] wine, spirit, liquor; ~खाना a bar, wine shop; ~खोर a drunkard, boozy; ~खोरी addiction to liquor, habitual drinking.

शराबी [*nm* and *a*] a drunkard; boozy; -कबाबी exercising no temperance in food and drinks.

शराबोर [*a*] thoroughly drenched/soaked.

शरार/त [*nf*] mischief/mischievousness; wickedness; ~ती naughty; hence ~ पन.

शरीअत [*nf*] divine law, religious law; justice.

शरीक [*a*] participating/ associating; partnering/ co-sharing; included.

शरीफ़ [*a*] gentlemanly; noble, virtuous.

शरीफ़ा [nm] the custard apple.

शरीर [*nm*] body, physique; [a] mischievous; —और आत्मा body and soul; -क्रिया Physiology; ~क्रिया विज्ञान Physiology; -रचना anatomy, physical structure; ~ विज्ञान/शास्त्र Anatomy; ~रचना-वैज्ञानिक an Anatomist; anatomical; ~विज्ञान/शास्त्र Physiology; ~वैज्ञानिक a physiologist; physiological; –शास्त्री a physiologist ~शास्त्रीय physiological; -संस्कार sixteen rituals or consecrations of physical purification prescribed by the Vedas.

शरीरांत [*nm*] death, demise.

शरीरी [*a*] physical, corporeal; concrete; [*nm*] an organism.

शर्करा [*nf*] sugar, saccharose.

शर्त [*nf*] a condition, term; provision; bet, wager; —बदना/लगाना to bet, to wager; —यह है कि provided that.

शर्तिया [*a* and *adv*] sure; unfailing [as —इलाज]; positively, definitely, without fail.

शर्म [*nf*] shame; bashfulness, shyness; ~नाक shameful, disgraceful; शर्माहजूरी through modesty/personal consideration.

शर्माना [*v*] to feel shy, to be abashed/ashamed, to blush; to put to shame.

शर्माशर्मी [*adv*] through shame, out of bashfulness/shyness.

शर्मि/न्दा [*a*] ashamed; ~न्दगी shame; shamefulness.

शर्मीला [*a*] shy, bashful; ~पन shyness, bashfulness.

शलज/म [*nm*] turnip; ~मी turnipy, resembling ~म.

शल्य [*nm*] a surgical instrument; a thorn; ~कर्म/क्रिया surgery. a surgical operation; -चिकित्सा surgical operation; surgery.

शव [*nm*] a corpse, dead body; ~दाह cremation; -परीक्षा autopsy, post-mortem; ~शाला mortuary.

शशांक [*nm*] the moon.

शशि [*nm*] the moon.

शस्त्र [*nm*] an arm, weapon; instrument, tool.

शस्त्रागार [*nm*] an armoury, arsenal.

शस्त्राभ्यास [*nm*] practice of arms, military exercise.

शस्त्रास्त्र [*nm*] arms [both used as missiles and for projecting].

शहंशाह [*nm*] an emperor, a king of kings.

शह—an allomorph of शाह; [nf] instigation, incitement; a check [in chess]; ~ज़ादा a prince; ~ज़ादी a princess; ~जोर powerful; strong; hence ~जोरी; ~तीर a beam, a girder; —मात the conclusive check [in chess]; to ~ करना to render helpless; ~सवार an adept horseman/rider; ~सवारी horsemanship.

शहद [*nm*] honey; [a] very sweet; —की छुरी a honey-tongued crook.

शहनाई [*nf*] a clarionet.

शहर [*nm*] a city, town.

शहादत [*nf*] evidence; martyrdom.

शहीद [*a* and *nm*] [a] martyr.

शांत [*a*] peaceful/pacific; still; silent, quiet, quiescent, tranquil, unperturbed.

शांति [*nf*] peace; calmness, quiet, tranquillity, quietude; silence; ~प्रिय peace-loving, peaceable; -भंग breach of peace, eruption of disturbances; ~मय peaceful, peaceable; ~वाद pacifism; ~वादी a pacifist; pacific; -सम्मेलन peace conference.

शाइ/स्ता [*a*] civil, modest, polite, gentle; hence ~स्तगी.

शाक [*nm*] vegetable.

शाकाहा/र [*nm*] vegetarian diet/food; ~री vegetarian.

शाक्त [*a* and *nm*] pertaining to शक्ति; a worshipper of शक्ति.

शाख़ [*nf*] a branch, twig, bough; an offshoot; lineage.

शाखा [*nf*] a branch; off-shoot; sect.

शाख़ा [*nf*] a twig, branch.

शागि/र्द [*nm*] a pupil, disciple; an apprentice; ~र्दी pupilage, discipleship; apprenticeship.

शातिर [*a*] cunning, crooked, guileful, vile.

शादी [*nf*] marriage, wedding.

शान [*nf*] magnificence, splendour, pomp, grandeur; a touchstone; whetting; ~दार magnificent; pompous, splendid, grand; -शौक़त pomp and show, grandeur and splendour; -बान grandeur, magnificence, pomp and show; –धरना to whet, to sharpen; —मारना to boast, to brag; —में बट्टा लगना a fair name to be tarnished.

शाप [*nm*] a curse, an imprecation.

शापित [*a*] cursed, accursed, imprecated.

शाबा/श [*int*] bravo!, well done!, excellent; attaboy; ~शी applause, praise;—देना to applaud.

शा/ब्द, ~ ब्दी [*a*] pertaining to a word/sound; literal, verbal; vocal.

शाब्दिक [*a*] verbal, vocal; literal/literalistic; —अनुवाद literal translation; -अर्थ literal meaning.

शाब्दिकता [*nf*] verbatism; literalism,literality.

शाम [*nf*] evening, dusk.

शामत [*nf*] misfortune, ill- luck, affliction; —आना to be in for an affliction, to be in the grip of misfortune.

शामियाना [*nm*] a canopy.

शामिल [*a*] included, associated, connected; annexed; united.

शामिला/त [*nf*] joint property; partnership; ~ती joint, held in partnership.

शायद [*ind*] perhaps probably, possibly.

शाय/र [nm] a poet; ~राना poetic, befitting a poet; ~री poetry, poetic composition.

शाया [*a*] published, brought to light.

शायिका [*nf*] a sleeper berth.

शारद [*a*] autumnal; born, produced in or pertaining to autumn; also शारदी.

शारदीया [*a*] autumnal, pertaining or belonging to the autumn.

शारीरिकी [*nm*] Anatomy; [a] anatomical, corporeal.

शारीरिक [*a*] physical, bodily, corporeal; concrete.

शार्दूल [nm] a tiger.

शाल [*nf*] a shawl; [*nm*] the sal tree.

शाला [*nf*] a house, residence; suffixed as the second member in compound words to denote a place dedicated to or meant for a particular purpose [as पाठशाला, धर्मशाला].

शाली—used as an adjectival suffix to mean one who or that which has or possesses [e.g. बलशाली, संपत्तिशाली etc.].

शालीन [*a*] modest, gentle, well-behaved, cultured; hence ~ता.

शाश्वत [*a*] eternal, immortal, perpetual; permanent; hence ~ ता.

शास/क [*nm*] a ruler; king; master; ~कीय governmental, public.

शासन [*nm*] government, administration; rule; command; -तंत्र polity, system of government; government, regime;-पद्धति/प्रणाली polity, system of government; -व्यवस्था government, system of government.

शासित [*a*] governed, ruled; administered.

शास्त्र [*nm*] scripture [s], a religious or scientific treatise, a composition of divine or secular authority; science; a discipline; literature of knowledge; ~कार the author of a shastra; ~ज्ञ one who is well-versed in shastras; -ज्ञान knowledge of a sha:stra or the sha:stra; -विधान a precept or prescription of the scriptures [shastras]; -विधि permission of the scriptures (शास्त्र); -सिद्धि proved by the scriptures, in accordance with the scriptures [शास्त्र].

शास्त्रार्थ [*nm*] discussion, contention or debate on the scriptures (शास्त्र); the purport or meaning of the scriptures (शास्त्र).

शास्त्री [*nm*] a scholar of or authority on the scriptures [or shastras]; ~य scriptural; academic; scientific, disciplinary; classical; ~ संगीत classical music.

शाहंशा/ह [*nm*] an emperor, a monarch; [*a*] very liberal; ~ही monarchical, royal; royalty; the royal throne or the duties thereof.

शाह [*nm*] a king; the king in playing cards or in chess; master; title or Mohammedan fakirs; ~कार a masterpiece; ~खर्च a spendthrift, extravagant;~ज़ादा a prince; ~ज़ादी princess.

शाहाना [*a*] kingly, royal, regal, magnificent.

शाही [*a*] royal, regal, majestic; liberal.

शिकंजा [*nm*] a clamp, pressing appliance; clasp, grasp, clutches.

शिकन [*nf*] wrinkle, shrivel; crease.

शिकमी [*a*] inherent, instinctive; [*nm*] sub-tenant [of a holding].

शिकवा [*nm*] a grudge, grouse, grievance.

शिकस्त [*nf*] a complaint, grievance; accusation, backbiting.

शिकायती [*a*] containing a complaint or grievance; [*nm*] a complaint.

शिकार [*nm*] a victim, prey.

शिकारा [*nm*] a long [partly covered] boat.

शिकारी [*a* and *nm*] hunting; a hunter, huntsman.

शिक्षक [*nm*] a teacher.

शिक्षण [*nm*] teaching, instruction, education; [a] academic, educational; -कला the art of teaching; -वृत्ति/व्यवसाय teaching profession.

शिक्षा [*nf*] education, instruction, teaching; moral; -दीक्षा education and initiation; education in general; -पद्धति system of education; -परिषद् academic council; -प्रणाली see -पद्धति; ~ प्रद educative; instructive, imparting a moral; -विभाग department of Education –व्यवस्था academic settup, educational system; -शास्त्र the science of Education.

शिक्षार्थी [*nm*] a student, pupil.

शिक्षालय [*nf*] a school, educational institution.

शिक्षित [*a*] educated.

शिखंडी [*nm*] an impotent man, eunuch.

शिखर [*nm*] a peak, top, summit, pinnacle; vortex, apex.

शिखा [*nf*] tuft or distinctive lock of hair on the crown of the head, traditionally worn by the Hindus, a top-knot; pointed flame; the crown of a cock or peacock; apex.

शिगूफ़ा [*nm*] a bud, blossom; a titbit, an anecdote; queer utterance.

शिथिल [*a*] loose, lax; slow, tardy, languid; slack; weary; not hard or compact, flaccid; ~ता looseness, laxity, lassitude; weariness, tardiness, slackness; flaccidity.

शिनाख़्त [*nf*] identification.

शिरकत [*nf*] partnership; participation; ~नामा partnership deed.

शिरा [nf] a vein.

शिरोधार्य [*a*] worthy of respect or to be respected, to be greatly honoured.

शिरोमणि [*nm*] the most outstanding person; the chief [of] [as कवि-शिरोमणि]; a jewel worn in a diadem or crown.

शिला [*nf*] a rock, large piece of stone; foundation stone; cliff; ~न्यास laying of the foundation stone; ~लिपि/लेख [rock] inscription, petrograph.

शिलिंग [*nm*] a shilling [British currency].

शिल्प [*nm*] craft; architecture; -कला technology; craft; ~कार a craftsman; an architect; ~कारी craftsmanship; -विद्या technology; craft; architecture; -विधि technique.

शिल्पी [*nm*] a craftsman; an artist; a sculptor.

शिव [*nm*] one of the divine trio (ब्रह्मा, विष्णु and महेश) of the Hindus; the good; well being, welfare; [*a*] happy; auspicious; ~लिंग phallus—worshipped as the symbol of Shiv.

शिवता [*nf*], ~त्व [nm] the good; well-being.

शिवा/लय, ~ ला [*nm*] a temple of Shiv.

शिविका [*nf*] a palanquin.

शिविर [*nm*] a camp, tent.

शिशि/र [nm] the winter; ~रांत the end of winter.

शिशु [nm] an infant; a baby; child; ~ता, ~ त्व childhood, infantilism.

शिश्न [*nm*] penis, phallus, male genital organ.

शिष्ट [*a*] civilised, courteous, gentle, decent, well-behaved; ~मंडल a delegation; deputation.

शिष्टता [*nf*] civility, courteousness, gentleness, good behaviour, decency.

शिष्टाचा/र [*nm*] etiquette; courtesy, decency, hence ~ री.

शिष्य [*nm*] a pupil, disciple; student; ~ता/त्व pupilage, discipleship; studentship.

शीघ्र [*adv*] immediately, soon, urgently; promptly, quickly, rapidly, sharp[ly], hurriedly speedily; ~ता quickness, rapidity, promptitude; hurry, haste/hastiness.

शीत [*a*] cold, frigid, chilly; [*nm*] the winter.

शीतल [*a*] cool; cold, frigid; ~ता coolness, frigidity.

शीतला [*nf*] small-pox.

शीतोष्ण [*a*] temperate, moderate.

शीत्कार [*nf*] the sound of shishi [supposed to indicate the thrill of intense pleasure or agony of severe pain].

शीरा [*nm*] syrup; molasses.

शीर्ण [*a*] broken; worn out; crushed, shattered; decayed; hence ~ता.

शीर्ष [*nm*] the head; top, summit; apex.

शीर्षक [*nm*] a title, heading.

शील [*nm*] modesty;piety, virtue, moral conduct; disposition; used as a suffix to denote natural or acquired disposition or aptitude [as प्रगतिशील, क्रोधशील etc.]; -भंग outrage of modesty; —तोड़ना to become harsh, to be blunt; to outrage the modesty [of].

शील/वान [*a*] modest; well-behaved, urbane, of good moral character, pious, virtuous; hence ~वती feminine form.

शीश [*nm*] the head; an allomorph of शीशा used as the first member in compound words; ~महल a palace fitted with mirrors all round.

शीशम [*nf*] the Indian rose-wood tree—Dalbergia sisso.

शीशा [nm] glass; a mirror, looking glass.

शीशी [*nf*] a small bottle, a phial, a vial.

शुक [*nm*] a parrot.

शुक्र [*nm*] semen; [the planet] Venus; Friday; thanks, an expression of gratitude; ~गुजार grateful, thankful; thanks-giver; hence~गुज़ारी; ~ वार Friday.

शुक्राणु [*nm*] a spermatozoon.

शुक्राना [*nm*] thanks-offering,—money paid by a client to one's pleader [and his clerks] over and above the usual remuneration [for winning a case].

शुक्राशय [*nm*] the vesicular seminalis.

शुक्रिया [*nm*] thanks [giving], [expression of] gratitude; [int] thanks! thank you!

शुक्ल [*a*] white, clean; [*nm*] a sub-division of Bra:hmans; -पक्ष the moonlit half of a lunar month.

शुग़ल [*nm*] hobby; fun; avocation.

शुचि [*a*] pure, sacred, virtuous; clean, hence ~ता/त्व.

शुतुरमुर्ग़ [*nm*] an ostrich.

शुद्ध [*a*] pure; unadulterated; sacred; uncorrupt; correct; rectified, amended; clean; natural [note—in music]; net [as—लाभ]; ~ता, ~ त्व purity; sacredness; state of being unadulterated/uncorrupted; correctness; rectification; cleanliness; naturality of a note [in music].

शुद्धि [*nf*] purity; correction/correctness; rectification; purification; -पत्र corrigendum; errata.

शुभ [*a*] auspicious; good; [nm] the good, well-being; ~कामनाएँ good wishes; ~चिंतक a well-wisher; -मुहूर्त auspicious moment/instant; —शकुन a good omen; —सूचना good news.

शुभाकांक्षी [*nm* and *a*] [*a*] well-wisher; well-wishing.

शुभागमन [*nm*] welcome, welcome arrival.

शुभाशीर्वाद [*nm*] blessings, benediction.

शुभाशीष [*nm*] see शुंभाशीर्वाद.

शुभाशुभ [*a*] good and evil; pleasant and unpleasant; agreeable and disagreeable.

शुभ्र [*a*] radiant, shining; clear, spotless [as कीर्ति]; brightcoloured; white; hence ~ता.

शुमार [*nm*] counting, accounting; computing; calculation, numbering.

शुरू [*nm*] beginning, commencement.

शुरुआत [*nf*] beginning, commencement; initiation.

शुक्ल [*nm*] fee; subscription; duty.

शुश्रूषा [nf] attendance, nursing.

शुष्क [*a*] dry/dried, withered, parched; arid; emaciated; tedious [as—कार्य]; prosaic; unfeeling; hard; hence ~ता.

शूकर [*nm*] a boar, hog, pig.

शू/द्र [*nm*] a member of the fourth of the four original classes or castes in the traditional hierarchical set-up of the Hindu society; hence ~ द्रा, ~ द्राणी [nf].

शून्य [*a*] empty, void; vacant [as—दृष्टि]; hollow; desolate; absent-minded; non-existent; [nm] a cipher, zero; void, viodance; vacuum, blank, emptiness; space; non-entity/absolute non-existence; hence ~ता/त्व; ~वाद nihilism; the Buddhist doctrine of non-existence [of any spirit -either supreme or human]; hence ~वादी.

शूर [*a* and *nm*] valiant, brave, heroic, gallant, mighty, valorous [man]; hero; a warrior; hence ~ता/त्व; -वीर brave and valorous, hero, valiant.

शूल [*nm*] sharp or acute pain [esp. in the stomach]; grief; sorrow; any sharp and pointed instrument; a spear; prong; ~हर removing or relieving pain.

शूलना [*v*] to inflict pain/sorrow, to torture/torment.

शृंखला [*nf*] a chain, fetters; series; order; connection; belt; ~वद्ध systematic, orderly; bound by a chain or fetters; hence शृंखलित;

शृंग [*nm*] top/summit [esp. of a mountain], peak; pinnacle, acme; horn [of an animal].

शृंगार [*nm*] love, the erotic sentiment, sexual passion or desire; elegant make-up; —रस one of the nine rasas —according to Indian Poetics, this one is the most comprehensive and extensive and is known as रसराज [the king of rasas].

शृंगारी [*a*] inspired by amorous passion/erotic feeling/love; disposed to prank/make-up.

शृंगा/ल [*nm*] a jackal; hence ~ली [*nf*].

शेखचिल्ली [*nm*] a conventional fool who builds castles in the air, a typical nitwit ever living in a fool's paradise.

शेख़ी [*nf*] boast, brag; ~खोर, खोरा/बाज boastful; a braggadocio, braggart, boaster; ~खोरी, ~बाजी boastfulness.

शेर [*nm*] a lion; couplet; [in Urdu poetry]: -बवर a lion; —के मुँह से शिकार छीन लेना to salvage somebody from the jaws of death; —बकरी का एक घाट पानी पीना to have rule of perfect equity; to have the same treatment meted out to high and low;—होना to become too cheeky; to be encouraged too far.

शेरवानी [*nf*] a typical long-tight coat.

शेष [*a* and *nm*] rest, remaining; outstanding; residue; balance; remainder; ~नाग name of the celebrated mythological thousand-headed serpent [regarded as an emblem of eternity].

शेषांश [*nm*] the remaining portion, remainder, residue.

शै [*nf*] a thing, article, object.

शैक्षिक [*a*] academic, educational; scholastic.

शैतान [*nm*] the Satan, devil; a mischief-monger; [*a*] naughty; mischievous, guileful, wicked.

शैतानी [*nf*] naughtiness; mischievousness, wickedness.

शैथिल्य [*nm*] see शिथिल(ता).

शैदा [*a*] love-crazy, erotomaniac.

शैल [*nm*] a rock; hill, mountain.

शैली [*nf*] style; diction; ~कार a stylist; -विज्ञान Stylistics.

शैव [*nm*] a worshipper/devotee of Lord Shiva; [*a*] pertaining or belonging to Lord Shiva.

शैशव [*nm*] childhood; infancy; infantilism.

शोक [*nm*] sorrow, grief; condolence; -संदेश a condolence message; —सभा a condolence meeting.

शोख़ [*a*] insolent; playful, sportive; coquettish; bright, loud [as—रंग].

शोख़ी [*nf*] insolence; playfulness, sportiveness; coquetry, brightness, loudness [as of रंग].

शोचनीय [*a*] critical; causing concern/anxiety.

शोणित [*nm*] blood; [*a*] red, bloody.

शोथ [*nm*] swelling, morbid intumescence.

शोध [*nf*] research; purification; cleansing, refinement; rectification, correction; setting right; [re-] payment; calculation regarding hour of marriage; ~न purification; cleansing, refinement; rectification, correction, setting right; [re] payment; treatment.

शोधना [*v*] to purify/cleanse/refine/correct; to work out an auspicious moment [for marriage etc.] by calculation.

शोभन [*a*] befitting, becoming; graceful.

शोभा [*nf*] grace, elegance, beauty; glamour, splendour, brilliance, lustre.

शोभायमान [*a*] looking graceful/pretty/splendid/brilliant, beautiful, lustrous.

शोभित [*a*] splendid, radiant, beautiful, adorned or embellished.

शोर [*nm*] noise; tumult, din, hue and cry; -गुल/शराबा noise, tumult, din, hue and cry.

शोरबा [*nm*] soup, broth.

शोरा [*nm*] soda, nitre [sodium nitrate].

शोला [*nm*] a flame of fire —भड़कना a flame to burst suddenly.

शोशा [*nm*] a projecting point [as in some Arabic letters]; queer thing; —छोड़ना to let off a squib.

शोषक [*nm*] an exploiter, one who exploits; an absorber, that which absorbs.

शोष/ण [*nm*] exploitation; soaking; hence ~णीय [*a*].

शोषित [*a*] exploited.

शोहदा [*nm*] a rogue, knave, scoundrel; libertine; hence ~पन.

शोहरत [*nf*] fame; renown, celebrity.

शौक़ [*nm*] fondness; fancy; hobby; —चर्राना to be extremely fond [of]; to manifest fondness for.

शौक़िया [*a* and *adv*] amateurish; as hobby; fondly, fashionably.

शौक़ी/न [*a*] fashionable; fond of fine things; foppish; dandy; ~नी fashionableness, fondness; foppishness, dandyism.

शौच [*nm*] evacuation of excrement, toilet, ablution; cleanliness; purification [esp. from defilement caused by the death of a relation].

शौचालय [*nm*] a latrine, lavatory.

शौरसेनी [a] a regional variation of the Prakrit [—प्राकृत] and the Apabhransh [—अपभ्रंश] languages.

शौर्य [*nm*] chivalry, gallantry, valour, heroism.

शौहर [*nm*] husband.

श्मशान [*nm*] the cremation ground, crematorium; -वैराग्य momentary detachment from mundane affairs aroused in the cremation ground.

श्मश्रु [*nm*] beard and moustache.

श्याम [*a*] black, dark-coloured; dark blue; [nm] Lord Krishnā.

श्याम/ल [*a*] dark-complexioned, dark-coloured, black; hence ~लता, ~ लिमा [*nf*].

श्रद्धांजलि [*nf*] tribute, homage.

श्रद्धा [*nf*] faith, veneration; reverence.

श्रद्धालु [*a*] having faith/veneration, trustful; hence ~ता.

श्रद्धावान [*a*] having faith, trustful, believing.

श्रद्धास्पद [*a*] venerable, worthy of or deserving faith/reverence.

श्रद्धेय [*a*] venerable, reverend; worthy of faith.

श्रम [*nm*] labour, toil, exertion; -कल्याण labour welfare; ~जीवी a labourer, one who lives by one's sweat; ~दान voluntary contribution of labour for a public cause; -विवाद a labour dispute; ~शील laborious, assiduous, hard-working; -संघ a labour union; ~साध्य arduous, strenuous.

श्रमण [*nm*] a Buddhist monk/mendicant.

श्रमिक [*nm* and *a*] a labourer; labour; -वर्ग labour class; -संघ a labour union.

श्रमी [*a* and *nm*] assiduous, hard-working, labourious. [person].

श्रव/ण [*nm*] an ear, organ of hearing; audition; ~णीय audible, perceptible through the ear, worth hearing; auditory; hence ~णता [*nf*].

श्रावण [*nm*] name of the fifth lunar month of the Hindu calendar July-August.

श्रवणेंद्रिय [*nf*] ear—the organ of hearing.

श्रव्य [*a*] audible; worth hearing; —काव्य one of the two main divisions of literautre in Sanskrit Poetics —literature that can be read and heard [the other being दृश्य काव्य —literature that is to be presented on the stage]; ~ता audibility; range of audibility.

श्रां/त [*a*] tired, wearied, fatigued, exhausted; ~ति tiredness, weariness, fatigue, exhaustion.

श्रेष्ठ [*a*] good; the best, most superior; hence ~तर, ~तम, ~ता.

श्रेष्ठता [*adj*] excellence, superiority, eminence, see श्रेष्ठ.

श्रोणि [*nf*] the waist; hip, buttocks.

श्रोता [*nm*] a listener, audience.

श्लथ [*a*] languid, slothful; flaccid; feeble; diffused.

श्लाघनीय [*a*] praise-worthy laudable, admirable, commendable.

श्लाघा [*nf*] praise, admiration, commendation.

श्लाघनीय [*adj*] praiseworthy.

श्लिष्ट [*a*] punned; equivocal, susceptible of double interpretation; clasped, joined together.

श्लील [*a*] clean, not vulgar.

श्लेष [*nm*] pun, paranomasia.

श्लेष्मा [*nm*] phlegm, mucus.

श्लोक [*nm*] a [Sanskrit] couplet; hymn of praise.

श्वान [*nm*] a dog; -निद्रा lit. dog's sleep—light slumber.

श्वानी [*nf*] a bitch.

श्वास [*nm*] breath, respiration; -क्रिया the act of breathing; -नली bronchial tube; -प्रश्वास breathing in and out.

श्वासोच्छ्वास [*nf*] deep inspiration and expiration, respiration.

श्वेत [*a*] white; bright; blemishless; spotless; fair-complexioned; -पत्र a white paper; ~प्रदर leucorrhoea.

श्वेतता [*nf*] whiteness.

ष—the second of the sibilantt rio (श, ष, स,) of the Devanagari: alphabet. In Modern Hindi sound-pattern, however, this one has lost its identity and is invariably pronounced as palatal sibilant (श) rather than as cerebral.

ष - देवनागरी वर्णमाला में व्यंजन का इकतीसवाँ वर्ण है। इसका उच्चारण स्थान मूर्द्धा है। इसलिए यह मूर्धन्य 'ष' कहलाता है।

षका/र [*nm*] the letter ष and its sound; ~रांत [a word] ending in ष [sh].

षट् [*a*] six; [nm] the number six; ~कोण a hexagon; six-angled; ~चक्र the six mysterious chakras [viz. मूलाधार, अधिष्ठान, मणिपूर, अनाहत, विशुद्ध and आज्ञा of the body according to हठयोग]; ~शास्त्र the six schools of Indian philosophy [viz. न्याय, सांख्य, योग, वैशेषिक, पूर्वमीमांसा and उत्तरमीमांसा].

षड् —an allomorph of षट् [six] appearing as the first member in some compound word; ~आनन/मुख six-faced, having six faces i.e. कार्तिकेय; ~ऋतु the six seasons of the year [viz. ग्रीष्म, वर्षा, शरत, हेमन्त, शिशिर, वसंत]; -दर्शन see षट्शास्त्र [under षट्]; ~भुज a hexagon; ~राग the six main tastes or flavours of food [viz. मीठा, नमकीन, कड़वा, तीता, कसैला, खट्टा]; the six main strains in Indian music [viz. भैरवी, मल्हार, श्री हिंडोल, मालकोस and दीपक]; see झंझट; ~रिपु the six internal enemies of man according to Indian tradition [viz. काम, क्रोध, मद, लोभ, मोह, मत्सर].

षड्यंत्र [*nm*] a conspiracy, plot, an intrigue; ~कारी a conspirator, an intriguer.

षष्टि [*a*] sixty; [*nm*] the number sixty; ~पूर्ति [observation or celebration of] the sixtieth birthday.

षष्ठ [*a*] sixth.

षष्ठी [*nf*] the sixth day of a fortnight; the sixth day from the day of child birth; possessive case.

षोडश [*a*] sixteen; [nm] the number sixteen; —श्रृंगार see सोलह सिंगार.

षोडशी [*nf*] a girl of sixteen years of age, a girl in the prime of youth.

स—the last of the sibilant-trio (श, ष, स) of the Devanagari: alphabet. In Hindi sound pattern, this one happens to be the most dominant of the three.

स – देवनागरी वर्णमाला का बत्तीसवाँ व्यंजन वर्ण इसका उच्चारण स्थान दंत है। इसलिए इसे दंत्य 'स' कहते हैं।

संकट [*nm*] a crisis, emergency; danger; hazard.

संकर [*a*] hybrid, cross; intergrade.

संकरा [*a*] narrow; strait.

संकलन [*nm*] compilation; collection; assemblage; summation; ~कर्ता a compiler, assembler.

संकलित [*a*] compiled, collected; amassed; assembled.

संकल्प [*nm*] determination, resolve; resolution, will; animus; -शक्ति will power; —करना to resolve; to gift away.

संकल्पना [*nf*] concept; [a] to make a resolve; to conceive [of]; ~वाची conceptual.

संकल्पित [*adj*] conceived, imagined a notion, intended; desired; resolved on.

संकल्पनात्मक [*a*] conceptual; pertaining to resolution/determination.

संकल्पित [*a*] imaginary, fancied, conceptual; gifted away.

संकीर्ण [*a*] parochial, narrow; ~ता parochialism, narrowness.

संकीर्तन [*nm*] [collective] singing of hymns/devotional songs.

संकुचित [*a*] parochial, narrow; mean; contracted.

संकुल [*a*] crowded; congested; confused, chaotic.

संकेत [*nm*] a sign, signal; indication, hint; tip; token.

संको/च [*nm*] hitch, hesitation; shyness; contraction; hence ~ची hesitant, shy, bashful.

संक्रमण [nm] infection; transition; transgression; -काल period of transition.

संक्रामक [a] infectious; —रोग an infectious disease.

संक्षिप्त [*a*] brief, short, summary; abridged.

संक्षेप [*nm*] a compendium; summary; abbreviation.

संखिया [*nf*] arsenic, white arsenic.

संख्या [*nf*] a number; numera: figure; strength; degree.

संग [*nm*] company, association, contact; stone ~तराश a stone-cutter/carver; ~तराशी stone-cutting/carving; ~मरमर marble; ~मरमरी white and gracious like marble.

संगठन [*nm*] [the act or process of] organizaion [or an organised body or system or society].

संगठित [*a*] organised.

संगत [*nf*] company; accompaniment; [a] relevant; logical, rational; compatible; —करना to accompany; ~कार an accompanist.

संगति [*nf*] company, association; consistency/consistence; compatibility; rationality; coherence, relevance.

संगत [*nm*] a confluence; union, junction; federation.

संगिनी [*nf*] a female companion.

संगी [*nm*] a companion, an associate; -साथी friends and companions.

संगीत [*nm*] music; -, कंठ vocal music; ~कार a composer; -नाटक an opera; —, वाद्य instrumental music.

संगीतज्ञ [*nm*] a musician, one well-versed in music.

संगीताचार्य [*nm*] master of musical art; a great musical composer.

संगीतात्मक [*a*] musical, hence ~ता.

संगीन [*nf*] bayonet; [*a*] serious; critical.

संगृहीत [*a*] collected; gathered; amassed; compiled.

संग्रह [*nm*] collection; compilation; compendium; repository, deposit; storage; reserve; hence ~कर्ता.

संग्रहण [*nm*] collection; reception.

संग्रहणी [*nf*] an acute form of chronic diarrhoea.

संग्रणीय [*a*] fit to be collected/preserved fit to be acquired.

संग्रहालय [*nm*] a museum.

संग्रही [*a* and *nm*] [one] given to collection/ accumulation, of a accumulative disposition.

संग्राम [*nm*] war, battle; fight, combat.

संघ [*nm*] a federation; union; league, organisation, association; ~चारी gregarian moving in groups; -भाव/भावना/वृत्ति esprit de corps, team spirit; ~वाद federalism; ~वादी a federalist; federalistic.

संघट/न [*nm*] organisation; formation; constitution, composition; ~कं component [part], constituent, ingredient.

संघर्ष [*nm*] struggle; conflict, strife, friction.

संघाराम [*nm*] a Buddhist monastery.

संघीय [*a*] federal; pertaining to union, union.

संचय [*nm*] accumulation, collection; reserve, deposit; hoard; hence ~न [*nm*].

संचयी [*a*] who accumulates/collects/saves.

संचरण [*nm*] transmission; movement [of a body etc.].

संचार [*nm*] communication; transmission; movement; hence ~ण; -व्यवस्था communication system.

संचारी [*a*] communicable; mobile, moving; an auxiliary sentiment in Poetics which strengthens the main sentiment [also called—भाव]; —रोग a communicable disease.

संचालक [*nm*] a director; conductor.

संचालन [*nm*] direction; conduction [as of a meeting etc.].

संचित [*a*] accumulated; collected, gathered; reserved; hoarded.

संजाफ़ [*nf*] a border cloth; border [in a quilt-cover etc.].

संजी/दा [*a*] solemn, serious, grave; sober; hence ~दगी.

संजीवनी [*nf*] an elixir; a kind of plant with powers to reanimate/revive or restore the dead to life.

संजोना [*v*] to put things systematically/in order; to arrange, to arrange in a presentable manner; to keep in good shape.

संज्ञा [*nf*] a noun; denomination, name, appellation; consciousness; —, जातिवाचक a common noun; —, भाववाचक an abstract noun; ~वान in sense, conscious; having a name;—, व्यक्तिवाचक a proper noun.

सँझला [*a*] younger than the middle [brother].

संड [*nm*] a bull; -मुसंड stout and robust fellow [said contemptuously].

संड़सी [*nf*] pincers, household iron forceps.

संडास [*nm*] a lavatory, latrine.

संत [*a* and *nm*] saintly; a saint.

संतत [*a*] continuous.

संतति [*nf*] offspring, progeny.

संतप्त [*a*] grieved, distressed, tormented, troubled.

संतरा [*nm*] an orange.

संतान [*nf*] issue, progeny.

संताप [*nm*] grief, distress, woe, sorrow, contrition; compunction.

संतु/लन [*nm*] balance, equilibrium, equipoise; hence ~ लित.

संतुष्ट [*a*] satisfied, gratified; content.

संतृ/प्त [*a*] saturated; satiated, gratified; hence ~ प्ति.

संतोष [*nm*] satisfaction, gratification; contentment; ~जनक/प्रद satisfactory.

संतोषी [*a* and *nm*] [a] contented [person].

सं/त्रास [*nm*] terror, horror, fright, alarm; hence ~ त्रस्त.

संदर्भ [*nm*] reference, context; -ग्रंथ a reference book/work; bibliography.

संदि/ग्ध [*a*] doubtful, uncertain; ambiguous, equivocal, amphibological; suspicious; hence ~ग्धता.

संदूक [*nm*] a box.

संदूक/चा [*nm*] a box; hence ~ ची feminine form.

संदेश [*nm*] a message.

संदेह [*nm*] a doubt, suspicion.

संधान [*nm*] searching; aiming at; joining together, uniting, union; fixing [as an arrow on the bow].

संधि [*nf*] a treaty; conjunction, union; joint; articulation; -पत्र a treaty; -विच्छेद separation of the constituents in a conjunct word.

संध्या [*nf*] evening, twilight; select Vedic hymns recited in the morning or evening prayers.

संध्योपासना [*nf*] evening prayers/meditation/adoration.

संन्या/स [*nm*] renunciation, asceticism; ~**सी** an ascetic, one who has renounced the world.

संपत्ति [*nf*] property; estate; wealth.

संपदा [*nf*] wealth, opulence.

संपन्न [*a*] prosperous, rich; well-off; completed, accomplished; ~ता prosperity, wealthiness.

संपर्क [*nm*] contact.

संपादक [*nm*] an editor; ~त्व editorship; -मंडल board of editors.

संपादकीय [*nm* and *a*] [an] editorial.

संपा/दन [*nm*] editing; accompishment; hence ~दित edited; accomplished.

संपीडन [*nm*] compression, pressing, squeezing: harassing.

संपुट [*nm*] a hemispherical bowl or any thing so shaped [as when the two palms are joined together leaving hollow space in between]; a posture of coitus.

संपूरक [*nm* and *a*] a supplement, supplementary.

संपूर्ण [*a*] whole; entire; complete; finished; total.

सँपेरा [*nm*] a snake-charmer.

संप्रति [*ind*] at present, now.

संप्रदान [*nm*] the act of giving or bestowing, handing over, the dative case [in Grammar]; —कारक the dative case.

संप्रदाय [*nm*] a community; sect; ~वाद communalism; sectarianism; ~ वादी [*a*] communalist: sectarian.

संप्रेष/ण [*nm*] communication; despatch; ~णीय communicable; to be communicated; ~णीयता communicability.

संप्रेष्य [*nm*] content [to be communicated]; [a] see संप्रेषणीय; ~ता see संप्रेषणीयता.

सम्बन्ध [*nm*] relation/relationship; connection; association; ~वाचक genitive, possessive [case].

संबंधित [*a*] related, connected, affiliated.

सम्बन्धी [*nm*] a relative/relation; used as a suffix to mean related with or pertaining to.

संबद्ध [*a*] jointed, connected, attached to; bound; affiliated, related; relevant.

संबल [*nm*] support, backing.

संबोधन [*nm*] address; calling aloud; the vocative case [in Grammar]; -कारक the vocative case.

संभरण [nm] supply.

सँभलना [*v*] to pull [oneself] together; to be alert to be supported; to save from a fall; to upstay, to be cautious.

संभव [*a*] possible.

संभवतः [*adv*] possibly, probably, perhaps.

सँभाल [*nf*] care-taking, upkeeping, maintenance; being in senses.

सँभालना [*v*] to take care of; to support; to hold; to keep in careful custody; to manage; to supervise.

संभावना [*nf*] possibility, probability, likelihood.

संभावित [*a*] probable, likely.

संभाषण [*nm*] dialogue, talks.

संभ्रांत [*a*] respectable, well-to-do; confused; hence ~ता [*nf*].

संभ्रांति [*nf*] respectability; confusion/perplexity.

संय/त [*a*] controlled restrained, guarded; sober; hence ~तता, ~ति.

संय/म [*nm*] [self] restraint, control, check; moderation, temperance; sobriety; ~मी who exercises control over self, moderate, temperate, abstemious; sober.

संयुक्त [*a*] united; joint; mixed, blended; [two or more consonants] combined.

संयोग [*nm*] coincidence, chance, accident, mixture; coalition, combination; conjunct consonant; communion, carnal contact, sexual union; —श्रृंगार in Poetics, one of the two kinds of श्रृंगार रस wherein the lover and the beloved are united.

संयोजक [*nm*] a convenor; cónjunction [in Grammar].

संयोजन [*nm*] the act of joining or uniting, conjugation; composition; assemblage/assembly; attachment.

संरक्षक [*nm*] a guardian; patron, protector; conservator; custodian; hence ~ ता.

संरक्ष/ण [*nm*] guardianship; patronage, protection; conservation, tutelage; hence ~क्षा, ~ क्षित.

संलग्न [*a*] attached, enclosed, appended; adjacent; engaged; associated.

संवत् [*nm*] a contraction of संवत्सर [see], a year, year [as Shak or Vikrami].

संवत्स/र [*nm*] a year; ~रीय annual, yearly.

संवरण [*nm*] selection, liking; subjugation of passions; complication [in a dramatic plot].

सँवरना [*v*] to be mended/amended/rectified; to be arranged, to be put in order; to be made up; to be decorated, to be tip-top.

सँवरिया [*nm*] an epithet of Lord Krishnā; a lover, hero.

संवर्ध/न [*nm*] magnification; enrichment; culture, promotion, increase, growth; hence ~क.

संवाद [*nm*] a dialogue; conversation, discussion; news, information, message; ~दाता a correspondent, pressman.

संवा/दी [*a*] concordant [as a note—संवादी स्वर in music]; agreeing or harmonising with.

सँवारना [*v*] to make up; to dress up neatly; to decorate; to arrange; to mend/amend/rectify; to channelize along successful lines.

संविदा [*nm*] a contract; compact.

संविधान [nm] constitution.

संविहित [*a*] constitutional, valid, tenable; prescribed, enjoined.

संवेग [*nm*] momentum; impetus; emotion; passion.

संवेदन [*nm*] sensation, feeling, sensitizing; the act or process of experiencing; ~शील sensitive, sensible; feeling.

संवेदना [*nf*] sensitivity, sensation; sensibility, feeling.

संवेद्य [*a*] sensible, perceptible [through senses]; worth experiencing.

संवैधानिक [*a*] constitutional; hence ~ ता.

संशय [*nm*] a suspicion, doubt; uncertainty.

संशयात्मक [*a*] doubtful; uncertain.

संशयालु [*a*] sceptic; suspicious; hence ~ता.

संशोधक [*nm* and *a*] a mendor/rectifier/purifier; who amends or corrects.

संशोधन [*nm*] amendment; correction, rectification; revision; purification; ~वाद revisionism; hence ~वादी a revisionist; revisionistic.

संशोधित [*a*] corrected; amended, revised; improved; purified.

संश्लिष्ट [*a*] synthetic; synthesised; mixed up.

संश्ले/षण [*nm*] synthesis, synthesism; ~षित synthesised; mixed up.

संस/द [*nf*] parliament; ~दीय parliamentary.

संसर्ग [*nm*] intercourse; association, commingling; contact; contagion; connection; conjunction.

संसार [*nm*] the world.

संसारी [*nm* and *a*] a mortal being; belonging to the world, mundane.

संसृति [*nf*] the world, course of mundane existence.

संस्करण [*nm*] an edition, issue [of a journal etc.]; correction; curing.

संस्कार [*nm*] mental impression[s] [forming the mind]; sacrament; rite/ritual, ceremony; purification; improvement, refinement; hence ~शील, ~ हीन.

संस्कृ/ति [*nf*] culture; ~ त cultured, refined; Sanskrit [language].

संस्था [*nf*] an institution; organisation, concern.

संस्थान [*nm*] an institute.

संस्थापक [*nm*] a founder.

संस्था/पन [*nm*] establishment/establishing, founding; ~पना establishment, founding; ~पित founded, established.

संस्मरण [*nm*] memoirs, reminiscences; ~शील reminiscent.

संहत [*a*] compact; assembled, collected, gathered.

संहति [*nf*] a mass; system; compactness.

संहार [*nm*] annihilation; massacre; hence ~क.

संहि/त [*a*] gathered, accumulated; heaped up; mixed; uninterrupted.

संहिता [*nf*] a code.

सइयाँ [*nm*] lover; husband.

सई/स [*nm*] a groom; ~सी the work or function of a groom.

सक/ता [*nm*] state of being confounded/flabbergasted; awe; ~ते की हालत में in a stunned state.

सकना [*v*] can; may; to be capable/competent.

सकपकाना [*v*] to be startled/amazed, to be confounded out of wits; to be overawed.

सकर्मक [*a*] transitive; —क्रिया a transitive verb.

सकल [*a*] whole, all, entire; total.

सकाम [*a*] desirous, inspired by a desire; lustful; hence ~ ता.

सका/र [nm] the letter स and its sound; acceptance; ~रना to accept; ~रांत [a word] ending in स; ~रात्मक positive.

सकारे [*adv*] early in the morning, at day-break.

सकु/चना, ~ चाना [*v*] to hesitate; to be abashed/ashamed; to wither [as a flower]; to shrink; hence ~ चाहट.

सक़्क़ा [*nm*] a water-bearer, one who carries water in a large leathern bag.

सक्रिय [*a*] active; ~ता activity.

सक्षम [*a*] competent; capable; hence ~ता.

सखा [*nm*] a friend, compear.

सखी [*nf*] a [female] friend, [female] companion.

सख़ी [*a*] bounteous, generous, open-handed.

सख़्त [*a*] hard; harsh [as अल्फ़ाज]; strong, stiff; strict; rigorous; serious [as—बीमार]; dire [as—जरूरत].

सख़्ती [*nf*] hardness; strictness harshness; stiffness; rigorousness; —करना to deal with strictly, to be strict; —से पेश आना to deal with strictly; to be harsh.

सगा [*a*] real, born of the same parents; kin; ~पन kinship, near relationship.

सगाई [*nf*] betrothal; engagement.

सगु/ण possessed of attributes [as—ब्रह्म]; endowed with qualities.

सगुन [*nm*] an omen, good omen; augury; see सगुण.

सगुनिया [*nm*] an augury, a soothsayer.

सगोत्र [*a*] belonging to or of the same गोत्र [clan], allied by blood.

सघन [*a*] dense, thick; intensive; overcast with clouds, cloudy; hence ~ता.

सच [*a*] true; right; [*nm*] the truth; [*ind*] really!; ~मुच actually; truly, really, surely, in fact.

सच्चाई [*nf*] truth; truthfulness; integrity.

सचित्र [*a*] pictorial, illustrated [with pictures].

सचिव [*nm*] secretary.

सचिवालय [*nm*] secretariat.

सचेत [*a*] conscious; careful, alert, attentive.

सचेतक [*nm*] a whip.

सचेतन [*a*] conscious.

सचेष्ट [*a*] alert, active; —attemptive.

सच्चरि/त, ~ त्र [*a*] virtuous, of good moral character or integrity; hence ~त्रता [*nf*].

सच्चा [*a*] true; genuine; sincere; loyal; faithful; real; ~ई/पन truth, truthfulness; reality.

सच्चिदानंद [*nm*] an epithet of the Supreme Soul [as the Ultimate resort of Truth, consciousness and happiness].

सज [*nf*] adornment/adorning; ornamentation; -धज/बज prank; ornamentation.

सजग [*a*] alert, cautious, vigilant, careful; hence ~ता.

सजन [*nm*] husband; lover.

सजना [*v*] to be adorned/decorated/embellished/beautified; to prank; to be made-up; to be neatly arranged; [nm] see सजन; -सँवरना to groom, to make-up, to prank.

सजनी [*nf*] beloved, sweetheart; wife.

सजल [*a*] full of water; tearful; hydrous, aqueous.

सज़ा [*nf*] punishment; penalty; ~याफ़्ता convicted, punished.

सजाना [*v*] to decorate, to adorn, to embellish, to beautify; to furnish; to arrange; to dress nealty; सजा-धजा made-up; well-adorned, decorated.

सजाव [*nm*] see सजावट.

सजाव/ट [*nf*] decoration, ornamentation; make-up; display, array; ~टी decorative; pranked.

सजीला [*a*] decorated; foppish, grand, graceful; hence ~पन.

सजीव [*a*] living, alive; lively; vivacious; hence ~ ता [*nf*].

सज्जन [*nm* and *a*] a gentleman; noble, gentle; ~ता gentility, nobility.

सज्जा [*nf*] embellishment, decoration, adorning; equipment.

सज्जित [*a*] decorated, adorned, embellished, beautified; equipped.

सटकना [*v*] to slip away; to turn tails, to make good one's escape.

सटना [*v*] to be in close proximity, to be in physical contact; to stick; to adhere to; to be adjacent.

सटा [*nf*] mane; thickened locks of hair; [*a*] see सटना.

सटीक [*a*] apt, befitting, correct and accurate; with commentary/annotation.

सटोरिया [*nm*] a speculator.

स/ट्टा [*nm*] speculation; ~ट्टेबाज a speculator; ~ट्टेबाजी speculation.

सठियाना [*v*] to suffer senile decay, to be in dotage; to be decrepit.

सड़क [*nf*] a road, street.

सड़न [*nf*] decay, decomposition; putrefaction; rot, rottenness.

सड़ना [*v*] to decay, to decompose; rot, to ferment, to putrefy; to be or fall in misery.

सड़सठ [*a*] sixty-seven; [*nm*] the number sixty-seven.

सड़ाँध [*nf*] stench, putrefaction, putrescence, putridity; mustiness.

सड़ा [*a*] rotten, decayed, putrid, putriscent; -गला rotten and decayed.

सड़ाक [*nf*] [sound produced by] cracking of a whip.

सड़ान [*nf*] decay/decaying, rot/rotting, putrefaction/putridity.

सड़ासड़ [*adv*] with repeated sounds of cracking [of a whip].

सड़ियल [*a*] rotten; putrid, putrescent; worthless, good for nothing.

सत [*nm*] essence, juice; strength, vitality; truth, truthfulness; an allomorph of सात used as the first member in certain compound words; ~गुना seven times; ~गुरु/true/good preceptor; God; ~युग/one and the first of the four yugas [the other being द्वापर, त्रेता, and कलि] of the universe according to Indian mythology. The सतयुग is said to be the best or golden period/age of creation; ~मासा of seven months; a ceremony performed about the seventh month of pregnancy; [a child] born in the seventh month of pregnancy; ~वंती [*a*] chaste [woman]; ~सई a collection of seven hundred [and odd] couplets [generally दोहा and सोरठा]; see सत्.

सतत [*adv* and *a*] incessantly, continuous; ever, always.

सतर [*nf*] a line; row.

सतर्क [*a* and *adv*] cautious, vigilant, alert, careful; argumentative; hence ~ता.

सत/ह [*nf*] surface; level; ~ही superficial.

सतहत्तर [*a*] seventy-seven; [*nm*] the number seventy-seven.

सताना [v] to trouble; to harass, to torment, to oppress; to victimise.

सती [*nf*] a chaste and faithful/loyal woman devoted to her husband; a woman who burns herself willingly on the funeral pyre (चिता) of her husband out of devotion; [*a*] chaste, virtuous [said of a married woman]; ~त्व/पन chastity, virtuousness; -साध्वी/सावित्री a women extremely devoted to her husband.

सतोगु/ण [*nm*] virtue, the quality of purity and goodness; one of the three gunas (सत्त्व, रजस् and तमस्); ~ णी having the qualities of goodness and purity, virtuous.

सत् [*a*] good; pious, virtuous; present; true.

सत्कार [*nm*] hospitality, welcome.

सत्त [*nm*] essence, extract; truth; integrity, chastity.

सत्तर [*a*] seventy; [*nm*] the number seventy.

सत्ता [*nm*] being, existence, entity; powers, sway, authority; reality, a playing card with seven pips; ~धारी ruling, [in] authority; a man of authority/power; ~रूढ़ ruling; wielding power; potentate.

सत्ताई(इ)स [*a*] twenty-seven; [*nm*] the number twenty-seven.

सत्तानवे [*a*] ninety-seven; [*nm*] the number ninety-seven.

सत्तावन [*a*] fifty-seven; [*nm*] the number fifty-seven.

सत्तासी [*a*] eighty-seven; [*nm*] the number eighty-seven.

सत्तू [*nm*] powder of parched gram, barley or other grains.

सत्त्व [*nm*] being, existence; entity; reality; substance; spiritual essence; quintessence; strength, vitality; quality of purity and goodness.

सत्य [*a*] true; veritable; [*nm*] veracity, truth, verity; ~ता truth; verity, veracity; ~निष्ठ verdical, dedicated to truth, solemn; ~वादी veridicious, speaking the truth; ~व्रत strictly truthful, who has taken a vow to be truthful.

सत्यनारायण [*nm*] name of a particular divinity.

सत्याग्र/ह [*nm*] insistence, on truth—passive resistance offered to uphold truth [a weapon made popular by Gandhiji during the Indian freedom movement]; ~ ही one who offers satyagrah.

सत्यानाश [*nm*] complete ruin, total destruction, devastation.

सत्यानाशी [*a*] ruining, devastating; destructive; [*nm*]; Argumone mexicana.

सत्र [*nm*] a session.

सत्रह [*a*] seventeen; [*nm*] the number seventeen.

सत्त्व [*nm*] see सत्त्व.

सत्सं/ग [*nm*] intercourse or association with good/pious men; hence ~गी.

सदन [*nm*] a house; house of legislature, chamber.

सदमा [*nm*] a blow, emotional stroke, shock.

सदर [*a*] head, main; [*nm*] chief, chairman; president; —मुकाम heaoqQuarters.

सदस्य [*nm*] a member; ~ता membership.

सदा [*adv*] always, ever; [*nf*] call; echo; ~बहार perennial, evergreen; a plant having pink or white flowers; ~वर्त pledge to distribute free food daily; free food so distributed; ~वर्ती one who distributes free food.

सदाचा/र [*nm*] morality, virtuous/moral conduct, rectitude; hence ~ रिता. ~री.

सदाश/य [*a*] genuine, of good faith; noble, magnanimous; [*nm*] good faith; hence ~ यता; ~यी.

सदी [*nf*] a century.

सदुपयोग [*nm*] good or proper use/usage.

सदृश [*a*] like, similar, alike, resembling; hence ~ ता.

सदैव [*adv*] always, ever.

सदोष [*a*] faulty; wrong.

सद् allomorph of सत् as it appears in numerous compounds; ~गुण virtue; merits, qualities; ~गुणी virtuous; meritorious; ~गुरु worthy preceptor/teacher; God; ~भाव goodwill kindly feeling; presence; ~वृत्ति [the] good, righteousness, moral disposition.

सद्यः [*adv*] at once, immediately; just, recently.

सधना [*v*] to be tamed; to be accomplished/ accustomed; to get habituated/accustomed; target to be hit; to be aligned [as निशाना].

सध/र्म, ~ र्मा, ~ र्मी [*nm* and *a*] [a] co-religionist; who follows the same religion.

सधवा [*a* and *nf*] [a woman] whose husband is living.

सन [*nm*] a year; an era; a kind; of jute, hemp; [*nf*] whizzing sound; [a] stupefied; ~सन whizzing sound.

सनक [*nf*] whim, caprice, eccentricity; craze, mania, frenzy; —आना, चढ़ना, —सवार होना to go crazy, to be overwhelmed by a whim/ craze, to be in a caprice.

सनकी [*a* and *nm*] capricious, crazy, crank, whimsical [person].

सनद [*nf*] a certificate, testimonial, deed.

सनना [*v*] to be kneaded/besmeared/stained/ soiled, to be drowned [as पाप में—].

सनम [*nm*] dear, beloved one; a statue.

सनसना/ना [*v*] to produce a whizzing sound; to have thrilling sensation; hence ~हट.

सनसनी [*nf*] thrilling sensation; excitement; ~खेज sensational.

सनातन [*a*] eternal; ancient, orthodox, time-honoured.

सनाय [*nf*] senna, a plant the leaves of which are used as purgative.

सनीचर [*nm*] Saturn; Saturday; an ominous person.

सन् [*nm*] an era, a year; —, ईसवी the Christian era; —, हिजरी Mohammedan era.

सन्न [*a*] stunned, stupefied, dumb-founded, flabbergasted; —रह/हो जाना to be stunned/ stupefied/dumb-founded/flabbergasted.

सन्नद्ध [*a*] ready, equipped.

सन्नाटा [*nm*] still; silence, quietude.

सन्निकट [*ind*] close, proximal, at hand, near by; imminent; approximate; hence ~ता.

सन्निहित [*a*] implied; vested; lying within.

सन्मार्ग [*nm*] path of virtue, moral/good course.

सन्मुख [ind] see सम्मुख.

संन्या/स [nm] renunciation, abandonment of worldly ties or mundane interests; ~सी an anchorite, a monk, one who has renounced the world.

सपत्नी [*nf*] a co-wife; ~क along with wife.

सपना [*nm*] a dream.

सपरिवार [a and *adv*] with family.

सपाट [*a*] flat; plain, smooth, level, even; ~पन flatness.

सपा/टा [nm] speed; expeditiousness; run; ~टे से quickly, expeditiously, with speed.

सपूत [*nm*] a worthy or dutiful son.

सपेरा [*nm*] a snake-charmer.

सप्त [*a*] seven; [*nm*] the number seven; ~पदी the ceremony of seven circumambulations of the sacred sacrificial fire as an integral part of the Hindu wedding process; ~म seventh; ~मी the seventh day of each half, of a lunar month; the locative case [in Grammar]; ~र्षि Ursa Major; the seven sages (मरीच, अत्रि, अंगिरा, पुलह, त्रतु, पुलस्त्य, वसिष्ठ,); ~ लोक the seven worlds (भूलोक, भुवलोक, स्वर्लोक: महर्लोक, ज़नलोक, तपलोक, सत्यलोक); ~ स्वर the seven notes of music (स रे ग म प ध नी).

सप्ता/ह [*nm*] a week; ~हांत week-end.

सफ़र [*nm*] travel, journey; ~नामा a travelogue, travel account.

सफ़रमैना [*nm*] sappers and miners.

सफ़री [*a*] pertaining to travel, convenient during a journey.

सफल [*a*] successful; effective, fruitful; ~ता success, achievement; —होना to succeed.

सफलीभूत [*a*] successful, succeeded.

सफ़ा [*nm*] a page; clean, white; ~चट blank; perfectly clean; ~या a clean sweep; end, ruination destruction.

सफ़ाई [*nf*] cleanliness; purity; conservancy; defence [in a law suit]; clarification; —पक्ष the defence [side]; —देना to justify; to clarify.

सफ़ीर [*nm*] an ambassador, envoy.

सफ़ेद [*a*] white; ~पोश whitecollared; dressed in white; —पड़ जाना to be rendered pallid; to be anaemic.

सफ़ेदा [*nm*] white lead.

सफ़ेदी [*nm*] whiteness; whitewash.

सब [*a*] all; entire; whole; [prefix]; sub; -कुछ all; all in all; -डिविजन a sub-division; —से भला चुप silence is gold.

सबक़ [*nm*] a lesson; moral; —पढ़ाना/सिखाना to teach a lesson.

सबब [*nm*] a reason; cause.

सबल [*a*] strong, powerful; valid.

सबूत [*nm*] a proof, an evidence.

सबे/रा [*nm*] the morning; dawn, day-break; ~रे in the morning.

सब्ज़ [*a*] green; -बाग़ दिखलाना to arouse high hopes in vain.

सब्जी [*nf*] vegetable; herbage; —मंडी a vegetable market.

सब्र [*nm*] patience, contentment.

सभा [nf] an assembly, association; a meeting; society; ~गार/गृह an assembly hall, chamber; ~पति chairman; ~पतित्व chairmanship; ~मंडप a pavilion; ~सद member of an assembly.

सभ्य [*a*] civilised/civil, courteous; ~ता civilization, courtesy, decency.

समंजन [*nm*] adjustment, coordination.

सम [*a*] even; equal; homogeneous; regular pro—; [*nm*] even number; first accented beat in a rhythmic cycle; ~कक्ष equal/equivalent; matching of the same stature.

समकालिक [*a*] synchronizing/synchronous; hence ~ ता.

समकालीन [*a*] contemporary/contemporaneous, ~ता contemporaneity.

समकोण [*nm*] a right angle; [*a*] having equal angles.

समक्ष [*adv*] before, in front of.

समग्र [*a*] total; whole, entire; ~ता totality;—रूप से at all points, on the whole, in entirety.

समझ [*nf*] understanding, intellect, sense; ~दार keen, intelligent, sensible, wise; -बूझ discretion; [keenness of] understanding.

समझना [*v*] to understand, to grasp, to comprehend, to catch, to follow; समझ-बूझकर deliberately, knowingly, wittingly.

समझाना [*v*] to persuade; to explain; -बुझाना to persuade; to cajole; to calm, down.

समझौता [*nm*] a compromise, understanding; pact, agreement, settlement.

समतल [*a* and *nm*] level, even; plain.

सम/ता [*nf*] equality; parity; equity, equanimity; similarity, likeness, resemblance; evenness; also ~त्व.

समतुल्य [*a*] equivalent; similar; hence ~ता.

समत्रिभुज [*nm*] an equilateral triangle.

समद/र्शी [*a*] equanimous; impartial; hence ~ र्शिता.

समदृष्टि [*nf*] equanimity; impartiality.

समधिन [*nf*] mother-in-law [or aunt-in-law etc.] of son or daughter.

समधिया/न, ~ ना [*nm*] place/abode of समधी.

समधी [*nf*] father-in-law [or uncle-in-law etc.] of son or daughter.

समन [*nm*] summons;—तामील करना to serve summons [on].

सम/न्वय [*nm*] coordination, harmony; ~न्वित coordinated, harmonized.

समबाहु [*a*] equilateral.

समय [*nm*] time, period; timings; occasion; leisure, a convention; —से in time.

समयोचित [*a*] opportune, timely.

समर [*nm*] a war; battle; -तंत्र strategy, tactics, war-tactics; ~तंत्री tactician, strategist; ~तंत्रीय, tactical, strategic; -नीति strategy;-भूमि battlefield.

समरस [*a*] equanimous; harmonious; ~ता equanimity; harmony.

समरांगण [*nm*] a battlefield.

समरू/प [*a*] pari passu, homogeneous; identical; similar; hence ~पता.

समर्थ [*a*] capable, competent; hence ~ता.

सम/र्थक [*nm*] a supporter; vindicator; ~र्थन support; vindication; corroboration; ~र्थित supported, vindicated.

सम/र्पण [*nm*] dedication; surrender; ~र्पित dedicated; surrendered.

समवयस्क [*a*] of the same age, equal in age; hence ~ता [*nf*].

समवर्ती [*a*] concurrent; adjacent, contiguous.

समवा/य [*nm*] collection, company; concourse; concomitance; ~ यी inseparable; concomitant.

समवेत [*a* and *adv*] collective [ly].

समवेदना [*nf*] condolence.

समशीतोष्ण [*a*] moderate, temperate.

समष्टि [*nf*] collectiveness, totality, aggregate; ~वाद collectivism; ~वादी a collectivist; collectivistic.

समसामयिक [*a*] contemporary, contemporaneous; ~ता contemporaneity.

समस्त [*a*] all; whole, complete, entire.

समस्या [*nf*] a problem; the last portion or line of a metrical composition which is meant for completion in the same metre by a competition; -नाटक problem play; -पूर्ति completing a metrical composition posed as a 'समस्या'.

समाँ [*nm*] occasion; weather; gaiety; finery; spectacle, —बँधना to be bound by a spell, a spellbinding performance to be occasioned.

समांतर [*a*] parallel; ~ता, ~ वाद parallelism.

समाई [*nf*] capacity; capability; patience.

समागम [*nm*] arrival; intercourse.

समाचार [*nm*] news; information.

समाज [*nm*] society; community; ~वाद socialism; ~वादी a socialist; socialistic; -व्यवस्था social order; ~शास्त्र Sociology; ~शास्त्रज्ञ/शास्त्री a sociologist; ~शास्त्रीय sociological; -सेवक a social worker; -सेवा social service; -सेवी rendering social service, social worker.

समाजी [*nm*] an instrumental musician who accompanics a singing and dancing girl; [a] social.

समादर [*nm*] reverence, honour, respect, veneration; hence ~णीय.

समादृत [*a*] respected, honoured.

समाधान [*nm*] solution [of a problem etc].

समाधि [*nf*] trance; intense meditation; a tomb.

समान [*a*] equal, equivalent; similar, alike, identical, tantamount; hence ~ता.

समानांतर [*a*] parallel; ~ता parallelism.

समाना [*v*] to be contained [in]; to enter; to fit [in].

समानाधिका/र [*nm*] equal rights; ~री possessing equal rights; joint heir.

समानार्थक [a] synonymous; ~ता synonymity.

समापन [*nm*] conclusion; completion; -समारोह closing/concluding function; hence समाप्य.

समाप्त [*a*] finished, ended, concluded, terminated; completed. ~प्राय almost finished/ended/concluded/completed/terminated.

समाप्ति [*nf*] the end, conclusion, termination; completion.

समायोजन [*nm*] adjustment.

समारंभ [*nm*] inauguration, commencement, beginning.

समारोह [*nm*] celebration, festivity, function.

समालोच/क [*nf*] a critic; ~न see समालोचना.

समालोचना [*nf*] criticism; -शास्त्र criticism.

समावर्तन [*nm*] returning home [esp. after completion of studies]; -संस्कार/समारोह a convocation.

समाविष्ट [*a*] included, entered, incorporated; pervaded, permeated.

समावेश [*nm*] inclusion, entry, incorporation; pervasion, permeation.

समास [*nm*] a compound [word]; abridgement; concision, terseness; —शैली terse style.

समा/हरण [*nm*] concentration, collection, accumulation; procuration; hence ~ हर्ता; ~ हार collection, accumulation concentration; procuration; sum, totality, aggregate; conjunction or connection of words or sentences, compounding of words.

समाहित [*a*] collected, concentrated; merged [into].

समिति [*nf*] a committee.

समिधा [*nf*] sacrificial fire- wood; an oblation to fuel or firewood.

समीकरण [*nm*] an equation.

समीक्षक [*nm*] a reviewer.

समी/क्षा [*nf*] a review; ~क्षाकार a reviewer; ~क्षय under review; worth reviewing.

समीचीन [*a*] proper, fit, right; equitable; hence ~ता.

समीप [*a*] near [in place or time], beside, proximate, close by at hand; hence ~ता; ~ वर्ती; ~ स्थ.

समीर [*nf*] air, breeze.

समुचित [*a*] proper, right, fit.

समुच्चय [*nm*] set; collection, aggregate/aggregation, totality, assemblage; conjunction of words or sentences.

समुदाय [*nm*] community; aggregate, collection.

समुद्र [*nm*] an ocean, a sea.

समुद्री [*a*] oceanic, marine; sea-borne; ~य oceanic, pertaining to the sea.

समुन्न/त [*a*] risen, elevated; progressed, developed; hence ~ति; ~यन [*nm*].

समुल्लास [*nm*] exhiliration; chapter [of a book].

समूचा [*a*] all, whole, entire.

समूल [*a*] having root[s]; wellfounded; [*adv*] from the root.

समूह [*nm*] a group; collection; aggregate, assemblage, multitude; community.

समृद्ध [*a*] prosperous, flourishing; affluent, rich; ~द्धि prosperity, flourish; affluence, richness.

समेटना [*v*] to wrap up, to roll up; to wind up; to gather/collect; to rally; to amass.

समेत [*a* and *adv*] with, together with, along with; accompanied by.

समोसा [*nm*] a kind of stuffed pie of a triangular shape.

सम्मत [*a*] supported [by], approved of [by], authenticated [by].

सम्मति [*nf*] opinion; consent; advice.

सम्मन [*nm*] summons.

सम्मान [*nm*] respect, honour; prestige.

सम्माननीय [*a*] honourable, respectable.

सम्मानित [*a*] honoured, respected.

सम्मान्य [*a*] see सम्माननीय.

सम्मिलन [*a*] coming together, union; coalescence.

सम्मिलित [*a*] united; mixed; included.

सम्मिश्रण [*nm*] the act or process of intermixing/commingling; combining.

सम्मुख [*a*] before, in front of; opposite; facing, confronting, being face to face; propitious.

सम्मेलन [*nm*] a conference; meeting; assembly.

सम्मो/ह [*nm*] hypnosis; fascination; stupefaction; beguilement; ~हन hypnosis, hypnotising; fascinating. stupefying; ~हन-विद्या hypnotism; ~हनी hypnotic spell; ~हित hypnotised; fascinated; stupefied.

सम्यक् [*adv* and *a*] thoroughly, completely, wholly; duly, well; due.

सम्राट [*nm*] an Emperor.

सयाना [*a*] grown up; clever; cunning; ~पन grown up state; cleverness, cunningness.

सरंजाम [*nm*] preparations, arrangements; accomplishment.

सर [*nm*] see सिर; a pond, pool; an arrow; one of the four top-valued playing cards; [*a*] conquered, subdued; ~कश mischief monger; impudent, rebellious; ~ख़त agreement of hiring a house; ~ग़ना leader [of a gang], ring-leader; ~गर्मी hectic activity; passionate effort; enthusiasm; ज़मीन country; territory; ~दर्द headache; botheration; ~दार a chieftain; leader; boss; a sikh; ~दारी the office, function or status of a सरदार; ~ नाम well-known, renowned, famous; ~नामा form of address and superscriptional formalities in a letter etc; ~पंच the head पंच; ~परस्त a patron; supporter; hence ~परस्ती; ~ फ़रोशी readiness to sacrifice life; intrepidness; ~सब्ज green, verdant; prosperous; ~शाम early in the evening, as soon as the evening sets in; —करना to conquer; to subdue; to vanquish; —मुँड़ाते ही ओले पड़े ill-luck overtaking at the very outset.

सरकंडा [*nm*] [a kind of] reed.

सरकना [*v*] to slip; to slide; to creep.

सरकार [*nf*] government; administration.

सरकारी [*a*] governmental; public; official; administrative.

सरगम [*nf*] the gamut; a syllabic form of musical composition.

सरपट [*a* and *adv*] galloping; apace.

सरमा/या [*nm*] capital; ~येदार a capitalist; ~येदारी capitalism.

सरल [*a*] easy, simple; straight; direct; straightforward; ingenuous; light; hence ~ता.

सरली/करण [*nm*] simplification; ~कृत simplified.

सरस [*a*] juicy; sweet; delicious, tasteful; relishable; hence ~ता [*nf*].

सरसठ [*a*] sixty seven; [*nm*] the number sixty-seven.

सरसना [*v*] to flourish, to prosper; to acquire fullness; to be in full bloom; to be full of relish/charm; hence सरसाना.

सरसरा/ना [*v*] to produce a rustling noise, to cause a frou-frou; ~हट frou-frou, rustle.

सरसरी [*a*] cursory; hurried.

सरसों [*nf*] mustard seed or plant; —का तेल mustard oil.

सरस्वती [*nf*] the goddess of learning/speech; speech; name of a river.

सरह/द [*nf*] boundary, frontier; ~दी pertaining to/related with or belonging to ~द.

सर्रा/फ़ [*nm*] a dealer in gold and silver jewellery; ~फ़ा gold and silver exchange market.

सर्राफ़ी [*nf*] the business of a सर्राफ़; the script used by Indian style accountants which is just an expedient variation of Devanagari:.

सराबोर [*a*] completely drenched; soaked.

सराय [*nf*] an inn, a tavern.

सरासर [*adv*] altogether, entirely; sheer.

सराह/ना [*v*] to praise, to applaud, to commend; to eulogize, to appreciate: [nf] praise, appreciation, applause; eulogy; ~नीय praiseworthy, laudable, commendable.

सरिता [*nf*] a river, stream.

सरिया [*nm*] an iron-bar.

सरीखा [*a*] like, resembling, identical.

सरेबाज़ार [*adv*] openly, publicly.

सरे/श, ~ स [*nf*] glue.

सरोकार [*nm*] concern, business.

सरोज [*nm*] a lotus flower.

सरोद [*nf*] sarod—a stringed musical instrument.

सरोवर [*nm*] a pond, pool.

सरौता [*nm*] a nut-cracker.

सर्कस [*nm*] a circus.

सर्ग [*nm*] a canto; world; ~बद्ध divided into cantos.

सर्जन [*nm*] creation; a surgeon; ~हार a creator.

सर्जना [*nf*] creation.

सर्द [*a*] cold; cool, frigid; lifeless; -गर्म ups and downs, whirligigs [of life].

सर्दी [*nf*] cold; winter; -गरमी winter and summer; vicissitudes of life; —खाना to be struck by cold.

सर्प [*nm*] a serpent, snake.

सर्व [*a*] all; whole, entire, complete; ~जनीन universal; applying to or concerned with all and sundry; ~ज्ञ a know all, omniscient; ~ज्ञता omniscience; ~देशीय cosmopolitan, universal; hence ~देशीयता; ~ नाम a pronoun; ~नाश holocaust, complete ruin, utter destruction/devastation; ~नाशी all-destroying, causing complete ruin; ~विद omniscient; ~व्यापक omnipresent; universal; ~व्यापकता omnipresence; universality; ~व्यापी ominipresent; universal; ~शक्तिमान omnipotent; ~श्री Messrs; ~सम्मत unanimous; ~सम्मति unanimity; ~साधारण the common man, people at large; ~सुलभ easily accessible to all.

सर्वत्र [*ind*] everywhere; always, in every case.

सर्वथा [*ind*] entirely, thoroughly, in all respects, in every way.

सर्वदा [*ind*] always, at all times.

सर्वस्व [*nm*] one's all, all one's belongings/possessions.

सर्वहारा [*nm*] the proletariat.

सर्वांग [*nm*] the whole person; all over; ~पूर्ण complete in all respects.

सर्वांगीण [*a*] permeating all parts, all-sided, all-round, in all respects.

सर्वाधिकार [*nm*] all rights; ~ सुरक्षित all rights reserved.

सर्वाधिकारी [*a*] plenipotentiary, wielding or vested with all rights.

सर्वेक्ष/ण [*nm*] survey; ~क a surveyor.

सर्वे/श, ~श्वर [*nm*] Master of all, God.

सर्वेसर्वा [*a*] all-in-all, all- powerful.

सर्वोत्तम [*a*] the best, most excellent; optimum.

सर्वोदय [*nm*] uplift of all; [-आन्दोलन] a non-violent movement in India meant for the uplift of all men without distinction of caste, creed, sex or status [led by Acharya Vinoba Bhave and Jaya Prakash Narayan].

सर्वोपरि [*a*] supreme, above all, ahead of all; ~ता supremacy.

सर्वोच्च [*a*] supreme, highest, best; ~ता supremacy.

सलज्ज [*a*] shy, bashful; modest.

सलमा [*nm*] a band of embroidery; -सितारा a kind of embroidery consisting of small shining stars between embroidered bands.

सलवार [*nf*] a kind of trousers.

सलहज [*nf*] wife of a साला –brother-in-law.

सलाई [*nf*] a knitting needle, needle; thin wire; stick.

सलाख़ [*nf*] a thin iron rod, bar.

सलाद [*nm*] salad.

सलाम [*nm*] salutation; adieu, good bye.

सलामत [*a*] safe, sound, well.

सलामती [*nf*] safety; well- being, welfare; —का जाम पीना to drink to the health [of]; —चाहना to wish well; —से safely, well.

सलामी [*nf*] salutation; salute [in honour of a guest, esp. by booming of guns]; guard of honour; —देना to present a guard of honour, to salute [esp. with the booming of guns].

सलाह [*nf*] advice, counsel; opinion; cordial relations; reconciliation.

सलाहकार [*nm*] an adviser; counsellor; [*a*] advisory.

सलिल [*nm*] water.

सली/क़ा [*nm*] manners, etiquette; ~क़ेदार mannerly; ~केमंद mannerly.

सलीब [*nf*] cross.

सलोतरी [*nm*] a veterinary doctor.

सलो(लौ)ना [*a*] charming, winsome; saltish; ~पन charm, winsomeness; saltishness.

सल्तनत [*nf*] sultanate, Empire.

सवर्ण [*a*] of the same colour/caste; caste; —हिंदू a caste Hindu.

सवा [*a* and *nm*] [the number] one and a quarter.

सवाक् [*a*] talking, gifted with speech; -चित्र talkie.

सवाया [*a*] one and a quarter times; more [than], ahead [of].

सवार [*nm*] a rider, horseman; person sitting in or in a carriage/vehicle; [*a*] mounted, riding.

सवारी [*nf*] a conveyance, vehicle; passenger; procession.

सवाल [*nm*] a question, query; an exercise/problem [in Mathematics]; demand; -जवाब question and answer;—करना to put a question; to put forth a demand;—कुछ जवाब कुछ, —दीगर जवाब दीगर the answer to be beside the question.

सवालात [*nm*] plural form of सवाल -questions.

सवालिया [*a*] interrogatory.

सविनय [*a* and *adv*] courteous[ly], modest[ly], polite [ly]; civil; —अवज्ञा civil disobedience; ~ आंदोलन Civil Disobedience Movement [launched by Gandhiji during the Indian freedom movement].

सवे/रा [*nm*] morning, daybreak; ~रे in the morning, at daybreak.

सवैया [*nm*] a popular metric composition in Hindi [during the mediaeval ages].

सशंक [*a*] suspicious, sceptic.

सशक्त [*a*] potential, powerful, strong, forceful.

सशस्त्र [*a*] armed, equipped with arms.

ससुर [*nm*] father-in-law; a term of abuse generally used by menfolk.

ससुरा [*nm*] see ससुर—generally used in the latter sense i.e. as a term of abuse.

ससुराल [*nf*] father-in-law's house, house/place of one's in-laws.

सस्ता [*a*] cheap; trash, inferior.

सस्ती [*nf*] cheapness; depression; feminine form of, see सस्ता.

सस्नेह [*adv* and *a*] with love; loving; affectionate.

सस्य [*nm*] crop; -क्रांति green revolution.

सह [*ind*] with, along with, simultaneously; co-; [a] enduring, bearing; proof [as जलसह—waterproof]; -अस्तित्व co-existence; ~कारिता cooperation; ~कारी cooperative; a colleague, junior colleague; assistant; ~गमन self-immolation of a widow with her deceased husband; hence -गामिनी; ~चर an associate; a companion, friend; a co-variant; hence ~चारी an associate, a companion, friend; associate element; gregarious, going together, ~धर्मिणी wife; ~धर्मी co-religionist; charged with the same duties; ~पाठी a class-fellow, class mate; ~भागिता partnership; complicity; ~भागी a partner; an accomplice; existing together; co-existence; ~भोज collective feasting/eating; ~मरण see ~गमन; ~यात्री a co-traveller, fellow passenger; companion; ~शिक्षा co-education; -सम्बन्ध correlation.

सहज [*a*] easy, simple; spontaneous; straightforward; ingenuous; innate, natural; congenital; hence ~ता; ~ वृत्ति instinct.

सहत्व [*nm*] co-existence, being together.

सहन [*nm*] patient endurance, forbearance; tolerance; a courtyard; -शक्ति endurance, forbearance, tolerance; ~शील enduring, forbearing, tolerant.

सह/ना [*v*] to endure, to forbear, to tolerate, to stand.

सहम/त [*a*] agreed; consented/concurred; ~ति agreement, concurrence, consent.

सहमना [*v*] to be panicked, to be struck with terror, to be nervous.

सहयो/ग [*nm*] cooperation; collaboration; ~गिता synergism; cooperation, collaboration; ~गी a colleague; supporter, one who extends cooperation.

सहलाना [*v*] to rub gently; to tickle, to titillate.

सहवास [*nm*] cohabitation.

सहसा [*ind*] suddenly, all of a sudden; unexpectedly.

सहस्र [*a*] one thousand; [*nm*] the number one thousand.

सहानुभूति [*nf*] sympathy; ~ शील sympathetic.

सहाय [*nm*] a helper, supporter.

सहायक [*nm*] a helper; an assistant; [*a*] auxiliary; assistant.

सहायता [*nf*] help, support; assistance; aid, relife.

सहार [*nm*] tolerance, endurance; ~ना to tolerate, to endure.

सहारा [*nm*] support; backing; aid, succour; a strut.

सहालग [*nm*] auspicious period for solemnization of marriages.

सहित [*ind*] with, together with, along with, accompanied by.

सहिष्णु [*a*] tolerant, enduring; ~ता tolerance, endurance.

सही [*a*] correct, right; true; accurate; authentic; -सलामत safe and sound, hale and hearty, secure.

सहूलियत [*nf*] convenience, facility.

सहृदय [*a*] humane, compassionate, tender-hearted; considerate; hence ~ता.

सहेजना [*v*] to keep securely; to keep with care; to entrust.

सहेतु, ~क [*a*] logical; having a reason/cause.

सहेली [*nf*] a female companion.

सहोदर [*nm*] a real brother; [*a*] real, born of the same mother.

सह्य [*a*] tolerable, endurable.

साँई [*nm*] God, Lord; master; husband; a title used for Mohammedan faqirs.

साँकल [*nf*] a chain.

सांकेतिक [*a*] token; nominal; symbolic; indicative.

सांख्य [*nm*] one of the six major Indian Philosophical systems.

सांख्यिकी [*nf*] [the science of] Statistics; ~य statistic [al].

सांगोपांग [*a*] complete [with limbs and parts], entire.

सांघातिक [*a*] fatal, mortal.

साँच [*a*] true, correct; [*nm*] truth; —को आँच नहीं/कहीं truth knows no fear.

साँचा [*nm*] a modellling tool; model; die, mould, moulding pattern.

साँझ [*nf*] evening, dusk.

साँझा [*nm*] see साझा.

साँट [*nm*] a cane.

साँठ-गाँठ [*nf*] a plunderbond, conspiratorial alliance; secret relationship; intrigue.

साँड़ [*nm*] a bull.

साँड़नी [*nf*] a fast-moving she- camel.

साँडा [*nm*] a species of sand-lizard.

सांत [*a*] finite, having an end.

सांत्वना [*nf*] consolation, solace.

सांध्य [*a*] pertaining to the evening, evening.

साँप [*nm*] a snake, serpent; [fig] a venomous person; —कलेजे या छाती पर लोटना to burn within on account of jealousy; —के सँपोले ही होंगे as the crow is, so the egg shall be; -छछूँदर की सी गति होना to be on the horns of a dilemma; —सूँघ जाना to be rendered still.

साँपिन [*nf*] a female snake/serpent.

सांप्रदायिक [*a*] communal; sectarian; ~ता communalism; sectarianism.

साँवला [*a*] slightly dark-complexioned; hence ~पन.

साँवलिया [*nm*] a lover; husband.

सांविधिक [*a*] statutory.

सांश्लेषिक [*a*] synthetic; ~ता synthetism.

साँस [*nf*] breath/breathing; —उखड़ना to be out of breath;—का रोग asthma; —गिनना to count the breaths; death to be imminent; —छूटना to be suffocated; —टूटना to pant; —तब तक आस, जब तक while there is life, there is hope; —फूलना to gasp; —रहते as long as living, till the last breath; —लेना to take breath, to breathe; —लेना, लंबी to heave a sigh; —लेने की फुर्सत breathing interval/respite.

साँसत [*nf*] distress, affliction, trouble.

सांसारिक [*a*] worldly, mundane, earthly, secular; hence ~ता.

सांस्कृतिक [*a*] cultural.

साइत [*nf*] moment, hour, time; auspicious moment.

साई [*nf*] earnest money, security; advance [money to fix a deal].

साई/स [*nm*] a horse-keeper, groom; ~सी horse-tending, grooming.

साका [*nm*] an era; overwhelming influence, eminence.

साकार [*a*] formal, having a form; concrete; —उपासना worshipping a formal deity, idol worship.

साकिन [*nm*] resident [of].

साक़ी [*nm*] a cup-bearer, one who serves a drink [liquor].

साक्षर [*a*] literate; ~ता literacy.

साक्षात् [*adv*] in the presence of, in person, visibly; [*a*] manifest, tangible, visible; ~कार an interview; ~कारी an interviewer; ~कृत interviewed.

साक्षी [*nm*] a witness, deponent; [*nf*] evidence, testimony.

साक्ष्य [*nm*] evidence, testimony; vouchment.

साख [*nf*] credit; reputation; trust; -पत्र letter of credit, credit note.

साखी [*nm*] a witness.

साग [*nm*] greens, vegetable; -पात vegetables and herbs; -सब्जी vegetables.

सागर [*nm*] the ocean, sea.

सागवान [*nf*] teak [wood]; also सागौन.

साज [*nm*] accoutrements, embellishment; appurtenance; —सजाना to organise a spectacle; to present in a particular manner.

साज़ [*nm*] a musical instrument, implement, equipment; harness; used as a suffix to mean—a mendor or manufacturer of, as ज़ीनसाज़; -बाज़ intrigue, conspiracy; paraphernalia; -सामान furnishings, appurtenance, equipment; necessaries.

साजन [*nm*] lover; husband.

साज़िंदा [*nm*] an instrumentalist, accompanyist.

साज़िश [*nf*] a conspiracy, plot, intrigue.

सा/झा [*nm*] partnership; share; [*a*] common; ~झेदार a partner, shareholder; ~झेदारी partnership; ~झे की हँड़िया चौराहे पर फूटती है a common horse is worst shod.

साझी [*nm*] a partner; ~दार see साझेदार under साझा; ~दारी see साझेदारी under साझा.

साटन [*nf*] satin [cloth].

साठ [*a*] sixty; [*nm*] the number sixty.

साठा [*a*] of sixty years of age; —सो पाठा youth sets in as one reaches sixty.

साड़ी [*nf*] a sari.

साढ़ू [*nm*] the husband of wife's sister.

साढ़े [*a*] plus half; ~साती [seven and a half year's] Saturian position foreboding evil.

सात [*a*] seven; [nm] the number seven; ~वाँ the seventh; -पाँच लगाना to higgle, to raise numerous objections; —परदों में रखना to keep away from all eyes, to keep well indoors; —समुंदर पार across the seven seas, very vcry far.

सातत्य [*nm*] continuity, uninterruptedness.

सात्त्विक [*a*] endowed with the quality of सत्त्व [purity and goodness], virtuous, righteous; hence ~ता [*nf*].

साथ [*adv*] with, together, along with, withal; by; [nm] company, association; support; —देना to keep company with; to stand by; —निबाहना to continue to be a loyal companion; to steadfastly stand by; —लेकर डूबना to involve someone in a sure tragedy; —सोना to share bed with; —ही साथ together.

साथी [*nm*] a companion, comrade; mate, associate, fellow; hence साथिन [*nf*].

सादगी [*nf*] simplicity, plainness.

सादर [*adv*] respectfully, with regards.

सादा [*a*] simple, plain; unadorned, artless; ~पन simplicity, plainess, artlessness; ~मिज़ाज plain and frank, artless; ~मिज़ाजी artlessness.

सादृश्य [*nm*] resemblance, likeness, analogy; affinity.

साध [*nf*] an ambition, a craving, longing.

साधक [*nm*] one engaged in or devoted to spiritual achievement/accomplishment; [*a*] effective, instrumental, conducive; engaged in or devoted to spiritual achievement/accomplishment; hence ~ता.

साधन [*nm*] medium, means; equipment, device, an implement; processing; solution; resources; realization.

साधना [*nf*] devotion; practice, mental training; spiritual endeavour or performance [esp. aspiring for an end]; [*v*] to tame; to aim; to train; to practise.

साधार [*a*] having a basis/ground.

साधारण [*a*] ordinary; simple; common, commonplace; usual, moderate; hence ~ ता [*nf*].

साधारणत: [*ind*] ordinarily, usually.

साधारणतया [*ind*] see साधारणतः

साधारणी/करण [*nm*] generalisation; impersonalisation; objectivisation; hence ~ कृत [*a*].

साधु [*nm*] a saint, saintly person; hermit; [*a*] good, noble, virtuous; -साधु good! excellent! well done!

साधुता [*nf*] saintliness; nobility, goodness, virtuousness, rectitude.

साधुवाद [*nm*] acclamation, applause.

साध्य [*nm*] the end; that which is to be proved; [*a*] practicable/feasible; [fit] to be achieved/accomplished; curable; hence ~ता; ~वाद teleology.

साध्वी [*a*] chaste [woman], virtuous.

सानंद [*a* and *adv*] happy/happily; pleased/ with pleasure.

सान [*nf*] whetting; sharpness; a whetstone.

सानना [*v*] to make into a paste; to besmear; to implicate.

सानी [*nf*] cattle-food [consisting of chaff and oilcake mixed together]; [*nm*] a match, an equal.

सानुनासिक [a] nasalised; ~ता nasalisation.

सान्निध्य [*nm*] proximity, nearness.

सापेक्ष [*a*] qualified, conditional; relative; ~ता relativity.

साप्ताहिक [*a*] weekly; [*nm*] a weekly journal.

साफ़ [*a*] clean, clear; slick; plain, frank; categorical, forthright, straight-forward; processed; refined; undefiled; distinct; unscathed; [adv] openly, frankly, plainly; fully; clearly; cleverly; ~गोई frankness; —जबाव a frank reply, forthright reply; ~दिल clean at heart; —बात a frank statement/word; -साफ़ openly, clearly, frankly, plainly; —करना to clean[se]; to sweep clean; to process, to refine; to clear [as बाधाएँ]; to clear off [as हिसाब—]; to claim life after life; to practise;—कहना to say plainly/frankly;—छूटना to go unscathed; to go scot free.

साफ़ा [*nm*] a turban.

साबित [*a*] entire, complete, unbroken; unwavering, steady; proved; ~क़दम steady; ~क़दमी steadiness.

साबुत [*a*] entire, complete; unbroken.

साबुन [*nm*] a soap.

साबूदाना [*nm*] sago.

साभार [*adv*] gratefully, with gratitude.

सामंजस्य [*nm*] harmony; consistence/consistency.

सामंत [*nm*] a feudal lord, feudatory, landlord; ~वाद feudalism; ~वादी a feudalist; feudalistic; ~शाही feudal [ism].

सामंती [*a*] feudal.

साम [*nm*] one of the four Vedas; tranquillizing, calming; gentle words intended to win over an adversary; conciliation; -नीति policy of conciliation [one of the four traditionally prescribed means used against an enemy].

सामग्री [*nf*] matter; material, things, stuff; data.

सामना [*nm*] confrontation, encounter, meeting; opposition; frontage.

सामने [*ind*] face to face; before, in front of; as compared with; against; in opposition; to; —आना to confront, to come fact to face; —की बात as seen by oneself.

सामयिक [*a*] opportune, timely; topical, periodic; casual; [*nm*] a periodical.

सामरिक [*a*] strategic [al]; military.

सामर्थ्य [*nf*] competence; capacity; power, strength; hence ~वान; ~हीन.

सामाजिक [*a*] social; [nm] a member of an assembly; —व्यवस्था social order.

सामान [*nm*] goods; luggage, bag and baggage; material, stuff; stock; ~घर luggage office.

सामान्य [*a*] general; common; usual, normal; routine; ~ता generality; commonness; usualness; normality; routine state or condition.

सामान्यत: [*ind*] generally; usually, normally; as a matter of routine.

सामीप्य [*nm*] proximity, nearness, vicinity.

सामुदायिक [*a*] collective; [pertaining to] community.

सामुद्रिक [*nm*] chiromancy; [*a*] oceanic.

सामूहिक [*a*] collective; community [~ wise].

साम्य [*nm*] community, equality; resemblance, similarity; equilibrium; ~वाद communism; ~वादी a communist; communistic.

साम्राज्य [*nm*] an empire; ~वाद imperialism; ~वादी an imperialist; imperialistic.

सायं [*nf*] see सायंकाल.

सायंकाल [*nm*] the evening, dusk.

सासत [*nf*] see साइत.

सायबान [*nm*] an awning, a shed.

सा/या [*nm*] shade; shadow; influence; shelter, protection; a petticoat; ~येदार shady; ~या उठना to be deprived of a proctective hand, a benevolent person to be no more; ~या पड़ना to be ifluenced by [a bad company], an association to have its ill effect; ~ये की तरह साथ-साथ रहना to always hang around like a shadow, to shadow somebody; साये में

रहना to live under the protection/patronage of; ~ये से बचना never to come near; to maintain a distance, to keep oneself at a safe distance [from].

सायुज्य [*nm*] complete union, a kind of मुक्ति [beatitude] where in the individual soul becomes one with the Supreme Soul.

सारंग [*nm*] a kind of antelope, deer; the bow of lord Vishnū; [*a*] variegated; ~पाणि an epithet of Lord Vishnū.

सारंगी [*nf*] a typical stringed Indian musical instrument.

सार [*nm*] substance, gist, purport, abstract; essence, extract; epitome; iron; ~गर्भित substantial, meaningful; full of pith/marrow; ~तत्त्व extract, substance; ~भूत essential; susbtantial; ~वान substantial, significant, meaningful; precious; useful.

सारणी [*nf*] a table; schedule; -समय time-table; ~वद्ध tabular.

सार/थि, ~थी [*nm*] a charioteer.

सारस [*nm*] a species of heron, a crane.

सारस्वत [*a*] pertaining to Sarawati:—the goddess of learning; [nm] ancient name for the tract of land lying on the bank of river Saraswati:.

सारांश [*nm*] abstract summary, gist, purport.

सारा [*a*] entire, whole; all; —जाता देखिए आधा लीजे बाँट better give the wool than the whole sheep.

सारिका [*nf*] a kind of Indian bird—Turdus salica [also called] मैना/ famous for its melodious note.

सारिणी [*nf*] see सारणी.

सारूप्य [*nm*] similarity of form, identity of appearance; a kind of भक्ति [beatitude] wherein the individual soul achieves formal identity with God.

सार्थक [*a*] articulate, meaningful, significant; effective, useful; hence ~ता.

सार्वज/निक, ~नीन, ~ न्य [*a*] universal; common; public, relating to public to general.

सार्वदेशिक [*a*] universal, pertaining/belonging to all lands or territories.

सार्वभौमिक [*a*] universal, pertaining or belonging to all beings/all places; ~ता universality.

सार्वभौम [*a*] universal.

सार्वलौकिक [*a*] universal, cosmopolitan.

साल [*nm*] an year; pain; the Sal tree; ~गिरह birthday.

सालन [*nm*] meat or fish or vegetable curry.

सालना [*v*] to torment, to torture; to fit a tenon in a mortise.

साला [*nm*] a brother-in-law—wife's brother; a term of abuse [directed to men]; hence साली [nf].

सालाना [*a*] yearly, annual.

सालारजंग [*nm*] a commander-in chief.

सालिम [*a*] complete, whole, entire.

सालियाना [*nm*] yearly gratuity; [a] yearly, annual.

सालोक्य [*nm*] a grade of मुक्ति [beatitude] which enables the soul to dwell in the company of God in the same लोक.

सावधा/न [*a*] careful, alert, cautious; attentive; [ind] attention! [in drill etc.]; hence ~नता/नी.

सावन [*nm*] the fifth month of the Hindu calendar.

साष्टांग [*a*] with the whole body or with all its members; —प्रणाम reverential prostration of the whole body.

सास [*nf*] mother-in-law, mother of [one's] wife or husband.

साह [*nm*] a good man or gentleman [as opposed to a thief—चोर]; a trader, merchant.

साहचर्य [*nm*] association, company; synergy/synergism.

साह/ब [*nm*] the Master, Lord; a whiteman, European; boss; gentleman, white-collared person; a title of courtesy; [vocative] word of respect; ~बज़ादा son of a साहब; a son; ~बज़ादी daughter of a साहब; a daughter; ~ब-बहादुर a [vocative] word of respect; ~बाना lordly; ~बी lordliness; ~ करना to live in a lordly manner; ~बीयत lordliness, lordly conduct.

साह/स [*nm*] courage, nerve, guts, boldness, daring; enterprise; ~सिक daring, bold, courageous; ~सी courageous; enterprising, adventurous.

साहि/त्य [*nm*] literature; ~त्यकार a litterateur, writer; ~त्यशास्त्र Poetics; ~त्यिक literary; ~त्यिकता literariness.

साहू [*nm*] see साह; a respectful vocative word used for a member of the Vaishya community.

साहूका/र [*nm*] a moneylender, private banker; a rich man, man of means; ~रा/री money lending business, banking.

सिंगार [*nm*] make-up, prank; ornamentation, embellishment; ~दान a dressing case.

सिंघाड़ा [*nm*] a waternut, water chestnut; a kind of firework.

सिंचाई [*nf*] irrigation; wages paid for irrigation.

सिंचित [*a*] irrigated; drenched.

सिंदूर [*nm*] vermillion.

सिंदू/रिया, ~री [*a*] vermillion-coloured, of the colour of vermillion.

सिंधी [*a*] belonging or pertaining to Sindh; [*nm*] a person belonging to the Province of Sindh; [nf] the Sindhi language.

सिंधु [*nm*] ocean, sea; the province of Sindh.

सिंह [*nm*] a lion; leo—the fifth sign of the zodiac [also सिंह राशि]; a caste-title amongst the kshattriyas; ~द्वार/पौर main gate; portal, propylon.

सिंहल [*nm*] an ancient name for Ceylon; also ~द्वीप.

सिंहली [*nf*] the Sinhali language; [nm] an inhabitant of Ceylon; [*a*] belonging or pertaining to Ceylon.

सिंहावलोकन [*nm*] retrospection.

सिंहासन [*nm*] a throne; —पर बैठना to ascend the throne; —से उतरना to dethrone.

सिंहिनी [*nf*] a lioness.

सिकंजबीन [*nm*] a typical sweet beverage prepared with fresh lemon-juice, water and sugar as ingredients.

सिकंदर [*nm*] Alexander; -तकदीर का exceptionally fortunate, a man of unusually good luck.

सिकता [*nf*] sand, sandy soil.

सिकुड़न [*nf*] shrinkage; contraction; a wrinkle, pucker.

सिकुड़ना [*v*] to contract; to shrink; to pucker, to wrinkle; to cower.

सिक्का [*nm*] a coin, coinage; lead; —जमना to acquire sway, to come to wield tremendous influence [over].

सिक्ख [*nm*] a Sikh [follower of Guru Nā:nak]; —धर्म/पंच the Sikh religion, Sikhism.

सिख [*nm*] see सिक्ख.

सिखाना [*v*] to train; to teach, to instruct, to school.

सिगरेट [*nf*] a cigarette.

सिगार [*nm*] a cigar.

सिजदा [*nm*] prostration, salutation, a process of Muslim prayers wherein the head, nose, knee, etc. of the worshipper touch the ground.

सिझना [*v*] to be cooked/boiled.

सिटकिनी [*nf*] a latch [of a door, window, etc.].

सिटपिटाना [*v*] to be stupefied, to be embarrassed, to be in a fix.

सिट्टी [*nf*] bragging; —गुम हो जाना,-पिट्टी गुम हो जाना, -पिट्टी भूल जाना–भूल जाना to be nervous, to be in a panic, to be stunned/stupefied.

सि/ड़ [*nf*] eccentricity, craziness, crankiness, whim; ~ड़ी eccentric, crazy, cranky, whimsical; hence ~ पन/पन.

सितंबर [*nm*] the month of September.

सितम [*nm*] tyranny, oppression; hence ~गर, ~गरी.

सितार [*nm*] a typical stringed Indian musical instrument; ~वादक one who plays on a सितार; ~वादन playing on a सितार.

सितारा [*nm*] a star, planet; small shining tablets of metal or mica which are studded on the cap, shoe, etc.; —चमकना, —बुलंद होना one's star to be in the ascendance, to have an advent/run of good fortune; —डूबना to be in the grip of adversity, adverse times to commence.

सिद्ध [*a*] proved; accomplished, perfected/perfect; endowed with supernatural powers; [*nm*] a saint; name of a special cult of saint; one who has acquired supernatural powers; hence ~ता/त्व perfection; the state of having achieved supernatural powers; accomplishment; ~हस्त proficient, skilful, expert.

सिद्धांत [*nm*] a principle; theory; doctrine; ~तः theoretically; as a matter of principle.

सिद्धांती [*a* and *nm*] [*a*] theoretician/theorist; dogmatic; a man of principles.

सिद्धि [*nf*] acquisition, accomplishment; proof; fulfilment, success; supernatural powers supposed to be acquired through Yogic practices [see अष्टसिद्धि].

सिधाई [*nf*] see सीधापन [under सीधा]; alignment.

सिधाना [*v*] to tame; to domesticate; to help acquire practice.

सिधारना [*v*] to go, to depart; to expire.

सिनेमा [*nm*] a cinema; ~ई cinematic; ~घर a cinema hall.

सिपाहियाना [*a*] soldierly, befitting a soldier.

सिपाही [*nm*] a soldier; sepoy, constable, policeman.

सिप्पा [*nm*] influence; approach; device; —जमाना/बैठाना/ भिड़ाना/लगाना/लड़ाना to make an approach, to manoeuvre; to see a scheme through.

सिफ़त [*nf*] a characteristic [quality]; attribute.

सिफ़र [*nm*] a cipher, zero; blank; —होना to be just blank.

सिफ़ारिश [*nf*] recommendation; ~शी recommendatory.

सियापा [*nm*] mourning, weeping and wailing over a death.

सियार [*nm*] a jackal; cunning fellow.

सिया/सत [*nf*] politics; ~सी political.

सिर [*nm*] head; top, apex, highest part or point; ~खपाई [the process of] taxing one's brain overmuch; too much of mental exertion; ~चढ़ा cheeky, given too much of lift; ~ताज [lit. and fig.] crown, the best [amongst]; diadem; chief; master, husband; ~नामा form of address [in a letter etc.]; ~मौर see ~ ताज; ~ हाना head-rest; the upper end of a bedstead; -आँखों पर with one's heart and soul; most willingly, most cordially; —उठाना to rise in revolt, to rebel; —उठाने की फ़ुरसत न होना not to have a moment's respite; —उड़ा देना to behead, to chop off the head; —उतारना to behead; —ऊँचा करना to be pround [of], to feel a sense of pride; —क़दमों पर रखना to bow in obeisance; to make a complete surrender; —क़लम करना to behead, to chop off the head; —की टली जान पर आई spared by one calamity, plagued by another; —के बल headlong; with due deference; —कोरे उस्तरे/छूरे से मूंड़ना to fleece ruthlessly; —खाना to pester, to plague, to go on bothering; —खुजलाना to be in for a beating/thrashing;—खुजलाने की फ़ुरसत/मुहलत न होना not to have even a breathing respite; —घूमना/चकराना to feel giddy, to suffer from vertigo; —चढ़ना to take too much liberty; to take much lift; —चढ़कर बोले, जादू वह जो a spell must somehow procure a tangible, expression; —चढ़ना to become too cheeky, to take too much liberty; —झुकना —to feel ashamed, to hang the head [in shame]; —टकराना to dash the head against; to suffer too much of mental exertion; ~तोड़ कोशिश करना to make a frantic/desperate bid; —थाम लेना to hold the head [as expressive of having suffered a tragic blow]; -थोपना to impose [upon]; to accuse; —दु:खना to suffer from headache; —देना to stake one's life, to die [for];—धुनना to beat the head as a mark of mourning, to weep and wail aloud;—न उठाने देना to allow no respite, to keep thoroughly engaged; to give no life/quarter; to give no opportunity to rise against; —न पाँव/पैर groundless, having no logic whatever, absolute absurdity; —नीचा करना to inflict a defeat; to cause embarrassment; to hang one's head in shame; —पकड़कर रह जाना to be stunned still by grief; —पटकना to make frantic efforts to mourn, to weep and wail; —पड़ना to be obliged to shoulder [a responsibility etc.], to be imposed on, to have [an obligation etc.] devolved on; —पर आ जाना to approach very near; to be imminent; to be face to face with; to devolve on; —पर आसमान/घर उठाना to create a havoc, to cause an uproar; to kick up a row; —पर आसमान टूटना to be in the grip of a terrible affliction, a calamity to befall; —पर क़यामत टूटना a great calamity to befall, to be in the grip of a terrible affliction; —पर कोई ना होना to have none to guide or to provide protection; —पर खून चढ़ना या सवार होना to be overwhelmed by murder-mania; —पर चढ़ाना

to spoil [as a child] out of fondness; to pamper a bit too much; to encourage into insolence; —पर डालना to shift a botheration; to put a responsibility over; —पर पड़ना [a responsibility etc.] to devolve upon, to have to be shouldered; —पर पाँव रखकर भागना या उड़ जाना to show a clean pair of heels; —पर बिठाना/बैठाना to extend respectful welcome, to receive with deference; —पर भूत सवार होना to be under an obsession, to turn into a maniac; to go crazy through an obstinate resolve; —पर लादकर ले जाना to carry along [to the next world]; —पर लेना to accept a responsibility, to own a responsibility; —पर शैतान चढ़ना or सवार होना to be overwhelmed by sinful mentality; to be obsessed by a sense of anger/obstinacy; —पर सनीचर सवार होना to be in adversity, to be under the sway of ominous times; —पर सवार रहना to ever hover around; to keep under constant watch; to behave in an insolent manner, to keep bullying; to keep under obsession; —पर साया रहना/होना to enjoy the shadow of a protective hand, to be under the protection of; —पर सेहरा बाँधना to earn a distinction; to be plumed; —पाँव न होना or —पैर न होना to make no head or tail, to make no sense; to be absurd, to be ridiculously illogical/incoherent; —पीट कर रोना to lament violently, to weep and wail; —फटा जाना/पड़ना the head to crack with pain, to have severe headache; —फिरना to go crazy, to run amuck; to be out of senses; —भारी होना to have headache; to have a heaviness in the head; —भिन्नाना to feel giddy, to suffer from vertigo; to have a fit of anger; —मारना to tax one's brain, to try to explain something to a nitwit, to make strenuous efforts, to try no end, to take great pains; —मुँड़ाते ही ओले पड़ना to be confronted with obstacles at the very first step, ill luck to overtake at the very outset; —रँगना to make one's head bleed, to break somebody's head; —लगना to be accused, to be faced with an accusation; —लेना to own up, to undertake a responsibility; —से कफ़न बाँधना to be ready to face death, to stake one's life; —से तिनका उतारने का अहसान मानना to be grateful even for the semblance of a good turn; —सेहरा बँधना to get the credit for [a success etc.], to get the applause for an achievement; —से बला टालना to get rid of an unpleasant context, to be done with somehow; —से बोझ उतारना to rid oneself of a burden; —हथेली पर धरना/रखना to be ever-ready to face death, to be never scared of death; —हाजिर है to be ready to risk life with pleasure, to be ready to take up a risk.

सिरका [*nm*] vinegar.

सिरजन [*nm*] creation; ~हार the Creator.

सि/रा [*nm*] an edge; end; head, top; ~रे extremities, ends.

सिर्फ़ [*a* and *adv*] only, mere[ly].

सिल [*nf*] a stone-slab on which spices etc. are ground; ~खरी/खड़ी chalk.

सिलना [*v*] to sew/stitch; to be sewn/stitched.

सिलवट [*nf*] a wrinkle; pucker.

सिलसि/ला [*nm*] a chain, series; line; arrangement; system; ~लेवार serial[ly]; consecutive[ly]; systematic[ally].

सिलाई [*nf*] the act or process of sewing/stitching; stitching charges.

सिल्ली [*nf*] a slab [of stone or wood etc.]; whetstone, hone.

सिव/इयाँ, ~ई [*nf*] vermicelli.

सिवा, ~य [*ind*] except, but.

सिवाला [*nm*] a temple dedicated to Lord Shiv.

सिसकना [*v*] to sob.

सिसका/रना [*v*] to hiss, to produce a hissing sound; ~री hissing [sound].

सिसकी [*nf*] a sob, sobbing; —भरना to sob.

सिहरन [*nf*] a thrill; shiver.

सिहरना [*v*] to be thrilled; to shiver.

सींक [*nf*] wicker of a broom; a spit, skewer.

सींकचा [*nm*] window-bars.

सींग [nm] a horn; —समाना to find accommodation/refuge; —होना, सिर पर या सिर में lit. to have horns over the head—to have a rare characteristic.

सींचना [*v*] to irrigate, to water.

सींव [*nf*] boundary.

सींवन [*nf*] seam.

सी [*ind*] feminine form of सा meaning-like, similar, resembling, identical with, etc; sibilance; muffled spirant sound expressive of intense joy or excessive pain; —सी करना to express intense joy or pain through muffled spirant sounds.

सीख [*nf*] teaching, advice; moral.

सीखना [*v*] to learn.

सीटी [*nf*] a whistle.

सीठा [*a*] insipid; ~पन insipidity.

सीढ़ी [*nf*] a ladder; stairs, staircase.

सीता [nf] the celebrated daughter of king Janak [of Mithila:] who was married to Ram, the hero of the renowned Indian epic of Ramayan; -स्वयंवर the episode of the स्वयंवर of सीता [in the Ramayan];~हरण the episode of the kidnapping of सीता by the demon-king रावण [in the Ramayan].

सीताफल [*nm*] see कद्दू—a custard apple.

सीत्कार [*nf*] sibilance, a muffled spirant sound expressive of intense joy or excessive pain.

सीध [*nf*] alignment, straightness.

सीधा [*a* and *adv*] straight; simple; erect, upright; direct; gentle; good; forthrightly; through; [nm] victuals earmarked for a Bra:hmān as alms; ~पन simplicity; straightness; uprightness; gentleness; -सादा/साधा simple, innocent; gentle; good; docile, —करना to put straight; to knock out one's haughtiness/conceit, to fix in one's proper place; to align; hence —होना.

सीधी [*a* and *adv*] feminine form of सीधा; -आँख favourable glance; —राह a straight path; moral course; —उँगली से घी नहीं निकलता softness does not evoke compliance.

सीधे [*adv*] straight; without a halt or detour; without protest; quietly; in a gentlemanly fashion; —मुँह with due courtesy; in an appropriate manner.

सीना [*v*] to sew; to stitch; [nm] chest; ~जोर exercising coercion, ever-assertive; unashamedly aggressive, hence ~जोरी; सीने पर पत्थर रखना to endure patiently, to suppress agony in a quiet manner.

सीप [*nf*] oyster shell, mother pearl.

सीमंत [nm] the parting line of the locks of hair on the head in combing.

सीम [*nf*] silver; see सीमा.

सीमांत [*a* and *nm*] frontier; limit; margin/marginal; extreme.

सीमा [*nf*] a border, boundary/bounds; frontier; limit, extent; verge; -रेखा border-line; line of demarcation.

सीमित [*a*] restricted, limited, bounded; qualified.

सीमेंट [*nm*] cement.

सीयन [*nf*] seam; stiching, sewing.

सीर [*nf*] self-cultivated land; [*nm*] a plough.

सीरा [*nm*] molasses.

सील [*nm*] see शील; [*nf*] damp/dampness, moisture; a seal.

सीलन [*nf*] dampness, moisture.

सीवन [*nf*] see सीयन.

सीस [*nm*] the head.

सीसम [*nm*] a particular tree [that yields a rich variety of timber for furniture etc.].

सीसा [*nm*] lead.

सीसी [*nf*] see सी-सी; see शीशी.

सुँघनी [*nf*] a snuff; sneeze-wort.

सुंदर [*a*] beautiful, handsome, pretty; fine; ~ता beauty, prettiness.

सु—a prefix imparting the meanings of good, beautiful, pretty, excellent, thorough, well, easy, etc.

सुकर [*a*] easy; ~ता easiness.

सुकुमा/र [*a*] delicate, tender; ~रता delicacy, tenderness; hence ~री.

सुकून [*nm*] peace, comfort; consolation.

सुकोमल [*a*] extremely soft, very delicate; ~ता extreme softness/delicacy.

सुख [*nm*] happiness, pleasure; comfort; felicity; contentment; -चैन happiness and comfort; ~द happy, pleasant, pleasurable; comfortable; ~दायी see ~ दुःख happiness and sorrow; pleasure and pain; ~ पूर्वक happily; comfortably; -भोग luxurious living, enjoyment; ~वाद hedonist; hedonistic; -शांति comfort/joy and peace, happiness and peace, felicity; -सौभाग्य pleasure and plenty, physical and mental happiness; —की नींद carefree sleep; —लूटना to enjoy, to make merry.

सुखांत [*a*] with a happy ending, ending happily; also ~क. सुखात्मक [*a*] happy; hedonic.

सुखी [*a*] happy; contented.

सुगंध [*nf*] scent, fragrance, perfume, aroma.

सुगंधि [*a*] scented, fragrant, perfumed; aromatic.

सुगठित [*a*] shapely, well-built; muscular; well-organised.

सुगम [*a*] easy; approachable, accessible; intelligible; hence ~ता.

सुग्गा [*a*] a parrot.

सुघड़ [*a*] shapely, well-built; elegant; dexterous; ~ता see सुघड़ाई; ~पन see सुघड़ाई.

सुघड़ाई [*nf*] concinnity; shapeliness, elegance; dexterousness.

सुचारु [*a*] charming, pretty, comely; hence ~ता.

सुजन [*nm*] a gentleman; ~ता gentlemanliness.

सुजान [*a*] wise, learned hence ~ता [*nf*].

सुझाना [*v*] to suggest; to propose; to indicate.

सुझाव [*nm*] a suggestion, proposal.

सुड़कना [*v*] to sniff up, to inhale with the breath; to drink noisily.

सुडौल [*a*] shapely, comely, well-built; hence ~ता [nf].

सु/त [*nm*] a son; hence ~ता [*nf*].

सुतरां [*ind*] moreover; thus, therefore; what more.

सुतली [*nf*] twine, thin rope.

सुथरा [*a*] clean, neat and tidy; refined; ~ई/पन cleanliness neatness and tidiness; refinement.

सुदी [*nf*] the moonlit fortnight of a lunar month.

सुदूर [*a*] very far, remote; ~पूर्व far east; ~वर्ती remote, far-flung.

सुदृढ़ [*a*] very strong; very firm; very rigid.

सुदौसी [*ind*] early.

सुध [*nf*] memory; consciousness, senses; ~ न रहना to forget; to lose or be out of senses; —बिसरना to forget; to lose or be out of senses;—लेना to remember; to enquire after.

सुधरना [*v*] to be reformed; to be improved; to be amended/corrected; to be repaired.

सुधवाना [*v*] to cause to be or to get calculated [as an auspicious moment]; to get purified.

सुधाना [*v*] to get calculated/purified.

सुधार [*nm*] reform/reformation; uplift; repair, amendment; modification; improvement; ~क a reformer; ameliorant; ~वाद reformism; meliorism.

सुधारना [*v*] see सुधरना.

सुधी [*a* and *nm*] [*a*] wise/learned [man]; the wise; ~जन learned people, the wise.

सुनना [*v*] to hear, to listen; to pay heed; [*nm*] hearing, audition; सुना-सुनाया hearsay, based on hearsay; सुनी-अनसुनी करना to pay no heed, to ignore.

सुनवाई [*nf*] hearing [of a case etc.].

सुनसान [*a*] desolate, deserted; lonely; [nm] loneliness; stillness.

सुनह/रा, ~ला [*a*] golden; ~रापन goldenness.

सुनाना [*v*] to cause to hear; to relate; to read out; to recite; to pronounce.

सुनार [*nm*] a goldsmith.

सुनिश्चित [*a*] assured; definite.

सुनीति [*nf*] equity.

सुन्न [*a*] still[ed]; insensitive, benumbed, etherised, stupefied.

सुन्नत [*nf*] circumcision.

सुपच [*a*] easily digestible.

सुपच्य [*a*] salubrious; [nm] salubrious diet.

सुपात्र [*nm*] a deserving [person], one who deserves; [a] deserving; hence ~ता [*nf*].

सुपारी [*nf*] betel-nut; arecanut.

सुपुर्द [*a*] entrusted, committed; charged [with]; ~गी trust; charge, care; delivery.

सुप्त [*a*] asleep, dormant; [rendered] senseless.

सुप्ति [*nf*] sleep, slumber.

सुप्रसिद्ध [*a*] reputed, renowned, famous, celebrated.

सुफल [*nm*] good/welcome result.

सुबह [*nf*] morning, dawn; -सुबह early [in the] morning, -सवेरे early [in the] morning, —का भूला शाम को आए veering round to the proper course at long last.

सुबुद्धि [*nf*] good/moral sense, wisdom; [*a*] wise, intelligent.

सुबोध [*a*] intelligible, easy; ~ता intelligibility, easiness.

सुभाग [*a*] beautiful; lucky.

सुभीता [*nm*] convenience; comfort.

सुमति [*nf*] unity/union; see सुबुद्धि [*nf* and *a*].

सुमधुर [*a*] very sweet, melodious.

सुमन [*nm*] a flower; [*a*] favourably disposed; happy.

सुमिरणी [*nf*] a rosary [of beads].

सुमुखी [*a* and *nm*] [a] pretty faced [woman], beautiful.

सुमेरु [*nm*] the mythological mountain of gold.

सुयोग [*nm*] a happy chance/coincidence.

सुयोग्य [*a*] very able, worthy.

सुरंग [*nf*] a tunnel; mine.

सुर [*nm*] tone; a note in music; vowel; a god; ~गण gods, the whole body of gods; -तान tone and tune; ~त्व godhood; ~दार melodious, harmonious; ~धाम the abode of gods; –मिलाना to attune, to harmonise.

सुर/क्षा [*nf*] protection, security; ~क्षित safe, secure, protected; reserved.

सुरति [*nf*] memory, recollection; amorous dalliance, sexual enjoyment.

सुरभि [*nf*] fragrance, aroma, perfume, scent; ~त fragrant, aromatic, perfumed, scented.

सुरमई [*a*] dark grey, of the colour of सुरमा.

सुरमा [*nm*] collyrium, antimony ground into fine powder.

सुरम्य [*a*] charming, attractive, beautiful.

सुरसुरा/ना [*v*] to rustle; to creep or crawl like an insect; to itch; hence ~हट.

सुरा [*nf*] wine, liquor.

सुराख़ [*nm*] a hole, cavity, an aperture.

सुराग [*nm*] a clue, trace.

सुराही [*nf*] a flagon, long-necked earthen water-pot; ~दार/~नुमा shaped like a surahi:

सुरीला [*nm*] sweet, melodious; ~पन sweetness, melodiousness; symphony.

सुरुचि [*nf*] refined taste, good taste.

सुरूर [*nm*] mild/slight intoxication; pleasant after-effects of mild slight intoxication.

सुर्ख [*a*] red, ruddy; ~रू reputed, having reputation; honourable.

सुर्ख़ाब [*nm*] a ruddy goose —Anas casarca; —के पर लगे होना to be blessed with an unusual feature, to have some remarkable characteristic; to be privileged.

सुर्ख़ी [*nf*] redness, ruddiness; a headline; brick-dust; lipstick.

सुलगना [*v*] to smoulder; to burn [esp. inwardly]; to begin to burn, to be ignited; hence सुलगाना.

सुलझना [*v*] to be disentangled; to be unravelled; to be solved; hence सुलझाना.

सुलझाव [*nm*] disentanglement; solution.

सुलतान [*nm*] a Sultan.

सुलफ़ा [*nm*] an intoxicating drug; crude tobacco smoked without using filter.

सुलभ [*a*] easy; accessible, available, handy; hence सुलभ्य.

सुलह [*nf*] an agreement; reconciliation, rapproachement; ~नामा [a written] agreement; compromise deed; peace-treaty.

सुलाना [*v*] to cause to sleep, to lull to sleep.

सुलूक [*nm*] treatment, behaviour.

सुलेख [*nm*] calligraphy; -कला [the art of] callligraphy, ~कार a calligraphist.

सुवर्ण [*nm*] gold; good colour; higher caste.

सुवार्ता [*nf*] good news.

सुवासित [*a*] fragrant, aromatic, perfumed, scented.

सुविदित [*a*] well-known.

सुविधा [*nf*] facility; convenience; ~पूर्वक conveniently.

सुव्यव/स्था [*nf*] order/orderliness, good organisation/administration; ~स्थित orderly; regular; well-organised; well-administered.

सुशिक्षित [*a*] well-educated.

सुशी/ल [*a*] courteous, suave; modest; hence ~लता.

सुशोभित [*a*] [well] adorned; graceful; hence— करना, —होना.

सुश्री [*a*] an honorofic prefixed to the name of a woman—married or otherwise.

सुषमा [*nf*] beauty, exceptional prettiness, charm.

सुषु/प्त [*a*] asleep, in deep slumber; ~प्तावस्था state of deep sleep; ~प्ति deep sleep.

सुषुम्ना [*nf*] one of the three principal or major nerves, according to the hathayogis, that plays an important role in the achievement of Supreme Bliss.

सुष्ठु [*a*] elegant; appropriate; hence ~ता.

सुसंग/त [*a*] very appropriate/logical, valid/temple/reasonable; concordant; relevant; ~ति good association; commendable company, validity; relevance; concord[ance].

सुसंस्कृत [*a*] cultured; refined.

सुसज्जित [*a*] well-adorned; well-equipped.

सुस्त [*a*] slow, languid; indolent; lazy, idle; in low spirit; spiritless, depressed.

सुस्ताना [*v*] to relax, to rest; to have a respite.

सुस्ती [*nf*] languor indolence; laziness, idleness; spiritlessness, depression.

सुहबत [*nf*] company, association; coition; —बिगड़ना to fall into bad company.

सुहबती [*a*] sociable, affable.

सुहाग [*nm*] the happy state of a woman when her husband is alive; husband; good fortune; ~रात the first night of a couple's union; —उजड़ना [said of a woman] to be widowed, to lose the protection of the husband.

सुहागा [*nm*] borax, plank.

सुहागि/न, ~नी, ~ल [*a* and *nm*] [a woman] whose husband is alive, who is ever-blessed with the protective care of her husband.

सुहाना [*v*] to be pleasing; to look charming, to be liked; [a] pleasing, charming, likeable.

सुहावना [*a*] pleasing; charming, likeable.

सुहृद [*a*] friendly, loving; [nm] a friend.

सूँघना [*v*] to smell, to scent; to sniff; to eat very little.

सूँड़ [*nf*] the trunk [of an elephant], proboscis.

सूँड़ी [*nf*] a grub.

सूअर [*nm*] a boar, pig; a word of abuse—swine; very dirty/thick skinned person.

सूआ [*nm*] a big needle.

सूई [*nf*] a needle; the hands of a watch/clock; —का भाला/फाबड़ा बना देना to make a mountain of a molehill, to exaggerate no end; —के नाके में से ऊँट निकालना to perform a miracle/an impossible feat.

सूक्त [*nm*] a mantra of the Vedas.

सूक्ति [*nf*] a maxim, an epigram, a pithy pointed saying.

सूक्ष्म [*a*] subtle, minute, fine; thin; ~ता subtlety, minuteness; fineness, thinness; precision; ~दर्शी a microscope; keen observer; keen-eyed; ~दृष्टि keensighted; keen sight.

सूखना [*v*] to dry up, to wither; to dwindle; to be attenuated; to evaporate; सूखकर काँटा हो जाना to become too tenuous, to be reduced to a skeleton.

सूखा [*a*] dry, sapless; blunt; flat [as जवाब;] all-told, with nothing extra: [nm] drought; [in children] cramp [also called—रोग]; —जबाव देना to refuse flatly; —टालना to say a flat 'no'.

सूचक [*nm*] an informant/informer; a pointer; [a] suggestive, symptomatic; indicative.

सूचकांक [*nm*] an index number.

सूचना [*nf*] information; intimation; notice, notification; -पट्ट a notice-board; ~पत्र a notification, circular; ~र्थ for information.

सूचित [*a*] informed, intimated.

सूची [*nf*] a list, catalogue; ~पत्र a catalogue.

सूजन [*nf*] swelling, inflammation.

सूजना [*v*] to swell.

सूजा [*nm*] a big needle, an awl, distaff; [*a*] swollen.

सूज़ाक [nm] gonorrhoea.

सूझ [nf] insight, vision, imagination, perception; -बूझ imagination, understanding, intelligence.

सूझना [*v*] to be visible, to be seen; to occur to one's mind.

सूत [*nm*] yarn, thread: length equal to one-eighth of an inch; a charioteer; one who relates ancient legends.

सूती [*a*] cotton-, made of cotton.

सूत्र [*nm*] a thread, yarn, fibre; source; aphorism; formula; sacred thread (जनेऊ); ~धार the stage manager [in a dramatic performance]; ~पात beginning, commencement; ~बद्ध formulated; integrated.

सूद [*nm*] interest; ~खोर usurer; usurrious; ~खोरी usury.

सूना [*a*] lonely, desolate; empty; ~पन loneliness, desolation; emptiness.

सूप [*nm*] a winnowing basket; soup, broth.

सूफ़ियाना [*a*] befitting a Sufi; plain and simple;—अंदाज in the manner of a Su:fi:

सूफ़ी [*nm*] a sect of Muslim saints [whose characteristic quality is their plain and simple ways]

सूबा [*nm*] a province.

सूबेदा/र [*nm*] a governor, head of a province; a non-commissioned army rank.

सूम [*a*] penurious, miser, niggardly; [*nm*] a miser; hence ~पन/पना.

सूर [*a*] brave; blind; [nm] the sun; ~दास [euphemistically] a blind person.

सूरज [*nm*] the sun; —पर थूकना, —पर धूल फेंकना to accuse the infallible and be self-debased.

सूरत [*nf*] countenance, face; appearance, looks, form; case; condition, state; -शक्ल appearance; —निकल आना to grow prettier; a solution [to a problem] to emerge; —बदलना to disguise; things to change; —से बेजार होना not to be able to stand the sight of, to be absolutely fed up of.

सूरमा [*a* and *nm*] brave; a hero; warrior; ~ई/पन bravery, heroism.

सूराख [*nm*] a hole, an aperture, orifice; a puncture; eyelet.

सूर्य [*nm*] the sun; ~ग्रहण solar eclipse; ~मुखी the sunflower—Helianthus annus; having the colour of the skin rendered white [through disease].

सूर्यास्त [*nm*] sunset.

सूर्योदय [*nm*] sunrise.

सूर्योपास/क [*nm*] a sun-worshipper, heliolater; hence ~ना.

सूली [*nm*] gallows, gibbet; —देना,—पर चढ़ना to hang to death, to execute by hanging.

सृजन [*nm*] creation; ~शील creative; hence ~शीलता; ~हार creator [of the world].

सृष्टि [*nf*] creation; the world.

सेंकना [*v*] to foment; to bake; to roast; to warm.

सेंत [a] gratis, free of charge/cost; —में gratis; -मेंत see सेंत; ~ में gatis; without any charge.

सेंध [*nf*] a hole [made] in a wall [by a burglar]; burglary, house-breaking.

सेंधा [*nm*] rock salt; —नमक rock salt.

से [*ind*] from; with; by; than; since; [*a*] similar, equal.

सेकना [*v*] see सेंकना.

सेकंड [*nm*] a second [one sixtieth of a minute].

सेज [*nf*] a bed, richly decorated bed.

सेठ [*nm*] a wealthy merchant, moneyed man; hence सेठानी [*nf*].

सेतु [*nm*] a bridge; causeway.

सेना [*nf*] army, military; [*v*] to hatch.

सेम [*nf*] bean, kidney-bean [name of a particular vegetable].

सेर [*nm*] a seer—weight equivalent to 16 chhataks or a little over 2 lbs.

सेलखड़ी [*nf*] soap-stone, silica, chalk, talc.

सेव [*nm*] an apple; a saltish/sweet vermicelli-like preparation of gram-flour.

सेवई [*nf*] vermicelli.

सेवक [*nm*] a servant, an attendant; hence सेविका [*nf*].

सेव/न [*nm*] taking [as medicine etc.], consuming; using, use; serving; hence ~नीय.

सेवा [*nf*] service, attendance; -टहल servitude, service; -निवृत्त retired; ~निवृत्ति retirement.

सेवी—a suffix used to impart the sense of using or doing service for, etc. [as स्वयंसेवी].

सेव्य [*a*] fit or deserving to be served; [*nm*] one to whom service is rendered; master.

सेहत [*nf*] health.

सेहरा [*nm*] a nuptial headwear, a head-dress worn by the bride groom at the time of marriage; eulogical verses read at a wedding; auspicious song sung at the time of wedding; —बँधना to be married; to get the credit for.

सैंतालीस [*a*] forthy-seven; [*nm*] the number forty-seven.

सैंतीस [*a*] thirty-seven; [*nm*] the number thirty-seven.

सैयाँ [*nm*] husband; lover.

सैकड़ा [*nm*] one hundred; a group of one hundred.

सैद्धांतिक [*a*] theoretical, pertaining to some theory or doctrine.

सैनिक [*nm*] a soldier; [a] military, pertaining to the army; solider-like; —क्रांति military revolution; —तानाशाही military dictatorship; —न्यायालय military court.

सैन्य [a] military, pertaining to army; ~नायक/पति/पाल a commander.

सैन्या/धिपति, ~ ध्यक्ष [*nm*] the commander/in chief [of an army].

सैर [*nf*] walking/walk; ramble; excursion; outing; stroll.

सैलानी [*nm*] a tourist; wanderer; holiday-maker; hence ~पन.

सैलाब [*nm*] flood.

सैलून [*nm*] a saloon [barber's shop or a rail-way carriage meant for high officials etc.].

सोंठ [*nf*] dry ginger.

सोंधा [*a*] aromatic; sweet-smelling; having the pleasant smell of just-wetted soil; hence ~पन.

सो [*ind*] therefore, thus; [pro] that, he.

सोखना [*v*] to dry up; to absorb.

सोख़्ता [*nm*] a blotting paper; blotter.

सोग [*nm*] mourning, bereavement.

सोच [*nm*] anxiety; brooding, musing, considera-tion, reflection; -विचार reflection, thinking, pondering, consideration; hesitation.

सोचना [*v*] to think/to reflect, to ponder over, to consider.

सोटा [*nm*] a cudgel, wandstick.

सोता [*a*] sleeping; [*nm*] a stream, spring, brook; source.

सोदाहरण [*a*] illustrated, exemplified, with example.

सोनजुही [*nf*] a kind of yellow jasmine.

सो/ना [*nm*] gold; an excellent thing; [v] to sleep; ~ना चाँदी gold and silver; wealth; ~ना चढ़ाना to gild; ~ने का घर मिट्टी कर देना to turn riches into ruins, to spell ruin on a prosperous household; ~ ने की चिड़िया an extremely rich victim; ~ने में सुगंध added excellence/richness; ~ने में सुहागा added excellence/richness, one excellence superimposed over another.

सोपान [*nm*] a stair, staircase.

सोफ़ा [*nm*] a sofa; ~सेट a sofaset.

सोफ़ियाना [*a*] elegant; simple but attractive; sophisticated.

सोम [*nm*] the moon; Monday; the moon creeper yielding an intoxicating juice which was drunk at sacrifice (यज्ञ) in ancient times; ~रस the intoxicating juice of the सोम creeper; ~वार/वासर Monday.

सोया [*nm*] a sweet smelling plant used for preparing a vegetable.

सोयाबीन [*nm*] soyabean.

सोरठा [*nm*] a particular metre [couplet] in Hindi poetry.

सोलह [a] sixteen; [nm] the number sixteen; -सिंगार made up in all the possible sixteen [traditional] ways, सोलहों आने completely, totally, fully.

सोसाइ(य)टी [*nf*] society.

सोहनहलवा [*nm*] a typical Indian sweetmeat.

सोहबत [*nf*] company, association; copulation, intercourse.

सोहर [nm] a typical song sung by women to celebrate the birth of a male child.

सौंदर्य [*nm*] beauty, charm, prettiness; ~बोध aesthetic sense; -शास्त्र aesthetics; ~शास्त्री an aesthetician, सौंदर्यानुभूति aesthetic experience/sensibility.

सौंध [*nf*] fragrance, sweet smell.

सौंपना [*v*] to hand over; to give, to entrust; to surrender; to delegate [as powers], to assign.

सौंफ़ [*nf*] anise; aniseed; fennel.

सौ [a] hundred; [nm] the number hundred; ~गुना hundred times; ~वाँ hundredth; —जान से whole heartedly; [with] heart and soul;

—बात की एक बात the long and short of a matter, the essence.

सौकुमार्य [*nm*] tenderness, delicacy.

सौगं/द, ~ध [nf] an oath, swearing; ~ध खाना to take an oath, to swear.

सौग़ात [*nf*] a present, gift.

सौजन्य [*nm*] goodness, courtesy; —से by courtesy.

सौड़ [*nm*] a quilt, sheet for covering oneself up while sleeping.

सौत [*nf*] a co-wife.

सौतेला [*a*] pertaining to or related with or born of सौत; half-blood.

सौदा [*nm*] a bargain, transaction; negotiation; goods, commodity; ~गर a trader, merchant; ~गरी business, trade, commerce; -सुलफ़/सुलुफ़ commodity, goods; —पटना a bargain to be settled/struck.

सौदामिनी [*nf*] lightning:

सौभाग्य [*nm*] good luck, fortune; ~वती a woman of good luck; fortunate in having one's husband alive; ~वान fortunate; ~शाली fortunate.

सौम्य [*a*] amiable, gentle; ~ता/त्व amiability, gentility.

सौर [*a*] solar; [*nm*] a [cotton] wrapper; —परिवार solar system.

सौरभ [*nm*] fragrance, aroma.

सौरी [*nf*] a lying in/confinement chamber.

सौष्ठव [nm] grace, elegance, charm.

सौहार्द [*nm*] amity; friendship, love, good relations.

स्कंध [*nm*] the shoulder; stem or trunk of a tree; division of an army; stock.

स्कंधावार [*nm*] royal camp/pavilion.

स्कूल [*nm*] a school.

स्ख/लन [*nm*] a lapse, slip; discharge; ~लन, वीर्य discharge of the semen.

स्टेशन [*nm*] a station; -मास्टर station master.

स्टैंड [*nm*] a stand.

स्तंभ [*nm*] a column; pillar; stem; stupefaction, torpor.

स्तंभन [*nm*] retention; astringency; restraining, stopping, arresting.

स्तंभित [*a*] stupefied, benumbed; wonder-struck,flabbergasted.

स्तन [*nm*] the female breast; udder; ~धारी a mammal.

स्तन्य [*nm*] milk [of the breast]; [*a*] contained in the breast.

स्तब्ध [*a*] stupefied; stilled; stunned, flabbergasted; spastic; hence ~ता/त्व.

स्तर [*nm*] standard, level; layer, stratum/strata; fold; grade; स्तरित/स्तरीकृत stratified; graded; levelled; स्तरीकरण levellizing; stratification; स्तरीय levelled; stratified.

स्तव [*nm*] praise, eulogy, panegyric.

स्तवक [*nm*] a bunch of flowers, bouquet; chapter of a book.

स्तव/न [*nm*] praising/praise, eulogy, panegyric; hence ~नीय.

स्तुति [*nf*] prayer, invocation; eulogy, praise.

स्तुत्य [*nm*] laudable, praise worthy, admirable.

स्तूप [*nm*] a [Buddhistic] monument [generally of a pyramidal or dome-like form and erected over the sacred relics of the Buddha or on spots consecrated as the scenes of his acts].

स्तोत्र [*nm*] a hymn [of praise]; eulogism, doxology.

स्त्री [*nf*] a woman, female; -जाति womenfolk; ~त्व womanhood, feminity/feminality; -प्रसंग/भोग/समागम/सेवन sexual intercourse; ~लिंग feminine [gender].

स्त्रैण [*a*] effeminate; feminine, womanish/womanly; henpecked.

स्थ—a Sanskrit suffix used in the sense of situated, residing, fixed, present or engaged, etc. [as तटस्थ, शीर्षस्थ, स्वस्थ etc.]

स्थगन [*nm*] postponement; adjournment; -प्रस्ताव adjournment motion.

स्थगित [*a*] postponed; adjourned.

स्थल [*nm*] land; place; site, location, venue; field [as as युद्धस्थल battlefield]; ~चर/चारी terrestrial; living on land.

स्थली [*nf*] land; place; spot, site; field [as युद्ध~]; ~य terrestrial, pertaining to land.

स्थविर [*nm*] a Buddhist monk.

स्थान [*nm*] place, spot; site; space, room; accommodation; post; position, station; premises, venue; residence; locality.

स्थानांत/र [*nm*] transfer; another or different place/position/post; displacement; hence ~रथ; रित.

स्थानापन्न [*a* and *nm*] acting, officiating; a substitute; locurs tenens.

स्थानिक [*a*] local; resident; endemic.

स्थानीकृत [*a*] localised.

स्थानीय [*a*] local, endemic; colloquial.

स्थापत्य [*nm*] architecture; -कला architecture.

स्थापना [*f*] propounding; setting up, founding, establishing; installing [an idol].

स्थापित [*a*] propounded; founded, established, instituted, set up; fixed, placed; erected; installed.

स्थायित्व [*nm*] permanency; stability, durability; ~ कारी stabiliser.

स्थायिवत् [*a*] quasi-permanent, as good as permanent.

स्थायी [*a*] permanent; stable, lasting, durable; regular, steady; the first part/line of a song usually confined to the lower and middle octavo and repeated again and again; —भाव enduring emotion, lasting state of mind [in Indian Poetics, the emotions that are enduring are called स्थायी भाव [as compared with संचारी भाव which are fleeting]].

स्थावर [*a*] immovable; stable, stationary; -जंगम immovable and movable.

स्थित [*a*] situated, located, placed; circumstanced.

स्थिति [*nf*] position; situation, location; place, site; state, condition, stage; phase; status, set-up; attitude.

स्थिर [*a*] stable, firm; steady; still, unmoved, motionless, immobile; constant; stationary; quiescent, calm, pacific; inflexible; hence ~चित्त/चिता/बुद्धि/मति/मना; ~ता/त्व steadiness, stability; quiescence, poise.

स्थिरीकरण [*nm*] stabilization.

स्थूल [*a*] plump, fat, bulky, corpulent; thick; massive; rough, crude, gross; hence ~ता/त्व.

स्थैतिक [*a*] static.

स्थैर्य [*nm*] steadiness, firmness stability.

स्नात/क [*nm*] a graduate; bachelor [as कला-]; ~कोत्तर postgraduate.

स्नान [*nm*] bath, ablution; ~गृह a bath, bathroom.

स्नानागार [*nm*] see स्नानगृह [under स्नान].

स्नायविक [*a*] nervous, pertaining to sinews/nerves, ligamentary.

स्नायु [*nm*] nerves, sinews, ligament.

स्निग्ध [*a*] affectionate; smooth, glossy; oily, greasy; hence ~ता.

स्नेह [*nm*] love, affection; oil, oily substance; -पात्र object of love, beloved; -योग्य lovable.

स्नेही [*nm*] a lover; [*a*] loving, affectionate.

स्पं/दन [*nm*] vibration, pulsation, throb[bing]; hence ~दित.

स्प/र्धा [*nf*] rivalry, envy; hence ~र्धी.

स्पर्श [*nm*] touch, contact, feel; -ज्ञान feeling.

स्पर्शेन्द्रिय [*nf*] sense of touch, the skin.

स्पष्ट [*a*] clear, vivid, lucid; evident, distinct; positive, unambiguous, apparent; obvious; articulate, conspicuous; intelligible; express; blunt, categorical, point blank; plain; ~तया plainly, clearly, lucidly; obviously; ~ता clarity, clearness, vividness, lucidity; obviousness; openness.

स्पष्टी/करण [*nm*] clarification; explanation; hence ~कृत.

स्पृश्य [*a*] touchable, perceptible through touch.

स्पृहणीय [*a*] covetable, worth craving for; hence ~ता.

स्पृ/हा [*nf*] covetousness, craving, wistful.

स्फटिक [nm] crystal, quartz.

स्फी/त [*a*] inflated; ~ति inflation.

स्फुट [*a*] miscellaneous; distinct; manifest; apparent; hence ~ता.

स्फु/रण [*nm*] spurt; throbbing, pulsation; scintillation, twitch; hence ~ रित [*a*].

स्फुलिंग [*nm*] a spark.

स्फूर्ति [*nf*] agility, smartness, quickness; tone.

स्मर [*nm*] Cupid—the god of love.

स्मरण [*nm*] memory; remembrance, recollection; पत्र/पत्रक a reminder; -शक्ति memory; स्मरणीय memorable.

स्मारक [*nm*] a monument, memorial.

स्मित [*nm*] a smile; [a] smiling.

स्मिति [*nf*] a smile.

स्मृति [*nf*] memory, remembrance; books of traditional code of Hindu law [as मनुस्मृति, याज्ञवल्क्य स्मृति, etc.] said to be 18 in number.

स्यंदन [*nm*] a chariot.

स्यात् [*ind*] perhaps.

स्यापा [*nm*] mourning, bewailing on a [relative's] death.

स्याह [*a*] black, dark.

स्याही [*nf*] ink; darkness, blackness; ~दान an inkpot; ~सोख a blotting paper.

स्रष्टा [*nm*] creator, maker; the Creator [of the universe].

स्राव [*nm*] flow, oozing; miscarriage.

स्रोत [*nm*] source, resource; a stream, current; ~स्विनी a river/stream.

स्व [*pro*] one's own, personal; self; ~त्व [one's] due.

स्वकीय [*a*] own, one's own, personal.

स्वकीया [*nm*] [In Indian Poetics] a loyal heroine; wife.

स्वगत [*a*] aside, speaking to oneself.

स्वचालित [*a*] automatic.

स्वच्छंद [*a*] self-willed; unrestrained.

स्वच्छ [*a*] clean, clear, neat; pure; transparent; hence ~ता.

स्वजन [*nm*] kith and kin, kinsfolk.

स्वतंत्र [*a*] independent, free, sui juris, autonomous; unrestrained, uncontrolled; separate; ~ता independence, freedom, liberty.

स्वतः [*adv*] of one's own accord, voluntarily; spontaneously; ipso facto; self.

स्व/त्व [*nm*] one's due, right; copyright; ~त्वाधिकारी owner, master; copyright-holder.

स्वदेश [*nm*] one's own country, motherland, homeland, native land: -प्रेम patriotism; -भक्ति patriotism.

स्वदेशी ~ **य** [*a*] native, indigenous, belonging to one's own country.

स्वधर्म [*nm*] one's own duty/religion.

स्वनाम [*nm*] one's own name; having a reputation through one's own self; ~धन्य celebrated [through one's own self].

स्वप्न [*nm*] a dream; ~दर्शी a dreamer, dreamy; a dream-visionary; ~, दिवा day-dreaming; ~दोष emission, pollution nocturnal; ~द्रष्टा see ~दर्शी; -लोक dreamland, dreamworld.

स्वप्निल [*a*] dreamy.

स्वभाव [*nm*] nature; temperament, disposition; habit; ~तः naturally, by nature; ~सिद्ध natural, innate.

स्वयं [*adv*] by oneself, of one's own accord; personally; automatically; ~प्रमाण/प्रमाणित self-evident; self-proved; ~वर lit. self-choice —an ancient custom where in a bride chose her husband of her own accord, selection by a bride of her husband from amongst a galaxy of suitors; ~सिद्ध a truism, an axiom; axiomatic; self-evident; ~सिद्ध a postulate, an axiom; ~सेवक a volunteer.

स्वयमेव [*adv*] by oneself; of one's own accord; in person.

स्वर [*nm*] a vowel; sound, voice; tone; gamut; note; ~बद्ध rhythmic, moulded in a rhythm; -भंग soreness/hoarseness [of the throat]; loss of voice; -माधुर्य melody; -यंत्र larynx; -लहरी melody; -संगति harmony of musical note; vowel harmony; -संधि [in Grammar] fusion of adjacent vowels into one; -सप्तक the gamut, seven notes of music; —चढ़ाना to raise the voice or the musical note; —साधना to practise mastery over musical notes.

स्वरांत [*a*] ending in a vowel; —अक्षर an open syllable.

स्वराघात [*nm*] pitch; accent.

स्वराज्य [*nm*] independence; autonomy; home-rule, self-government.

स्वराष्ट्र [*nm*] homeland, one's own country.

स्वरूप [*nm*] shape, form; appearance; character, nature.

स्वर्ग [*nm*] paradise, heaven, abode of gods; ~वास heavenly abode—death; ~ होना to die, to pass away; ~वासी late; —सिधारना to die; to pass away.

स्वर्गारोहण [*nm*] ascendance into the heaven/paradise, death.

स्वर्गिक [*a*] divine, transcendental; late.

स्वर्गीय [*a*] late, dead.

स्वर्ण [*nm*] gold; ~कार a goldsmith; -जयंती golden jubilee; -युग the golden age.

स्वर्णिम [*a*] golden.

स्वल्प [*a*] little, very little; very small.

स्ववश [*a*] under one's own control.

स्वशासन [*nm*] self-rule, home-rule, self government.

स्वस्ति [*int*] [a word of benediction] May you be happy!; [*nf*] well-being, prosperity.

स्वस्तिक [*nm*] a benedictory or auspicious mark. [卐].

स्वस्थ [*a*] healthy, hale; robust; ~चित sane, mentally healthy.

स्वाँग [*nm*] mimicry; farce, sham; —बनाना to mimic; —भरना, का to impersonate for, to mimic.

स्वागत [*nm*] welcome, reception; -कक्ष reception room; -समिति reception committee; -समारोह a reception.

स्वातंत्र्य [*nm*] freedom, independence, liberty.

स्वा/ति, ~ती [nf] the fifteenth of the twenty-seven traditional nakshatras; ~ बिंदु a rain drop in the स्वाति नक्षत्र.

स्वाद [*nm*] taste, flavour, relish.

स्वादिष्ट [*a*] tasteful, delicious, dainty, palatable, relishable; hence ~ता.

स्वादु [*a*] see स्वादिष्ट.

स्वाधीन [*a*] free, independent, sui juris; ~ ता freedom, independence, liberty.

स्वाध्या/य [*nm*] self study; ~ यी studious.

स्वानुभूति [*nf*] self-experience, personal/individual sensibilities.

स्वाभाविक [*a*] natural; innate, inherent, inborn; ~ ता naturality, inartificiality.

स्वाभिमा/न [*nm*] self-respect; ~ नी self-respecting.

स्वामित्व [*nm*] ownership, proprietorship.

स्वामिनी [*nf*] mistress; female proprietor, proprietress; patroness.

स्वा/मी [*nm*] master, lord; proprietor, owner; husband; a title used with the name of saints and ascetics [as स्वामी दयानंद]; ~ मिभक्त loyal, faithful [to the master].

स्वायत्त [*a*] autonomous; ~ ता autonomy.

स्वार्थ [*nm*] selfishness, self-interest; -त्याग self-denial; ~ त्यागी selfless; ~ पर/परायण selfish, self-seeking; ~ लिप्सा self interested-ness; ~ वाद egoism; ~ वादी an egoist; egoistic; ~ साधक a self-seeker; ~ साधन (ना) self-seeking; -सिद्धि accomplishment of self-interest; ~ हीन selfless.

स्वार्थी [*a* and *nm*] selfish, self-seeking; an egoist.

स्वावलं/बन [*nm*] self-reliance; self-sufficiency; voluntarism; hence ~ बिता; ~ बी self-relying, self-sufficient.

स्वास्थ्य [*nm*] health.

स्वाहा [ind] a word uttered while offering oblation to sacrificial fire; [*a*] burnt; -करना to ruin/destroy, to burn to ashes.

स्वीकार [*a*] accepted; confessed; granted; [*nm*] acceptance; confession; hence—करना/~ना [*v*].

स्वीकारोक्ति [*nf*] confession.

स्वीकारना [*v.t.*] to accept.

स्वीकार्य [*adj*] deserving or requiring acceptance, see स्वीकार.

स्वीकृति [*nf*] acceptance, sanction, approbation; acknowledgement, consent.

स्वेच्छ [*a*] arbitrary; voluntary; ~ या arbitrarily; voluntarily.

स्वेच्छा [*nf*] one's own will, free will. ~ चारी self-willed, autocratic; arbitrary.

स्वैच्छिक [*a*] voluntary; arbitrary; hence ~ ता.

स्वेद [*nm*] sweat, perspiration.

स्वेदन [*nm*] sweating.

स्वेदित [*adj*] steamed; made dim from sweat or steam the sight.

स्वैर [*a*] licentious, self-willed; ~ ता licentiousness, self-willedness; ~ वृत्ति liberum arbitrium, self-willedness.

स्वैराचार [*nm*] licentious/self-willed conduct, licentiousness.

ह

ह—the last and the thirty-third letter of the Devanagari: alphabet—aspirated in sound.

ह - देवनागरी वर्णमाला का तैंतीसवाँ और उष्मवर्ण का अन्तिम व्यंजन वर्ण है। इसका उच्चारण स्थान कठ है।

हँकड़ना [*v.i.*] to bellow; to low cattle.

हंगामा [*nm*] uproar, tumult; affray, riotous scene.

हंटर [*nm*] a whip, flog, lash.

हंडा [*nm*] a huge brass pot [for storing water etc.]

हँड़ि(डि)या [*nf*] a small earthen pot.

हंडी [*nf*] हँड़िया.

हंत [*int*] an interjectional word for expressing sorrow, regret, grief, etc.

हंता [*nm*] a slayer, murderer.

हंतव्य [*adj*] to be struck down, or killed; deserving death.

हंस [*nm*] a swan, goose; noble/liberated soul; the sun; ~ गमन/गति graceful gait as that of a swan; ~ गामिनी [a woman] blessed with a graceful [swan like] gait; ~ वाहिनी the goddess Saraswati:.

हँसना [*v*] to laugh; to deride, to ridicule; to joke; हँसकर बात उड़ाना to laugh away; हँसते-बोलते while joking, in jokes; हँसते-हँसते पेट में बल पड़ जाना to laugh into cramps; हँसते-हँसते लोट-पोट हो जाना to burst into an uncontrollable fit of laughter; हँसना-बोलना to exchange pleasantries; to exchange jokes, to talk happily.

हँसनुआ [*nm*] reg. a laughing-stock.

हँसमुख [*a*] gay, cheerful, having a smiling face.

हँसली [*nf*] the collar-bone; an ornament worn around the neck.

हँसाई [*nf*] derision, ridicule.

हँसिया [*nm*] a sickle.

हँसी [*nm*] laughter; joke; derision, ridicule; -खुशी happily; happiness; -खेल an easy job; fun, fun and frolic; -ठट्ठा an easy job; joking and jesting; -उड़ाना to make fun of, to ridicule/deride; —में उड़ाना/उड़ा देना to laugh off; —में टालना to laugh away; —समझना to treat as an easy job or as a joke.

हँसोड़ [*a*] jolly, humorou; [*nm*] jester.

हँसाऊ [*adj*] laughable, ridiculous.

हक [*a*] stunned, still; [*nm*] palpitation.

हक़ [*nm*] right; entitlement; due return [as नमक का हक़ अदा करना); ~ दार rightful, entitled; one who has a right; —अदा करना to perform one's duty;—लड़ना to fight for one's right;—मारना to deprive of one's due; to usurp ones's dues; to usurp one's right; —में in respect of; for.

हकबकाना [*v*] to be stunned, to be non-plussed.

हकला [*a* and *nm*] stammering; one who stammers; a stammerer; hence ~ पन, ~ हट.

हकलाना [*v.i.*] to stutter, to stammer, हकलाकर बोलना.

हकारना [*v.t.*] हँकारना.

हका/र [*nm*] the letter 'ह' and its sound; ~ रांत [a word] ending in ह.

हक़ारत [*nf*] contempt.

हक़ीक़त [*nf*] reality, fact, truth.

हकीम [*nm*] a physician [trained in the unani system].

हकीमी [*nm*] medical, the practice or profession of medicine, — करना, to practise medicine.

हक्काबक्का [*a*] stunned, stupefied.

हगना [*v*] to discharge faeces.

हगाना [*v.t.*] to cause to defecate; to get a child to relieve itself. to act as a purgative.

हगास [*nf*] a feeling like discharing faeces; inclination to evacuate the bowels.

हज [*nm*] a pilgrimage to Mecca.

हज़म [*a*] digested; usurped; —करना to digest; to usurp, to misappropriate.

हज़रत [*int*] a vocative term of honour, Sir; [*nm*] a title for eminent men; prophet Mohammed; [*a*] mischievous, cunning.

हजामत [*nf*] shaving; haircutting.

हज़ार [*a*] one thousand; [*nm*] the number one thousand.

हजारों [*a*] thousands.

हजूम [*nm*] a crowd, multitude.

हज्जाम [*nm*] a barber.

हटना [*v*] to move/go away; to recede; to withdraw; hence हटाना.

हट्टा-कट्टा [*a*] strong and sturdy, well-built; hale and hearty.

हठ [*nm*] obstinacy, stubbornness; ~ धर्मी intransigence; ~ योग a type of Yoga; ~ योगी one who practises हठयोग;—रखना to yield or submit to ones's obstinate demand.

हठात् [*ind*] forcibly, suddenly, all of a sudden.

हठी [*a*] obstinate, stubborn.

हठीला [*a*] refractory; of obstinate disposition, temperamentally stubborn; hence ~ पन.

हड़ [*nf*] myrobalan; an allomorph of हाड़ used as the first member of certain compound words; ~ कंप turmoil, panic; terror.

हड़ता/ल [*nf*] a strike; ~ ली a striker.

हड़पना [*v*] to swallow, to gulp; to purloin, to usurp.

हड़बड़ाना [*v*] to be impetuous; to act hastily/ in a hurry; to be non-plussed/confused/ perplexed.

हड़बड़िया [*a*] impetuous, hasty, rashness.

हड़बड़ी [*nf*] impetuosity, hastiness, rashness.

हड्डी [*nf*] a bone; —खुजाना to feel like being thrashed, a beating to be imminent; -पसली एक करना to thrash thoroughly.

हत [*a*] killed; stuck; ~बुद्धि rendered senseless/ witless, stupid; ~प्रभ out of wits, non-plussed; ~भाग्य/भागा/भागी unfortunate, luckless.

हतक [*nf*] insult; defamation; -इज्जत defamation.

हता/श [*a*] despondent, hopeless; ~शा despondency, dejection.

हताहत [*a*] casualties, killed and wounded.

हतोत्साह [*a*] demoralised, disheartened.

हत्था [*nm*] a handle; butt, batten; arm [of a chair].

हत्थमहत्था [*nf*] hand to hand fight [ing].

हत्थी [*nf*] a handle; palm [of the hand]; —टेकना to yield, to submit; to lend support.

हत्थे [*ind*] in hand; —चढ़ना/पड़ना to fall into the clutches [of]; —लगना to obtain, to acquire.

हत्या [*nf*] murder, assassination; —सवार होना to be roused to the point of readiness to kill; to be murderously enraged; —सिर मढ़ना to level an accusation; to impose an affliction/ botheration.

हत्या/रा [*nm*] a murderer, an assassin; hence ~रिन, ~री [*nf*].

हथ—an allomorph of हाथ [as in हथकड़ी] and हाथी [as in हथसार]; as it appears in many compound words; ~कंडा sleight; trick, tactics, intrigue; ~कड़ी handcuffs; ~गोला a hand-grenade; ~छुट in the habit of striking forthwith out of provocation.

हथिनी [*nf*] a she-elephant.

हथियाना [*v*] to usurp, to grab, to seize, to acquire by force.

हथियार [*nm*] a weapon, arms; ~घर an arsenal, armoury; ~बंद armed, equipped with arms.

हथेली [*nf*] palm of the hand; —पर जान रखना या लेना to risk one's life; —पर सरसों जमाना to accomplish a task within an impossible span of time; —पर सरसों नहीं जमती Rome was not built in a day.

हथौड़ा [*nm*] a hammer, malleus.

हद [*nf*] limit/limitation, boundary; extent; ~बंदी delimitation.

हनन [*nm*] slaughter, killing, assassination, murder.

हफ़्ता [*nm*] a week; ~तेवार weekly.

हब्शी [*nm*] a Negro.

हम [*pro*] we—plural form of the first person pronoun मैं; [a] similar; equal; together; ~उम्र contemporary; of equal age; ~जोली associate or companion of the same age-group; ~दर्द sympathetic; a sympathizer; ~दर्दी sympathy; ~पेशा co-professional; ~राह travelling together; ~राही a co-traveller; ~वतन a compatriot; ~वार even; ~सफर a co-traveller, travelling together; ~साया a neighbour.

हमल [*nm*] conception, pregnancy.

हमला [*nm*] attack, assault; ~वर an invader, an assailant, aggressor.

हमारा [*pro*] possessive form of हम—our, ours.

हमें [*pro*] the objective and dative form of the first person plural pronoun हम —to us.

हमेशा [*ind*] always, ever.

हम्माम [*nm*] a warm-bath, bagnio.

हया [*nf*] shame; sense of shame; modesty; ~दार modest; ~दारी modesty.

हर [*a*] each, every; [*nm*] a denominator; a suffix imparting the meaning of one who or that which takes away, deprives, seizes; ~चंद however much; ~जाई flirt, disloyal [woman]; —तरह in every way/manner; ~दम always, ever; —फ़नमौला jack of all trades.

हरकत [*nf*] movement, activity; mischief.

हरकारा [*nm*] a courier; dak-runner.

हरगिज [*ind*] ever, under any circumstances; —नहीं never, under no circumstances.

हरड़ [*nf*] myrobalan.

हरण [*nm*] kidnapping, abduction, forcible carrying away, seizing; as a suffix it imparts the meaning of one who or that which carries away, seizes or takes by force, rids, etc; hence हर्ता.

हरताल [*nf*] yellow orpiment.

हरदा [*nm*] yellow rust.

हरना [*v*] to kidnap, to abduct, to carry away by force, to seize.

हरबा [*nm*] arms, tools.

हरम [*nm*] harem, female apartment.

हरमज़दगी [*nf*] bastardy, rascality, scoundrelism.

हरसिंगार [*nm*] a particular sweet-smelling flower and its plant.

हरा [*a*] green, verdant; fresh; gay, delighted; ~पन. greenness; verdancy; -भरा verdant; prosperous, flourishing; gay; —होना, (मन) to be delighted, to be gay.

हराना [*v*] to defeat, to vanquish.

हराम [*a*] ill-begotten; unlawful, forbidden; improper; ~खोर subsisting on ill-begotten resources or on other's earnings; slothful, basely indolent; ~खोरी subsistence on ill-begotten resources; slothfulness, base indolence; ~ज़ादा ill-begotten; bastard; rascal, scoundrel; hence ~जादी; ~जादापन see हरमज़दगी; —कर देना to make[things] difficult/impossible; —का ill-begotten; —का माल illegitimate earnings; —की कमाई ill-begotten earnings/money.

हरामी [*a*] ill-begotten, illegitimate; unscrupulous; doing just nothing, utterly indolent; [*nm*] a bastard, rascal scoundrel; ~पन illegitimacy; unscrupulousness; utter indolence.

हरारत [*nf*] temperature; feverishness.

हरावल [*nm*] vanguard.

हरि [*nm*] Lord Vishnū/Krishnā: —इच्छा the will of God; ~ बलवान inevitable is the will of God; -कीर्तन individual or collective singing of the eulogies of हरि; ~नाम name[s] of हरि; ~ स्मरण remembering the name of हरि; -स्मरण remembering हरि.

हरिजन [*nm*] an untouchable.

हरिण [*nm*] a deer; hence ~णी [*nf*].

हरित [*a*] green, verdant; delighted, gay.

हरियल [*nm*] greenish; unripe [as a fruit].

हरियाना [*v*] to turn green, to be full of verdure; to be delighted; [*nm*] one of the northern Hindi-Speaking states of the Union of India.

हरियाली [*nf*] greenery; verdure; vegetation.

हरीतिमा [*nf*] greenery, verdure, verdancy.

हरे [*int*] O God! —कृष्ण O Krishnā!, O God~; —राम O Ra:m, O God!

ह/र्जे, ~र्जा [*nm*] harm; loss, damage.

हर्ज़ाना [*nm*] damages, compensation, indemnity.

हर्फ़ [*nm*] a letter [of the alphabet]; -ब-हर्फ़ literal; letter by letter.

हर्र [*nf*] myrobalan; —लगे न फिटकरी रंग चोखा आये to invest nothing, to gain everything.

हर्ष [*nm*] joy, jubilation, mirth, delight, happiness; ~ध्वनि/नाद/स्वन cry of joy/jubilation; ~विह्वल overwhelmed by joy.

हर्षातिरेक [*nm*] ecstasy, rapture.

हर्षातिशय [*nm*] see हर्षातिरेक.

हर्षित [*a*] joyous, delighted, cheerful.

हर्षोन्माद [*nm*] ecstasy, rapture.

हलंत [*a*] [a word] ending in a consonant [and not a vowel].

हल [*nm*] a plough; solution; ~जीवी/ a farmer/ peasant; ~धर/~वाहा a farmer, peasant.

हलक़ [*nm*] the throat; wind pipe; —पर छुरी फेरना to cut somebody's throat; to cause immense loss; —से नीचे उतरना to be comprehensible [as बात], to appear reasonable.

हलका [*a*] light; cheap; thin [as कपड़ा]; faint; [*nm*] a circle, area; ~पन lightness; cheapness; thinness; —करना to insult, to cause humiliation; —पड़ना to prove lesser; —बनना/ होना to be cheap; to be disgraced.

हलक़ान [*a*] troubled, bothered.

हलकोर [*nf*] a massive billow.

हलचल [*nm*] commotion, hustle; agitation, movement; —मचना a commotion to be created; —होना movement to take place; commotion to be caused.

हलदिया [*a*] yellow; [*nm*] jaundice; a variety of big yellowish frog.

हलदी [*nf*] turmeric, curcuma; —के हाथ होना marriage to take place; —लगाकर बैठना to sit idle.

हलफ़ [*nm*] an oath; ~दरोगी self-contradiction; ~नामा an affidavit.

हलफ़न [adv] on oath.

हलफ़िया [*a*] see हलफ़ी.

हलफ़ी [*a*] [statement etc. given] on oath.

हलवा [*nm*] a typical Indian pudding; ~सोहन a celebrated Indian sweetmeat.

हलवाई [*nm*] a sweetmeat manufacturer/seller, confectioner.

हलाक [*a*] slaughtered, slain; —-करना to slaughter, to slay; hence —होना.

हलाल [*a*] legitimate; hard-earned, well-begotten; [*nm*] an animal slaughtered in accordance with conventional prescription; ~खोर subsisting on scrupulous earnings/well-begotten earnings; a sweeper; hence ~खोरी; —करके खाना to subsist on hard-earned money; —करना to slaughter in the conventionally prescribed manner; to do slowly to death —का legitimate; scrupulous, well-begotten; —की कमाई hard-earned income.

हलाहल [*nm*] deadly poison.

हलोर [*nf*] a heave; billow.

हल् [*nm*] a pure consonant; a symbol appended at the foot of a letter to denote devowelized consonant [्].

हल्दी [*nf*] see हलदी.

हल्ला [*nm*] noise, uproar, tumult, tumultuous activity; -गुल्ला uproarious scene, tumult and uproar; —बोलना to raid; —मचाना to create a noise/uproar; to cause a tumultuous scene.

हवन [*nm*] a fire sacrifice; ~कुंड a sacrificial pit.

हवलदार [*nm*] a havildar; ~री the job or office of a havildar.

हवस [*nf*] lust, passion, passionate longing; —बुझना a passion to subside, longing to die out.

हवा [*nf*] air, wind, breeze; ~खोरी a stroll, walk; ~दार airy; well-ventilated; -पानी climate; ~बाज़ an airman; a tall-talker, braggadocio; ~बाज़ी airmanship; tall talk, bragging; ~मार anti-aircraft; ~मार तोप an anti-aircraft gun; —उड़ना a rumour to be afloat; news to go round; hence —उड़ाना; —का रुख जानना to know which way the wind is blowing; —का रुख़ देखना to wait and watch; to move according to the whirligig of time; —का रुख़ बताना to forecast the shape of things to come; —के घोड़े पर सवार होना to be in a terrible hurry; —के रुख़ जाना to move in the direction of the wind; to move according to the times; —खाना to go for a walk, to enjoy fresh air; to fail to achieve; —गरम होना the air to have a touch of warmth; to be in great demand; —देना to instigate, to provoke; —पलटना the shape of things to undergo a change; the direction of the wind to change; —पीकर/फाँक कर रहना to go without meals [said ironically]; ~बंद airtight; —बँधना the air to become still; a reputation/name to be earned; hence —बाँधना; —बिगड़ना the atmosphere to be polluted/ poisoned; to be in a tight corner; —भर जाना to be inflated; to be puffed up, to be full of pride; —लगना to feel the touch of air; to be possessed [by an evil spirit]; to be puffed up, to be influenced by; —से

बातें करना to be moving at a terrible speed; to talk in the air; —से लड़ना to be out to pick up a quarrel; to fight without any provocation/without the existence of a second party; to be too truculent; —हो जाना to disappear; to flee to run away.

हवाई [*a*] aerial; false, imaginary; —अड्डा an aerodrome, airport; —करतब aerobatics; —किले बनाना to build castles in the air —जहाज an aeroplane, aircraft; —डाक airmail; —मार्ग/रास्ता airways, air-passage; —यात्रा air journey; —हमला an air raid/attack; हवाइयाँ उड़ना, मुँह पर the face to lose all lustre, to appear non-plussed.

हवाल [*nm*] conditions; news.

हवा/ला [*nm*] a reference; trust, custody; ~ला देना to cite a reference; ~ले करना to entrust, to hand over [to].

हवालात [*nf*] lock-up, [police] custody; ~ती under [police] custody, in [police] lock-up.

हवाली-मवाली [*nm*] [in a derogatory sense] comrades and companions.

हवास [*nm*] senses [used only as the second member in the compound होश-हवास].

हविष्य [*a* and *nm*] [oblations] offered to gods or to the sacrificial fire.

हवेली [*nf*] a [palatial] mansion.

हव्य [*a* and *nm*] [fit to be offered as] oblation [to the sacrificial fire].

हशमत [*nf*] glory and grandeur; huge paraphernalia.

हश्र [*nm*] consequence, result.

हसद [*nf*] jealousy, malice.

हसरत [*nf*] wistfulness, longing, craving; —निकलना/पूरी होना a longing/craving to find its fulfilment; —निकालना to have it out; to see one's longing/craving materialised; —बाक़ी रहना a longing/craving to remain unfulfilled.

हसीन [*a*] beautiful, pretty; charming.

हस्त [*nm*] a hand; trunk of an elephant; —कला handicraft;—कौशल manual skill; ~गत in hand, obtained, received; ~रेखा the lines of one's palm [supposed to signify one's destiny]; ~लिखित hand-written, in manuscript form; ~लिपि/लेख hand, handwriting; manuscript.

हस्तक्षेप [*nm*] interference.

हस्तां/तरण [*nm*] transfer transference; hence ~रित.

हस्ताक्षर [*nm*] signature; hand-writing.

हस्तामलक [*nm*] lit. 'the fruit or seed of the emblic myrobalan in the hand' —absolutely clear and readily comprehensible; ~वत् like—, clear and readily comprehensible.

हस्ती [*nf*] existence, being; worth; personage; [*nm*] an elephant; —मिटना to be ruined, to be forced out of existence; —होना to be existent; to be worth reckoning.

हस्ते [*ind*] through, through the agency of.

ह/स्ब [*ind*] according to, in accordance with; ~स्बे-मामूल as usual.

हाँ [*nf*] yes, yea; [ind] a word denoting agreement, fulfilment, affirmation etc.; हाँ-हाँ yes, yes; a word expressing negation/affirmation that would depend on its intonation; —में हाँ मिलाना to keep on flattering, to say 'yes' to everything to chime in.

हाँक [*nf*] bawling; calling aloud; ~ना to drive [an animal or an animal-driven vehicle]; to goad, to urge on; to call aloud.

हाँका [*nm*] in hunting, an uproar [through beating of drums, cans etc.] to drive the prey towards the spot where the hunter is seated.

हाँड़ी [*nf*] a small earthen pot.

हाँफना [*v*] to pant; to breathe heavily.

हाँफनी [*nf*] panting; —छूटना to start panting, to be breathing heavily.

हा [*int*] oh!, Gosh!, a particle expressive of pleasure, pain, regret, contempt, amazement, etc.

हाकि/म [*nm*] a ruler; boss; ~माना befitting a ruler/officer/boss; ~मी rule, ruling; work as an officer.

हाकी, हाँकी [*nf*] hockey.

हाजत [*nf*] need, requirement; pressure in the bowels.

हाज़मा [*nm*] digestion.

हाज़िर [*a*] present; ready; ~जवाब quick-witted, witty; hence ~जवाबी; -नाज़िर present and watching; —में हुज्जत नहीं to be in my hands is to be at your disposal.

हाज़िरी [*nf*] presence; attendance, roll call; breakfast; —देना to notify/intimate one's presence; —बजाना to dance attendance upon; —लेना to have the roll call, to mark attendance.

हाजी [*nm*] a Mohammedan who has been to the haj pilgrimage.

हाट [*nf*] a temporary and periodic market; [improvised] market-place, bazar, mart;-बाजार करना to go out making purchases, to go out marketing; —लगना marketing activity to commence; a bazar to come up.

हाड़ [*nm*] a bone; —पेलना to work assiduously/very hard.

हाता [*nm*] see अहाता.

हाथ [*nm*] a hand; manual skill; the skill to strike; turn in a game of cards; handle; arm [of a chair]; —आजमाना to try one's hand; —आना to have in hand, —उठाना, किसी पर to beat, to inflict a beating; —उठा बैठना to strike all of a sudden; —उतरना the arm-bone to be dislocated; —ऊँचा रहना to have an upper hand; to be in a position to oblige; —कट जाना to be helpless, to be helpless on account of a commitment; —का झूठा dishonest in dealings; in the habit of pinching things; unreliable in money matters; —कानों पर रखना to vow not to repeat; to vow never to do again; to swear incompetence to do; —का सच्चा honest in one's dealings, reliable in money matters; —की सफाई manual skill; nimbleness of the hand; finnesse in one's stroke; —खाना to be slapped/struck; —खाली जाना a stroke/chance to be missed; a trick/device not to work; —खाली न होना to be busy; to have no time; —खाली होना to be penniless/in utter penury, —खींचना to withdraw support/active association; to refrain from financial aid/support; —खुजलाना to be a good augury for incoming money; to feel like slapping/beating, —खुलना to be bounteous; to be a spendthrift; to have money in hand; to be in the habit of striking readily; — चढ़ना to fall into the clutches of, to come under the control [of]: —चलना to be nimble-fingered to be quick at work; to be in the habit of beating/striking [others]; —चूमना lit. to kiss one's hand —to be all praise for somebody's handiwork; —छोड़ना to begin to strike; —जड़ना to implant a slap, to strike; —जमना a slap to be implanted, a stroke to be given; to have one's hand firmly [in]; finnesse/perfection in a handwork to be acquired; hence —जमाना; —जोड़ देना to fold hands [—as symbolic of acceptance of defeat]; to beg pardon; —जोड़ना to salute by folded hands; to present one's compliments, to entreat, to make an entreaty; to request forgiveness; [ironically] to have nothing to do any more; —झाड़ना to give a slap; to go on striking; —झूठा पड़ना to miss a stroke; an expert hand to lose its efficaciousness; to be rendered incapable for manual work; —डालना (किसी काम में) to take in hand, to undertake a work; —तंग होना to be tight, to be in a financial stringency; —दिखाना to give a proof of one's efficacy, to get one's palm read [by a palmist]; hence —देखना; —धोकर पीछे पड़ना to go heart and soul after; to concentrate all efforts to inflict harm on; —धोना,—धो बैठना to lose, to write off; —न धरने देना to yield to no persuasion/entreaties/arguments; to allow no quarter whatever; —पकड़ते पहुँचा पकड़ना to try to turn small concession into big liberties; to strive for ever bigger benefits out of someone; —पड़ जाना to fall into the hands [of], to come one's way; to obtain without effort; —दबना to be in a crisis; to be in hot waters; to be in a tight corner; —पर कुरान/पर गंगाजली रखना to swear by the Qoran/by the holy water of the Ganges, —पर हाथ धर कर बैठ जाना to be complacent; to be frustrated; —पसारना to beg; to make an entreaty for help; —पसारे जाना to go empty-handed [to the other world]; -पाँव का जवाब देना to be incapacitated, to be rendered incapable [through disease or old age]; -पाँव चलना to be industrious; to be capable to work; -पाँव ठंडे होना to be on the verge of death; to pass away; to be stupefied/stunned; -पाँव फूलना to lose one's wits; -पाँव फैलाना to extend one's gather more and more power;

to grow; -पाँव बचाना to keep oneself secure, to keep out of risk; -पाँव मारना to make [frantic] efforts; to try one's level best; -पाँव सीधे करना to relax the limbs; पीले करना to give away in marriage; —फेर देना to pinch, to pilfer; —फेरना to fondle, to caress; —फैलाना to beg, to extend a needy hand for help; —बाँटना to cooperate, to help; to extend cooperation; —बढ़ाना to extend a hand; —बाँधें (खड़े) रहना to be always in attendance, to be at the service of; —बिकना/बिकाना to be a slave to, to be in utter subservience; —बेचना to sell out to; —भर का कलेजा होना to have immense courage; to be in raptures; —भर की जबान होना to be too intemperate in speech, to be insolently outspoken; —भरना the hands to be wearied; —भेजना, (के) to send through; —मँजना to acquire a finnesse [in doing a thing]; —मलना to be remorseful; —मारना to pinch; to case a bet; to acquire control over/possession of; —मिलाना to shake hands [with]; —में लेना to take up; —में सनीचर होना to be prone to lose everything; —में हाथ hand in hand; —में हाथ देना to give away in marriage; —में होना के to be under the sway of; —रँगना to stain one's hands with a sin/misdeed; to take a bribe; —रखना, सिर पर to give protection to; —लगाना to touch; to commence a work; to slap; —लगाये कुम्हलाना to be as tender as touch-me-not; —लगा मैला होना to be as shining as to be rendered untidy by mere touch; -साफ़ करना to polish off, to consume; to misappropriate; to put to death; —सिर पर रखना to swear by; —से जाना/निकलना to slip out of hand; to lose; —हिलाते आना to come empty-handed; —होना to have a hand in; (दोनों) हाथों समेटना to amass huge wealth; हाथों-हाथ from hand to hand; in no time; ~ बिक जाना to h ave a hot sale; हाथों-हाथ लेना to receive with great warmth; to extend a very cordial reception.

हाथा/पाई, ~बाँही [*nf*] a scuffle, skirmish, tussle.

हाथी [*nm*] an elephant; a jumbo; castle/rook [in the game of chess]; ~दाँत ivory; ~वान a mahout; —बाँधना to maintain an elephant; —हो जाना to become very corpulent/plump.

हादसा [*nm*] an accident, a mishap.

हानि [*nf*] loss; damage; detriment harm; ~कर/कारक/कारी damaging; harmful; detrimental.

हाफ़िज [*nm*] a protector; a Mohammedan who remembers the whole of the Qoran by heart.

हामिला [*a*] pregnant [woman].

हामी [*nf*] assent; acceptance; [*nm*] a supporter; champion [of]; ~दार an underwriter; ~दारी underwriting; —भरना to say' yes', to give assent [for].

हाय [*int*] oh! ah me!, alas!; also a particle expressive of mental or physical agony; [*nf*] curse [as किसी की हाय न लो]; -हाय see हाय; affliction; rush [of work etc.—as हर वक्त हाय-हाय पड़ी रहती है]; panic and confusion; -हाय करना to be rushed; to be afflicted; —करके रह जाना to be obliged to suffer mental or physical agony; —पड़ना a curse to come true.

हार [*nf*] defeat; loss; a garland, necklace; a suffix meaning one who or that which carries away per force or usurps, charms, etc; or else it denotes a doer [as सिरजनहार.]

हारना [*v*] to be defeated, to lose; to be wearied; हारा-थका worn and wearied.

हारमोनियम [*nm*] a harmonium, a music intrument

हारा —a suffix carrying the sense of a doer [as सिरजनहारा]; [a] defeated; wearied.

हार्दिक [*a*] cordial hearty.

हाल [*nm*] state, condition; account, news; a hoop, metallic tyre over a wooden wheel; turmoil; violent vibration/agitation, a hall; [a] present, current; ~चाल general condition, state of affairs; news; —का recent; fresh.

हाल/त [*nf*] state; condition; ~लात conditions, circumstances.

हालाँकि [*ind*] though, although.

हाला [*nf*] wine, liquor.

हाली [*a*] current, contemporary.

हाव [*nm*]; -भाव gestures, blandishments; amorous dalliance [of a woman].

हावी [*a*] dominant.

हाशिया [*nm*] margin; border.

हास [*nm*] laughter/laughing, derisive laughter; fun, joke; the abiding emotion of हास्य रस; -परिहास fun and humour.

हासिल [*a*] acquired, obtained; what is carried forward; —करना to acquire, to obtain; hence —होना.

हास्य [*nm*] humour; ridicule, fun; ~का/कारक/जनक humorous; provoking laughter; ~चित्र a cartoon; —चित्रकार a cartoonist; —भाव sense of humour; —रस the final and successful culmination of the sense of humour (हास्य) into a rasa; ~रसात्मक full of or abounding in हास्य रस.

हास्यापद [*a*] ludicrous, ridiculous, funny; hence ~ता [*nf*].

हास्योत्पादक [*a*] ludicrous, ridiculous, funny; hence ~ता [*nf*].

हाहा [*nf*] [sound produced by] loud laughter; entreaties, humble supplication; [int] a particle expressive of amazement, grief etc; -ठीठी joke and jest, fun and humour; -हीही see -ठीठी; ~ करना to have humour and hilarity; -हूहू loud laughter and hilarity; -करना/खाना to make humble entreaties/supplication.

हाहाकार [*nm*] loud lamentation, distressful commotion, tumult, uproar.

हिंडो/रा, ~ला [*nm*] a swing, sway.

हिंद [*nm*] India.

हिंदवी [*nf*] a name used for the Hindi language by mediaeval writers.

हिंदी [*nf*] the Hindi language; [*a*] Indian.

हिंदुत्व [*nm*] Hinduism; the state of being or characteristics of a Hindu.

हिंदुस्तान [*nm*] India.

हिंदुस्तानी [*a*] Indian; [*nm*] an Indian, native of India; [*nf*] a theoretically existent style of the Hindi language which is supposed to consist of current and simple words of whatever sources and is neither too much biased in favour of Perso-Arabic elements nor has any place for too much high-flown Sanskritized vocabulary.

हिंदुस्था/न [*nm*] India; ~नी [an] Indian.

हिंदू [*nm* and *a*] a Hindu; ~पन/~पना Hinduism; the state of being, or characteristics of, a Hindu.

हिंदोस्तान [*nm*] see हिंदुस्तान.

हिंदोस्तानी [*nm* and a] see हिंदुस्तानी.

हिंसक [*a*] [animate thing] violent; ferocious, fierce; [*nm*] a murderer, killer.

हिंसा [*nf*] violence; ~त्मक violent [act etc.].

हिंस्र [*a*] violent, fierce, ferocious; ~ता violence; fierceness.

हिकमत [*nf*] medical practice under the Unani system; a contrivance; manoeuvring; hence ~ती.

हिक़ारत [*nf*] contempt.

हिचक [*nf*] hitch, hesitation; shilly-shally.

हिचकना [v] to hesitate, to hitch; to shrink; to shilly-shally.

हिचकिचा/ना [v] see हिचकना; ~हट hesitation, hitch; shilly-shally.

हिचकी [*nf*] hiccup; —बँध जाना/हिचकियाँ बँध जाना/हिचकियाँ लेना to have a fit of hiccup; to have non-stop hiccuping; to sob bitterly.

हिचकोला [*nm*] a jerk; jolt.

हिजड़ा [*nm*] eunuch; [*a*] impotent.

हिजरी [*nf*] the Mohammedan era [which commences from the day of Prophet Mohammed's flight from Mecca to Medina on the 15th July, 622 A.D.].

हिज्जे [*nm*] spelling.

हिज्र [*nm*] separation.

हित [*nm*] welfare, well-being; interest; gain, benefit; ~कर/कारक/कारी beneficial; useful, advantageous; ~चिंतक a well-wisher, benefactor.

हिताहित [*nm*] good and bad.

हितू [*a*] see हितैषी.

हितैषी [*a* and *nm*] well-wishing; a well-wisher.

हिदायत [*nf*] instruction; ~नामा a manual of instructions, series of instructions.

हिनहिना/ना [*v*] to neigh, to whinny; ~हट neighing, whinnying.

हिना [*nf*] myrtle.

हिफ़ाजत [*nf*] protection, security, safety.

हिफ़ाजती [*nm*] protective.

हिफ़्ज [*a*] memorised, committed to memory.

हिम [*nm*] snow, ice; frost; ~कण a snow-particle; ~कर the moon; ~गिरि the Himalayas; ~नदी a glacier, an ice-river; ~पात/पात ice/snow-fall; -मानव snowman; ~युग the ice-age; ~वृष्टि snow-fall;—शैल an iceberg; ~श्वेत snowhite.

हिमवान [*nm*] the Himalayas.

हिमांशु [*nm*] [an epithet of] the moon.

हिमाक़त [*nf*] stupidity, foolishness, idiocy.

हिमाचल [*nm*] the Himalayas; -प्रदेश a northern state of the Union of India.

हिमाच्छन्न [*a*] snow-clad, snow-covered.

हिमाद्रि [*nm*] see हिमालय.

हिमानी [*nf*] a glacier; an avalanche.

हिमाय/त [*nf*] support, backing; defence, protection; ~ती a supporter; defender, protector, patron.

हिमालय [*nm*] the Himalayas.

हिमावृत [a] snow-capped, snow-clad.

हिम्मत [*nf*] courage, boldness; —बढ़ाना to encourage; to allow liberty, to cause to be cheeky; —हारना to lose courage, to be demoralised.

हिम्मती [*a*] courageous, bold.

हिय, ~रा [*nm*] the heart, bosom.

हिया [*nm*] the heart, bosom; courage; —काँपना to be terribly fear-stricken, to be struck with extreme terror; —जलना to be angry; to be full of jealousy; to suffer extreme agony; —ठंडा होना to be gratified, to feel assuaged [on account of an adversary's distress]; —फटना to have the heart rent by deep sorrow; —भर आना to be moved by emotion; हिये की फूटना to lose one's senses/wits, to become absolutely witless.

हिरण [*nm*] a deer, an antelope.

हिरण्य [*nm*] gold.

हिरन [*nm*] a deer, an antelope; —हो जाना to take to heels, to flee; to disappear.

हिरासत [*nf*] custody.

हि/र्स [*nf*] [spirit of] competition, envy; greed.

हिलको/र, ~रा [*nm*] a surge, billow.

हिलना [*v*] to move; to shake; to swing; to get very familiar; -डोलना to move; to be physically active; -मिलना to have intimacy with, to associate with; हिल-मिलकर in a friendly/co-operative spirit.

हिलाना [*v*] to move; to shake; to jolt; to swing; to cause to get very intimate.

हिलो/र, ~रा [*nf*] ~ [*nm*] a surge, billow; हिलोरें लेना to surge.

हिल्लोल [*nf*] a surge, billow.

हिसाब [*nm*] arithmetic; account; calculation, rate; manner, custom; -किताब account[s]; ~ करना to account for, to settle or work out the accounts; —, टेढ़ा difficult affair; -वही an account book, a ledger; —करना, पाक/बेबाक to pay off, to clear the account; —चुकता करना to clear off all the accounts or dues; —तलब करना to call for accounts; to ask for an explanation; —देना to render accounts; —बैठना the account to tally; things to veer round; hence —बैठाना; -साफ़ करना to clear off the account [of]; —से properly, proportionately; considering all the pros and cons.

हिसाबी [*a*] calculative; well-versed in arithmetic/calculations.

हिस्टीरिया [*nm*] hysteria.

हि/स्सा [*nm*] part, portion; share; division; ~स्सेदार a co-sharer, partener; shareholder; ~स्सेदारी partnership; co-sharing.

हींग [*nf*] asafoetida.

हीं-हीं [*nf*] grinning, sound of subdued laughter.

ही [ind] only, solely, alone; none but.

हीक [*nf*] stench.

हीन [*a*] inferior, worthless, deficient; used as the second member in compound words to mean devoid or divested of; —ग्रंथि inferiority complex; ~ता/त्व inferiority; deficiency; —पक्ष weak side, weak aspect; —भावना inferiority complex, feeling of inferiority.

हीर [*nm*] a pith, essence, quintessence; see हीरा.

हीरक [*nm*] a diamond; —जयंती diamond jubilee.

हीरा [*nm*] a diamond;—चाटना/हीरे की कनी चाटना

to commit suicide [by licking a diamond or diamond particle].

हीरो [*nm*] a hero.

हीरोइन [*nf*] a heroine.

हीला [*nm*] evasion; pretext; pretence/pretension; -हवाला dilly-dally, shilly-shally, evasion; pretence.

हुँ [*int*] a particle denoting assent, yes.

हुंकार [*nm*] roaring, bellowing; loud sound produced by a man to express menacing disposition or readiness to fight/strike.

हुंकारी [*nf*] to show assent by uttering 'हुँ'; —भरना to utter 'हुँ' for expressing assent.

हुंकृति [*nf*] see हुंकार.

हुंडी [*nf*] a bill of exchange, draft;—सकारना to honour/accept [a bill of exchange].

हुक [*nm*] a hook.

हुकुम [*nm*] see हुक्म.

हुकूमत [*nf*] government; rule; jurisdiction;—करना to govern, to rule; —चलना to run a government; to order about; —जताना to show one's authority/eminence; to try to order about.

हुक़्क़ा [*nm*] a hubble-bubble; -पानी social intercourse; ~ बन्द करना to excommunicate, to cease to have social intercourse.

हुक्काम [*nm*] plural form of हाकिम—officers; rulers.

हुक्म [*nm*] order, command; one of the suits in playing cards—the spade; ~नामा an edict, a written order; ~रान rulers; commanding authority; ~रानी rule, government; —तामील करना to obey or carry out one's order; —चलाना to issue an order; to order about; to rule/govern; —बजाना to carry out one's order; —मानना to obey one's order.

हुक्मी [*a*] imperative, mandatory; pertaining to an order; —बंदा obedient servant.

हुजूम [*nm*] a crowd, multitude.

हुजूर [*int*] your honour, your majesty, your lordship!; Sir!; [*nm*] gracious! Presence-ए-वाला your lordship! your honour!; —में in the court [of], in the gracious presence of, in attendance.

हुजूरी [*nf*]; ~,जी sycophancy, servile attitude.

हुज्ज/त [*nf*] altercation; wrangling; pugnacity; hence ~ती.

हुड़कना [*v*] to pine, to fret.

हुड़दं/ग [*nm*] commotion, uproar, tumult; ~गी uproarious, riotous, commotive.

हुतात्मा [*nm*] a martyr.

हुनर [*nf*] art, craft; skill; ~मंद an artist; skilful, skilled; ~मंदी artistry; skilfulness.

हुमकना [*v*] to thrust; to dance about with joy, to be hilarious.

हुर्रा [*int*] hurrah!

हुलसना [*v*] to be hilarious, to be full of joy/aspirations; to look pretty.

हुलास [*nm*] hilarity, joy; aspiration.

हुलिया [*nf*] physical features; description; -तंग होना to be in very hot waters; to be terribly afflicted; —बिगाड़ना to harass no end; to put into very hot waters.

हुल्लड़ [*nm*] shemozzle, tumult, uproar; ~बाज़ी causing tumultuous scenes/shemozzle; —करना/मचाना to raise a tumult, to kick up a row.

हुश [int] hush!; keep silent!; don't do!.

हुस्न [*nm*] beauty, prettiness; ~परस्त a lover of beauty; hence ~परस्ती; —का आलम age of superb beauty; times or world of superb beauty.

हूँ [*ind*] yes; [v] am.

हूँठा [*nm*] three and a half.

हूक [*nf*] haunting agony, smarting pain/affliction.

हूकना [*v*] to have smarting pain; to suffer from a haunting agony.

हूबहू [*a*] exactly alike, similar in all respects.

हूर [*nf*] a fairy; beauty, beautiful woman; —की परी a superb beauty.

हूश [*a*] rustic, rude, uncivil; ~पन rusticity, rudeness, incivility.

हृत [*a*] taken away, stolen, pilfered; ~सर्वस्व rendered penniless, deprived of all.

हृदयंगम [*a*] taken to heart; mentally assimilated.

हृदय [*nm*] the heart; core, best part; darling [person]; ~गत/स्थ taken to heart, mentally assimilated; ~ग्राही captivating, charming; ~विदारक heart-rending; ~वेधी heart-piercing;

~शून्य/हीन dry, hard-hearted, unfeeling; ~स्पर्शी pathetic, touching, moving; ~हारी charming, attractive, gripping; —फटना/विदीर्ण होना the heart to rend, to be anguished.

हृदये/श, ~श्वर [*nm*] lit. the lord of one's heart —dear one; dear husband/lover; hence ~श्वरी [*nf*].

हृदयरोग [*nm*] heart-disease.

हृषीकेश [*nm*] an epithet of Lord Vishnū or Krishnā.

हृष्ट [*a*] glad, delighted, pleased; -पुष्ट stout, robust.

हें-हें [*nf*] grinning sound [of laughter]; making humble entreaties, imploring.

हे [ind] a vocative particle.

हेकड़ [*a*] hubristic; unyielding, stubborn; exercising force.

हेकड़ी [*nf*] hubris, arrogance; stubbornness; exercise of coercion, show of force/strength —जताना/दिखाना to show arrogance, to be hubristic; to apply coercion; —भूल जाना hubristic attitude to be shed away; to lose all one's wits.

हेच [*a*] worthless, trifling.

हेठा [*a*] inferior, low, mean; ~पन inferiority, meanness, lowness.

हेठी [*nf*] humiliation, insult, indignity; —करना to humiliate/insult, to heap indignity on; hence —होना.

हेड [*a*] head; -ऑफ़िस head office; ~क्वार्टर heaoqQuarter; ~मास्टर head-master; ~मास्टरी headmastership.

हेतु [*nm*] reason, cause; motive; ~ता/त्व causation, causativeness, existence of cause or motive; ~वाद statement of reasons or arguments, assigning of cause.

हेत्वाभास [*nm*] a fallacy, sophism.

हेमंत [*nm*] the winter season.

हेम [*nm*] gold.

हेर-फेर [*nm*] interchange; change; rotation; manipulation, unscrupulousness.

हेराफेरी [*nf*] manipulation, unscrupulous activity.

हेलमेल [*nm*] intimacy, close relationship.

हैं [*v*] are; [ind] no, what is this; a particle showing, astonishment, negation or non-acceptance.

हैंडबैग [*nm*] a handbag.

हैंडिल [*nm*] a handle.

है [*v*] is.

हैज़ा [*nm*] cholera.

हैट [*nm*] a hat.

हैरत [*nf*] amazement, astonishment; ~अंगेज़ amazing, astonishing; ~ज़दा amazed, astonished.

हैरान [*a*] tired, wearied; perplexed, confounded; amazed, astonished.

हैरानी [*nf*] surprise, amazement; botheration, trouble; weariness.

हैवा/न [*nm*] an animal; savage; brute, beast; ~नियत beastliness, brutality, savagery; हैवानी beastly, savage, brutal.

हैसियत [*nf*] status; capacity; ~, ब in the capacity of; ~दार having a status.

होंठ [*nf*] see ओंठ; -काटना/चबाना to be full of wrath; —सो जाना to be dumb-founded, to be speechless; —हिलाना to move the lips, to commence speech.

हो/टल, ~ टेल [*nm*] a hotel.

होठ [*nm*] lip.

होड़ [*nm*] competition; race; bet; —लगाना to enter into a competition, to have a race/rivalry.

होड़ा-होड़ी [*nf*] competition; [*adv*] by way of or through competition rivalry.

होता [*nm*] one who offers oblation [to the sacrificial fire].

होनहार [*a*] promising; [*nm*] the inevttable, destiny; —बिरवान के होत चीकने पात coming events cast their shadows before.

होना [v] to be; to occur, to happen; to exist; to be born; हो न हो probably, perhaps, in all likelihood, may be.

होनी [*nf*] destiny, predestination; the inevitable; —के बस में, तीन लोक the entire universe is bound by destiny.

होम [*nm*] a sacrifice; an oblation fire; ~कुंड a pit for oblation fire; —करते हाथ जलना do a good turn and earn a bad name—करना to perform a sacrifice, to offer ablation to fire.

होमियोपै/थ [*nm*] a homoeopath; ~थिक homoeopathic; ~थी the science of homoeopathy; practising medicine through the homoeopathic system.

होला [*nm*] green gram.

होलिका [*nf*] the होली festival; ~दहंन burning of the pile of fuel on the occasion of होली.

होली [*nf*] a Hindu festival celebrated on the last day of the month of फागुन when coloured water is thrown on one another; —खेलना to throw coloured water [on].

होल्डऑल/होल्डाल [*nm*] a hold-all.

होल्डर [*nm*] a holder.

होश [*nm*] sense, consciousness; —हवास see होश; -आना to come to senses; to regain consciousness; उड़ना/उड़ जाना/काफ़ूर या गुम होना/जाते रहना/फाख्ता होना/ हवा होना/ हिरन होना to be at one's wit's end, to lose wits, to be thoroughly confounded; —की दवा करो come to senses; talk sense!; —ठिकाने आना/होना to come to senses; to be fixed in one's proper place, to learn a lesson; —न रहना to be unconscious, to lose senses;—में आना to come to senses; to gain consciousness; —सँभालना to gain consciousness; to come of age.

होशयार [*adj*] होशियार.

होशियार [*a*] clever, wise, intelligent; careful.

होशियारी [*nf*] cleverness, wisdom, intelligence; carefulness.

हौंकना [*v.i.*] to pant, to roar.

हौंस [*nf*] craving, longing; deep aspiration.

हौआ [*nm*] see हौवा.

हौज़ [*nm*] a tank reservoir [of water etc.]; sink.

हौद [*nm*] see हौज.

हौदा [*nm*] an open or covered seat placed over an elephant; a pond; see हौज.

हौदी [*nf*] a small tank, reservoir; sink.

हौल [*nm*] fear, dread; a hall; ~दिल stunned, terrified; ~नाक stunning, fearful, dreadful.

हौले-हौले [*adv*] slowly; gently; quietly.

हौवा [*nm*] a bogey, bugbear; scare-crow; a scare-word used for frightening children.

हौसला [*nm*] courage; morale; हौसलेमंद courageous; —करना to take courage, to pluck courage —तोड़ना to demoralise, to discourage; —पस्त होना to be demoralised.

ह्रस्व [*a*] short, small; —स्वर short vowel.

ह्रस्वता [*nf*] shortness, see ह्रस्व.

ह्रास [*nm*] decay; fall, down fall; diminution; ~मान decaying, falling, suffering a downfall.

ह्रासोन्मुख [*a*] decaying, diminishing, decadent; ~ता decadence.

ह्री [*nf*] shame, modesty.

ह्वेल [*nf*] a whale.

परिशिष्ट–1/Appendix-1

बैंकिंग शब्दावली और अंग्रेजी पर्याय

(Banking Terminologies and English Meanings)

अ

अंक	figure, point
अंकगणितीय परिवर्तन	arithmetical, conversion
अंकित करना	record mark
अंकित मूल्य	face value
अंकित राशि	face amount
अंगीकार करना, गोद लेना	adopt
अँगूठा निशान	thumb impression
अंचल	zone circle
अंचल प्रशिक्षण केन्द्र	zonal training centre
अन्तरक बैंकिग कम्पनी	transfer banking company
अन्तरण	transfer
अन्तरण अदायगी, भुगतान	transfer payment
अन्तरण आदेश	transfer order
अन्तरण इन्दराज	transfer entry
अन्तरण कर्ता	transferor
अन्तरणका प्रमाणन	certification of transfer
अन्तरण चैक	transfer cheque
अन्तरण टीप	transfer entry
अन्तरण विलेख	deed of transfer
अन्तरणीय लेखा	transferable amount
अन्तरिम अधिनिर्णय	interim award
अन्तर्देशीय प्रलेखी, हुण्डियाँ	inland documentary bills
अन्तर्नियम	article
अन्तर्निहित	implicit
अन्तर्बैंक	inter-bank
अन्तर्बैंक माँग मुद्रा पर	inter-bank call money rate
अन्तर्राष्ट्रीय प्रारक्षित निधियाँ	international reserve funds
अन्तर्राष्ट्रीय–मुद्रा	international currency
अन्तर्राष्ट्रीय–व्यापार	international trade
अन्तर्विभागीय अन्तरण सूची	inter-deptt. transfer scroll
अन्तर्शाखा लेनदेन	inter-branch transactions
अन्तर्शाखा लेखों का समाधान	reconcilation of inter-branches' account
अन्तिम उत्तरजीवी पॉलिसी	last survivor policy
अन्तिम ऋणदाता	last debteor
अन्तिम टीप/प्रविष्ट	last/closing entry
अन्तिम वेतनपत्र	last pay certificate
अन्तिम वैध धारक	last legal holder
अन्तिम शेष	final balance
अंशकालिक कर्मचारी	part time worker
अक्षम	incompetent
अक्षरांकीय पंच	alpha-numeric punch
अग्रणी बैंक	lead bank
अग्रता सूची	priority list
अग्रदाय लेखा	imprest account
अग्रिम	advance
अग्रेषण	forward/onward transmission
अचल सम्पत्ति	immovable proerty
अटल मुख्तारेआम	irrevocable power of attorney
अतिथि वक्ता	guest speaker
अतिदेय किश्तें	overdue instalments

अतिदेय हुण्डी	overdue bill
अतिरिक्त जोखिम	extra risk
अतिरिक्त प्रभार	additional charges
अतिशीघ्र	most urgent
अर्जन, उपार्जन	earning
अधशेष	opening balance
अदत्त	unpaid
अदाकर्ता बैंकर	paying banker
अदायगी आदेश	pay order
आकस्मिक/खर्च	unforseen expenditure
अधिक राशि निकालना	overdraw
अधिकारक्षेत्र	jurisdiction
अधिकारों का आवंटन	delegation of power
अधिकृत	authorised
अधिदेश	mandate
अधिनिर्णय	award
अधिपत्र	warrant
अधिप्रमाणन	authentication
अधिमान	preference
अधिमूल्यन	overvaluation
अधिवर्षनिधि	superannuation fund
अधिसूचित बैंक	notified bank
अधिस्थगन आदेश	order of moratorium
अधीनस्थ कर्मचारी	subordinate staff
अधीन कार्यालय	subordinate office
अनन्तरणीय	non-transferable
अनन्तिम आँकड़े	provisional figure
अनधिकृत	unauthorised
अनुसूचित बैंक	scheduled bank
अनलिखित	unrecorded
अनलिखित छुट्‌टी	leave-not-earned
अनाचार	malpractice
अनापत्ति प्रमाणपत्र	no-objection certificate
अनियत रिक्तस्थापन	casual vacancy
अनियमित अग्रिम	irregular advances
अनियमित बेचान	irregular endorsement
अनिवार्य योग्यता	essential qualification
अनिवार्य सेवानिवृत्ति/ अवकाश ग्रहण	compulsory retirement
अनिवासी	non-resident
अनुकूल विनिमय दर	favourable rate of exchange
अनुकूत व्यापार शेष	favourable balance of trade
अनुग्रह अवधि	grace period
अनुज्ञप्ति (लाइसेंस)	licence
अनुज्ञापत्र	permit
अनुदान	grant
अनुदेश	instruction
अनुदेश पुस्तक	book of instruction
अनुदेश पुस्तिका	manual of instruction
अनुपात	ratio
अनुपातन	compliance
अनुमानित लागत	estimated cost
अनुमोदन	approval
अनुमोदित निर्दिष्ट साख संस्था	approved specified credit inst.
अनुरोध पत्र	letter of request
अनुवर्ती कारवाई	follow-up-action
अनुलग्नक	enclosure
अनुलिपि	duplicate
अनुशासनात्मक कार्रवाई	disciplinary action
अनुसंगी	ancillary, subsidiary, satellite
अनुस्मारक	reminder
अन्य पक्ष की गारण्टी	a third party guarantee
अपचार	act of misconduct
अप्राक्राम्य अविनियमसाध्य	not negotiable
अप्राक्राम्य रेखन	non-negotiable crossing
अप्रचलित देयताएँ	non-current liabilities
अप्रचलित सिक्का	obsolete coin

अब्याजी	non-interest bearing	अवकाश	leave, interval, leisure
अभिकरण	agency	अवधि की समाप्ति	expiry of term
अभिकरण व्यवस्था	agency arrangements	अवधि पूर्णता की तारीख	date maturity
अभिकरण उधार	agency loans	अवयस्क खाता	minor account
अभिनन्दन पत्र	welcome recitation	अवरुद्ध परिसम्पत्तियाँ	frozen assets
अभिभावक	guardian	अवांछित आहरण	unwanted drawals
अभिलिखित प्रतिभूति	inscribed security	अविभक्त हिन्दू परिवार	undivided Hindu family
अभिलेख	record	अविमुक्त दिवालिया	undischarged bankrupt
अभिव्यक्त प्राधिकार	express authority	अवेतन छुट्टी	leave without pay
अभ्यावेदन	representation	अवैधधारक	unlawful holder
अमान्यकरण	invalidation	अवैध हड़ताल	illegal strike
अमुक बैंक	particualar bank	अव्यावहारिक हुण्डी बिल	non-mercantile bill
अयोग्यता	disqualification	अनाधिकारिक	unofficial
अर्जन क्षमता	earning capacity	अशोध्य ऋण	irrecoverable
अर्जित छुट्टी	earned leave	असंगति	advances/bad debts
अर्णोपाय स्थिति	ways and means position	असाधारण छुट्टी	extraordinary leave
अर्धनिर्मित माल	semi-manufactured product	अस्थायी अग्रिम	temporary advance
अर्धवार्षिक संवरण	half-yearly closings	अस्थायी व्यवस्था	temporary arrangement
अल्पकालीन ऋण	short-term loans	अस्वस्थता प्रमाणपत्र	medical certificate of sickness
अल्प बचत	small savings	अस्वीकृति सूचना	notice of dishonour
अल्प ब्याज धन	cheap money	अहस्तान्तरणीय	non-transferable
अल्प सुविधा प्राप्त	under privileged		

आ

आँकड़े	figures	आदाता	payee, reciever
आन्तरिक लेखा परीक्षा	internal audit	आदाता खाता रेखन	payee's a/c
आंशिक अदायगी	part payment	आदाता खजांची की सूची	receiving cashier's scroll
आकस्मिक देयता	contingent liability	आदिष्ट चेक	order cheque
आकस्मिक व्यय बिल	contingent bill	आद्यक्षर	initials
आगे लाया गया	brought forward	आधार अवधि	base period
आगे ले जाया गया	carried over	आनुपातिक व्यय	proportional expenditure
आचार नियमावली	conduct rules	आनुमानित दर	appropriate rate
आज्ञापरक	mandatory	आपत्ति सहित	under protest
आतिथ्य भत्ता	entertainment allowance	आपाती उधार	credit emergency
आदतन चूककर्ता	habitual defaulter	आबण्टन	allotment

आय उत्पादक क्षमता	income generating capacity	आवधिक जमा	fixed deposits
आयात बिलों पर अग्रिम	advance against import bill	आवधिक जाँच	periodical checking
आयात व्यापार नियन्त्रण	import restrictions	आवधिक विवरिणियाँ	periodical returns
आरक्षण	reservation	आवर्ती जमा	recurring deposits
आर्थिक संकट	economic crisis	आस्तियों का मूल्यांकन	evaluation of assets
आलोच्य वर्ष	year under review	आस्थगित अदायगी	deferred payments
आवक/जावक नकदी रजिस्टर	cash inward/outward register	आस्थगित प्राप्त बिल	deferred bill
आवक नकदी प्रेषण	incoming cash remittance	आहरण अधिकार	drawing power
		आहरण पर्ची	drawing form
		आहरण सीमा	drawing limits

इ

इण्डेण्टकर्ता	indentor	इक्विटी शेयर	equity share
इन्दराज	entry, posting	इकहरी प्रविष्ट	single-entry system
इतिशेष	closing balance	इन्वायस बही	invoice book

उ

उगाही हुण्डी दर	realisation levy rate	उत्पादक कीमत	producer's price
उचन्त लेखा/खाता	bills for collection rate	उत्पादन कार्यकलाप	production activity
उचित प्राधिकारी	appropriate authority	उत्पादन क्षमता	production capacity
उचित समय	reasonable time	उत्पादन लागत	cost of production
उच्च प्राथमिकता	top priority	उत्पादन शुल्क	excise duty
उच्चतम निर्धारित कीमत	ceiling price	उद्गम प्रमाणपत्र	ceritficate of origin
उच्चाधिकारी	higher authority	उद्यमकर्ता/उद्यमी	entrepreneur
उतराई खर्च	unloading charges	उद्योगपति	industrialist
उतराई प्रभार	unloading charges	उधार अन्तराल	credit gap
उतराई प्रमाण पत्र	unloading certificate	उधार अधिसंकुचन	credit squeeze
उतार-चढ़ाव	fluctuation	उधार की दरें	lending rate
उत्कृष्ट	outstanding	उधार की मियाद	currency of loan
उत्तरजीवी	survivor, surviving	उधार दाता/ऋणदाता	lender, creditor
उत्तरदिनांकित चेक	post-dated cheque	उधार पद्धति	lending pattern/ system
उत्तरवर्ती	succeeding, subsequent	उपक्रम	undertaking
उपसाधन, सहायक उपकरण	accessories	उपज के आँकड़े	field statistics
उत्तराधिकार प्रमाणपत्र	succession certificate	उपच क्षेत्र	area under crop

उपदान	subsidy
उपबन्ध	provision
उपभोक्ता कीमत सूचकांक	consumer-price-index
उपयोग में लायी गयी क्षमता	utilization capacity
उपरिव्यय/ऊपरी खर्चे	overhead expenses
उपस्कर	equipment
उपस्थिति प्रमाणपत्र	fitness/eligibility certificate
उपहार चेक	gift cheque
उपर लिखित	above mentioned

ऋ

ऋण अनुबन्ध	loan agreement
ऋण आवेदन	loan application
ऋण का प्रतिदान	redemption of debt
ऋण की पुनर्व्यवस्था	rescheduling of loan
ऋण गारण्टी योजनाएँ	credit gaurantee scheme
ऋणदाता	creditor, lendor
ऋणदात्री संस्थाएँ	lending institutions
ऋण नकार/अस्वीकरण	debt repudiation
ऋण प्रलेख/दस्तावेज	loan documents
ऋण प्राधिकरण योजना	credit authorization scheme

ए

एक पक्षीय/एकतरफा	unilateral
एक मुश्त	lump sum
एकल स्वामित्व	individual proprietorship
एक समान दर	flat rate
एक मात्र अभिकर्ता	sole agent
एकाधिकार नियन्त्रण	monopoly control
एकीकृत साख प्रणाली	integrated credit system
एकीकृत ग्रामीण विकास कार्यक्रम	integrated rural developement scheme
एजेंसी प्रबन्ध	agency arrangement
एवजी	substitute
एच्छिक सेवा निवृत्ति	voluntary retirement

ओ, औ

ओवरड्राफ्ट/अधिविकर्ष सीमा	O.D. limit
औद्योगिक उत्पादन	industrial production
औद्योगिक अधिकरण	industrial tribunal
औद्योगिक विवाद	industrial dispute
औद्योगिक सम्बन्ध	industrial relation
औपचारिक अनुमोदन	formal approval
औसत अग्रिम	average advances
औसत आय	average revenue

क

कम्पनी का व्यय रजिस्टर	company's register of charges
कम्पनी प्रतिभूति	corporate security
कच्चा माल	raw material
कटाफटा चेक	mutilated cheque
कदाचार	misconduct
कपटपूर्ण समझौता	fraudulent settlement
कर्तव्य भंग	breach of duty
कम कूतना/आँकना	under-estimate

कम पोत लदान	under-shipments
कर की वसूली	recovery of tax
कर निर्धारण वर्ष	assessment year
कर मुक्त आय	tax-free income
कर योग्य आय	taxable income
कर योग्य लाभ	taxable profits
करार निष्पादन	execution of agreement
कर्मचारी अंशदान	employee's contribution
कल्पित क़ीमत	shadow price
कागजी लेन-देन	paper transaction
कारीगर	craftsman
कामगार	workman
कारोबार का प्रकार	nature of transaction
कारोबार परिमाण	volume of business
कार्मिक नीति	personnel policy
कार्मिक प्रबन्ध	personnel management
कार्यकारी अधिकार	executive power
कार्यक्रम का क्रियान्वयन	implementation of programme
कार्यक्षेत्र	area of operation
कार्य ग्रहण की तिथि	date of joining
कार्य ग्रहण रिपोर्ट/प्रतिवेदन	joining report
कार्यमूल्यन	performance rating
कार्यमूल्यांकन	job evaluation
कार्यवाही	proceedings
कार्यवृत्त पुस्तक	minutes book
कार्यशाला	workshop
कार्यशील पूँजी अग्रिम	working captial advance
कार्यसाधक ज्ञान	working knowledge
कार्यसूची	agenda
कार्यालय आदेश	office order
कार्य समय	business hours
कार्यकारक	job-factor
कार्यावर्तन	job-rotation
कार्यालय क्रियाविधि	office procedure
कार्यालय ज्ञापन	office memorandum
कार्यालय टिप्पणी	office note
कार्यालय प्रति	office copy
कालाधन	black money
काश्तकार	farmer tenant
किश्त उधार	credit instalment
किराया खरीद अदायगी	hire purchase payment
कुंजी रजिस्टर	key register
कुक्कुट पालन	poultry farming
कुछ नहीं 'विवरणी'	nil return
कुटीर और लघुउद्योग	cottage and small industries
कुर्क करना	attach
कुर्की आदेश	attachment order
कुल मूल्य	aggregate value
कूट लेखन	encoding
कृषि अग्रिम	agricultural advance
कृषि आधारित उद्योग	agro-based industries
कृषि उत्पादक	agricultrural producers
कृषि उत्पादन वित्तपोषण	agricultural advance
कृषि उपकरण	agricultural implement
कृषि ऋण निगम	agricultural credit corporation
कृषि विस्तार सेवा	agricultural extension services
कृषि सरकारी संस्था	farm co-operative
कृषि सेवा केन्द्र	agro-services centre
कृषि विपणन	agricultural marketing
केन्द्रीय बैंक	central bank, banker's bank
क्रेता	buyer

क्रेता के अधिकार से	by authority of buyer	क्रेता के देय/के कारण	due to buyer
क्रेता के अधिकरण में	in supersession of buyer	क्रेता तिथि पर देय	due on buyer
क्रेता के अनुसार	in accordance with buyer	क्रेता को सम्बोधित	addressed to buyer
क्रेता के आदेश	by command, by order	क्रेता को समाप्त लेखा अवधि	accounting period ended
क्रेता के नाते	by virtue of buyer	क्रेता को समाप्त हुई तिमाही	quarter ended on buyer
क्रेता के नाम	addressed to buyer	कोटि/किस्म नियन्त्रण	quality control
क्रेता के नाम आहरण करना	drawing in favour of buyer	कोरा फार्म	blank form
क्रेता के निपटान में	in satisfaction of buyer	कोरा अन्तरंग	blank transfer
क्रेता के विपरीत	in contrast	कोरी हुण्डी	blank bill
क्रेता के सिवाय	save	कोषयान	cash van
क्रेता के स्थान पर	in lieu of buyer	क्रमबद्ध	in order
क्रेता के हित में	in the interest of buyer	क्रमिक जोड़	progressive total
		क्षतिपूर्ति मुआवजा	indemnification, compensation
		क्षमता	capacity
		क्षेत्रफल	area
		क्षेत्राधिकार	jurisdiction

ख

खरीदी गयी हुण्डी	bill purchased	खुदरा कीमत	retail price
खाता पन्ना	ledger folio	खुला टेण्डर	open tender
खाता बही क्लावी	ledger clerk	खुला बाजार कार्रवाई	open market operation

ग

गम्भीर अनियमितताएँ	grave irregularities	गहन कृषि क्षेत्र जिला	intensive agricultural district
गणक	teller	गिरवी	pledge
गणना करना	count, calculate	गिरवी कर्ता	pledger
गणना मशन परिचालक	accounting machine operator	गिरवी ग्राही	pledgee
गत महीने का	ultimo	गुजारा भत्ता	subsistence allowance
गतावधि	out of date	गुणानुक्रम	order of merits
गतावधि ऋण	expired loan	गुणावगुण	merits and demerits
गतावति चैक	stale cheque	गुप्त जाँच	secret enquiry
गवाह	witness		

गुणवत्ता नियन्त्रण	quality control	गौण उद्योग	ancillary industry
गृहनिर्माण अर्द्ध सहायता	housing subsidy	ग्रहणाधिकार	lien
गृह निर्माण ऋण	housing loan	ग्राम और कुटीर उद्योग	village and cottage industries
गृहीता	receiver	ग्रामीण अर्थ व्यवस्था	rural economy
गैर जमानती ऋण	unsecured loan	ग्रामीण अर्थशास्त्र	rural economics
गैर टिकाऊ माल	non-durable goods	ग्रामीण ऋणग्रस्तता	rural indebtedness
गैर बैंकिंग कम्पनियाँ	non-banking companies	ग्राहक	client, customer
गोचर परिसम्पत्तियाँ	tangible assets	ग्रहण करना	taking over
गोदाम रसीदें	warehouse receipts	ग्राहक सेवा ईकाई	customer service unit

घ

घटक	constituent	घाटे की जोत	uneconomical holding
घटबढ़ का विश्लेषण	analysis of variance	घोर चूक	gross negligence
घरेलू उत्पाद/खपत	domestic product	घोर दुराचरण	gross misconduct
घाट किराया	wharf rent	घोषित मूल्य	declared value

च

चकबन्दी	consolidation of holding	चालू माँग	current demand
		चालू वित्तवर्ष	current finacial year
चक्रवृद्धि दर	compound rate of interest	चिकित्सा-अवकाश	medical leave
		चिकित्सा प्रमाणपत्र	medical certificate
चयन का मानदण्ड	criteria for selection	चिकित्सा व्यय	medical expenses
चयनात्मक	selective	चिरउत्तराधिकार	perpetual succession
चर्म उद्योग	leather industry	चिह्नित चेक	crossed cheque
चल अस्तियाँ	movable assets	चुंगी शुल्क	octroi
चल प्रतिभूति	floating security	चुकायी गयी हुण्डी/बिल	discharged bill
चल सम्पत्ति	movable property	चुकौती कार्यक्रम	repayment
चलन अवधि	period of currency	चेक का रेखन	crossing of cheque
चालू आय	current income		

छ

छपाई तथा लेखन सामग्री	writing and printing stationery	छुट्टी यात्रा रियायत	leave travel concession
छलपूर्ण दावा	fraudulent claim	छुट्टी वेतन अग्रिम	leave salary advance
छानबीन	scrutiny, searching	छूट अवधि	grace period
छिद्रित	perforated	छूट प्राप्त वर्ग	exempted category

ज

जकात	octroi	जानकारी और विकास	knowledge and belief
जनजातीय क्षेत्र	tribal area	जानबूझकर ऋण न चुकाने वाला	wilful defaulter
जरशक्ति प्रबन्धन	manpower management	जामिन	security
जबानी गारण्टी	oral guarantee	जारी करने की दर	rate of issue
जमाकर्ता	depositor	जालसाजी करना	forge
जमानती ऋण	secured loan	जाली दस्तावेज बनाना	fabrication of documents, forged documents
जमा-पर्ची	pay-in-slip	जावक डाक अन्तरण	outward mail transfer
जमाराशि का संघटन	composition of deposits	जावन निकासी	outward clearance
जमाराशियों की वृद्धि	growth of deposits	जीवन निर्वाह के प्रकट साधन	ostensible means of subsistence
जमा शेष	credit balance	जोखिम उठाना	risk taking
जमा ह्रास	deposite erosion	जोखिम प्रीमियम	risk premium
जर्नल प्रविष्टि	journal entry	जोत क्षेत्र	holdings
जहाज तक निःशुल्क	f.o.b. (free on board)	ज्ञापन	memorandum
जहाज भाड़ा	shipping freight		
जाँच अधिकारी	enquiry officer		
जाँच प्रमाणपत्र	test certificate		

ट, ठ

टकसाल	mint	ट्रक चालक	truck drivers
टनभरक्षमता	tonnage capacity	ठोस निर्यात आदेश	firm export order
टिप्पण और प्रारूपण	noting and drafting	ठोस प्रतिभूति	substantantial security
टेक कीमत	support price		

ड, ढ

डाक द्वारा लेनदेन	postal transaction	ड्राफ्ट और डाक अन्तरण	draft and mail transfer
डाक पता	postal address	ढुलाई	transportaion
डाक्टरी परीक्षा	medical examination	ढुलाई शुल्क	transport charges
डायरी में चढ़ाना	enter in diary		
डेरी उद्योग	dairy farming		

त

तन्त्र	system	तकनीकी संभावनाएँ	technical feasibilities
तकनीकी सलाह	technical advice	तट व्यापार	coastal trade

तटस्थ बाजार	neutral market	तिजारती अभिकरण	mercantile agency
तत्काल	immediate	तिजोरी	chest currency chest
तत्काल नकदी अदायगी	down payment	तुड़ाना/भुनाना	encashment
तत्काल हड़ताल	lightening strike	तुलन पत्र	balance sheet
तथ्यत:	factually, de facto	तैनाती	posting
तथ्यपूर्ण	factual	तैयार माल लेखे	finished goods account
तथाकथित असमानता	alleged disparity	तोल सूचना	weightment advice
तदर्थ ऋण	ad-hoc loan	त्रिपक्षीय करार	tripartite agreement
तरल परिसम्पत्तियाँ	liquid assets	तैयार उत्पादन	finished products
तार सन्देश कोड	telegraphic message code		

थ

थोक कीमत	wholesale price	थोक व्यापारी	wholesale dealer
थोक माँगपत्र	bulk indent		

द

दण्डनीय	punishable	दावे का निपटारा	settlement of claim
दण्डराशि	penal sum	दावेदार	claimant
दण्डात्मक कारवाई	penal action	दिवाला	insolvency, bankruptcy
दण्डात्मक हर्जाना	punitive damages	दीर्घकालिक उपाय	longterm measure
दखल अधिकारी	occupancy rights	दीर्घावधि ऋण	longterm credit
दखल पट्टा	occupancy tenure	दुधारू पशु योजना	milk cattle scheme
दफ्तरी हिदायतें	official instructions	दुर्लभ मुद्रा क्षेत्र	hard currency area
दर अनुसूची	rate schedule	दुहरी/दोहरी फसल	double crop
दर संविदा	rate contract	दोहरा वित्तपोषण	double financing
दर सूची	tariff	दृष्टिबन्धन अनुबन्ध	hypothecation agreement
दर्शनी हुण्डी	sight bill	देनदार की योग्यताएँ	debtor's qualification
दलाल	broker	देनदारी	liability
दलाली	brokerage	देय ड्राफ्ट पंजिका	draft payable register
दस्तकारी	handicraft	देय बिल	bill payment
दस्तावेज	document	देय ब्याज	interest payable
दस्तावेजी/प्रलेखी साक्ष्य	documentary evidence	देय हुण्डियों पर अग्रिम	advance against bills payable
दावा प्रपत्र	claim form		
दावा दायर करना	filing of claim		

देयता	liability
देयता आधार पर समायोजन	adjust mention liability basis
देशी माँग	indigenous demand
देशी बिल	inland bills
देशी व्यापार आँकड़े	inland trade statistics
दैनिक काउण्टर अदायगी बही	daily counter pay ment book
दैनिक बही	day book
दैनिक रिपोर्ट	daily report
दोहर प्रविष्टि पद्धति	double-entry system
दौरा कार्यक्रम	tour programme
द्विपक्षीय व्यापार लेख	bilateral trade accounts

ध

धन्धा	business, occupation
धन ऋण प्रविष्टियाँ	credit debit entries
धनी जोग चेक	bearer cheque
धातु मुद्रा	metal money coin
धारक चेक	bearer cheque
धारक/वाहक	holder/bearer

न

नकद अदा किया	paid in cash
नकद आर्थिक सहायता	cash subsidy
नकद उपदान	cash subsidy
नकद बट्टा	cash discount
नकद भुगतान मोहर	pay cash stamp
नकद लेन-देन	cash transaction
नकद सौदा	cash transactions
नकद जमा जमा अनुपात	cash deposit ratio
नकदी रसीद	cash receipt
नकदी फसल	cash crop
नकदी बाज़ार	cash market
नकार सूचना	dishonour advice
नकारा गया चेक	dishonoured cheque
नकारात्मक आय प्रभाव	negative income effect
नकारात्मक ग्रहणाधिकार	negative lien
नक्शा	map, blue print
नक्शानवीस	draftsman
नगर प्रतिकार भत्ता	city compensatory allowance
नगरीय जनसंख्या	urban population
नमूना जाँच	test check
नमूना हस्ताक्षर पर्ची	specimen signature slip
नलकूप	tubewell
नवीकरण प्रस्ताव	renewal proposal
नाबालिग खाता	minor account
नामजद सदस्य	nominated member
नामजोग चेक	debit account
नामांकन	nomination
नामित सदस्य	nominated member
नामे खाते	debit account
नामे डालने की सूचना	debit advice
नामे बाकी	debit balance
निकासी अभिकर्ता	agent clearing
निक्षेप	deposit
निगमन प्रमाणपत्र	certificate of incorporation
निगमित निकाय	corporate body
निजी अन्तरण अदायगियाँ	private transfer
निजी क्षेत्र	private sector
निजी जोखिम	own risk
निजी व्यवसाय करने वाला	self-employed persons
निजी संसाधन	own resources
निजी स्वामित्व	private ownership
निदेशक मण्डल	board of directors

निधि निर्माण	generation of funds
निधियों का अन्तर्गणन	interlocking of founds
निपटान की प्रक्रिया	procedure of settlement
निपटान की शर्तें	terms of settlement
निभावपत्र हुण्डी/बिल	accommodation paper bill
निम्नतर दर	lower rate
नियन्त्रक मूल कम्पनी	holding company
नियत तिथि	due date
नियत पत्र	letter of allotment
नियम	rule
निर्यात अभिकर्ता	agent exporting
नियुक्त उत्तराधिकारी	appointed heir
नियुक्ति की शर्तें	terms of appointment
नियुक्ति प्राधिकारी	appointing authority
नियुक्ति शाखा	appointment branch
निरीक्षण कार्यक्रम	inspection programme
निरीक्षण रिपोर्ट/प्रतिवेदन	inspection reports
निरुद्ध खाते	blocked accounts
निर्गम रजिस्टर	issue register
निर्दिष्ट गारण्टी	specified gaurantee
निर्धारित अवधि	prescribed time/ period
निर्धारित दर	prescribed rate
निर्धारित ब्याज	scheduled interest
निर्धारित रीति	prescribed manner
निर्बाध स्वीकृति/सकार	clean acceptance
निर्बाध ओवरड्राफ्ट	clean overdraft
निर्माण उद्योग लागत	manufacturing/ industry cost
निर्माता	manufacturer
निर्यात ऋण	export credit
निर्यात औपचारिकता से छूट	waiver from export formalities
निर्यात के लिए अग्रिम	advances to exports
निर्यात नियन्त्रण	export control
निर्यात निष्पादन गारण्टी	export performance guarantee
निर्यात बिल	export bill
निर्यात लदान पत्र	export bill of lading
निर्यात लाइसेंस शुल्क	export licence fee
निर्यात विकास योजना	export promotion scheme
निर्यात व्यापार नियन्त्रण	export trade control
निर्यात व्यापारी	export merchant
निर्यात सहायता	export subsidy
निर्यात साखपत्र	export letter of credit
निर्यातित माल	exported goods
निर्यात वित्त पोषण	export financing
निर्यातोन्मुख उद्योग	export-oriented industry
निर्वाह भत्ता	subsistence allowance
निलम्बित	suspended
नीलाम	auction
नीलामकर्त्ता	auctioneer
निलम्बित करना	suspend
निवल उत्पादन	net production
निवल सम्पत्ति	net worth
निविदा	tender
निवृतिपूर्व अवकाश	leave preparatory to retirement
निवेश छूट	investment allowance
निवेश लागत	investment cost
निषेधाज्ञा	injunction, prohibitory order
निष्क्रिय भागीदार	dormant partner
निष्ठाशपथ	oath of alleginace
निष्पादन गारण्टी	performance guarantee
नेमी आदेश	routine orders

नोटों की गड्डी	wad of notes/ currency notes	न्यूनतम जोत	minimum holding
न्यास	trust	न्यूनतम वसूली निष्पादन	minimum recoveries performance
नौसिखिया	apprentice	न्यूनतम पूँजीगत आवश्यकता	minimum capital requirement
न्यून पोतलदान	short snipment	न्यूनतम वेतन	minimum wages
न्यून मूल्यांकन करना	under value		

प

पंच निर्णय/पंचाट	award	परियोजना रिपोर्ट	project report
पंचवर्षीय योजना	five-year plan	परियोजना रूपरेखा	project profiles
पंचवार्षिक	quinquennial	परिलब्धियाँ	emoluments
पंजीयन प्रतिभूतियाँ	registered securities	परिवर्तन ऋण	conversion loan
पक्का पट्टा	permanent lease	परिवहन चालक	transport operator
पट्टा विलेख	deed of lease	परिवाद	complaint, grievances
पट्टेदार	lessee	परिवार का प्रमुख	head of household
पट्टेदार प्रणाली	land tenure	परिवीक्षा	probation
पट्टे वाली भूमि	leasehold land	परिशोधित ऋण	amortized loan
पड़ताल कर्त्ता	checker	परिसमापन कार्यवाही	liquidation prceedings
पण्यावर्त	turnover		
पदच्चुति	dismissal	परिसमापनाधीन बैंक	bank under liquidation
पदावनति	reversion, demotion		
पदोन्नति के अवसर	chances of promotion	परीक्षण चालन	test run
परम्परा	practice	परीक्षित लेखा	audited accounts
पराक्राम्य	negotiation	परोक्ष उत्पादन	indirect production
पराक्राम्य लिखत	negotiable instruments	परोक्ष कर	indirect tax
		पर्यवेक्षक	observer, supervisor
परमावश्यक	absolutely necessary	पर्याप्त प्रतिभूति	adequate securtiy
परम गोपनीय	most secret	पर्याप्त समय	reasonable time
परम विवेक	absolute discretion	पश्चलेख	post-script
परांकन पर्ची	allonge	पहचानपत्र	identity card
पशुधन	livestock	पहरेदार (वाचमैन)	watchman
परिचय पत्र	letter of identification	पहाड़ भत्ता	hill allowance
परिचालन लागत	operational cost	पात्रता आँकना	assessing the eligibility
परिणत छुट्टी	converted leave		
परिपक्वता की तारीख	date of maturity	पात्रबिल	eligible bills
परिपत्र संख्या	circular number	पाने वाला	payee, addressee
		पाबन्दी	ban

पारम्परिक प्रकार	conventional type
पारदर्शी लिफाफा	window envelope
परिवहन	transport
पारम्परिक	mutual
पारम्परिक हित	mutual interest
पारित करना	pass
पारिश्रमिक	honorarium, remuneration
पार्टीवार/दलानुसार	partywise
पालन	compliance, observance
पालिसीधारक	policy holder
पावतीकार्ड	acknowledgement card
पावती सहित/बाकी	acknowledgement due
पिछली आदिम जातियाँ	backward tribes
पिछला क्षेत्र	backward area
पिछला वर्ग	backward classes
पिसाई	crushing
पुन: जारी करना	re-issue
पुन: पूर्तियोजना	re-plenishment scheme
पुन: पृष्ठांकित	re-endorsed
पुन: स्थापित करना	reinstate
पुनरावृत्ति	recurrence, repetition
पुनरीक्षण	revision
पुनर्गठन	reorganisation, reconstitution
पुनर्निर्माण	reconstruction
पुनर्भुनाई	rediscounting
पुनर्ग्रहणाधिकार	lien
पुनर्वासा वित्त	rehabilitation finance
पुनर्वित	refinance
पुरस्कार योजना	price scheme
पुष्टि	confirmation
पूँजी और प्रारक्षित निधियाँ	capital and reserve fund

पूँजी जमा अनुपात	capital deposit ratio
पूँजी निर्माण शुद्ध	capital formation/net
सकल	gross
पूँजी श्रम अनुपात	capital labourration
पूँजीगत अदायगी	capital payments
पूँजीगत माल	capital goods
पूँजीगत व्यय	capital expenditure
पूर्ण और शर्तरहित	absolute and unconditional
पूर्ण कालिक	whole time
पूर्ण बेचना	full endorsement
पूर्ण स्वामित्व	absolute ownership
पूर्णत: आश्रित	wholly dependent
पूर्णत: गारण्टीकृत	fully guaranteed
पूर्णत: चुकता	fully paid up
पूर्तिकार लेखा	supplier's account
पूर्वदत्त बाउचर	pre-paid vouchers
पूर्व दिनांकित चेक	antedated cheque
पूर्वमंजूरी/स्वीकृत	previous sanction
पूर्वोक्त	aforesaid
पूर्वोदाहरण	precedent
पूर्वोपाय	precautionary measures
पृष्ठांकन	endorsement
पृष्ठांकिती	endorsee
पैतृक व्यवसाय	ancestral profession
पोत प्राधिकरण	shipping authority
पोत लदान दस्तावेज	shipment document
पोत लदानोत्तर ऋण	post-shipment credit
प्रक्रिया नियम	rules of procedure
प्रक्रियात्मक	procedural
अनियमितताएँ	irregularities
प्रचल परिसम्पत्तियाँ	circulating assets
प्रचार सामग्री	publicity material
प्रतिउत्तर	counter reply
प्रतिकूल टिप्पणियाँ	unfavourable remarks

प्रतिपर्ण	counterfoil
प्रतिपूरक भत्ता	compensatory allowance
प्रतिपूर्ति	reimbursement
प्रतिबन्ध	restriction/ prohibition
प्रतिबन्धित सम्पत्तियाँ	restricted assets
प्रतिबन्धी बेचान	restrictive endorsement
प्रतिभू	surety
प्रतिभूति	security
प्रतिभूति बाण्ड	security bond
प्रतिभूमि रहित अग्रिम	clean advance
प्रतिभूतियों पर ब्याज	interest on securities
प्रतिवेदन	report
प्रतिव्यक्ति आय	per capita income
प्रतिशत	percent
प्रतिस्थापक	substitute
प्रतिस्पर्धी दर	competitive rate
प्रति हस्ताक्षर	counter-signature
प्रतीक्षा सूची	waiting list
प्रत्यक्ष वित्त	direct finance
प्रत्याभूति गारण्टी की सीमा	extent of guarantee
प्रत्याशित प्रतिफल	expected returns
प्रथम दृष्टया	prima facie
प्रथा	custom
प्रबन्ध तकनीकी	management technique
प्रबन्ध निदेशक	managing director
प्रथम प्रभार	first charge
प्रदत्त पूँजी	paid up captital
प्रभार निर्माण	creation of charge
प्रभारी अधिकारी	officer incharge
प्रभावी कब्जा	effective occupation
प्रमाणक पृष्ठांकन	certifying endorsement
प्रमाणित चैक	certified cheque
प्रमुख शीर्ष	main head
प्रलेखों (दस्तावेजों) का निष्पादन	stamping of documents
प्रवासी	migrant
प्रविष्टि (टीप)	entry
प्रशासन प्रबन्ध	administration
प्रशासनिक योग्यता	administrative ability
प्रस्तुत करना	submit
प्राकृतिक विपत्ति	natural calamity
प्राथमिक सहकारी समिति	primary co-oprative society
प्राथमिकता	priority
प्राथमिकता के क्रम से	in order of priority
प्रारम्भिक टीप/प्रविष्टि	opening entry
प्रारम्भिक नकदी	opening cash
प्रारक्षित अनुपात	reserve ratio
प्रारक्षित मूल्य	reserve price
प्रासंगित व्यय	incidental expenses
प्रेषण की सूचना	advice of dispatch
प्रेषक/परेषक	sender/consigner
प्रेषिती	addressee, remittee
प्रेस विज्ञप्ति	press release
प्रोद्भूत आय और व्यय उपचित	accrued income and expenditure
प्रेषण अभिकर्त्ता	agent forwarding

फ

फार्म का नमूना	specimen form
फुटकर जमा	sundry diposit
फुटकर नकद बही	petty cash book
फुटकर रोकड़ प्राप्तियाँ	petty cash receipts
फेरीवाला	hawker

ब

बन्द खाते/लेखे	dead accounts, closed accounts
बन्दोबस्त विलेख	deed of settlement
बन्ध पत्र और ऋण पत्र	bonds and debentures
बन्धक	mortagages, pledge
बन्धक कर्त्ता	mortgagers, pledger
बन्धक ग्राही	mortgagere, pledgee
बन्धक नामा	mortgage deed
बकाया चुकौती	repayment of outstanding
बकाया देनदारी/देयता	outstanding liability
बकाया राशि/वेतन	amount outstanding
बट्टा काटना	discounting
बट्टाकृत/बट्टागत मूल्य	discounted value
बट्टे पर विनिमय	exchange at a discount
बर्खास्तगी आदेश	dismissal orders
बहाली	reinstatement
बहीखाता रखना	book-keeping
बही मूल्य	book-value
बहुउद्देश्यीय समितियाँ	multipurpose societies
बहुमूल्य धातु	precious metal, bullion
बहुविध वित्तपोषण	multiple financing
बहुविध विनिमय दरें	multiple exchange rate
बाकीदारों की सूची	defaulters list
बाकी पड़ना	fall into arrears
बाकी देयताएँ	outstanding liabilities
बकाया शेष	outstanding balance
बाजार प्रतिस्पर्धा	market competetion
बजट प्रवधान	budget provision
बजट लीकेज	budget leakage
बफर स्टॉक	buffer stock
बहुविध वित्त	multiple finance
बाजार मुद्रा	money market
बाजार मूल्य	market value
बालिग	major
बाहरी चेक	outstation cheque
बाह्य अलंकरण	window dressing
बाह्य स्थान भत्ता	external audit
बिक्री मूल्य	sale value
बिक्री योग्यता	market ability
बिजली चालित करघे	powerlooms
बिना अनुमति के अनुपस्थिति	unauthorised absence
बिना वेतन छुट्टी	leave without pay
बिल का नवीकरण	renewal of bill
बिल का बेचान करना	enorsement of bill
बिल का भुगतान	retirement of bill
बिल भुनाना	bill discounting
बिल समर्पन	bill backing
बिल स्वीकृत बही	acceptance book
बिल छुड़ाना	retirement of bill
बीजक	invoice
बीमाकृत	insured
बीमा प्रमाणपत्र	certificate of insurance
बीमारी की छुट्टी	medical leave
बीते समय का चैक	stale cheque
बुनकर	weaver
बेचान किया गया चैक	endorsed cheque
बेचान पर्ची	allonge
बेचनीय	negotiable
बेजमानती कर्ज	clean loans
बैंक अधिकारीगण	bank staff
बैंक उधार	bank credit
बैंक की रोकड़ सूची	bank's cash scroll
बैंक गारण्टी योजना	bank gaurantee statement

बैंक समाधान विवरण	bank reconcilation statement	बैंकों के सेवा-शुल्क	bank service charge
बैंकर की सम्पत्ति	bankers' opinion	बोली	bid
बैंकरों का चेक	banker cheque	ब्याज उचित लेखा	interest suspense account
बैंकों के पास रोकड़	cash in hand with banks	ब्याज उपदान	interest subsidy
बैंकिंग व्यवस्था	banking system	ब्याज मुक्त अग्रिम	interest free advances

भ

भण्डार माल	stock in trade	भारतीय बैंक संस्थापन	indian institute of bankers
भण्डार रजिस्टर	stock register	भुगतान आदेश	pay orders
भरण-पोषण भत्ता	maintenance allowance	भुगतान करना	pay
भर्ती	recruitment	भुगतान सुविधा	payment facility
भविष्य निधि निवेश	provident fund investment	भुनाई सूची	encashement schedule
भागीदार	partner	भुनाये गये गिल	bills discounted
भार (वजन)	freight	भूमि का किराया	ground rent
भारग्रस्त सम्पदा	relieve	भूमिबन्धक चेक	land mortgage cheque
भारमुक्त करना	indian bank	भूल-चूक	errors and omissions
भारतीय बैंक संघ	indian bank association	भृत्य	peon
		भौतिक माल	material goods

म

मंच मंचूर वेतनमान	plateform, forum	मरम्मत और नवीकरण	repair and renovation
मण्डल प्रस्ताव	sanctioned pay scale	मसौदा/मसविदा	draft
मकान किराया भत्ता	board resolution	मँहगा मुद्रा बाजार	tight meney market
मजदूर संघ	labour union	महत्त्वपूर्ण परिवर्तन	material alteration
मझोले खेतिहर	medium cultivators	माँग का संकुचन	contraction of demand
मध्यकालिक ऋण	intermediate loans		
मध्यकालीन ऋण	medium term loans	माँग जमा	demand deposit
मध्य मूल्य	middle price	माँग देयता	demand liability
मध्यवर्ती उपभोग	intermediate consumption	माँग पर्ची	requisition slip
		माँग बाजार मुद्रा	call money market
मध्यवर्ती बन्धक	intermediate mortgage	माँगने पर अदा करें	pay on demand
		माँगने पर देय	payable on demand
मनोनीत निदेशक	nominated director	मानकीकरण	standardisation

मानद	honorary
मानेदय	honorarium
मानार्थ स्वीकृति	acceptance for honour
मामले की जाँच	investigation of the cases
मार्ग पत्रक	way bill
मार्ग में हुई हानि	loss in transit
मार्गदर्शी सिद्धान्त	guidelines
मार्जिन की अपेक्षाएँ	margin requirements
मार्जिन राशि	margin money
माल गोदामी कर्ज	warehousing loan
माल पाने वाला	consignee
माल भेजने वाला	consignor
मासिक तलपट	monthly trial balance
मितव्ययिता उपाय	economy measures
मिलान करना	tally
मिश्रित पूँजी कम्पनी	joint stock copany
मीयादी ऋण	term loans
मीयादी जमा रसीद	fixed deposit receipt
मीयादी देयताएँ	time liabilities
मीयादी मिद्‌पत्री	usance bill
मुअत्तिल करना	suspend
मुक्त व्यापार क्षेत्र	free-trade zones
मुख्तारनामा	power of attorney
मुख्य आय शीर्ष	main income heads
मुख्य ऋणी/ऋणकर्ता	principal debtor
मुख्य प्रतिभूति	principal security
मुख्य लक्षण	salient features
मुद्रांक शुल्क	stamp duty
मुद्रा	currency, money
मुद्रा का अवमूल्यन	devaluation of currency
मुद्रा की क्रयशक्ति	purchasing power of currency
मुद्रा नीति	monetary policy
मुद्रा प्रणाली	monetary systems
मुख्य मदें	main heads
मुख्य अधिकारी	chief officer
मुद्रा रिजर्व	monetary reserve
मुद्रास्फीति	inflation
मुद्राओं का पुनर्मूल्यन	revaluation of currency
मुर्गीपालन	poulry farming
मूर्त जमानत	tangible security
मूलधन की वापसी	repayment of principal
मूल पद वेतन	substantive pay
मूल प्रति	original copy
मूल्य घटबढ़ (मूल्य अस्थिरता)	price fluctuation
मूल्य निर्धारण	price determination
मूल्य आँकना	appraise
मूल्य प्राप्त	value received
मूल्य रेखा	price line
मूल्यवर्गानुसार	denomination-wise
वर्गीकरण	clsasification
मूल्यवृद्धि	price-escalation
मूल्य सूचकांक	price index
मूल्य सूची	price list
मूल्यह्रास लागत	depreciation cost
मूल्यांकन	evaluation
मूल्यानुसार कर	ad-valorem tax
मृत जमाकर्ता	deceased depositor
मौखिक	oral, verbal
मौसमी अग्रिम	seasonal advances
मौसमी धन्धा	seasonal occupation

य

यथानुपात अदायगी	pro-rata payments
यथामूल्य शुल्क	ad-valorm duty

यथा समय भुगतान	payment in due course
यथोचित समय	reasonalbe time
यूरोपीय आर्थिक समुदाय	european economic community
योग्य बिल/हुण्डियाँ	eligible bill
योग्यताक्रम	order of merit
यथामूल्य	ad-valorem
यात्रा बिल	way bill
योग्यता सूची	merit list
योग्यता प्राप्त उम्मीदवार	qualified candidates
योजना का क्रियान्वयन	implementaion of paln

र

रकमवार	amount-wise
रक्षित ऋण	secured loan
राजकोष	exchequer, treasury, fisc
राजनिष्ठा शपथ	oath of allegiance
राजपत्र अधिसूचना	gazette notification
राजभाषा	official language
राजस्व की छूट	remission of revenue
राजस्व स्टाम्प	revenue stamp
राज्य वित्त निगम	state financial corporation
राशि का अन्तिम उपयोग	end use of the
रात्रि ड्यूटी भत्ता	amount
राष्ट्रीय करण	nationalisation
राहत ऋण	relief loan
रिक्त पद	vaccant post
रिपोर्ट प्राधिकारी	reporting authority
रियायती ब्याज दर	concessional rate of interest
रुक्का/वचनपत्र	promissory note
रूई ओटना	cotton ginning
रूढ़िगत बेचनीयता	negotiability by custom
रूपान्तरित छुट्टी	coummuted leave
रेखन मोहर	crossing stamp
रेखित चेक	crossed cheque
रोक रखा गया	held in abeyance
रोक सूचना	notice of stoppage
रोकड़िया की सूची	cashier's scroll
रोकड़ का हिसाब करना	accounting of cash
रोकड़ जमा	cash deposit
रोकड़ बाकी	cash balance
रोजगार पूर्व प्रशिक्षण	pre-employment training
रोजनामचा	day book

ल

लक्षण	symptoms, features, characteristics
लक्ष्य	target, goal, mission
लघु उद्योग	small scale industries
लघु सिंचाई परियोजना	minor irrigation project
लदाई-उतराई	loading, unloading
लदान आदेश	shipping order
लदान बिल पत्र	bill of loading
लदान प्राप्त क्षमता	licenced capacity
लाकर सुविधा	locker facility
लागत और निर्माण लेखाकार	cost and work accountants
लागत की वसूली	recovery of cost
लागत निर्धारण	costing
लापता ड्राफ्ट	lost draft

लापरवाही से हुआ	occasioned by negligence
लाभकारी उपक्रम	advantageous enterprise
लाभकारी उद्यम	remunerative enterprise
लाभकारी धन्धा	gainful occupation
लाभ की गुंजाइश	margin of profit
लाभप्रद परिणाम	salutory effect
लाभहानि लेखा	profit and loss account
लाभांश	dividend
लावारिस प्रतिभूति	unclaimed security
लिखित साक्ष्य	written evidence
लेखन सामग्री	stationery
लेखा पुस्तकें	book of accounts
लेखा शीर्ष	account head
लेखा समाधान	adjustments of accounts
लेखा परीक्षक का प्रमाणपत्र	certification of auditor
लेखा परीक्षक प्रतिवेदन	auditor's report
लेखा परीक्षित तुलनपत्र	audited balance sheet
लेखा वर्ष	accounting year
लेखों का वार्षिक समापन	annual closing of accounts
लेखों में हेर-फेर करना	manipulation of accounts
लोकऋण की व्यवस्था	management of public debt

व

वंशगत अधिकार	hereditary rights
वचनपत्र	promissory note
श्रेष्ठ हुण्डी	first class bill
वरिष्ठता सूची	seniority list
वर्णक्रम	alphabetical order
वर्तमान बाजार मूल्य	current market price
वर्तमान वित्त वर्ष	current financial year/fiscal year
वर्धमान जोड़	progressive total
वर्धमान सीमान्त लागत	increasing marginal
वर्धिता दर	enhanced rate
वयस्कता	majority, adulthood
वसीयत	will, testament
वसीयत प्रमाणपत्र	probate
वसूली	recovery
वसूली पर्यन्त	pending realisation
वस्तु के रूप में चुकाया गया	repaid in kind
वस्तु विनिमय पद्धति	banker system
वस्तुकर	tax commodity
वस्तु:त	de facto
वाणिज्य और उद्योग	commerce and industry
वाणिज्य साख	commercial credit
वापस माँगे गये अग्रिम	recalled advances
वापसी डाक से	by return of post
वायदा बाजार	forward market
वायदा विनिमय सौदा	forward exchange transaction
वारिस	heir
वार्धत्य निवर्तन	superannuation
वार्षिक किराया निर्धारण	annual rental valuation
वार्षिक चुकौती क्षमता	annual repaying capacity
वार्षिक निरीक्षण	annual inspection
वार्षिक प्रतिफल	annual returns
वार्षिक वेतन वृद्धि	annual increments
वार्षिक निधि	annuity fund
वार्षिक लेखाबन्दी	yearly closing of accounts

वार्षिक लेखा समापन	yearly closing of accounts
वार्षिक संवरण	annuual clsings
वार्षिक लेखा	annual accounts
वास्तविक खरीददार	bonafide purchaser
वास्तविक पूँजी	real capital
वास्तविक मूल्य	actual cost
वास्तविक हर्जाना	actual damages
वाहक चेक	bearer cheque
वाहक द्वारा	per bearer
वाहक प्रतिभूतियाँ	bearer securities
वाहक व्यवस्था	courier arrangements
वाहन भत्ता	conveyance allowance
विकलांग कामगार	handicapped workman (labour)
विकृत सिक्का	defaced coins
विक्रेताधीन बाजार	seller's market
विक्रेय प्रतिभूति	marketable securities
विकेन्द्रित ऋण	decentralized loans
विचार किये बिना	irrespective of
विचाराधीन	under consideration
विचारार्थ	for consideration
वितरण	disbursement
वित्तनिभाव	financial accommodation
वित्त पोषक	financier
वित्त वर्ष	financial year
वित्तीय अनुशासन	financial discipline
वित्तीय दण्ड	financial penalty
वित्तीय दृष्टि से दुरस्त	financial sound
वित्तीय वचनबद्धता	financial commitment
वित्तीय हैसियत	finacial position
विदेशों में संयुक्त उद्यम	joint venture abroad
विदेश व्यापार क्षेत्र	foreign trade zone
विदेशी ऋण	external loan
विदेशी प्रेषण	foreign remittance
विदेशी बिल	external bill
विदेशी मुद्रा व्यापार	foreign exchange business
विदेशी मुद्रागत मूल्य	exchange value
विदेशी हुण्डी	external bill
विधि परामर्शदाता	legal advisor
विधिक संरक्षण	legal protection
विधिवत संरक्षण	legal protection
विधिवत हस्ताक्षरित	duly signed
विनिमय दर	exchange rate
विनिमेय मुद्रा	converible currency
विनियन्त्रण	decontrol
विनियोजन	appropriation
विपणन पद्धति	marketing method
विभागीय जाँच	departmental enquiry
विभेदक ब्याजदर	differential interest rate
विमुक्त दिवालिया	discharged bankrupt
विमोचित	retired
विराम भत्ता	halting allowance
विरासत कर	inheritance tax
विलम्बित भुगतान	delayed payment
विलम्ब शुल्क	late fee
विवरण	statements
विवरण का सत्यापन	verification of statements
विवरणी	return
विवादग्रस्त हुण्डी	disputed bill
विवेकाधीन ऋण सीमाएँ	discretionary credit limit
विशिष्ट माल	specified goods
विशेष अनुदान	special grant
विशेष औसत	particular average
विशेषकार्य अधिकारी	officer on special duty
विशेष रियासत	special concession
विशेष राय	expert opinion

विशेषाधिकार	privilege
विसंगत	irrelevant
विसंगति	discrepency
वृद्धि का उच्च दर	high rate of growth
वेतन और भत्ता	pay and allowance
वेतनमान	scale of pay
वेतन वृद्धि	increment
वेतन सहित छुट्टी	leave with pay
वैकल्पिक माँग	alternate demand
वैध उत्तराधिकारी	legal successor heir
वैध-निविदा	legal tender
वैध धारक	lawful holder
वैधता अवधि	validity period
वैयक्तिक गारण्टी	personal guarantee
वैयक्तिक जमानत	personal security
व्यक्त प्राधिकार	express authority
व्यवसाय	business, occupation
व्यवसाय का मुख्य स्थान	principle place of business
व्यवसाय का परिमाण	volume of business
व्यवसायिक प्रतिष्ठान	business establishment
व्यवसाय संगठन	business organisation
व्यवस्थित	sytematic
व्यवहार्य	viable, workable
व्यापार ऋण	trade credit
व्यापार घाटा	trade deficit
व्यांपार चिह्न प्रथा	trade mark
व्यापार बट्टा	trade discount
व्यापारिक अभिकरण	mercantile agency
व्यापारी बैंक	merchant banking
व्यावसायिक	professional
व्यावहारिक कठिनाई	practical difficulty

श

शक्ति चालित करघे (मशीन चालित करघा)	powerlooms
शक्ति चालित हल	power tillers
शपथ पत्र	affidavit
शहरी आबादी	urban population
शाखा अन्तरण सूची	branch transfer scroll
शब्द और अंकों में अन्तर	words and figures difference
शाखा प्रबन्धक	branch manager
शाखावार आँकड़े	branch-wise figure
शाखा विस्तार कक्ष	branch expansion cell
शाखा समायोजन	branch clearing code
शाखाओं का आपसी लेन-देन	inter-branch transaction
शाब्दिक/मौखिक	verbal/oral
शिकायतों का निवारण	redressal of grievances
शिक्षित बेकारी	educated unemployment
शिखर बुनकर समिति	apex weaver society
शिकायत हीन क्षेत्र	zero complaint region
शिनाख्त निशान	identification mark
शिल्पकार	sculptor
शिष्टमण्डल	delegation
शिष्टाचार	courtesy
शीघ्रावधि द्रव्य बाजार	call money market
शीर्ष/शिखर	apex
शीर्ष प्रबन्धन	top management
शुद्ध अचल आस्तियाँ	net fixed assets
शुद्ध अर्जन	net earning
शुद्ध आय	net income
शुद्ध कार्यशील पूँजी	net working capital
शुद्ध तरलता अनुपात	net liquidity ratio
शुद्ध देशी उत्पाद	net domestic product
शुद्ध प्रतिफल	net returns
शुष्क कृषि	dry farming
शून्य लागत	zero investment

श्रम आयुक्त	labour commissioner
श्रम कानून	labour laws
श्रम की अकुशलता	inefficiency of labour
श्रम लागत	zero investment
श्रम विवाद	labour disputes
श्रम शक्ति आयोजन	manpower mobilisation
श्रमिक वर्ग	working class, proletariat
श्रेणी	category rank
श्रेष्ठ प्रतिमूर्ति	gilt edged security

स

संकाय सदस्य	faculty member
संक्षिप्त विवरण	resume
संगठन और पद्धति	organisation and method
संगत उद्धरण	relevant extract
संग्रहण	mobilization
संघ के अन्तर्नियम	articles of association
संचालन करना (प्रोग्राम/गाड़ी)	conduct, handle, steer
संचित हानि	accumulated loss
सन्तुलन मूल्य	equilibrium price
सन्तुलित बजट	balanced budget
सन्तोषजनक	satisfactory
सन्दर्भ पुस्तकालय	reference library
सन्दर्भाधीन	under reference
सन्देशवाहक	messenger
सन्देह लाभ	benefit of doubt
सम्पत्ति का अधिकार	right to property
सम्पत्ति की कुर्की	attachment of property
सम्पर्क अधिकारी	liaison officer
सम्पार्श्विक प्रतिभूति	collateral security
सम्पूर्ण अधिकार	absolute title
सम्बद्ध उद्धरण	relevant extract
सम्बन्धित उपबन्ध	relevant provision
सम्भावी क्रेता	potential buyer
सम्भाव्य माँग	potential demand
सम्भाव्यता अध्ययन	feasibility studies
सम्मिश्र अग्रिम	composite advance
संयन्त्र और मशीन लेखा	plant and machinery account
संयुक्त परिवार सम्पत्ति	joint family property
संरक्षित काश्तकार	protected tenants
संलग्न करना	attach
संवर्गेत्तर पद	ex-cadre post
संवितरण पश्चात् निरीक्षण	post-disbursement inspection
संविदा दायित्व	obligation of contract
संविधि पुस्तक	statute book
संसाधन करना	processing
संस्तुति	recommendation
संस्तुतिपरक	recommendatory note
स्वीकृति	sanction
सकल आय	gross income
सकल हानि	gross loss
सकारने पर देय प्रलेख	documents against acceptance
सकारात्मक	positive
सक्रिय भागीदार	active partner
सक्रिय ऋण	active loan
सक्षम प्राधिकारी	competent authority
सट्टा प्रतिभूतियाँ	speculative securities
सतत प्रतिभूति	continuing security
सतर्कता अधिकारी	vigilance officer
सत्कार भत्ता	entertainemt allowance
सत्यनिष्ठा पूर्वक	solemnly
सत्यापन	verification
सदस्य सचिव	member-secretary

सदाचार	good conduct
सद्भाव से कार्य करते हुए	acting in good faith
सनदी लेखाकार	chartered accountant
समकक्ष	equivalent
समग्र व्यापार शेष	overall balance of trade
समझौता	agreement
समता सिद्धान्त	parity principle
सममूल्य पर	at par
समय पालन	punctuality
समयपूर्व आहरण	premature withdrawal
समय बद्ध कार्यक्रम	time bound programme
समय सारणी	schedule, time table
समयोपरि	overtime
समरूप कूट	uniform code
समर्थ प्राधिकारी	competent authority
समर्थन मूल्य	support price
समनुदेशिती	assignee
समर्पित	dedicated
समादेश याचिका	writ petition
समाधान विवरण	reconciliation statement
समापन	closing, concluding
समापनाधीन	under liquidation
समाप्ति सूचना	termination notice
समामेलित बैंकिंग कम्पनी	amalgamated banking company
समायोजन भत्ता	adjustment
समायोज्य अग्रिम	adjustable advance
समाशोधन करार	clearing agreement
समाशोधन गृह	clearing house
संचयित भण्डार योजना	buffer stock plan
समीक्षाधीन	under review
समुचित प्रतिफल	good consideration
समुद्रपारीय कार्यालय	overseas office
समुद्री जोखिम	marine risk
समुद्री व्यापार	maritime trade
समूह अग्रिम	group advance
समूह प्रणाली	pool system
समेकन	consolidation
समेकित दर	composite rate
समेटना	wind up
सरकारी आदाता	official receiver
सरकारी टिकट	service stamp
सरकारी प्रलेख	official document
सरकारी वित्त	public finance
सरकारी समापक	official liquidation
सर्राफा बाजार	bullion market
सराहना	appreciation
सराहनीय सेवा	meritorious service
सर्वाधिकार सुरक्षित	all rights reserved
सर्वेक्षण रिपोर्ट	survey report
सर्वेक्षण प्राधिकरण	supreme authority
सलाहकार मण्डल	advisory board
सवारी भत्ता	conveyance allowance
सवेतन अवकाश	leave with pay
सशर्त अदायगी	conditional payments
सहकारी बैंक	co-operative bank
सहकारी उद्यम	co-operative enterprises
सहकारी ऋण ढाँचा	co-operative credit structure
सहकारी सामूहिक कृषि समिति	co-operative collective farming society
सहभागिता प्रमाणपत्र	participation certificate
सहभागी ऋण	participation loan
सहयोगी संस्था	sister concern
सहज अधिकार	inherent rights
सहज विकास दर	nutural growth rate

सहमत	agreed
सहमति	consent, concurrence
सहायक उद्योग	ancillary industry
सहायक संस्था	subsidiary unit/ organization
सहायक बल	auxiliary force
सहायता अनुदान	grant in aid
सहायता ऋण	relief loan
सहायता संघ	aid-consortium
सांख्यकीय त्रुटि	statistical error
सांयोगिक दायित्व	contingent obligation
सांविधिक आदेश	statutory order
साक्ष्य सत्यापन	verification of testimony
साख सूचना	credit information
साधन	resource
साधारण बन्धक	ordinary mortgage
साधिकार अर्जित अवकाश	privilege leave
साधिकार धारक	holder in due course
सापेक्ष प्रतिवेदन	qualified report
साप्ताहिक बकाया विवरण	weekly arrears report
साम्यिक बन्धक	equitable mortgage
सामाजिक आर्थिक विकास	socio-economic development
सामाजिक नियन्त्रण	social control
सामान का बही मूल्य	book value of stores
सामान्य ऋण नियन्त्रण	general credit control
सामान्य ग्रहणाधिकार	general lien
सामान्य भविष्य निधि	general provident fund
सामान्य रक्षोपाय	usual safeguard
सामान्य व्यवहार	normal behaviour
सामान्यीकरण	generalization
सामान्य खाता बही	general ledger
सामुदायिक विकास योजना	community development project
सामूहिक खेती	collective farming
सामूहिक बीमा	group insurance
सारणीकरण	tabulation
सारवृत्त	resume
सार्वजनिक ऋण	public debt
सावधि बिल	time bill
सावधि जमा पर ऋण	loan against fixed deposits
सावधि रसीद का परिपक्वता	maturity of F.D.R.
सावधि निर्यात ऋण	term export credit
सहकार अधिनियम	money lenders act
सिक्का ढलाई	minting
सिद्धान्ततः	in principle
सिफारिश	recommendation
सीधा लदान-पत्र	through bill of lading
सीधी भर्ती	direct recruitment
सीमान्त	margin
सीमान्त उपज	marginal yield
सीमाएँ	limits
सीमा शुल्क निकासी परमिट	custom clearance permit
सीमित देनदारी	limited liability
सीमित देयल प्रतिष्ठान	limited company
सुअर पालन	piggery
सुदृढ़ पार्टी	sound party
सुनियोजित	systematic
सुपुर्दगी का स्थान	place of delivery
सुपुर्दगी द्वारा आक्रमण	negotiation by delivery
सुरक्षा उपाय	security measures
सुरक्षित जमाकक्ष	safe deposit value
सूखा	drought
सूचक कार्ड	index card
सूचकांक	index numbers

सूचना नहीं	no advice
सूचना पट्ट	notice board
सूचना प्रणाली	information system
सूचना रहित प्रदत्त	paid without advice
सूचीगत प्रतिभूति	listed security
सूत का व्यापार	trading in yarn
सूती वस्त्र उद्योग	cotton textile
सेवा की सराहना	appreciation of service
सेवा पूँजी	service book
सौंपना	entrust
स्टाम्प शुल्क की छूट	remission of stamp duty
स्टाक आवर्त अनुपात	stock turnover ratio
स्टाक मूल्य वृद्धि	stock appreciation
स्टाफ प्रशिक्षण केन्द्र	staff training centre
स्थगन आदेश	stay order
स्थानान्तरण भत्ता	transfer allowance
स्थान पर	at sight
स्थानापन्न	substitute
स्थानापन्न हैसियत	officiating capacity
स्थानीय ढुलाई	local cartage
स्थानीय प्राधिकार	local authority
स्थानीय वितरण	local distribution
स्थापन लागत व्यय	set-up-cost
स्रोत पर	at source
स्थाना व्यय	establishment expenses
स्थायी अनुदेश	standing instruction
स्थायी देनदारी	fixed liability
स्थायी पट्टा	permanent lease
स्थायी परिसम्पत्तियाँ	fixed assets
स्थायीवत्	quasi permanent
स्थिर कीमतें	stable price
स्थिर माँग	stable demand
स्रोत पर कटौती	deduction at source
स्वनियोजन	self-employment
स्वग्रहणाधिकार	possessory title
स्वचालित	automatic
ऋण गारण्टी योजना	credit gaurantee
स्वभावत: चूक कर्त्ता	habitual defaulter
स्वयं अदा करें	pay to self
स्वयं को देय	payble to self
स्वर्णाभूषणों पर अग्रिम	advance against gold ornaments
स्वस्थ्य बैंक प्रणाली	sound banking system
स्वास्थ्यता प्रमाणपत्र	medical certificate
स्वागत	reception
स्वामित्व पर प्रकार	pattern of ownership
स्वीकार्य सीमा	permissible limit
स्वीकृत ऋण सीमाएँ	sanctioned limits on loan
स्वीकृत प्रतिभूति	approved security
स्वीकृति पत्र	letter of acceptance

ह

हड़ताल निषेध धारा	no-strike clause
हथकरघा उद्योग	handloom industry
हलफनामा	affidavit
हवाई डाक सेवा	air mail service
हस्तलिखित दस्तावेज	hand written document

हस्तान्तरण विलेख	transfer deed
हस्तान्तरणीय	transferable
हस्तान्तरी	transferee
हाजिरी रजिस्टर	muster roll
हानि निर्धारण	assessment of loss
हामीदार	underwritten
हुण्डीकर्त्ता	drawer
हुण्डी की अवधि	term of bill
हुण्डी की चुकौती	discharge of bill
हैसियत	status
हुण्डी सरकारी खाता	acceptors' ledger

परिशिष्ट–2/Appendix-2

भारतीय संविधान विषयक हिन्दी शब्दावली एवं अंग्रेजी पर्याय

(Hindi Terms and their English Equivalents used in Indian Constitution)

अ

अक्षम	inompetent
अक्षमता	inompetency
अग्रिम धन	advance
अतिक्रमण	violation, transgression, encroachment
न्यायाधीश	judge
अतिरिक्त न्यायाधीश	additional judge
अतिरिक्त लाभ	excess profit
अधिकरण	tribunal
अधिकार	right
अधिकार-अभिलेख	record of rights
अधिकार-पृच्छा	quo waranto
अधिग्रहण	requisition
अधिनियम (सं.)	act
अधिनियम (क्रि.)	enact
अधिपत्र	warrant
अधिभार	surcharge
अधिमान	preference
अधिवक्ता	advocate
अधिवास	domicile
अधिवासी	domiciled
अधिष्ठाता	presiding officer
अधिसूचना	notification
अधीक्षक	superintendent
अधीक्षण	superintendence
अधीन	subject
अधीनस्थ अधिकारी	subordinate officer
अधीनस्थ न्यायालय	subordinate court
अध्यक्ष	speaker
अध्यादेश	ordinance
अध्यासीन होना	preside
एक क्षेत्राधिकार	exclusive jurisdiction
अनर्हता	disqualification
अनर्हीकरण	disqualify
अनियमितता	irregularity
अनुकूलन	adaptation
अनुच्छेद	article
अनुज्ञप्ति/लाइसेंस	licence
अनुज्ञा (क्रि.)	permit
अनुज्ञा (संज्ञा)	permission
अनुदान	grant
अनुदेश (न.)	instruction
अनन्मुक्त	undischarged
अनुपाती प्रतिनिधित्व	proportional representation
अनुपूरक अनुदान	supplementary
अनुमति	assent
अनुमोदन (क्रि.)	approve
अनुमोदन (संज्ञा)	approval
अनुशासन	discipline
अनुशासन सम्बन्धी	disciplinary
अनुषक्ति	adherence
अनुष्ठान	rites, rituals
अनुसमर्थन (संज्ञा)	ratification
अनुसमर्थन (क्रि.)	ratify
अनुसन्धान (क्रि.)	investigate
अनुसन्धान (संज्ञा)	investigation
अनुस्मारक	reminder
अनुसूचित क्षेत्र	scheduled area

अनुसूचित जन जाति	scheduled tribe
अनुसूचित जाति	scheduled caste
अनुसूची	schedule
अन्तर्गसन	involvement
अन्तर्गस्त	involved
अन्र्देशीय जलपथ	inland waterway
अन्तर्राष्ट्रीय	international
अन्त:करण	onscience
अन्यदेशीय	aliens
अन्य संक्रामण (क्रि.)	alienate
अन्य संक्रामण (संज्ञा)	alienation
अपमान लेख	libel
अपमान वचन	slander
अपमिश्रण	adulteration
अपर न्यायाधीश	additional judge
अपराध	crime, offence
अपराधी	criminal
अपवर्जन (क्रि.)	exclude
अपवर्जन (संज्ञा)	exclusion
अपात्र	ineligible
अपात्रता	ineligibility
अपील	appeal
अपील न्यायालय	court of appeal
अपवृत्त	inoperative
अभिकथन	allegation
अभिरण	agency
अभिकर्त्ता	agent
अभिप्राय	opinion
अभियाचना	demand
अभियुक्त	accused
अभियुक्ति	charge
अभियोग	prosecution
अभियोजन	prosecution
अभियोज्य दोष	cognizable offence
अभिरक्षा	custody
अभिलेख	record
अभिलेख न्यायालय	court of record
अभिलेख कक्ष	record room
अभिशप्त	cursed
अभिशप्ति/अभिशक्ति	curse
अभिसमय	convention
अभ्यर्थी	candidate
अमान्य	invalid
अयुक्त प्रभाव	undue influence
अर्जन	acquisition
अर्जी	petition
अर्थकरना	construe
अर्थदण्ड	fine
अर्हता	qualification
अल्पसंख्यक वर्ग	minority
अल्पीकरण	derogation
अवधिदान	adjourn
अवमान/अवमानना	contempt
अवयस्क	minor
अविभाजित कुटुम्ब/परिवार	joint family
अविश्वास प्रस्ताव	motion of no confidence
अवैध	illegal
अवैधाचरण	illegal practice
असमर्थता	incapacity
असमर्थता निवृत्ति वेतन	invalidity pension
असैनिक	civil
असैनिक शक्ति	civil power
अहितकारी	detrimental
अंकन	endorsement
अंकित	endorsed
अंग/इकाई	unit
अंश	share
अंशदान	contribution

आ

आकलन (क्रि.)	scrutiny	आयकर	income tax
आकस्मिकता निधि	contingency fund	आयात शुल्क	import duty
आचार	custom	आयुक्त	commissioner
आजादी	freedom	आयोग	commission
आजीविका	profession, vocation	आरक्षक	police
आजीविका-कर	professional tax	आरक्षक बल	police force
आज्ञप्ति	decree	आरोप	allegation
आदेश	order	आरोपण करना	allege
आदेशिका	process	आर्थिक	economic
आनुषंगिक	consequential	आर्थिक क्षेत्राधिकार	pecuniary
आपराधिक	criminal	आवर्तक	recurring
आपात	emergency	आवारागर्दी	vagrancy
आपाती	emergent	आवेदन पत्र	application
आपात की घोषणा	proclamation of emergency	आस्ति	property
आभार	obligation	आहिंडन	vagrancy
		आह्वान	summon
		आँकना	estimate

इ, उ

इच्छापत्र/वसीयत/विल	will, testament	उद्भव	descent
इच्छा-पत्र हीन	intestate	उद्यम	enterprise
इच्छा-पत्र हीनत्व	intestacy	उद्योग	industry
उगाहना (क्रि.)	collect, levy	उधार/ऋण	loan
उच्चतम न्यायालय	supreme court	उधार ग्रहण	borrowing
उच्च न्यायालय	high court	उन्मत्त	lunatic
उत्तराधिकार	succession	उन्माद	lunacy
उत्तराधिकार शुल्क	succession duty	उन्मुक्ति/प्रतिरक्षा	immunity
उत्तराधिकारी	successor, heir	उपकर	cess
उत्तरवादिता	liability	उपक्रमण	initiate
उत्पादन	production	उपचार	remedy
उत्पादन शुल्क	excise duty	उपजीविका	occupation
उत्प्रवास	emigration	उपदान	gratuity
उत्प्रेक्षण लेख	certiorari	उपदेश/परामर्श	homily/advisory
उद्ग्रहण (संज्ञा)	levy	उपनिर्वाचन	by-election
उद्घोषणा	proclamation	उपनिवेशन	colonization

उपबन्ध	provision
उपभोग/उपभोक्ता	consumption/ consumer
उपराज्यपाल	lieutenant governor
उपराष्ट्रपति	vice president
उपलब्धि	emolument
उपविभाग	subdivision
उपवेशन/बैठक	sitting
उपविधि	bye law
उपसभापति	vice chairman
उपस्थित होना	appear
उपाध्यक्ष	deputy speaker
उपायुक्त	deputy commissioner
उपायोजन/रोजगार	employment
उपार्जित/प्रोद्भूत	accrued
उम्मीदवार/प्रत्याशी	candidate
उल्लंघन	contravention

ऋ, ए

ऋण	debt
ऋण ग्रस्तता	indebtedness
ऋणपत्र	debenture
एकक	unit
एकल निगम	corporation, sole
एकल संक्रमणीय मत	single transferable vote
एकस्व	patent

क

कटक (सैन्यबल स्थायी निवास/छावनी)	cantonment
कदाचार	misbehaviour, misdemeanour
कब्जा	possession
कम्पनी	company
कर	tax
करारनामा	agreement
कर्तव्य	duty
कर्तुमभिप्रेत	purporting to be done
कर्मचारी गण	staff
कानूनी	legal
कारखाना	factory
कारबार/कारोबार	business
कारागार	prison
काराबन्दी	prisoner
कारावास	imprisonment
कार्मिक संघ	trade union
कार्य	business
कार्यकारी	acting
कार्यपालिका अधिकार	executive power
कार्यपालिका	executive
कालदान	adjourn
कावल	custody
काँची हाउस/मवेशीखाना	cattle pound
किराया	fare
किसान	land tenant
कुर्की	attachment
कूटनीति	diplomacy
कृतिस्वाम्य	copyrigth
कृत्य	function
केन्द्रीय गुप्तचर विभाग	central
कैद	imprisonment
कैदी	prisoner
क्षति	injury damage
क्षति पूरक बिल	bill of indemnity

क्षमताशाली	competent	क्षेत्र	area
क्षमा	pardon	क्षेत्राधिकार	jurisdiction

ख

खनिज	mineral	खर्च	cost
खनिज सम्पत्	mineral resources	खण्ड	clause

ग, घ

गणना	account	ग्राम परिषद्	village counil
गणना परीक्षा	vote on account	ग्रास	admissible
गणपूर्ति	audit	घोषणा	declaration, proclamation
गवेषणा	resarch		
गूढ़-पत्र/मत-पत्र	ballot paper		

च

चर्चा	discussion	चिह्न	mark
चालू मुद्रा	currency	चुने हुए	selected
चित्त विकृति	unsoundness of mind	चुंगी	octroi
		चेक	cheque

छ, ज

छावनी	cantonment	जिला निधि	district fund
जगह, षद	post	जिला न्यायालय	district court
जनगणना	census	जिला परिषद्/काउन्सिल	distrit council/board
जनजाति परिषद	tribal council	जीविका	livelihood
जल दस्युता	piracy	जुआ	gambling
जल प्रांगण	territorial waters	जुर्माना	fine
जामिन	bail	जेल	prison
जाँच करना	inquire	ज्वार-जल	tidal waters
जिला	district	ज्ञाप	memo
जिला गण	district board	ज्ञापन	memorandum

ट

टंकण — coinage/type
टाँच — attach
ट्राम — tram car
ट्राम गाड़ी — tram car

त, थ

तत्सम — for the time being
तदर्थ — ad-hoc
तत्स्थली/अनुरूप — corresponding
तृतीय-पठन — third reading
त्रैवार्षिक — triennial
थाना — police station

द

दत्तक ग्रहण — adoption
दत्तक स्वीकरण — adoption
दस्तकारी — handicraft
दस्तावेज — document
दंड देना — punish
दंड न्यायालय — criminal court
दंड-विधि — criminal law
दंड विषयक — criminal
दंडादेश — sentence
दंडाधिकारी न्यायालय — magistrate's court
दाखिल — entry
दातव्य — charities
दाय (भाग) — inheritance
दायित्व — liability
दावा — claim
दिवाला — bankrupt
दिवाला — insolvency
दीवानी — civil
दीवानी-अदालत — civil court
दृष्टांत — visas
देय — fee
दोहरा/द्विगृही — bicameral
दोष प्रमाणित — convicted
दोष सिद्धि — conviction
दोषारोप — charge
द्यूत — gambling
द्वितीय-पठन — second reading

ध

धन — money
धन विधेयक — money bill
धर्म — faith/religion
धन्धा — occupation

न

नक्ष — design
नगर क्षेत्र — municipal area
नगर-ट्राम वे — municipal tram way
नगर निगम — municipal corporation
नगर पालिका — municipality
नगर रथ्यायान — municipal tram way
नगर समिति — municipal commitee
नागरिकता — citizenship

नाम निर्देशन/नामित	nominate	निर्वाचन (क्रि.)	elect
नावाधिकरण	admiralty	निर्वाचन (संज्ञा)	election
निकाय	body	निर्वाचनाधिकरण	election tribunal
निक्षेपनिधि	sinking fund	निर्वाचन-आयुक्त	election commissioner
निखात निधि	treasure trove	निर्वाचन क्षेत्र	constituency
निगम कर	corporation tax	निर्वाचित	elected
निगमन	incorporation	निर्वासन	transportation, punishment
निगम-निकाय	body/corporate	निर्वाह मजदूरी	subsistence wages
निदेश	direction	निलम्बित करना (क्रि.)	suspend
निधि	fund	निलम्बन (संज्ञा)	supension
निबद्ध/पंजीकृत	registered	निवारक निरोध/नजरबन्दी	preventive detention
निबन्धक	term	निवृत्त होना	retire
निबन्धन	registration	निवृति	retirement
नियन्त्रक महालेखा परीक्षक	comptroller and auditor general	निवृत्ति वेतन	pension
नियन्त्रण	control	निषेध	forbid, prohibit
नियम	rule	निषिद्ध	forbidden, prohibited
नियुक्ति	appointment	निष्ठा	alleginace
नियोजन उत्तरदायित्व	employers liability	नौकरी	employment, service
निरसन	repeal	नौकरी-कर	employment tax
निराकरण करना	abrogate	नौकाधिकरण	admiralty
निरोध	custody	नौपरिवहन	navigation
निरोधा/संक्रमण रोगावधि	quarantine	नौसेना विषयक	naval
निर्णायक मत	casting vote	न्यस्त करना	entrust
निर्देश/सन्दर्भ	reference	न्यायपालिका	judiciary
निर्धारण	assessment	न्यायाधिकरण	tribunal
निर्माण	construction	न्यायाधिपति	justice
निर्यात	export	न्यायाधीश	judge
निर्यात शुल्क	export duty	न्यायालय अवमानना	contempt of court
निर्योग्यता/अपंगता	disability	न्यायिक कार्यवाही	judical proceeding
निर्वचन	interpretation	न्यायिक मुद्रांक	judicial stamp
निर्वसीयत	intestate	न्यायिक अधिकार	judicial power
निर्वसीयता	intestacy	न्यास	trust
निर्वहन करना	discharge	न्यूनन	abridge
निर्वाचक गण	electoral college		
निर्वाचन नामावली	electoral rolls		

प

पक्ष	party
पण लगाना	bet
पणक्रिया	betting
पण्य चिह्न	merchandise mark
पत्तन निरोध	port qurantine
पथ कर	toll
पथ नियम	road rules
पद/पदस्थान	post, office
पदच्युत करना	dismiss
पदत्याग/पद त्याग करना	resignation/demise
पदधारी	incumbent
पदावधि	tenure
पदआवास	official residence
पदेन	ex-officio
पराया करण	alienation
परमादेश	mandamus
परन्तु	provided
परमिट (संज्ञा)	permit
परामर्श	consultation
परित्यजन/परित्यांग	abandonment
परित्राण	safeguard
परिपालन	implement
परिप्रश्न	enquiry
परिलब्धि	perquisite
परिवहन	transport
परिव्यय	cost
परिषद्	council
परिषद् आदेश	order in council
परिसीमन (क्षेत्र का)/ (चुनाव क्षेत्र का)	delimitation/ delineation
परिसीमा	delimitation
परिहार	remission
परिहार विधेयक	bill of indemnity
परोक्ष-निर्वाचन	indirect election
पर्यवेक्षण	inspection
पर्यालोचन	deliberate
पंचाट	award
पात्रता	eligibility
पात्र	eligible
पारपत्र	passport
पारण	pass
पारित	passed
पारितोषिक	reward
पारिश्रमिक	remuneration
पावती	receipt
पीठासीन	preside
पीठासीन अधिकारी	presiding officer
पुनरीक्षण	revision
पुनर्विचार न्यायालय	court of appeal
पुनर्विलोकन/पुनरावलोकन	review
पुरः स्थापन	introduce
पुरः स्थापना	introduction
पूर्त	charity
पूर्तधार्मिक धर्मस्व	charitable and religious endowment
पूर्त संस्था	charitable institution
पूर्व-मंजूरी	previous sanction
पूर्वसम्मति	previous consent
पूंजी	capital
पृष्ठांकन	endorse
पृष्ठांकित	endorsed
पेशगी/अग्रिम धन	advance
पेशा	profession
पोषण	maintenance
पोषण करना	maintain
पौरत्व/नागरिकता	citizenship
खोज/अन्वेषण	discovery
प्रकाशन	publication
प्रक्रिया	procedure
प्रख्यापन	promulgate

प्रग्रहण/गिरफ्तार	arrest
प्रचलित	current
प्रचार करना	propagate
प्रतिकार	compensation
प्रतिकूल असर डालना	affect prejudicially
प्रतिकूलता	contravention
पूर्वमति ग्राहयता	prejudice
प्रतिकृति/प्रतिलिपि	copy
प्रतिज्ञान	affirmation
प्रतिनिधि	representation
प्रतिपत्री	proxy
प्रतिपालक अधिकरण	court of wards
प्रतिभूति	security
प्रतिरक्षा	defence
प्रतिलिप्याधिकार	copyright
प्रतिवेदन	report
प्रतिव्यक्ति कर	capitation tax
प्रतिषिद्ध	prohibited
प्रतिषेध	prohibition
प्रतिशुल्क	counter vailing duties
प्रतिषेधलेख	writ of prohibition
प्रतिसंहरण	revoke
प्रत्यक्ष निर्वाचन	direct election
प्रत्यय	credit
प्रत्यय-पत्र	letter of credit
प्रत्ययानुदान	votes of credit
प्रत्यर्पण	extradition
प्रत्याभूति	guarantee
प्रथम पठन (निचला) सदन	lower house
प्रधानमन्त्री	prime minister
प्रपत्र/फारम	form
प्रभाव	influence
प्रभुसत्ता	sovereign
प्रंभुता	sovereignty
प्रमाणपत्र	certificate
प्रमाणीकरण	authentication
प्रमोदकर	entertainment tax
प्रयुक्ति/प्रयोग	application
प्रयोग/अभ्यास	exercise
प्रति विलम्बन	reprive
प्रवर समिति	select commitee
प्रविष्टि	entry
प्रवेश	access
प्रवेशन	accession
प्रव्रजन	migration
प्रशान्ति	tranquility
प्रशासन	administration
प्रशासनिक कार्यक्षमता	efficiency of administration
प्रशासकीय	administrative
प्रशासित	administered
प्रशिक्षण	training
प्रसंग/सन्दर्भ	context
प्रसारण	broadcasting
प्रसूति राहत	maternity relief
प्रस्ताव	motion, proposal
प्रस्तावना	preamble
प्रस्थापना	proposal
प्राक्कलन	estimate
प्रादेशिक आयुक्त	regional commissioner
प्रादेशिक क्षेत्राधिकार	regional jurisdiction
प्रादेशिक निधि	regional fund
प्रादेशिक निर्वाचन क्षेत्र	territorial constituency
प्रादेशिक परिषद्	regional council
प्रादेशिक भार	territorial charges
प्राधिकार	authority
प्राधिकारी	authority
प्राधिकृत	authorised
प्रान्त	province
प्रापण/प्राप्त होना	accrue
प्राप्ति	receipt
प्रोमिजरी नोट/वचन-पत्र	promissory note
प्रासंगिक/अनुषंशिक	incidental
प्रोद्भूत	accrued

फ

फरियाद comptaint
फीस देय fee
फेडरल न्यायालय federal court

ब

बँटवारा allocation
बनाये रखना (क्रि.) maintain
बनाये रखना (संज्ञा) maintenance
बन्दी प्रत्यक्षीकरण habeas corpus
बन्धक mortgage, hostage
बल forces
बहि शुल्क customs duty
बहुमत majority/plurality
बिल bill
बीमापत्र policy of insurance
बेकारी unemployment
बैठक sitting
बैंक bank
बोर्ड board

भ

भत्ता allowance
भविष्यनिधि provident fund
भर्ती recruitment
भागिता partnership
भाटक rent
भाड़ा/किराया fare
भार charge
भारग्रस्त सम्पदा encumbered estate
भारत सरकार government of india
भारित करना charge
भू-अभिलेख land records
भू-धृति land tenures
भू-राजस्व land revenue
भ्रष्ट corrupt

म

मजदूरी wage
मण्डल जिला district
जिला न्यायालय district court
मण्डलाधीश/मण्डलायुक्त deputy commissioner
मण्डली परिषद् board
मत vote
मतदाता voter
मतदान voting
मतदाता सूची voter list
मताधिकार suffrage
मतिमन्द dullness
मध्यस्थ न्यायालय arbitral tribunal
मध्यस्थ arbitrator
मध्यस्थ निर्णय/मध्यस्थता arbitration
मनोदौर्बल्य mental weakness
मनोनयन nominate
मनोवैकल्य mental deficiency
मन्त्रणा advice
मन्त्रणापरिषद् advisory council
मन्त्रि परिषद् council of ministers
मन्त्री minister
मरण शुल्क death duty
महाजनी usury
महाधिवक्ता advoate general

महान्यायावदी	attorney general	मुक्त	exempt
महाप्रशासक	administrator general	मुखिया	headman
महालेखा परीक्षक	auditor general	मुख्य	chief
महाभियोग	impeachment	मुख्य आयुक्त	chief commissioner
मानदेय	honorarium	मुख्य निर्वाचन आयुक्त	chief election commissioner
मानव पण्य	traffic in human being	मुख्य न्यायाधिपति	chief justice
मानहानि	defamation	मुख्यमन्त्री	chief minister
मान्यता	validity	मुद्रा/मोहर	seal
मार्ग प्रदर्शन	guidance	मुद्रांक शुल्क	stamp duty
माँग	demand	मूलधन	capital
मीनक्षेत्र	fishery	मूलधन मूल्य	capital value
मछली पकड़ना	fishery		

य

यथास्थिति	status quo	यातायात	traffic
यन्त्रशास्त्र/अभिमन्त्रण	engineering	योगदान काल	joining time
याचिका	petition		

र

रक्षण/आरक्षण	reservation	राय	opinion
रक्षा कवच	safeguard	राशि	amount
रक्षित वन	reserved forest	राष्ट्र	nation
रद्द करना	annulment	राष्ट्र ऋण	public debt
रसीद	receipt	राष्ट्रपति	president
राजकोष गामी	escheat	राष्ट्रपति-प्रसाद पर्यन्त	during the pleasure of the president
राजस्व	revenue		
राजस्व न्यायालय	revenue court	राष्ट्रीय राजपथ	national highways
राज्य	state	राष्ट्रों की विधि	laws of nations
राज्य सरकार	state government	रिक्त स्थान/रिक्तता	vacancy
राज्य क्षेत्र	territory	रिक्थ	property
राज्य क्षेत्रातीत प्रवर्तन	extra territorial operation	रुकावट	bar, ban
		रूढ़ि	custom
राज्यनिधि	state fund	रूप, भेद	modification
राज्यपरिषद्	council of states	रूपांकन	design
राज्यपाल	governor	रेल	railway
राज्यसूची	state list		

ल

लगान	levy
लादना (थोपना)	impose
लम्बित	pending
लागत	cost
लागू करना	apply
लाभ	profit
लाभांश	dividend
लिखित	written instrument
लिखित सूचना	notice in writing
लिखित आदेश	writ
लेखा	account
लेखा परीक्षा	audit
लेखानुदान	vote on account
लेख्य (आलेख)	document
लेना-देना	dealings/concern
लोक	people
लोक अधिसूचना	public notification
लोकसभा	house of the people, parliament
लोक समाज	community
लोक सेवाएँ	public service
लोक सेवा आयोग	public service commission
लोक स्वास्थ्य	public health

व

वकालत करना	plead
वकील	pleader
वचनबद्ध	commited
वधिक् पोत	merchant ship
वयस्क	major, adult
वयस्क मताधिकार	adult suffrage
वस्तुभाड़ा/मालभाड़ा	freight
वहनपत्र	bill of lading
वाक्स्वातन्त्र्य	freedom of speech
वाणिज्य	commerce
वाणिज्य दूत	consul
वाणिज्य विषयक	commercial
वाद	cause
वाद पद	issue
वाद प्रतिवाद	controversy
वादमूल	cause of action
वाद-विवाद	debate
वाद विषय	subject matter
वायदा बाजार	future market
वायुपथ	airways
वार्षिक	annual
वार्षिक वित्त विवरण	annual financial statement
वार्षिकी	annuities
विकलन	debit
विकृत चित्त	unsound mind
विक्रय	sale
विक्रय कर	sales tax
विघटन	dissolution
विचार	onsideration
विचारार्थ प्रस्ताव	motion for consideration
वितरण	distribution
वित्त	finance
वित्त विधेयक	finance bill
वित्त आयोग	finance commission
वित्तीय	financial
वित्तीय भार	finacial obligation
वित्तीय विवरण	financial statement
विदेशीय कार्य/मामले	foreign affairs

विदेशीय विनिमय	foreign exchange
विधान	legislation
विधान परिषद्	legislative council
विधान मण्डल	legislature
विधान सभा	legislative assembly
विधायिनी शक्ति	legislative power
विधि	law
विधि व्यवस्था	law and order
विधि प्रश्न	question of law
विधिमान्य	legal tender
विधियों का समान संरक्षण	equal protection of law
विधि विषयक	legal
विधेयक	bill
विनिमय	regulation
विनिमयन	regulate
विनिमय-पत्र	bill of exchange
विनियोग	appropriation
विनियोग विधेयक	appropriation bill
विनिश्चय	decision
विभाग	section
विभाजन	distribution
विभेद	discrimination
विमति	dissent
विमान परिवहन	air navigation
विमान यातायात	air traffic
विमान बल	air force
विमोचन	redemption
विमोचन भार	redemption charges
वियुक्त/वंचित	deprived
विराम	respite
विलेख	deed
विवरणी	return
विवाद	dispute
विवाह विच्छेद	divorce
विशेषाधिकार	privilege
विश्वास प्रस्ताव	motion of confidance
विश्वास का अभाव	want of confidence
विसर्जन	disperse
विसंगत	irrelevant
विस्तार करना	extend
विस्फोटक	explosive
वीसा	visas
वृत्ति	profession
वृत्तिकर	profession tax
वृद्धि/सूद	interest
वेतन	pay/salary
वेलई/रोजगार	employment
वैदेशिक कार्य	external affairs
व्ययगत होना (अवधि समाप्त होना)	lapse
व्यय	expenditure/expense
व्यवसाय	vocation
व्यवस्था	order
व्यवहार	civil/dealings
व्यवहार अदालत/ व्यवहारालय/व्यवहार न्यायालय	civil court
व्यवहार प्रक्रिया (दिवानी)	civil procedure
व्यवहार प्रक्रिया संहिता	civil procedure code
व्यवहार में घसीटना	sue
व्यवहार वाद	civil suit
व्यवहार विषयक अपकृत्य/दोष	civil wrong
व्यवहार शक्ति	civil power
व्याख्या	explanation
व्यापार	trade
व्यापार कर	trade tax
व्यापार चिह्न	trade mark
व्यापार संघ	trade union
व्यावृत्ति	savings

श

शक्ति अधिकार	power
शर्त	condition/proviso
शलाका/शलाका पद्धति	ballot
शान्ति	peace
शाश्वत उत्तराधिकार	perpetual succession
शासक	ruler
शासन	governance/ government
शासी निकाय	governing body
शास्ति	penalty
शिक्षा	education/instruction
शिल्पी प्रशिक्षण	technical training
शिविर	camp
शिशु	infant
शिस्त	disciplinary
शुल्क	duty/tax/levy
शुल्क सीमान्त	custom frontiers
शून्य	void
शैरिफ	sheriff
शोधना	research
श्रम	labour
श्रमिक संघ	labour union

स

सत्र	session
सत्र न्यायालय	sessions court
सत्रावसान करना/सत्रावसान (सदन का)	prorogue/ prorogation
सदन	house
सदस्य	member
सदाचरण पर्यन्त	duration of good behaviour
सदाचार (नैतिक)/ सैद्धान्तिक	morality/probity/ ethics
संस्था	association
सन्धि	treaty
सभा	assembly
सभापति	chairman
समता	equality
समर्पण करना/समर्पण	dedicate/dedication
समवर्ती सूची	concurrent list
समवाय	company
समवाय संस्था/सहकारी संस्था	cooperative society
समवेत होना	assemble
समागम	intercourse
समापन	winding up
समिति	committee
समुदाय	community
समुद्र नौवहन	maritime shipping
सम्पदा	estate
सम्पदा शुल्क	estate duty
सम्पूर्ण प्रभत्व सम्पन्न गणराज्य	sovereign
सम्मेलन	conference
सरकार	government
सरकारी अभियाचना	public demand
सर्वक्षमा	amnesty
सर्वोच्च समादेश	supreme command
सलाह	advice
सशस्त्र बल	armed forces
सहमति	concurrence
सहायक	ancillary
सहायक अनुदान	grant in aid
संकटमय	hazardous
संकल्प	resolution
संक्रमण	transition
संगणना	compute

संघ	union
संघटन	organization
संघ सूची	union list
संचार	communication
संचार करना	communicate
संचार साधन	means of communication
संचितनिधि	consolidated fund
सन्दर्भ	context
सन्देश	message
सम्बोधित सम्पत्ति	addressed
सम्पत्ति हस्तान्तरण पत्र	assurances of property
सम्पर्क	contact
सम्मति	consent
सम्भावना	possibility
संरक्षक	guardian
संलग्न	append
संविदा	contract
संविधान	constitution
संविधान सभा	constituent assembly
संशोधन	amendment
संसद	parliament
संस्थापन	establishment
संहिता	code
साक्ष्य	evidence
साख	credit
साधारण निर्वाचन	general election
सामर्थ्य	capacity
सामाजिक बीमा	social insurance
सामाजिक रूढ़ि	social custom
सामाजिक सेवा	social service
सामान्य मुद्रा/मुहर	common seal
सार्वजनिक अधिसूचना	public notification
सार्वजनिक अभियाचना	public demand
सार्वजनिक कल्याण	common good
सार्वजनिक व्यवस्था	public order
साहूकार	money lender
साहूकारी	money lending
सांसर्गिक	contagious
सांक्रामिक	infectious
सिद्धदोष	convicted
सिफारिश	recommendation
सिफारिश करना	recommend
सीमा	boundary
सीमाकर	terminal tax
सीमान्त	frontiers
सीमाशुल्क	custom duty
सीमांकन	demarcation
सुधार प्रयास	improvement trust
सुधारालय	reformatory
सुसंगति	relevancy
सूचना/सूचना पत्र	notice
सूची	list
सूत्र	formula
सूत्रित	formulated
सेना/सैनिक	military
सेना न्यायालय	court martial
सेवा	service
सेवा शर्तें	conditions of service
सेवानियोजन	employment
सेवाभार	service charges
सैन्यविभाजन	demobilization
सौंपना	assign/entrust
स्थगन	adjourn
स्थान	seat
स्थानान्तरण	transfer
स्थानीय क्षेत्र	local area
स्थानीय गण/मण्डली	local board
स्थानीय निकाय	local body
स्थानीय प्राधिकारी	local authority
स्थानीय स्वशासन	local self-government
स्थापना	establishment
स्थापित करना	establish

स्थायी आदेश	standing orders	स्वाधीनता	liberty
स्थायी समिति	standing committee	स्वामित्व	ownership
स्पष्टीकरण	clarification/ explanation	स्वामिलभ्य	royalties
स्मारक	memorial	स्वामी	owner
स्वतन्त्रता/स्वातन्त्र्य	freedom	स्वामिहीनत्व	bona vacancia
स्ववश	possession	स्वामी होना	own
स्वविवेक	discretion	स्वायत्तता	autonomy

ह

हक्क	title	हस्तान्तर पत्र	conveyance
हक्क होना	entitled	हस्तान्तरण	transfer
हटाना	removal	हिदायतें	instructions
हस्तशिल्प	handicraft		

परिशिष्ट–3/Appendix-3

कुछ पदनाम (Designations)

अध्यक्ष एवं प्रबन्ध निदेशक	chairman & managing director
कार्यपालक निदेशक	executive director
महाप्रबन्धक	general manager
संयुक्त महाप्रबन्धक	joint-general manger
उपमहाप्रबन्धक	deputy general manager
सचिव	secretary
प्रबन्धक	manager
मुख्य प्रबन्धक	chief manager
शाखा प्रबन्धक	branch manager
मण्डल प्रबन्धक	divisional manager
मुख्य अधिकारी	chief officer
लेखाकार	accountant
सुरक्षा अधिकारी	security officer
चिकित्साधिकारी	medical officer
विधि अधिकारी	law officer
जाँच अधिकारी	investigation officer
प्रधानलिपिक	head clerk
अनुवादक	translator
टंकण	typist
खजांची	cashier
बिल संग्राहक	bill collector
प्रकाशन	publication
प्रकाशक	publisher
प्रकाशन व्यवसाय	publishing
पुस्तक लेखक/रचयिता	author
लेखक	writer
सम्पादक	editor
समाचार सम्पादक	news editor
मुख्य उप-सम्पादक	chief sub-editor
उप-सम्पादक	sub editor
लेख त्रुटि शोधक	proof reader
मुद्रक	printer
पुलिस अधीक्षक	superintendent of police

परिशिष्ट–4/Appendix-4

विज्ञान शब्दावली

(Terms used in Science)

अकार्न	पु.	बाँझ फल, बंजू फल, बलूत के पेड़ का फल।
अकास्टिक	वि.	ध्वनिक; सुनने या ध्वनि की अनुभूति से सम्बन्धित।
अकिलीज टेण्डन	पु.	टाँग के अन्दर का मजबूत और महीन पदार्थ जो पिण्डली को ऐड़ी से जोड़ता है।
अकिलीज हील	पु.	किसी वस्तु या व्यक्ति का कमजोर पक्ष।
अक्रिलिक	पु.	एक कृत्रिम पदार्थ जो वस्त्र और पेंट बनाने में काम आता है।
अकैडमी	पु.	विशेष प्रशिक्षण देने वाली संस्था, विज्ञान, कला या साहित्य के क्षेत्र में सुप्रतिष्ठित व्यक्तियों का मान्यता प्राप्त अधिकारी वर्ग।
अकैशिया	पु.	बबूल, कीकर जिसके पीले या सफेद फूल होते हैं। इस पेड़ के अनेक प्रकार होते हैं, कुछ पेड़ों में से चिपचिपा द्रव निकलता है।
अक्वीडक्ट	पु.	पुल के समान बना एक ढाँचा जिसके माध्यम से पानी को घाटी के पार ले जाया जाता है, कृत्रिम जलप्रणाली।
अक्वेटिक	वि.	जल में रहने वाला, जल में होने वाला।
अक्वेरिअम	पु.	पानी से भरी शीशे की टंकी जिसमें मछली आदि जलजीवों को रखा जाता है, मछली घर, जलजीवशाला।
अक्सीलिरेट	क्रि.	गति का गढ़ाना, किसी वस्तु, घटना आदि की गति को बढ़ाना।
अक्सीलिरेशन	पु.	वाहन का वह नियन्त्रक यन्त्र जिसे वेग बढ़ाने के लिए पैर से दबाते हैं, एक्सिलिरेटर।
अटामिक	वि.	परमाणविक।
अटामिक एनर्जी	स्त्री.	परमाणु ऊर्जा।
अटामिक मॉस	पु.	परमाणु पिण्ड, परमाणु की मात्रा, द्रव्यमान।
अटामिक नम्बर	पु.	किसी रासायनिक तत्त्व के नाभि में स्थित धनात्मक विद्युत आवेश वाले प्रोटॉनों की संख्या, परमाणु संख्या।
अट्रॉफी	स्त्री.	रक्ताल्पता के कारण शरीर के क्षीण हो जाने की स्थित।
अट्रोसिटी	स्त्री.	पाशविक कृत्य, अत्याचार, अतिक्रूर व्यवहार।
अडल्टरेट	क्रि.	अपमिश्रण करना, खाद्यपदार्थ में मिलावट करना।
अडल्टरी	स्त्री.	परस्त्री या परपुरुष के साथ यौन सम्बन्ध, परस्त्रीगमन, परपुरुषगमन, व्यभिचार।

अडैप्टर	पु.	वह यन्त्र जिससे विद्युत के स्रोत के साथ एक से अधिक विद्युत उपकरणों को जोड़ा जा सकता है, एडॉप्टर, एक प्रकार का यन्त्र है जो विद्युत उपकरणों के अलग-अलग पुर्जों को जोड़ता है, जो एक-दूसरे के साथ जोड़े जाने के उद्देश्य से नहीं बनाये गये।
अर्थवार्म	पु.	केंचुआ।
अनाइण्ट	पु.	शरीर पर या चोट आदि पर मरहम या तेल आदि लगाना।
अनीमिया	स्त्री.	रक्त में लाल कणों की कमी, रक्ताल्पता, खून की कमी।
अपेण्डिक्स	पु.	उदर के निकट का एक छोटा अंग, उण्डुक पुच्छ।
अपेण्डिसाइटिस	स्त्री.	एक बीमारी जिसमें उदर के पास स्थित एक अंग में दर्द उत्पन्न होता है और इस अंग को निकालना पड़ता है।
अप्रेण्टिस	पु.	प्रशिक्षु, प्रशिणार्थी, किसी विशेष हुनर को सीखने के लिए कम वेतनमान पर काम करने को तैयार व्यक्ति।
अप्रेण्टिसशिप	पु.	प्रशिक्षुता, प्रशिखणार्थिता, प्रशिक्षु की अवस्था।
अबजार्ब	क्रि.	(द्रव पदार्थ, ताप आदि को) अपने में सोख लेना, अवशोषित करना, आत्मसात करना, अपने में समा लेना किसी के यान या रुचि को आकृष्ट करना, अचानक पहुँचे तीव्र आघात के प्रभाव को कम करना।
अबजार्बेट	वि.	द्रव को सोख लेने की क्षमता रखते हुए।
अबजार्पशन	पु.	द्रव, गैस या अन्य पदार्थ के अवशोषित होने की प्रक्रिया।
अबसलूट जीरो	पु.	परम शून्य, न्यूनतम सम्भव तापमान, निरपेक्ष शून्य तापमान।
अबॉर्ट	क्रि.	गर्भपात कराना, भूणहत्या कराना।
अबर्शिन	पु.	गर्भपात कराने लिए शल्य क्रिया।
अबैकस	पु.	एक धातु या लकड़ी का बना ऐसा चौखटा जिसमें तार लगे होते हैं और उन तारों में धातु, लकड़ी या रबर की बनी गोलियाँ पिरोयी होती हैं। इसका प्रयोग बच्चे गिनती सीखने के लिए करते हैं, गिनतारा।
अब्रीविएशन	पु.	किसी शब्द या पदबन्ध का संक्षिप्त रूप।
अमीनो एसिड	पु.	एक प्रकार का अम्ल जो पशुओं और पौधों में पाये जाने वाले तत्त्वों से मिलकर प्रोटीन का निर्माण करता है। प्रोटीन शारीरिक स्वास्थ्य और विकास के लिए आवश्यक होता है।
अमोनियम	पु.	अमोनियायुक्त पदार्थों में पाया जाने वाला एक विशेष रसायन, यह धनावेशयुक्त होता है।
अमोनिया	स्त्री	एक तेज गन्धयुक्त रंगहीन गैस, अमोनियायुक्त एक तरल पदार्थ जो सफाई के काम आता है।

अम्बिलिकल कार्ड	पु.	नाभि रज्जु, गर्भस्थ शिशु को माँ से जोड़ने वाली नलिका।
अरिथमेटिक	पु.	अंकगणित।
अरिथमेटिक प्रोग्रेशन	पु.	समान अन्तर से संख्याओं के बढ़ने या घटने की एक गणना विधि, समान्तर श्रेणी।
अर्थ्राइटिस	पु.	सन्धिवात, गठिया रोग।
अर्थ्रोपॉड	पु.	सन्धिपाद, मेरुदण्ड रहित कठोर शरीर वाला कोई भी प्राणी, इन प्राणियों के टाँगों में कई जोड़ होते हैं और प्रत्येक जोड़ पर मुड़ जाती है।
अलना	पु.	कलाई और कोहनी के बीच बाँह के नीचे की दो में से एक लम्बी हड्डी, अतः प्रकोष्ठिका।
अल्कलाइड	पु.	पौधों में पाया जाने वाला एक विषैला पदार्थ जिसका प्रयोग औषधियाँ बनाने के लिए किया जाता है।
अल्कोहलिक	वि.	मादक, मादक पेय का अभ्यस्त।
अल्कोहलिज्म	पु.	अत्यधिक अल्कोहल के सेवन के कारण उत्पन्न शारीरिक अक्षमता।
अल्जेबरा	पु.	बीजगणित।
अल्ट्रासाउण्ड	पु.	शरीर की आन्तरकि भाग का चित्र प्रस्तुत करने वाली डाक्टरी प्रक्रिया, ऐसी ध्वनि जो मानव की श्रवण क्षमता से परे हो।
अल्ट्रासोनिक	वि.	मानव की श्रवण क्षमता से परे, पराश्रव्य, पराध्वनिक।
अल्ट्रावायलेट	वि.	एक तरह का प्रकाश जिसके प्रभाव से मनुष्य की त्वचा काली पड़ जाती है, इस प्रकाश की अधिक मात्रा बहुत हानिकारक होती है, पराबैंगनी।
अल्सर	पु.	फोड़ा, व्रण, नासूर।
असेक्शुअल	वि.	यौन क्रिया से असम्बद्ध, अलिंगी, यौन लक्षणों से वंचित, यौन क्रिया का अनिच्छुक।
असेप्टिक	वि.	हानिकारक जीवाणुओं से रहित।
अस्कार्बिक एसिड	पु.	नींबू, सन्तरे व हरी सब्जियों में पाया जाने वाला एक प्राकृतिक पदार्थ, जो स्वास्थ्यवर्द्धक होता है।
अस्ट्रॉलॉजी	स्त्री.	सौरग्रहों तथा तारों की स्थिति और उनकी गति तथा उनका मानव जीवन पर पड़ने वाला प्रभाव का अध्ययन, फलित ज्योतिष।
अस्टिमेटिज्म	पु.	दृष्टि वैषम्य, अविन्दुकता, आँख का एक ऐसा बेडौलपन जिसके कारण साफ दिखायी नहीं देता।
अस्ट्रोनॉट	पु.	अन्तरिक्ष यात्री।
अस्ट्रोनॉमर	पु.	खगोलविद, ज्योतिर्विद।

अस्ट्रोनॉमी	स्त्री.	नक्षत्रों, सूर्य, ग्रहों तथा चन्द्रमा का वैज्ञानिक अध्ययन, खगोलविज्ञान।
अस्थमा	पु.	एक प्रकार का श्वास रोग, दमा।
अस्थमेटिक	पु.	दमे का रोगी।
अस्पैरागस	पु.	सतावरी, सतावर, नागदौन नामक वनस्पति।
अस्लीप	वि.	नींद में सोया हुआ।
आइण्टमेण्ट	पु.	मलहम जिसे चोट आदि पर लगाते हैं।
ऑक्साइड	पु.	ऑक्सीजन और अन्य रासायनिक तत्त्वों का संयोजन, ऑक्साइड।
ऑक्सीजन	पु.	एक जीवनदायी गैस जिसे आप न देख सकते हैं और न सुन सकते हैं, जीवधारी बिना ऑक्सीजन के जीवित नहीं रह सकते।
ऑटोमेटिक	पु.	स्वचालित मशीन।
आटोप्सी	स्त्री.	मृत्यु का कारण जाने के लिए की गयी शव परीक्षा।
ऑपरेटिंग थियेटर	पु.	शल्यकाक्ष, ऑपरेशन कक्ष।
ऑपरेटिंग सिस्टम	पु.	कम्प्यूटर प्रोग्राम जो अन्य प्रोग्रामों को व्यवस्थित करता है एवं संचालित करता है, प्रचालन तन्त्र।
ऑपरेशन	पु.	शल्यक्रिया।
आबट्यूज	वि.	मन्द बुद्धि।
आबट्यूज एंगिल	पु.	अधिक कोण, 90 और 180 डिग्री का कोण।
आरिकल	पु.	हृदय का उपरिगह्वर जिसमें से रक्त प्रवाहित होकर सारे शरीर में जाता है, कान का बाहरी भाग, बहिकर्ण।
आरिन्थोलॉजी	स्त्री.	पक्षियों वैज्ञानिक अध्ययन, पक्षी विज्ञान।
आर्किओलॉजिकल	वि.	पुरातत्त्व विज्ञान से सम्बन्धित, पुरातत्त्वीय।
आर्किटोलॉजिस्ट	पु.	पुरातत्त्वज्ञ, पुरातत्त्व विज्ञान विशेषज्ञ।
आर्किटोलॉजी	स्त्री.	पुरातत्त्व विज्ञान।
आर्कीटेक्चर	पु.	वास्तुकला, भवननिर्माण विज्ञान, स्थापत्य कला, वास्तुशैली।
आर्कीटेक्ट	पु.	वास्तुशिल्पी, स्थापत्यविद्, भवन निर्माण का नक्शा बनाने वाला।
आर्कीपेल्गो	पु.	(भूगोल में) द्वीप समूह।
आर्गाज्म	पु.	कामोत्तेजना का चरम बिन्दु, रति निष्पत्ति।
आर्गेनिज्म	पु.	अतिसूक्ष्म जीव, जिन्हें माइक्रोस्कोप से देखा जा सकता है।
आर्च	पु.	चाप, मेहराब, तोरण, पैर के तलवे की चाप।
आर्चरी	स्त्री.	धनुर्विद्या, तीरन्दाजी।
आर्टिलरी	पु.	तोपखाना।

आर्टीफीशियल इण्टेलिजेंस	पु.	ऐसी युक्ति जिसे कम्प्यूटर को मानव बुद्धि की नकल करने में सक्षम बनाया जा सके, यान्त्रिक बुद्धि।
आर्टीफीशियल इंसेमिनेशन	पु.	कृत्रिम गर्भाधान।
आर्टीफीशियल	पु.	कृत्रिम श्वसन क्रिया।
आर्थोपीडिक्स	पु.	विकलांग चिकित्सा, इस चिकित्सा पद्धति में अस्थियों या मांसपेशियों की क्षति से सम्बन्धित रोगों की चिकित्सा की जाती है।
आर्म	पु.	बाँह, भुजा, बाहु।
आल्टरनेट करेण्ट	पु.	नियमित रूप से बार-बार दिशा परिवर्तन करने वाली विद्युतधारा, प्रत्यावर्ती विद्युतधारा।
आल्टरनेट	पु.	कार में प्रयोग किया जाने वाला वह कम्पोनेण्ट जो विभिन्न दिशाओं में जाने वाली विद्युतधारा उत्पन्न करता है, प्रत्यावर्तित।
आसिलेट	क्रि.	विद्युत या रेडियो तरंगों का लगातार शक्ति या दिशा बदलना, झूलना, दोलायमान होना।
आसिलोस्कोप	पु.	दोलनदर्शी, विद्युतधारा की तरंगों को परदे पर एक रेखा के रूप में दर्शाने वाला यन्त्र।
आस्टियोपैथ	पु.	अस्थि चिकित्सक।
आस्टियोपोरोसिस	स्त्री.	अस्थियों की दुर्बलता एवं भंगुरता का रोग।
इंजक्ट	क्रि.	सिरिंज में लगी सुई के द्वारा शरीर में त्वचा के अन्दर दवा पहुँचाना, सूई लगाना, इंजेक्शकन लगाना, टीका लगाना।
इंजिन	पु.	गति उत्पादक यन्त्र, इंजन।
इंजीनियर	पु.	अभियन्ता, इंजीनियर।
इंजीनियरिंग	पु.	अभियान्त्रिकी, इंजीनियरी विद्या।
इंजेक्शन	पु.	सिरिंज व सूई से मनुष्य के त्वचा के अन्दर दवा पहुँचाने की क्रिया।
इण्टर कनेक्ट	क्रि.	एक समान वस्तुओं को आपस में परस्पर जोड़ना।
इण्टरकॉम	पु.	किसी कार्यालय, विमान आदि में रेडियो या टेलीफोन द्वारा संचालित संचार प्रणाली, इस प्रणाली को प्रयोग में लाने वाला उपकरण।
इण्ट्रानेट	पु.	एक ही संगठन के अन्दर का कम्प्यूटर तन्त्र, आन्तरिक कम्प्यूटर तन्त्र।
इण्ट्रावेनस	वि.	नसों के अन्दर जाने वाली दवा, शिरा अभ्यान्तर।
इण्टेगर	पु.	पूर्ण संख्या।
इण्टोमोलॉजी	पु.	कीटविज्ञान, एण्टोमालॉजी।

इंसुलिन	पु.	शरीर में स्वयं उत्पन्न होने वाला एक पदार्थ, जो रक्त में ग्लूकोज की मात्रा को नियन्त्रित करता है।
इंसुलेटर	पु.	ताप, विद्युत रोधक यन्त्र।
इंसुलेटिंग टेप	पु.	बिजली के आघात से बचने के लिए बिजली के तारों पर चढ़ाया गया विद्युतरोधी टेप।
इको	पु.	गूँज, प्रतिध्वनि।
इकोलॉजी	स्त्री.	पर्यावरण विज्ञान, पर्यावरण का अध्ययन।
इक्लिप्स	पु.	चन्द्रमा या सूर्य का कुछ देरी के लिए पूर्ण या आंशिक रूप से पृथ्वी पर दिखायी न पड़ना, सूर्य या चन्द्र ग्रहण का लगना।
इक्वीलिब्रियम	पु.	संतुलन की स्थिति।
इक्वीलैट्रल	वि.	समान लम्बाई की भुजाओं वाला त्रिभुज।
इक्वेशन	पु.	समीकरण।
इजेक्ट	क्रि.	किसी मशीन से बटन दबाकर टेप, डिस्क आदि को बाहर निकाल देना।
इजैकुलेशन	पु.	वीर्य स्खलन।
इटियोलॉजी	स्त्री.	रोगों के कारणों का अध्ययन करने वाला शास्त्र, रोगहेतु विज्ञान।
इग्नियस	वि.	आग्नेय।
इग्निशन	पु.	इंजन आदि स्टार्ट करने वाली प्रणाली, ज्वलन क्रिया, जलने या जलाने की क्रिया।
इनएडिबल	वि.	आखाद्य जो खाने लायक न हो।
इनडक्शन	पु.	एक प्रकार की क्रिया जिसके द्वारा विद्युत या चुम्बक शक्ति एक वस्तु से दूसरी वस्तु तक बिना स्पर्श किये पहुँचती है, प्रेरण, प्रवर्तन।
इनडाइजेशन	पु.	भोजन पचने में कठिनाई के कारण उत्पन्न होने वाला उदरशूल, बदहजमी, अपच।
इनफर्टाइल	वि.	सन्तानोत्पादन में असमर्थ, बाँझ या बन्ध्या, अनुपजाऊ, अनुर्वर।
इनफर्टिलिटी	स्त्री.	बाँझपन, बन्ध्या।
इनफार्मेशन टेक्नॉलॉजी	पु.	सूचना प्रोद्यौगिकी, कम्प्यूटर के माध्यम से सूचनाओं के सम्प्रेषण के विषय में अध्ययन और उनका प्रयोग।
इनफेक्शन	पु.	संक्रमण, रोगसंचार, हानिकारक बैक्टीरिया या हानिकारक कीटाणुओं के सम्पर्क से उत्पन्न होने वाली बीमारी, रोगाणु ग्रस्तता।
इनफेक्शस	वि.	छुतहा, संक्रामक।
इनफैंट	पु.	अबोध शिशु।

इनफ्यूजन	पु.	अनुप्रेरण, निषेचन, काढ़ा, क्वाथ, शरीर की नसों में द्रव पदार्थ को प्रविष्ट करना।
इनबार्न	वि.	जन्मजात, नैसर्गिक।
इनब्रीडिंग	पु.	अन्तः प्रजनन।
इनर्ट	वि.	रासायनिक गुणरहित, निष्क्रिय, अन्य रसायनों के प्रति क्रियाहीन।
इनवर्टेब्रेट	पु.	बिना रीढ़ का प्राणी, मेरुदण्ड रहित प्राणी।
इनवेंशन	पु.	आविष्कार, खोज, आविष्करण।
इनर्शिया	स्त्री.	जड़ता, ऊर्जा की न्यूनता, शक्तिहीनता, निष्क्रियता वस्तु की स्थिति स्थिरता, गतिस्थिरता, वस्तु की स्थिरता शक्ति।
इनसीजन	पु.	शल्य क्रिया के दौरान सावधानीपूर्वक लगाया गया चीरा।
इंसुलिन	स्त्री.	शरीर में उत्पन्न एक पदार्थ जो शरीर में शक्कर की मात्रा को नियन्त्रित करता है।
इनसेक्टीसाइड	स्त्री.	कीटनाशक पदार्थ
इनसेफलाइटिस	स्त्री.	मस्तिष्क में सूजन का एक रोग, मस्तिष्क शोथ।
इनहेलर	पु.	प्रश्वसन यन्त्र, औषधियुक्त छोटी नली के आकार की वस्तु जिसे आप नाक पर रखकर साँस अन्दर खींचते हैं, यह साँस के रोगियों के लिए बहुत उपयोगी है।
इनार्गेनिक	वि.	अजैव, जो सजीवों से प्राप्त या निर्मित नहीं होते हैं।
इनैमल	पु.	एक चमकीला पदार्थ जो धातुओं को सुरक्षित रखने के काम आता है।
इंजाइम	पु.	एक प्रकार का पदार्थ जो रासायनिक परिवर्तन के घटित होने में सहायता करता है किन्तु स्वयं परिवर्तित नहीं होता।
इफिकेशी	स्त्री.	किसी औषधि या चिकित्सीय उपचार की प्रभावोत्पादकता।
इमर्सन	पु.	किसी वस्तु को द्रव में पूरी तरह से डुबा देने की क्रिया; द्रव में पूरी तरह से डूबे होने की स्थिति।
इमल्शन	पु.	प्रायः मिश्रित न होने वाले द्रवों का मिश्रण; फोटोग्राफिक फिल्म पर लगा एक पदार्थ, जिससे फिल्म प्रकाश के प्रति संवेदनशील हो जाते हैं।
इम्पोटेण्ट	वि.	नपुसंक।
इम्प्रेसन	पु.	प्रभाव, छाप।
इम्प्योर	वि.	अशुद्ध, मिलावटी, अनैतिक।
इम्प्योरिटी	स्त्री.	अशुद्धता, मिलावट।
इम्मिजरेबुल	वि.	अमापनीय, अपरिमित।
इम्यूनाइजेशन	पु.	प्रतिरक्षीकरण।

इयर	पु.	कान, श्रवणेन्द्रिय।
इयरऐक	पु.	कान में दर्द, कर्णशूल।
इयरड्रम	पु.	कर्णपटल, कान का पर्दा।
इयरफोन	पु.	सुनने के लिए कान पर लगाया जाने वाला उपकरण, इयरफोन।
इलास्टिक	वि.	लचीला, लचकदार, ऐसा लचीला पदार्थ जो खींचने के बाद बड़ा होता है किन्तु छोड़ने पर अपनी पूर्व अवस्था में लौट आता है।
इलास्टीसिटी	स्त्री.	लचीलापन, प्रत्यास्थता।
इलेक्ट्रॉन	पु.	परमाणु के तीन मूल कणों में से एक जिस पर ऋणात्म विद्युत आवेश होता है।
इलेक्ट्रॉनिक	वि.	इलेक्ट्रॉनिक्स के प्रयोग से युक्त, इलेक्ट्रॉनिक्स पर आधारित।
इलेक्ट्रानिक्स	पु.	एक प्रकार की प्रोद्यौगिकी जो इलेक्ट्रॉन पर आधारित होती है, जिसकी सहायता से कम्प्यूटर और दूसरे विभिन्न प्रकार के उपकरण तैयार किये जाते हैं, आजकल यह प्रोद्यौगिकी बहुत विकसित हो गयी है और नित नई–नई सम्भावनाएँ ढूँढ़ी जा रही है।
इलेक्ट्रिक	वि.	विद्युत उत्पन्न करने वाला, विद्युत से चलने वाला।
इलेक्ट्रिक शाक	पु.	बिजली से लगने वाला झटका।
इलेक्ट्रीफाई	क्रि.	विद्युतीकरण करना।
इलेक्ट्रीशियन	पु.	बिजली का मिस्त्री, बिजली के उपकरणों की मरम्मत करने वाला।
इलेक्ट्रीसिटी	स्त्री.	विद्युत, बिजली, विद्युतधारा।
इलेक्ट्रोस्टेटिक्स	वि.	स्थिर विद्युत आवेशों से सम्बन्धित।
इलेक्ट्रोड	पु.	बैटरी का बिन्दु जहाँ से विद्युतधारा आती या जाती है।
इलेक्ट्रोमैगनेटिक	वि.	विद्युत के लक्षणों के साथ चुम्बकीय क्षमता से युक्त, विद्युत चुम्बकीय।
इलेक्ट्रोलाइट	पु.	एक द्रव जिसमें से विद्युतधारा प्रवाहित की जा सकती है।
इलेक्ट्रोलिसिस	पु.	विद्युत के प्रयोग से द्रव के विभिन्न रासायनिक अंशों को पृथक् करने की विधि, विद्युत अपघटन; विद्युत के प्रयोग से शरीर के बालों से स्थायी रूप से साफ करने की प्रक्रिया।
इस्थीट	स्त्री.	सौन्दर्य संवेदी, सौन्दर्यवादी; सुन्दर वस्तुओं में रुचि रखने वाला व्यक्ति।
इस्थेटिक	वि.	सौन्दर्यात्मक, सुरुचिपूर्ण।
इस्थेटिक्स	पु.	सौन्दर्य शास्त्र, कला और सौन्दर्य का विश्लेषण करने वाला शास्त्र।

ईको साउण्डर	पु.	बोलने वाले के पास प्रतिध्वनि के लौट आने में लगे समय के माप के अनुसार समुद्र की गहराई या समुद्र में पड़ी वस्तुओं की जानकारी के लिए बना एक यन्त्र।
ईको सिस्टम	पु.	क्षेत्र विशेष में पाये जाने वाले व अपने परिवेश से सम्बन्धित सभी पौधे व पशु; पारिस्थितिकी तन्त्र।
ई-मेल	पु.	एक कम्प्यूटर से दूसरे कम्प्यूटर को इलेक्ट्रॉनिक संदेश या सूचना भेजने की विधि।
ईथेन	पु.	एक रंगहीन, गंधहीन, ज्वलनशील प्राकृतिक गैस।
ईफीकेसी	पु.	किसी औषधि या चिकित्सीय उपचार की प्रभावोत्पादकता।
ईफेक्ट	पु.	प्रभाव।
ईवैपोरेट	क्रि.	वाष्पीकरण होना, भाप बन जाना।
ईवोलूशन	पु.	परिवर्तन और विकास की क्रमिक प्रक्रिया।
ईशोफेगस	पु.	भोजन की नली, जो भोजन को मुख से आमाशय तक पहुँचाती है।
ईस्ट्रजन	पु.	अण्डाशय रस, एक प्रकार का रस जो हार्मोन के प्रभाव से बनता है जिसे स्त्री अत्यधिक कामुक होकर गर्भ धारण के लिए तैयार हो जाती है।
एअरेट	क्रि.	वायु को मिट्टी, पानी आदि में मिश्रित करना; किसी द्रव पदार्थ में दबाव के साथ गैस मिलाना।
एरियल	पु.	मकान के ऊपर धातु की लगी लम्बी छड़ जो रेडियो या टेली. विजन की तरंगे ग्रहण करती हैं; आकाशकीय, हवाई।
एअरोडॉयनॉमिक्स		वायुगति विज्ञान, वायुगतिकी।
एअरोनाटिक्स	पु.	विमान के निर्माण और उसके उड़ाने की शिक्षा देने वाला शास्त्र, विमान विज्ञान।
एअरोबिक	पु.	ऑक्सीजन पर आधारित, ऑक्सीजन से सम्बन्धित।
एअरोसाल	पु.	एक पात्र जो द्रव पदार्थों को दाब में रखकर फव्वारे के रूप में दवा को छिड़कने के काम आता है।
एअरोस्पेस	पु.	वायुयान और अन्तरिक्षयान बनाने का उद्योग।
एक्यूट	वि.	तीव्र, प्रखर; कुशाग्र, तेज।
एक्यूट एंगिल	पु.	न्यूनकोण, वह कोण जो 90° से कम होता है।
एक्यूपंक्चर	पु.	शरीर में बारीक सूइयों से छेद करके रोग को ठीक करने की चिकित्सा करने की प्रणाली।
एक्यूमेन	पु.	स्थिति को तत्काल और स्पष्ट रूप से समझ लेने की योग्यता, विदग्धता, कुशाग्र बुद्धि।

एक्वामैरीन	पु.	हलका हरापन लिए नीला रत्न; हरितनील; हलका हरापन लिए नीला रंग।
एगोनाइज	क्रि.	किसी कठिन समस्या या कठिन परिस्थिति में सोचना या चिन्तित होना।
एगोनी	स्त्री.	तीव्र पीड़ा, तीव्र वेदना, अत्यधिक व्यथा, कष्ट।
एगोराफोबिया	पु.	भीड़-भाड़ वाले स्थान पर जाने से भय; विवृत्त स्थान-भीति।
एग्रीकल्चर	पु.	कृषि, खेती।
एग्रोकेमिकल	पु.	कृषि रसायन, खेती में प्रयोग किये जाने वाले रसायन।
एग्रोनामिस्ट	पु.	शस्यविज्ञानी, कृषिशास्त्री।
एग्रोनामी	स्त्री.	कृषि शास्त्र, शस्यविज्ञानी।
एज	पु.	उम्र, आयु, वय।
एजलिमिट	पु.	कुछ करने के लिए निर्धारित न्यूनतम आयु सीमा।
एजिटेट	क्रि.	आन्दोलन करना।
एजीज्म	पु.	अतिवृद्ध मानकर किसी के साथ किया गया अनुचित व्यवहार।
एण्डोथर्मिक	पु.	ताप से निस्पन्न होने वाली एक रासायनिक क्रिया ऊष्माशोषी।
एण्डोस्केलटन	पु.	पशुओं का अन्तः कंकाल, पशुओं के अन्दर की हड्डी का ढाँचा।
एण्डोस्कोप	पु.	शरीर के अन्दरूनी भाग को देखने का यन्त्र।
एण्डोस्पर्म	पु.	पौधों के बीज का वह भाग जो पौधे के विकास के लिए भोजन को संचित रखता है, भ्रूणकोष।
एडल्ट	पु.	वयस्क, बालिग, पूर्णतया विकसित।
एडल्ट एजूकेशन	पु.	वयस्कों के लिए गैर औपचारिक शिक्षा।
एडिक्ट	पु.	वह व्यक्ति जिसे हानिकारक या नशीली वस्तुओं की आदत है।
एडिनॉयड्स	पु.	बच्चों के नाक और गले का पिछला भाग जो कभी-कभी सूज जाता है, जिससे साँस लेने और छोड़ने में कठिनाई होती है।
एडोलसेंस	पु.	किशोरावस्था, 13 से 17 वर्ष के बीच की उम्र।
एडोलसेण्ट	पु.	तेरह से सत्तरह वर्ष के बीच की उम्र के लड़के व लड़की, किशोर, किशोरी।
एथलीट	पु.	खेल-कूद प्रतियोगिताओं में भाग लेने वाले व्यक्ति।
एनर्जी	पु.	ऊर्जा, सक्रिय रहने की क्षमता; कोयला, विद्युत, गैस आदि से उत्पन्न होने वाली शक्ति, ऊर्जा, जैसे-परमाणविक ऊर्जा।
एनलजेशिक	पु.	पीड़ाहारी पदार्थ, पीड़ानाशक पदार्थ।
एनलजेशिय	पु.	पीड़ा शून्यता; पीड़ा शून्य करने वाली दवा।
एनस	पु.	गुदाद्वार, मलद्वार।

एनाइन	पु.	रसायन शास्त्र में ऋणात्मक आयन।
एनाबोलिकइस्टेरॉयड	पु.	एक रसायन जिसका प्रयोग करने से मांसपेशियों के आकार में वृद्धि होती है।
एनीमामीटर	पु.	पवन वेग मापी यन्त्र।
एनीमेशन	पु.	ऐसी फिल्में, कम्प्यूटर गेम आदि बनाने की तकनीक, जिसमें चित्र चलते हुए दिखायी देते हैं।
एनोड	पु.	धनाग्र; बैटरी का वह भाग जिससे विद्युत प्रवेश करती है।
एनोरक्सिया	स्त्री.	स्त्रियों को होने वाला एक रोग जिसमें मोटा हो जाने की अस्वाभाविक भय पैदा हो जाता है और रोगिणी खाना-पीना बन्द कर देती है।
एपिटाइट	पु.	भूख, क्षुधा, बुभुक्षा।
एपिलेप्सी	स्त्री.	मिरगी रोग।
एपीग्लाटिस	स्त्री.	गले की घण्टी, कौआ, उपजिह्वा।
एपीडर्मिस	स्त्री.	बाहरी त्वचा।
एपीडेमियोलॉजी	स्त्री.	रोगों के फैलने और उन पर नियन्त्रण का वैज्ञानिक अध्ययन, महामारी विज्ञान।
एमीनोसेण्टेसिस	पु.	एक प्रकार का डाक्टरी परीक्षण जिसमें गर्भाशय के तरल पदार्थ की जाँच कर गर्भस्थ शिशु के स्वास्थ्य की जाँच की जाती है।
एम्नियोटिक फ्लूड	पु.	गर्भस्थ शिशु के चारों ओर का तरल पदार्थ।
एम्नीजिया	पु.	याददाश्त खो बैठने की अवस्था; स्मृति लोप।
एम्पूल	पु.	दवा से युक्त शीशे का छोटा पात्र, जिसे सुई द्वारा शरीर में चढ़ाया जाता है।
एम्प्लीट्यूड	पु.	ध्वनि तरंगों के कम्पन का अधिकतम आयाम।
एम्प्लीफायर	पु.	ध्वनि विस्तारक यन्त्र; विद्युत शक्ति प्रवर्धक यन्त्र।
एम्फीबियन	पु.	जल और थल दोनों जगह रहने वाले प्राणी।
एयरकण्डिशनर	पु.	वातानुकूलन यन्त्र।
एयरक्राफ्ट	पु.	वायु में उड़ने वाला यान।
एयरक्रू	पु.	विमानकर्मी दल, वायुसेना दल।
एयरटाइट	पु.	वायुरुद्ध।
एयरबेस	पु.	सैनिक विमानों के लिए हवाई अड्डा।
एपियरी	पु.	मधुवाटिका।
एपैथेटिक	वि.	उदासीन, अनिच्छुक।
एपैथी	पु.	उदासीनता, अनिच्छा।

एपैरेटस	पु.	किसी कार्य में प्रयोग आने वाले उपकरणों का सेट।
एफिड	पु.	पौधों के लिए हानिकर एक बहुत छोटा कीड़ा माहू।
एयरवेब्ज	पु.	रेडियो तरंगें जिनके माध्यम से रेडियो और टीवी कार्यक्रम प्रसारित किया जाता है।
एयरसिक	पु.	विमान यात्रा के समय जी मिचलाने का रोग, उड्डयन अस्वस्थता।
एरिया	स्त्री.	क्षेत्र, इलाका, क्षेत्रफल।
एलर्जन	पु.	ऐसी वस्तु जिसे खाने, छूने या साँस लेने पर कुछ लोग बीमार हो जाते हैं।
एलाय	पु.	मिश्र धातु।
एलिविएट	क्रि.	पीड़ा या कष्ट के प्रभाव को कम करना।
एलीमेण्ट	पु.	तत्त्व किसी वस्तु की अल्प मात्रा; किसी विद्युत उपकरण का ताप उत्पादक धातु निर्मित अंश।
एलीमेण्ट्रीकैनाल	पु.	आहारनाल, आमाशय, पाचन संस्थान।
एलूमिनियम	पु.	एल्यूमिनियम नामक धातु।
एल्कलाई	पु.	अम्ल के साथ अभिक्रिया होने पर लवण का निर्माण करने वाला एक रसायन; क्षार।
एल्कीन	पु.	हाइड्रोजन और कार्बन से युक्त कोई भी गैस, जिसमें अणुओं को जोड़े रखने की सामान्य से अधिक शक्ति होती है।
एल्केन	पु.	हाइड्रोजन और कार्बन से युक्त कोई भी गैस।
एल्केमी	पु.	प्राचीनकाल का रसायन शास्त्र जिसमें सामान्य धातुओं को सोने में बदलने की विधि ढूँढ़ी जाती थी।
एल्टसाइमजडिजीज	पु.	एक प्रकार का मस्तिष्क को प्रभावित करने वाला रोग, जिसमें आयु बढ़ने के साथ-साथ व्यक्ति की चिन्तनशक्ति भी प्रभावित होती है; अल्जाइमर रोग।
एल्टीमीटर	पु.	समुद्रतल से ऊँचाई नापने वाला यन्त्र, तुंगतामापी यन्त्र।
एल्ब्यूमिन	पु.	श्वेतक।
एवियेशन	पु.	वैमानिकी, विमान बनाने व उड़ाने की विद्या।
एसिटिक एसिड	पु.	सिरके में पाया जाने वाला एक अम्ल।
एसिटिलीन	पु.	एक चमकीली ज्वाला देने वाली गैस जिसका प्रयोग धातुओं को काटने के लिए किया जाता है।
एसिटेट	पु.	एक रासायनिक यौगिक जो एसिटिक एसिड से बनता है। इसका प्रयोग प्लास्टिक बनाने के लिए किया जाता है; रासायनिक तत्त्वों से बना एक चिकना कपड़ा।

एसिटोन	पु.	एक रंगहीन द्रव जो तीखी गन्ध वाला होता है। इसका प्रयोग वस्तुओं को साफ करने, एनैमल पेंट को पतला करने एवं अनेक प्रकार के रासायनिक पदार्थों को बनाने के काम में लाया जाता है।
एसिड	पु.	रसायन शास्त्र में एक तेजाब अम्ल। इस द्रव में धातुएँ गल जाती हैं। त्वचा पर पड़ने से त्वचा झुलस सकती है। इसका pH मान 7 से कम होता है। यह स्वाद में खट्टा होता है।
एसिड रेन	पु.	एक प्रकार की वर्षा जिसमें कारखानों आदि से निकले रसायन होते हैं और जो वनस्पतियों और पेड़-पौधों को बहुत क्षति पहुँचाती हैं।
एसिडिटी	स्त्री.	एक प्रकार का आमाशयिक रोग जिसमें पेट में खट्टापन बनता है और पाचन क्रिया खराब हो जाती है।
एसी	पु.	एयरकण्डिशनर, एक वातानुकूलन यन्त्र; आल्टरनेटिंग करेण्ट।
ऐंगल	पु.	दो रेखाओं के बीच का कोण।
ऐंजाइटी	पु.	चिन्ता या भय की या अनिश्चय की भावना।
ऐण्टइटर	पु.	चींटी खाने वाला एक जानवर।
ऐण्टीकाबुलेण्ट	पु.	रक्त को गाढ़ा होने और थक्का बनने से रोकने वाला पदार्थ; स्कन्दरोधी।
ऐण्टीक्लाइन	पु.	वह भूक्षेत्र जहाँ पृथ्वी की सतह पर स्थित चट्टान की परतें मेहराब के आकार में मुड़ी हों।
ऐण्टीडॉट	पु.	किसी भी अप्रिय प्रभाव से निपटने में सहायक कोई अन्य वस्तु; प्रतिकारक; प्रत्यौषध।
ऐण्टीडिप्रेसेण्ट	पु.	निराशा, विषाद उदासी आदि दूर करने वाली दवा।
ऐण्टीपर्सपिरेण्ट	पु.	पसीना कम करने के लिए प्रयोग किया जाने वाला तरल पदार्थ
ऐण्टीफ्रीज	पु.	रेडियेटर में पानी को जमने से रोकने वाला रसायन; जमावरोधी रसायन।
ऐण्टीबॉडी	पु.	रक्त में उत्पन्न होने वाला रोग निरोधक पदार्थ
ऐण्टीबायोटिक	पु.	जीवाणु नाशक औषधि, प्रतिजैविक।
ऐण्टीबैक्टीरियल	वि.	जीवाणु निरोधक, प्रति जीवाणु।
ऐण्टीलोप	पु.	बारहसिंगा।
ऐण्टीसेप्टिक	पु.	रोगाणुरोधक दवा या मरहम।
ऐण्टीहिस्टेमाइन	पु.	एलर्जी दूर करने वाली दवा।
ऐक्रिड	वि.	गन्ध और स्वाद में कड़वा, तीव्र और तीखा।

ऐक्ने	पु.	युवावस्था में होने वाला चेहरे का एक रोग जिसमें चेहरे पर छोटी-छोटी फुंसियाँ निकल आती हैं।
ऐक्सीडेण्ट	पु.	दुर्घटना।
ऐक्सीडेण्ट प्रोन	वि.	दुर्घटना आशंकित स्थान, वह स्थान जहाँ अधिकतर दुर्घटनाएँ होती हैं।
ऐटमास्फेयर	पु.	वायुमण्डल; किसी स्थान का वातावरण; मन:स्थिति, मनोदशा।
ऐटम	पु.	परमाणु; किसी तत्त्व का सबसे सूक्ष्म भाग।
ऐड	क्रि.	संख्याओं या राशियों को जोड़ना, योग करना।
ऐडहेसन	पु.	आसंजन, चिपकाव; किसी के साथ चिपकने की क्रिया।
ऐडहेसिव	पु.	आसंजक, आपस में चिपकाने वाला पदार्थ।
ऐड्स (AIDS)	पु.	यह एक्वायर्ड इम्यून डिफीशियंसी सिण्ड्रोम का संक्षिप्त रूप है। यह एक प्रकार का रोग है, जो शरीर की रोग प्रतिरोधक क्षमता को पूर्णतया समाप्त कर देता है।
ऐनेरोबिक	वि.	जिसे ऑक्सीजन की जरूरत न हो, ऑक्सीजन निरपेक्ष।
ऐनेस्थीजिया	स्त्री.	संवेदनाहरण; एक प्रकार की औषधि जो शल्य चिकित्सा से पूर्व रोगी को संवेदन शून्य करने के लिए दी जाती है।
ऐनेस्थेटिक	पु.	संवेदनहीनता उत्पन्न करने वाला रसायन या पदार्थ; संवेदनहारी पदार्थ।
ऐनेस्थेटिस्ट	पु.	संवेदनाहरक, निश्चेतना विज्ञानी।
ऐन्थ्रासाइट	पु.	एक कठोर प्रकृति का कोयला जिसकी ज्वलनशीलता बहुत कम होती है और जो धुआँहीन होता है।
ऐन्थ्रैक्स	पु.	गाय, बैलों और भेड़ों आदि को होने वाला गम्भीर रोग जिसमें मृत्यु सम्भव है।
ऐन्थ्रोपोलोजी	स्त्री.	मानव की उत्पत्ति उसके विकास का वैज्ञानिक अध्ययन मानव विज्ञान के द्वारा होता है।
ऐप	पु.	एक प्रकार का बड़ा पूँछहीन बन्दर।
ऐप्रीशियेशन	पु.	गुण ग्रहण, गुणदोष विवेचन; आभार, कृतज्ञता; किसी समस्या स्थिति आदि का बोध, परिबोध।
ऐब्सट्रैक्शन	पु.	सार ग्रहण; पृथक्करण; किसी वस्तु को किसी अन्य वस्तु से अलग करना।
ऐस्ट्रोफिजिक्स	पु.	खगोल भौतिकी।
ऐस्पिरिन	स्त्री.	ज्वर कम करने और दर्द कम करने की एक औषधि।
ऐस्फाल्ट	पु.	एक काला गाढ़ा पदार्थ जिसे सड़कों को रंगने के काम में लिया जाता है, अलकतरा, कोलतार, डामर।

ऐस्फिक्सिया	स्त्री.	साँस न ले पाने की स्थिति, जो मृत्यु का कारण भी बन सकती है; श्वास रोग।
ओजोन	पु.	एक जहरीली गैस है। यह भी ऑक्सीजन का एक दूसरा रूप है।
ओजोन लेयर	पु.	वायुमण्डल में बहुत ऊँचाई पर ओजोन गैस की एक मोटी सतह जो कि सूर्य की हानिकारक किरणों से पृथ्वी को बचाने में सहायक होती है।
ओडोर	पु.	गन्ध।
ओबरी	स्त्री.	अण्डाशय; पौधे में बीच उत्पन्न करने वाला अंश।
ओम	पु.	विद्युत की प्रतिरोध शक्ति को मापने की इकाई, वैद्युत प्रतिरोध मात्रक।
ओविपैरस	वि.	अण्डज प्राणी, ऐसे प्राणी जो शिशु न पैदा कर अण्डा देते हैं।
ओवम	पु.	अण्डाणु।
ओव्यूल	पु.	बीज वाले पौधों में बीजास्म का वह भाग जिसमें मादा कोशिका रहती है, जो कि आगे चलकर बीच बनता है; डिम्ब।
ओव्यूलेट	क्रि.	अण्डा देना, अण्डाणु उत्पन्न करना।
ओव्यूलेशन	पु.	अण्डोत्सर्ग।
कण्टाजियस	वि.	संसर्गज रोग; सम्पर्क या स्पर्श के द्वारा फैलने वाला रोग।
कण्डक्टर	पु.	वह पदार्थ जो ताप या विद्युत को अपने में से गुजरने दे; संवाहक पदार्थ, चालक।
कनफिगरेशन	पु.	किसी कम्प्यूटर पद्यति का निर्माण करने वाले उपकरण और प्रोग्राम तथा उनकी विशिष्ट संरूपण व्यवस्था।
कम्पाउण्ड	पु.	यौगिक पदार्थ; दीवार से घेरा गया भूक्षेत्र जिस पर अनेक भवन बने हों।
कम्पास	पु.	कुतुबनुमा, दिक्सूचक।
कम्प्यूटर	पु.	एक प्रकार की अत्याधुनिक इलेक्ट्रॉनिक मशीन जिसमें जानकारी संचित करने, ढूँढ़ने, उसे व्यवस्थित करने, परिकलन करने व अन्य मशीनों पर नियन्त्रण रखने के लिए तैयार किया गया है।
कम्प्यूटराइजेशन	पु.	कम्प्यूटरीकरण।
कम्प्यूटरलिटरेट	वि.	कम्प्यूटरदक्ष; कम्प्यूटर के प्रयोग का जानकार।
कम्प्यूटिंग	पु.	कम्प्यूटर का प्रयोग।
कम्पोनेण्ट	पु.	अवयव।
कम्बस्टिबल	वि.	आसानी से ज्वलनशील, सुदाह्य।
कम्बस्टन	पु.	आग से जलने की क्रिया।

कम्युनिकेशन	पु.	सूचनाओं, भावनाओं और विचारों के आदान-प्रदान की क्रिया; सन्देश-प्रेषण, संचार व्यवस्था।
कलवर्ट	पु.	सड़क आदि के नीचे से जाने वाला पानी का नाला या नाली; पुलिया।
काण्टैक्ट लेंस	पु.	आँख पर लगाया जाने वाला शीशे या प्लास्टिक का बना पतला टुकड़ा जिससे दृष्टि में सुधार होता है; संस्पर्श लेंस।
कांस्टीपेशन	पु.	कब्ज, भोजन का अच्छी तरह से न पचना।
काक्लिआ	पु.	कान के अन्दर सीपी के समान एक भाग जो सुनने में सहायता करता है; कर्णावर्त।
काक्सिक्स	पु.	रीढ़ की हड्डी के अधोभाग की छोटी हड्डी।
कॉनकेव	वि.	अवतल, नतोदर, अन्दर की तरफ मुड़ती हुई।
कॉनवेक्स	वि.	उन्नतोदर, उत्तल बाहर की ओर निकलती हुई।
काम्प्लेक्शन	पु.	चेहरे की त्वचा का प्राकृतिक रंग और गुण किसी वस्तु का सामान्य स्वरूप।
कार्टरिज	पु.	किसी मशीन में प्रयोग होने वाली सामग्री जैसे, प्रिण्टर में लगने वाली स्याही की कार्टरीज, कैमरे की फिल्म आदि।
कॉयल	पु.	कुण्डलाकृति।
कार्क	पु.	एक प्रकार का हल्का मुलायम पदार्थ जो विशेष प्रकार की पेड़ की छाल से बनाया जाता है और बोतल को बन्द करने के लिए डॉट के रूप में प्रयोग होता है।
कार्कस्क्रू	पु.	बोतलों पर लगी डॉट को खोलने के लिए एक उपकरण।
कार्टिलेज	पु.	हड्डियों के जोड़ों पर पाया जाने वाला सुदृढ़ पदार्थ।
कार्टोग्राफर	पु.	मानचित्र निर्माता; नक्शानवीस।
कार्प्सकल	पु.	लाल या सफेद रक्तकणिका।
कार्बन	पु.	एक रासायनिक तत्त्व। यह तत्त्व कोयला और हीरे में भी तथा सजीवों में पाया जाता है।
कार्बन कॉपी	पु.	मसि-पत्र लगाकर बनायी गयी प्रति; किसी वस्तु या दस्तावेज की एक दम सही प्रतिलिपि।
कार्बन डाइऑक्साइड	पु.	एक रंगहीन व गन्धहीन गैस जो जीवधारियों के स्वास्थ्य के लिए हानिकारक होती है।
कार्बोनेट	पु.	कार्बन डाइऑक्साइड और किसी अन्य रासायनिक तत्त्व से प्रतिक्रिया करने के परिणाम स्वरूप निर्मित लवण।
कार्बोहाइड्रेड	पु.	भोजन में उपलब्ध एक तत्त्व जो शरीर को ऊर्जा प्रदान करता है।

कार्ब्यूरेटर	पु.	कारों, मोटरसाइकिल आदि में लगा एक उपकरण जो पेट्रोल और हवा को मिश्रित कर इंजन में भेजता है।
कार्डियक	वि.	हृदय से सम्बन्धित।
कार्डियक अरेस्ट	पु.	हृदय गति के रुक जाने की गम्भीर स्थिति।
कार्सिनोंजेन	पु.	कैंसर पैदा करने वाला एक तत्त्व।
कॉलरबोन	पु.	कन्धे को छाती की हड्डियों से जोड़ने वाली हड्डी।
कास्टिक सोडा	पु.	साबुन बनाने के काम आने वाला पदार्थ।
किलोग्राम	पु.	भार मापने की एक इकाई। यह 1000 ग्राम के बराबर होता है।
किलोजूल	पु.	भोजन से मिलने वाली ऊर्जा को माने की एक इकाई। 1000 जूल बराबर 1 किलो जूल।
किलोमीटर	पु.	लम्बाई की एक माप। यह एक हजार मीटर के बराबर होता हैं।
किलोवाट	पु.	विद्युत शक्ति को मापने की इकाई। यह एक हजार वॉट के बराबर होता है।
क्रिप्टॉन	पु.	फ्लूरोसेण्ट ट्यूबों में प्रयोग की जाने वाली प्रतिक्रियाहीन और रंगहीन गैस।
क्रिस्टल	पु.	रवा; ठोस हो जाने पर पदार्थों की सुनिश्चित आकृति; स्फटिक; उच्चगुणवत्ता की काँच।
क्रिस्टलाइन	वि.	रवेदार, रवे जैसा।
की-बोर्ड	पु.	कम्प्यूटर का कुंजीपटल; पियानों का कुंजीपटल।
कूलम्ब	पु.	विद्युत चार्ज की इकाई।
के एच जेड		यह किलोहर्ट्ज का संक्षिप्त रूप है। इसका प्रयोग रेडियो तरंगों की फ्रिक्वेंसी की इकाई के रूप मं किया जाता है।
केबल	पु.	मोटा मजबूत धातुनिर्मित तार जिस पर प्लास्टिक का कवर चढ़ा होता है; विद्युत धारा के प्रवाहित होने के लिए प्लास्टिक से ढका तारों का समूह।
केबल कार	पु.	पहाड़ों पर आने जाने के लिए तार के मोटे रस्सों पर चलने वाल केबिनयुक्त गाड़ी।
केबल टेलीविजन	पु.	रेडियो तरंगों के स्थान पर केबल द्वारा टेलीविजन कार्यक्रम प्रसारित करने की पद्वति।
केमिकल	वि.	रासायनिक; रसायन शास्त्र विषयक। पु. रसायन; रासायनिक प्रक्रिया से बना पदार्थ।
केमिस्ट	पु.	औषधि निर्माता।
केमिस्ट्री	स्त्री	रसायन शास्त्र।
केमोथिरेपी	स्त्री.	रासायनिक पदार्थों द्वारा चिकित्सा, रसचिकित्सा।

कल्विन पु. ताप मापने की एक इकाई, केल्विन एक डिग्री सेल्सियस के बराबर होता है।

कैण्टिलीवर पु. डॉट, लकड़ी या धातु का लम्बा टुकड़ा जो दीवार से बाहर की तरफ निकला होता है और पुल के छोर या अन्य ढाँचे को बल देता है; बाहुधरण।

कैनन पु. स्वीकृत नियम, मापदण्ड या सिद्धान्त जिससे किसी वस्तु का मूल्यांकन होता है।

कैनबिस पु. भाँग की जाति का एक पौधा ओर उससे निर्मित एक नशीला पदार्थ जिसका सेवन कुछ लोग आन्दद उठाने के लिए करते हैं।

कैंसर पु. एक प्राणघातक गम्भीर रोग जिसमें शरीर के किसी भाग की कोशिकाओं की संख्या में असामान्य रूप से वृद्धि होने लगती है।

कैंसरस वि. कैंसर रोग से ग्रस्त।

कैक्टस पु. नागफनी, सेहुँड़।

कैजुअलिटी स्त्री. आपातकालीन विभाग।

कैटरपिलर पु. सूँड़ी, इल्ली।

कैटरैक्ट पु. मोतियाबिन्द।

कैटलाइज क्रि. रासायनिक प्रतिक्रिया को उत्प्रेरित करना।

कैटलिसिस पु. उत्प्रेरण।

कैटालिटिक कनवर्टर पु. मोटरकारों में लगा उपकरण जो विषैली गैसों से होने वाली पर्यावरण की हानि को कम करता है।

कैडमियम पु. एक सफेद-नीली विषैली धातु जिसका प्रयोग उद्योगों में बैटरी बनाने में किया जाता है।

कैथार्सिस पु. विरेचन; भावनाओं का समन।

कैथेटर पु. शरीर में से अनावश्यक द्रव पदार्थ को बाहर निकालने के लिए नलिका के समान यन्त्र।

कैथोड पु. बैटरी में वह बिन्दु जहाँ से होकर विद्युतधारा बाहर निकलती है।

कैथेड-रे ट्यूब पु. टेलीविजन, कम्प्यूटर स्क्रीन आदि के अन्दर की नली जिसके अन्तर्गत बनने वाले इलेक्ट्रॉनों के कारण परदे पर चित्र बनते हैं; कैथोड किरण नलिका।

कैपासिटर पु. विद्युत आवेश को संचित करने वाला उपकरण, सन्धारित्र।

कैपेसिटी स्त्री. क्षमता, धारण शक्ति; किसी मशीन की उत्पादन क्षमता।

कैप्सूल पु. दवा से भरी छोटी सम्पुटिका; सीलबन्द डिब्बा जिसमें वायु, नमी आदि न प्रवेश कर सके।

कैफीन	स्त्री.	चाय और कॉफ़ी में पाया जाने वाला एक पदार्थ।
कैमरा	पु.	फोटोग्राफी या चलचित्र रिकॉर्ड करने के लिए एक यन्त्र।
कैमकॉर्डर	पु.	सचल वीडियो कैमरा जिससे ध्वनि भी रिकॉर्ड की जा सकती है।
कैलिडोस्कोप	पु.	रंगीन काँच के टुकड़ों से भरी दर्पणों वाली नली का खिलौना जिसे घुमाने से रंग-बिरंगी दृश्यावली दिखायी देती है; बहुमूर्तिदर्शी।
कैलीब्रेशन	पु.	किसी उपकरण पर मापन इकाइयों के निर्धारण की क्रिया, अंशांकन; किसी उपकरण (जैसे थर्मामीटर आदि) पर अंकित मापन इकाइयाँ।
कैलोरिफिक	पु.	ऊर्जा या ऊर्जा उत्पादन से सम्बन्धित।
कैलोरी	स्त्री.	ऊर्जा की इकाई; उष्मा की इकाई, उष्मा की उतनी मात्र जिससे एक ग्राम जल का तापमान एक डिग्री बढ़ जाये।
कैल्कुलस	पु.	गणित की एक शाखा, जिसका मूल विषय परिवर्तन मात्राएँ होती है।
कैल्कुलेटर	पु.	गणना करने वाला एक इलेक्ट्रॉनिक यन्त्र, परिकलक।
कैल्सिफिकेशन	पु.	कैल्शिम के प्रयोग से किसी वस्तु को कठोर करने की क्रिया।
कैल्शियम	पु.	एक रासायनिक तत्त्व जो शरीर की हड्डियों और दाँतों को मजबूत कराने में सहायक होता है।
कैल्शियम	पु.	खड़िया, चूने और संगमरमर में पाया जाने वाला सफेद ठोस पदार्थ।
कैशे	पु.	कम्प्यूटर स्मृति का वह भाग जहाँ सूचना सामग्री की प्रतिलिपि संचित रहती है।
कैबिज	पु.	बन्दगोभी, करमकल्ला।
कैस्ट्रेट	क्रि.	बधिया करना।
कोइफीशियट	पु.	3X गुणांक, जैसे 3X में; किसी पदार्थ की विशिष्टता का मापक गुणांक।
कोऐगुलेट	क्रि.	(द्रव पदार्थ का) गाढ़ा और कुछ ठोस हो जाना, जम जाना।
कोडीन	पु.	एक दर्द निवारक औषधि।
कोबाल्ट	पु.	एक कड़ी चाँदी जैसी सफेद धातु।
कोरियोग्राफी	पु.	नृत्यरचना।
कोरोनरी	वि.	हृदय से सम्बन्धित, हृदय का। पु. एक प्रकार का दिल का दौरा।
कोलाइड	क्रि.	गतिमान वस्तुओं का टकराना, टकराव होना।
कोलेस्ट्राल	पु.	मनुष्यों व पशुओं के रक्त में पाया जाने वाला एक पदार्थ जिसकी मात्रा बढ़ जाने पर हृदय रोग होने की सम्भावना होती है।

कोसाइन	पु.	कोज्या, कोटिज्या, किसी समकोण त्रिभुज में न्यूनकोण के साथ की भुजा का सबसे लम्बी भुजा से अनुपात।
कौलीफ्लावर	स्त्री.	फूलगोभी।
कोल्ड सोर	पु.	विषाणु (वायरस) द्वारा संक्रमण से होंठ या मुख के अन्दर पड़ा दर्द युक्त छाला।
क्यूब	पु.	घनाकृति, समान पार्श्वों वाला ठोस पिण्ड; (गणित में) घनफल।
क्यूबरूट	पु.	(गणित में) घनमूल।
क्यूबिक	पु.	घनीय।
क्लाइटोरिस	स्त्री.	भगशिश्न; स्त्री के जननेन्द्रिय का एक भाग।
क्लाइमेट	पु.	जलवायु, वातावरण आबोहावा।
क्लाइमटोलॉजी	स्त्री.	जलवायु विज्ञान।
क्लाट	पु.	खून का थक्का।
क्लीनिक	पु.	चिकित्सा सुविधा प्रदान करने वाला छोटा अस्पताल।
क्लीनिकल	वि.	रोगियों के परीक्षण और चिकित्सा से सम्बन्धित; नैदानिक, उपचारात्मक।
क्लोज्ड सर्किट टेलीविजन	पु.	अपराध पर नियन्त्रण रखने के लिए किसी भवन में लगायी गयी एक प्रकार की टेलीविजन व्यवस्था।
क्लोन	पु.	किसी पौधे या पशु की कोशिका से वैज्ञानिक पद्धति द्वारा बनी उसकी सही अनुकृति।
क्लोरोफार्म	पु.	एक तीव्रगन्ध वाला रंगहीन द्रव पदार्थ जिसका प्रयोग कर मरीज को शल्यचिकित्सा से पूर्व बेहोश किया जाता है।
क्लोरोफिल	पु.	पौधों में पाया जाने वाला हरा पदार्थ जो सूर्य की किरणों को ग्रहण कर पौधों की वृद्धि में सहायता करता है; पर्णरहित।
क्लोरोप्लास्ट	पु.	पौधों की कोशिका का क्लोरोफिल वाला वह भाग जहाँ प्रकाश संश्लेषण होता है।
गामा	पु.	ग्रीक वर्णमाला का तीसरा अक्षर।
गामारेडिएशन	पु.	रेडियो सक्रिय पदार्थों से निकलने वाली किरणें।
गार्गल	पु.	किसी रासायनिक द्रव पदार्थ से गरारे करना।
गालब्लैडर	पु.	शरीर में यकृत से जुड़ा पित्त को संचित करने वाला एक अंग; पित्ताशय।
गाल स्टोन	पु.	पित्ताशय में पायी जाने वाली पथरी, जो बहुत कष्टदायी होती है।
ग्राइण्डर	पु.	पीसने की मशीन।
ग्राफ	पु.	एक आरेख जिसमें दो मात्राओं, मापों आदि के बीच सम्बन्ध को सीधी या वक्र रेखाओं में दिखाया जाता है, लेखाचित्र।

ग्राफिक्स	पु.	आरेखन चित्रों आरेखों आदि का निर्माण।
ग्रिड	स्त्री.	मानचित्र पर बनी वर्ग प्रणाली जिस पर किसी स्थान की स्थिति अंकित की जा सकती है या पता लगाया जा सकता है; विद्युत वितरण के लिए बिजली के तारों की व्यवस्था।
गीयर	पु.	किसी वाहन या मशीन का वह पुर्जा जिससे वाहन या मशीन चलती है।
गीयर लीवर	पु.	गीयर बदलने की छड़।
ग्रेफाइट	पु.	पेंसिलों में प्रयुक्त कोमल काला पदार्थ।
ग्रेविटी	पु.	गुरुत्वाकर्षण बल।
गेज	पु.	किसी वस्तु की चौड़ाई या दो वस्तुओं के बीच की दूरी की माप।
गैंगरीन	पु.	किसी रोग या चोट के कारण शरीर के किसी अंग में रक्त रुक जाने से अंग का निष्क्रिय और निष्प्राण हो जाना।
गैमीट	पु.	नर या मादा कोशिका जो विपरीत लिंग के साथ मिलकर शिशु का निर्माण करने वाली कोशिका बनाती है; युग्मक कोशिका।
गैलन	पु.	द्रव को मापने का एक माप।
गैलेक्सी	स्त्री.	सूर्य और ग्रहों का तारापथ जो रात्रिकालीन आकाश में प्रकाशित पट्टी जैसा दिखायी देता है; आकाश गंगा।
गैलवैनाइज	पु.	लोहे पर या इस्पात पर जस्ता चढ़ाना जिसमें उसमें जंग न लगे।
गैस	पु.	वायु के समान पदार्थ जो न ठोस हो न द्रव; भोजन बनाने या किसी धातु को गलाने में प्रयोग आने वाली एक प्रकार की प्राकृत गैस।
गैसकिट	पु.	रबर आदि का समतल टुकड़ा जिसे पाइप या इंजन की दो धातुई सतहों के बीच में रख देते हैं जिससे भाप या तेल बाहर न निकले।
गैस्ट्राइटिस	स्त्री.	आमाशय में सूजन और दर्द की बीमारी।
गैस्ट्रो-इण्ट्राइटिस	स्त्री.	आमाशय और आँतों में सूजन और दर्द की बीमारी।
गैस्ट्रोपॉड		कोमल शरीर और कड़े आवरण वाला प्राणी जो भूमि और जल में रह सकता है, जठरपाद।
गैसमीटर	पु.	घरों में प्रयोग की जाने वाली गैस की मात्रा को मापने का मीटर; मैस मीटर।
ग्लिसरीन	स्त्री.	चरबी और तेलों से बना एक गाढ़ा मीठा रंगहीन द्रव पदार्थ, जो विस्फोटकों में और सौन्दर्य प्रसाधनों में प्रयोग किया जाता है।
ग्लौकॉमा	पु.	एक नेत्र रोग जिसमें क्रमशः दृष्टि क्षीणता होती है, काला मोतिया।

चारकोल	पु.	लकड़ी का कोयला, काठ कोयला।
चार्ज	पु.	किसी वस्तु में विद्युत आवेश।
चिकेनपाक्स	पु.	चेचक, खसरा। इस रोग में रोगी के शरीर पर छोटे-छोटे, लाल दाने उभर आते हैं।
चेनरिएक्शन	पु.	रसायन विज्ञान में रासायनिक क्रियाओं की शृंखला, शृंखलाबद्ध प्रक्रिया।
चैनल	पु.	टेलीविजन स्टेशन, चैनल; रेडियो या टेलीविजन कार्यक्रमों के प्रसारण के लिए प्रयुक्त तरंगदैर्ध्य, द्रवों आदि के बहने के लिए मार्ग।
जर्म	पु.	रोग उत्पन्न करने वाले बहुत छोटे जीवाणु।
जाइरोस्कोप	पु.	घूर्णाक्षदर्शी।
जिप्सम	पु.	एक खड़िया जैसा सफेद, मुलायम खनिज।
जीओथर्मल	वि.	जमीन की गहराई में चट्टानों के प्राकृतिक ताप से सम्बन्धित।
जीओमेट्रिक	वि.	रेखागणित, ज्यामिति सम्बन्धी।
जीओमेट्रिक प्रोग्रेशन	पु.	1, 3, 9, 27, 81 आदि संख्याओं की शृंखला जिसमें प्रत्येक को एक निश्चित संख्या से गुणा या भाग किया जाता है जिसके परिणाम स्वरूप अगली संख्या आती है।
जीओमेट्री	स्त्री.	गणित के अन्तर्गत रेखाओं, आकृतियों आदि का अध्ययन।
जीओलॉजी	स्त्री.	भूविज्ञान।
जीनोम	पु.	कोशिका या सजीव में स्थित पूर्ण जीन समुच्चय।
जेनरेटर	पु.	विद्युत उत्पन्न होने वाली मशीन।
जेनिओलॉजी	स्त्री.	स्त्रीरोग विज्ञान।
जेनिटल	पु.	जनन सम्बन्धी।
जेनेटिक	वि.	आनुवंशिक विज्ञान, अनुवांशिकी।
जेनिटिक इंजिनियरिंग	पु.	जीन परिवर्तन के द्वारा मनुष्य, पशु या पौधे के विकास में परिवर्तन का वैज्ञानिक अध्ययन।
जेनेटिक्स	पु.	सजीवों में विभिन्न लक्षणों का माता-पिता से उनकी सन्तान तक पहुँचाने की विकास प्रक्रिया का वैज्ञानिक अध्ययन; आनुवंशिकता विज्ञान, जनन विज्ञान।
जेरिएट्रिक्स	पु.	जरा चिकित्सा; बूढ़ों, बुजुर्गों के स्वास्थ्य की देखभाल।
जेलिग्नाइट	पु.	विस्फोटकों को बनाने के लिए प्रयोग में आने वाला पदार्थ।
टंगस्टन	पु.	एक कड़ी स्लेटी रंग की धातु या इस्पात जिससे बिजली के बल्ब के तार बनते हैं।
टरबाइन	पु.	एक मशीन जो पानी, वायु, गैस के दाब से चलने वाले पहिए के सहारे चलती है।

टरमरिक	स्त्री.	हल्दी, हरिद्रा।
टाइपराइटर	पु.	टाइप करने की मशीन, टंकण मशीन।
टाइफाइड	पु.	आन्त्रज्वर, एक प्राणघातक ज्वर।
ट्रांजिस्टर	पु.	रेडियो, कम्प्यूटर में लगने वाला एक छोटा उपकरण।
ट्रांसपिरेशन	पु.	पौधे या पत्ते की सतह पर जलकण या वाष्प प्रकट होने की क्रिया; वाष्पोत्सर्जन।
ट्रांसपैरेण्ट	वि.	पारदर्शी।
ट्रांसपैरेसी	पु.	पारदर्शी प्लास्टिक खण्ड जिस पर कुछ लिखा हो, आरेख या चित्र बना हो और जिसे प्रोजेक्ट द्वारा प्रकाश फेंक कर देखा जा सके; दृश्यता।
ट्रांसप्लाण्ट	पु.	किसी एक व्यक्ति के शरीर से शल्यक्रिया द्वारा कोई अंग निकालकर दूसरे के शरीर में प्रत्यारोपित करने की क्रिया।
ट्रांसफार्मर	पु.	बिजली की शक्ति को बढ़ाने या घटाने का यन्त्र; बिलजी का ट्रांसफार्मर।
ट्रांसफ्यूजन	पु.	रक्ताधान करना; किसी के शरीर में रक्त चढ़ाने की क्रिया।
ट्रांसमिशन	पु.	कोई सूचना या डेटा एक व्यक्ति या स्थान से दूसरे व्यक्ति या स्थान को संचारित करने की क्रिया; संचारण, सम्प्रेषण।
ट्रांसल्यूसेण्ट	पु.	पारभाषक, जिसमें से प्रकाश पार तो कर जाये पर स्पष्ट दिखायी न दे।
ट्रांसवर्सवेब	पु.	अंश को कोण पर कम्पन करने वाली लहर; अनुप्रस्थ तरंग।
ट्राईसेप्स	पु.	बाँह के ऊपरी भाग के पीछे की मांसपेशी, त्रिशिरस्क।
टिटैनस	पु.	एक प्रकार का रोग जिसमें रोगी की शरीर में अकड़न आ जाती है। यह बैक्टीरिया जनक रोग है।
ट्रिग्नोमेट्री	स्त्री.	(गणित) त्रिकोणमिति।
ट्रिलियन	पु.	दस खरब की संख्या या एक लाख करोड़ की संख्या।
ट्रीटमेण्ट	पु.	किसी बीमार या घायल व्यक्ति का उपचार।
टेक्नीकल	वि.	विज्ञान और उद्योग के क्षेत्र में मशीनों आदि के व्यावहारिक उपयोग से सम्बन्धित तकनीक की जानकारी वाला।
टेक्नीशियन	पु.	मशीनों आदि की जानकारी से युक्त क्षमता वाला व्यक्ति, तकनीकी कारीगर।
टेक्नोलॉजी	स्त्री.	किसी उद्योग आदि के लिए आवश्यक वैज्ञानिक जानकारी।
टेक्नोलॉजिस्ट	पु.	प्रौद्योगिकीवेत्ता, शिल्प विज्ञानी।

टेप	पु.	संगीत, वीडियो आदि को रिकॉर्ड करने वाला कैसेट; रिकॉर्डर का टेप।
टेपरिकार्डर	पु.	ध्वनी को टेप पर रिकॉर्ड करने और सुनाने वाली मशीन।
टेपवार्म	पु.	आँतों में रहने वाला एक कीड़ा; फीताकृमि।
टेलीकम्युनिकेशंस	पु.	दूरसंचार प्रणाली।
टेलीकास्ट	पु.	दूरदर्शन पर प्रसारण।
टेलीग्राफ	पु.	तारों की सहायता से विद्युत संकेतों को दूर भेजने की प्रेषण प्रणाली।
टेलीग्राम	पु.	टेलीफोन प्रणाली द्वारा किसी को भेजा गया लिखित सन्देश; तार।
टेलीफोन	पु.	एक ऐसा इलेक्ट्रो इलेक्ट्रॉनिक उपकरण जिससे हम दूरदराज में रहने वाले व्यक्तियों से सीधे वार्तलाप कर सकते हैं।
टेलीस्कोप	पु.	दूरबीन, दूरदर्शक यन्त्र, दूर की वस्तुओं को साफ-साफ देखने वाला यन्त्र।
टेस्टट्यूब	स्त्री.	परखनली।
टेस्टोस्टेरोन	पु.	पुरुष के शरीर में उत्पन्न विशेष हार्मोन जो पुरुष के विशिष्ट शारीरिक और लैंगिक गुणों का विकास करता है।
ट्रेनर	पु.	प्रशिक्षण देने वाला, शिक्षक।
ट्रेनी	पु.	प्रशिक्षणार्थी, प्रशिक्षु।
ट्रेमर	पु.	अँगुलियों आदि में हल्का कम्पन।
टैंजेण्ट	पु.	(गणित) स्पर्शज्या; किसी 90 डिग्री कोण वाले त्रिकोण के सामने और बगल वाली विकर्ण से भिन्न भुजाओं की लम्बाइयों का अनुपात।
टैक्सोनॉमी	पु.	वस्तुओं को वर्गीकरण करने की वैज्ञानिक प्रक्रिया।
टैबलेट	पु.	औषधि की गोली, टिकिया।
ट्रैंक्विलाइजर	पु.	रोगी को या अनिद्रा रोग से ग्रस्त व्यक्तियों को सोने के लिए दी जाने वाली औषधि; दर्दनाशक औषधि।
ट्रैक्टर	पु.	खेतों में जोताई आदि करने की मशीन; भारी मशीनें खींचने के लिए बड़ी मशीन।
ट्रैक्शन	पु.	टूटी हुई हड्डी को जोड़ने का ढंग; अंगकर्षण; वाहन के पहियों आदि को फिसलने से रोकने वाली शक्ति; सतह पर खींचने की क्रिया, कर्षण।
ट्रैचिया	स्त्री.	श्वास नली।
ट्रैपेजियम	पु.	समलम्बाभ चतुर्भुज; वह चतुर्भुज जिसकी आमने-सामने की भुजा समानान्तर होती हैं।

ट्रैवेलसिक	वि.	वाहन के निरन्तर हिलने-डुलने के कारण उल्टी आने या मतली आने की बीमारी।
ट्रौमा	पु.	गहरा आघात और खिन्नता की स्थिति।
ट्यूब	पु.	नली।
ट्यूबर क्यूलोसिस	पु.	क्षय रोग, टीवी।
डर्मेटाइटिस	पु.	एक त्वचारोग, जिसमें त्वचा लाल, सूजनयुक्त और दर्द युक्त हो जाती है।
डर्मेटोलॉजिस्ट	पु.	चर्मरोग विशेषज्ञ, त्वचा विशेषज्ञ।
डर्मेटोलॉजी	स्त्री.	त्वचा विज्ञान, चर्मरोग विज्ञान।
डाइअटामिक	वि.	द्विअंशी, दो अंशों वाला।
डाइटेटिक्स	पु.	आहार शास्त्र, भोजन और स्वास्थ्य पर उसके प्रभाव का वैज्ञानिक अध्ययन।
डाउंजसिण्ड्रोम	पु.	एक जन्मजात विकृति जिसमें रोगी का चेहरा सपाट और चौड़ा तथा बुद्धि मन्द हो जाती है।
डाक्टर	पु.	चिकित्सक।
डॉक्टरिन	पु.	सिद्धान्त।
डॉयगोनल	पु.	विकर्ण रेंखा; वर्ग के सामने कोणों को मिलाने वाली सीधी रेखा अथवा वर्ग के एक कोण से दूसरे कोण तक खींची गयी सीधी रेखा।
डायग्राम	पु.	आरेख, रेखाचित्र।
डायग्नोसिस	स्त्री.	रोगी के रोग सम्बन्धी समस्या के कारण को पहचाने की क्रिया, निदान क्रिया।
डायबिटीज	पु.	मधुमेह का एक रोग।
डायबेटिक	स्त्री.	मधुमेह रोगी।
डायरिया	पु.	अतिसार रोग, दस्त की बीमारी।
डॉयलसिस	स्त्री.	क्षतिग्रस्त गुर्दों के रोगियों के लिए एक रक्त शोधन प्रक्रिया।
डायलॉगबॉक्स	पु.	कम्प्यूटर स्क्रीन पर उभरने वाला बॉक्स जो प्रयोगकर्ता को अगली क्रिया सम्पादित करने का निर्देश देता है।
डायाफ्रैग्म	पु.	फेफड़ों और पेट के बीच की मांसपेशी जो श्वसन क्रिया में सहायक होती है।
डायोड	पु.	एक इलेक्ट्रॉनिक उपकरण जिसमें विद्युतधारा केवल एक दिशा में प्रवाहित होती है।
ड्राइव	स्त्री.	कम्प्यूटर का वह भाग जो सूचना को ग्रहण और संचित करता है; वाहन का ऐसा उपकरण जो इंजन द्वारा उत्पन्न शक्ति को उसके पहियों तक पहुँचाता है।

डिकम्पोज क्रि. विघटित होना, प्राकृतिक रासायनिक प्रक्रियाओं द्वारा क्रमशः नष्ट हो जाना।

डिजिट पु. 0 से 9 तक की संख्या।

डिटेक्टर पु. किसी वस्तु (धातु या विस्फोटक आदि का) पता लगाने वाली मशीन।

डिटोनेट क्रि. बम आदि का विस्फोट होना या करना।

डिटोनेटर पु. विस्फोट करने वाला उपकरण।

डिनामिनेटर पु. (गणित में) भिन्न में हर को व्यक्त करने वाली संख्या, जैसे–3/4 भिन्न में 4 संख्या।

डिप्लायड वि. दो पूर्ण गुणसूत्र सेटों वाली कोशिका।

डिफलेक्ट क्रि. किसी से टक्कर खाकर दिशा बदल देना।

डिफलेक्शन पु. (टकराने से) दिशा परिवर्तन।

डिफिब्रिलेटर पु. हृदय की मांपपेशियों की हरकत को बिजली के झटके देकर नियन्त्रित करने की क्रिया।

डिफ्रैक्ट क्रि. भौतिक शास्त्र में बहुत पतले छिद्र से या किनारे के आर-पार जाती हुई प्रकाश की किरणों या प्रकाश की लहर की शृंखला का बहुरंगी पैटर्न में विभाजन करना।

डिफ्यूज क्रि. किसी गैस या द्रव का अन्य दूसरी वस्तु में मिल जाना या मिलकर एक हो जाना।

डिमेंशिया पु. मस्तिष्क रोग या आघात के कारण होने वाला एक गम्भीर मानसिक विकार जो व्यक्ति को सोचने, याद रखने और सामान्य व्यवहार करने की क्षमता नष्ट हो जाती है।

डिलीरियम पु. अत्यधिक ज्वर से उत्पन्न मस्तिष्क विभ्रम।

डिलीरियस वि. उन्मादग्रस्त, उन्मत्त; अत्यधिक प्रसन्न।

डिवाइस स्त्री. उपकरण मशीन।

डिसएबिलिटी स्त्री. शारीरिक रूप से असक्त होने की स्थिति।

डिस्इंफेक्शन पु. रोगाणुनाशन।

डिस्क स्त्री. कम्प्यूटर में प्रयोग की जाने वाली सूचना संचित करने वाली प्लास्टिक की बनी एक गोलाकार वस्तु।

डिस्कड्राइव स्त्री विद्युत से चलने वाला कम्प्यूटर में लगा एक इलेक्ट्रॉनिक उपकरण जो डिस्क से सूचना ग्रहण करता है या डिस्क में सूचना संगृहीत करता है।

डिस्कवरी स्त्री. खोज, अनुसंधान।

डिस्टेस्ट पु. अरुचि, स्वादहीन, नापसन्द।

डिस्टिल	क्रि.	द्रव को शुद्ध करने के लिए उसे भाप बनाना और फिर ठण्डा करके पुनः द्रव में बदलना।
डिस्टिलरी	स्त्री.	आसवनशाला; मद्यनिर्माणशाला।
डिस्टिलेशन	पु.	द्रवशोधन, आसवन।
डिस्पेंसरी	स्त्री.	अस्पताल, औषधालय, दवाघर।
डिस्प्रपोर्शनेट	पु.	अन्यु वस्तु की तुलना में बहुत बड़ा या छोटा, असंगत, बेमेल, अनुपातहीन।
डिहाइड्रेशन	पु.	निर्जलीकरण।
डीएनए	पु.	किसी सजीव प्राणी या पौधे की कोशिकाओं में विद्यमान रसायन जो उसके गुण-धर्म को निर्धारित करता है।
डीजे	पु.	रेडियो पर संगीत कार्यक्रम को प्रस्तुत करने वाला व्यक्ति।
डेण्टिस्ट्री	पु.	दाँत और मुख के विषय में अध्ययन; दन्त चिकित्सा।
डेंसिटी	स्त्री.	घनत्व, किसी स्थान के क्षेत्रफल का, वहाँ के व्यक्तियों व वस्तुओं की संख्या का आनुपातिक सम्बन्ध; सघनता।
डेक्सट्रोज	पु.	ग्लूकोज का एक रूप।
डेसीमल	वि.	दशमलव पद्धति से सम्बद्ध, दस या दसवें इकाइयों में परिगणित। पु. दशमलव भिन्न।
डेसिमल प्वाइण्ट	पु.	दशमलव बिन्दु।
डेसीमीटर	पु.	लम्बाई मापने की इकाई। यह मीटर का दसवाँ हिस्सा होता है।
डेस्कटॉप	पु.	कम्प्यूटर की स्क्रीन जिस पर कम्प्यूटर में उपलब्ध प्रोग्रामों के संकेत चित्र होते हैं।
डेस्कटॉप पब्लिशिंग	पु.	पुस्तक आदि मुद्रित करने के लिए कम्प्यूटर और प्रिण्टर का प्रयोग।
ड्यूडोनियम	स्त्री.	छोटी आँत का आगे का भाग, ग्रहणी।
ड्यूप्वाइण्ट	पु.	ओसांक, तापमान का वह बिन्दु जहाँ वायु में जल का अंश नहीं रहता। इस तापमान से नीचे के बिन्दु पर जल ओस बनकर वायु में से निकल जाता है।
थर्मामीटर	पु.	तापमामी, ताप मापने का उपकरण।
थर्मोस	पु.	द्रव को ठण्डा या गरम रखने के लिए प्रयोग में आने वाली बोतल, थर्मस बोतल।
थर्मोस्टेट	पु.	किसी मशीन के तापमान को नियन्त्रित करने वाला उपकरण, तापस्थिरिक।
थर्मोस्फीयर	पु.	वाह्य वायुमण्डल।
थाईबोन	पु.	जाँघ की हड्डी।

थ्राम्बोसिस	पु.	हृदय या रक्तनली में थक्का जमने का गम्भीर रोग, शिरावरोध।
थियोडोलाइट	स्त्री.	कोणों को मापने का उपकरण, कोणमापी।
थिरेपी	स्त्री.	शारीरिक रोगों की चिकित्सा।
थोरेक्स	पु.	छाती, वक्ष, सीना (आदि की चिकित्सा)।
थ्रोट	पु.	गला, कण्ठ।
थ्योरम	पु.	प्रमेय, सत्यसिद्ध किया जाने वाला नियम या सिद्धान्त।
नर्व	पु.	स्नायु तन्त्र, नस, तन्त्रिका।
नर्वस	वि.	स्नायु विषयक, स्नायु स्नायविक।
नाइट्रिक एसिड	पु.	यह एक शक्तिशाली अम्ल है, इसका प्रयोग विनाशकारी और विस्फोटक पदार्थों में किया जाता है।
नाइट्रेट	पु.	नाइट्रोजन से बना एक यौगिक। यह मिट्टी को बहुत उपजाऊ बनाने में सहायता करता है।
नाइट्रोजन	पु.	एक गैस जो रंग, स्वाद और गन्धरहित होती है। यह वायुमण्डल में 80 प्रतिशत के अनुपात में मौजूद होता है।
नाटिकलमाइल	पु.	समुद्र में दूरी नापने की इकाई समुद्री मील।
नार्कोटिक	पु.	शक्तिशाली नशीला पदार्थ; स्वापक; ऐसी दवा या पदार्थ जो तनाव को दूर करे, दर्द मिटाये और नींद लाये।
नास्ट्रिल	पु.	नासाछिद्र, नथुना।
नासा	पु.	यह नेशनल एयरोनॉटिक्स एण्ड स्पेस ऐडमिनिस्ट्रेशन का संक्षिप्त रूप है। यह अमेरिकी सरकार का एक संगठन है जो अन्तरिक्ष अनुसन्धान तथा अन्तरिक्ष यात्रा का आयोजन करता है।
निआन	पु.	एक प्रकार की प्रतिक्रियाहीन गैस जो लैम्पों और विज्ञापन पट्टों को चमकदार बनाती है।
निकिल	पु.	एक धातु जो चाँदी के समान सफेद होती है और दूसरे धातुओं में अकसर मिलायी जाती है।
निकोटीन	पु.	तम्बाकू में पाया जाने वाला एक विषैला रसायन।
नेप्थालीन	पु.	पेट्रोलियम और तारकोल के आसवन से बनी फिनायल की गोलियाँ जिनका प्रयोग कीटनाशक दवाओं के निर्माण में किया जाता है।
नोज	पु.	नाक, नासिका।
नोज ब्लीड	पु.	नक्सीर, नाक से खून का गिरना।
नोड	पु.	वह बिन्दु जहाँ दो रेखाएँ मिलती हैं या एक-दूसरे को काटती हैं; मानव शरीर में हड्डियों के जोड़ के निकट एक ठोस मांसपिण्ड होता है।
न्यूक्लियर	वि.	आणविक या नाभिकीय ऊर्जा; परमाणु के नाभिक से सम्बन्धित।

न्यूक्लियर डिसआर्मामेंण्ट	पु.	परमाणुविक नि:शस्त्रीकरण; परमाणु अस्त्रों के विकास और प्रयोग पर रोक
न्यूक्लियर फिजिक्स	पु.	परमाणु नाभिकों का वैज्ञानिक अध्ययन; परमाणुविक भौतिकी।
न्यूक्लियर रिऐक्टर	पु.	परमाणु ऊर्जा उत्पन्न करने का संयन्त्र।
न्यूक्लियस	पु.	परमाणु या कोशिकाओं का केन्द्रीय भाग।
न्यूक्लेयिक एसिड	पु.	सभी सजीव कोशिकाओं में उपस्थिकत दो प्रकार के एसिड–डीएनए और आरएनए में से कोई एक।
न्यूटर	क्रि.	किसी पशु या मनुष्य को नपुंसक बनाना।
न्यूट्रान	पु.	परमाणु के तीन घटकों में से एक। न्यूट्रान में कोई विद्युत आवेश नहीं होता है।
न्यूट्रिएण्ट	पु.	पोषक तत्त्व।
न्यूट्रिशन	पु.	स्वास्थ्य को पुष्ट करने वाला आहार, पोषाहार।
न्यूमरल	पु.	मात्रा या संख्या का सूचक चिह्न या प्रतीक अंक।
न्यूमरेटर	पु.	भिन्न में रेखा के ऊपर की संख्या, अंश जैसे 3/4 की संख्या अंश है।
न्यूरोलॉजिस्ट	पु.	स्नायुरोग विशेषज्ञ, स्नायु विज्ञानी।
न्यूरोलॉजी	स्त्री.	स्नायु विज्ञान।
न्यूरोसिस	पु.	मनस्ताप का स्नायुरोग जिसमें भय और चिन्ता की बहुलता होती है।
न्यूरोसिस्टम	पु.	मस्तिष्क तथा समस्त स्नायुमण्डल।
फंक्शन–की	पु.	कम्प्यूटर के की–बोर्ड पर एक कुंजी जिससे विशेष प्रक्रिया सम्पन्न की जाती है।
फन्नीबोन	पु.	कोहनी की हड्डी।
फरटाइल	वि.	मनुष्य, पशु या पौधे सन्तान उत्पत्ति में सक्षम, फलोत्पादन में सक्षम नये पौधों आदि के उत्पादन में सक्षम।
फरटिलिटी	स्त्री.	उत्पादन क्षमता; उर्वरता।
फाइबरऑप्टिक्स	पु.	प्रकाश संकेतों के यप में सूचना सम्प्रेषण के लिए फाइबर का प्रयोग; तन्तु प्रकाशिकी।
फाइब्रिन	पु.	रक्त में पाया जाने वाला पदार्थ जिससे फाइब्रिन बनता है।
फाइब्रिनोजन	पु.	ताप मापने का एक पैमाना; ताप मापेन की एक इकाई।
फॉरेनहाइट	पु.	अपराध सम्बन्धी जाँच के लिए वैज्ञानिक परीक्षणों का प्रयोग करने वाला।

फीबुला पु. घुटने से टखने के बीच की दो हड्डियों में से बाहरी हड्डी; बहिजंघिका।

फिलामेण्ट पु. विद्युतधारा प्रवाहित होने पर बल्ब में प्रकाश उत्पन्न करने वाला महीन तार; फूल के बीच का रेसा।

फिल्टर पु. कैमरे के साथ प्रयोग होने वाला एक छोटा रंगीन शीशा ज़ो कुछ प्रकार की प्रकाश रेखाओं को पार नहीं होने देता; द्रव या गैस को छानने का उपकरण, छननी।

फिल्टरेशन पु. फिल्टर द्वारा द्रव या गैस को छानने की क्रिया।

फीमर स्त्री. जाँघ की हड्डी उर्विका।

फीसीज स्त्री. विष्ठा, मल।

फुलफ्रेम पु. वह आधार बिन्दु जिस पर कोई वस्तु घूमती है या जिस पर किसी वस्तु को टिकाया जाता है; टेक, आधार।

फूडप्रोसेसर पु. विद्युत चालित मशीन जो भोज्य पदार्थों को काटती और मिश्रित करती है।

फेल्ड्रस्पार पु. (भूविज्ञान) एक प्रकार की सफेद या लाल चट्टान।

फैक्टर पु. (गणित) गुणक; एक को छोड़कर वह पूर्ण संख्या जिससे बड़ी संख्या विभाजित हो सके।

फैक्टरी स्त्री. कारखाना, उद्योग।

फैलोपियन ट्यूब स्त्री. यह मादा पशु के शरीर में दो नलियाँ जिनमें से होकर डिम्ब अण्डाशय से गर्भाशय तक पहुँचता है; डिम्बवाही नलियाँ।

फ्रैक्चर पु. अस्थिभंग; किसी कठोर वस्तु में छूट।

फ्रैक्शन पु. छोटा अंश या छोटी मात्रा।

फ्रैक्शन डिक्टिनेशन पु. द्रव मिश्रण को तपाकर उसके अंश विभाजन की प्रक्रिया ताप बढ़ने के साथ प्रत्येक अंश गैस में बदल जाता है और फिर ठण्डा होकर नली में से गुजरते हुए द्रव बन जाता है।

फोकलप्वाइण्ट पु. अभिरुचि या क्रियाकलाप का केन्द्र बिन्दु; वह बिन्दु जहाँ किरणें या प्रकाश की तरंगें परावर्तन या अनुवर्तन के बाद मिलती है।

फोकललेन्थ पु. दर्पण या लेंस के केन्द्र बिन्दु से उसके फोकस की नाभीय दूरी।

फोकस क्रि. आँखों या कैमरे का वस्तुओं से ऐसा मेल होना बैठना कि वस्तुएँ साफ दिखायी दें।

फोयटस पु. भ्रूण; स्त्री या मादा पशु के शरीर में बढ़ता बच्चा।

फ्लाइंगसासर पु. उड़नतश्तरी; एक गोलाकार अन्तरिक्षयान जिसे कुछ लोग देखने का दावा करते हैं और मानते हैं कि यह यान किसी ग्रह से आया है।

फ्लापी डिस्क	पु.	कम्प्यूटर से सूचना संचित करने वाली प्लास्टिक की चौकोर तस्तरी।
फ्लक	पु.	पशुओं या पक्षियों के शिशुओं के शरीर पर आने वाली नयी रोयेंदार खाल।
फ्लैमेबल	वि.	प्रज्वलनशील, जिसमें आग आसानी से लग सके।
फ्लोचार्ट	पु.	क्रमदर्शी आरेख, प्रवाह चार्ट।
फ्लोराइड	पु.	एक रासायनिक पदार्थ जिसे दाँतों की रक्षा के लिए पानी या टूथपेस्ट में मिलाया जा सकता है।
फ्लोरीन	स्त्री.	एक विषैली हलके पीले रंग की गैस।
बम्ब	पु.	बम, गोला, विस्फोटक पदार्थों से भरा पात्र; परमाणु अस्त्र।
बर्ड	स्त्री.	चिड़िया।
बर्थ	पु.	जन्म; माँ के शरीर से बाहर आने की क्रिया।
बर्थकण्ट्रोल	पु.	सन्तति निग्रह।
बर्नर	पु.	चूल्हे का वह भाग जिसमें से आग निकलती है।
बल्ब	पु.	बिजली के लैम्प का शीशे वाला हिस्सा, जिसमें से प्रकाश फैलता है।
बाण्ड	पु.	किसी रासायनिक मिश्रण में अणुओं के संयोजित होने की विधि।
बाइल	पु.	पित्त।
बाइसेप्ट	क्रि.	विभाजन करना, दो खण्डों में बाँटना।
बाइसेप्स	पु.	भुजा के शिखर पर बड़ी मांसपेशी।
बाईकार्बोनेट	पु.	कार्बनडाई ऑक्साइड की दुगनी मात्रा वाला लवण।
बाईफोकल	पु.	दो हिस्सों वाले लेंस का चश्मा।
बाक्साइट	पु.	एक मुलायम चट्टान जिससे एल्युमिनियम प्राप्त होता है।
बाटनिस्ट	पु.	वनस्पति शास्त्री।
बाटनी	स्त्री.	वनस्पति शास्त्र।
बॉटलगोर्ड	पु.	लौकी।
बायोकेमिस्ट	पु.	जीव रसायनविद्।
बायोकेमेस्ट्री	स्त्री.	जैवीय रसायन का वैज्ञानिक अध्ययन, जीव रसायन।
बायोगैस	पु.	पौधे और पशुओं के अपघटन से निर्मित मिथेन तथा कार्बन ऑक्साइड गैस का मिश्रण।
बायोडायवर्सिटी	पु.	जैव विविधता।
बायोप्सी	पु.	रोग की परख के लिए शरीर से किसी ऊतक को निकालने की क्रिया।
बायोमास	पु.	जैव पिण्ड।

बॉयोलाजी	पु.	सजीवों का वैज्ञानिक अध्ययन; जीव विज्ञान।
बायोलाजिकल वारफेयर	पु.	हानिकारक जीवाणुओं का युद्ध के अस्त्रों के रूप में प्रयोग; जैविकयुद्ध।
बायोफिजिक्स	पु.	भौतिकी के नियमों पर जीव विज्ञान का अध्ययन; जैव भौतिकी।
बायोरिद्म	पु.	सजीवों के जीवन में होने वाले परिवर्तनों की नियमित शृंखला; जैवीय लय।
बार्ली	स्त्री.	जौ, यव।
बॉलबियरिंग	पु.	धातु निर्मित गोली जो मशीन के पुर्जों के बीच लगती है ताकि मशीन आसानी से चलती रहे।
बाल्ड	वि.	गंजा।
बिटरगोर्ड	पु.	करेला।
बिटूमेन	पु.	सड़कों को रंगने वाला तारकोल, डामर।
बीकर	पु.	वैज्ञानिक प्रयोगों में काम आने वाला एक काँच का बना बर्तन जिसमें द्रव रखते हैं।
बीजवैक्स	पु.	मधुमक्खी का मोम, इसका प्रयोग लकड़ी की पालिश करने और मोमबत्तियाँ बनाने में होता है।
बीटल	पु.	एक प्रकार का बड़ा काला और चमकीला कीट, जिसके पंखों का आवरण बहुत कठोर होता है; भौंरा।
बुलमिया	पु.	एक प्रकार का रोग जिसमें रोगी अपने भोजन पर नियन्त्रण नहीं रख पाता; क्षुधातिशयता।
बुल्डोजर	पु.	भूमि को समतल बनाने की एक भारी एवं शक्तिशाली मशीन।
बूटेन	पु.	पेट्रोल से बनी और द्रव रूप में प्रयोग की जाने वाली एक गैस।
बेंजीन	पु.	पेट्रोलियम से प्राप्त एक रंगहीन द्रव पदार्थ जिससे प्लास्टिक या विभिन्न रासायनिक पदार्थ बनते हैं।
बेंजीन रिंग	पु.	बेंजीन एंव अन्य यौगिकों में उपलब्ध छः कार्बन अणुओं का वलय।
बेकिंग पाउडर	पु.	एक रासायनिक मिश्रण जिसे केक बनाते समय प्रयोग किया जाता है।
बेबीइश	वि.	शिशु समान, शिशु के समान आचरण करते हुए।
बेबीहुड	पु.	बचपन, शैशव।
बेरियम	पु.	एक चाँदी जैसी मुलायम धातु।
बेरीलियम	पु.	एक सफेद कठोर धातु जिससे विभिन्न मिश्र धातुएँ बनती हैं।
बेस	पु.	एक रसायन; क्षार।
बेसिल	पु.	तुलसी का पौधा।

बैण्डविड्थ	पु.	इलेक्ट्रॉनिक सन्देश भेजने में प्रयुक्त की जाने वाली तरंग पट्टिका में आवृत्तियों का परास, बैण्ड चौड़ाई; कम्प्यूटर के नेटवर्क या इण्टरनेट के कनेक्यान द्वारा एक विशेष अवधि में भेजी जा सकने वाली सूचना की माप, इसे बिट्स प्रति सेकंड में मापा जाता है।
बैण्ड़ेज	पु.	चोट पर बाँधने के लिए पट्टी।
बैकबोन	पु.	रीढ़ की हड्डी।
बैक्टीरिया	स्त्री.	ऐसे जीवाणु जो बड़ी संख्या में वायु, जल, मिट्टी और प्राणियों में पाये जाते हैं।
बैटरी	स्त्री.	विद्युत उत्पन्न करने वाला एक यन्त्र।
बैरोमीटर	पु.	वायुदाब मापी, वायु का दाब मापने और मौसम में परिवर्तन देने वाला यन्त्र।
बैलास्ट	पु.	हवा के गुब्बारे या जहाज को स्थिर रखने के लिए उसमें रखा गया भारी सामान।
बैलिस्टिक्स	पु.	वायु में प्रक्षेपित होने वाली वस्तुओं का वैज्ञानिक अध्ययन, जैसे बुलेट।
बैलून	पु.	गुब्बारा; आकाश में उड़ाया जाने वाला गैस का गुब्बारा जिसके नीचे एक बड़ी टोकरी लगी रहती है जिसमें बैठकर लोग उड़ते हैं।
बैलेंस	पु.	तराजू, तुला, काँटा।
बैसिलस	पु.	बहुत छोटे जीवाणु जो रोगजनक होते हैं।
बोन	पु.	हड्डी, अस्थि।
बोल्ट	पु.	धातु का बना चूड़ीदार उपकरण जिससे किसी पुर्जे आदि को कसते हैं।
ब्रांकस	पु.	फेफड़ों तक हवा ले जाने वाली नली।
ब्रांकइटिस	पु.	श्वासनली की एक बीमारी जिसके कारण बहुत खाँसी आती है; श्वसनी शोथ।
ब्रांकियल	वि.	श्वसनी, श्वासनली के मुख्य दो शाखाओं से सम्बन्धित।
ब्रांज	पु.	ताँबे और टिन के मिश्रण से बनी धातु।
ब्रीड	पु.	किसी पशु की विशेष नस्ल।
ब्रीद	पु.	श्वास, साँस; श्वसन क्रिया।
ब्रीद टेस्ट	पु.	शराब पीकर चलाने वाले वाहन चालक की जाँच के लिए श्वास परीक्षण।
ब्रीस्ट	पु.	स्त्री का स्तन, स्त्री की छाती।

ब्रीस्ट बोन	पु.	छाती के मध्य स्थित लम्बी चपटी हड्डी जिससे पसलियाँ जुड़ी होती हैं।
ब्रोमाइड	पु.	औषधियों में प्रयोग किया जाने वाला एक रासायनिक मिश्रण जो उपशामक होता है।
ब्रोमीन	पु.	एक विषैली तेज गन्ध वाली लाल रंग की गैस।
ब्लड	पु.	खून, रक्त, रुधिर।
ब्लडग्रुप	पु.	रुधिर वर्ग, रक्त के चार प्रकार।
ब्लडप्वाइजनिंग	पु.	रक्तविषाक्तता; रक्त में जीवाणुओं के संक्रमण से उत्पन्न होने वाला रोग।
ब्लडट्रांसफ्यूजन	पु.	किसी के शरीर में रक्त चढ़ाना।
ब्लडवेसल	पु.	रक्तवाहिका, शिरा।
ब्लीच	पु.	कपड़ों आदि को अधिक सफेद या वस्तुओं को साफ करने वाला शक्तिशाली रासायनिक पदार्थ।
ब्लैडर	पु.	मूत्राशय।
ब्वायल	पु.	वह तापमान जिसपर कोई द्रव उबलने लगता है; व्रण, फोड़ा।
ब्वायलर	पु.	वाष्पित्र, ब्वायलर; एक बहुत बड़ा पात्र या चैम्बर जिसमें ताप द्वारा पानी को उबालकर भाप बनाते हैं।
ब्वायलिंग प्वाइण्ट	पु.	वह तापमान जिसपर कोई द्रव उबलना शुरू कर देता है; क्वथनांक।
मर्करी	पु.	बुध ग्रह; चाँदी के रंग की एक धातु जो द्रव रूप में होती है और जिसका प्रयोग मानक उपकरणों जैसे, थर्मामीटर आदि के लिए किया जाता है, पारा।
मलेरिया	पु.	मच्छरों के काटने से होने वाली एक जानलेवा बीमारी जिसमें बहुत कंपकंपी के साथ बहुत तेज ज्वर होता है।
मशीन	पु.	यन्त्र, मशीन।
मशीन कोड	पु.	प्रोग्राम के लिए प्रयुक्त (विशेष) भाषा जिसमें निर्देशों को संख्याओं के रूप में लिखा जाता है ताकि कम्प्यूटर उसे समझकर तद्नुसार कार्य कर सके, अंक-भाषा।
मशीनगन	पु.	मशीनगन ऐसी बन्दूक जो लगातार गोलियाँ निकालती हो।
मशीनटूल	पु.	मशीन में प्रयोग किये जाने वाले औजार।
मशीनरी	स्त्री.	सभी प्रकार की मशीनें, मशीन के चलने वाले पुर्जे, यन्त्रों का समूह।
मशीनिस्ट	पु.	मशीन चलाने वाला व्यक्ति; मशीनें बनाने वाला व्यक्ति; यन्त्राकार।
माइक्रो कम्प्यूटर	पु.	माइक्रोप्रोसेसर युक्त छोटा कम्प्यूटर।

माइक्रोचिप	पु.	कम्प्यूटर के अन्दर प्रयुक्त सिलिकान का सूक्ष्म कण, जो कम्प्यूटर को सक्रिय करता है।
माइक्रोप्रोसेसर	पु.	कम्प्यूटर का वह भाग जो सेण्ट्रल प्रोसेसिंग यूनिट का काम करता है।
माइक्रोफोन	पु.	ध्वनिवर्द्धक या एसे रिकॉर्ड करने वाला विद्युत उपकरण।
माइक्रोब	पु.	अति सूक्ष्म जीवाणु; रोगाणु।
माइक्रोबायोलाजिस्ट	पु.	सूक्ष्म जीवों का वैज्ञानिक अध्ययन करने वाला; सूक्ष्मजीव विज्ञानी
माइक्रोबायोलाजी	स्त्री.	सूक्ष्म जीव विज्ञान; सूक्ष्म जीवों का वैज्ञानिक अध्ययन।
माइक्रोमीटर	पु.	लम्बाई नापने की इकाई।
माइक्रोवेब	पु.	रेडियो संकेतों को भेजने के लिए प्रयुक्त सूक्ष्म विद्युत तरंग।
माइक्रोस्कोप	पु.	सूक्ष्मदर्शी यन्त्र जिसमें न दिखायी देने योग्य वस्तुएँ भी इसके द्वारा दिखायी देती हैं।
माइनस	पु.	घटना, घटाना; शून्य से कम या नीचे; गणित में प्रयुक्त ऋण चिह्न जो यह व्यक्त करता है कि संख्या शून्य से कम या नीचे है, किसी दूसरी संख्या को पहली संख्या को घटाने के लिए प्रयोग किया जाने वाला चिह्न (–)।
माल्टोज	पु.	शरीर के रसायनों द्वारा स्टार्च से बनायी गयी शर्करा।
मिक्सर	पु.	मिश्रित करने वाली मशीन।
मिक्सचर	पु.	मिश्रण; कई वस्तुओं को मिलाकर बनायी गयी एक वस्तु।
मिथेन	पु.	एक रंगहीन, गन्धहीन ज्वलनशील गैस जो बहुत ताप उत्पन्न करती है।
मीजर	पु.	किसी वस्तु का आकार, मात्रा आदि बताने का पैमाना।
मीटर	पु.	दूरी या गहराई को मापने वाला मात्रक।
मीटरिक	वि.	जिसमें मीटरिक पद्धति पर आधारित मापन प्रणाली का प्रयोग हुआ है।
मीटरिक सिस्टम	पु.	मीटर, किलोग्राम और लीटर को मूल इकाइयों के रूप में प्रयुक्त करने वाली मापन, प्रणाली मीटरिक पद्धति।
मीडियम वेब	पु.	रेडियो संकेतों को प्रसारित करने की प्रणाली जिसमें 100 और 1000 मीटर के बीच की ध्वनि तरंगों का प्रयोग होता है।
मेंस्टुअल	वि.	मासिकधर्म सम्बन्धी।
मेकेनिक	पु.	यन्त्रों या मशीनों की मरम्मत करने वाला व्यक्ति, मिस्त्री।
मेकेनिज्म	पु.	कुछ करने या संचालित होने की विधि; विशेष काम करने वाले मशीन के सचल कलपुर्जे।
मेटलर्जिस्ट	पु.	धातु विज्ञानी।

मेटलर्जी	पु.	धातु विज्ञान।
मेटाबोलिज्म	पु.	पेड़-पौधों और जन्तुओं में होने वाली रासायनिक प्रक्रियाएँ जो भोजन को ऊर्जा में परिवर्तित कर देती है जिससे उनकी वृद्धि होती है; चयापचन।
मेटामार्फोसिस	पु.	प्राकृतिक विकास प्रक्रिया के अन्तर्गत पूर्णरूप से आकृति में परिवर्तन।
मेटिअरोलॉजी	स्त्री.	मौसम विज्ञान।
मेटिओर	पु.	उल्का, एक आकाशीय पिण्ड जिसका पृथ्वी के वातावरण में प्रवेश करने पर आकाश में प्रकाशमयी रेखा बन जाती है।
मेथड	पु.	रीति, विधि।
मेथडोलॉजी	स्त्री.	विशेष सिद्धान्तों और विधियों पर आधारित कार्यप्रणाली।
मेथनाल	पु.	अलकोहल का विषैला रूप जो रंग और गन्ध से रहित होता है और आसानी से गैस में बदल जाता है।
मेथिलेटेड स्प्रिट	पु.	एक प्रकार का अपेय अलकोहल, जिसका प्रयोग गन्दे धब्बे को दूर करने, जलाने या गरम करने के लिए किया जाता है।
मेनोपाज	पु.	रजोनिवृत्ति; उम्र के साथ महिलाओं का मासिकधर्म का बन्द हो जाना।
मेमोरी	स्त्री.	स्मरणशक्ति, याददाश्त; स्मृतिकोश; कम्प्यूटर का वह भाग जहाँ सूचना संग्रहीत रहती है।
मेसोफिल	पु.	वह तत्त्व जिससे पत्ती का आन्तरिक भाग बना होता है; मध्यपर्ण।
मैंगनीज	पु.	एक प्रकार की कठोर या भूरी धातु।
मैण्डिबल	पु.	जबड़ा, अधोहनु, चिबुकास्थि।
मैटरनिटी	वि.	आसन्न प्रसवा या सद्यः प्रसूता माता से सम्बन्धित।
मैटीरियल	पु.	कुछ बनाने या कुछ करने के लिए प्रयुक्त पदार्थ।
मैटीरियलिज्म	पु.	धन आदि भौतिक वस्तुओं को सर्वाधिक मानने की प्रवृत्ति; भौतिकवाद।
मैटीरियलिस्ट	पु.	भौतिकवादी।
मैथमेटिक्स	पु.	गणितशास्त्र।
मैथमेटीशियन	पु.	गणितज्ञ।
मैक्रो	पु.	कम्प्यूटर के लिए अकेला बड़ा निर्देश जिसे वह स्वचालित रूप से निर्देश समुच्चय के रूप में ग्रहण करता है। ताकि विशिष्ट कार्य को सम्पन्न किया जा सके।
मैक्रोबायोटिक	पु.	ऐसा खाद्य पदार्थ जो रसायन के प्रयोग से मुक्त होता है और आयुवर्द्धक माना जाता है।

मैगनीफाइंग ग्लास	पु.	छोटी वस्तुओं या छोटे अक्षर को बड़े आकार में देखने के लिए मूठ लगा एक लेंस; आवर्द्धक लेंस।
मैग्नीशियम	पु.	एक हल्की चाँदी जैसी सफेद धातु जिसमें से चमकदार सफेद लौ निकलती है।
मैगनेट	पु.	चुम्बक।
मैगनेटिक	वि.	चुम्बकीय।
मैगनेटिक फील्ड	पु.	चुम्बकीय क्षेत्र; चुम्बक या चुम्बकत्व वस्तुओं का प्रभाव क्षेत्र।
मैगनेटिज्म	पु.	चुम्बकत्व; चुम्बक शक्ति।
मोटर	पु.	पेट्रोल, गैस, विद्युत आदि से चलने वाला यन्त्र जिसमें मशीनें आदि चलती हैं।
मोडेम	पु.	टेलीफोन लाइनों द्वारा कम्प्यूटरों को परस्पर जोड़ने वाला यन्त्र।
मोबाइल फोन	पु.	एक प्रकार का टेलीफोन जिसे कहीं आते-जाते समय भी आप अपने पास रख सकते हैं और उसका प्रयोग कर सकते हैं।
मोलस्क	पु.	मृदु कवचधारी जन्तु जो सामान्यतया कठोर आवरण युक्त कोष में रहते हैं।
मोशन	पु.	गति।
म्यूकस मेम्बरेन	पु.	श्लेष्मल झिल्ली। यह नाक और मुँह के अन्दर त्वचा की महीन परत होती है। जिससे श्लेष्मा उत्पन्न होता है जो इन अंगों को सूखने नहीं देता।
रडार	पु.	रेडियो तरंगों का प्रयोग कर चलते जहाज, उड़ते विमान आदि की स्थिति का पता लगाने की एक प्रणाली।
रिफ्लेक्स एंगिल	पु.	108° से बड़ा कोण।
रिफ्लेक्टिव	वि.	परावर्तनशील, प्रकाश या ताप को लौटाने वाला।
रिफ्रैक्ट	क्रि.	(भौतिक विज्ञान) पानी, काँच आदि में प्रकाश रेखा का दिशा परिवर्तन, अपवर्तन करना।
रिसिस्टर	पु.	विद्युत शक्ति को परिपथ पर खुलकर प्रवाहित हरेने वाला उपकरण।
रिसिस्टेण्ट	वि.	प्रतिरोधी।
रिस्पीरेशन	पु.	श्वसन; साँस लेने व छोड़ने की क्रिया।
रेडिएण्ट	वि.	प्रकाश या ताप को बिखेरने वाला, विकिणकारी।
रेडिएटर	पु.	कमरे को गरम करने के उद्देश्य से धातु का बना हुआ उपकरण जिसमें गरम पानी भरकर दीवार पर लगाया जाता है; कार के इंजन को ठण्डा करने के लिए उसके आगे लगाया गया एक उपकरण जिसमें पानी भरा जाता है और इंजन को शीतल करता है।

रेडिएशन	पु.	कुछ पदार्थों से निकलकर फैलने वाली शक्तिशाली और हानिकारक किरणें। इन किरणों को हम देख या महसूस नहीं कर सकते, किन्तु इन किरणों के प्रभाव से गम्भीर रोग हो सकता है जो मृत्यु का कारक हो सकता है।
रेडियम	पु.	एक रासायनिक तत्त्व। यह सफेद रंग का एक विकिरणशील तत्त्व है। इसका प्रयोग गम्भीर रोगों के उपचार में भी किया जाता है।
रेडियस	पु.	वृत्त या व्यासार्भ; त्रिज्या; वृत्त के केन्द्र से परिधि तक की दूरी; बाँह की कलाई से कुहनी तक की छोटी हड्डी; बहि: प्रकोष्ठिका।
रेडियो	पु.	विद्युत संकेतों या रेडियो तरंगों द्वारा वायु के माध्यम से सन्देशों को भेजने या प्राप्त करने की क्रिया।
रेडियोएक्टिव	वि.	विकिरणशील या रेडियो सक्रिय। अणु विखण्डन के कारण उत्पन्न होने वाली शक्तिशाली और हानिकारक किरणें जो गम्भीर रोगों अन्त: मृत्यु का कारण होती हैं।
रेडियोग्राफर	पु.	अस्पताल में शरीर के अंगों का एक्स-रे लेने वाला व्यक्ति।
रेफ्रिजरेशन	पु.	प्रशीतन।
रोटेन	वि.	सड़ा गला।
रोटेशन	पु.	धुरी पर वृत्ताकार आवर्तन, घूर्णन।
रोम	पु.	इसका पूर्णरूप रीड ओनली मेमोरी है। इसमें आवश्यक सामग्री स्थाई रूप से संचित की जाती है और उसमें किसी भी प्रकार का परिवर्तन नहीं किया जा सकता है।
रोलर	पु.	एक बेलनाकार उपकरण या मशीन का भाग जो किसी चीज को दबाकर उसकी सतह समतल करे।
लांगीट्यूड	पु.	उत्तर से दक्षिणी ध्रुव तक जाने वाली रेखा के पूर्व या पश्चिम में उस रेखा से किसी स्थान की दूरी; देशान्तर रेखा। इसे डिग्री में मापा जाता है।
लांगीट्यूडनल वेब	पु.	देशान्तरीय लहर।
लाइट	पु.	सुप्रकाशित, रोशनीदार, प्रकाशमय।
लाइट ईयर	पु.	प्रकाश वर्ष, एक वर्ष में प्रकाश द्वारा तय की जाने वाली दूरी जो लगभग 9.46×10^{12} किलोमीटर होती है।
लाउडस्पीकर	पु.	रेडियो, सीडी प्लेयर आदि में लगा स्पीकर; ध्वनि विस्तारक यन्त्र।
लॉग-आउट/लॉग-ऑफ	क्रि.	कम्प्यूटर प्रणाली को निष्क्रिय करने के लिए आवश्यक क्रियाएँ करना।
लॉगैरिथ्म	पु.	लघुगणक; लघुगणक तालिका में क्रम से संख्याएँ दी हुई होती हैं। यहाँ संख्याओं में गुणा या भाग करने के लिए संख्याओं के

		सामने दिये गये अंकों को जोड़ा या घटाया जाता है। तत्पश्चात् एक अन्य तालिका से गुणनफल या भागफल प्राप्त हो जाता है।
लिक्विड क्रिस्टल डिस्प्ले (एलसीडी)	पु.	एक प्रकार की इलेक्ट्रॉनिक मशीन जिसमें एक विशेष द्रव में विद्युतधारा को प्रवाहित किया जाता है और छोटे परदे पर संख्याएँ और अक्षर दिखायी देते हैं।
लिगामेंट	पु.	मनुष्य या पशु के शरीर के अन्दर एक ऊतक जो हड्डियों को जोड़ती है; स्नायु अस्थिबन्ध।
लिग्नाइट	पु.	भूरा कोयला।
लिटमस	पु.	एक विशेष पदार्थ जो अम्ल के स्पर्श से लाल और क्षार के स्पर्श से नीला हो जाता है।
लिम्फ	पु.	मानव शरीर में श्वेत रक्त कोशिकाओं वाला रंगहीन द्रव, जो संक्रमण को रोकता है।
लिम्फनोड	पु.	शरीर में गाँठ जिसमें से होकर लसीका प्रवाहित होती है।
लिम्फोसाइट	स्त्री.	एक प्रकार की छोटी श्वेत रक्त कोशिका, लसीका कोशिका।
लुब्रीकेण्ट	पु.	चिकना पदार्थ जिसको लगाने से मशीन के पुर्जे बिना रुकावट के आसानी से कार्य करते हैं।
लेंस	पु.	आँख में पुतली के पीछे एक पारदर्शी अंग जो प्रकाश को नियन्त्रित करने के लिए अपनी आकृति बदलता है।
लेजर	पु.	अत्यधिक शक्तिशाली प्रकाशपुंज उत्पन्न करने वाली क्रिया जिसका प्रयोग उपकरण के रूप में भी किया जा सकता है।
लेजर प्रिण्टर	पु.	कम्प्यूटर से संयुकत लेजर किरणों के सहायता से प्रिण्ट करने वाला एक मुद्रण यन्त्र।
लेथर्जी	पु.	बहुत थकान या कमजोरी।
लैक्टोज	पु.	दूध में पायी जाने वाली शर्करा, जिसका प्रयोग शिशु आहारों में किया जाता है।
लैक्सेटिव	पु.	विरेचक औषधि, पेट साफ करने में सहायक औषधि, दस्तावर औषधि।
लैक्टिक एसिड	पु.	एक विशेष प्रकार का अम्ल जो दूध के बासी हो जाने पर उसमें उत्पन्न होता है। यह शारीरिक कठोर श्रम करने के फलस्वरूप मांसपेशियों में भी उत्पन्न हो जाता है, दुग्धाम्ल।
लैंगुयेज लैबोरेटरी	पु.	भाषा प्रयोगशाला; इलेक्ट्रॉनिक उपकरणों टेप, वीडियो आदि की सहायता से भाषा सीखने की प्रयोगशाला।
लैण्टर्न	पु.	लालटेन।
लैण्डस्लाइड	पु.	भूस्खलन, चट्टानों आदि का टूटकर गिरना।

लैडर पु. सीढ़ी, जीना।

लैपटॉप पु. एक छोटा अत्याधुनिक कम्प्यूटर जिसे बिजली न होने पर बैटरी से भी चलाया जा सकता है।

लैबरिन्थ पु. आन्तरकर्ण।

लैबियल पु. ओष्ठ्य ध्वनि, ओठों से उत्पन्न ध्वनि।

लैबोरेटरी पु. विज्ञान की प्रयोगशाला।

लैरिंक्स पु. कण्ठ, स्वरयन्त्र, गले का ऊपरी भाग जिसमें ध्वनि उत्पादक मांसपेशियाँ होती हैं।

लैरिंजाइटिस पु. गले का एक रोग जिसके कारण बोलने में कठिनाई होती है; गले की सूजन, कण्ठ शोथ, स्वरयन्त्र शोथ।

लोलेवल वि. कम्प्यूटर में सामान्य भाषा में विभिन्न अंकों की पद्धति जिसे कम्प्यूटर समझता है, कम्प्यूटर ग्राह्य अंक पद्धति की भाषा।

लोवेस्टकॉमन डिनामिनेटर पु. (गणित) लघुत्तम समापवर्त्य।

ल्यूकेमिया स्त्री. रक्त का एक गम्भीर रोग जो मृत्यु का कारण भी हो सकता है।

ल्यूकोसाइट पु. रक्त का श्वेतकण; रक्त की श्वेत कोशिका।

सरकमफरेंस पु. परिधि, घेरा।

सर्कल पु. गोल आकृति, वृत्त, घेरा, गोला।

सर्किट पु. विद्युतधारा का परिपथ।

सर्किटबोर्ड पु. विद्युत यन्त्रों के अन्दर का विद्युत परिपथ।

सर्कुलेशन पु. शरीर में रक्त का संचरण; परिचालन।

साइकल पु. घटना श्रृंखलाओं या प्रक्रियाओं की उसी क्रम में अनेक बार पुनरावृत्ति होना।

साइक्लोन पु. चक्रवात, बवण्डर।

साइटोलॉजी पु. पौधों और पशुओं की कोशिकाओं का वैज्ञानिक अध्ययन; कोशिका विज्ञान।

साइटोप्लाज्म पु. वह पदार्थ या द्रव्य जिससे कोशिका का निर्माण होता है।

साइबर कैफे पु. जहाँ भाड़े पर इण्टरनेट व कम्प्यूटर के प्रयोग की सुविधा हो।

साइबरनेटिक्स पु. सम्प्रेषण और नियन्त्रण की प्रक्रियाओं का वैज्ञानिक अध्ययन जिसमें उदाहरण के लिए पशु के मस्तिष्क का मशीन और इलेक्ट्रॉनिक उपकरण से तुलना की जाती है।

साइबर स्पेस पु. एक अभौतिक स्थल जहाँ एक से दूसरे कम्प्यूटर को भेजे जा रहे इलेक्ट्रॉनिक सन्देश स्थिर होते हैं।

सायनाइड पु. एक विषैला रसायन।

सिरोसिस	पु.	यकृत को प्रभावित करने वाला एक विशेष रोग। यह रोग मदिरापान के कारण होता है।
सिलेण्डर	पु.	बेलन की आकार की वस्तु; किसी इंजन का बेलनाकार पुर्जा।
सिस्ट	स्त्री.	शरीर के अन्दर बन जाने वाली एक खोखली गाँठ जिसमें द्रव पदार्थ जमा हो जाता है।
सिस्टिकफाइब्रोसिस	पु.	एक गम्भीर जन्मजात प्राणघातक रोग जिसमें रोगी के कुछ अंग ठीक से काम नहीं करते।
सिस्टाइसिस	पु.	मूत्राशय की सूजन।
सीडी	पु.	इसका पूरा रूप कम्पैक्ट डिस्क है। यह प्लास्टिक का गोल आकार में बना एक चपटा टुकड़ा है जिस पर सूचना सामग्री व ध्वनि रिकॉर्ड किया जाता है।
सीडी रोम	पु.	कम्प्यूटर में प्रयोग की जाने वाली सीडी जिसमें सूचना सामग्री संगृहीत होती है किन्तु इसमें किसी प्रकार का बदलाव नहीं किया जा सकता और न ही इसे मिटाया जा सकता है।
सेण्टीमीटर	पु.	लम्बाई मापने की एक इकाई, 100 सेमी के बराबर 1 मीटर होता है।
सेण्ट्रल प्रोसेसिंग यूनिट	पु.	कम्प्यूटर के विभिन्न भागों को नियन्त्रित करने वाला केन्द्रीय अंश या भाग। इसे संक्षिप्त में सीपीयू भी कहा जाता है।
सेण्ट्रल हीटिंग	पु.	केन्द्रीय तापन प्रणाली।
सेण्ट्रीपेटल	वि.	अभिकेन्द्रीय; केन्द्र की ओर जाते हुए।
सेण्ट्रीफ्यूगल	वि.	अपकेन्द्री; केन्द्रबिन्दु से दूर हटते हुए।
सेरेबेलम	पु.	मस्तिष्क के पिछले हिस्से का वह भाग जो मांसपेशियों की गतिविधियों को नियन्त्रित करता है।
सेरेब्रल	वि.	प्रमस्तिष्कीय; मस्तिष्क विषयक।
सेरेब्रल पाल्सी	पु.	जन्म के समय या पहले हुई मस्तिष्क क्षति जिसके कारण भुजाओं और टाँगों पर नियन्त्रण भी क्षतिग्रस्त हो जाता है; प्रमस्तिष्क विषयक।
सेरेविक्स	पु.	गर्भाशय ग्रीवा; गर्भाशय के विवर का संकीर्ण मार्ग
सेल्यूलोज	पु.	एक प्राकृतिक पदार्थ जो प्राणियों की कोशिका भित्तियों को बनाता है। इस पदार्थ से प्लास्टिक कागज आदि भी बनाये जाते हैं।
सेल्सियस	पु.	तापमान मापने की एक प्रणाली जिसमें पानी का हिमांक 0° और क्वथनांक 100° पर होता है।
हर्ट	पु.	हृदय, दिल; मनुष्य के मनोभावों का केन्द्र।
हर्ट अटैक	पु.	दिल का दौरा; हृदयगति का अनियमित होना।
हर्टऐच	पु.	मनोवेदना।

हर्पीच	पु.	एक संक्रामक त्वचा रोग जिसमें त्वचा पर विशेष रूप से गुप्तांगों पर अत्यधिक कष्टदायी चकत्ते पड़ जाते हैं, बिसर्पिका।
हर्ब	पु.	जड़ी-बूटी।
हर्बीसाइड	स्त्री.	अनावश्यक पौधों के उगने पर उनको नष्ट करने का रसायन।
हर्माफ्रोडाइट	पु.	व्यक्ति, पशु या पुष्प जिनमें नर और मादा दोनों के लक्षण हों, उभयलिंगी।
हाइजीन	पु.	मानव शरीर और उसके परिवेश की स्वच्छता, साफ-सफाई।
हाइड्राक्साइड	पु.	एक यौगिक रसायन जिसमें किसी धातु और ऑक्सीजन एवं हाइड्रोजन का मिश्रण होता है।
हाइड्रोइलेक्ट्रिक	वि.	जल की शक्ति से उत्पन्न किया हुआ; विद्युत उत्पादन में जल की शक्ति का प्रयोग करने वाला।
हाइड्रोकार्बन	पु.	(रसायन शास्त्र) हाइड्रोजन और क्लोरीन युक्त अम्ल।
हाइड्रोजन	पु.	एक हलकी रंगहीन गैस।
हाइड्रोजन बम	पु.	बहुत शक्तिशाली नाभिकीय बम।
हाइड्रोलॉजी	पु.	भूजल का वैज्ञानिक अध्ययन, भूजल विज्ञान।
हाईटेक	वि.	अत्याधुनिक मशीनों और तकनीकों का प्रयोग करने वाले।
हाइपर लिंक	पु.	कम्प्यूटर स्थित इलेक्ट्रॉनिक डॉक्यूमेण्ट में एक स्थान जो दूसरे इलेक्ट्रॉनिक डाक्यूमेण्ट से जुड़ा हो।
हाइपोकॉण्ड्रिया	स्त्री.	वास्तविकता के विपरीत रोगी होने का भ्रम, रोगभ्रम।
हाइपोटेन्यूज	पु.	समकोण त्रिभुज का कर्ण।
हाइपोडर्मिक	वि.	त्वचा के नीचे इंजेक्शन लगाने के लिए प्रयुक्त यन्त्र।
हाइपोथेटिकल	वि.	प्राक्कल्पना पूर्वक; प्राकल्पित रूप से।
हाइपोथर्मिया	पु.	शरीर का तापमान सामान्य से बहुत कम हो जाने की दशा।
हाइपोथेसिस	स्त्री.	किसी तथ्य को समझने के लिए मान ली जाने वाली बात, अनुमान पर आधारित विचार; प्राक्कल्पना।
हाईब्रिड	पु.	दो विभिन्न प्रजातियों के जनकों से उत्पन्न पशु या पौधा, संकर पशु या पौधा; वर्णसंकर।
हाईड्रण्ट	पु.	सड़क पर लगा नल जिससे पानी लेकर सड़क साफ करने या आग बुझाने का कार्य किया जाता है।
हाईड्रेट	पु.	किसी को जलयुक्त करना; कोई ऐसा उपाय करना जिससे पानी अन्दर जाये।
हाईड्रौलिक	वि.	दाब की स्थिति में पाइप आदि में से बहते पानी या अन्य द्रव से चलने वाला द्रव चालित।
हाउंचेज	पु.	पशु का पुट्ठा; पुरुष का नितम्ब।

हाटलाइन	पु.	किसी संगठन की या व्यापार केन्द्र की सीधी टेलीफोन लाइन।
हॉरिजेण्टल	वि.	क्षितिज के समानान्तर; समतल।
हार्डकॉपी	पु.	कागज पर मुद्रित कम्प्यूटर संचित जानकारी, पढ़ने योग्य कॉपी।
हार्डडिस्क	पु.	कम्प्यूटर के अन्दर लगी एक डिस्क जिसमें आँकड़े और प्रोग्राम स्थायी रूप से संचित रहते हैं।
हार्डड्रग	स्त्री.	शक्तिशाली और गैरकानूनी मादक पदार्थ जिसका सेवन करना एक आदत बन जाती है।
हार्डवेयर	पु.	कम्प्यूटर में प्रयोग की जाने वाली कम्पोनेण्ट्स एवं डिवाइस, जिनके सहयोग से कम्प्यूटर चलता है।
हिस्टामिन	पु.	घायल होने पर या स्पर्श आदि की प्रतिकूल प्रतिक्रिया स्वरूप शरीर में उत्पन्न रसायन।
हिस्टीरिया	स्त्री.	भावोन्माद; व्यक्ति की अपनी भावनाओं पर नियन्त्रण खो बैठने की दशा।
हिस्टेरिक्स	पु.	उन्माद का रोग; हिस्टीरिया का दौरा।
हीटर	पु.	पानी या कमरे को गरम करने के लिए प्रयोग की जाने वाली मशीन।
हीमोफिलिया	स्त्री.	अधिक रक्तस्राव का रोग।
हील	पु.	एड़ी, पैर के पीछे का भाग।
हेक्सागॉन	पु.	छः फलकों वाली आकृति।
हेटरोजाइगोट	पु.	जीवधारी, जिसमें जीव के विशेष दो रूप हैं; विषम, युग्मज प्राणी।
हेटरोसेक्सुअल	वि.	विपरीत लिंगी व्यक्ति के प्रति कामुक भाव से आकृष्ट होना।
हेडलाइट	पु.	किसी वाहन के अग्रभाग में चमकने वाला तेज प्रकाश का स्रोत।
हेपेटाइटिस	स्त्री.	यकृतशोथ।
हेमीस्फीयर	पु.	पृथ्वी का आधाभाग, गोलार्द्ध।
हेरेडिटी	पु.	वह प्रक्रिया जिसके द्वारा माता-पिता के शारीरिक व मानसिक गुण सन्तान तक पहुँचते हैं; आनुवंशिकता।
हेलिक्स	पु.	कुण्डली मारे सर्प जैसी आकृति, सिलेण्डर या कोन।
हेल्थ	पु.	मनुष्य के शरीर व मन की दशा; स्वास्थ्य, शरीर के स्वस्थ एवं रोगमुक्त होने की स्थिति।
हेल्थ सर्विस	स्त्री.	स्वास्थ्य सेवा, चिकित्सा सेवा।
हेल्थ सेण्टर	पु.	स्वास्थ्य केन्द्र, अस्पताल।
हैकर	पु.	कम्प्यूटर में संचित सूचना की चोरी करने वाला व्यक्ति।
हैक्सॉ	पु.	धातुओं को काटने वाली आरी।

हैमर	पु.	हथौड़ा।
हैमराइड्स	पु.	बवासीर, अर्श।
हैमरेज	पु.	शरीर के अन्दर किसी नलिका के फटने से अधिक रक्तस्राव होना।
हैमस्ट्रिंग	पु.	घुटने की पीछे की नस जो टाँग के ऊपर के हिस्से की मांसपेशियों के नीचे की हड्डियों से जोड़ती है; घुटनस।
हैमोग्लोबिन	पु.	रक्त में पाये जाने वाले लालकण जिसमें आयरन की मात्रा अधिक होती है और ये लाल कण ऑक्सीजन का वहन करते हैं।
हैलूसिनेशन	पु.	दृष्टिभ्रम या मतिभ्रम।
हैलोजन	पु.	पाँच रसायनों में से कोई एक जो हाइड्रोजन के साथ मिलकर शक्तिशाली अंग का निर्माण करते हैं।
होमियोपैथ	पु.	होम्योपैथी का डॉक्टर।
होमियोपैथी	स्त्री.	होम्योपैथी चिकित्सा पद्धति।
होमियोस्टैटिस	पु.	परिवर्तनों के प्रति शारीरिक प्रतिक्रिया की प्रक्रिया जिसमें शरीर की अन्दरूनी दशाएँ स्थिर रहती हैं।
होमोजाइगोट	पु.	सयुग्मज प्राणी; ऐसा प्राणी जिसमें एक विशेष जीन का केवल एक ही रूप होता है।
होलोग्राम	पु.	किसी सतह पर लगी कोई लघु छवि या चित्र जो प्रकाश मिलने पर अलग से चमकती और उभरती है।

परिशिष्ट–5/Appendix-5

रोजमर्रा के उपयोग के लिए आवश्यक शब्दावली

शरीर के अंग (Parts of the Body)

अनामिका–Capital-finger
अँगुली–(पैर की)–Toe
अँगुली–(हाथ की)–Finger
अँगूठा–(हाथ का)–Thumb
आँख–Eye
आँत–Intestine
ओंठ–Lip
एड़ी–Heel
कन्धा–Shoulder
कनपटी–Temple
कमर–Waist
कलाई–Wrist
कान–Ear
कानी अँगली–Little-finger
काँख–Arm-pit
कोहुनी–Elbow
खोपड़ी–Skull
गर्दन–Neck
गर्भ–Womb
गर्भाशय–Uterus
गलमुच्छा–Whiskers
गला–Throat
गाल–Cheek
गुदा–Anus
गोद–Lap
घुटना–Knee
चमड़ा–Skin
चूचूक–Nipple
चूतड़–Buttock

चेहरा–Face
चोटी–(बालों की)–Braid
छाती–(मनुष्य की)–Chest
छाती–(स्त्री की)–Breast
जाँघ–Thigh
जिगर–Liver
जीभ–Tongue
जूड़ा (बालों का)–Lock
जोड़–Joint
ठुड्डी–Chin
तर्जनी–Index-finger
तलवा–Sole
तालु–Palate
दाढ़–Jaw
दाढ़ी–Beard
दाँत–Tooth
दिमाग–Brain
धमनी–Artery
नख–Nail
नथुना–Nostril
नरेटी–Gullet
नली (पैर की)–Calf
नस–Vein
नाक–Nose
नाभि–Navel
पलक–Eyelid
पसली–Rib
पोर (अँगुली की)–Phalange
प्लीहा–Spleen

पीठ–Back
पेट–Belly stomach
पेडू–Abdomen
पुतली (आँख की)–Eyeball
पेशी (पुट्ठा)–Muscle
पैर–Foot
फेफड़ा–Lung
बगल–Arm-pit
बरौनी–Eyelash
बाल–Hair
बाँह–Arm
भेजा–Brain
भौंह–Eyebrow
मध्यमा–Middle finger
मसूढ़ा–Gum
मुट्ठी–Fist
मुख–Mouth
मूत्राशय–Kidney
मोंछ–Moustache
योनि–Vagina
रीढ़–Backbone
रोमकूप–Pore
रोवाँ–Hair
ललाट–Borehead
लोहू–Blood
शिश्न–Penis
हड्डी–Bone
हथेली–Palm (of hand)
हँसिया–Collar-bone
हृदय–Heart

शरीर के विकार तथा रोग
(Conditions of the Body and Ailments)

अण्डवृद्धि–Hydrocele
अन्धा–Blind
अल्पदृष्टि–Shortsight
अम्लपित्त–Acidity
अतिसार–Diarrhoea
आतशक–Syphilis
आँख आना–Conjunctivitis
आँत उतरना–Hernia
आँसू–Tears
उबासी–Yawn
ओकाई–Nausea
ऐंचा–Squint-eyed
कखौरी–Boubo
अण्ठमाला–Goitre
कद–Stature
कफ–Phlegm
कय करना –Vomit
कामला –Jaundice
काला ज्वर–Typhus
कास–Bronchitis
काना–One-eyed
कुबड़ा–Hunchbacked
कोढ़–Leprosy
कोष्ठबद्धता–Constipation
कृमि–Worms
खसरा–Eczema
खाँसी–Cough
खून की कमी–Anaemia
खून बहना–Haemorrhage

गठिया–Rheumatism
गर्भपात–Abortion
गरमी–Syphilis
गलका–Whitlow
गला बैठना–Hoarseness
गाँठ–Tumour
गिलटी–Tumour
गूँगा–Dumb
गंजा–Bald
घाव–Wound
चक्कर–Giddiness
चकोता–Botch
चर्बी बढ़ना–Obesity
चोट–Hurt
छींक–Sneeze
छोटा–Short
जलोदर–Dropsy
जवान–Young
जहरबाद–Carbuncle
जुकाम–Cold
जूड़ी–Ague
जंभाई–Yawn
ज्वर–Fever
ठण्ड–Chill
डकार–Belch
मुँहासे–Pimple
तन्दुरुस्ती–Health
थूक–Spittle
दमा–Asthma

दर्द–Pain
दर्द (सिर का)–Headache
दस्त–Stool
दाँत बैठना–Lock-jaw
दाद–Ringworm
दुबला–Lean
दूरदृष्टि–Long-sight
नस चटकना–Sprain
नासूर–Sinus
नींद–Sleep
नींद न आना–Insomnia
पथरी–Stone
पसीना–Sweat
पागल–Mad
पागलपन–Insanity
पित्त–Bile
पिब–Pus
पेचिश–Dysentery
प्रदर–Leucorrhoea
प्यास–Thirst
फीलपाँव–Elephantiasis
फुन्सी–Pimple
फोड़ा–Boil
बलगम–Phlegm
बवासीर–Piles
बहुमूत्र–Diabetes
बाघी–Bubo
बुड्ढा–Old
बुखार–Fever

बेवाय–Chilblain

बौना–Dwarf

भगन्दर–Fistula

भूख–Hunger

मन्दाग्नि–Dyspepsia

मरोड़–Giiping

मस्सा–Mole

महामारी–Pestilence

मिरगी–Epilepsy

मूत्र–Urine

मोटा–Fat

मोतियाबिन्द–Cataract

मोतीझरा–Influenza

मुँहासे–Acne

लकवा–Paralysis

लार–Saliva

विष्ठा–Stool

राजयक्ष्मा–Phthisis, Tuberculosis

रोग–Disease

लँगड़ा–Lame

लँगड़ा बुखार–Dengue

लम्बा–Tall

लू लगना–Sunstroke

शीतला–Small-pox

श्वेत कुष्ठ-Leucoderma

साँस-Breath

सूजन-Swelling

सूरजमुखी-Albino

सूजाक-Gonorrhoea

संग्रहणी-Sprue

स्वर-Voice

स्वस्थ-Healthy

हिचकी-Hiccough

हैजा-Cholera

क्षय-Consumption

सम्बन्धी (Relations)

अतिथि-Guest
अध्यापक-Teacher
अम्मा-Mamma
असामी-Tenant
उपपत्नी-Co-wife
गुरु-Preceptor
ग्राहक-Customer
चाचा-Uncle
चाची-Aunt
चेला-Disciple
जमींदार-Landowner
जेठानी (देवरानी)-Sister-in-law
दत्तक पुत्र-Adopted son
दत्तक कन्या-Adopted daughter
दादा-Grandfather
दादी-Grandmother
दामाद-Son-in-law
नाना-Grand-father
नानी-Grand-mother

पति-Husband
पत्नी-Wife
पतोहू-Daughter-in-law
परीक्षक-Examiner
परीक्षार्थी-Examinee
पिता-Father
पुत्र-Son
पुत्री-Daughter
बहन-Sister
भतीजा-Nephew
भतीजी-Niece
भाई-Brother
भांजा-Nephew
भांजी-Niece
महलती-Landlord
माता-Mother
मामा-Maternal Uncle
मामी-Maternal Aunt
मुवक्किल-Client

मौसी-Mother's sister
यजमान-Host
यार-Paramour
रखनी-Concubine
रोगी-Patient
वकील-Pleader
वारिस-Heir
वैद्य-Physician
व्यापारी-Merchant
शिष्य-Pupil
ससुर-Father-in-law
सास-Mother-in-law
सम्बन्धी-Relation
सौतेली कन्या-Step-daughter
सौतेला पुत्र-Step-son
सौतेला पिता-Step-father
सौतेली बहन-Step-sister
सौतेला भाई-Step-brother
सौतेली माता-Step-mother

पहनने-ओढ़ने के वस्त्र
(Clothes and Apparel)

अस्तर-Lining
अस्तीन-Sleeve
अँगरखा-Tunic
अँगिया-Bodice
अंग्रेजी टोपी-Hat
अँगोछा-Napkin
ऊन-Wool
कपड़ा-Clothes
कमरबन्द-belt
कमीज-Shirt
कम्बल-Blanket
कश्मीरा-Cashmira
कामदानी-HaDiaper
किनारा-Border
किरमिच-Canvas
कोट-Coat
गद्दा-Cushion
गुलूबन्द-Muffler
घूँघट-Veil

चादर-Sheet
चिकन-Lappet
छींट-Chintz
जाली-Gauze
जाँघिया-Half-pant
जीन-Drill
जेब-Pocket
टोपी Cap
डुपट्टा Scarf
तागा-Thread
तोशक-Quilt
तौलिया -Towel
दस्ताना-Gloves
रूमाल-Hand-kerehief
दुशाना-Shawl
नयनसुख-Jaconet
पट्टा-Lace
पतलून-Pantaloon
पायजामा-Trousers

पेवन-Patch
फतुही-Waistcoat
फलालीन-Flannel
फीता-Tape
बटन-Button
बनात-Broadcloth
मखमल-Velvet
मगजी-Hem
मलमल-Linen
माटापुलाम-Madapollam
मुरेठा-Turban
मोजा-Stockings
रफू-Darning
रूई-Cotton
रेशम-Silk
लबादा-Cloak, Gown
लहँगा-Petti-coat
साफा-Turban
सूत-Yarn

फल-फूल और वनस्पतियाँ
(Fruts and Vegetables)

अखरोट Chestnut
अनन्नास Pine-apple
अनार Pomegranate
आम Mango
आलू Potato
अंगूर Grape
अंजीर Fig
इमली Tamarind
ऊख Sugarcane
ककड़ी Cucumber
कटहल Jack-fruit
कमल Lotus
कमलिनी Lily
कद्दू Pumpkin
काजू Cashewnut
कुकुरमुत्ता Mushroom
केतकी Pandanus
केला Plantain
कोई Lily
कोंहड़ा Squash
खजूर Date
खरबूजा Muskmelon
खीरा Gourd
खूबानी Apricot
गाजर Carrot
गुलदाउदी–Chrysanthemum
गुलमेंहदी–Balsam
गुलबहार–Daisy
गुलाब–Rose

गुलाबजामुन–Roseberry
गेंदा–Marigold
घास–Grass
चकोतरा–Citron
चमेली–Jasmine
चम्पा–Magnolia
चिड़चिड़ा–Snake-gourd
चुकन्दर–Beet
जामुन–Blackberry
जैतून–Olive
तम्बाकू–Tobacco
तरबूज–Watermelon
दाख–Currant
धतूरा–Stramonium
नारियल–Cocoanut
नारंगी–Orange
नाशपाती–Pear
नरगिस–Narcissus
नीबू–Lemon
नील–Indigo
पटुआ–Hemp
पपीता–Papaya
पान–Betel
पालक–Spinach
पिस्ता–Pistachio
पुदीना–Mint
पोस्ता–Poppy
पौधा–Plant
प्याज–Onion

फूलगोभी–Cauliflower
बकाइन–Lilac
बदाम–Almond
बनफशा–Violet
बन्दगोभी–Cabbage
बबूल–Acacia
बेर–Plum
बेंत–Cane
बैंगन–Brinjal
भिंडी–Okra, Lady finger
मिरचा–Chilli
मुनक्का–Raisin
मूँगफली–Groundnut
मूली–Radish
मेंहदी–Myrtle
रतालू–Yam
रूई–Cotton
लता–Creeper
लहसुन–Garlic
शरीफा–Custard apple
शहतूत–Mulberry
शकरकन्द–Sweet-potato
सतालू–Peach
सन–Flax
साबूदाना–Sago
सिरपचा–Ivy
सुपारी–Betel-nut
सेब–Apple
सेम–Bean
सेमल–Silk-cotton

अन्न तथा भोजन के पदार्थ
(Cereals and Eatables)

अचार-Pickle
अरारूट-Arrowroot
आटा-Flour
कढ़ी-Curry
कहवा-Coffee
कुल्फी-Ice-cream
गेहूँ-Wheat
घी-Clarified butter
चटनी-Sauce
चना-Gram
चपाती-Cake
चावल Rice
चाय-Tea
चिवड़ा-Beaten rice
चीनी-Sugar
चोंकर-Bran
जलखावा-Tiffin
जलपान-Lunch
जई-Oat
जई का आटा-Oatmeal
जव-Barley
जूस-Broth
जूसी-Treacle

तरकारी Vegetable
तिल Sesame
तेल Oil
दलिया Mash
दही Curd
दाल Pulse
दिन का भोजन Lunch
दूध Milk
धान Paddy
पनीर Cheese
पावरोटी Loaf
बरफ-Ice
बाजरा Millet
बिसकुट Biscuit
भुट्टा Maize
भोज Feast
भोजन-Food
मकई-Maize
मक्खन-Butter
मट्ठा-Whey
मलाई-Cream
मसूरी-Lentil
माँड़-Gruel

मांस-Meat
मांस गाय का-Beef
मांस बकरे का-Mutton
मांस सुअर का-Pork
मांस हिरन का-Venison
मिठाई-Sweetmeat
मिश्री-Sugar-candy
मुरब्बा-Jam
मूँग-Kidney-bean
मैदा-Flour (fine)
मोथी-Buck-wheat
राब-Molasses
रात का भोजन-Supper
रेंडी-Castor-seed
रोटी-Bread
लायचीदाना-Comfit
लावा-Parched rice
शक्कर-Loaf-sugar
शर्बत-Syrup
शराब-Wine
शहद-Honey
सरसों-Mustard

वृक्ष और उनके अवयव
(Trees and their Parts)

अंकुर-Germ
अमरूद-Guava
आम-Mango
इमली–Tamarind
कलम–Graft
कली–Bud
काठ–Wood
काँटा–Thorn
गुठली–Stone
गोंद-Gum
चीड़-Pine

छाल-Bark
छिलका-Skin, Rind
जटा (नारियल की)-Coir
जड़-Root
जीरा-Stamen
टहनी-Branch
धड़-Stem
नस-Fibre
पत्ती-Leaf
फूल-Flower
बरगद-Banyan

बबूल-Acacia
बीज-Seed
बाँस-Bamboo
भोजपत्र-Birch
महोगनी-Mahogany
रस-Juice
रेशा-Pulp
शाखा-Branch
सरो-Cypress
सागवान-Teak
सेंहुड़-Cactus

मसाले और औषधियाँ
(Spices and Medicines)

अजवाइन का सत्त–Thymol
अदरक–Ginger
अफीम–Opium
अम्बर–Amber
कपूर–Camphor
कबाब चीची–Cubeb
कस्तूरी–Musk
कालीमिर्च–Black-pepper
केशर–Saffron
खमीर–Yeast
कत्था–Catechu
खड़िया–Chalk
गरू–Ruddle
चन्दन–Sandal
छबीला–Madder
जायफल–Nutmeg
जावित्री–Mace

जीरा–Cumin-seed
तुलसी–Basil
तूतिया–Copperas, Copper Sulphate
तेजपात–Cassia
दालचीनी–Cinnamon
फिटकरी–Alum
नमक–Salt
मजीठ–Madder
माजूफल–Gall-nut
मिर्चा–Pepper
मुसब्बर–Aloe
राल–Bitumen
रीठी–Soap-nut
लवाँग–Cloves
लाइची–Cardamom
लाल फिटकरी–Chrome alum

लोहबान–Benzoin
शोरा–Salipetre
सज्जीखार–Alkali
सफेदा–Litharge
सिगरिफ–Chinnabar
सुपारी–Betel-nut
सनाय–Senna
सिरका–Vinegar
संखिया–Arsenic
सोंठ–Dry ginger
सोहागा–Borax
सौंफ–Aniseed
सेतखली–Alabaster
साबूदाना–Sago
हल्दी–Turmeric
हर–Myrobalan
हींग –Asafoetida

औजार (Hand Tools)

आरी–Saw

करघा–Loom

करनी–Trowel

कुतुबनुमा–Compass

कुल्हाड़ी–Axe

कैंची–Scissors

कोल्हू (तेली)–Oil Mill

कोल्हू (गन्ने का)–Sugar Mill

गोनियाँ–Trying-angle

गोलची–Gauge

छुरा–Razor

छेनी–Cold chisel

टेकुवा–Awl

ढ़िबरी–Nut

तराजू–Balance

निहाई–Anvil

पतवार–Rudder

परकाल–Divider

पाराबटाम–Spirit-level

पाहू–Clamp

पिचकारी–Syringe

पेंच–Bolt

पेंचकस–Screw-driver

फरसा–Spade

फार–Colter

फुँकनी–Blowpipe

फावड़ा–Shovel

बरमा–Auger

बरमी–Drill

बसूला–Adze

बंसी–Fishing-angle

बादिया–Stock and diesr

बाँक–Vice

भभका–Still

भाथी–Bellows

मुँगरी–Mallet

रन्दा (छोटा)–Trving-plane

रन्दा (बड़ा)–Jack-plane

रुखानी–Chisel

रेती–File

रंभा–Lever

लंगर–Anchor

सबरी–Jemmy

सिल्ली–Hone

साहुल–Plumbline

हथकल–Spanner

हथौड़ी–Hammer

हल–Plough

हल का फार–Plough-share

हाथ बाँक–Hand-vice

रत्न और आभूषण

(Gems, Jewels and Ornaments)

अँगुठी–Ring
कंगन–Bracelet
कड़ा–Bangle
कड़ी–Link
कमीज का बटन–Stud
करनफूल–Ear-ring
काँटा (बाल का)–Hair-pin
काँटा (साड़ी का)–Brooch
कील नाक की–Nose-pin
गोमेके–Zircon
चिमटी–Clip
चूड़ी–Bangle
जवाहरात–Gems
जोसन–Armlet
तमगा–Medal
तल्ला (कान का)–Ear-stud
तोड़ा–Wristlet
नथुनी–Nose-ring
नीलम–Sapphire
पन्ना–Emerald
पेटी–Belt
पैजनी–Anklet
पखराज–Topaz
पोलकी–Opal
फीरोजा–Turquoise
मानिक–Ruby
माला–Garland
मुकुट–Tiara
मूँगा–Coral
मोती–Pearl
मोती सीप–Mother of pearl
लटकन–Locket
लोलक–Pendant
सिकड़ी–Chain
सुलेमानी पत्थर–Agate
लहसुनियाँ–Cat's eye
हार–Necklace
हीरा–Diamond
हँसुली–Neckband

खनिज पदार्थ

(Minerals and Metals)

अकीक–Cornellan
अभ्रक–Mica
कांस्य–Bronze
कुरुन–Emery
कोयला (पत्थर का)–Coal
खड़िया–Chalk
खान–Mine
गंधक–Sulphur
गेरू–Ochre
चकमक पत्थर–Flint
चाँदी–Silver
जस्ता–Zinc
ताँबा–Copper
तूतिया–Blue vitriol
पक्का लोहा–Steel
पारा–Mercury
पीतल–Brass
राँगा–Tin
शिलाजीत–Bitumen
सूरमा–Antimony
संखिया–Arsenic
सज्जी–Fuller's earth
सज्जीखार–Natron
सिंगरिफ–Cinnabar
सीसा–Lead
सफेदा–White lead
सिन्दूर–Vermilion
संगमरमर–Marble
लोहा–Iron
हड़ताल–Orpiment

व्यवसाय (Occupation)

अखबार वाला–News-agent
अध्यापक–Professor
अहिरिन–Milkmaid
अहीर–Milkman
इंजीनियर–Engineer
कसाई–Butcher
कारीगर–Artist
किसान–Farmer
किताब फरोश–Book-seller
कुली–Coolie
कोचवान–Coachman
कोठीवाल–Banker
खजांची–Treasurer
खरादने वाला–Turner
खुदरा विक्रेता–Retailer
गन्धी–Perfumer
गाड़ीवान–Coachman
ग्रन्थकार–Author
चिट्ठीरसाँ–Postman
जर्राह–Surgeon
जहाजी–Sailor
जादूगर–Magician
जिल्दसाज–Book-binder
जुलाहा–Weaver
जूता बनाने वाला–Shoe-maker
जौहरी–Jeweller
टाइप बैठाने वाला–Compositor
ठठेरा–Brasier
ठीकेदार–Contractor
डाक्टर–Doctor
तबलची–Drummer

तमोली–Betel-seller
तेली–Oil-man
तान्त्रिक–Sorcerer
दर्जी–Tailor
दलाल–Broker
दवा विक्रेता–Druggist
दाई–Midwife
दाँत बनाने वाला–Dentist
दुकानदार–Shopkeeper
धाय–Nurse
धुनियाँ–Carder
धोबिन–Washerwoman
धोबी–Washerman
नानबाई–Baker
पनभरा–Waterman
परीक्षक–Examiner
पहरेदार–Watchman
प्रकाशक–Publisher
प्रबन्धकर्ता–Manager
फेरी वाला–Hawker
फोटो वाला–Photographer
बढ़ई–Carpenter
बजाज–Draper
बारिस्टर–Barrister
बीच–विक्रेता–Seeds-man
भिक्षुक–Beggar
भूँजा–Parcher
भंडारी–Butler
मछुवा–Fisherman
मरम्त करने वाला–Repairer
मल्लाह–Boatman

मालिक–Proprietor
माली–Gardener
मीनाकार–Enamellet
मुनीम–Agent
मुद्रक–Printer
मुंशी–Clerk
मेहतर–Sweeper
मोची–Cobbler
मोदी–Grocer
मोहर्रिर–Writer
रसायनी–Chemist
रसोइयादार–Cook
रोकड़िया–Cashier
रोशनाई वाला–Inkman
रंगसाज–Painter
रंगरेज–Dyer
लादने वाला–Carrier
लेखक–Writer
लोहार–Blacksmith
वकील–Pleader
वैद्य–Physician
शिक्षक–Teacher
साईस–Groom
सीतला छापने वाला–Vaccinator
सिकलीगर–Glazier
सोनार–Goldsmith
संगतराश–Sculptor
सम्पादक–Editor
हज्जाम–barber
हलवाई–Confectioner

जानवर (Animals)

ऊँट–Camel
कस्तूरी मृग–Musk-deer
कुत्ता–Dog
कुतिया–Bitch
खच्चर–Mule
खरगोश–Rabbit
खरहा–Hare
गदहा–Ass
गाय–Cow
गिलहरी–Squirrel
गैंड़ा–Rhinoceros
गोरखर–Zebra
घोड़ा–Horse
घोड़ी–Mare
चीता–Panther
चूहा–Mouse
छछूँदर–Mole
जंगली सुअर–Boar
झबरा कुत्ता–Spaniel
टट्टू–Pony
तेंदुआ–Leopard

नेवला–Mongoose
दुम–Tail
पशु–Beast
पंजा–CIaw
पिल्ला–Puppy
बकरा–He-goat
बकरी–She-goat
बकरी का बच्चा–Kid
बछड़ा–Calf
बछिया–She-calf, Heifer
बछेड़ा–Colt
बछेड़ी–Filly
बिल्ली–Cat
बिल्ली का बच्चा–Kitten
बन्दर–Monkey
बनमानुस–Orang-outang
बैल–Ox
बारहसिंगा–Antelope, Stag
बारहसिंगी–Hind
भालू–Bear
भेंड़–Sheep

भेंड़ी–Ewe
भेंड़ी का बच्चा–Fawn
भैंसा–Buffalo
माँद–Den
मेमना–Lamb
मूसा–Rat
मृग–Stag
लोमड़ी–Fox
लकड़बग्घा–Hyena
लंगूर–Ape
व्याघ्र–Tiger
शिकारी कुत्ता–Hound
साँड़–Bull
साही–Porcupine
सियार–Jackal
सिंह–Lion
सींग–Horn
सुअर–Hog, Pig
सुअरी–Swine
हरिन–Deer
हाथी–Elephant

पक्षी (Birds)

अबाबील–Swallow
अड्डा–Perch
अण्डा–Egg
उल्लू–Owl
कठफोड़वा–Wood-pecker
कबूतर–Pigeon
काकातुआ–Cockatoo
काला (डोम) कौवा–Raven
कोयल–Cuckoo
कौवा–Crow
गरुड़–Eagle
गिद्ध–Vulture
गौरैया–Sparrow
घोंसला–Nest
चमगादड़–Bat

चील–Kite
चोंच–Beak
चोटी–Crest
डैना–Wing
तीतर–Partridge
नीलकण्ठ–Magpie
पर–Feather
पिंजड़ा–Cage
पंख–Plume
पेड़की–Dove
बत्तक–Drake
बत्तक का बच्चा–Duckling
बत्तकी–Duck
बुलबुल–Nightingale
बया–Weaverbird

बटेर–Quail
बाज–Falcon
मुर्गा–Cock
मुर्गी–Hen
मुर्ग–Fowl
मुर्गी का बच्चा–Chicken
मोर–Peacock
मोरनी–Peahen
लवा–Lark
शुतुर्मुर्ग–Ostrich
सारस–Crane
सुग्गा–Parrot
सेना (अण्डे का)–Hatching
हिरामन तोता–Macaw
हंस–Swan

कीड़े, मकोड़े

(Reptiles, Worms and Insects)

अजगर–Boa
कछुवा–Turtle
काला साँप–Adder
केचुली–Slough
केंचुवा–Earthworm
केकड़ा–Crab
खटमल–Bug
गिरगिट–Chameleon
गेहुवन साँप–Cobra
गोजर–Centipede
घड़ियाल–Beetle
घोंघा–Alligator
छिपकली–Snail
जहर–Lizard
जहर का दाँत–Fang

चींटी–Ant
जुगनू–Firefly
जू–Louse
जोंक–Leech
झींगुर–Cricket
टिड्डी–Locust
तितली–Butterfly
दरियाई घोड़ा–Hippoptamus
बिच्छू–Scorpion
मछली–Fish
दीमक–White ant
मछली का बच्चा–Spawn
मधुमक्खी (नर)–Drone
मधुमक्खी (मादा)–Bee
मेढक–Forg

मेढक का बच्चा–Tadpole
फन–Hood
फतंगा–Grasshopper
मकड़ा–Spider
मकड़े का जाला–Web
मक्खी–Fly
मगर–Crocodile
मच्छड़–Mosquito
बर्रे–Wasp
रेशम का कीड़ा–Silkworm
रेशम का कोआ–Cocoon
लीख–Nit
साँप–Snake
शंख–Conch
सीप–Oyster
सुफना (मछली का)–Fin

लिखने-पढ़ने तथा दफ़्तर के सामान

(Stationery and Office Requisites)

अक्सी कागज–Tracing paper

अलमारी–Newspaper

आधी रसीद–Counterfoil

आरामकुर्सी–Easy Chair

आलपीन–Pin

आलपीन गद्दी–Pin cushion

कलम–Pen

कागज–Paper

कागजदाब–Paper-weight

काग–Cork

कार्ड–Card

कोश–Dictionary

खड़िया पेंसिल–Crayon

खाता–Register

गड्डी–File

गोंद–Gum

चिमटी–Clip

चौकी–Bench

जेबी पोथी–Pocket Book

टिकट (स्टाम्प)–Postage stamp

टेबुल–Table

डोरी कीलदार–Tag

ड्राइंग पिन्–Drawing Pin

तार–Wire

तार की डोलची–Office Tray

तिपाई–Stool

दवात–Inkpot

दैनिक पत्र–Daily Paper

नकल करने का कागज–Carbon paper

नकल करने की स्याही–Copying ink

नकल करने की पेंसिल–Copying pencil

नक्शा–Map

निमन्त्रणपत्र–Invitation card

नीली स्याही–Blue Ink

परकाल–Divider

पुकारने की घंटी–Call-bell

पेंसिल–Pencil

पेंसिल पकड़–Crayon

पोस्टकार्ड–Post Card

फाइल–File

फीता–Tape

भेंट कार्ड–Visiting Card

मासिक पत्रिका–Magazine

मोहर–Seal

रबड़–Eraser

रबड़ की मोहर–Rubber-stamp

रद्दी की टोकरी–Waster basket

रसीद बही–Receipt-Book

रूलर–Ruler

रोशनाई–Ink

रोशनाई का गद्दा–Ink-pad

लपेटने का कागज–Packing paper

लाल रोशनाई–Red ink

लिखने की पट्टी–Writing pad

लिफाफा–Envelope

लेखाबही–Ledger

साप्ताहिक पत्र–Weekly paper

सरेस–Glue

सादा कागज–Blank paper

सोखता–Blotting-paper

होल्डर–Holder

परिशिष्ट–7/Appendix-7

शासकीय शब्दावली

(Terms used in Government Notifications)

अ

अकारण करते हुए	In supersession of.
अकिंचन अपील	Pauper appeal.
अकिंचनता का मद	Forma pauperis.
अकिंचन वाद	Pauper suit.
अक्षधुरी	Axis
अक्षरोटी	Spelling
अक्षिकप	Orbit
अखाद्य फसल	Non-food crops
अग्नि प्रशामक	Fireman, Fire-extin guisher.
अग्नि–इष्टिका	Fire-brick.
अग्नि सुरक्षित तिजोरी	Fire-proof safe.
अग्र ऋण	Advance, Taqavi-advance.
अग्रतम (प्रमुख)	Foremost
अग्रधन	Imprest
अग्रहार–दान	Endowment
अग्राह्य दावा	Inadmissible claims
अग्रीव	Flange
अचल सम्पत्ति	Immovable property
अढ़वाल (कसनी)	Brace
अणु–कण	Corpuscles
अण्डवृत्त	Ellipse
अतिवृत्त	Lapse
अतिरिक्त अनुदान	Additional grant
अतिरिक्त कर	Cess
अतिरिक्त कर्तव्य	Extraneous duties
अतिरिक्त खेती	Intermittent cultivation
अतिरिक्त नियमपत्र	Collateral agreement
अतिरिक्त प्रविष्टि	Additional entry
अतिरेक (वचत)	Surplus
अत्यधिक	Excessive
अत्यन्त छोटा	Infinitesimal
अत्वस्थान	Overstay
अदह	Asbestos
अधस्तन	Lower
अधिकतम उन्नति के लिए योग्यता	Fitness for further advance
अधिकतम माँग–सूचक	Maximum demand indicatory
अधिक बलन	Reinforcement
अधिक भार का कारण पत्र	Instrument of furthep charge
अधिक भुगतान	Overpayment
अधिक मूल्य पर	Above par
अधिकरण	Article, Bench
अधिकरणिक	Magistrate
अधिकरणिक वर्ग	Bench of magistrates
अधिक व्यय	Overcharge
अधिकार	Power
अधिकार क्षेत्र	Jurisdiction
अधिकार घोषक न्यायपत्र	Declaratory decree
अधिकार त्यागपत्र	Duty on release

अधिकार सीमा	Purview
अधिकारवर्ग सूची	Civil list
अधिकारी	Authority, Officer
अधिकृत	Authorise
अधिकोष (धनागार)	Bank
अधिक्षेत्र	Commanded area
अधिगमन	Acquisition
अधिनियम	Act
अधिपत्र	Warrant
अधिपत्र-अधिकारी	Warrant-officer
अधिभार	Overcharge, Surcharge
अधिमान	Preference
अधिमूल्यन	Appreciation
अधियाचक	Claimant
अधियाचन (दावा)	Claim
अधिवक्ता	Advocate
अधिष्ठाता	Rector
अधीनस्थ	Subordinate
अधीनस्थ पशुचिकित्सा सेवा	Subordinate Veterinary service
अध्यादेश	Ordinance (law)
अध्ययन-छुट्टी	Study-leave
अनन्य	Identical
अनाधिकारिक	Non-official
अनामक	Anonymous
अनायुक्त अधिकारी	Non-commissioned officer
अनावर्ती व्यय	Non-recurring expenditure
अनावृष्टि	Drought
अनावासिक	Non-residential
अनावासिक छात्र	Day scholar.
अनियत	Non-contract
अनियम	Anomaly
अनियमता	Irregularity
अनिर्दय पशुवध-यन्त्र	Humane cattle killer
अनिवार्य निवृत्ति	Compulsory retirement
अनिवार्य भर्ती	Conscription
अनिश्चित	Erratic
अनुक्रम (परम्परा)	Succession
अनुक्रमणिका	Index
अनुग्रह-धन	Compassionate Gratuity
अनुग्रह रूप सहायता	Ex-gratia relief
अनुचित दबाव	Coercion
अनुचित्रक	Tracer
अनुच्छेद	Para
अनुज्ञप्ति खण्डन	Revocation of licence
अनुज्ञा-पत्र	Licence
अनुज्ञा पत्र दायक	Licencing authorities
अनुज्ञाधारी	Licensee
अनुज्ञेय	Permissible
अनुतर	Freight
अनुत्पादक	Unproductive
अनुदर्शन (जाँच)	Survey
अनुदान	Grant
अनुदेश	Instruction
अनुधावन (अनुसरण)	Pursuance
अनुपत्र	Enclosure
अनुप्रस्थ छेद	Crosssection
अनुपस्थान	Default
अनुपस्थित (नादिहन्द)	Defaulter
अनुपस्थिति विवरणपत्र	Absentee statement
अनुपात	Proportion
अनुपाततः	Pro-rata
अनुपालन	Maintenance

अनुपूरक	Supplementary	अपरिगणित	Non-scheduled
अनुमति	Approval	अपरिश्रमी	Non-labouring
अनुमतिपत्र	Permit	अपर्याप्त	Inadequate
अनुमानिक (वेतन)	Presumptive (pay)	अपलाभ (जरे वासलात)	Mesne profit
अनुमानित अभ्युद्देश	Speculative reference	अपवाद	Exception
अनुमोदन	Endorsement, Approval	अपसृत	Escapee
		अपहरण	Abduction, Kidnapping
अनुमोदित सेवा	Approved service		
अनुरूपता	Conformity	अपहरण	Forfeiture
अनुरेखण	Tracings	अपहार	Embezzlement
अनुलेख	Postscript	अपाकरण (दिवाला)	Liquidation
अनुशासन	Discipline	अपाहरण	Misappropriation
अनुशासनात्मक कार्यवाही	Disciplinary action	अपील	Appeal
		अपीलकर्ता	Appellant
अनुसंधेय	Cognizable	अपील के आधार	Grounds of appeal
अनुसंधान	Investigation	अपीली	Appellate
अनुसविच	Under-secretary	अपेक्षण	Requisition
अनुशासन की कार्यवाही	Disciplinary action	अप्रगुणता	Inefficiency
अनुशासित	Disciplined	अप्रचलित मुद्रा	Uncurrent coin
अनुशीलन	In pursuit of	अप्रचिलत स्टाम्प	Obsolete stamp
अनुसूची	Schedule	अप्रतिलक्ष्य	Irrecoverable
अनुस्मारक	Reminder	अप्रवीण	Unskilled
अनेकार्थ (वाद)	Multifarious (suit)	अप्रवेश्य	Impervious
अनैतिक पण	Immoral traffic	अप्रिय (थकाऊ)	Irksome
अनैयमिक	Anomalous	अबन्धित आज्ञा	Remain at large
अन्वायाम काट	Long section	अबाधित करना	Absolute order
अपमार्जन	Deletion	अभाव	Lack, Want
अपमृत्यु-मीमांसक	Coroner	अभिकर्ता	Agent
अपराध	Crime, Offence	अभिकर्तापत्र	Power of attorney
अपराध (बुरा काम)	Perpetration, Delinquency	अभिप्रेषण	Deputation
		अभिभाषक	Pleader
अपराध रोधक पुलिस	Crime police	अभिभाषक परिषद्	Bar Council
अपराध वृत्त	History sheet	अभिभाषक संघ	Bar Association, Bar

अभियुक्त	Accused
अभियोक्ता	Complainant
अभियोग	Prosecution
अभियोग	Charge
अभियोग (चलान)	Prosecute
अभियोग (दोषण)	Accusation
अभियोग पक्ष	Prosecution
अभियोग फलक	Charge sheet
अभियोग मुक्त	Discharged
अभियोग साक्षी	P.W. (Prosecution witness)
अभियोगी	Complainant
अभिलेख	Record
अभिलेख पाल	Record-keeper
अभिलेख संशोधन	Record operation
अभिलेखाधिकृत	Record-in-charge
अभिशून्यन	Annuling
अभिहरण अधिपत्र	Distress warrant
अभिहस्तांकन (बेंची)	Assignment (of land)
अभिहस्तांकिती	Assignee
अभ्यर्थना (याचिका)	Petition
अभ्यर्थी	Petitioner
अभ्युक्ति (कैफियत)	Remarks
अभ्युद्देश	Reference
अमान्य लेख	Discredited document
अमूर्त सम्पत्ति	Intangible property
अयोग्यता	Disqualification
अराजपत्रित (अधिकारी)	Non-gazetted (officer)
अरिष्ठि	Security
अरिष्ठ गुणक	Safety factor
अर्गल	Bar (as in efficiency bar), Bolt, Latch
अर्थदण्ड	Fine
अर्थ पुस्तिका	Financial hand book
अर्थमन्त्री	Finance Minister
अर्धसरकारी	Demi-official
अर्ध सरकारी पत्र	D. O. letter
अर्थ स्थायी	Quasi-permanent
अर्धोपान्त	Half-margin
अलगाव	Segregation
अलपेट	Kink
अलाव	Fire-place
अलोनी	Eaves
अल्पकाल ऋण	Floating debt
अल्पवयस्क	Minor
अल्पवयस्क अपराधी	Juvenile offender
अल्पवाद न्यायालय	Small Causes Court
अल्पशुल्क	Moiety fees
अवकाश	Recess, Vacation
अवक्रमण	Devolution
अवक्षेपण (विवरण पत्र)	Objection (statement)
अवतरण (उद्धरण)	Extract
अवधि	Limitation
अवधिताकाल	Period of limitation
अवधि बाधित	Barred by limitation
अवलूल्यन	Depreciation
अवयव	Component parts
अवर कर्मचारी वर्ग	Inferior staff
अवरुद्ध	Detenue
अवरोध	Detention
अवगीकृत	Unclassified
अवधि वद्धि	Extension
अवशिष्ट	Arrears
अवशिष्ट के प्राप्य	Arrear claims
अवशेष	Residue
अवहार (छूट)	Rebate

अविनय	Misbehaviour
अविभक्त जोत	Joint holding
अविभक्त परिवार सम्पत्ति	Joint family property
अविभाज्य लेन-देन	Indivisible transaction
अविरत सक्रिय सेवा	Continuous active service
अविरत सेवा	Continuous service
अविवेकी, अविवेकपूर्ण	Indiscriminate
अवेक्षक	Overseer
अवेक्षा	Care (regard)
अवैतनिक	Honorary
अवैध	Illegal
अवैध समुदाय	Unlawful assembly
अव्यवस्था	Random
अशक्त	Infirm
अशक्तता छुट्टी	Disability leave
अशुद्ध वर्णन	Mis-description
अशुद्धि शोधन	Rectification of error
अशुद्धि-सूची	Errata list
अश्रु-धूम टुकड़ी	Tear-smoke squad
अश्व-शक्ति	Horse power
असमर्थता	Infirmity
असलम्ब चतुर्भुज	Trapezoid (with no sides parallel)
असली काश्तकार	Tenant-in-chief
असाधारण छुट्टी	Extraordinary leave
असाध्य	Unmanageable
असावधानी	Negligence
असिग्रन्थि	Sword knot
असैनिक कर्मचारी	Civil employee
असोख	Non-porous
असंगत	Irrelevant
असंगति	Discrepancy
असम्बन्धित इच्छापत्र	Non-testamentary
अस्थायी	Provisional
अस्थायी पद	Temporary post
अस्थि-मज्जा	Bone marrow
अस्थायी मूल	Provisional substantive
अस्पष्ट (अप्रसिद्ध)	Obscure
अस्वस्थ	Unsound
अस्वाभाविक	Unnatural
अस्वाभाविक धन	Escheat
अस्वामिक	Unclaimed
अस्वामिक लेखपत्र	Unclaimed documeat
अस्वास्थ्यकर	Unwholesome
अस्वास्थ्यकरदा	Unhealthiness
अहस्तक्षेप्य	Incognizable

आ

आकल्प (सज्जा)	Accoutrement
आकस्मिक	Emergency
आकस्मिक छुट्टी	Casual Leave
आकस्मिक घृतदल	Contingent Reserve
आकस्मिक व्यय	Contingencies
आकाश (रिताई)	Space
आक्रमण	Assault
आखेट (खेल)	Sport
आगणन	Estimate
आगमपत्र	Title-deed
आगामी	Forthcoming
आघात	Injury
आचरण	Conduct
आजीवन पट्टा	Life-tenure
आज्ञा नस्ती	Order file
आज्ञापत्र (फरमाना)	Writ

आज्ञा पुस्तक	Order book
आज्ञा फलक	Order sheet
आज्ञासार संग्रह	Manual of orders
आड	Hypothecation
आतति (तनाव)	Tension
आतान	Strain
आतिथि	Up-to-date
आतुरालय	Infirmary
आत्ययिक	Urgent
आत्ययिक पर्ची	Urgent slip
आदाता	Recipient
आदिता (पूर्वता)	Priority
आदेय	Assets (as opposed to liability)
आदेश	Provision, Instructions (law)
आदेश पत्र वाहक	Process server
आदेश-पंजी	Order-book
आदेशात्मक	Mandatory
आधर्षण	Conviction
आधर्षित	Convict
आधारभूत	Fundamental
आधार-रेखा	Base line
आधि (गिरवी)	Pawn, Pledge
आधिकारिक (सरकारी)	Official
आनियम (नियमन)	Regulation
आनुपातिक	Proportionate
आनुषंगिक व्यय	Incidental charge
आपत्ति	Objection
आपत्तिकर्ता	Objector
आपराधिक षड्यन्त्र	Criminal conspiracy
आपात	Incidence
आपेक्षिक	Specific
आप्त (प्रामाणिक)	Authentic
आबकारी विभाग	Excise department
आबनूस	Ebony
आभ्यासिक अपराधी	Habitual offender
आमान	Gauge
आयकर	Income-tax
आयत (याताकार)	Oblong
आयतन (खंड)	Volume
आयति	Budget
आयव्ययक (बजट)	Budget
आयव्ययक सारसंग्रह	Budget manual
आयात	Import
आयात-निर्यात कर	Tariff, Customs-duty.
आयुक्त	Commissioner
आयुधक	Armourer
आयुधकार	Armourer
आयुधपाल	Retainer
आयोग	Commission
आयोजक	Organiser
आरोप	Allegation, Imposition
आरंभ	Commencement
आरंभ और क्षणिक	Commencement and transitory
आरंभिक	Opening balance
आरंभिक निर्णय	Original award
आरंभिक वेतन	Initial pay
आर्थिक	Pecuniary, Monetary
आर्थिक दिष्टि	Monetary allotment
आलेख (नक्शा)	Draft
आलेखक	Draftsman
आलोचन	Observation
आलोचना	Comment

आलंब (टक)	Fulcrum
आवक्ष भित्ति	Breast wall
आवधिक	Terminal
आवरक	Cover
आवर्ती	Recurring
आवश्यक परिवर्तनों सहित	Mutatis Mutandis
आवारागर्द	Vagrant
आवारगर्दी	Vagrancy
आवास	Residence, Quarter
आवासिक	Resident
आवेदक	Memorialist, Applicant
आवेदन पत्र	Representation
आशु	Express
आशुपत्र	Express letter
आश्वासन	Assurance
आसजन	Co-ordinate
आसेध	Warrant of arrest
आस्थगित वेतन	Deferred pay
आस्थान	Site
आस्पद (पदवी)	Rank
आस्मारक (अभिरक्षित)	Protected monument
आह्वान पत्र	Summons
आँकड़े	Figures, Statistics
आँकड़े का संकलन	Compilation of statistics
आँकना	Assess
आंशिक पूर्ति	Part performance, Part supply
आह्वान शुल्क	Process fees

इ

इकबारा	Casual (As in casual prisoner)
इकसार	Uniform
इच्छापत्र कर्ता	Testator
इच्छापत्र की प्रमाणित प्रतिलिपि	Probate
इच्छापत्र साधक	Executor
इजरा की कार्रवाई करना	Taking up execution proceedings
इष्टिका	Brick

उ

उगाही (वसूली)	Realization
उग्रवादी	Extremist
उचन्त (अवर्गित)	Suspense
उच्च न्यायालय	High Court
उच्च अधिकारी	Higher authority
उच्चदारी (इत्तलानामा)	Caveat
उतार-चढ़ाव	Fluctuation
उत्केन्द्र	Eccentric
उत्तरदायी	Liable
उत्तरदायी	Respondent
उत्तर पक्ष	Defence
उत्तर रोध	Estopped
उत्तरवादी और सहोत्तरवादी	Respondent and Co-respondent
उत्तराधिकार प्रमाणपत्र	Succession certificate
उत्तराधिकार (विरासत) का प्रमाणपत्र	Letter of administration
उत्तराधिकारी	Successor
उत्तरी भारत	Northern India
घाट विधान	Ferries Act

उत्पाद कर	Excise duty
उत्पादन	Production
उत्प्रवासी संरक्षक	Protector of emigrants
उदरकीट का विरु	Bots & warble
उदासीनता	Apathy
उदाहृत	Illustrated, Illustrate
उदाहुत करना	Exemplify
उद्गम कार्यजात	Head works
उद्देश्य	Object
उद्यान	Park
उद्विकास	Evolution
उद्धरण	Extract
उद्धावन	Flush
उन्मूलन	Abolition
उप अनुच्छेद	Sub-paragraph
उपकर	Cess
उपकरण	Implement, Tools
उपज	Yield
उपजीवन (निर्वाह)	Subsistence
उपदान	Offer
उपदंश कानून	Dourine Act
उपधारा	Sub-section
उपनिधान	Deposit
उपनियम	Bye-laws
उपनिवेशी सेवा	Colonial service
उप प्रमाणक	Sub-voucher
उपभाग	Sub-division
उपभोक्ता	Consumer
उपयुक्त	Appropriate
उपराज्यपाल	Lieutenant Governor
उपरिव्यय	Overhead charges
उपलब्ध	Available
उपविभाग	Section
उपशिक्षा	Training
उपशीर्षक	Sub-head
उपसंक्षेप	Abstract
उपसंक्षेप पुस्तक	Abstract book
उपसंस्थान	Sub-station
उपसन्न	Approximate
उपसमिति	Sub-committee
उपस्कर	Furniture
उपस्थापन	Submission
उपस्थित होना	Appear
उपस्थिति	Appearance
उपस्थिति का स्मृतिपत्र	Memo of appearance
उपस्थिति के लिए सफीना	Citation
उपस्वामी	Sub-proprietor
उपाधिक	Additional
उपाधि प्राप्ति	Predication
उपात	Margin
उपांत शीर्षक (पार्श्व शीर्षक)	Marginal heading
उपांत लिखित	Marginally noted
उभयपक्ष	Parties
उभार	Relief (Carving)
उल्लंघन	Infringement, Contravention

ऊ

ऊपर	Supra
ऊपरिक	Formal (superficial)
ऊसर	Barren

ए

एकड़ों में क्षेत्रफल	Acreage
एकपक्षीय	Exparte

एकमत निर्णय	Concurrent judgment
एकमत्य	Accord
एकराशि	Lump sum
एक सार (वर्दी)	Uniform
एक स्थानीय चौराहा ड्यूटी	Fixed point duty
एकस्थीकरण	Consolidation
एकस्थीकृत	Consolidated
एकस्व भेषज	Patent medicine
एकाधिकार	Monopoly
एकीकरण	Amalgamation, Coordination
एकीकृत पूर्वानुमान	Consolidated forecast
एकीकृत वेतन	Consolidated pay
एड़ी जोड़ा	Heel file
एतदर्थ	Ad Hoc

ए, ओ, औ

ऐतिहासिक क्रम	Chronological order
ओरी कोल	Sector (Radius Vector)
औद्योगिक	Technical
औद्योगीकरण	Industrialization
औपाधिक आदेश	Conditional Order
औपान्तिक	Marginal
औरस	Legitimate (as in legitimate child)
औसत	Average
औसत परिलाभ	Average emoluments

अं

अंकनी	Pencil
अंकित मूल्य से कम	Below par
अंग	Member (Roof)
अँगुली छाप	Finger Print
अंगुष्ठ भित्ति	Toe wall
अंडाकार क्षेत्र तथा वक्र क्षेत्र	Eliptic and curved figures
अंतराल	Interval
अंतरिक्ष विज्ञान मान-मन्दिर	Meteorological observatory
अंतरिक्ष विद्या	Space Science
अंतर्कालीन (अंतरिम)	Interim
अंतर्गतपत्र	Enclosure
अंतर्परजीवी	Entozoa
अंतर्न्यास	Insertion
अंतर्वस्तु	Content
अंत:स्थायी	Intermediary, Intermediate
अंतिम डिगरी	Decree absolute
अंतिम रूप से निर्णीत	Finally disposed of (decided)
अंतिम शेष	Closing balance
अंश	Numerator, Share
अंश (घटक द्रव्य)	Ingredient
अंश कालिक	Part time
अंश दान	Contribution
अंश हस्तांतरण	Transfer of share
अंशाधिपत्र	Share warrant
अंशी	Co-parcener
अंशुक वकीय (रोग)	Actinomycosis

ऋ

ऋण (उधार)	Credit
ऋणग्रस्त	Encumbered
ऋणशोधन (किश्तों में)	Amortization
ऋणात्मक	Negative
ऋण चुकाव कोष	Sinking fund

ऋणपत्र	Debenture

क

कक्ष (ग्रहपथ)	Orbit
कक्षस्थ (गुप्त)	In Camera
कच्चा काश्तकार	Tenant at will
कच्चा माल	Raw material
कछार	Alluvion
कटहरा	Balustrade
कट्टा	Segment
कटौती	Cut, Deduction
कड़ा	Ankle, Ring
कड़ाबीन आधार	Carbine bucket
कड़ी (धरणी)	Rafter
कड़ी	Link
कनकत	Appraisement
कपट (कूट, छल, धोखा)	Fraud
कपास का गोला	Cotton balls
कब्जा आराजी	Tenancy
कमरकोटा (मुँडेर)	Parapet
कमी का स्मृतिपत्र	Discrepancy memo
कम्पनी का विधान नियम	Article of Association
करघटा	Railings, Rack
करणपत्र	Instrument (in writing)
करनिर्धारक जज	Taxing Judge
कर निर्धारण	Assessment, Assess
कर्जे में दिया गया रुपया	Subscription for the loan
कर्ण	Hypotenuse
कर्ण शिक्षा	Aural education
कर्तनी चिह्न	Cross mark
कर्तव्य पालन	Discharge of duties
कर्तव्य भत्ता	Duty allowance
कर्मचारी	Official
कर्मशाला	Workshop
कर्मचारी वर्ग	Staff
कलश (शिखर)	Finial
कलादीर्घा	Art gallery
कल्पना	Hypothesis
कल्याण-केन्द्र	Welfare centre
कागजात का नुकसान	Injury to records
कागजात तलब करना	Calling for the record
काचावृत रचनाएँ	Cover glass preparation
काट (खाड़ी और खंबानी)	Section (Cross & long)
काठी	Harness
कानून-व्यवस्था	Statute
काम (ठेके का)	Job
कामगर	Workman
कारगर चौड़ाई	Effective span
कारण से	By virtue of
कारापाल	Jailor
कारा शिविर	Concentration camp
कारोपान्त	Jail premises.
कार्य पद्धति	Procedure
कार्य पीठ	Bureau
कार्यत्यक्त	Discharged
कार्यग्रहण अवधि	Joining time
कार्यभार प्रमाणपत्र	Charge certificate
काय्र योग्यता प्रमाणपत्र	Fitness certificate
कार्यवाह नियुक्ति	Acting appointment
कार्यवाही	Proceedings, Action
कार्यवाही का रजिस्टर	Minute book
कार्यवाही	Minutes
कार्यविधि	Procedure

कार्यविवरण पत्र	Business statement	कुल चिह्न	Coat of arms
कार्यसमिति	Standard of work	कुलाह	Turban
कार्यस्तर	Standard at work	कूटकरण (बाल कल्पना)	Forgery
कार्यान्वयन	Implementation	कूट रचना	Forgery
कार्यावली	Agenda	कूट वेधन	Well boring
कालकाठरी	Solitary confinement, Dungeon	कृत्य	Function
कालक्रम	Time Scale	कृषक	Cultivator
कालतिरोहित	Time-barred	कृषक ऋण एक्ट	Agriculturists Loan Act
कालव्यतिक्रम (तारीख की गलती)	Anachronism	कृषि उपकरण	Agricultural implements
कालातीत	Lapsed	कृषि पट्टा	Agricultural lease
काश्त में	Under cultivation	कृषि योग्य बंजर	Culturable waste
काजी हाउस	Cattle house	कृषि विषयक	Agricultural
काँटा (ठोकर)	Spur	केन्द्राभि	Centripetal
किराये का नक्शा	Rent statement	केन्द्रायग	Centrifugal
किराये की गाड़ी	Public conveyance	केन्दीय अभिलेखालय	Central Record Office
किरायेदार की दर	Occupiers' rate	केन्द्रीय उत्पादकर और नमक	Central Excise & Salt
किशोर अपराधी	Juvenile offender	केन्द्रीय विवरणपत्र	Central division
कोट (कृषि)	Maggot	केन्द्रीय राजस्व मुद्रांक	Central Revenue Stamp
कीटाणु नाशक	Disinfectant	कैंची, डंडा, बेड़ी	Cross, bar, fetter
कीटाणु परीक्षा	Bacteriological examination	कोई शब्द छल से लिख देना	Interpolating
कुछवाजिबी अधिक	In moderate excess	कोटि	Ordinate, Grade
कुड़क करना	Attach (Legal Term)	कोटिक्रम	Gradation list
कुड़क कराना	Distrain	कोर्ट साहिब	Gradation
कुड़की	Seizure, Attachment	कोषस्थीकरण	Prosecuting inspector
कुत्ता	Ratchet	कोष	Encasing
कुत्ते का संक्रामक पाण्डुरोग	Infections, Jaundice of the dogs	कोष्ठीय	Cellular
कुन्द	Lathe	कंकड़ी (छोटी-छोटी)	Shingle
कुन्दकार	Turner		
कुन्दा कब्जा	Hasp		

कंटक (बाधा)	Nuisance
क्रमिक	Serial
क्रयविक्रय योग्य सरकारी हुण्डी	Marketable security
क्रेता	Transferee
क्रोड़पत्र	Codicil
क्लीवाक्ष	Neutral axis
क्षणिक	Transitory
क्षतिपूर्ति	Indemnity, Compensation
क्षत मुद्रांक	Injured stamp
क्षतिपूरक बंध	Bond of indemnity
क्षतिपूरक प्रतिज्ञापत्र	Indemnity bond
क्षतिपूर्ति का वाद	Damages suit
क्षमा	Condonation
क्षप (क)	Addendum
क्षेत्रमिति	Mensuration
क्षमता	Calibre
क्षय	Decay
क्षय रोग सम्बन्धी	Tubercular
क्षुद्र प्रासंगिक व्यय	Petty contingent expenditure

ख

खजाना	Treasure vault
खड़ा लम्ब	King post
खपत	Absorption
खराद	Lathe
खलीता	Satchel
खसरा	Field-book
खाँचा	Mould
खाद	Fertiliser, manure
खाद्य कोष्ठ	Pantry
खाद्य मन्त्री	Minister of food
खाद्य सामग्री भण्डार	Larder
खारिज करना	Dismiss, Weed out, Set side
खुजली	Demodectic scabies
खुजीला	Scarbutic
खुला रखना	Exposure
खुली हुई रूई	Loose cotton
खेल-कूद	Athletic
खंड	Volume, Bay (division of roof)

ग

गजनिमीजिका	Connivance
गट्ठा	Bamboo measuring rod
गणना	Calculation
गणनाकार	Computer
गणनाधिकारी	Accounts officer
कणनाध्यक्ष	Accountant
गणना परीक्षा विवरण	Audit report
गणवेश	Uniform
गतस्वामित्व	Ex-proprietary
गतिशास्त्र	Dynamics
गति सीमा	Speed limit
गत्ताकारी	Book craft
गबन	Embezzlement
गवाक्ष	Fenestra
गर्भपात	Miscarriage
गर्भाधान	Insemination
गश्त	Beet (Patrolling), Patrol
गश्ती दस्ता	Mobile squad
गार्टर	Girder
गाभिन करना (या कराना)	To cover

गाभिन फार्म	Covering farm
गाभिन विवरण पत्र	Covering return
गारद	Escort
गादद और कमान	Guards & Escorts
गारा	Mud mortar
गिट्टी	Ballast
गिनती की किताब	Muster-roll
गिनती (हाजिरी)	Muster
गुट (समूह)	Group
गुणक	Factor
गुनिया	Offset piece
गुप्त अक्ष विचार	En-camera trial
गुप्तमत	Ballot
गुप्त सेवा व्यय	Secret service Charges
गुरुत्व	Gravity
गुंडा	Bully
गुंबज	Vault
गूल	Guts, Water course
गृहोपान्त	Premises
गैरदखिलकारी असामी	Non-occupancy tenant
गैर वसूल लागत	Cost outstanding
गोला	Sphere
गोला-गारूद	Ammunition
गोली	Ammunition
गोली रोक	Bullet-proof
गोप्य	Confidential
गोष्ठ	Stable
गौण उत्तरवादी	Proforma-respondent
गौण प्रतिवादी	Proforma-defendant
गंदा नाला	Sewer
ग्रस्त (प्रभावित)	Affected
ग्रहणाधिकार	Lien
ग्राम रक्षा समिति	Village defence society
ग्राम्य	Rural
ग्राहक-पुस्तिका (पासबुक)	Pass-book
ग्राह्य	Admissible

घ

घटना (घटाया जाना)	Abatement
घटबढ़	Variation
घटाव	Subtraction
घटोत्तरी	Set off
घन	Cube
घनमूल	Cube-root
घाट	Ferries
घुड़सवार पुलिस	Mounted police
घुन लगना	Weeviling
घोल	Solution (chemistry)
घोषणा	Proclamation, Declaration
घोषणापत्र	Manifesto
घोष विक्रय (नीलाम)	Auction

च

चकबंदी	Consolidation of holdings
चकबंदी अधिकारी	Consolidation Officer
चकबंदीकर्ता	Consolidator
चक्राधिकारी	Circle officer
चढ़ता	Sliding scale
चतुष्पथ	Crossing
चरित्रवर्ति (चरित्रावली)	Character-roll
चर्बी रहित	Grease free
चर्भसार (पन्छा)	Scrum

चर्मीय	Cutaneous
चलता विवरण	Running statement
चल सम्पत्ति	Movable property, Movable effect
चहला (कीचड़)	Silt
चालक	Operator
चालान-व्यय	Propulsion charges
चालू	Current
चालू कर्तव्य	Current duty
चिकित्सकीय छुट्टी	Medical leave
चित्रसम (प्रक्षेप)	Isometric
चिह्न	Identification mark
चुनाव आन्दोलन	Election Campaign
चुनावपद	Selection post
चुंगीकर	Octroi duty
चूना (टपकना)	Ooze
चूल (जिस पर कोई वस्तु घूमे)	Pivot
चूसण	Suction
चेक चुकाई एजेन्ट	Clearing agent
चेक चुकाई कार्यलय	Clearing office
चेतावनी	Warning
चोपे की भूमि	Water-logged land
चोर घंटी	Burglar Alarm
चोरबत्ती	Torch
चौक (चबूतरा, बाजार, कचहरी)	Square
चौकसी	Vigilance
चौकी	Outpost (Police)
चौकी पुलिस	Watch & ward (Police)
चौपार (डेवढ़ी)	Lobby, Chaupal
चौर्यपण	Smuggling
चौसाला	Quadrennial

छ

छटनी	Retrenchment
छत्ता	Arcade
छद (आवरण)	Cover
छद्मव्यक्तिता	Impersonation, False personation
छर्रा	Buck ammunition
छल (हरण, गबन)	Embezzlement
छलनी परीक्षा	Sieve test
छल्ला	Ferrule
छाप	Impression
छायांकित	Adumbrated
छावनी कानून	Cantonment Act
छिद्र पक्ष	Jambs
छिद्र व्यास	Calibre
छिपटी (खपच्ची)	Splinter
छीलन	Scrap
छुटकारा	Exoneration
छुट्टी बढ़ाना	Extension of leave
छुट्टी वेतन	Leave salary
छुट्टी से वापस बुलाना	Recall from leave
छूट	Remission
छेद	Aperture
छेदा	Logarithm
छेदिका	Secant

ज

जड़ता	Inertia
जड़ता प्रवृत्ति	Moment of inertia
जत्था	Batch
जनगणना	Census
जनजाति	Tribe

जन-सुरक्षा	Public safety
जन-सेवक	Public servant
जनित्र (जनक)	Generator
जब्त करना	Forfeit
जब्त किये हुए लेख पत्र	Impounded documents
जब्ती	Confiscation, Forfeiture
जमा	Credit
जमा की सूचना	Credit advice
जमानत दाखिल करना	Furnish security
जमीन बढ़ाना	Encroachment
जमीन का उठाना	Letting
जरीब	Chain (measuring)
जल	Hydro
जल चालित	Hydraulic
जलतोड़	Groyne
जलनियन्त्रक पुल	Aquaduct
जल निर्गमन मार्ग	Spill way
जलमग्न	Submerged
जल विद्युत तारजाल	Hydro-electric grid
जलाशय (टंकी, हौज)	Reservoir
जलांतक चिकित्सा	Anti-rabies treatmerit
जलोत्सारण	Drainage
जहरबाद	Farcy
जहाज का किराया नाम	Charter party
जस्ता चढ़ी	Galvanized
जागरण	Vigil
जागर नियन्त्रण	Vigilant control
जाब्ता फौजदारी	Criminal procedure
जारी करना	Issue, Code
जाल (जालि का छेद)	Mesh
जाली (झँझरी)	Gratings
जाँच	Verification
जाँच आयोग	Commission of inquiry
जिरह	Cross examination
जीवा	Chord
जूरी पंच	Foreman of the Jury
जेवनार	Banquet
ज्येष्ठता	Seniority
जोड़पत्र	Addendum
जोत	Tillage, Holdings
जोत का बँटवारा	Division of holdings
ज्ञानमन्दिर (ज्ञानालय)	Institute
ज्ञान वृद्ध	Veteran

झ

झगड़ालू	Violent
झालर (नीली)	Blue fringe
झिलमिली	Louvre
झूका	Inclined
झोंक	Momentum

ट

टंकन	Coinage
टिड्डी	Locust
टिप्पणी लेखक तथा पाण्डु लेखक	Noter and Drafter
टीका	Inoculation, Comments, Notes
टीपें और आज्ञाएँ	Notes and orders
टीला	Mound
टूट-फूट	Wear and tear
टोंटी	Bib cock, Cock stop
टोली नायक	Group leader
टोटा भरना	Make restoration, Compensate

ठ

ठेका	Contract
ठेके का काम	Piece work

ड

डंडा	Main wall (Jail ward), Baton, Bludgeon
डंडा बेड़ी	Bar-fetters
डाक	Dak
डाक सवार	Despatch Rider
डाट का पार्श्व	Rib of an arc
डामर	Asphalt
डाँट-फटकार	Admonition
डाँड़	Penalty farm
डाँस	Biting
डिग्री	Decree
डिग्री इजरा करना	To execute decree
डेरी फार्म	Dairy farm
ड्यूटी का रजिस्टर	Register of duty

ढ

ढाल	Run off, Gradient
ढाल चालित नहर	Gravity canal
ढूला (नौशय्या)	Berth
ढोर पालक	Breeder

त

तड़ित संवाहक	Lightning conductor
तत्वावधान में	Under the auspices
तन्य	Tensile
तरपल (तिरपाल)	Tarpaulin
तर्क	Argument
तली	Exhaust
तवा (लपरी)	Gridiron
तंग	Girth
तंग मोड़	Sharp curve, Hairpin
तानक	Stretcher
तापमापक	Thermometer
तामील	Execution
तामील किया गया	Served
तारण गृह	Rescue Home
तार काट	Cable Crossing
तार जोड़	Cable jointers
तारा चिह्न	Asterisk
तावान देना	Indemnification
त्याग	Relinquishment, Abandonment, Surrender
त्यागपत्र	Resignation
तिर्यक्	Oblique
तीव्र अनुधावन	Hot-pursuit
त्रिपाद	Tripod
त्रैमासिक विवरण	Quarterly statement
तुकमा और हुक	Eye and hook
तुच्छ	Insignificant
तुषार	Blight
तैनाती	Posting
तोड़ना (भंग करना)	Violate
तोरण शीर्ष	Crown of an arc
तोरणाधार	Abutment

थ

थानेदार (बड़े)	Station officer
थानेदार	Sub-Inspector
थोक	Bluk
थोक भाव	Wholesale price
थोप चेप मरम्मत	Patch repairs

द

दखील असामी — Occupancy tenant
दग्ध भाग — Branded portion
गग्धांकन प्रमाणपत्र — Branding Gertificate
दत्तक पत्र — Adoption deed
दत्तक ग्रहण का अधिकारपत्र — Authentication of power of attorney
दमकल — Fire brigade
दमकल भृत्या — Fire service
दलत्यागी — Deserter
दया की अभ्यर्थना — Mercy petition
दवामूलक — Compassionate
दरअनुसूची — Schedule of rates
दलेल — Fatigue
दशमलव भिन्न — Decimal fraction
दशा — Condition
दहन — Combustion
दहन वर्ति — Fuse
दहनागार — Combustion chamber
दहेहकारणपत्र — Instrument of dowery
दंड (धुरा) — Shaft
दंड — Punishment, Penalty
दंड आज्ञा देने वाले प्राधिकारी — Sentencing authority
दंडनायक — Magistrate
दंडनीय (अपराध) — Culpable
दंड विधि संग्रह — Criminal Procedure Code
दंड विषयक — Penal
दंडअपराध — Criminal offence
दंडशास्त्र — Penology
दंडात्मक श्रम — Servitude
दंड विधि — Term of Sentence
दाखिल खारिज रजिस्टर — Mutation register
दानपत्र — Deed of gift
दान्ता — Notch
दाय (बपौती) — Heritage, Inheritance
दाय वंचित करना — Disinherit
दायर करने की तारीख — Date of institution
दायरा क्लर्क — Suits clerk
दायित्व — Liability
दायरा का करणपत्र — Obligation instrument
दारा-भूति — Alimony
दावा छोड़ने वाला — Disclaimer
दावा छोड़ देना — Yield
दावेदार — Claimant
दिक स्थिति — Bearing, (Direction)
दिलाहा — Panel (architecture)
दिवालिया ठहराना — Adjudication
दिष्टि — Allotment
दीर्घा — Gallery
दीवानी के सामान्य नियम — General Rules, Civil
दीवारगीर — Bracket
दीवार पकड़ रंग — Distemper
दी हुई बात — Data
दुग्धशाला — Dairy
दुर्भिक्ष कर्तव्य — Famine-duty
दुर्भिक्ष संहिता — Famine-code
दुरुत्साहन — Abetment
दुहरा — Duplicate
दुर्वचनीय कापी — Illegible copy
दूती (संचारिका) — Procuress
दूधा — Emulsion
दूरदर्शी — Provident
दूरभाष (टेंलीफोन) — Telephone

दृढ़ कोष्ठ	Strong room
दृष्टांत	Visa
देखिए	Vide
देन विक्रेता	Ex-officio vendor
देय	Chargeable
देशांतर (लंबान)	Longitude
देशित	Indicator
देशीकरण (नागरिकीकरण)	Naturalization
देशी भाषा विभाग	Vernacular Department
दैनंदिनी (दिन पंजी)	Diary
दोष	Default
दोष मुक्त	Discharged
दोष मुक्ति	Acquittal
दोषी (अपराधी)	Delinquent
दोषी (दोष प्राप्त)	Guilty
दौरा	Sessions
दौरा अदालत में मुकदमा	Sessions trial
दौरा का प्रोग्राम	Tour programme
दौराजज	Sessions Judge
दौरा न्यायगृह	Sessions House
द्राष्टिक संकेत	Visual signalling
उपविभाग	Section
द्वारपट	Leaves of door
द्विपारी प्रथा	Double shift system
द्विमुखी कृमि	Amphistome worm
द्विवर्षीय	Biennial
द्विवार्षिक	Biennial
द्विविभाजन	Bifurcation
द्वेषजनक	Invidious

ध

धन तथा ऋण का स्मृति पत्र	Plus & minus memo
धनात्मक	Positive
धनादेश	Cheque
धनुर्वाद	Tetanus
धमनी	Artery
धरणी	Joist
धरोहर	Deposit
धर्म-मूर्ति	My Lord
धवनी	Flush latrine
धारा	Section
धारा के अधीन	Under section
धावक (हरकारा)	Runner
धूलरोक	Dust-proof
धृतवार्डर	Warder reserve
धृतदल रक्षिगण	Reservists
ध्वनि शास्त्र	Acoustics
धोखादेही से बचाने की रोकथाम	Check against fraud

न

नई परती	New fallow
नकद फीस	A fee in cash
नकद भुगतान	Cash payment
नकदी लगान	Cash rents
नगदी लगान	Cash Outlay
नगरपालिका	Municipality
नगर योजक सड़क	Arterial road
नजीर का हवाला	Citations
नत्थी (मिसिल, नस्ती)	File
नत्थी	Annexure
नदमट (कछार)	Alluvial

न पालन करना	Non-compliance
नभ-सेना	Air-force
नमना	Representative fraction
नये सिरे से	De Novp
नरमी (तार खींचे जाने की क्षमता)	Ductility
नलकूप	Tube well
नवीकर कोर्स	Refresher's course
नवीकरण	Renewal
नस्ती पंजी	File register
नस्या (टग)	Tag
नहर की सिंचाई	Canal irrigation
नहर डिविजन अधिकारी	Divisional canal Officer
नाक (टोंटी)	Nozzle
नागरिक (दीवानी)	Civil
नाप पुस्तक	Measurement book
नाभि	Focus
नाम सूची	Nominal roll
नाम निवेश	Enrolment
नामकरण	Nomenclature
नाम की सूचना	Debit advice
नाम और जमा	Debit and Credit
नाम संक्रम सूचना	Advice of Credit Transfer
नाल (टोंटी)	Jet
नालीदार	Corrugated
नावन्तरण	Trans-shipment
नाविक सेना	Naval Force
निकम्मा	Unserviceable
निकाली हुई धनराशि	Withdrawal of amount
निकास	Outlet
निकासा	Bay window
निकासी	Discharge of water
निक्षेपण	Bailment
निकृन्त (स्टेन्सिल)	Stencil
निगरानी	Surveillance, Revision
निचय	Stock
निधि	Fund
निनाल	Syphon
निन्दा	Censure
निपटारा पत्र	Composition deed
निबटाया	Disposed off
नियत	Prescribed
नियतन	Allocation
नियत फारम	Prescribed form
नियत भत्ता	Contract allowance
नियन्त्रक अधिकारी	Controlling Officer
नियन्त्रण परिवर्तन	Transfer of control
नियम पत्र	Deed of agreement
नियमबद्ध विक्रय	Contract of sale
नियम भंजन	Breach of rule
नियम विरुद्ध	Abnormal, Irregular
नियमानुरूप	Pro-forma
नियामक	Regulator
नियुक्ति विभाग	human resources department
निरर्थक किया हुआ (मंसूख किया हुआ)	Annulled
निरसन (मंसूखी)	Revocation, Cancellation
निरस्त करना	Revoke
निराई	Weeding
निरीक्षक	Visitor, Inspector

निरीक्षण	Inspection
निरीक्षण पुस्तक	Visitors' book
निरीक्षण शुल्क	Inspection fee
निरोगिता प्रमाणपत्र	Fitness certificate
निरोध करना	Impound
निरंतर	Consecutive
निलंबन	Suspension
निवारक	Preventive
निवास प्रतिबंध	Obligation of residence
निविदा (टेंडर)	Tender
निवेश	Impression (copy)
निवेशन (छावनी)	Encampment
निवेशन	Halt
निवेशन (भत्ता)	Halting (allowance)
निवेश संभार	Camp equipage
निवेश स्थल	Encamping ground
निवेश सज्जा	Camp equipment
निवृत्ति	Retirement
निवृत्ति पूर्व छुट्टी	Leave preparatory to retirement
निवृत्ति वेतन	Pension
निवृत्ति वेतनी	Pensioner
निर्गम मूल्य	Issue Price
निर्गमन	Issues
निर्णय	Decision, Finding, Judgment
निर्णय लेखक	Judgment writer
निर्णय का पुनर्निरीक्षण	Review of judgment
निर्णीत	Decided
निर्णीत ऋणी	Judgment-debtor
निर्दान (निराई)	Weeding
निर्दान चिप्पी	Weeding label
निर्दान सूची	Weeding list
निर्दिष्ट	Specific
निर्दिष्ट करना	Earmark
निर्दिष्ट भाग	Allotment
निर्देश	Direction
निर्देशिनी	Directory
निर्दान पर्ची	Weeding slip
निर्धन	Indigent
निर्धारित वेतन क्रम	Scale prescribed
निर्मुक्ति (बेदखली)	Ejectment
निर्माण	Manufiicture
निर्माण क्रिया	Manufacturing process
निर्यात	Export
निर्वर्तन योग्य	Executable
निवर्तन	Disposal
निर्वाचनाध्यक्ष	Presiding officer
निर्वासन (देश निकाला)	Deportation
निर्वाह अनुदान	Subsistance grant
निर्वाह भत्ता	Subsistence allowance
निर्वाही	Executive
निष्क्रयवर्ति, (वेतन चिट्ठा)	Acquittance roll
निष्कास	Egress
निष्पादन	Execution (as of decree)
निष्पादन की इन्कारी	Denial of execution
निष्प्रभाव और निरर्थक	Null and void
निषेध	Prohibition
निषेधाधिकार	Veto
निषेधाज्ञा	Injunction
न्यायालय	Court of law

न्यायालय अपमान	Contempt of Court
न्यायालय की आज्ञा से	By order of the Court
न्यायालय उपस्थितिपत्र	Appearance slips
न्यायालय द्वारा रोक	Restraint by Court
न्यायालय सम्बन्धी	Forensic
न्यायालयिक प्राधिकारी	Judicial authority
न्यायाधिकार	Judicature
न्यायाधिकारी वर्ग	Judiciary
न्यायिक कार्यवाही	Judicial proceeding
न्यायिक निर्णय	Adjudication
न्यायिक विचारण	Judicial investigation
न्यायेतर स्टाम्प	Non Judicial Stamp
न्यायोचित दातव्य	Legitimate dues
न्याय्य	Legitimate
न्यायता	Equity
न्यूनकोण	Acute angle
न्याय पत्रग्राही (डिगरीदार)	Decree-holder
न्याय विभाग	Judicial Department
न्याय वैफल्य	Miscarriage of Justice
न्याय शुल्क	Court fees
न्याय शुल्क चिप्पी	Court fee label
न्याय सम्बन्धी	Judicial
न्याय शुल्क विधान	Court fees act
न्यायाधीश गण	Full Bench
न्यायालयेत्तर	Non Judicial
न्याय पत्र	Decree
नीचे	Infra
नीला थोथा (तूतिया)	Blue Vitriol
नींव	Basement
नौकरी की शर्त	Condition of service
नौचालन	Navigation
नौभार	Cargo

प

पक्का करना	Confirmation
पक्की (सड़क)	Metalled (Road)
पक्षपात	Prejudice
पक्षियों की यक्ष्मा परीक्षा	A vain Tuberculosis test
पचपन साला	Superannuation
पचपन साले की तारीख	Superannuation (date of)
पटरी (पाया)	Stave
पटीरन	Lintel
पट्टा	Lease
पट्टा इस्तमरारी	Tenure in perpetuity
पट्टा करने वाला	Lessor
पट्टा समर्पण पत्र	Surrender of lease
पट्टिका	Plate
पट्टीदारी	Tenure in severality
पट्टे	Leases
पट्टे की भूमि	Lease hold
पट्टेदार	Lessee
पड़ोस	Vicinity
पणायन (लेनदेन)	Transaction
पतला अनाज	Shrivelled grain
पताका दंड	Flag staff
पत्री वर्ष	Calendar year
पथदर्शक योजना	Pilot scheme
पद (ओहदा)	Post, Rank
पद कर्तव्य	Function
पद कारणात्	Ex-officio
पदकारणात् उपपंजीयक	Ex-officio Sub-Registrar
पदच्यूति	Dismissal
पद धारणा	Incumbency
पदनाम, ओहदा	Designation

पदभार	Charge of office
पद स्थापन	Creation (of post)
पदाति	Infantry
पदावनति	Reduction
पदिक	Pedestrian
पदेन	Ex-officio
पदोन्नति	Promotion
परकार	Compass (pair of)
पर नोटिस तामील करना	To serve notice on
परम पूज्य	Reverend
पर राष्ट्रिक	Foreigner
पर हितकारी प्रन्यास	Benevolent trust
पराकृत (करना)	Set aside
परिकल्पक	Designer
परिकल्पना	Design
परिकल्पित	Designed
परिगणित	Scheduled
परिचर	Attendant
परिचारक	Attendant
परिणामस्वरूप	In consequence
परितोष	Gratification
परित्याग दस्तबरदारी	Relinquishment
परिदेवना	Complaint
परिधिस्थ	Aide-de-camp
परिपक्वता	Maturity
परिपत्र	Circular (letter)
परिमाप	Perimeter
परिमाण	Quantity, Volume
परिमार्जक	Cleaner
परिरक्षा	Preservation
परिलाभ	Emoluments
परिवाह	Escape (for surplus water)
परिव्यय उपसंक्षेप	Abstract of cost
परिशिष्ट	Appendix
परिश्रम	Industry, Labour
परिषद्	Council, Board
परिषद्यता	Fellowship
परिसम्पत (संपत्ति)	Assets
परीक्षण	Probation
परीक्ष्यमाण	Probationer
परीवर्त	Turbine
परेषणी	Consignee
पर्चीपुस्त	Slip book
पर्ण	Folio
पर्यवेक्षक	Supervisor
पर्याण	Saddle
पर्यादान	Appropriation
पलट	Conversion
पलटा करना	Commutation
पल्वल (पोखर)	Pool
पलायित दोषी	Fugitive criminal
पशुओं की नसलकशी का फार्म	Cattle Breeding farm
पशुचिकित्सा सहायक सर्जन	Veterinary Assistant Surgeon
पशुधन	Live stock
पशुपालन विभाग	Animal Husbandry Department
पशु प्रर्वधन क्रिया	Breeding operation
पशुवध यन्त्र	Cattle killer
पशुविज्ञान महाविद्यालय	Veterinary College
पहली दृष्टि में	Prima facie
पहचान	Identification
पहुँच	Access
पाक विषयक	Culinarv

पाताल जलपुंज	Ground water supplied
पात्रता	Eligibility
पाद	Quadrant
पपड़ी	Flake
पाया (संभा)	Pier
पारपत्र	Passport
पारप्रेषण	Transmit
पारस्परिक संविदा	Covenanty
पारस्परिकता	Reciprocity
पारिणामिक	Consequential
पारितोषिक प्रतिज्ञापत्र	Prize bonds
पारितोषिक व्यवस्थापन	Family arrangement
पारिश्रमिक	Remuneration
पारेषण	Transmission
पारंपरीय (पैतृक)	Hereditary
पार्श्व भित्ति	Side wall
पालन करते हुए	In compliance with
पालन करना	Abide by
पालनादेश	Compliance
पावती-पावनी	Acknowledgment due
पावती	Acknowledgment, Receipt
पांडुलेख (मसविदा)	Draft
पाँचा	Rake
पिघलाकर जोड़ना	Welding
पिचक	Stear
पिचकारी	Syringe
पिजापट्ट	Switch-board
पिंड	Lump
पिंडराशि	Lump-sum
पिटवा	Apron
पिठर (बायलर)	Boiler
पिस्सू	Fleas
पीठभू (कुर्सी)	Plinth
पीड़ित	Rolled (steel)
पीट्ट (चरबी)	Tallow
पुनर्ग्रहण	Resumption
पुनर्दर्शन	Review
पुनर्नवीकरण	Renovation
पुनर्नियुक्त	Re-employed
पुनर्नियक्ति	Re-employment
पुनर्योग	Re-totalling
पुनरवलोकन	Review
पुनरावृत्ति	Revision
पुनः पर्यादान	Re-appropriation
पुनः पंजीयन	Re-registration
पुनः रचना	Re-constitution
पुनः शस्त्रीकरण	Re-armament
पुनः स्थापन	Re-establishment, Re-instatement
पुनः संगठन	Re-organisation
पुरातत्त्व विभाग	Archaeological department
पुरानी परती	Old fallow
पुरीप (विष्ठा)	Excreta
पुरः स्थापना	Introduction
पुश्तीवान	Batten
पुस्त संक्रम	Book transfer
पूँजीकृत	Capitalized
पूँजी परिव्यय	Capital, Cash
पूज्य	Reverend
पूतिक	Rotten
पूरक लेख्य	Supplemental deed
पूरी तरह उपचार करना	Deal thoroughly

पूर्णता (अंतिमता)	Finality
पूर्णयोग	Grand total
पूर्ण बिक्री	Turn over
पूर्व	Ante
पूर्वक्रयाधिकार (हकशफा)	Pre-emption, Right of pre-emption
पूर्वतटीय ज्वर	East coast fever
पूर्वता (आदिता)	Precedence
पूर्वता अधिपत्र	Warrant of precedence
पूर्व दृष्टांत	Antecedent, precedent
पूर्वदोष वेंचन	Pre-censorship
पूर्व प्रभाव	Retrospective effect
पूर्व प्रभाव सहित	With retrospective effect
पूर्वानुदर्शन	Reconnaissance
पूर्वानुमान	Forecast
पूर्वाह्न	Fore-noon
पूर्वी	Oriental
पूर्वोपाय	Precaution
पूर्वापायी कोष	Provident fund
पृष्ठ लेख	Endorsement
पृष्ठ विवरण	Topography
पृष्ठांकन	Endorsement
पेंशन का संराशिकरण	Commutation of pension
पैत्तिक ज्वर (अश्व)	Bilious fever (horse)
पैतृक संपत्ति	Ancestral property
पोट्टलिका (पार्सल)	Parcel
पोतपति	Master of ship
पोषक	Feeder
पोषक क्षेत्र	Catchment
पोषक माध्यम	Culture medium
पौधशाला	Nursery

पंककिट्ट	Silt
पंकार (बंध)	Embankment
पंक्ति	Alignment
पंक्तिकरण	Alignment
पंक्तिमध्य लेख	Interlination
पंच (मध्यस्थ)	Arbitrator
पंच निर्णय	Award
पंचमंडल	Arbitration, Tribunal
पंचवर्षीय	Quinquennial
पंचायत	Arbitration
पंचांग मास	Calendar month
पंजी	Register
पंजीयक	Registrar
पंजीयन	Registration
पंजीयित	Registered
प्रकाशना (प्रख्यापना)	Publicity
प्रकीर्ण (विविध)	Miscellaneous
प्रक्रम	Procedure
प्रक्षेपण	Projection
प्रगति	Headway
प्रगाढ़ता	Intensity
प्रगुणता अर्गल	Efficiency bar
प्रचंड	Virulent
प्रचार	Propaganda
प्रच्छना	Interrogation, Inquiry
प्रति (बनाम)	Versus
प्रति आपत्ति	Cross objection
प्रति उपकुलपति	Pro-vice-chancellor
प्रतिकर (क्षतिपूर्ति)	Compensation
प्रतिकर भत्ता	Compensatory allowance
प्रतिकाश	Reflection
प्रतिकाशक	Reflector

प्रतिग्राहक	Receiver
प्रतिज्ञा, प्रतिज्ञान	Affirmation
प्रतिज्ञापत्र	Bond
प्रतिदान	Returning
प्रतिधारण	Retention
प्रतिनिधि	Representative
प्रतिनिधि पत्र	Power of attorney
प्रतिनियुक्ति (प्रतिनिधि मण्डल)	Deputation
प्रतिनियुक्ति भत्ता	Deputation (duty) allowance
प्रतिपक्ष	Opposite party
प्रतिपरीक्षा	Cross examination
प्रतिपर्ण (मुसन्ना)	Counterfoil
प्रतिपुरुष	Proxy, Locum tenens
प्रतिबन्ध	Ban
प्रतिबन्धात्मक वाक्य खण्ड	Proviso
प्रतिबन्धित न्यायपत्र	Decree nisi
प्रतिभाव्य	Bailable
प्रतिभू	Security (of a person) Bail order
प्रतिभूति	Security, Bail, Surety
प्रतिभू पत्र	Bail bond, Security bond
प्रतिमान	Pattern
प्रतियोगिता परीक्षा	Competitive examination
प्रतिरक्षा विभाग	Defence Department
प्रतिरक्षा	Defence
प्रतिरूप	Counterpart
प्रतिरोध	Resistance
प्रतिलब्धि	Recovery
प्रतिलिपि (मुसन्ना)	Counterpart, Copy
प्रतिलिपिक	Copyist
प्रतिलिपिक यन्त्र	Pantographer
प्रतिलिपि पर शुल्क	Duty on counterpart or duplicate
प्रतिलिपि मुद्रित पत्र	Copy stamped papers
प्रतिलिपि विभाग	Copying Department
प्रतिलेखन	Transcription
प्रतिवाद साक्षी	Defence witness
प्रतिवादी	Defendant
प्रतिवेदन	Renort
प्रतिव्यक्ति प्रभार	Capitation charges
प्रतिशपथ पत्र	Counter affidavit
प्रतिष्ठापन	Installation
प्रतिष्ठापनिक	Inaugural
प्रतिसेकंड घनफुट	Cusecs
प्रतिस्थापन	Replacement
प्रतिस्थानी बनने के लिए प्रार्थनापत्र	Substitution application
प्रतिहस्ताक्षर	Counter signature
प्रतीक	Token
प्रतीप दर	Inverse rate
प्रत्यक्ष व्यय	Direct charge
प्रत्यक्ष रोगग्रस्त	Clinically affected
प्रत्युत्तर	Rejoinder
प्रत्यय	Suffix
प्रत्यधिकार	Encroachment
प्रत्ययपत्र	Letter of credit
प्रत्याक्षेप	Cross objection
प्रत्यादान	Resumption
प्रत्यायुक्त	Depute
प्रत्यायुक्ति	Delegation
प्रत्यावर्तन	Reversion

प्रत्याशा	Anticipation
प्रत्याशिक	Anticipator
प्रत्याशित	Anticipated
प्रत्याशित अधिक व्यय और बचत	Anticipated excess and savings
प्रत्यासन्न	Imminent
प्रामि दृष्टि सिद्ध	Prima facie
प्रथमोपचार	First aid
प्रथानुसार	Conventionally
प्रदर्शन	Display
प्रदर्शित वस्तु	Exhibit
प्रदान	Vesting
प्रदान पत्र	Instrument of gift
प्रदेश	Region
प्रधान	Preponderance
प्रधान प्रेरक	Prime mover
प्रन्यास घोषणा	Declaration of trust
प्रन्यास वृत्तिदान	Trust endowment
प्रन्यास सम्पत्ति	Trust property
प्रबंधक	Manager
प्रबंधक विवरण पत्र	Return
प्रबंधाधिकार पत्र	Letter of administration
प्रभार शीर्षक पर डाला जाये	The charge should be debited to the head
प्रभार	Charge
प्रभाव रेखा	Influence line
प्रभावित करना	Affect
प्रमाणक	Voucher
प्रमाण भार	Burden of proof
प्रमाणित अवतरण	Certified extract
प्रमाणीकरण	Verification, Authentication, Certification
प्रमाण	Standard
प्रमाण से ऊपर	Above standard
प्रमेय (साध्य)	Theorem
प्रयोगात्मक	Experimental
प्रलंबन	Suspension
प्रवर समिति	Select committee
प्रवर स्थापना	Superior staff
प्रवाहमान ईक्षण	Stream gauging observation
प्रविधि	Technique
प्रविष्टि	Entry
प्रवीण	Proficient
प्रवीण श्रम	Skilled labour
प्रवेश (द्वार)	Ingress, Inlets
प्रवेश परिषद्	Admission board
प्रशासक	Administrator
प्रशासकीय	Administrative
प्रशासकीय प्रतिज्ञापत्र	Administrative bond
प्रशासकीय विभाग	Administrative department
प्रशासन	Administration
प्रश्नावली	Questionnaire
प्रसूति छुट्टी	Maternity leave
प्रसूति चिकित्सालय	Maternity hospital
प्रसंग	Context
प्रसंधि	Confederacy
प्रस्ताव	Resolution, Proposal
प्रस्तावना	Preamble, Introduction
प्रस्तावित नकशा	Proposition statement
प्रस्तावित विवरण	Proposition statement
प्रस्तुत	Presented, Submitted

प्रस्तुति	Production (as a document)
प्रहरी	Sentry
प्राङ्‌गन्याय	Res-Judicata
प्राचीन अवशेष	Antiquities
प्राणदण्ड	Capital sentence
प्रणिधि	Care (attention)
प्राथमिक इकाई	Primary unit
प्रादेशिक	Regional
प्रादेशिक ढंग पर लागू होना	Territorial application
प्राधिकारी वर्ग	Authority
प्राधिकृत अभिकर्ता	Authorised agent
प्राप्ति	Acquisition
प्राप्ति पंजी	Receipt register
प्राप्ति स्वीकार	Acknowledgment
प्राप्य	Dues
प्रामाणिक	Standard, Bonafide
प्रामणिक करना	Standardization
प्रारंभिक	Preliminary
प्रारंभिक सूचना रपट	First Information Report
प्रार्थी	Applicant
प्राविधिक	Technical
प्राविधिक स्वीकृति	Technical sanction
प्रासंगिक	Contingent
प्रासंगिक व्यय	Contingency
प्रिवी कौंसिल	Privy Council
प्रेरणा (प्रलोभन)	Inducement
प्रेषण	Consignment
प्रेषित	Forwarded
प्रोत्साहन	Stimulus
प्रौढ़ (परिपक्व)	Mature

फ

फटकन	Cleaning losses
फटाव	Rupture
फन्नी	Wedge
फरार	Absconding
फसल की प्रत्याशा	Crop prospects
फालतू	Spare
फार्मों का संरक्षण और दिया जाना	Custody & Supply of forms
फाँसी	Execution
फाँसी का (कैदी)	Condemned
फोड़ा	Tumour
फौज, फौजी दस्ते	Troops
फौजी टोपी	Cap
फीता	Fillet
फीसमाफी	Sizarship

ब

बचन पत्र	Pronote
बटमारी	Dacoity
बटालियन	Battalion
बट्टे की जाँच पड़ताल	Check of discount
बट्टा	Discount
बट्टे खाते डालना	Write-off
बट्टे पर (से)	At a discount
बड़ा शीर्षक	Major head
बढ़ती पर (से)	At a premium
बदरावण रोग	Coccidiosis
बदली	Transfer
बधिया करना	Castration
बन्दूक की मक्खी	Sight
बन्दूकदार छड़ी	Walking stick gun
बन्दीकरण	Apprehension

बन्दी करना	Apprehend
बन्धक कर्ता	Mortgagor
बन्धक ग्राही	Mortgagee
बम्बा (पटी हुई नाली)	Conduit
बरमा	Auger
बरसाती	Water proof
बराबर करना	Counter balance
बलात ग्रहण	Extortion
बसन्त (ऋतुराज)	Florescence
बस्ताबरदार	Bundle Lifter
बहाव	Aflux
बहिर्परजीवी	Ectozoa
बहीखाता	Ledger
बहुभुज	Polygon
बहुमत	Majority
बहुविधवाद	Multifarious suit
बाद की कार्यवाही	Subsequent proceeding
बाँध	Weir, Barrage
बारद्योतक	Co-efficient
बारूद	Gunpowder
बारंग (डंडी)	Shank
बालबीर (सेनोछात्र)	Cadet
बाप्प शील	Volatile
बिगाड़ना	Enfacement
बिरंजी	Tack
बिलकुल	In toto
बिल्ला	Chevron, Badge, Stripe
बिसहरिया	Authrax
बीच का पूर्वानुमान	Intermediate forecast
बीजक	Invoice
बीज छाग	Stud buck
बीजाज	Stud ram
बीजाश्व (घुड़साँड़)	Horse stallion
बुलेटिन	Bulletin
बेगार	Forced labour
गेड़ी	Fetter
बेतार तार चालक	Wireless operator
बेदखली	Ejectment
बेदन	Rinderpest
बेब्याज	Interest-free
बेलन	Cylinder
बैंक की हुंडी	Bank draft
बैठक (बरोठा)	Parlour
बोझ	Weighment
बोया हुआ क्षेत्रफल	Cropped area
ब्योरेवार बिल	Detailed bill
बौछार	Volley
बंध (बमस्सुक)	Bond
बंधक	Mortgage
बंधक पत्र	Mortgage bond
बंधक मोक्षण प्रतिरोध	Foreclosure of mortgage
बंधकमोचन	Redemption of mortgage
बंधन (कैद)	Confinement

भ

भगोड़ा	Absconder
भत्ता	Allowance
भबका	Boiler
भरती	Recruitment
भरती रोगी	Indoor patient
भवन भाग (घर)	Tenement
भवन्निष्ठ	Yours truly, Yours sincerely, faithfully

भस्त्रका	Bellows
भंडक (माल)	Goods
मांडकशुल्क	Tariff
भांडागारिक	Storeman
भाजन (आधान)	Receptacle
भाड़ाक्रय	Hire purchase
भारतवासी	Native of India
भारतीय उत्तराधिकार विधान	Indian Succession Act
भारतीय जनपद भृत्या	Indian Civil Service
भारतीय दण्ड संहिता	Indian Penal Code
भारतीय विवाह विच्छेद विधान	Indian Divorce Act
भारतीय शस्त्र विधान	Indian Arms Act
भारतीय साक्ष्य विधान	Indian Evidence Act
भारतीय सेना विधान	Indian Army Act
भारधारक बढ़ाव	Corbel
भार-वृद्धि	Extension of load
भारित	Loaded
भारी प्रमाद	Gross negligence
भावी	Prospective
भित्ति भीतर	Intramural
भिन्नता	Discrepancy
भिश्ती	Water carrier
भुगतान	Payment
भुगतानकारी अधिकारी	Disbursing officer
भुगतान प्राधिकारी	Disbursing authority
भूअभिलेख लेखक	Land record clerk
भूअभिलेख सार संग्रह	Land record manual
भूगर्भ अनुदर्शन	Geological survey
भूतपूर्व असामी	Ex-tenant
भूमाप और भूव्यवस्था	Survey and Settlement
भूमाप फलक	Survey sheet
भूमाक शिक्षक	Survey instructor
भूमि अधिकार	Tenancy
भूमि का अधिकारत्याग	Relinquishment of land
भूमि खण्ड	Tract
भूमि प्रविष्ट पुल	Pile bridge
भूमि वर्गीकारक	Soil classifier
भूमि सुधार ऋण विधान	Land Improvement Loans Act
भूमि सुधारार्थ ऋण	Land Improvement loan
भू राजस्व	Land revenue
भू लेखा	Land record
भू लेखा विभाग	Land record department
भूव्यवस्था	Settlement
भूसम्पत्ति	Landed property, Estate
भूस्वामी	Landlord
भृति	Wage
भृति अर्जन योजना	Wage earning scheme
भेंट	Visitation
भेदगुणक	Diversity factor
भोगोधिकार (दखीलकारी)	Occupancy right
भोजन व्यय	Diet money
भौतिक परिसम्पत्	Physical assets
भंग करना	Infringement
भ्रष्टाचार	Corruption

म

मकान किराया भत्ता	House rent allowance
मक्खन-मलाई शाला	Creamery
मक्खी रोक	Fly-proof

मजदूर	Wage earner
मतदत्त दिष्टि	Voted allotment
मतभेद	Difference of opinion
मत्स्य पट्टिका	Fish plate
मत्स्यारौह सीढ़ी	Fish ladder
मद	Item
मद्यनिषेध	Prohibition
मध्यम भार	Medium pressure
मध्यवर्ती	Interim
मध्वर्ती स्थगन	Interim stay
मनोनीत	Designate
मरणासन्न कथन	Dying declaration
मरोड़ (ऐंठन)	Torsion
मलकूप	Sink
मलत्याग	Faecal discharge
मवाद पड़ा हुआ घाव	Supporating lesion
मसूरी, मसूरी लाल	Vaccine
महराब	Intrados
महाअधिवक्ता	Advocate General
महाकारानिरीक्षक	Inspector General of Prisons
महानिरीक्षक	Inspector General
महामान्य (महामहिम)	His Excellency
महामारी	Epidemic disease
महा प्रबंधक	Administrator General
महाप्लवस्तर चिह्न	High flood level
महालेखाकार	Accountant General
महाशिला	Boulders
माँग	Demand, Requisition
माँग पत्र	Indent
मातृका	Matron
मादक द्रव्य	Intoxicating drug
माध्य (औसत)	Mean
माध्यमिक	Intermediate
माध्य वेतन	Average pay
मानचित्र	Plan
मानचित्र	Ribands (of decorations & medals), Sash and banner
मानदेय	Honorarium
मानहानि	Defamation, Contempt
माना हुआ लगान	Assumed rent
मान्यता	Recognition
मान्यता प्राप्त अभिकर्ता	Recognised agent
माप	Modulus
मापक (मीटर)	Meter
माल	Revenue
माल अधिपत्र	Warrant for goods
माल का स्टाम्प	Revenue stamp
मालगुजारी	Land revenue
माल प्रशासक	Revenue administrator
माल बोर्ड	Board of revenue
माल विभाग की रिपोर्ट	Revenue administration report
मालस्थापना	Revenue Establishment
मालियत जमाबन्दी	Rental
मालीयत्त	Valuation
मासिक उपसंक्षेप	Monthly abstract
मासिक विवरणपत्र	Monthly return
मियान	Scabbard
मिलावट	Adulteration

मिल्कियत अमीन	Tenure, Land tenure
मिश्रक	Compounder, Mixer
मीटर वाचक	Meter reader
मुकदमे का प्रकार	Nature of the case
मुकदम की पैरवी करना	To defend the case
मुकदम में कागजात दाखिल करना	Filing of document
मुकदमों को सूचीगत करना	Listing of cases
मुकाबिल दावा	Counter claim
मुक्ति (छूट)	Exemption
मुखचित्र	Frontis piece
मुख्य आयुक्त	Chief Commissioner
मुख्य धरणी	Principal rafter
मुखावरण	Mask
मुख्य नियन्त्रक राजस्व प्राधिकारी	Chief controlling revenue authority
मुख्य न्यायाधीश	Chief Justice
मुख्य परिवर्तन	Material change
मुख्य स्थान	Headquarter
मुख्यालय	Headquarters
मुचलका	Recognizance
मुद्रलेखक	Typist
मुद्रलेखन	Type writing
मुद्रा (आसन)	Posture
मुद्रांक नियन्त्रक	Controller of stamps
मुद्रांकित स्टाम्प	Impressed stamp
मुद्रास्फीति	Inflation
मुद्रास्फीतिरोधक	Anti-inflatory
मुवक्किल	Client
मुहर	Seal
मूर्तिकर्म	Sculpture
मूल	Original
मूलकूपन	Basic coupon
मूलधन	Principal money
मूलपद	Substantive post
मूल रचना	Cadre
मूल वेतन	Substantive pay
मूल्य	Value
मूल्यवान	Denomination
मूल्यानुसार	Ad valorem
मृत्यु विचारणा	Inquest
मौखिक	Verbal
मौखिक परीक्षा	Viva voce
मौखिक साक्ष्य	Oral evidence
मौलिक	Fundamental
मौलिक नियम	Fundamental rule
मौलिक पथप्रदर्शनी	Fundamental guide book
मंडूर (जंग)	Rust
मंत्रण	Counsel
मंत्रणा अधिकारी	Advisory officer
मंसूखी	Repeal

य

यक्ष्मा परीक्षा	Tuberculin test
यथाचार	Formal
यथानियम उत्तरवादी	Proforma respondent
यथानियम चेतावनी	Formal warning
यथापूर्व कर देना	Restitution
यथावत्	Duly
यथाविधि स्वीकृति	Duly approved
यथाशीघ्र	At your earliest convenience, As early as possible

यथासमय	In due course
यथोचित	Adequate
यथोचित टिकट लगा हुआ	Duly stamped
यन्त्र (औजार)	Appliance
यन्त्र-कलाप	Apparatus
यन्त्रजात	Apparatus (for a particular experiment)
यन्त्रजाल (यन्त्र कलाप)	Apparatus (as a whole)
यातायात	Traffic, Communication
यात्रा भत्ता	Travelling allowance
युद्धोत्तर	Post-war
योग	Aggregate
योग पंजी	Totalling register
योग्यकारी सेवा की शर्त	Condition of qualifying service
योग्यता	Competency
योग्य (समर्थ)	Competent
योग्य पात्र	Eligible
योजना	Project, Scheme
योधागार	Barrack

र

रकाब	Stirrup
रक्त तन्तु	Fibrin
रक्षक वर्ग	Escort
रक्षा	Protection
रक्षित	Reserve
रक्षी (तिलंगा)	Constable
रखरखाव	Maintenance
रखरखाव निरीक्षक	Maintenance Inspector
रखरखाव अधिकारी	Maintenance officer
रचनात्मक	Creative
रजबहा	Distributory
रद्द किया गया	Cancelled
रद्द किया हुआ लेखपत्र	Discredited document
रद्द करने वाला अधिकारी	Cancelling officer
रपट	Report
रसकपूर	Corrosive sublimate
रसीद बही	Receipt book
रेहन बन्धक	Mortgage
रंगमान (रंग)	Shade
रंजक	Painter
राखिया	Ashman
राज	Mason
राजक्षमा	Amnesty
राजगीरी	Masonry
राजच्युत करना	Depose
राजदया	Clemency
राजदया अपील	Letters patent appeal
राजद्रोह	Sedition
राजपत्र (गजट)	Gazette
राजपत्रित अधिकारी	Gazetted Officer
राजमन्त्री	Secretary of state
राजमार्ग	Highway
राजस्व	Revenue
राजस्व विषयक	Fiscal
राजसंघ	Confederacy
राजसाक्षी	Approver
साजसात् किया माल	Escheat
राजसात्करण	Confiscation
राज्य निष्ठा शपथ	Oath of allegiance

राज्य परषिद्	Council of State
राज्यपाल	Governor
राल	Bitumen
राष्ट्रीयकरण	Nationalization
राष्ट्रीय सेवा	National Service
रास्ता	Post
रास्ते से हटना	Deviate
रिक्त स्थान	Vacancy
रिक्ति	Vacancy
रिक्थ (वसीयत)	Will
रिक्थपत्रों का संरक्षण	Custody of wills
रिक्थ साधक	Executor of will
रिक्थी	Legatee
रियायतें	Concessions
रियायती छुट्टी	Privilege leave
रीति	Process
रुक्का	Pronote
रुचि	Option
रुझान	Affinity
रुद्धगति	Brake speed
रुपये का बँटवारा	Allocation of fund
रुपये का लगाना	Investment
रुपये की वापसी	Refund
रूप (ढाँचा)	Skeleton form
रूपपत्र (फार्म)	Form
रूपपरिवर्तक	Transformer
रूपान्तर	Transformation
रोक	Strut
रोकना	Withhold
रोकड़ की पेटी	Cash chest
रोकड़ बही	Cash book
रोकड़ बाकी	Cash balance
रोक रखने की लागत	Holding cost
रोग फैलाने का स्थान	Scene of outbreak
रोगज वृद्धि	Malignant growth
रोग विषयक	Clinical
रोग विषयक नमूने	Pathological specimens
रोगशास्त्र	Pathology
रोगहर उपाय	Curative measure
रोगाणु नाशक	Disinfectant
रोटी कपड़े का दावा	Suit for maintenance
रोड़ा (कंकड़)	Gravel
रोड़ी (छान)	Pebble

ल

लकीरी	Linear
लक्षण	Symptoms
लगभग क्षेत्रफल	Approximate areas
लगान उगाहना	Levy
लगान का नकशा	Rent statement
लगान में कमी	Abatement of rent
लगाम (दहाना)	Bit, Bit-Head, Bit-Rims
लघु स्थापना	Petty establishment
लघुवाद न्यायालय	Small Causes Court
लघुहस्ताक्षरित	Initialled
लटकन (झूमका)	Pendant, Hanger
लसीका ग्रन्थि	Lymphatic glands
लंगर	Anchor bolt
लँगड़िया	Black quarter
अम्बमान	Pending
लम्बमानता	Pendency
लाइन के बीच में लिखना	Inter-lineation
लागत	Outlay
लाघवकारक	Derogatory

लाठी	Truncheon
लाभांश	Bonus
लालमूत्र रोग	Cattle prioplasmose, or Red water
लिखा-पढ़ा गया लेखपत्र	Executed document
लिखित उत्तरवाद	Written statement
लिपि	Script
लेखन सामग्री	Stationery
लेखपत्र (लेख्य)	Document
लेख्यप्रमाणक	Notary public
लेख्यात्मक	Documentary
लेखा (गणना)	Account
लेखा परीक्षा अधिकारी	Audit officer
लेखा परीक्षा आपत्ति	Audit objection
लेखा परीक्षक	Auditor
लेखा महापरीक्षक	Auditor General
लेखा परीक्षा	Audit
लेखा शीर्षक	Head of account
लोप	Disappearance
लौटकालर	Turn down collar

व

वक्फ	Waqf
वक्र	Curve
वक्र (पीछे को, उलटा)	Retrograde (Motion)
वक्षस्थल	Thorax
वधस्थान	Gallows
वयस प्रतिबंध	Age limit
वयस्क	Major
वरण	Selection
वरणीयता	Eligibility
वरीवत मिस्त्री	Turbine mistri
वर्ग समीकरण	Quadratic equation
वर्गीकरण	Classification
वर्जित	Excepted
वर्णन	Statement
वर्णनवर्ति	Descriptive roll
वर्तमान पड़ती	Current fallow
वर्तमान स्टाक	Stock-in-hand
वर्तुलाकार जीव	Oval or rounded creature
वर्दी	Uniform
वर्धमान वेतन	Progressive pay
वर्षा की दशा	Character of rainfall
वर्षामापक	Rain gauge
वसूल लागत	Cost realized
वसूली छोड़ देना	Waive the recovery
वहन पत्र	Bill of lading
वाक्य खण्ड	Clause
वाणिज्य विभाग	Commercial department
वाणिज्य सम्बन्धी	Commercial
वाद	Suit, case
वाद, अर्जीदावा	Plaint
वाद (नालिश)	Suit
वादपत्र (अर्जी दावा)	Plaint
वादमूल्य विधान	Suit Valuation Act
वाद स्थगन	Stay of suit
वादी	Plaintiff
वापसी	Withdrawal
वायुसंचालित बन्दूक	Air gun
वायु संचार	Ventilation
वायुभार मापक	Barometer
वारंवारता	Frequency
वार्डर	Warder
वार्षिक वृत्ति प्रतिज्ञापत्र	Annuity Bond
वास्तविक अन्याय	Material injustice

वास्तविक आँकड़े	Actuals
वास्तविक क्षमता	Effective capacity
वास्तविक यात्रा व्यय	Actual travelling allowance
वास्तविक सम्पत्ति	Net assets
वास्तु विद्या (स्थापत्य)	Architecture
वाहन	Transport
विकलन	Debit
विकल्प	Option, Alternative
विकास मन्त्री	Development minister
विकेन्द्रीकरण	Decentralization
विकेन्द्रीकरण (समिति)	Decentralization committee
विक्रयपत्र, पट्टा	Deed (Sale, Lease)
विक्रय प्रमाणपत्र	Sale certificate
विकृत कायिक पदार्थ	Morbid material
विक्री का प्रस्ताव	Sale proposal
विक्षिप्त दोषी	Lunatic criminal
विखंडन करना	Repeal
विचारकालिक दाराभृति	Alimony pendentilite
विचार न्यायालय	Trial court
विचारार्थ	For consideration
विचाराधिकार	Authority of consideration
विचाराधिकार विधान	Jurisdiction Act
विचाराधीन	Under consideration
विचाराधीन बन्दी	Undertrial prisoner
विज्ञप्ति	Notification, Communique
वितरण	Disbursement, Distribution
विदेशी अपराधी का प्रत्यर्पण	Extradition
विदेशी मुद्रा	Foreign currency
विदेशी शाखा	Alien's branch
विद्यापरिषद्	Academy
विद्युत उत्पादन संस्थान	Generating station
विद्युत् प्रतिष्ठापन	Electrical installation
विद्युत् सज्जा	Electrical equipment
विधान	Act
विधानत:	De jure
विधायन (कानून)	Enactment
विधि	Procedure
विधि अनुकूल सभा	Lawful assembly
विधिकरण, विधिनिर्माण	Enactment
विधि प्रक्रम	Course of law
विधि भंग	Breach of law
विधि वक्ता	Barrister, Advocate, Lawyer
विधिविहित फार्म	Statutory form
विधेयक	Bill
विध्युपजीवी अभिभाषक	Legal practitioner
विनिमय	Exchange
विनिमयकरण पत्र	Exchange instrument
विनिमय क्षतिपूरक भत्ता	Exchange of compensation allowance
विनिमय दर	Rate of exchange
विनिमय पत्र	Exchange deed
विन्दुरेख	Graph
विन्दु रेखा	Dotted line
विपक्ष	Opposite party
विपत्ति	Calamity, Distress
विपरीत	Repugnant

विपणी (आपण)	Market
विप्रेषित धनराशि	Remittance
विभागाध्यक्ष	Head of the department
विभाजन	Allocation
विभिन्न	Various
विभेदक अक्षर	Distinguishing letter
विमोचन	Redemption
विरुद्ध	Against
विलापन	Cancellation
विलामत:	Vice versa
विवरण	Particular, Statement
विवरण प्रतिवेदन	Report
विवरण पत्र	Return (Statistics)
विवाद	Litigation
विवाद प्रश्नों को स्थिर करना	Framing of issues
विवादास्पद	Disputed
विवाह का रद्द किया जाना	Annulment of Marriage
विवाह प्रमाणपत्र	Marriage certificate
विवाह भंग	Marriage (Dissolution of)
विवाह विषयक पेशकार	Matrimonial reader
विवेक	Discretion
विवेकाधीन रजिस्टरी	Discretional registration
विषम	Odd
विषमार	Antidote
मवषय	Combination
विशिष्ट (सविशेष)	Particular
विशिष्ट अनुष्ठान	Specific performance
विशिष्ट क्षेत्र	Specific area
विशेष अभियोग अधिकारी	Special prosecuting officer
विशेष कार्य	Special duty
विशेष कार्यार्थ	On special duty
विशेष कार्याधिकारी	Officer on special duty
विशेषज्ञ	Expert
विशेष दूत	Special messenger
विशेष विषयक वेतन	Technical pay
विशेष वेतन	Special pay
विश्लेषक	Analyst
विश्लेषण	Analysis
विशेषाधिकार	Privilege
विशुद्ध प्रतिलिपि	Fair copy
विश्वास	Belief
विश्राम (छुट्टी)	Recess
विश्रामकोण	Angle of repose
विसंवाहक	Insulator
विसंवाहकस्तर	Insulation layer
विसहारिया	Anthrax
विस्फोटक पदार्थ विधान	Explosives Act
विहित (निर्धारित)	Prescribed
वृक्षरोपण विद्या	Arboriculture
वृत्त (व्यवसाय)	Profession
वृत्तान्त	Narrative
वृत्ति, पेशा	Occupation
वृद्धि	Enhancement
वेग	Velocity
वेगक्षय	Retardation
वेगवृद्धिकर	Acceleration
वेतन	Pay
वेतन कालक्रम	Time scale of pay
वेतन क्रम	Scale of pay
वेतन क्रम का संशोधन	Revision of scale of pay

वेतन लेखा	Pay account
वेतन वृद्धि	Increment
वेधनी	Perforator
वेष, वस्त्र	Dress
वेष नियमावली	Dress regulation
वैक्सीन भण्डार	Vaccine depot
वैक्सीन लसीका	Vaccinal lymph
वैतनिक	Stipendiary
वैद्युतिक	Electrician
वैधता	Validity
वैधानिक	Statuary
वैधानिक उत्तरदायित्व	Statuary Responsibility
वैध उद्बोधक	Legal Rememberancer
वैधिक	Legal
वैभागिक	Departmental
वैभागिक लेखा	Departmental account
वैयक्तिक प्रपंजी	Personal ledger
वैयक्तिक वेतन	Personal pay
वैयक्तिक स्वतन्त्रतारक्षक	Habeas Corpus
वैवाहिक अधिकार	Conjugal right
व्यक्तिगत उपस्थिति	Personal appearance
व्यय	Charge, Expenditure
व्यय पर नियन्त्रण	Control over expenditure
व्यय विवरण	Statement of expenditure
व्ययहरण	Defalcation
व्यवसाय वेतन	Trade pay
व्यवस्था	Provision (Budget)
व्यवस्था (नजीर)	Ruling
व्यवस्थापिका विभाग	Legislative department
व्यवस्थापिका सभा	Legislative assembly
व्यवस्था खण्डन पत्र	Settlement, revocation of
व्यवस्थान	Settlement
व्यवस्थापत्र	Instrument of Settlement
व्यवसाय	Vocation
व्यवस्था पुलिस	Traffic Police
व्यवहार (लेनदेन)	Transaction
व्याख्या	Interpretation
व्याख्यानात्मक अनुपूरक	Explanatory supplement
व्यापक संक्रामक रोग (पशु)	Epizootic
व्यापक संक्रामक रोग (मनुष्य)	Epidemic
व्यापार चिह्न	Trade mark
व्यायाम शिक्षक	P. T. Instructor
व्यायामशाला	Gymnasium
व्यांवसायिक	Vocational
व्यासिद्ध (विनिषिद्ध)	Contraband
व्यौरा	Specification

श

शक्त प्राधिकारी	Competent authority
शक्ति	Energy
शपथ पत्र	Affidavit
शपथपूर्वक साक्ष्य देना	Depose
शमन (न्यूनीकरण)	Mitigation
शरणार्थी	Refugee
शर्त	Condition
श्रमिकों का दैनिक नकशा	Daily labour return
शल्यवैद्य (सर्जन)	Surgeon

शवपरीक्षा	Post-mortem
शस्त्रागार	Magazine
शहरी	Urban
शंकु	Cone
शंकुकक्ष	Axis of a cone
शाखा	Faculty
शाखाकोठार	Branch depot
शांत होना	Abate
शांति	Peace
शांति-रक्षा दण्डनायक	Justice of the peace
शांति रक्षा आधिकरणिक	Justice of the Peace
शांति-भंग	Breach of peace
शारीरिक दण्ड	Corporal punishment
शाश्वत भत्ता	Perpetual allowance
शासित	Governed
शिक्षणाधीन अधिकारी	Officer under training
शिक्ष्यमाण	Apprentice
शिक्षण पाठचर्या	Courses of training
शिखर	Crest
शिखर खण्ड	Crown post
शिथिलता	Relaxation
शिथिलीकरण	Relaxation
शिथिलीकृत	Relaxed
शिररज्जु	Head rope
शिरस्त्राण	Helmet
शिलालेख	Inscription
शिल्पकार	Artisan
शिविर	Camp
शिशुवध	Infanticide
शिष्टमडण्ल	Delegation
शीर्ष	Vertex
शीर्षक और उपशीर्षक	Head and Sub-head
शीर्षस्तर नियामक	Head Regulator
शीर्ष शहतीर	Hip rafter
शुद्ध	Net
शुद्ध परिलाभ	Net emoluments
शुद्ध लाभ	Net profit
शुद्धिपत्र	Corrigendum
शुद्धि पर्ची	Correction slip
शुल्क	Duty
शुल्क गणना	Computation of fees
शून्य	Void
शून्यक (रिक्त)	Vacuum
शेष	Unexpired
श्रेणी	Category
श्लेष्क मुद्रांक	Adhesive stamp
शैथिल्य	Relaxation
शोधन (सुधार)	Correction

ष

षष्टक	Sextant

स

सकपट रजिस्ट्री को बचा लेना	Evasion of registration
सकल	Aggregate
सकल भार	Gross load
सकल वेतन	Gross salary
सक्रिय भत्ता	Active allowance
सगोत्र	Cognate
सचिव	Secretary
सज्जा	Equipment
सज्जा सूची	Equipment catalogue
सज्जा सारणी	Equipment table
सजातीय (समाधान)	Homogeneous
सटीक	Annotated
सड़न रोक रस	Antiseptic fluid

सत्यकार (बयाना)	Earnest money
सत्यशीलता	Integrity
सतर्कता	Caution
सद्भाव	Good Faith
सदाचार	Good behaviour
सत्यापन (जाँच)	Verification
सप्रतिबन्धक विक्रय	Conditional sale
सफाई का रजिस्टर	Cleaning register
सभाकक्ष	Lobby
सभाभवन	Auditorium
समकालिक	Concurrent
समतल	Plane
समता	Par
समतोल	Equilibrium
सम्मन	Summons
समय के बाहर	Beyond time
समय लेखक	Time-keeper
समय विभाग	Time table
समय-समय पर पूरा किया जाय	To be recouped from time to time
समय सार्गल	Time barred
समयोत्तर (काम)	Overtime
समर्थ न्यायालय	Competent court
समर्पण (कारागार भेजना)	Commitment
समर्पित	Delivered
समलम्ब चतुर्भुज	Trapezium (with only two sides parallel)
समादेश	Command
समादेशक	Commandant
समाधान	Adjustment
समाधेय अपराध	Compoundable offences
समान कार्यविधि	Uniform procedure
समान प्रभार	Flat charge
समान्तर	Parallel
समानुपात	Proportion
समानुपात नियम	Rule of proportion
समाप्त	Ceased
समाप्ति	Termination, Abolition
समाप्ताधिकार	Functus officio
समापन	Completion
समारम्भ	Undertaking
समावेश	Merger
समाहरण	Collection
समाहरणकारी सरकार	Collecting government
समाहर्ता	Collector
समहिति	Lay out
समिति	Committee
समीपस्थ (आसन्न)	Adjacent
समुद्र पार का वेतन	Overseas pay
समुद्री पालिसी	Maritime policy
समुद्री अधिकारी	Marine Officer
सरकार	Government, Crown
सरकारी अधिवक्ता	Government pleader
सरकारी अभिभावक	Government pleader
सरकारी अधिहस्तांकिती	Official Assignee
सरकारी आज्ञा	Government order
सरकारी ऋण पत्र	Security
सरकार-चालित मुकदमा	Public Prosecution
सरकार द्वारा जारी की हुई हुंडी	Treasury, bill
सरकी प्रन्यासी	Official trustee
सरदल	Bressummer

सरसरी तौर पर खारिज	Dismissed sum-marily
सरसरी निर्णय	Summary Judgement
सर्पीली (सँपेनी)	Serpentine
सरेस	Glue
सवारी	Conveyance
सशपथ कथन	Deposition
सशस्त्र रक्षकगण	Armed guard
सहकारिता (सहयोग)	Co-operation
सहकारी	Co-operative
सहकारी समितियाँ	Co-operative societies
सहकृषक	Co-tenant
सहतावारिक	Barrack
सहमति	Concurrence
सहवर्ति (संगामी)	Concurrent
सहयोग	Collaboration
सहस्वामी	Co-owner
सहायक	Accessory, Subsidiary
सहायक अनुदान	Grant-in-aid
सहायक नियम	Subsidiary rule
सहायक महानिरीक्षक	Asstt. Inspector General
सहायक पुलिस अधीक्षक	Asstt. Supdt. fo Police
सहायक वस्तुएँ	Accessories
संकट (पुलिस)	Emergency (Police)
संकटकाल (आपत्, विपत्ति)	Emergency
संकट कालीन	Emergency
संकलन	Compilation
संकल्प	Assignment (of Property)
संकल्प	Resolution
संकीर्णनिगम मार्ग	Bottle-neck
संकेत लिपिक	Bottle-neck
संकेन्द्र	Stenographer
संक्रम	Transfer, Transit
संक्रमण	Transition
संक्रामक रोग	Contagious disease
संक्षिप्त	Abbreviated
संक्षिप्त संग्रह	Digest
संख्यात	Numbered
संख्याशास्त्र	Statistics
संख्या शास्त्रीय सहायक	Statistical assistant
संख्या शास्त्रीय सारिणी	Statistical table
संगठन	Organisation
संगत	Consistent
संगम	Junction
संगर	Parole
संगर-बद्ध	On parole
संगीन	Bayonet
संग्रहालय संरक्षक	Custodian of museum
संघ	Federation, Union
संघटन	Organisation
संघटनकर्ता	Organiser
संघानी	Foundry
संचय	Savings
संचयन	Storage
संचयन में माल की हानियाँ	Storage losses
संडास	Water closet
संतोषजनक	Satisfactory
संदर्भ ग्रन्थ	Books of reference
संदिग्ध	Suspect, Suspected
संधाता	Welder

संपत्ति का पृथक् पूर्ण अधिकार	Severality
सम्पर्क	Contact
संपीड़न	Compression
सम्पूर्ण	Whole
संप्राप्त अधिकार	Power-vested
संप्रेषक	Despatcher
संबक	Plumb (mason)
संबद्धता	Affiliation
सम्बन्ध रखना	Pertain
संभार	Equipage
संभूत वेतन वृद्धि	Accrual increment
संमन्त्रण	Consultation
संयात्रा	Passage (voyage by sea)
संयोजक	Convener
संरक्षक	Patron, Custodian
संरक्षण	Custody
संरक्षतावाद	Suits for guardianship
संरक्षा	Care Protection
संराशि	Commuted value
संराशिदान	Commutation
संलग्नशीलता	Viscosity
संवर (बाँध)	Dam
संवातन	Ventilation
संवाहन	Conduction
संविदा	Covenant
संविद्जनित सम्बन्ध	Contractual relation
संविधान	Constitution
संविभाग	Apportionment
संशोधक अधिकारी	Revision Officer
संशोधक विधान	Amendment Act
संशोधन	Modification, Amendment
संशोधित	Revised
संशोधित अनुदान	Modified grant
संशोधित आगणन	Revised estimate
संसर्ग	Intercourse
संस्थान	Station
संस्थापित	Stationed
संहिता	Code
साइक्लोस्टाइल	Cyclostyle
साक्षी	Witness
साक्षीकरण	Attestation
साक्षी का बयान	Deposition
साक्षीकृत	Attested
साक्ष्य	Evidence
साक्ष्य में ग्राहिता	Admissibility in evidence
साख	Credit
साझाभंग पत्र	Dissolution of partnership
साधारण	Normal
साधारण वेष	Mufti
साधारण सैनिक वर्ग	Rank and file
सान	Grind-stone
सामयिक	Periodical
सामान	Paraphernalia
सामान अस्तबल	Stable gear
सामान्य	Normal, General
सामान्य नियम	General rules
सामान्य प्रासंगिक व्यय	Common contingent charges
सामान्य पूर्वोपायी कोष	General Provident fund
सामूहिक चन्दा	Collective subscription

सारिणी	Table
सार-संग्रह	Manual (books)
सारा वृत्तान्त	Full particulars
सार्वजनिक अधिकारी	Public Officer
सार्वजनकि उपयोगिता	Public utility
सार्वजनिक ऋण	Public debt
सार्वजनिक निर्माण विभाग	Public works Department
सार्वजनिक मामले	Public affairs
सार्वजनिक हितोन्नति	In furtherance of a common cause
सावधान	Caveat
सार्वधिक पद	Tenure of post
साहित्यादि विद्यालय	Arts college
सिकिजा	Clamp
सिंचाई आदेश सारसंग्रह	Manual of Irrigation Order
सिद्ध करना	Establishing
सिद्धान्त	Theory
सिरा (चोटी)	Apex
सीका (कगार)	Cornice
सीटी	Whistle
सीढ़ी	Tread of steps
सीधी देखभाल	Direct supervision
सीमाकर	Terminal tax
सीमा-भंजन	Encroachment
सीमांकित	Terminal
सीसागर	Plumber
सुखाधिकार का वाद	Suit of easement
सुधरा हुआ	Improved
सुना भाग	Part-heard
सुनवाई	Hearing
सुनवाई के लिए नियत की गयी	Fixed for hearing
सुनवाई के लिए स्वीकृत	Admitted for hearing
सुपुर्दगी का अधिपत्र	Warrant of commitment
सुपुर्दगी लेने वाला	Assignee
सुवहनीय	Portable
सुरक्षापत्र	Guarantee letter
सुरक्षित भूमि	Protected land
सुलझान	Solution (Math)
सुक्ष्मदर्शकीय परीक्षा	Microscopical examination
सूक्ष्म परीक्षा	Scrutiny
सूक्ष्माकार (लघुचित्र)	Miniature
सूख	Dryage
सूचना	Intimation
सूची	Pyramid (ancient world)
सूची	Inventory
सूजा	Arrows
सूत्र	Formula
सेतु	Viaduct
सेंध लगाना	Burglary
सेना	Troops
सेनापति	Commander
सेवानियम पत्र	Agreement for service
सेवा नियमावली	Service-rules
सेवा पुस्तिका	Service-book
सेवाभिलेख	Record of service
सेवावर्ति	Service roll
सेवोपहार	Gratuity
सैनिक अधिकारी	Military officer
सैनिक कोषागार	Military stores
सैनिक चिह्न	Decorations

सैनिक सेवा	Military service
सोना-चाँदी	Bullion
सोपाधिक दीर्घकालीन बन्दोबस्त	Conditional long settlements
सोपाधिक मुक्ति	Conditional release
सौंप	Committal
सौंप पत्र	Consignment
स्टाम्प निरीक्षणाधिकारी वर्ग	Inspectorate of stamp
स्टाम्प रजिस्टरों की जाँच-पड़ताल	Check of stamp register
स्टाम्प विक्रेता	Stamp vendor
स्टाम्प व्यवहरण	Stamp defalcation
स्टाम्प शुल्क	Stamp duty
स्टाम्प का संरक्षण	Custody of stamp
स्तरमापक दण्ड	Levelling staff
स्तरांक	Bench mark
स्थगन	Adjournment
स्थगन	Suspension
स्थगन आज्ञा	Stay order
स्थगित करना	Suspend
स्थगन प्रार्थनापत्र	Stay application
स्थगित ग्रहणाधिकार	Lien suspended
स्थपति	Architect
स्थल चित्र	Site plan
स्थानाधिकार	Locus standi
स्थानान्तरण	Transfer
स्थानापन्न	Officiating, Substitute
स्थानापन्न नियुक्ति	Officiating appointment
स्थानिक (स्थानीय)	Local
स्थानीय कर	Local cess
स्थानीय कोठार	Local depot
स्थानीय निकाय	Local bodies
स्थानीय भत्ता	Local allowance
स्थानीय सरकार	Local government
स्थानीय संस्थाकोष	Local funds
स्थापना	Establishment
स्थायी अग्रधन	Permanent advance
स्थायी आदेश	Standing Order
स्थायी दाराभूति	Permanent alimony
स्थायी निवास	Domicile
स्थायी पद	Permanent post
स्थायी बन्दोबस्ती	Permanently settled
स्थायी भू भुक्तिधारी	Permanent tenure holder
स्थायी वकील	Standing counsel
स्थावर सम्पत्ति	Immovable property
स्थिर	Stationary
स्थिर जमा	Fixed deposit
स्थिर यन्त्र और मशीनें	Plant and machinery
स्थिरीकरण	Stabilization
स्पर्शवर्जन	Quarantine
स्पर्शवर्जन छुट्टी	Quarantine leave
स्मारक ग्रन्थ	Commemoration volume
स्मारकपत्र	Reminder
स्मृतिपत्र	Memorandum
स्राव	Exudation
स्रोतस्तर	Spring level
स्वत:	Automatically
स्वत: व्याख्यात्मक	Self-explanatory
स्वत: सिद्ध	Ipso facto
स्वत्वाधिकार	Title
स्वत्वाधिकार पूर्ववर्ती	Predecessor-in-title
स्वदेशार्पण	Repatriation

स्वधर्म शास्त्र	Personal law
स्वनिष्ठित	Substantive
स्वभाव विकृत	Denaturalised
स्वयंचल	Automatic
स्वामी	Proprietor
स्वार्थोत्पादक करणपत्र	Instruments creating interest
स्वास्थ्य प्रमाणपत्र	Health certificate
स्वीकारात्मक	Affirmative
स्वीकृत अनुदान	Sanctioned grant
स्वीकृत आगणन	Sanctioned estimate
स्वीकृत उम्मीदवार	Approved candidate
स्वीकृति	Acknowledgment, Sanction, Approval
स्वेच्छापूर्ण चंदा	Voluntary contribution

ह

हथगोला	Hand grenade
हथचिट्ट	Hand slip
हरजाना	Damage
हलका	Circle
हवाई बेड़ा	Air force
हवालात	Lock-up
हवालाती	Undertrial prisoner
हस्तक्षेप्य	Cognizable
हस्तलिपि	Hand writing
हस्तांतरण	Alienatipn
हस्तांतरण पत्र	Conveyance
हस्तांतरहण व्यय	Transfer charge
हस्तांतरण शुल्क	Duty of transfer
हाथ गाड़ी (ठेला)	Barrow
हाथ समन	Summon dasti
हानिपूरक नियमपत्र	Indemnity bond
हितकारी ट्रस्ट	Benevolent trust
हिताधिकारी	Beneficiary
हिन्दू उत्तरभोगी	Hindu reversioner
हिन्दू विधवा का जीवन निर्वाह	Hindu widow's maintenance
हिंसा	Violence
हृदय संपुट	Ventricle
हीनता	Turpitude
हुंडी मुद्रांक	Hundi, Stamp
होमगार्ड	Home guard
हौज (टंकी)	Cistern

परिशिष्ट–8/Appendix-8

भारतीय गणतन्त्र के संविधान में प्रयुक्त हिन्दी और अंग्रेजी के पारिभाषिक शब्द

(Hindi and English Equivalents of terms used in Indian Constitution)

अ

अक्षम	Incompetent
अक्षमता	Incompetency
अग्रिम धन	Advance
अतिक्रमण	Violation
अतिरिक्त न्यायाधीश	Additional Judge
अतिरिक्त लाभ	Excess profit
अधिकरण	Tribunal
अधिकार	Right
अधिकार अभिलेख	Record of rights
अधिकार-पृच्छा	Quo warranto
अधिग्रहण	Requisition
अधिनियम	Act
अधिनियमन	Enactment
अधिपत्र	Warrant
अधिभार	Surcharge
अधिमान	Preference
अधिवक्ता	Advocate
अधिवास	Domicile
अधिवासी	Domiciled
अधिष्ठाता	Presiding officer
अधिसूचना	Notification
अधीक्षक	Superintendent
अधीक्षण	Superintendence
अधीन	Subject
अधीन-अधिकारी	Subordinate Officer
अधीन-न्यायालय	Subordinate Court
अध्यक्ष	Speaker
अध्यादेश	Ordinance
अध्यासीन होना	Preside
अनन्य क्षेत्राधिकार	Exclusive jurisdiction
अनर्हता	Disqualification
अनर्हीकरण	Disqualification
अनियमितता	Irregularity
अनुकूलन	Adaptation
अनुच्छेद	Article
अनुज्ञप्ति	Licence
अनुज्ञा	Permit
अनुदान	Grant
अनुदेश	Instruction
अनुन्मुक्त	Undischarged
अनुपाती-प्रतिनिधित्व	Proportional representation
अनुपूरक	Supplementary
अनुपूरक अनुदान	Supplementary grant
अनुमति	Assent
अनुमोदन	Approval
अनुशासन	Discipline
अनुशासन-सम्बन्धी	Disciplinary
अनुशक्ति	Adherence
अनुष्ठान	Exercise

अनुसमर्थन	Ratification
अनुसंधान	Investigation
अनुस्मारक	Reminder
अनुसूचित-क्षेत्र	Scheduled area
अनुसूचित-जनजाति	Scheduled tribe
अनुसूचित जाति	Scheduled caste
अनुसूची	Schedule
अन्तर्ग्रसन	Involvement
अन्तर्ग्रस्त	Involved
अन्तर्देशीय जलपथ	Inland waterway
अन्तर्राष्ट्रीय	International
अन्तःकरण	Conscience
अन्यदेशीय	Aliens
अन्य-संक्रामण	Alienate
अन्य-संक्रामण	Alienation
अपमान लेख	Libel
अपमान-वचन	Slander
अपमिश्रण	Adulteration
अपर-न्यायाधीश	Additional Judge
अपराध	Crime, offence
अपराधी	Criminal
अण्वर्जन करना	Exclude
अपवर्जन	Exclusion
अपात्र	Ineligible
अपात्रता	Ineligibility
अपील	Appeal
अपील न्यायालय	Court of Appeal
अप्रवृत्त	Inoperative
अभिकथन	Allegation
अभिकरण	Agency
अभिकर्त्ता	Agent
अभिप्राय	Opinion
अभियाचना	Demand
अभियुक्त	Accused
अभियुक्ति	Charge
अभियुक्ति	Prosecution
अभियोग	Accusation
अभियोजन	Prosecution
अभियोज्य दोष	Actionable wrong
अभिरक्षा	Custody
अभिलेख	Record
अभिलेख न्यायालय	Court of record
अभिशस्त	Convicted
अभिशस्ति	Conviction
अभिसमय	Convention
अभ्यर्थी	Candidate
अमान्य	Invalid
अयुक्त प्रभाव	Undue influence
अर्जन अर्जी	Acquisition
अर्थ करना	Petition
अर्थ-दण्ड	Construe
अर्हता	Qualification
अल्पसंख्यक वर्ग	Minority
अल्पीकरण	Derogation
अवधिदान	Adjourn
अवमान	Contempt
अवयस्क	Minor
अवभिक्त कुटुम्ब	Joint-family
अविभक्त परिवार	Joint-family
अविश्वास प्रस्ताव	Motion of no-confidence
अवैध	Illegal
अवैधाचरण	Illegal practice
असमर्थता	Incapacity
असमर्थता निवृत्ति वेतन	Invalidity pension
असैनिक	Civil

असैनिक शक्ति	Civil power
अहितकारी	Detrimental
अंकन	Endorsement
अंकित	Endorsed
अंग	Unit
अंश	Share
अंशदान	Contribution

आ

आकलन	Estimate
आक्स्मिकता निधि	Contingency Fund
आचार	Custom
आजादी	Freedom
आजीविका	Callings
आजीविका कर	Callings tax
आज्ञप्ति	Decree
आदेश	Order
आदेशिका	Process
आनुषंगिक	Incidental, Ancillary
आपराधिक	Criminal
आपात	Emergency
आपाती	Emergent
आपातकाल उद्घोषणा	Proclamation of emergency
आभार	Obligation
आयकर	Income Tax
आयात शुल्क	Import duty
आयुक्त	Commissioner
आयोग	Commission
आरक्षक	Police
आरक्षक बल	Police force
आरोप	Allegation
आरोपण करना	Impose
आरोपण	Levy
आर्थिक	Economic
आर्थिक क्षेत्राधिकार	Pecuniary Jurisdiction
आवर्त्तक	Recurring
आवारागर्दी	Vagrancy
आह्वान	Summons
आहूत	Summoned
आँक	Estimate

इ

इच्छा पत्र	Will
इच्छा पत्रहीन	Intestate
इच्छा पत्रहीनत्व	Intestacy

उ

उगाहना	Levy
उच्चतम न्यायालय	Supreme Court
उच्च न्यायालय	High Court
उत्तराधिकार	Succession
उत्तराधिकार शुल्क	Succession duty
उत्तराधिकारी	Successor
उत्तरवादिता	Liability
उत्पादन	Production
उत्पादन शुल्क	Excise duty
उत्प्रवास	Emigration
उत्प्रेषण लेख	Certiorarl
उद्ग्रहण	Levy
उद्घोषणा	Proclamation
उद्भव	Descent
उद्यम	Enterprise
उद्योग	Industry
उधार	Loan
उधार ग्रहण	Borrowing

उन्मत्त	Lunatic
उन्माद	Lunacy
उन्मुक्ति	Immunity
उपकर	Cess
उपक्रमण करना	To initiate
उपचार	Remedy
उपजीविका	Occupation
उपदान	Gratuity
उपदेश	Advice, Instruction
उपनिर्वाचन	Bye-election
उपनिवेशन	Colonization
उपबन्ध	Provision
उपभोग	Consumption
उपराज्यपाल	Lieutenant, Governor
उपराष्ट्रपति	Vice President
उपलब्धि	Emolument
उपविभाग	Sub-division
उपवेशन	Sitting
उपविधि	Bye-law
उपसभापति	Deputy Chairman
उपस्थित होना	Appear
उपाध्यक्ष	Deputy Speaker
उपायुक्त	Deputy Commissioner
उपायोजन	Employment
उपार्जित	Accrued
उम्मीदवार	Candidate
उल्लंघन	Contravention

ऋ

ऋण	Debt
ऋणग्रस्तता	Indebtedness
ऋणपत्र	Debenture

ए

एकक	Unit
एकल निगम	Corporation sole
एकल संक्रमणीय मत	Single transferable vote
एकस्व	Patent
एकांश	Unit

क

कदाचार	Misbehaviour
कब्जा	Possession
कम्पनी	Company
कर	Tax
करार	Agreement
कर्तव्य	Duty
कर्तुमभिप्रेत	Purporting to be done
कर्मचारी वृन्द	Staff
कानून सम्बन्धी	Legal
कारखाना	Factory
कारबार	Business
कारागार	Prison
काराबन्दी	Prisoner
कारावास	Imprisoament
कार्मिक संघ	Trade union
कार्य	Business
कार्यकारी	Acting
कार्यपालिका शक्ति	Executive power
कार्यपालिका	Executive
कावल	Custody
काँजी हौस	Cattle pound
किराया	Fare
किसान	Tenant
कुर्की	Attachment

कृत्य Function
केन्द्रीय गुप्तवार्ता विभाग Central Intelligence Bureau
कैद Imprisonment
कैदी Prisoner
क्षति Injury
क्षतिपूर्ति बिल Bill of Indemnity
क्षमताशाली Competent
क्षमा Pardon
क्षेत्र Area
क्षेत्राधिकार Jurisdiction

ख

खनिज Mineral
खनिज सम्पत Mineral resources
खर्च Cost
खण्ड Clause

ग, घ

गजट Gazette
गणना Calculation
गणपूर्ति Quorum
गवेषणा Research
ग्राम परिषद् Village Council
ग्राह्य Admissible
घोषणा Declaration

च

चर्चा Discussion
चित्त विकृति Unsoundness of mind
चिह्न Mark
चुकती Agreement
चुने हुए Elected
चुंगी Octroi
चेक Cheque

छ, ज

छावनी Cantonment
जगह Post
जनगणना Census
जनजाति Tribe
जनजाति क्षेत्र Tribal area
जनजाति परिषद् Tribal Council
जलदस्युता Piracy
जल प्रांगण Territorial waters
जामिन Bail
जाँच करना Inquire
जिला District
जिलागण District Board
जिलाधीश District Magistrate
जिला निधि District Fund
जिला न्यायालय District Court
जिला परिषद् District Council
जिला मंडली District Board
जीविका Livelihood
जुआ Gambling
जुर्माना किया Fined
जेल Prison
ज्वार जल Tidal water
ज्ञापक Memo
ज्ञापन Memorandum

ट, ड

टंगण Typewriting
ट्राम Tramway
ट्रामगाड़ी Tram car
डिक्री Decree

त

तदर्थ Ad hoc

तृतीय-पठन	Third reading
त्रैवार्षिक	Triennial

थ

थाना	Police Station
थानेदार	Police Station Officer

द

दत्तक ग्रहण	Adoption
दत्तक स्वीकरण	Adoption
दस्तकारी	Handicraft
दस्तावेज	Document
दंड देना	Punish
दंड न्यायालय	Criminal Court
दंड विधि	Criminal Law
दंड सम्बन्धी	Criminal
दंडादेश	Sentence
दंडाधिकारी न्यायालय	Magistrate's Court
दाखिला	Entry
दातव्य	Charities
दाय	Inheritance
दायित्व	Liability
दावा	Claim
दिवाला	Bankruptcy, insolvency
दीवानी	Civil
दीवानी अदालत	Civil Court
देय	Due, Payable
देशीयकरण	Naturalization
दोष-प्रमाणित	Convicted
दोष सिद्धि	Conviction
दोषारोप	Charge
द्यूत	Gambling
द्विगृही	Bicameral
द्वितीय पठन	Second reading

ध

धन	Money
धन विधेयक	Money-bill
धर्म	Faith
धर्मस्व	Endowment
धंधा	Occupation

न

नगर क्षेत्र	Municipal area
नगर ट्रामवे	Municipal tramway
नगर निगम	Municipal Corporation
नगर पालिका	Municipality
नगर समिति	Municipal Committee
नागरिकता	Citizenship
नाम निदर्शन	Nomination
नावाधिकरण	Admiralty
निकाय	Body
निक्षेप निधि	Sinking Fund
निखात निधि	Treasure trove
निगम	Corporation
निगम कर	Corporation tax
निगमन	Incorporation
निगम निकाय	Body, Corporate
निर्देश	Direction
निधि	Fund
निबद्ध	Registered
निबन्धन	Registration
निबंधन	Term
नियन्त्रक महालेखा परीक्षक	Controller & Auditor General
नियन्त्रण	Control

नियम	Rule
नियुक्ति	Appointment
नियोजक उत्तरवादिता	Employer's liability
नियोजक दात्व्य	Employer's Liability
निरसन	Repeal
निराकरण करना	Abrogate
निरोध	Prevention
निर्णय	Judgment
निर्णायक मत	Casting vote
निर्देश	Reference
निर्धारण	Assessment
निर्गन्धिन	Restriction
निर्माण	Manufacture
निर्यात	Export
निर्यात कर	Export Tax
निर्यात शुल्क	Export duty
निर्योग्यता	Disability
निर्वचन	Interpretation
निर्वसीयत	Intestate
निर्वसीयता	Intestacy
निर्वहन	Discharge
निर्वाचक गण	Electoral rolls
निर्वाचक नामावली	Electoral rolls
निर्वाचन (करना)	Fleet
निर्वाचन	Election
निर्वाचन अधिकरण	Election Tribunal
निर्वाचन आयुक्त	Election Commissioner
निर्वाचन क्षेत्र	Constituency
निर्वाचित	Elected
निर्वासन	Transportation
निर्वाह मजूरी	Living-wage
निलम्बन करना	To suspend
निलम्बन	Suspension
निवारक निरोध	Preventive detention
निवृत्त होना	Retire
निवृत्ति	Retirement
निवृत्ति वेतन	Pension
निषेध	Forbid
निषिद्ध	Forbidden
निष्ठा	Allegiance
नौकरी	Employment
नौकरी कर	Employment tax
नौकाधिकरण	Admiralty
नौ-परिवहन	Navigation
नौसेना सम्बन्धी	Naval
न्यस्त करना	Entrust
न्यायपालिका	Judiciary
न्यायाधिकरण	Tribunal
न्यायाधिपति	Justice
न्यायाधीश	Judge
न्यायालय	Court
न्यायालय अवमान	Contempt of Court
न्यायिक कार्यरीति	Judicial proceeding
न्यायिक कार्यवाही	Judicial proceeding
न्यायिक मुद्रांक	Judicial stamp
न्यायिक शक्ति	Judicial power
न्यास	Trust
न्यूनन	Abridgement

प

पक्ष	Party
पण लगाना	Bet
पण क्रिया	Betting
पण्य चिह्न	Trademark
पत	Credit

पत्तन निरोध	Port quarantine	पर्यवेक्षण	Inspection
पथ कर	Rule of the road	पर्यालोचन	Deliberate
पथ नियम	Toll	पशु अवरोध	Cattle pound
पद	Post	पंचाझा	Award
पद	Office	पंजी	Register
पदच्युत करना	Dismiss	पंजीबद्ध	Registered
पदत्याग	Resignation	पंजीबन्धन	Registration
पदधारी	Incumbent of an office	पंजीयन	Registration
		पात्र	Eligible
पदाधिकारी	Officer	पात्रता	Eligibility
पदावधि	Tenure	पार पत्र	Passport
पदावास	Official residence	पारित	Passed
पदेन	Ex-officio	पारितोषिक	Reward
परकीकरण	Alienation	पारिश्रमिक	Remuneration
परमादेश	Mandamus	पावती	Receipt (Paper)
परन्तु	Provided	पीठासीन होना	Preside
परमिट	Permit	पीठासीन पदाधिकारी	Presiding Officer
परामर्श	Consultation	पुनर्निरीक्षण	Revision
परित्यजन	Abandonment	पुनर्विचार न्यायालय	Court of Appeal
परित्याग	Abandonment	पुनर्विलोकन	Review
परित्राण	Safeguard	पुरःस्थापन करना	To introduce
परिपालन	Implement	पुरःस्थापना	Introduction
परिप्रश्न	Enquiry	पूर्व मंजूरी	Previous sanction
परिलब्धि	Perquisite	पूर्व सम्मति	Previous consent
परिवहन	Transport	पूँजी	Capital
परिव्यय	Cost	पृष्ठांकन	Endorsement
परिषद्	Council	पृष्ठांकित	Endorsed
पदिषद् आदेश	Order-in-Council	पेशगी	Advance
परिसीमन	Delimitation	पेशा	Profession
परिसीमा	Limitation	पोषण	Maintenance
परिहार	Remission	पोषण करना	Maintain
परिहार विधेयक	Bill of indemuity	प्रकट करना	Discover
परोक्ष निर्वाचन	Indirect election	प्रकाशन	Publication

प्रक्रिया	Procedure
प्रख्यापन	Promulgation
प्रग्रहण	Arrest
प्रचलित	Current
प्रचार करना	Propagate
प्रतिकर	Compensation
प्रतिकूल असर डालना	Affect prejudicially
प्रतिकूलता	Contravention
प्रतिकूल प्रभाव	Prejudice
प्रतिकूल प्रभाव डालना	Affect prejudicially
प्रतिकृति	Copy
प्रतिज्ञान	Affirmation
प्रतिनिधि	Representative
प्रतिनिधित्व	Representation
प्रतिपत्री	Proxy
प्रतिपालक अधिकरण	Court of Wards
प्रतिभूति	Security
प्रतिरक्षा	Defence
प्रतिलिपि	Copy
प्रतिवेदन	Report
प्रतिव्यक्ति कर	Capitation tax
प्रतिषिद्ध	Prohibited
प्रतिषेध	Prohibition
प्रति शुल्क	Countervailing duties
प्रतिषेध लेख	Writ of prohibition
प्रतिसंहरण	Revoke
प्रत्यक्ष निर्वाचन	Direct election
प्रत्यर्पण	Extradition
प्रत्याभूति	Guarantee
प्रथम पठन	First reading
प्रधानमन्त्री	Prime Minister
प्रपत्र	Form
प्रभाव	Influence

प्रभु	Sovereign
प्रभुता	Sovereignty
प्रमाण पत्र	Certificate
प्रमाणीकरण	Authentication
प्रयोग	Application exercise
प्रविलम्बन	Reprieve
प्रवर समिति	Select Committee
प्रविष्टि	Entry
प्रवेश	Access
प्रवेशन	Accession
प्रव्रजन	Migration
प्रशान्ति	Tranquillity
प्रशासन	Administration
प्रशासन कार्यक्षमता	Efficiency of administration
प्रशासन कार्यपटुता	Efficiency of administration
प्रशासनीय	Administrative
प्रशासनीय कृत्य	Administrative functions
प्रशासित	Administered
प्रशिक्षण	Training
प्रसंग	Context
प्रसारण	Broadcasting
प्रसूति साहाय्य	Maternity relief
प्रसूति सहायता	Maternity relief
प्रस्ताव	Motion
प्रस्तावना	Preamble
प्रस्थापना	Proposal
प्राक्कलन	Estimate
प्रादेशिक आयुक्त	Regional Commissioner
प्रादेशिक क्षेत्राधिकार	Territorial jurisdiction

प्रादेशिक निधि	Regional Fund
प्रादेशिक परिषद्	Regional Council
प्रादेशिक भार	Territorial Charges
प्राधिकरण	Authority
प्राधिकारी	Authority
प्राधिकृत	Authorised
प्रान्त	Province
प्राप्त होना	Accrue
प्राप्ति	Receipt
प्रामिसरी नोट	Promissory note
प्रासंगिक	Incidental
प्रोद्भवन	Accretion
प्रोद्भूत	Accrued

फ

फरियाद	Complaint
फारम	Form
फीस	Fees
फेडरल न्यायालय	Federal Court

ब

बटवारा	Allocation
बनाये रखना	Maintain
बन्दी करना	To arrest
बन्दी प्रत्यक्षीकरण	Habeous Corpus
बन्धक	Mortgage
बल	Forces
बहि:शुल्क	Custom duty
बहुमत	Majority
बाँट	Allotment
बिल	Bill
बीमा	Insurance
बीमा पत्र	Policy of insurance
बेकारी	Unemployment
बैठक	Sitting
बैंक	Bank
बोर्ड	Board

भ

भत्ता	Allowance
भविष्य निधि	Provident Fund
भर्ती	Recruitment
भागिता	Partnership
भाड़ा	Fare
भार	Charge
भारग्रस्त संपदा	Encumbered estate
भारत सरकार	Government of India
भारित करना	To charge
भू-अभिलेख	Land records
भू-राजस्व	Land revenue
भ्रष्ट	Corrupt

म

मजूरी	Wage
मत	Vote
मतदाता	Voter
मतदान	Voting
मताधिकार	Suffrage
मतिमान्द्य	Dullness
मध्यस्थ न्यायाधिकरण	Arbitrator Tribunal
मध्यस्थ	Arbitrator
मध्यस्थ निर्णय	Arbitration
मनोदौर्बल्य	Mental weakness
मनोनयन	Nomination
मनोवैकल्य	Mental deficiency
मन्त्रणा	Advice
मन्त्रणा देना	Advise
मन्त्रणा परिषद्	Advisory Council

मन्त्रि परिषद्	Council of Ministers
मन्त्री	Minister
मरण शुल्क	Death duty
महाजनी	Banking
महाधिवक्ता	Advocate General
महान्यायवादा	Attorney General
महालेखापरीक्षक	Auditor General
महाभियोग	Impeachment
मंजूरी	Sanction
मानेदय	Honorarium
मानवी पण्य	Traffic in human beings
मानहानि	Defamation
मान्यता	Validity
मार्ग प्रदर्शन	Guidance
माँग	Demand
मीन क्षेत्र	Fishery
मुक्त	Exempt
मुखिया	Headman
मुख्य	Chief
मुख्य आयुक्त	Chief Commissioner
मुख्य निर्वाचन आयुक्त	Chief Election Commissioner
मुख्य न्यायाधिपति	Chief Justice
मुख्य न्यायाधीश	Chief Judge
मुख्यमन्त्री	Chief Minister
मुद्रा	Seal
मुद्रांक शुल्क	Stamp duty
मूलधन	Capital
मुलधन मुल्य	Capital value

य

यथास्थिति	As the case may be
यन्त्र शास्त्र	Engineering
याचिका	Petition
यातायात	Traffic

र

रक्षण	Reservation
रक्षाकवच	Safeguard
रक्षित वन	Reserved forest
रद्द करना	Annulment
रसीद	Receipt
राजनय	Diplomacy
राजस्व	Revenue
राजस्व न्यायालय	Revenue Court
राज्य	State
राज्य क्षेत्र	Territory
राज्य क्षेत्रातीत प्रवत्तन	Extraterritorial operation
राज्य निधि	State Fund
राज्य परिषद्	Council of States
राज्यपाल	Governor
राज्य सूची	State-list
राय	Opinion
राशि	Amount
राष्ट्र	Nation
राष्ट्र ऋण	Public debt
राष्ट्रपति	President
राष्ट्रपति प्रसाद पर्यन्त	During the pleasure of the President
राष्ट्रीय राजपथ	National highway
राष्ट्रों की विधि	Laws of Nations
रिक्तता	Vacancy
रिक्त स्थान	Vacancy
रिक्ति	Vacancy
रुकावट	Bar
रूढ़ि	Custom

रूप	Form
रूपभेद	Modification
रूपांकन	Design
रेल	Railway

ल

लगान	Rent
लगाना	Impose
लघुकरण	Commute
लम्बमान	Pending
लम्बित	Pending
लाइसेन्स	License
लागत	Cost
लागू होना	Application
लाभ	Profit
लाभांश	Dividend
लिखित	Instrument
लिखित सूचना	Notice in writing
लेख	Writ
लेखा	Account
लेखा परीक्षा	Audit
लेखानुदान	Votes on accounts
लेक्ष्य	Document
लेना-देना	Dealings
लोक	People
लोक अधिसूचना	Public notification
लोकसभा	Lok Sabha
लोक समाज	Community
लोक सेवाएँ	Public Services
लोक सेवा आयोग	Public Service Commission
लोक स्वास्थ्य	Public health

व

वकालत करना	Plead
वकील	Pleader
वचन पत्र	Promissory note
वचन बन्ध	Engagement
वणिक पोत	Merchant marine
वयस्क	Major
वयस्क मताधिकार	Adult suffrage
वसीयत	Will
वस्तु भाड़ा	Freight
वंटन	Allot
वाक्स्वातंत्र्य	Freedom of speech
वाणिज्य	Commerce
वाणिज्यदूत	Consul
वाणिज्य सम्बन्धी	Commercial
वाद	Cause
वाद-पद	Issue
वाद प्रतिवाद	Controversy
वादमूल	Cause of action
वाद-विवाद	Debate
वाद-विषय	Subject matter
वायदा-बाजार	Future market
वायु-पथ	Airway
वार्षिक	Annual
वार्षिक वित्त विवरण	Annual financial statement
वार्षिकी	Annuities
विकृत चित्त	Unsound mind
विक्रय कर	Sales tax
विघटन	Dissolution
विचार	Consideration
विचारार्थ प्रस्ताव	Motion for consideration

वितरण	Distribution
वित्त	Finance
वित्त विधेयक	Finance bill
वित्तायोग	Finance Commission
वित्तीय	Financial
वित्तीय भार	Financial obligation
वित्तीय विवरण	Financial statement
विदेशीय कार्य	Foreign affairs
विदेशीय विनिमय	Foreign exchange
विधान	Legislation
विधान परिषद्	Legislative Council
विधान मण्डल	Legislative
विधान सभा	Legislative Assembly
विधायिनी शक्ति	Legislative power
विधि प्रश्न	Question of law
विधि मान्य	Legal tender
विधियों का समान संरक्षण	Equal protection of law
विधि सम्बन्धी	Legal
विधेयक	Bill
विनियम	Regulation
विनियमन करना	Regulate
विनिमय पत्र	Bill of exchange
विनियोग	Appropriation
विनियोग विधेयक	Appropriation bill
विनिश्च	Decision
विभाजन	Distribution
विभेद	Discrimination
विमति	Dissent
विमान परिवहन	Air navigation
विमान यातायात	Air traffic
विमान बल	Air Force
विमोचन	Redemption
विमोचन भार	Redemption charges
वियुक्त करना	Deprive
विराम	Respite
विरुद्ध	Repugnant
विरोध	Repugnance
विरोध	Repugnancy
विलेख	Deed
विवरणी	Return
विवाद	Dispute
विवाह-विच्छेद	Divorce
विशेषाधिकार	Privilege
विश्वास प्रस्ताव	Motion of confidence
विश्वास का अभाव	Want of confidence
विषय	Subject
विसर्जन	Dispersion
विसंगत	Irrelevant
विस्तार	Extent
विस्फोटक	Explosive
वृत्ति	Profession
वृत्ति कर	Profession Tax
वृद्धि	Interest
वेतन	Pay, Salary
वैदेशिक कार्य	External affairs
वंचित करना	Deprive
व्यक्ति	Person
व्यपयत होना	Lapse
व्यय	Expenditure
व्यवसाय	Vocation
व्यवस्था	Order
व्यवहार	Civil
व्यवहार	Dealing
व्यापार	Trade
व्यापार कर	Commercial Tax

व्यापार चिह्न	Trade mark
व्यापार संघ	Trade association

श

शक्ति	Power
शर्त	Condition
शान्ति	Peace
शाश्वत उत्तराधिकार	Perpetual succession
शासक	Ruler
शासन	Governance
शासन करना	Govern
शासी निकाय	Governing body
शास्ति	Penalty
शिक्षा	Instruction, Education
शिल्पी प्रशिक्षण	Technical training
शिविर	Camp
शिशु	Infant
शुल्क	Duty
शुल्क सीमान्त	Customs duty
शून्य	Void
शेरीफ	Sheriff
शोध, शोधना	Research
श्रद्धा	Faith
श्रम	Labour
श्रमिक संघ	Labour Union

स

सक्षम	Competent
सत्र	Session
सत्र न्यायालय	Sessions Court
सत्रावसान	Prorogue
सदाचरण पर्यन्त	During good behaviour
सदाचार	Morality
संस्था	Association
सन्धि	Treaty
सभा	Assembly
समता	Equality
समर्पण	Dedicate
समवर्ती सूची	Concurrent list
समवाय	Company
समवाय संस्था	Co-operative society
समवेत होना	Assemble
समागम	Intercourse
समापन	Winding up
समुदाय	Community
समुद्र नौवहन	Maritime shipping
सम्पदा	Estate
सम्पदा शुल्क	Estate duty
सम्पूर्ण प्रभुत्व सम्पन्न लोकतंत्रात्मक गणराज्य	Sovereign democratic republic
सम्मेलन	Conference
सरकार	Government
सरकारी अभियाचना	Public demand
सर्वक्षमा	Amnesty
सर्वोच्य समादेश	Supreme Command
सलाह	Advice
सशस्त्र बल	Armed forces
सहकारी संस्था	Co-operative Society
सहमति	Concurrence
सहायक	Auxiliary
सहायक अनुदान	Grants-in-aid
संकटमय	Hazardous
संकल्प	Resolution
संक्रमण	Transition
संगणना	Computation
संघ	Union

संघ-सूची	Union List
संचार	Communication
संचार करना	Communicate
संचार साधन	Means of Communications
संचित निधि	Consolidated Fund
सम्बोधित	Addressed
संपत्ति हस्तांतरण पत्र	Assurances of transfer of property
सम्पर्क	Contact
सम्मति	Consent
संरक्षक संलग्न	Appended
संविदा	Contract
संविधान	Constitution
संविधान सभा	Constituent Assembly
संशोधन	Amendment
संसद	Parliament
संस्था	Institution
संस्थापन	Establishment
संहिता	Code
साक्ष्य	Evidence
साधारण निर्वाचन	General election
सामाजिक बीमा	Social insurance
सामाजिक रूढ़ि	Social custom
सामाजिक मुद्रा	Social service
सामान्य मुहर	Common seal
सार्वजनिक अभिसूचना	Common seal
सार्वजनिक अभियाचना	Public notification
सार्वजनिक कल्याण	Public demand
सार्वजनिक व्यवस्था	Common good
साहूकार	Public order
साहूकारी	Money lender
सांसर्गिक	Money lending
सांक्रामिक	Infectious
सिद्ध दोष	Convicted
सीमाकर	Terminal Tax
सीमान्त	Frontiers
सीमा शुल्क	Custom duty
सीमांकन	Demarcation
सुधार प्रन्यास	Improvement Trust
सुधारालय	Reformatory
सुसंगत	Relevant
सुसंगति	Relevancy
सूद	Interest
सूत्र	Formula
सूत्रित	Formulated
सेना न्यायालय	Court Martial
सेवा	Service
सेवा की शर्त	Condition of service
सेवा नियोजन	Employment
सेवा भार	Service charges
सैनिक	Military
सैन्य वियोजन	Demobilization
सौंपना	Assign, Entrust
स्थानान्तरण	Transfer
स्थानीय क्षेत्र	Local area
स्थानीय निकाय	Local body
स्थानीय प्राधिकारी	Local Authority
स्थानीय मण्डली	Local Board
स्थानीय शासन	Local Government
स्थानीय स्वशासन	Self Governmen
स्थापना	Establishment
स्थापित करना	Establish
स्थायी करना	Standing Orders
स्थायी समिति	Standing Committee
स्पष्टीकरण	Clarification

स्पष्टीकारण	Explanation
स्मारक	Memorial
स्वतंत्रता	Freedom
स्वविवेक	Discretion
स्वातंत्र्य	Freedom
स्वाधीनता	Liberty
स्वामित्व	Ownership, Royalty
स्वामी	Owner
स्वामी होना	Own
स्वायत्तता	Autonomy
स्वीय विधि	Personal law

ह

हक्क	Entitled
हक्क होना	Entitled
हटाना	Removal
हस्त शिल्प	Handicraft
हस्तांतरण	Transfer
हिदायतें	Instructions

परिशिष्ट–9/Appendix-9

भारतीय गणतन्त्र के संविधान में प्रयुक्त अंग्रेजी के पारिभाषिक शब्दों और पदों के हिन्दी समानार्थक शब्द व पद

(Terms defined in English and their Hindi Equivalents in the Indian Constitution)

A

Abandonment	परित्यजन, परित्याग
Abridgement	न्यूनन
Abrogate	निराकरण
Access	प्रवेश
Account	लेखा, गणना
Accrue	प्रापण, प्रोद्‌भवन
Accrued	प्राप्त, प्रोद्‌भूत उपार्जित
Accusation	अभियोग
Accused	अभियुक्त
Acquisition	अर्जन
Act	अधिनियम
Acting	कार्यकारी
Actionable wrong	अभियोज्य दोष
Adaptation	अनुकूलन
Addressed	सम्बोधित
Adherence	अनुषक्ति
Ad hoc	तदर्थ
Adjourn	स्थगन, स्थापित करना, अवधिदाब, कालदान
Administer	प्रशासन करना
Administration	प्रशासित
Administrative	प्रशासन
Administrative function	प्रशासकीय
Admiralty	नौसेना प्रमुख
Admissible	स्वीकार्य
Adoption	ग्राह्य

Adulteration	दत्तक ग्रहण, दत्तक स्वीकरण
Adulteration	अपमिश्रण
Adult suffrage	वयस्क मताधिकार
Advance	अग्रिम धन, पेशगी
Advice	मन्त्रणा, उपदेश, सलाह
Advise	मन्त्रणा देना
Advisory Council	मन्त्रणा परिषद्
Advocate	अधिवक्ता
Advocate General	महाधिवक्ता
Affect prejudicially	प्रतिकूल प्रभाव डालना
Affirmation	प्रतिज्ञान
Agency	अभिकरण
Agent	अभिकर्त्ता
Agreement	करार
Air Force	विमान बल
Air navigation	विमान परिवहन
Air traffic	विमान यातायात
Air ways	वायु पथ
Alien	अन्यदेशीय
Alienate	अन्य संक्रामण करना
Alienation	अन्य संक्रामण, परकीयकरण
Allegation	अभिकथन, आरोप
Allegiance	निष्ठा
Allocation	बँटवारा
Allot	बाँट लगाना
Allotment	बाँट

Allowances	भत्ता
Amendment	संशोधन
Amnesty	सर्वक्षमा
Amount	राशि
Annual	वार्षिक
Annual financial statement	वार्षिक वित्त-विवरण
Annuity	वार्षिकी
Annulment	रद्द करना
Appeal	अपील
Appear	उपस्थित होना
Appended	संलग्न
Application	प्रयुक्ति, लागू होना, आवेदन पत्र
Appointment	नियुक्ति
Appropriation	विनियोग
Appropriation bill	विनियोग-विधेयक
Approve	अनुमोदन करना
Approval	अनुमोदन
Arbitral Tribunal	मध्यस्थ न्यायाधीशकरण
Arbitration	मध्यस्थ निर्णय
Arbitrator	मध्यस्थ
Area	क्षेत्र
Armed Forces	सशस्त्र बल
Arrest	बन्दी करना
Article	अनुच्छेद
Assemble	समवेत होना, सम्मिलित होना
Assembly	सभा
Assent	अनुमति
Assessment	निर्धारण
Assignment	सौंपना
Association	संस्था
Assurance of property	संपत्ति हस्तांतरण पत्र
As the case may	यथास्थिति, यथाप्रसंग
Attach	कुर्की
Attorney General	महा-न्यायवादी
Audit	लेखा परीक्षा
Auditor-General	महालेखा परीक्षक
Authentication	प्रमाणीकरण
Authorize	प्राधिकृत करना
Authority	प्राधिकारी
Autonomous	स्वायत्त
Autonomy	स्वायत्तता
Award	पंचाज्ञा

B

Bail	प्रतिभू, जमानत
Ballot	मतपत्र
Bank	बैंक
Banking	महाजनी
Bankruptcy	दिवाला
Bar	रुकावट
Benefit	हित
Betting	पण लगाना, पण क्रिया
Bicameral	दोघरा, द्विगृही
Bill	विधेयक, बिल
Bill of exchange	विनिमय पत्र
Bill of indemnity	परिहार-विधेयक, क्षतिपूर्ति बिल
Bill of lading	वहन पत्र
Board	परिषद्
Body	निकाय
Body, Corporate	निगमनिकाय
Body governing	शासीनिकाय
Borrowing	उधार ग्रहण
Boundary	सीमा
Broadcasting	प्रसारण
Business	कारबार
Bye-election	उपनिर्वाचन
Bye-law	उपनियम

C

Calling	आजीविका
Camp	शिविर
Candidate	अभ्यर्थी, उम्मीदवार
Cantonment	छावनी
Capacity	सामर्थ्य
Capital	मूलधन, पूँजी
Capital Value	मूलधन-मूल्य
Capitation tax	प्रतिव्यक्ति कर
Carriage	परिवहन
Casting vote	निर्णायक मत
Cattle pound	पशु अवरोध, कांजीहौस
Cause	वाद
Cause of Action	वादमूलक
Census	जनगणना
Central Bureau of Intelligence	केन्द्रीय जाँच ब्यूरो विभाग
Certificate	प्रमाण पत्र
Certiorari	उत्प्रेषण-लेख
Cess	उपकर
Chairman	सभापति
Charge	दोषारोप, अभियुक्ति
Charge	भार, भारित करना
Charity	पूर्त, दातव्य
Charitable and endowments	दातव्य तथा धार्मिक धर्मस्व
Charitable institution	दातव्य संस्था
Cheque	चेक
Chief	मुख्य
Chief Commissioner	मुख्य आयुक्त
Chief Election-Commissioner	मुख्य निर्वाचन आयुक्त
Chief Judge	मुख्य न्यायाधीश
Chief Justice	मुख्य न्यायाधिपति
Chief Minister	मुख्यमन्त्री
Citizenship	नागरिकता
Civil	व्यवहारिक, असैनिक
Civil Court	दीवानी अदालत
Civil power	असैनिक शक्ति
Claim	दावा
Clarification	स्पष्टीकरण
Clause	खण्ड
Code	संहिता
Coinage	टंकण
Colonization	उपनिवेशन
Commerce	वाणिज्य
Commercial	वाणिज्य सम्बन्धी
Commission	आयोग
Commissioner	आयुक्त
Committee	समिति
Committee, Select	प्रवर समिति
Committee, Standing	स्थायी समिति
Common good	सार्वजनिक कल्याण
Common Seal	सामान्य मुद्रा, सामान्य मुहर
Communicate	संचार करना
Communication, Means of	संचार साधन
Community	लोकसमाज समुदाय
Commute	लघुकरण
Company	कम्पनी
Compensation	प्रतिकर
Competent	सक्षम
Complaint	फरियाद
Comptroller and Auditor General	नियंत्रक महालेखा परीक्षक
Compute	संगणना
Concurrence	सहमति
Concurrent list	समवर्ती सूची
Condition	शर्त
Conditions of service	सेवा की शर्तें

Conference	सम्मेलन
Confidence, want of	विश्वास का अभाव
Conscience	अन्तःकरण
Consent	सम्मति
Consent, Previous	पूर्व सम्मति
Consequential	आनुषंगिक
Consideration	विचार
Consolidated Fund	संचित निधि
Constituency	निर्वाचन क्षेत्र
Constituency, territorial	प्रादेशिक निर्वाचन क्षेत्र
Constituent Assembly	संविधान सभा
Constitution	संविधान
Consul	वाणिज्य-दूत
Consultation	परामर्श
Construe	अर्थ करना
Consumption	उपभाग
Contact	सम्पर्क
Contagious	सांसर्गिक
Contempt	अवमान
Contempt of Court	न्यायालय अवमान
Context	संदर्भ, प्रसंग
Contingency-Fund	आकस्मिकता निधि
Contract	संविदा
Contravention	प्रतिकूलता, उल्लंघन
Contribution	अर्थदान
Control	नियंत्रण
Controversy	प्रतिवाद
Convention	प्रथा, परम्परा
Conveyance	सम्पत्ति हस्तांतरण
Convicted	दोषसिद्ध, अभिशस्त, दोष प्रमाणित
Conviction	दोषसिद्धि, अभिशस्ति
Co-operative	सहकारी संस्था
Copy	प्रतिलिपि, प्रतिकृति
Copyright	प्रकाशनाधिकार
Corporation	निगम
Corporation, Sole	एकल निगम
Corporation Tax	निगम-कर
Corresponding	तत्स्थानी
Corrupt	भ्रष्ट
Cost	परिव्यय, खर्च, लागत
Council	परिषद्
Council of Ministers	मन्त्रिपरिषद्
Council of State	राज्यपरिषद्
Council Regional	प्रादेशिक परिषद्
Council, Tribal	जनजाति-परिषद्
Countervailing duty	प्रति शुल्क
Court	न्यायालय
Court of Appeal	पुनर्विचार न्यायालय
Court, Civil	दीवानी अदालत
Court, District	जिला न्यायालय
Court, High	उच्च-न्यायालय
Court, Magistrate	दंडाधिकारी न्यायालय
Court, Martial	सेना न्यायालय
Court of Wards	प्रतिपालक अधिकरण
Court, Revenue	राजस्व न्यायालय
Court, Sessions	सत्र न्यायालय
Court, Subordinate	अधीन न्यायालय
Court, Supreme	उच्चतम न्यायालय
Credit	प्रत्यय, साख, पत्त
Crime	अपराध
Criminal	अपराधी, आपराधिक, दण्ड सम्बन्धी
Criminal Law	दण्ड-विधि
Currency	प्रचलित मुद्रा
Custody	अभिरक्षा
Custom duty	सीमा शुल्क
Customs duty	शुल्क, सीमान्त
Custom	रूढ़ि, आचार

D

Dealing	व्यवहार, लेना-देना

Debate	वाद-विवाद
Debenture	ऋण-पत्र
Debt	ऋण
Decision	विनिश्चय
Declaration	घोषणा
Decree	आज्ञप्ति, डिगरी
Dedicate	समर्पण
Deed	विलेख
Detamation	मानहानि
Defence	प्रतिरक्षा
Deliberation	पर्यालोचन
Demand	माँग, अभियाचना
Demarcation	सीमांकन
Demobilisation	सैन्य-वियोजन
Deprive	वंचित करना
Deputy Chairman	उपसभापति
Deputy Commissioner	उपायुक्त
Deputy Speaker	उपाध्यक्ष
Descent	उद्भव
Derogation	अल्पीकरण
Design	रूपांकरण
Detrimental	अहितकारी
Diplomacy	राजनय
Direction	निर्देश
Disability	निर्योग्यता
Discharge	निर्वहन
Discipline	अनुशासन
Disciplinary	अनुशासन सम्बन्धी
Discovery	अन्वेषण, खोज
Discretion	स्वविवेक
Discrimination	विभेद
Discussion	चर्चा
Dismiss	पदच्युत करना
Disperse	विसर्जन करना
Dicpute	विवाद
Disqualification	अनर्हता
Disqualify	अयोग्य ठहराना
Dissent	विमति
Dissolution	विघटन
Distribution	वितरण, विभाजन
District	जिला
District Board	जिला परिषद्
District Council	जिलापरिषद्
District Fund	जिलानिधि
Dividend	लाभांश
Divorce	विवाह-विच्छेद
Documents	लेख्य, दस्तावेज
Domicile	अधिवांस
Domiciled	अधिवासी
Dullness	प्रतिमान्द्य
During good behaviour	सदाचारपर्यन्त
During the pleasure of the President	राष्ट्रपति-प्रसाद पर्यन्त
Duty	शुल्क, कर्तव्य
Duty, Custom	सीमा-शुल्क
Duty, Death	मरण शुल्क
Duly, Estate	सम्पत्ति शुल्क
Duty, Excise	उत्पादन शुल्क
Duty, Export	निर्यात शुल्क
Duty, Import	आयात शुल्क
Duty, Stamp	मुद्रांक शुल्क
Duty, Succession	उत्तराधिकार शुल्क

E

Economic	आर्थिक
Education	शिक्षा
Efficiency of administration	प्रशासन कार्य क्षमता
Elect	निर्वाचित करना
Elected	निर्वाचित चुने हुए
Election	निर्वाचन
Election Commissioner	निर्वाचन आयुक्त

Election, Direct प्रत्यक्ष निर्वाचन
Election, General साधारण निर्वाचन
Election, Indirect परोक्ष निर्वाचन
Election Tribunal निर्वाचन अधिकरण
Electoral roll निर्वाचन नामवली
Eligibility पात्रता
Eligible पात्र होना
Emergency आपात
Emergent आपाती
Emigration उत्प्रवास
Emoluments उपलब्धियाँ
Employer's liability नियोजक दात्व्य, नियोजक उत्तरवादिता
Enact अधिनियम
Encumbered estate भारग्रस्त सम्पदा
Endorse पृष्ठांकन
Endorsed पृष्ठांकित
Endowment धर्मस्व
Engagements वचनबद्ध
Engineering यन्त्र शास्त्र
Enterprise उद्यम
Entitled हक्क होना
Entrust सौंपना
Entry प्रविष्टि, दाखला
Equality समता
Equal protection of laws विधियों का समान संरक्षण
Escheat राजगामी
Establishment स्थापना, संस्थापन, स्थापना करना
Estates संपदा
Estimates आँक, प्राक्कलन
Evidence साक्ष्य
Excess profit अतिरिक्त लाभ
Exclude अपवर्जन करना
Exclusion अपवर्जन
Exclusive jurisdiction अनन्य क्षेत्राधिकार
Executive कार्यपालिका
Executive power कार्यपालिका शक्ति
Exempt मुक्त
Exercise प्रयोग, अनुष्ठान
Ex-officio पदेन
Expenditure व्यय
Explanation व्याख्या, स्पष्टीकरण
Explosives विस्फोटक
Export निर्यात
Extent विस्तार
External Affairs वैदेशिक कार्य
Extradition प्रत्यर्पण
Extra territorial operations राज्य क्षेत्रातीत प्रवर्तन

F

Factory कारखाना
Faith धर्म-श्रद्धा
Fare भाड़ा, किराया
Finance Bill देय शुल्क
Finance वित्त
Financial bill वित्त विधेयक
Financial Commission वित्तायोग
Financial वित्तीय
Financial obligation वित्तीय भार
Finance statement वित्तीय विवरण
Fine अर्थदण्ड
Fishery मीन क्षेत्र, मीन पण्य
Forbid निषेध
Forbidden निषिद्ध
Forces बल
Foreign affairs विदेशीय कार्य
Foreign exchange विदेशीय विनिमय
Form रूप, प्रपत्र, फारम
Formula सूत्र
Formulated सूत्रित

For the time being	तत्समय
Freedom	स्वतंत्रता, स्वातंत्र्य, आजादी
Freight	वस्तु भाड़ा
Frontiers	सीमान्त
Function	कृत्य
Function, Administrative	प्रशासकीय कृत्य
Fund	निधि
Fund sinking	निक्षेप निधि
Future market	वायदा बाजार

G

Gambling	द्यूत, जुआ
Gaztte	सूचना–पत्र, राजपत्र
General election	साधारण निर्वाचन
Govern	शासन करना
Governance	शासन
Government	सरकार, शासन
Government of State	राज्य की सरकार
Government of India	भारत सरकार
Governor	राज्यपाल
Grant	अनुदान
Grant-in-aid	सहायक अनुदान
Gratuity	उपदान
Guarantee	प्रत्याभूति
Guardian	संरक्षक
Guidance	मार्ग प्रदर्शन

H

Habeas Corpus	बन्दी प्रत्यक्षीकरण
Handicrafts	हस्तशिल्प, दस्तकारी
Hazardous	संकटमय
Headman	मुखिया
High Court	उच्च न्यायालय
Honorarium	मानदेय
House	सदन
House of People	लोकसभा

I

Illegal	अवैध
Illegal practice	अवैधाचरण
Immunity	उन्मुक्ति
Impeachment	महाभियोग
Implementing	परिपालन
Impose	आरोपण लगाना
Imprisonment	कारावास, कैद
Improvement Trust	सुधार प्रन्यास
Incapacity	असमर्थता
Incidental	प्रासंगिक
Incompetency	अक्षमता
Incompetent	अक्षम
Incorporation	निगमन
Incumbent of an office	पदधारी
Indebtedness	ऋणग्रस्तता
Industry	उद्योग
Ineligibility	अपात्रता
Ineligible	अपात्र
Infectious	सांक्रामिक
Inheritance	दाय
Initiate	उपक्रमण करना, दीक्षा देना
Injury	क्षति
Inland waterways	अन्तर्देशीय जलपथ
Inoperative	अप्रवृत्त
Inquiry	परिप्रश्न, जाँच
Insolvency	दिवाला
Inspection	पर्यवेक्षण
Institution	संस्था
Instruction	शिक्षा, अनुदेश, हिदायत
Instrument	संविदा, विलेख, उपकरण, साधन
Insurance	बीमा
Intercourse	समागम

Interest	ब्याज, सूद
International	अन्तर्राष्ट्रीय
Interpretation	निर्वचन, व्याख्या
Intestacy	इच्छापत्र-हीनत्व, निर्वसीयत
Intestate	इच्छापत्र-हीनत्व, निर्वसीयता
Introduce	पुरःस्थापन करना
Introduction	पुरःस्थापना
Invalid	अमान्य, असमर्थ
Invalidity pension	असमर्थता निवृत्ति वेतन
Investigation	अनुसंधान
Involve	अन्तर्ग्रस्त
Involved	अन्तर्ग्रस्त
Irregularity	अनियमितता
Issue	बाद-पद

J

Joint family	अवभिक्त कुटुम्ब, अविभक्त परिवार
Judge	न्यायाधीश
Judge, Additional	अतिरिक्त न्यायाधीश
Judgement	निर्णय
Judicial power	न्यायिक शक्ति
Judicial proceeding	न्यायिक कार्यवाही, न्यायिक कार्यरीति
Judicial stamp	न्यायिक मुद्रांक
Judiciary	न्यायपालिका
Jurisdiction	क्षेत्राधिकार
Justice, Chief	मुख्य न्यायाधीश

L

Labour	श्रम
Labour union	श्रमिक संघ
Land records	भू-अभिलेख
Land revenue	भू-राजस्व
Land tenures	भू-धृति
Law	विधि
Law of Nations	राष्ट्रों की विधि
Legal	विधि सम्बन्धी
Legislation	विधान
Legislative power	विधायिनी शक्ति
Legislative Assembly	विधान सभा
Legislative Legislature	विधान परिषद्
Legislature	विधान-मण्डल
Letters of credit	प्रत्ययपत्र
Levy	आरोपण, उद्ग्रहण, उगाहना
Liability	दायित्व
Libel	अपमान लेख
Liberty	स्वाधीनता
Licence	अनुज्ञप्ति, लाइसेन्स
Lieutenant Governor	उप राज्यपाल
Limitation	परिसीमा
List	सूची
List, Concurrent	समवर्ती सूची
List, State	राज्य सूची
List, Union	संघ सूची
Livelihood	जीविका
Loan	उधार, ऋण
Local area	स्थानीय क्षेत्र
Local authorities	स्थानीय प्राधिकारी
Local Board	स्थानीय मण्डली
Local body	स्थानीय निकाय
Local Government	स्थानीय शासन
Local Self Government	स्थानीय स्वशासन
Lock up	बन्दीखाना

M

Maintain	पोषण, बनाये रखना
Maintenance	पोषण
Major	वयस्क
Majority	बहुमत
Mandamus	परमादेश

Manufacture	निर्माण
Maritime shipping	समुद्र–नौवहन
Maternity relief	प्रसूति सहायता, प्रसूति साहाय्य
Member	सदस्य
Memo	ज्ञाप, स्मृति पत्र
Memorandum	ज्ञापन
Memorial	स्मारक
Mental deficiency	मनोवैकल्प
Mental weakness	मनोदौर्वल्य
Merchandise marks	पण्य–चिह्न
Merchant Ship	वणिक–पोत
Migration	प्रव्रजन
Mind, unsound	विकृतचित्त
Mineral	खनिज
Mineral resources	खनिज–सम्पत्
Minor	अवयस्क
Minority	अल्पसंख्यक वर्ग
Misbehaviour	कदाचार
Modification	रूपभेद
Money bill	धन–विधेयक
Morality	सदाचार
Motion of confidence	विश्वास–प्रस्ताव
Motion of no-confidence	अविश्वास–प्रस्ताव
Municipal area	नगर–क्षेत्र
Municipal Committee	नगर–समिति
Municipal Corporation	नगरनिगम

N

National highways	राष्ट्रीय राजपथ
Naturalization	देशीयकरण
Naval	नौसेना–सम्बन्धी
Navigation	नौ–परिवहन
Newspaper	समाचार–पत्र
Nominate	नामनिर्देशन, मनोनयन
Notice in writing	लिखित सूचना

O

Obligation	अधिसूचना
Occupation	आभार
Official residence	उपजीविका, धंधा
Officer	पदाधिकारी
Official residence	पदावास
Opinion	अभिप्राय, राय
Order in Council	परिषद्–आदेश
Order, Standing	स्थायी आदेश
Ordinance	अध्यादेश
Organization	संघटन
Owner	स्वामी

P

Parliament	संसद
Partnership	भागिता
Pass	पारण, आदेश, परिचयपत्र
Passed	पारित
Passport	पारपत्र
Patent	एकस्व
Pecuniary jurisdiction	आर्थिक क्षेत्राधिकार
Penalty	शास्ति, दण्ड
Pending	रुका हुआ
Pension	निवृत्ति वेतन
Permission	अनुज्ञा
Perpetual succession	शाश्वत उत्तराधिकार
Perquisite	परिलब्धि
Personal law	स्वीय विधि
Piracy	जल–दस्युता
Plead	वकालत करना
Police	आरक्षक, पुलिस
Police Force	आरक्षक बल
Policy of insurance	बीमा–पत्र
Port-quarantine	पत्तन–निरोधा
Possession	स्ववश, कब्जा
Preamble	प्रस्तावना

Preference	अधिमान
Prejudice	प्रतिकूल प्रभाव
Preside	पीठासीन होना, सभापतित्व करना
President	राष्ट्रपति
Presiding Officer	पीठाधीश
Preventive detention	निवारक निरोध
Prisoner	बन्दी, कैदी
Privileges	विशेषाधिकार
Process	आदेशिका
Proclamation	उद्घोषणा
Proclamation of emergency	आपतकाल उद्घोषण
Prohibited	प्रतिषिद्ध
Prohibition	प्रतिषेध, निषेध
Promulgation	प्रख्यापन
Proportional representation	अनुपाती प्रतिनिधित्व
Proposal	प्रस्ताव
Prorogue	सत्रावसान
Provided	परन्तु
Proxy	प्रतिपत्री
Publication	प्रकाशन
Public debt	राष्ट्र-ऋण
Public demand	सार्वजनिक अभियाचना
Public health	लोक-स्वास्थ्य
Public notification	सार्वजनिक अधिसूचना, लोक-अधिसूचना
Public order	सार्वजनिक व्यवस्था
Public Service Commission	लोक सेवा आयोग
Public service	लोक सेवा

Q

Qualification	अर्हता
Quarantine	निरोधा
Question of Law	विधि प्रश्न
Quorum	गणपूर्ति
Quo warranto	अधिकारपृच्छा

R

Ratification	अनुसमर्थन
Reading first	प्रथम वाचन
Receipt (paper)	पावती रसीद
Recommend	सिफारिश करना
Recommendation	सिफारिश
Records, Court of	अभिलेख न्यायालय
Record of rights	अधिकाराभिलेख
Recruitment	भर्ती
Recurring	आवर्तक
Redemption charges	विमोचन भार
Reference	निर्देश
Reformatory	सुधारालय
Refundable to	लौटाई जाने वाली
Regional Commissioners	प्रादेशिक आयुक्त
Regional Councils	प्रादेशिक परिषद्
Regional Fund	प्रादेशिक निधि
Registered	पंजीबद्ध, निबद्ध
Registration	पंजीयन, पंजी-बन्धन, निबन्धन
Regulation	विनिमय
Relevancy	सुसंगति
Relevant	सुसंगत
Remission	परिहार
Remuneration	पारिश्रमिक
Repeal	निरसन
Representation	प्रतिनिधित्व
Representative	प्रतिनिधि
Repreive	प्रविलम्बन करना
Repugnancy	विरोध
Repugnant	विरुद्ध
Requisition	अधिग्रहण
Reservation	रक्षण

Reserved forest	रक्षित वन
Respite	विराम
Restriction	निबन्धन
Retire	निवृत्त होना
Retirement	निवृत्ति
Review	पुनर्विलोकन
Revoke	प्रतिसंहरण
Reward	पारितोषिक
Rule of the road	पथ-नियम
Ruler	शासक

S

Safeguard	रक्षा
Sale	विक्रय
Sanction, previous	पूर्व मंजूरी
Savings	बचत
Security	प्रतिभूति
Sentence	दण्डादेश
Service charges	सेवा भार
Session	सत्र
Single transferable vote	एकल संक्रमणीय मत
Sinking Fund	निक्षेप निधि
Slander	अपमान वचन
Social custom	सामाजिक रूढ़ि
Social insurance	सामाजिक बीमा
Social service	सामजिक सेवा
Sovereign	प्रभु
Sovereign Democratic Republic	सम्पूर्ण प्रभुत्व-संपन्न लोकतन्त्रात्मक गणतन्त्र
Speaker	अध्यक्ष
Speech, Freedom of	वाक्स्वातन्त्र्य
Staff	कर्मचारी-वृन्द
Stamp duties	मुद्रांक-शुल्क
Standing orders	स्थायी आदेश
State Funds	राज्य-निधि
Stock exchange	श्रेष्ठि-चत्वर
Subject matter	वाद-विषय
Subordinate officer	अधीन अधिकारी
Succession	उत्तराधिकार
Successor	उत्तराधिकारी
Sue	व्यवहार लाना
Suffrage	मताधिकार
Suit, Civil	दीवानी मुकदमा
Summon	आह्वान
Superintendence	अधीक्षण
Supplementary grant	अनुपूरक अनुदान
Supreme Command	सर्वोच्च समादेश
Suspend	निलम्बन

T

Tax, Callings	आजीविका कर
Tax; Capitation	प्रतिव्यक्ति कर
Tax, Corporation	निगम कर
Tax, Employment	नौकरी कर
Tax, Entertainment	मनोरंजन कर
Tax, Export	निर्यात कर
Tax, Profession	वृत्तिकर
Tax, Income	आयकर
Tax, Sale	विक्रयकर
Tax, Terminal	सीमा कर
Tax, Commercial	व्यापार कर
Technical training	शिल्पी प्रशिक्षण
Tenant	किसान
Tender, Legal	विधि मान्य
Tenure	पदावधि
Term	अवधि
Territorial charges	प्रादेशिक भार
Territorial Jurisdiction	प्रादेशिक क्षेत्राधिकार
Territorial waters	जल-प्रांगण
Territory	राज्य-क्षेत्र
Tidal waters	वेला-जी, ज्वार-जी
Tolls	पथ-कर
Trade marks	व्यापार चिह्न

Trade Union	कार्मिक-संघ
Traffic	यातायात
Traffic (human)	मानव-पणन
Training	प्रशिक्षण
Transfer	स्थानान्तरण, हस्तान्तरण
Transition	संक्रमण
Transport	परिवहन
Transportation	निर्वासन
Treasure troves	निखात निधि
Treaty	ंधि
Tribal area	जनजाति क्षेत्र
Tribe	जनजाति
Tribunal	न्यायाधिकरण
Triennial	त्रैवार्षिक
Trust	न्यास

U

Undischarged	अनुन्मुक्त
Unemployment	बेकारी
Union	संघ
Unity	एकता
Unsoundness of mind	चित्त-विकृति

V

Vacancy	रिक्ति, रिक्तता
Vagrancy	अवारागर्दी
Validity	मान्यता
Vice-President	उप-राष्ट्रपति
Village Council	ग्राम-परिषद्
Violation	अतिक्रमण
Vocation	व्यवसाय
Vote, Casting	निर्णायक-मत
Voter	मतदाता, वोटदाता
Votes on account	लेखानुदान
Votes of credit	प्रत्ययानुदान

W

Wage	मजूरी
Wage, Living	निर्वाह मजूरी
Warrant	अधिपत्र
Will	इच्छा-पत्र, बिल, वसीयत
Winding up	समापन
Writ	लेख

परिशिष्ट–10/Appendix-10

उपसर्ग (Prefixes)

English Prefixes

A—signifies in, on, asleep, abroad, ashore, aside, away ; away from, far away: arise, awake, avert, abide, ago; in intensive meaning : athirst, afresh, aweary.

Al—all : altogether : almighty.

Be—identical with the meaning of by in the senses (1) adding intensive force to transitive verb : bedaub, besmear. (2) making intransitive verbs transitive : become. (3) when prefixed to transitive verbs, it changes the object of the transi¬tive relation : bethink, becalm, bespeak. (4) in the privative meaning : behead. (5) in conver¬ting nouns into transitive verbs : befriend. (6) in converting adjec¬tives into transitive verbs : bedim, becalm. (7) in forming adverbs and prepositions from nouns: beside, because. By—by, by the side of: bypath, bystander.

Em— form of en before p or b: if the sense of 'to make' enlighten, embitter.

For—through, completely, away, oppo¬site : forbear, forgive, forswear, forget, forbid.

Fore—in advance of : foretell, foresight.

Forth—forward: /forthcoming. Fro—from, away: /reward.

Gain—against: gainsay.

In—into, in : inside, insight, incision.

Mis—in the sense of wrong, mistake, mislead.

Off—of Offspring, offshoot. Out-t-beyond : outbreak, outside; denoting excess; outrun, outbid, outshine. Over—above, beyond : overhang, overflow, overhold, overdo.

Un—not : unnatural, untrue, unbro¬ken in sense of reversal : unloose, undress; against back : untie, undo, unwind.

Under—lower, below, beneath : under¬sell, underwear,' underlie, under-ground.

With—from, back, against : withdraw, withhold, withstand.

परिशिष्ट–11/Appendix-11

प्रत्यय (Suffixes)

English Suffixes

संज्ञा के अर्थ

-ard$_r$ —*art*—to form nouns, one who; *drunkard,* braggart.

-dom—dominion, state or jurisdiction : martyrdom, kingdom, freedom.

-er—male agent : painter, gardener.

-hood—state or rank, nature: man-*hood;* likeli*hood,* false*hood*, neigh-bour*hood.*

-head—rank: godhead,

-kin—diminutive: napkin, lamb*kin,*

-let—diminutive: eyelet, streamlet.

-ling—diminutive: duckling, codling,

-ledge, lock—state: knowledge, wedlock.

-ness—state of: mildness, redness.

-ock—diminutive: *bullock,*

-ow—diminutive: shadow.

-red—state: kindred.

-ship, -skip, -sc condition : counsel-*ship,* land*skip,* land*scape.*

-ster—(one who), agent : spinster, huckster.

-ther—agent or instrument : *feather, father.*

-wright—a workman : wheelwright.

-y—state or quality, place of; smithy, dirty.

विशेषण के अर्थ

-fast—firm : steadfast.

-fold—repetition : manifold, twofold.

-ish—in sense of (1) like : *childish,* waspish (2) designating nationalities : *English* (3) joined to adjectives with weakened effect; yellow-*ish, sweetish.*

-less—without : shoeless, fearless.

-ly—like, in manner of: manly, silently.

-some—same, full of : gladsome, frolicsome.

-wise—manner or position : lengthwise.

-worth—worth : stalworth.

क्रियापद के प्रत्यय

-ate—to make : variegate, captivate, invalidate.

-en, -er—to make of: broaden, lighten, hinder, potter.

-el, -le—turning into frequentative verbs: grovel, nipple.

-fy (Fr.)—to make : clarify, mollify.

-ize (Gr.)–to make: patronize, monopolize, dogmatize, philosophize, Christianize.

Latin and Greek Suffixes

क्रियापद के प्रत्यय

-able, -ible—able to : eatable, receivable, legible.

-aceous—distinguished by: herbaceous.

-age—collective sense: parsonage, assemblage.

-ary, -ier, -eer, -er—place or profession: seminary, parliamentary,

grenad. *ier,* engineer, painter, falconer.

-ee—object of acquisition: examinee.

-ery, -ry—an art, collective: cookery poultry.

—ferous—producing: cupriferous.

-ic (Gr.)—art or science: Physic.

-ic—belonging to: metallic, sulphuric.

-icle—diminutive: particle.

-ism (Gr.)—state or doctrine: *egoism* barbarism, spiritualism.

-ist (Gr.)—agent: artist.

-ive—that which is operative: explosive, pensive.

-scle—diminutive : corpuscle.

-ment—state of: concealment, pavement.

-sque—like: picturesque.

-tery—condition: mastery.

-five—able to: sensitive.

-tory, -sory—place: dormitory, illusory.

-ose, -ous—full of: bellicose, glorious.

परिशिष्ट–12/Appendix-12
भार, तौल तथा माप
(Weights and Measures)

अंग्रेजी चालू तौल
(Avoirdupois Weight)

27.32 grains make 1 dram.
16 drams ... 1 ounce.
16 ounces. ... 1 pound (1b.)
28 pounds ... 1 quarter (qr.)
4 quarters ... 1 hundred weight (cwt)

अंग्रेजी जौहरियों की तौल सोना, चाँदी और मणियों के लिए
(Troy Weight)

4 grains make 1 carat.
24 grains ... 1 penny weight (dwt).
20 dwts. ... 1 ounce troy
12 ounces troy... 1 pound troy
25 lbs. ... 1 quarter.
100 lbs. ... 1 cwt.
20 cwts 1 Ton of gold or silver

सूखी औषधियों की अंग्रेजी तौल
(Apothecaries Weight (Dry)

20 grains make 1 scruple.
3 scruples ... 1 drachm.
8 drachms ... 1 ounce.
12 ounces. ... 1 pound (lb.)

तरल औषधायों की अंग्रेजी तौल
(Apothecaries Fluid Measure)

60 minims (drops) make 1 dra fluid
8 dra fluid ... 1 fluid ounce.
16 ounces make ... 1 pint.
8 pints ...1 gallon.

भूमि के क्षेत्रफल का माप या वर्ग परिमाण
(Measurement of Area)

144 sq. inches = 1 sq. foot.
1296 sq. inches = 9 sq. ft. = 1 sq. yd.

काल या समय माप
(Measurement of Time)

60 seconds = 1 minute.
60 minutes = 1 hour.
24 hours = 1 day.
7 days = 1 week.
28 days = 1 Lunar Month.
28 to 31 days = 1 Calender Month.
12 Calender Months = 1 Year.
365 ¼ days = 1 Common Year.
366 days = 1 Leap Year.

भारतीय लम्बाई का परिमाप
(Indian Measurement of Length)

72 बिन्दु या 3 लम्बे जव = 1 इंच
9 इंच = 1 बित्ता (Span) या बालिश्त
2 बित्ता या 18 इंच = 1 हाथ
2 हाथ = 1 गज

भारतीय भूमि या धरती की लम्बाई नापने का परिमाण
(Indian Measurement of Area)

22 गज या चार पोप या लाठा = 1 जरीब या चेन
1 जरीब = 100 कड़ी (Links)

भारतीय काल या समय परिमाण

(Indian Measurement of Time)

60 अनुपल	= 1 विपल
60 विपल	= 1 पल या 24 सेंकड
60 पल	= 1 घड़ी या दण्ड या 24 मिनट
2।। घड़ी	= 1 घण्टा
7।। घड़ी	= 1 पहर (प्रहर)
8 पहर या 60 घड़ी	= 1 दिन (दिवस)

1 चन्द्र मास = 29 दिन, 31 घड़ी, 50 पल और 7 विपल

7 दिन	= 1 सप्ताह
15 दिन	= 1 पक्ष या पाख
30 दिन	= 1 मास या महीना
12 मास	= 1 युग
100 वर्ष	= 1 शताब्दी या सदी

भारतीय काल या समय परिमाण

12 units = 1 dozen या 12 इकाई = 1 दर्जन

12 dozen = 1 gross या 12 इकाई = 1 ग्रोस

20 units = kori या 12 इकाई = 1 कोड़ी

20 sheets of paper = quire

या 20 ताव कागज = 1 दस्ता या जिस्ता

20 qrires of paper = 1 ream

या 20 दस्ता = 1 रीम

10 reams of paper = 1 gattha

या 20 रीम = 1 गट्ठा

परिवर्तन सारिणी—बीच वाले कालम में मोटे अक्षरों में छपे अंक मीट्रिक या ब्रिटिश पैमाने के हैं। अतः 1 मीटर = 1.09 गज या 1 गज = 0.91 मीटर।

मीटर		गज	लीटर		पिन्ट्स	किग्रा		पाउंड
0.91	1	1.09	0.28	½	0.88	0.11	¼	0.55
1.83	2	2.19	0.57	1	1.76	0.23	½	1.10
2.74	3	3.28	1.14	2	3.52	0.45	1	2.20
3.66	4	4.37	1.70	3	5.28	0.68	1	3.31
4.57	5	4.47	2.27	4	7.04	0.91	2	4.41
			2.84	5	8.80	2.27	5	11.02
						2.72	6	13.23
						3.17	7	15.47
कि.मी		**मील**	**सें.ग्रे.**		**फा.हाईट**	**लिटर**		**गैलन**
1.61	1	0.62	−18	0	32	4.55	1	0.22
3.22	2	1.24	−14	6	43	6.82	1½	0.33
4.83	3	1.86	−11	12	54	9.09	2	0.44
6.44	4	2.48	−4	24	75	11.36	2½	0.55
8.05	5	3.11	0	32	90	13.64	3	0.66
9.65	6	3.73	2	36	97	15.91	3½	0.77
11.26	7	4.35	9	48	118	18.18	4	0.88
12.87	8	4.97	16	60	140	20.46	4½	0.99
14.48	9	5.59	22	72	162	22.73	5	1.10
			29	84	183	27.28	6	1.32
			36	96	205	31.82	7	1.54
			38	100	212	36.37	8	1.76
						40.91	9	1.98

रोमन अंक प्रणाली
(Roman Numerals)

1	एक	I
2	दो	II
3	तीन	I I I
4	चार	IV
5	पाँच	V
6	छः	VI
7	सात	VII
8	आठ	VIII
9	नौ	I X
10	दस	X
11	ग्यारह	XI
12	बारह	XII
13	तेरह	XIII
14	चौदह	XIV
15	पन्द्रह	XV
16	सोलह	XVI
17	सत्रह	XVII
18	अठारह	XVIII
19	उन्नीस	XIX
20	बीस	XX
21	इक्कीस	XXI
22	बाइस	XXII
23	तेइस	XXIII
24	चौबीस	XXIV
25	पच्चीस	XXV
26	छब्बीस	XXVI
27	सत्ताइस	XXVII
28	अट्ठाइस	XXVIII
29	उन्तीस	XXIX
30	तीस	XXX
31	इक्तीस	XXXI
32	बत्तीस	XXXII
33	तैंतीस	XXXIII
34	चौंतीस	XXXIV
35	पैंतीस	XXXV
36	छत्तीस	XXXVI
37	सैंतीस	XXXVII
38	अड़तीस	XXXVIII
39	उन्तालिस	XXXIX
40	चालीस	XL
41	इकतालिस	XLI
42	बयालिस	XLII
43	तैतालिस	XLIII
44	चौवालिस	XLIV
45	पैंतालिस	XLV
46	छियालिस	XLVI
47	सैंतालिस	XLVII
48	अड़तालिस	XLVIII
49	उन्चास	XLIX
50	पचास	L
51	इक्यावन	LI
52	बावन	LII
53	तीरपन	LIII
54	चौवन	LIV
55	पचपन	LV
56	छप्पन	LVI
57	सत्तावन	LVII
58	अट्ठावन	LVIII
59	उनसठ	LIX
60	साठ	LX
61	एकसठ	LXI
62	बासठ	LXII

63	तिरसठ	LXIII
64	चौंसठ	LXIV
65	पैंसठ	LXV
66	छियासठ	LXVI
67	सड़सठ	LXVII
68	अड़सठ	LXVIII
69	उनहत्तर	LXIX
70	सत्तर	LXX
71	इकहत्तर	LXXI
72	बहत्तर	LXXII
73	तिहत्तर	LXXIII
74	चौहत्तर	LXXIV
75	पचहत्तर	LXXV
76	छिहत्तर	LXXVI.
77	सतहत्तर	LXXVII
78	अठहत्तर	LXXIII
79	उन्यासी	LXXIX
80	अस्सी	LXXX
81	इक्यासी	LXXXI
82	बयासी	LXXXII
83	तिरासी	LXXXIII
84	चौरासी	LXXXIV
85	पचासी	LXXXV
86	छियासी	LXXXVI
87	सत्तासी	LXXXVII
88	अट्ठासी	LXXXVIII
89	नवासी	LXXXIX
90	नब्बे	XC
91	इक्यानबे	XCI
92	बानवे	XCII
93	तिरानवे	XCIII
94	चौरानबे	XCIV
95	पंचानबे	XCV
96	छियानवे	XCVI
97	सत्तानबे	XCVII
98	अट्ठानवे	XCVIII
99	निन्यानवे	XCIX
100	सौ	C
200	दो सौ	CC
300	तीन सौ	CCC
400	चार सौ	CD
500	पाँच सौ	D
600	छः सौ	DC
700	सात सौ	DCC
800	आठ सौ	DCCC
900	नौ सौ	CM
1000	एक हजार	M
2000	दो हजार	MM
3000	पाँच हजार	MMM

परिशिष्ट–13/Appendix-13

लोकोक्तियाँ तथा हिन्दी मुहावरें

1.	अंगूर खट्टे हैं	:	The grapes are sour.
2.	अंत भला, सो सब भला।	:	All is well that ends well.
3.	अंधा क्या चाहे, दो आँखें।	:	A blind person needs but two eyes.
4.	अंधा क्या जाने बसंत की बहार।	:	A blind man is no judge of colours.
5.	अंधेर नगरी चौपट राजा, टके सेर भाजी, टके सेर खाजा।	:	Knaves alone reign in the kingdom of fools.
6.	अंधे को सब अंधे ही जान पड़ते हैं।	:	Everything looks yellow to the jaundiced eye.
7.	अंधेरे में हर औरत सुन्दर होती है।	:	(i) In the dark all cats are grey. (ii) In the dark every woman seems sexy.
8.	अंधों में काना राजा।	:	(i) A figure among ciphers. (ii) In the kingdom of the blind the one-eyed man is king.
9.	अक्ल घास चरने गई है।	:	His senses have taken leave.
10.	अकेला चना भाड़ नहीं फोड़ सकता।	:	One swallow does not make a summer.
11.	अक्ल बड़ी या भैंस ?	:	The pen is mightier than the sword.
12.	अक्लमंद को इशारा, अहमक को फटकारा।	:	A nod to the wise and a rod to the foolish.
13.	अक्लमंद को इशारा ही काफी है।	:	The wise need just a nod.
14.	अच्छा साथी, रास्ता आसान।	:	A good companion makes the journey pleasant.

15. अच्छी चीज खुद बोलती है। : Quality speaks for itself.

16. अति किसी भी चीज की बुरी होती है। : An excess of anything is bad.

17. अधजल गगरी छलकत जाए। : An empty vessel makes more noise.

18. अपना-अपना, पराया-पराया। : Blood is thicker than water.

19. अपना पूत सभी को प्यारा। : Every potter praises his own pot.

20. अपना-सा मुँह लेकर बैठना। : To cut a sorry figure.

21. अपना हाथ जगन्नाथ। : Self-help is the best help.

22. अपनी गली में कुत्ता शेर। : (i) Every cock fights best on its own dunghill.
(ii) Every dog is a lion in his backyard.

23. अपने काम से काम रखना। : To mind one's own business.

24. अपने दही को कोई खट्टा नहीं कहता। : Every cook commends his own sauce.

25. अपने मुँह मियां मिट्ठू। : Self-praise is no recommendation.

26. अभी दिल्ली दूर है। : The destination is still far off.

27. अभी नहीं, तो कभी नहीं। : Now or never.

28. अल्प विद्या भयंकरी। : A little knowledge is a dangerous thing.

29. अवसर हाथ से न जाने दो। : Don't let opportunity pass by.

30. असलियत छिपती नहीं, सामने आ ही जाती है। : The truth is never hidden.

31. आँख का अंधा नाम नैनसुख। : Blind of sight, called Mr Bright.

32. आग से खेलना खतरे से खाली नहीं। : Don't play with fire.

33. आगे कुआँ, पीछे खाई। : Between the devil and the deep sea.

34. आज की कसौटी बीता हुआ कल है। : Things present are judged by the things past.

35. आज मेरी, कल तेरी। : Better today than tomorrow.

36. आदमी अपनी संगति से पहचाना जाता है। : Man is known by the company he keeps.

37. आदमी अपने भाग्य का निर्माण स्वयं करता है। : Man is the architect of his own fate.

38. आदमी अपने सलीके से पहचाना जाता है। : A man is known by his manners.

39. आप काज महाकाज। : Self effort, self gain.

40. आप भला तो जग भला। : Good mind, good find.

41. आ बैल मुझे मार। : To ask for trouble.

42. आम के आम, गुठलियों के दाम। : A dime a dozen.

43. आमने-सामने झूठ नहीं बोला जाता। : Face to face the truth comes out.

44. आरंभ अच्छा तो काम हुआ ही समझो। : Well begun is half done.

45. आलस्य गरीबी की जड़ है। : Indolence is the root cause of poverty.

46. आवश्यकता आविष्कार की जननी है। : Necessity is the mother of invention.

47. आसमान पर थूका मुंह पर आता है।	:	Slander rebounds on the slanderer.
48. आसमान से गिरा, खजूर में अटका।	:	From the frying pan into the fire.
49. इंतजार का फल मीठा।	:	The rewards of patience are sweet.
50. इंतजार की घड़ियां लम्बी।	:	A watched kettle never boils.
51. इंतजाम ऐसा कि परिंदा भी पर न मार सके।	:	A foolproof arrangement.
52. इलाज से परहेज अच्छा।	:	Prevention is better than cure.
53. इन्सान कमजोरी का पुतला है।	:	Man is a bundle of faults.
54. इच्छाओं का अंत नहीं।	:	A beggar's bowl is bottomless.
55. इश्क अंधा होता है।	:	Love is blind.
56. इश्क और मुश्क छिपाए नहीं छिपते।	:	Love and smoke cannot be concealed.
57. इस हाथ दे, उस हाथ ले।	:	Give with one hand and take with the other.
58. ईद का चाँद होना।	:	Once in a blue moon.
59. ईमानदारी सबसे अच्छी नीति है।	:	Honesty is the best policy.
60. ईर्ष्या कभी तृप्त नहीं होती।	:	Jealousy is the canker of the heart.
61. ईश्वर की माया, कहीं धूप कहीं छाया।	:	Ups and downs are part and parcel of life.
62. ईश्वर के दरबार में देर है, पर अंधेर नहीं।	:	God's justice may be delayed, but never
63. ईश्वर की इच्छा बलवान है।	:	God's great power is in the gentle breeze, not in the storm.

64. उँगली दी तो पहुँचा पकड़ा। : Give him an inch and he will take a yard.

65. उतावला, सो बावला। : Haste makes waste.

66. उतने पाँव पसारिए जितनी चादर होय। : Cut your coat according to your cloth.

67. उन्नति के पीछे अवनति। : Every rise has a fall.

68. उचित समय पर ही कार्य कर लेना बेहतर है। : A stitch in time saves nine.

69. उम्मीद पर दुनिया कायम है। : Hope sustains life.

70. उल्टा चोर कोतवाल को डांटे। : The pot calls the kettle black.

71. ऊँची दुकान, फीका पकवान। : Great cry, little wool.

72. ऊँट किस करवट बैठेगा? : See which way the wind blows.

73. ऊँट के मुँह में जीरा। : A drop in the ocean.

74. ऊधो का लेना न माधो का देना। : To mind one's own business.

75. उसकी अक्ल चरने गई। : His wits are gone wool-gathering.

76. एक अनार सौ बीमार। : One woman and a hundred suitors.

77. राम मिलाई जोड़ी, एक अंधा एक कोढ़ी। : Adversity brings in strange bedfellows.

78. एक और एक ग्यारह होते हैं। : Unity is strength.

79. एक तो करेला, दूजे नीम चढ़ा। : (i) A pimple upon an ulcer.
(ii) A bad man in bad company.

80. एक तन्दुरुस्ती हजार नेमत। : Health is wealth.

81. एक नजीर, सौ नसीहत। : An ounce of example is better than a ton of precept.

82. एक पंथ दो काज। : To kill two birds with one stone.

83. एक पापी सारी नाव डुबाए। : One bad apple spoils the basket.

84. एक फूल के खिलने से बहार नहीं आती। : One swallow does not make a summer.

85. एक बिल वाला चूहा आसानी से पकड़ा जाता है। : To live under a cat's foot.

86. एक मछली सारे तालाब को गंदा कर देती है। : A black sheep infects the whole flock.

87. एक म्यान में दो तलवारें। : (i) Two swords in one scabbard.
(ii) Two suns in the sky.

88. एक से दो भले। : Two heads are better than one.

89. एक हाथ से ताली नहीं बजती। : (i) It takes two to make a quarrel.
(ii) You can't clap with one hand.

90. एक ही साधन पर निर्भर करने वाला पछताता है। : Never keep all your eggs in one : basket.

91. एकै साधे सब सधे, सब साधे सब जाय। : All covet, all lose.

92. एड़ियाँ रगड़-रगड़ कर मरना। : To die a lingering death.

93. ऐरे-गैरे नत्थू खैरे। : Tom, Dick and Harry.

94. ओखली में सिर दिया तो मूसलों का क्या डर। : (i) He who would catch fish must not mind getting wet.
(ii) Those who handle thorns must suffer pain.
(iii) What cannot be cured, must be endured.

95. ओस चाटे प्यास नहीं बुझती। : (i) The dew can never slake one's thirst.
(ii) The chicken have to be first slaughtered before the curry can be enjoyed.

96. कंगाली में आटा गीला। : Misfortunes never come alone.

97. कथनी और करनी में बड़ा अन्तर है। : (i) There is a world of difference between precept and practice.
(ii) Example is better than precept.
(iii) It is not easy to walk the talk.

98. कब्जा सच्चा, मुकदमा झूठा। : Possession is nine points of the law.

99. कभी घी घना, कभी मुट्ठी भर चना, कभी वह भी मना। : All times are not alike.

100. कभी नाव गाड़ी पर, कभी गाड़ी नाव पर। : (i) Life is full of ups and downs.
(ii) Every dog has its day.

101. कम बोलना सभ्यता की निशानी है। : A quiet tongue shows a wise head.

102. कमान से निकला तीर और मुँह से निकली बात वापस नहीं आती। : (i) Wounds heal but not ill words.
(ii) Words and arrows can never be recalled.

103. कमाई में हाथ गंदे करने ही पड़ते हैं। : You have to soil your hands to earn a livelihood.

104. कर्म ही पूजा है। : Work is worship.

105. बुरे काम का बुरा नतीजा। : (i) Evil begets evil.
(ii) You reap as you sow.

106. कर भला, हो भला। : One good turn deserves another.

107. करनी न खाक की, बात मारे लाख की। : All talk, no work.

108. करिये मन की, सुनिये सब की। : (i) Dogs bark, but the caravan moves on.
(ii) Age considers, youth ventures.

109. करे सो डरे। : A guilty conscience needs no excuse.

110. कल किसने देखा है! : Who has seen tomorrow!

111. कहीं गधा भी घोड़ा बन सकता है। : An ass can never become a horse.

112. कहीं पर निगाहें कहीं पर निशाना। : To look one way, and row another.

113. कहीं बूढ़े तोते भी पढ़ते हैं। : An old dog learns no new tricks.

114. कहीं की ईंट कहीं का रोड़ा, भानुमती ने कुनबा जोड़ा : A marriage of convenience.

115. का वर्षा जब कृषि सुखाने। : After death, the doctor.

116. कांटे से कांटा निकलता है। : Use a thorn to remove a thorn.

117. काठ की हंडिया बार-बार नहीं चढ़ती। : You cannot fool all the people all the time.

118. काठ का उल्लू। : Bloody fool!

119. कानी के ब्याह में सौ जोखम। : There is many a slip between the cup and the lip.

120. काम नहीं तो दाम कैसा।	:	A horse that will not carry a saddle must have no oats.
121. काम प्यारा है, चाम नहीं।	:	Handsome is as handsome does.
122. काम से ही कारीगर की पहचान होती है।	:	A carpenter is known by his tools.
123. कायर जीवन में कई बार मरते हैं।	:	Cowards die a thousand deaths.
124. काल के पेट में हर चीज समा जाती है।	:	Time devours all things.
125. काला अक्षर भैंस बराबर।	:	This is Greek to me.
126. काली माँ के गोरे बच्चे।	:	A black hen also lays white eggs.
127. किसी के भी दिन सदा एक-जैसे नहीं रहते।	:	All days are never the same.
128. कुछ खोकर ही सीखते हैं।	:	One learns through one's failures.
129. कुछ न होने से तो कुछ होना अच्छा।	:	Something is better than nothing.
130. कुछ नहीं से थोड़ा भला।	:	Half a loaf is better than none.
131. जहाँ आग वहीं धुँआ।	:	No smoke without fire.
132. कुत्ते की दुम बारह बरस गाड़ो, फिर भी टेढ़ी की टेढ़ी।	:	A dog's tail is always crooked.
133. कुत्ते के भौंकने से हाथी नहीं डरता।	:	Dogs bark but the caravan moves on.
134. कुत्ते को घी नहीं पचता।	:	An upstart always grows haughty.
135. कुत्ते की मौत मरना।	:	To die a dog's death.

136. कुसंगत से अकेला ही भला। : No company is better than bad company.

137. कोई काम अधूरा मत करो। : Never do things by halves.

138. कोई काम तब तक आरंभ मत करो जब तक उसकी पूरी तैयारी नहीं हो। : Draw not your bow till your arrow is fixed.

139. कोई दूध का धोया नहीं है। : Nobody is pure as milk.

140. कोई भी व्यक्ति एक समय में दो काम नहीं कर सकता। : Always do one thing at a time.

141. कोई भी सर्वगुणसम्पन्न नहीं। : No one is perfect.

142. कौड़ियों के मोल। : At a throwaway price.

143. कौआ चला हंस की चाल, अपनी भी भूल गया। : Shining in borrowed plumes.

144. कौवों के कोसे ढोर नहीं मरते। : Solid worth is not sullied by slander.

145. खग ही जाने खग की भाषा। : Few save the poor feel for the poor.

146. खरबूजे को देखकर खरबूजा रंग बदलता है। : Association inevitably breeds affinity.

147. खरी मजूरी, चोखा काम। : A fair day's work for a fair day's wage.

148. खाने के बिना किसी का भी काम नहीं चलता। : Lips, however rosy, must be fed.

149. खाने के दांत और, दिखाने के और। : (i) A sheep in wolf's clothing.
(ii) An ass in a lion's skin.

150. खामोश नीम रजा। : Silence is half-consent.

151. खाली दिमाग शैतान का घर। : An empty mind is the devil's workshop.

152. खाली बातों से पेट भरना।	:	Empty words cannot fill one's stomach.
153. खूबसूरती गहनों की मोहताज नहीं।	:	Beauty needs no ornaments.
154. खूबसूरती विरासत में नहीं मिलती।	:	Beauty is not inherited.
155. खोदा पहाड़, निकली चुहिया।	:	(i) Great boast, little roast. (ii) Much ado about nothing.
156. गड़े मुर्दे मत उखाड़ो।	:	(i) Let bygones be bygones. (ii) Let sleeping dogs lie.
157. गधे से घोड़े का काम नहीं लिया जा सकता।	:	You can't make a silk piece out of a sow's skin.
158. गया वक्त फिर हाथ नहीं आता।	:	Time and tide wait for none.
159. गए थे नमाज बख्शवाने, रोजे गले पड़े।	:	Go for wool and come home shorn.
160. गरज आदमी को सभी तरह का नाच नचाती है।	:	Need makes a man dance to different tunes.
161. गरीब की जोरू सबकी भाभी।	:	Adversity makes strange bed-fellows.
162. गरीबी झगड़े की जड़ है।	:	Poverty breeds strife.
163. गरीबी सौ ऐबों का एक ऐब है।	:	Poverty is the greatest sin.
164. गलती अच्छे-अच्छों से भी हो जाती है। गलती इन्सान से ही होती है।	:	No one is born without faults, he is best who is beset by fewest.
165. गया वक्त फिर हाथ नहीं आता।	:	A lost opportunity never returns.

166. गुनाह का अंजाम मौत है।	:	The wages of sin is death.
167. गूदड़ में लाल नहीं छिपता।	:	Myrtle shines among nettles.
168. गेहूँ के साथ घुन भी पिस जाता है।	:	When bulls fight, it is the grass that gets trampled.
169. गोद में छोरा, शहर में ढिंढोरा।	:	To miss something right under one's nose.
170. घमंडी का सिर नीचा।	:	Pride has a fall.
171. घर का जोगी जोगड़ा, आन गांव का सिद्ध।	:	No prophet is honoured in his own land.
172. घर का भेदी लंका ढाए।	:	A small leak will sink a great ship.
173. घर की फूट घर को खाय।	:	United we stand, divided we fall.
174. घर की मुर्गी दाल बराबर।	:	Familiarity breeds contempt.
175. घर फूँक तमाशा देखना।	:	To kill the goose that lays the golden eggs.
176. घोड़ा घास से यारी करे तो खाए क्या?	:	The horse that befriends the grass starves.
177. चंदन विष व्यापत नहीं, लिपटे रहत भुजंग।	:	Sludge doesn't corrupt gold.
178. चंद्रमा में भी कलंक (दाग) है।	:	Nothing is perfect. (ii) Even the moon has spots.
179. चढ़ते सूरज को नमस्कार।	:	Salute the rising sun.
180. चलते घोड़े को चाबुक न मारें।	:	Do not whip a willing horse.
181. चाँद को भी ग्रहण लगता है।	:	Every white will have its black, every sweet its sour.

182. चाँद पर थूका मुँह पर आता है। : Spit directed at the heavens falls on one's face.

183. चापलूसी का ही जमाना है। : It is the age of flattery.

184. चार दिन की चाँदनी, फिर अंधियारी रात। : (i) The brightest day is followed by the darkest night.
(ii) Every spring is followed by autumn.

185. चाह है तो राह भी। : Where there is a will, there is a way.

186. चिंता चिता समान है। चिंता बुरी बला है। : Curiosity killed the cat.

187. चिकनी-चुपड़ी बातों से पेट नहीं भरता। : Fine words butter no parsnips.

188. चिकने घड़े पर पानी नहीं ठहरता। : Water doesn't stay on a duck's back.

189. चित भी मेरी, पट भी मेरी। : Heads I win, tails you lose.

190. चुल्लू भर पानी में डूबना। : To drown in shame.

191. चुप्पा आदमी गहरा होता है। : Still waters run deep.

192. चोर की दाढ़ी में तिनका। : A guilty conscience needs no

193. चोर के घर मोर। : Catch a weasel asleep.

194. चोर-चोर मौसेरे भाई। : Birds of a feather flock together.

195. चोर चोरी से जाए, हेराफेरी से न जाए। : Wolves may lose their teeth but not their temper.

196. चोरी का माल मोरी में। : Ill got, ill spent.

197. चौबे जी गये छब्बे बनने, दूबे ही रह गये। : Go for wool and come home shorn.

198. छुपे रुस्तम निकले। : You turned out to be a sly man.

199. छोटा मुँह, बड़ी बात। : Small wit, great brag.

200. जब तक साँस तब तक आस। : (i) Man lives on hope.
(ii) Hope rests eternal.

201. जब ईश्वर देता है तो छप्पर फाड़ कर देता है। : The gifts of God sometimes choose strange channels.

202. जबान का कड़वा, मन का साफ। : Clean at heart but harsh of tongue.

203. जल में रहकर मगर से बैर। : Never quarrel with the crocodile when in the river.

204. जवानी की अपनी ही मस्ती होती है। : (i) The young will sow their wild oats.
(ii) Youth has its own charm.

205. जहाँ काम आवे सुई, कहाँ करे तलवार। : Little sticks kindle the fire, but big ones put it out.

206. जहाँ गुड़ होगा, वहाँ मक्खियाँ आएंगी। : Wherever there is a flame burning, there are moths ready to die.

207. जहाँ चाह, वहाँ राह। : Where there is a will, there is a way.

208. जहाँ फूल, वहाँ काँटा। : No rose is without a thorn.

209. जहाँ सुख, वहाँ दुःख : Joy and sorrow go hand in hand.

210. जागते को जगाना मुश्किल है। : None so deaf as those that won't hear.

211. जादू वह जो सिर चढ़ कर बोले। : The proof of the pudding is in the eating.

212. जिंदगी का मजा काम करते रहने में है।	:	(i) Work is worship. (ii) Life is action not contemplation. (iii) Work is the salt of life.
213. जिन्दगी छोटी-छोटी चीजों से बनती है।	:	Life is made up of little things.
214. जितना गुड़ डालोगे, उतना ही मीठा होगा।	:	The harder you work, the sweeter the rewards.
215. जितना ज्यादा, उतना मजा।	:	The more the merrier.
216. जितने मुँह, उतनी बातें।	:	As many mouths, as much gossip.
217. जिधर रब उधर सब।	:	Who has God, hath all.
218. जिन खोजा तिन पाइयाँ गहरे पानी पैठ।	:	(i) The best fish swim near the bottom. (ii) The feather floats high, and the pearl lies below.
219. जिसकी गोद में बैठे, उसी की दाढ़ी नोचे।	:	To bite the hand that feeds.
220. जिस बर्तन में खाना, उसी में छेद करना।	:	To spit into one's own plate.
221. जिसकी जूती, उसी का सिर।	:	Beat one with his own staff.
222. जिसने की शरम, उसके फूटे करम।	:	He who hesitates is lost.
223. जिसने चोंच दी, वह चारा भी देगा।	:	God gives both mouth and meat.
224. जिसका खाइए, उसका गुण गाइए।	:	Sing for the one who pays.

225. जिसकी लाठी, उसकी भैंस। : Might is right.

226. जिसके पास रुपैया वह सबका भैया। : A full purse never lacks friends.

227. जिसे अपनी जबान पर नियंत्रण है उसे बहुत बतियाना नहीं आता। : It is the wise head that makes the still tongue.

228. जियो और जीने दो। : Live and let live.

229. जीती मक्खी निगली नहीं जाती। : One does not eat the spoils of war.

230. जीवन वह, जो दूसरों के काम आए। : Live a life of service to others.

231. जीने के लिए खाओ, खाने के लिए न जिओ। : Eat to live, not live to eat.

232. जेब खाली, मन उदास। : A light purse makes a heavy heart.

233. जेब भारी, तो चेहरे पर हँसी। : A heavy purse makes a light heart.

234. जैसा अन्न, वैसा मन। : A drunkard is qualified for all vices.

235. जैसा आया, वैसा गया। : (i) Easy come, easy go.
(ii) Ill got, ill spent.

236. जैसा कर्म, वैसा फल। : As you sow, so shall you reap.

237. जैसा गुरु, वैसा चेला। : Like master, like servant.

238. जैसा दाम, वैसा काम। : (i) Like offerings, like blessings.
(ii) Fair work for fair wages.

239. जैसा देवता, वैसी पूजा। : As the Gods, so the worshippers.

240. जैसा बाप, वैसा पूत।	:	Like father, like son.
241. जैसे को तैसा।	:	(i) Tit for tat. (ii) Eye for an eye. (iii) To pay back in the same coin.
242. जैसे नागनाथ, वैसे साँपनाथ।	:	Hawk and hog go together.
243. उधार खाए, दुःख बुलाए।	:	He who borrows attracts
244. जो कमाए, सो खाए।	:	He who would eat the fruit must climb the tree.
245. जो काम करेगा वह गलती भी करेगा।	:	He who works is bound to make a few mistakes.
246. जो कर नहीं सकता वही उपदेश देता है।	:	He who talks a lot accomplishes little.
247. जो सोया, सो खोया।	:	A sleeping fox catches no poultry.
248. जो गरजते हैं, वे बरसते नहीं।	:	Barking dogs don't bite.
249. जो चमकता है, सोना नहीं होता।	:	All that glitters is not gold.
250. जो जागत है, सो पावत है।	:	The early bird catches the worm.
251. जो देखना नहीं चाहता, वही सबसे बड़ा अंधा है।	:	None so blind as one who won't see.
252. जो बात मधुर शब्दों से हो जाती है, कड़वे शब्दों से नहीं होती।	:	A drop of honey catches more flies than a barrel of vinegar.
252. जो बीत गई सो बात गई।	:	Let bygones be bygones.
253. जो मुर्गी सोने का अंडा दे उसे मारना नहीं चाहिए।	:	Kill not the goose that lays the golden eggs.

254. जो गलतियों से सबक नहीं लेते, उन्हें दोहराते हैं। : (i) Those who forget history are condemned to repeat it.
(ii) Those who don't learn from their mistakes repeat them.

255. जो मनुष्य अपने काम की देखभाल नहीं करता, उसको हानि पहुँचती है। : A sleeping fox catches no poultry.

256. जो होना है, होगा ही। : Whatever is destined to happen will happen.

257. झूठ बोलना पाप है। : To tell a lie is a sin.

258. झूठे का बोला हुआ सच भी अविश्वसनीय होता है। : Speak the truth and shame the devil.

259. झूठे दोस्त से सच्चा दुश्मन अच्छा। : Better a known enemy than a false friend.

260. टका सा जवाब। : Flat refusal.

261. टाँय-टाँय फिस्स। : To end up in smoke.

262. डंडा सबका पीर है। : The rod tames every brute.

263. डायन भी सात घर छोड़कर खाती है। : A wise fox will never rob his neighbour's hen.

264. डूबते को तिनके का सहारा। : A drowning man clutches at a straw.

265. तंदुरुस्ती हजार नेमत। : Health is wealth.

266. तन सुखी तो मन सुखी। : Sound mind in a sound body.

267. तर्कबुद्धि आदमी को अनुशासित करती है। : Reason disciplines the man.

268. तरकश में कई तीर होना। : To have many arrows in the scabbard.

269. तलवार के घाव से बात का घाव गहरा होता है।	:	Evil words cut worse than a sword.
270. तह तक पहुँचना।	:	To get to the bottom of an issue.
271. ताकत झूठ को भी सच करवा लेती है।	:	Might is right.
272. तिल का ताड़ बनाना।	:	To make a mountain out of a molehill.
273. तुम जो काम कर नहीं सकते, उसमें हाथ मत डालो।	:	Don't try to fly without wings.
274. तुम भगवान और शैतान दोनों को एक साथ खुश नहीं कर सकते।	:	One can't serve two masters at the same time.
275. तुरंत दान महाकल्याण।	:	He gives twice who gives in a trice.
276. तेरा माल मेरा मेरा तो है ही मेरा।	:	Heads I win, tails you lose.
277. तेल देखो, तेल की धार देखो।	:	(i) See which way the wind blows. (ii) Let us see how the cat jumps.
278. तैराक ही प्रायः डूबते हैं।	:	It is a good horse that stumbles.
279. थूक से सत्तू नहीं साना जाता।	:	You cannot make a horn out of a pig's tail.
280. थोड़ा-थोड़ा करके बहुत हो जाता है।	:	Many a little makes a mickle.
281. थोथा चना, बाजे घना।	:	Empty vessels make the most noise.

282. दरबार तक पहुँच हो तो दरबारी के पास क्यों जाएं। : He is a fool that kisses the maid when he may kiss the mistress.

283. दरिद्रता कलह की जड़ है। : Poverty breeds strife.

284. दरिद्रता बूढ़ा बना देती है। : Wrinkled purses make wrinkled faces.

285. दरिया में रहके मगर से बैर। : Never quarrel with the crocodile when in the river.

286. दाई से पेट नहीं छिपाया जा सकता। : Wear one's heart upon one's sleeve.

287. दाँत काटी रोटी। : Intimate friendship.

288. दान की बछिया के दाँत नहीं देखे जाते। : Never look a gift horse in the mouth.

289. दाल-भात में मूसलचंद। : An unwelcome person or an intruder.

290. दाल में कुछ काला है। : (i) Nigger in the woodpile.
(ii) There is something fishy.
(iii) I smell a rat.

291. दिल को दिल से राह। दिल का दिल साखी है। : Love begets love.

292. दिल्ली दूर है। : The goal is distant.

293. दीपक तले अँधेरा। : Nearer the church, farther from God.

294. दीवार के भी कान होते हैं। : Even walls have ears.

295. दीवाली साल में एक बार आती है। : Christmas comes but once a year.

296. दुर्जन व्यक्ति की मृत्यु देर से होती है। : Sinners die late.

297. दुर्दिन के समान और कोई शिक्षा नहीं। : Sweet are the uses of adversity.

298. दुश्मन को भेद की बात कभी न बताएं। : Never tell an enemy that your foot aches.

299. दुष्ट का स्वभाव कभी नहीं बदलता। : The wolf may lose his teeth, but never his temper.

300. दूध का दूध, पानी का पानी। : To sift the chaff from the grain.

301. दूध का जला छाछ को भी फूँक-फूँक कर पीता है। : (i) A burnt child dreads fire.
(ii) Once bitten twice shy.

302. दूर के ढोल सुहावने। : Distant mountains always look green.

303. दुश्मन के साथ भी न्याय करो। : Give the devil his due.

304. दूसरों के इशारे पर नाचना। : To dance to the tune of others.

305. देखो, ऊँट किस करवट बैठता है। : See which way the wind blows.

306. दो घरों का पाहुना भूखा सोये। : Between two stools one falls to the ground.

307. दो जोरुओं का खसम फूँके चूल्हा। : Between two stools one falls to the ground.

308. दो नावों का सवार डूबता है। : He who pursues two hares catches neither.

309. दो लड़े, तीसरा ले उड़े। : When two cats fight, the third benefits.

310. दोनों एक जैसे हैं। : Both are alike.

311. दो हाथों से ताली बजती है। : It takes two to quarrel.

312. दोनों हाथों में लड्डू हैं।	:	To butter one's bread on both sides.
313. दो मुल्लाओं में मुर्गी हराम।	:	Too many cooks spoil the broth.
314. दोस्त की पहचान मुसीबत पड़ने पर होती है।	:	Prosperity gains friends, adversity tries them.
315. दोस्त वही जो मुसीबत में काम आए।	:	A friend in need is a friend indeed.
316. दौड़ के चले सो मुँह के बल गिरे।	:	Hasty climbers have sudden falls.
317. दौलत आज मेरी, कल तेरी।	:	Riches have wings.
318. दौलत से इज्जत कहीं अच्छी होती है।	:	A good name is better than a golden girdle.
319. धन मित्र बनाता है, दुख उनकी परख करता है।	:	Prosperity gains friends, adversity tries them.
319. धागा जहां सबसे कमजोर होता है, वहीं से टूटता है।	:	The rope breaks from the weakest point.
320. धीरज से सब कुछ मिलता है।	:	Patience is the plaster for all sores.
321. धोबी का कुत्ता, न घर का न घाट का।	:	(i) A rolling stone gathers no moss. (ii) Whistling maid and crowing hen are neither fit for Gods nor for men.
322. नंगी नहाएगी क्या, और निचोड़ेगी क्या!	:	(i) To keep body and soul together. (ii) To live from hand to mouth.

323. न इधर के रहे, न उधर के।	:	Neither here nor there.
324. नई बहू नौ दिन की।	:	(i) Glamour doesn't last long. (ii) Nine days' wonder.
325. न खाए, न खाने दे।	:	Dog in the manger.
326. न देने के हजारों बहाने।	:	An ill payer never needs an excuse.
327. नपी–तुली प्रशंसा।	:	Qualified praise or remark.
328. नदी में रहे और मगर से बैर।	:	Never quarrel with the crocodile when in the river.
329. न नौ मन तेल होगा, न राधा नाचेगी।	:	When the sky will fall, we shall gather larks.
330. न निगला जाय, न उगला जाय।	:	(i) Between two fires. (ii) On the horns of a dilemma.
331. न बाप बड़ा न भैया, सबसे बड़ा रुपैया।	:	Money is paramount in life.
332. नया नवाब, आसमान पर दिमाग।	:	The newly rich easily fly off the handle.
333. नया नौ दिन, पुराना सौ दिन।	:	(i) An old cart outlives a new one. (ii) Old is gold.
334. नया नौकर तीरंदाज। नया मुल्ला प्याज ज्यादा खाता है।	:	A new broom sweeps clean.
335. नये आविष्कार का जन्म अभाव से होता है।	:	Necessity is the mother of invention.

336. नरम उत्तर से गुस्सा भी नरम हो जाता है। : (i) Politeness cools temper.
(ii) A soft answer turns away wrath.

337. न रहेगा बाँस, न बजेगी बाँसुरी। : Take away the fuel, take away the flame.

338. नशे में आदमी सच बोलता है। : A drunk man speaks the truth.

339. नहले पे दहला। : To go one better.

340. नाच न जाने आंगन टेढ़ा। : A bad workman quarrels with his tools.

341. नाम बड़े, दर्शन छोटे। : (i) Much cry, little wool.
(ii) Much ado about nothing.

342. नाम में क्या रखा है। : What's in a name?

343. निर्बल के बल राम। : God tempers the wind to the shorn lamb.

344. नीम-हकीम खतरा-ए-जान। : A little knowledge is a dangerous thing.

345. नौ नकद न तेरह उधार। : Neither a borrower nor a lender be.

346. परमेश्वर की माया, कहीं धूप, कहीं छाया। : Life has its ups and downs.

347. पराधीन सपनेहुं सुख नाहीं। : It is better to rule in hell than serve in heaven.

348. पसंद अपनी-अपनी, स्वभाव अपना-अपना। : Many men, many minds.

349. पहले आत्मा, फिर परमात्मा। : First self, then God.

350. पहले पहुँचे, मन भर खाए। : The early bird catches the worm.

351. पाँचों उँगलियाँ बराबर नहीं होतीं।	: All five fingers are not alike.
352. पानी का बुलबुला।	: Nine days' wonder.
353. पापी से घृणा मत करो, पाप से डरो।	: Hate the sin and not the sinner.
354. पुरानी मछली, पुराना तेल।	: Old is gold.
355. पूत के पाँव पालने में ही पहचाने जाते हैं।	: Coming events cast their shadows long before.
356. पैसा सबको अंधा कर देता है।	: Lust for money is a blinding passion.
357. प्यार अंधा होता है।	: Love is blind.
358. प्यार और लड़ाई में सब कुछ उचित है।	: All is fair in love and war.
359. प्यार को प्यार खींचता है।	: Love begets love.
360. प्यासे को ही कुएँ के पास जाना पड़ता है।	: The mountain will not come to Mohammed; Mohammed must go to the mountain.
361. प्रभु जब चाहता है तो मिट्टी भी सोना हो जाती है।	: When God wills, all winds bring rain.
362. प्रयास से ही काम सधता है।	: Only effort leads to success.
363. प्रेम का पुरस्कार प्रेम है।	: Love is its own reward.
364. फिजूलखर्ची से फकीरी।	: (i) Waste not, want not. (ii) Burn the candle at both ends.
365. फिक्र में हाथी भी घुल जाता है।	: Worry kills the cat.
366. बंदर क्या जाने अदरक का स्वाद!	: A blind man is no judge of colours.

367. बगल में छोरा, शहर में ढिंढोरा।	:	To miss something right under one's nose.
368. बड़ों की बड़ी बात।	:	High winds blow on high hills.
369. बद अच्छा, बदनाम बुरा।	:	(i) Give the dog a bad name and hang it. (ii) A bad name is worse than bad deeds.
370. बदनाम होंगे, तो क्या नाम न होगा!	:	Notoriety also makes one known.
371. बदमिजाज का कोई न साथी।	:	The ill tempered have no friends.
372. बंदर के गले में मोतियों की माला।	:	(i) To cast pearls before a swine. (ii) Honey is not for the ass's mouth.
373. बलवान का भगवान भी साथी।	:	Fortune favours the brave.
374. बहती गंगा में हाथ धोना। बहते दरिया में हाथ धोना।	:	Make hay while the sun shines.
375. बांझ क्या जाने प्रसूति की पीड़ा!	:	(i) Only the wearer knows where the shoe pinches. (ii) One who dives, knows the depth of the sea.
376. बातों से पेट नहीं भरता।	:	Bare words buy no barley.
377. बाप बड़ा न भइया, सबसे बड़ा रुपैया।	:	Money is paramount in life.
378. बालू से तेल नहीं निकलता।	:	You cannot draw blood from a stone.
379. बिना आग धुआँ नहीं उठता।	:	There is no smoke without fire.
380. बिना खर्च किए कुछ नहीं मिलता।	:	No pain, no gain.

381. बिना दान कैसा प्रतिदान?	:	An empty hand is no lure for a hawk.
382. बिना दूध के दही नहीं बनता।	:	You cannot make curd without milk.
383. बिना परिश्रम के कुछ नहीं मिलता।	:	(i) Patience and perseverance overcome mountains. (ii) Perseverance conquers all difficulties.
384. बिना मथे मक्खन नहीं निकलता।	:	Nothing ventured, nothing gained.
385. बिन मांगे मोती मिले, मांगे मिले न भीख।	:	Those who desire nothing get everything, while those who hanker get nothing.
386. बिना रोये माँ भी बच्चे को दूध नहीं पिलाती।	:	A closed mouth catches no flies.
387. बिना विचारे जो करे, सो पाछे पछताए।	:	Think before you speak.
388. बिना सेवा मेवा नहीं।	:	No pain, no gain.
389. बिना मरे स्वर्ग नहीं मिलता। बिना हाथ-पैर हिलाए रोजी नहीं मिलती।	:	Nothing ventured, nothing gained.
390. बिल्ली के सर पे छीका नहीं टूटता।	:	Cattle do not die from a crow's curses.
391. बिल्ली के भागों छीका टूटा।	:	To secure a windfall.
392. बिल्ली, और दूध की रखवाली!	:	Set a wolf to guard the sheep.
393. बुरी आदत बड़ी मुश्किल से छूटती है।	:	Old habits die hard.

394. बुरी आदतें जल्दी पड़ जाती है। बुरी आदतें पड़ना आसान है। : Bad habits are contagious.

395. बुरे का अंत बुरा। : Evil begets evil.

396. बुरे की भी अच्छाई पहचानो। : (i) Give the devil his due.
(ii) There is a soul of goodness in all things evil.

397. बुरे काम का बुरा नतीजा। : Evil begets evil.

398. बूँद-बूँद करके घड़ा खाली हो जाता है। : Drop by drop the lake is drained.

399. बूँद-बूँद से घड़ा भरता है। : Many drops make the ocean.

400. बूढ़ा होने से स्वभाव तो नहीं बदलता। : The wolf may lose his teeth but never his temper.

401. बोए कोई, काटे कोई। : One sows the seed, another reaps the corn.

402. बोए पेड़ बबूल का, आम कहां से खाय! : (i) To sow thistles and expect figs.
(ii) As you sow, so shall you reap.

403. बोलने से मौन भला। : (i) Silence is the best policy.
(ii) Silence is golden, speech is silvern.

404. भगवान के यहाँ देर है पर अंधेर नहीं। : The mills of God grind slowly, but surely.

405. भगवे कपड़े पहनने से कोई साधु नहीं बन जाता। : (i) It is not the cowl that makes a monk.
(ii) Borrowed garments never fit well.

406. भले आदमी जल्दी ही अल्लाह को प्यारे हो जाते हैं। : Whom the Gods love, die young.

407. भागने से पहले चलना सीखो।	:	Learn to walk before you run.
408. भाग्य के लिखे को कौन टाल सकता है।	:	What is lotted cannot be blotted.
409. भूल-चूक लेनी-देनी।	:	Errors and omissions accepted.
410. भैंस के आगे बीन बजाए, भैंस खड़ी पगुराय।	:	(i) Honey is not for the ass's mouth. (ii) Casting pearls before swines.
411. भौंकते कुत्ते को रोटी का टुकड़ा।	:	To give one a bone to pick.
412. मंजिल एक, राह अनेक।	:	All roads lead to Rome.
413. मखमल में टाट का बखिया।	:	Even the lion has to defend himself against flies.
414. मरता क्या न करता।	:	The drowning man clutches at straws.
415. मनुष्य अपने काम से जाना जाता है।	:	A man is known by his deeds.
416. महँगा रोये एक बार, सस्ता रोये बार-बार।	:	The cheap buyer takes the bad meat.
417. मान न मान, मैं तेरा मेहमान।	:	Welcome or not, I am your guest.
418. मित्र वही जो समय पर काम आए।	:	A friend in need is a friend indeed.
419. मुँह में राम, बगल में छुरी।	:	(i) A fair face may be a foul bargain. (ii) A fair face may have a foul heart.
420. मुँह से निकली बात वापस नहीं आ सकती।	:	Words once spoken cannot be recalled.

421. मुफलिसी में आटा गीला। मुसीबतें कभी अकेली नहीं आतीं। : Misfortunes never come alone.

422. मुफलिसी में दोस्त भी साथ छोड़ देते हैं। : When misfortune strikes even friends leave your side.

423. मुँह तोड़ जवाब। : A fitting response.

424. मृत्यु का कोई समय नहीं। : Death keeps no calendar.

425. मौका बार-बार हाथ नहीं आता। : Opportunity does not knock twice.

426. मौन का अर्थ है आपकी 'हाँ'। : Silence means half consent.

427. यथा नाम तथा गुण। यथा राजा तथा प्रजा। : Like ruler like subjects.

428. यह मुँह और मूसर की दाल। : First deserve then desire.

429. यहाँ उल्टी गंगा बहती है। : (i) Here everything is topsy-turvy.
(ii) Putting the cart before the horse.

430. राई का पहाड़। : To make a mountain out of a molehill.

431. राजा किसी को सामंत बना सकता है किंतु शरीफ नहीं। : The king can make a knight, but not a gentleman.

432. राजा के घर मोतियों का क्या टोटा (अकाल)! : A great ship needs deep waters.

433. राजा गलती नहीं करता। : The boss is always right.

434. राम नाम जपना, पराया माल अपना। : (i) A devil in the garb of a saint.
(ii) Cross on the chest and devil in the heart.

435. राम मिलाई जोड़ी, एक अन्धा एक कोढ़ी।	:	A deaf husband and a blind wife always make a happy couple.
436. राष्ट्र का भविष्य माँ के हाथ में होता है।	:	The hand that rocks the cradle rules the world.
437. रोज कुआँ खोदना, रोज पानी पीना।	:	Living from hand to mouth.
438. राम की माया, कहीं धूप कहीं छाया।	:	Life is full of shade and sunlight.
439. लकीर के फकीर होना।	:	To tow the dotted line.
440. लक्ष्मी चंचल है।	:	Riches have wings.
441. जिसकी लाठी, उसकी भैंस।	:	Might is right.
442. लातों के भूत बातों से नहीं मानते।	:	Some only understand the language of force.
443. लेन-देन में लाज कैसी!	:	Fair exchange is no robbery.
444. लेना एक न देना दो।	:	To burn daylight.
445. लोहा लोहे को काटता है।	:	Diamond cuts diamond.
446. लौट के बुद्धू घर को आए।	:	A bad penny always returns to the owner.
447. लोहे के चने चबाना।	:	A hard nut to crack.
448. वक्त बड़े-से-बड़े घाव को भर देता है।	:	Time is the best healer.
449. वही होता है जो मंजूर-ए-खुदा होता है।	:	God's will reigns supreme.
450. वही ढाक के तीन पात।	:	King's breakfast, queen's lunch, a beggar's dinner.
451. विनाश काले विपरीत बुद्धि।	:	Those whom God wants to destroy, He first makes mad.

452. विष की दवा विष है।	: Diamond cuts diamond.
453. वैसा ही व्यवहार करो जैसा तुम अपने लिए चाहते हो।	: Do unto others as you would have others do unto you.
454. व्यापार में शर्म कैसी!	: Fair exchange is no robbery.
455. शर्म घोल कर पीना।	: To loose all sense of shame.
456. शिष्टाचार का ध्यान रखो।	: Mind your P's and Q's.
457. शेर चूहे का शिकार नहीं करता।	: The eagle does not hunt flies.
458. शैतान को याद करो, शैतान हाजिर।	: Think of the devil and there he appears.
459. संगठन में बड़ी ताकत है।	: Unity is strength.
460. सच का बोलबाला और झूठे का मुँह काला।	: Tell the truth and shame the devil.
461. सच्चाई कड़वी होती है।	: Truth is always bitter.
462. सदा न फूले केतकी, सदा न सावन होय।	: Death and decay spare none.
463. सबका खून लाल होता है।	: The colour of blood is always red.
464. सबको एक आँख से देखो।	: You must measure all by the same criteria.
465. सबसे भली चुप।	: Silence is the biggest virtue.
466. सब्र का फल मीठा।	: Slow and steady wins the race.
467. सभी अपने फायदे की बात सोचते हैं।	: Everyone sees their own interests.
468. सभी से दोस्ती करने वाला किसी का दोस्त नहीं।	: (i) One who tries to please everybody, pleases none. (ii) Everybody's friend is nobody's friend.

469. समझदार को इशारा काफी है। : The wise can read between the lines.

470. समय किसी की प्रतीक्षा नहीं करता। : Time and tide wait for none.

471. समय को दोष देना अपने को ही दोष देना है। : There never was a good war or a bad peace.

472. सरसों हथेली पर नहीं जमती। : Rome was not built in a day.

473. सवेरे का भूला साँझ को घर आए तो भूला नहीं कहलाता। : It is never too late to mend one's ways.

474. सस्ता रोए बार-बार महँगा रोए एक बार। : The cheap buyer takes the bad meat.

475. साँच को आँच नहीं। : Truth fears no examination.

476. सारी से आधी भली। : Half a loaf is better than no bread.

477. सावन के अंधे को हरा ही हरा दिखाई देता है। : Everything looks pale to the jaundiced eye.

478. सिर मुंड़ाते ही ओले पड़े। : Misfortune in the very first adventure.

479. सिर पर कफन बाँधे फिरते हैं। : To always be prepared for the worst.

480. सिर्फ मौजमस्ती का नाम जिंदगी नहीं है। : Life is not a bed of roses.

481. सीखने की भी एक उम्र होती है। : You cannot teach your grandmother to suck eggs.

482. सीधी उंगली से घी नहीं निकलता। : Softness evokes no compliance.

483. सीधे का मुँह कुत्ता चाटे। : All lay loads on a willing horse.

484. सुअवसर एक ही बार हाथ आता है।	: Opportunity never knocks twice.
485. सूम का धन शैतान खाय।	: Ill got, ill spent.
486. सूरज पूरब में ही उगेगा।	: Water seeks its own level.
487. सेब का पेड़ जितना पुराना, उतने ही अधिक फल देता है।	: Old is gold.
488. सेवा बिना मेवा नहीं। सेवा करे सो मेवा पावे।	: No pain, no gain.
489. सोने से पहले एक सेब खाए, डॉक्टर के पास कभी न जाए।	: An apple a day keeps the doctor away.
490. सौ सयानों का एक मत।	: Great men think alike.
491. सौ सुनार की, एक लुहार की।	: The stroke of a hammer equals hundred strokes of a chisel.
492. स्वर्ग की गुलामी से नरक का राज भला।	: Better to reign in hell than to serve in heaven.
493. स्वार्थ आदमी को अंधा बना देता है।	: Selfishness turns a man blind.
494. सबसे बड़ा सुख, निरोग काया।	: Health is wealth.
495. हंस कभी कीचड़ नहीं खाता।	: True blue will never stain.
496. हड़बड़ का काम शैतान का।	: Haste makes waste.
497. हताशा गीदड़ को भी शेर बना देती है।	: Silent dogs and still waters are dangerous.
498. हर आदमी को अपनी ही चीज अच्छी लगती है।	: The owl thinks her own young fairest.
499. हर आदमी खरीदा जा सकता है।	: Every man has a price.
500. हर आदमी में बुराइयाँ होती हैं।	: No garden is without weeds.

परिशिष्ट–14/Appendix-14

भिन्नार्थक शब्द

हिन्दी में अनेक ऐसे शब्द हैं, जिनमें अर्थ की दृष्टि से भिन्नता होती है, किन्तु लोग भ्रमवश उनका प्रयोग प्रायः समान अर्थ में कर देते हैं। ऐसे शब्दों का अर्थगत सूक्ष्म अन्तर जानना जरूरी है, ताकि उनके प्रयोग में गलती न हो। इसी दृष्टि से यहाँ आमतौर पर प्रयोग किये जाने वाले शब्दों की सूची प्रस्तुत है :

अबला : अबला स्त्री मात्र को कहते हैं।
निर्बला : बलहीन नारी।

अभिमान : सच्चा वर्ग।
अहंकार : झूठा घमंड।

दर्प : नियम के विरुद्ध काम करने पर भी घमंड।
घमंड : सभी परिस्थितियों में अपने को बड़ा और दूसरे को हीन समझना।

अवस्था : उम्र, जीवन के कुछ बीते समय।
आयु : जीवन की पूरी गणना।

अलौकिक : अद्‌भुत, उत्तम गुणवाला।
अस्वाभाविक : प्रकृति के विरुद्ध।

ईर्ष्या : दूसरे की उन्नति से जलना।
द्वेष : वैर–भाव।

उद्योग : उद्यम, परिश्रम।
उपाय : समस्या सुलझाने का तरीका या तरकीब।

कृपा : किसी के कष्ट दूर करने की साधारण चेष्टा या किसी की सहायता।

दया : दीन–दुःखी पर पिघलना अथवा दुःखियों के दुःख दूर करने की स्वाभाविक इच्छा।

खेद : मन का खिन्न होना।
शोक : मृत्यु आदि पर अफसोस।

कष्ट : साधारण तकलीफ।
दुःख : तन–मन या आत्मा का दुःखी होना।

निर्णय : फैसला।
न्याय : इनसाफ।

पाप : धर्म के विरुद्ध कार्य।
अपराध : कानून के विरुद्ध कार्य करना।

देखना : साधारण अर्थ में देखना।
दर्शन देना : सम्मान के अर्थ में।

श्रद्धा : महात्माओं, धार्मों के प्रति।
भक्ति : ईश्वर के प्रति।

भिन्न : अलग।
विपरीत : उलटा।

भ्रम : जो नहीं है उसे समझ बैठना, जैसे– रस्सी को साँप समझना।

संदेह : दुविधा, जैसे– साँप है या रस्सी।

धर्म : सत्य आदि मानवता के आदर्श।

मत : मजहब।

मूर्ख : मुढ़ बुद्धिहीन।

अनभिज्ञ : जिसे पता न हो।

अज्ञात : जिसका पता न हो।

अपरिचित : नावाकिफ।

स्त्री : सम्पूर्ण नारी जाति।

पत्नी : किसी की विवाहिता।

लज्जा : शर्म।

ग्लानि : किसी पाप या अपराध का अफसोस।

शंका : शक।

आशंका : खतरा।

भय : साधारण डर।

त्रास : भयंकर भय।

बहुमूल्य : बहुत कीमती।

अमूल्य : जिसका मूल्य न आँका जा सके।

यत्न : कोशिश।

चेष्टा : हरकत।

वेदना : शारीरिक कष्ट।

व्यथा : मानसिक कष्ट

कलंक : भारी दोष लगना।

अपयश : अपकीर्ति।

प्रलाप : बकना, बकवाद।

विलाप : किसी के मरने पर रोना।

परिचर्या : रोगी की सेवा।

सेवा : किसी की भी सेवा।

अनुग्रह : कृपा करना।

अनुकंपा : बहुत कृपा।

अनुरोध : बराबर वालों से अनुरोध किया जाता है।

प्रार्थना : ईश्वर या अपने से बड़ों से प्रार्थना की जाती है।

अस्त्र : वह हथियार जो फेंककर चलाया जाता है।

शस्त्र : वह हथियार जो हाथ में लेकर चलाया जाता है।

अधिक : आवश्यकता से ज्यादा।

काफी : पर्याप्त।

अनुराग : किसी विषय-वस्तु पर शुद्ध भाव से मन का केन्द्रित होना।

आसक्ति : मोहजनित प्रेम।

अंतःकरण : विशुद्ध मन की केन्द्रीय शक्ति।

आत्मा : अनश्वर, जीवों की चेतना।

अध्यक्ष : किसी गोष्ठी, समिति या संस्था के स्थायी प्रधान।

सभापति : अस्थायी प्रधान।

अर्चना : धूप, दीप, फूल इत्यादि से पूजा करना।

पूजा : बिना किसी सामग्री के भी भक्तिपूर्ण विनय अथवा प्रार्थना।

अभिनंदन : किसी श्रेष्ठ का मान या स्वागत।

स्वागत : अपनी सभ्यता-संस्कृति से सम्बन्धित किसी को सम्मान देना।

आदि : साधारणत: एक या दो उदाहरण के बाद।
इत्यादि : दो से अधिक या पूरे उदाहरण के बाद।
आज्ञा : पूज्य व्यक्ति द्वारा दिया गया कार्य-निर्देश।
आदेश : किसी अधिकारी द्वारा दिया गया कार्य-निर्देश।
आदरणीय : अपने से बड़ों या महान् व्यक्तियों के प्रति सम्मान सूचक शब्द।
पूजनीय : पिता, गुरु या महान् पुरुषों के प्रति सम्मान सूचक शब्द।
इच्छा : साधारण चाह।
अभिलाषा : किसी विशेष वस्तु की हार्दिक इच्छा।
उत्साह : काम करने की बढ़ती हुई इच्छा।
साहस : भय पर विजय प्राप्त करना।
कंगाल : जिसे पेट पालने के लिए भीख माँगनी पड़े।
दीन : निर्धनता के कारण जो दया का पात्र हो।
ग्रन्थ : इससे पुस्तक के आकार की गुरुता और विषय के गांभीर्य का बोध होता है।
पुस्तक : साधारणत: सभी प्रकार की किताबें।
दक्ष : जो हाथ से किये जाने वाले काम को अच्छी तरह और जल्दी करें।
निपुण : जिसने अपने कार्य विषय का पूरा-पूरा ज्ञान प्राप्त कर लिया हो।
कुशल : जो हर काम में मानसिक तथा शारीरिक शक्तियों का अच्छा प्रयोग करना जानता है।
कर्मठ : जिस काम पर लगाया जाये उस पर लगा रहने वाला।
निबंध : ऐसी गद्य रचना जिसमें विषय गौण और लेखक का व्यक्तित्त्व एवं शैली प्रधान हो।
लेख : ऐसी गद्य रचना जिसमें वस्तु या विषय की ही प्रधानता हो।
निधन : महान् और लोकप्रिय व्यक्ति की मृत्यु।
मृत्यु : सामान्य शारीरांत की मृत्यु।
निकट : सामीप्य का बोध।
पास : अधिकार के सामीप्य का बोध।
प्रणाम : बड़ों को प्रणाम किया जाता है।
नमस्कार : बराबर वालों को।
नमस्ते : बराबर वालों को।
पारितोषिक : किसी प्रतियोगिता में विजयी होने पर।
पुरस्कार : किसी व्यक्ति के अच्छे काम या सेवा पर।
पुत्र : अपना बेटा।
बालक : कोई भी लड़का।
बड़ा : आकार का बोधक।
बहुत : परिणाम का बोधक।

बुद्धि : प्रज्ञा कर्तव्य का निश्चय करती है।

ज्ञान : इन्द्रियों द्वारा प्राप्त अनुभव।

मित्र : वह पराया व्यक्ति जिसके साथ आत्मीयता हो जाती है।

बन्धु : आत्मीय मित्र, सम्बन्धी।

मन : जहाँ संकल्प-विकल्प हो।

चित्त : जहाँ बातों का स्मरण-विस्मरण हो।

महाशय : सामान्य लोगों के लिए महाशय का प्रयोग होता है।

महोदय : अपने से बड़ों या अधि-कारिकयों को महोदय कहा जाता हे।

यन्त्रणा : असहाय दुःख का अनुभव।

यातना : आघात से उत्पन्न कष्ट की अनुभूति, विशेषकर शारीरिक क्षेत्र में या रूप में।

विषाद : अतिशय दुःखी होने के कारण किंकर्तव्यविमूढ़ होना।

व्यथा : किसी आघात के कारण मानसिक कष्ट या पीड़ा।

सेवा : गुरुजनों की टहल।

शुश्रुषा : दीन-दुःखियों या रोगियों की सेवा।

साधारण : जो वस्तु या व्यक्ति एक ही आधार पर आश्रित हो।

सामान्य : जो बात दो अथवा कई वस्तुओं तथा व्यक्तियों आदि में समान रूप से पायी जाती है।

सहानुभूति : दूसरे के दुःख को निज दुःख मानना।

स्नेह : छोटों के प्रति प्रेम-भाव रखना।

सम्राट : राजाओं का राजा।

राजा : साधारण राजा।

अनुरूप : रूप के अनुसार।

अनुकूल : अपने पक्ष के मुताबिक।

अनुभव : अभ्यासादि द्वारा प्राप्त ज्ञान।

अनुभूति : चिंतन मननादि द्वारा प्राप्त आंतरिक ज्ञान।

अनबन : दो व्यक्तियों का आपस में नहीं बनना।

खटपट : दो पात्रों या व्यक्तियों में साधारण झगड़ा।

अर्पण : अपने से बड़े को जो भेंट दी जाती है।

प्रदान : बड़ों की ओर से छोटों को दिया जाना।

अन्वेषण : अज्ञात पदार्थ, स्थानादि का पता लगाना।

अनुसंधान : छानबीन, जाँच-पड़ताल करना।

गवेषणा : किसी गूढ़ विषय की मूल स्थिति जानने के लिए गम्भीर अध्ययन-मननादि।

अशुद्धि : लायी गयी भूल।

भूल : कार्य–व्यवहारादि में किसी चीज का छूट जाना, रह जाना।

आधि : मानसिक कष्ट।

व्याधि : शारीरिक कष्ट।

आह्लाद : वह प्रसन्नता जो क्षणिक, पर तीव्र भावों से समन्वित हो।

उल्लास : किसी अभिलषित पदार्थ की प्राप्ति की आशा में जो आनंद आता है।

आगामी : आगे आने वाला समय।

भावी : भविष्य का बोध हो जाना।

आराधाना : किसी देवता या गुरुजन के समक्ष दया की याचना।

उपासना : अपने इष्टदेव से किसी उद्देश्य की पूर्ति के लिए एकनिष्ठ साधना करना।

उपकरण : वह सामग्री जो किसी कार्य की सिद्धि के लिए जुटाई जाती है।

उपादान : किसी पदार्थ के निर्माण की सामग्री।

उदाहरण : किसी पदार्थ को सिद्ध करने के लिए दिया गया प्रमाण आदि।

दृष्टांत : किसी बात की परिपुष्टि के लिए दिया गया तथ्य।

अभिनेत्री : रंगमंच पर नारी की भूमिका अदा करने वाली अभिनेत्री कहलाती है।

नायिका : नाटक या उपन्यासादि की मुख्य नारी पात्र।

त्रुटि : कमी का भाव प्रकट होना।

दोष : उचित–अनुचित का भाव।

निवेदन : अधिकारी व्यक्ति के समक्ष नम्रता का भाव बरतना।

आवेदन : दरख्वास्त।

क्रांति : जनसाधारण द्वारा शासन को उलटने के लिए संघर्ष।

विद्रोह : शासन के विरुद्ध कार्य।

आज्ञा : किसी गुरुजन की आज्ञा।

अनुज्ञा : अनुमति स्वीकृति।

आमंत्रण : किसी समारोह में सम्मिलित होने के लिए बुलावा।

निमंत्रण : कहीं भोजन करने के लिए बुलाहट।

ऋषि : सत्य का साक्षात्कार, आविष्कार करने वाला।

मुनि : सत्य का मनन करने वाला।

संत : पवित्र, निष्काम तथा निर्विरोध जीवन बिताने वाला।

बालक : अल्पवयस्क मानव, शिशु से अधिक उम्र वाला।

लड़का : बालक और बेटा दोनों अर्थों में प्रसंगानुसार प्रयुक्त।

बचपन : बच्चे की अवस्था।

बचपना : बच्चों का स्वभाव, बच्चे जैसी चेष्टा।

धन्यवाद : किसी की सहायता पाकर उसके प्रति कृतज्ञता का भाव प्रकट करना।

बधाई : किसी की उपलब्धि से अपनी प्रसन्नता प्रकट करते हुए उसकी उन्नति की शुभकामना।

सहयोग : किसी काम को मिल-जुलकर करना।

सहायता : किसी काम में मदद, हाथ बँटाना।

परिशिष्ट–15/Appendix-15

समोच्चरित शब्द

कुछ शब्द उच्चारण और वर्तनी की दृष्टि से प्रायः समान प्रतीत होते हैं, किन्तु उनके अर्थ पर्याप्त भिन्न होते हैं। उदाहरण के लिए 'शाखा' और 'साख' शब्दों को लिया जा सकता है। 'शाख' शब्द का अर्थ है वृक्ष की डाली, जबकि 'साख' शब्द का अर्थ है प्रतिष्ठा। ऐसे शब्दों का अर्थगत सूक्ष्म अंतर जानना जरूरी है, ताकि उनके प्रयोग में गलती न हो। इसी दृष्टि से यहाँ आमतौर पर प्रयोग किये जाने वाले शब्दयुग्मों की सूची प्रस्तुत है:

अंब : आम
अंभ : जल
अंश : हिस्सा
अंस : कंधा
अधम : नीच
अधर्म : पाप
अनल : आग
अनिल : हवा
अणु : कण
अनु : पीछे
अनुदित : नहीं उगा
अनूदित : अनुवादित
अनुप्राश : भोजन
अनुप्रास : एक शब्दालंकार
अन्न : अनाज
अन्य : दूसरा
अपत्य : संतान
अपथ्य : अहितकर
अपेक्षा : इच्छा, आवश्यकता
उपेक्षा : निरादर
अभय : निर्भय
उभय : दोनों
अभिज्ञ : जानने वाला
अनभिज्ञ : अनजान

अभिराम : सुन्दर
अविराम : लगातार
अयश : अपकीर्ति
अयस : लोहा
अरि : शत्रु
अरी : सम्बोधन स्त्री के लिए
अर्घ्य : पूजनीय, पूजा में देने योग्य वस्तु
अर्ध : आधा
अलि : भौंरा
अली : सखी
अवधि : काल
अवधी : अवध की भाषा
अवश : विवश
अवश्य : निश्चय
अशक्त : असमर्थ, शक्तिहीन
असक्त : विरक्त
आदि : आरम्भ
आदी : अभ्यस्त, अदरक
आभास : अनुमान
आवास : वास स्थान
आस्तिक : ईश्वरवादी
आस्ती : एक ऋषि

आहुत	:	यज्ञ	कृति	:	रचना
आहूत	:	आमन्त्रित	कृती	:	यशस्वी
इतर	:	अन्य	केशर	:	कुंकुम
इत्र	:	सुगन्धित पदार्थ	केसर	:	सिंह के गर्दन के बाल
ईशा	:	ऐश्वर्य, दुर्गा	कोर	:	किनारा
ईषा	:	हल की लम्बी लकड़ी	कौर	:	ग्रास
उपपति	:	पति भिन्न प्रेमी	कोश	:	शब्दकोश
उपपत्ति	:	सिद्धि	कोष	:	खजाना
उपयुक्त	:	उचित	क्षत्र	:	क्षत्रिय
उपर्युक्त	:	ऊपर कहा हुआ	छत्र	:	छाता
उद्धत	:	उद्दंड	खोआ	:	दूध का बना ठोस पदार्थ
उद्यत	:	तैयार	खोया	:	भूल गया, खो गया
एतवार	:	रविवार	गज	:	हाथी
उतबार	:	विश्वास	गज	:	मापक
कंकाल	:	ठटरी	गुड़	:	शक्कर
कंगाल	:	गरीब	गूढ़	:	गम्भीर
कंटीली	:	काँटेदार	गृह	:	घर
कटीली	:	तीक्ष्ण	ग्रह	:	सूर्य, चन्द्र आदि
कपशि	:	मटमैला	चक्रवात	:	बवंडर
कपीश	:	हनुमान, सुग्रीव	चक्रवाल	:	चकवा पक्षी
करकट	:	कूड़ा	चषक	:	शराब पीने का प्याला
कर्कट	:	केकड़ा	चसक	:	चस्का, लत
कर्म	:	कार्य	चिर	:	देर/पुराना
क्रम	:	सिलसिला	चीर	:	कपड़ा
कलि	:	कलियुग	जगत	:	कुएँ का चौतरा
कली	:	अधखिला फूल	जगत्	:	संसार
काश	:	शायद, खास	जब	:	जिस समय
कास	:	खासी	जव	:	वेग/जौ
कीला	:	गाड़ा या बँधा	जबान	:	जीभ
किला	:	गढ़	जवान	:	युवा/सैनिक
कुच	:	स्तन	जाया	:	व्यर्थ
कूच	:	प्रस्थान	जाया	:	पत्नी
कुल	:	वंश			
कूल	:	किनारा			

जिन : सूर्य/महावीर
जिन्न : प्रेतात्मा
जोश : आवेश
जोष : सुख, आराम
तक्र : मट्ठा
तर्क : बहस
तड़ाक : जल्दी
तड़ाग : तालाब
तप्त : गरम
तृप्त : संतुष्ट
तरंग : लहर
तुरंग : घोड़ा
तरणि : सूर्य
तरणी : नाव
तरुणी : युवती
तब : उसके बाद
तव : तुम्हारा
थाती : धरोहर
थाति : स्थिरता
दाई : धात्री, दासी
दायी : देने वाला
दारा : स्त्री
द्वारा : माध्यम, मारुत
दूत : संवादवाहक
द्यूत : जुआ
देव : देवता
दैव : भाग्य
दौड़ : दौड़ने की कला
दौर : चक्कर
द्रव : तरल
द्रव्य : पदार्थ, धान
द्विप : हाथी
द्वीप : टापू
परिक्षा : कीचड़
परीक्षा : इम्तिहान
पुरी : नगरी
पूड़ी/पूरी : एक व्यंजन
पूरी : सारी
प्रहर : पहर (समय)
प्रहार : चोट (आघात)
[illegible]न : साँप का फण
[illegible]न : कला, सुन्दर
बदन : शरीर
वदन : मुख
बन : बनना/मजदूरी
वन : जंगल
बलि : बलिदान
बली : वीर
बहन : बहिन
वहन : ढोना
बाईं : बायाँ का स्त्री रूप
बाई : वेश्या
बात : वचन
वात : हवा
बाण : तीर
बान : लत, आदत
बार : दफा
वार : चोट
बाला : लड़की
वाला : एक प्रत्यय
बाह्य : बाहरी
वाह्य : वहन करने योग्य
भारती : सरस्वती
भारतीय : भारत के निवासी
मद : अहंकार/नशा
मद्य : शराब
मरिचि : किरण
मरीचि : सूर्य/चन्द्र
मल : पखाना
मैल : गन्दगी

वरण	:	चुनाव/ब्याह करना
वरन्	:	बल्कि
वर्ण	:	रंग
व्रण	:	घाव
वसन	:	कपड़ा
व्यसन	:	लत
संग	:	साथ
संघ	:	समूह/दल
संभावना	:	संदेह, आशा
समभावना	:	तुल्यता की भावना
सन	:	पटुआ/सनुई
सन्	:	साल
सन्मति	:	अच्छी मति
सम्मति	:	परामर्श
सर्ग	:	अध्याय
स्वर्ग	:	देवलोक
साँस	:	प्राणवायु
सास	:	पति/पत्नी की माँ
सुधि	:	स्मरण
सुधी	:	विद्वान
सुत	:	बेटा
सूत	:	सारथि/धागा
सुर	:	देवता/लय
सूर	:	अंधा/सूर्य
सूचि	:	शूची, सूई
सूची	:	विषयक्रम
सेब	:	एक फल
सेव	:	बेसन का पकवान
श्याम	:	श्रीकृष्ण/काला
स्याम	:	एशिया का एक देश
हरि	:	विष्णु
हरी	:	एक वर्णवृत्त
ओटना	:	कपास से बिनौले निकालना/रुई धुनना।
औटना	:	दूध को बार-बार उबालने की क्रिया।
ओर	:	एक तरु/किनारा
और	:	एक से अधिाक वस्तु
खोलना	:	किसी बन्द वस्तु को खोलना।
खौलना	:	किसी तरल पदार्थ का उबलना।
पाश	:	बंधन
पास	:	नजदीक/करीब
मेला	:	अवसर विशेष पर एकत्र होने वाला जनसमुदाय।
मैला	:	मल/गन्दगी
मोर	:	हमारा राष्ट्रीय पक्षी।
मौर	:	विवाह के वक्त सिर पर पहना जाने वाला एक विशेष प्रकार का अलंकरण।

लोटना	:	धूल में लेटना
लौटना	:	वापस आना
संकर	:	मिश्रित/दोगला
शंकर	:	महादेव
सकल	:	सब/पूरा/सम्पूर्ण
शक्ल	:	सूरत/चेहरा/रूपसर
सर	:	तालाब/सिर
शर	:	वाण/तीर
सादी	:	सादा/साधाारण
शादी	:	विवाह/परिणय सूत्र
साला	:	पत्नी का भाई
शाला	:	घर, मकान
शोक	:	दु:खी होना/किसी प्रिय की मृत्यु पर होने वाला दु:ख।
शौक	:	रुचि/अभिरुचि
सेर	:	तौल का एक पुराना मापक (वाट)
सैर	:	घूमना/टहलना

परिशिष्ट–16/Appendix-16

सहचर शब्द

हिन्दी में कुछ शब्द प्रायः विरोधाभासी होने के बावजूद साथ-साथ प्रयोग किये जाते हैं। यहाँ ऐसे ही कुछ शब्दों का संग्रह प्रस्तु है :

अंधा – काना
अच्छा – भला
अता – पता
आकुल – व्याकुल
आटा – दाल
आदर – सत्कार
आन – बान
आब – भगत
ईंट – पत्थर
ऊबड़ – खाबड़
ऐसा – वैसा
कभी – कभार
कलम – दवात
कागज – कलम
खट्टा – मीठा
खाना – पीना
गोर – चिट्ठा
घास – पात
चकला – बेलन
चाल – ढाल
चोर – उचक्का
छेड़ – छाड़
छैल – छबीला
जूता – चप्पल
झगड़ा – टंटा

टेढ़ा – मेढ़ा
ढोल – मजीरा
थाली – लोटा
दंगा – फसाद
दवा – दारू
नदी – नाला
पूछ – ताछ
पैसा – कौड़ी
बाग – बगीचा
बाप – दादा
बाल – गोपाल
भला – चंगा
मकान – दुकान
मार – पीट
यत्र – तत्र
यदा – कदा
यहाँ – वहाँ
रख – रखाव
रुपया – पैसा
रोक – टोक
रोग – शोक
रोना – गाना
लड़ाई – झगड़ा
लाल – पीला
लूला – लंगड़ा

शाक – भाजी
शोर – शराबा
सड़ा – गला
सर्दी – जुकाम
सीधा – सादा

हक्का – बक्का
हल्ला – गुल्ला
हाथ – पैर
हाथी – घोड़ा
हिसाब – किताब

परिशिष्ट–17/Appendix-17

पशु-पक्षियों की बोलियाँ

उल्लू – घुघुआना
ऊँट – बलबलाना
कबूतर – गुटर गूँ करना
कुत्ता – भौंकना, भूँकना
कोयल – कूकना, कुहकना
कौआ – काँव-काँव करना
गधा – रेंकना
गाय – रंभाना
घोड़ा – हिनहिनाना
चिड़िया – चहचहाना
चूहा – चूँ-चूँ करना
तोता – टें-टें करना
पपीहा – पिउ-पिउ करना
बन्दर – खी-खी करना
बकरी – मिमियाना
बत्तख – कें-कें करना

बाघ – दहाड़ना, गुर्राना
बिल्ली – म्याऊँ-म्याऊँ करना
भालू – खों-खों करना
भेड़ा – भें-भें करना
भौंरा – गुँजारना
मक्खियाँ – भिनभिनाना
मुर्गा – बाँग देना
मेंढक – टर्र-टर्र करना
मोर – मेह आओ मेह आओ करना
शेर – दहाड़ना, गरजना
साँड़ – डकारना
साँप – फुफकारना
सियार – हुआँ-हुआँ करना
हाथी – चिंघाड़ना

परिशिष्ट – 18/Appendix-18

अनेक शब्दों के लिए एक शब्द

अंडे से उत्पन्न होने वाला–**अंडज**
अनिश्चित जीविका–**आकाशवृत्ति**
अनुचित बात के लिए आग्रह–**दुराग्रह**
अपनी हत्या–**आत्महत्या**
आँखों के सामने–**प्रत्यक्ष**
आकाश को चूमने वाला–**गगनचुम्बी**
आत्मा से सम्बन्ध रखने वाला–अध्यात्म
इन्द्रियों को जीतने वाला–**जितेन्द्रिय**
उच्च कुल में उत्पन्न हुआ–**कुलीन**
उपकार के बदले किया गया उपकार–**प्रत्युपकार**
एक ही माता से जन्म लेने वाला–**सहोदर**
एक ही समय में रहने वाला–**समसामयिक**
ओछी जाति में जन्म लेने वाला–**अंत्यज**
कम बोलने वाला–**अल्पभाषी**
काँटों से भरा हुआ–**कंटकाकीर्ण**
कानून के विरुद्ध–**गैरकानूनी**
घुटने तक जिसके हाथ हों–**आजानुबाहु**
जन्म लेते ही मर जाना–**आदंडपात**
जल की सवारी–**जलयान**
जानने की इच्छा रखने वाला–**जिज्ञासु**
जिसका शत्रु जनमा ही न हो–**अजातुशत्रु**
जिसका पति मर गया हो–**विधवा**
जिसका जन्म पीछे हुआ हो–**अनुज**
जिसका जन्म पहले हुआ हो–**अग्रज**
जिसका दमन करना कठिन हो–**दुर्दम्य**
जिसका मूल न हो–**निर्मूल**
जिसका आधार न हो–**निराधार**
जिसकी आशा नहीं की गयी हो–**अप्रत्याशित**
जिसकी उपमा न हो–**अनुपम**
जिसकी गर्दन कबूतर की तरह (सुन्दर) हो–**कपोतग्रीव**
जिसकी चार भुजाएँ हैं–**चतुर्भुज**
जिस स्त्री को सूर्य भी न देख सके–**असूर्यपश्या**
जिसे टाला न जा सके–**अनिवार्य**
जिसे कोई जीत न सके–**अजेय**
जिसे छेड़ा या तोड़ा न जा सके–**अभेद्य**
जिसके हाथ में चक्र है–**चक्रपाणि**
जिसके चार पैर हों–**चतुष्पद**
जिसके दशमुख हैं–**दशानन**
जिसके आर-पार देखा जा सके–**पारदर्शक**
जिसके हाथ में वज्र हो–**वज्रपाणि**
जिसके हाथ में वीणा हो–**वीणापाणि**
जिसके हाथ में शूल हो–**शूलपाणि**
जिसके बराबर दूसरा न हो–**अद्वितीय**
जिसकी पत्नी मर गयी हो–**विधुर**
जिसके आर-पार न देख जा सके–**अपारदर्शक**
जिसे लाँघना कठिन हो–**दुर्लंघ्य**
जिसे समझना कठिन हो–**दुर्बोध**
जिसे कभी बुढ़ापा न आये–**अजर**
जिसे ईश्वर में विश्वास हो–**आस्तिक**
जो कहा न जा सके–**अकथनीय**
जो मापा न जा सके–**अपरिमेय**
जो प्रमाण द्वारा सिद्ध न हो सके–**अगोचर**
जो दूर या भविष्य की बात सोचता है–**अग्रशोची**

जो सबसे आगे रहे–**अग्रणी, अग्रसर**
जो देखा न जा सके–**अलक्ष्य**
जो छाती के बल चलता है–**उदग**
जो इच्छा के अधीन हो–**ऐच्छिक**
जो उपकार मानता हो–**कृतज्ञ**
जो कल्पना से परे हो–**कल्पनातीत**
जो इन्द्रियों के ज्ञान के बाहर हो–**गोतीत**
जो बहुत समय तक ठहरे–**चिरस्थायी**
जो उपकार नहीं मानता है–**कृतघ्न**
जो ठेंगे के समान नाटा हो–**ठिंगना**
जो जन्म से अन्धा हो–**जन्मांध**
जो देखने योग्य हो–**द्रष्टव्य**
जहाँ जाना कठिन हो–**दुर्गम्य**
जो देखने में प्रिय लगे–**प्रियदर्शी**
जो परदे के भीतर रहे–**परनादर्शी**
जो पृथ्वी के भीतर का हाल जानता हो–**भूगर्भवेत्ता**
जो पहले था या हुआ–**भूतपूर्व**
जो आसानी से पच जाये–लघुपाक/**सुपाच्य**
जो बुरी आदतों में फँसा हो–**विषयासक्त**
जो सब कुछ जानता हो–**सर्वज्ञ**
जो वेद जानता हो–**वेदज्ञ**
जो मांस नहीं खाता–**निरामिष**
जो मांस खाता हो–**मांसाहारी**
जो बहुत बोलता हो–**वाचाल**
जानने की इच्छा–**जिज्ञासा**
जो क्षमा करने योग्य हो–**क्षम्य**
जो अनुकरण करने योग्य हो–**अनुकरणीय**
जहाँ पहुँचा न जा सके–**अगम्य**
जो नया आया हुआ हो–**नवागंतुक**
जो मर न सके–**अमर**
जो दूसरे के अधीन हो–**पराधीन**
जो नष्ट होने वाला हो–**नश्वर**
जो दूसरों का उपकार करे–**परोपकारी**
जो सोचने योग्य न हो–**अचिंत्य**
तालाब में उत्पन्न होने वाला–**सरसिज**
तेज या प्रतिभा से रहित–**निस्तेज**
थोड़ा जानने वाला–**अल्पज्ञ**
दिल खोलकर कहना या गाना–**मुक्तकंठ**
दिल खोलकर (खुले हाथ)–**मुक्तहस्त**
न बहुत ठण्डा और न बहुत गरम–**समशीतोष्ण**
धन का देवता–**कुबेर**
पति के द्वारा त्याग दी गयी स्त्री–**परित्यक्ता**
परम अर्थ अर्थात् मोक्ष या ब्रह्म–**परमार्थ**
परलोक का हो–**पारलौकिक**
पसीने से उत्पन्न जीव–**स्वेदज**
पेट की आग (भूख)–**जठराग्नि**
प्राणदायक अथवा जीवन देने वाली–**प्राणदा**
बहुत बढ़कर कहना–**अतिशयोक्ति**
बहुत तेज चलने वाला–**द्रुतगामी**
बहुत दूर तक देखने वाला–**दूरदर्शी**
बार-बार कही गयी बात–**पुनरुक्ति**
बिना वेतन का–**अवैतनिक**
बिना पलक गिराये, एकटक–**निर्निमेष**
बिजली की तरह चमक वाला–**विद्युत्प्रभ**
बिना विचारे किया गया विश्वास–**अंधविश्वास**
बहुत तेज बुद्धि वाला–**कुशाग्रबुद्धि**
पृथ्वी से संबद्ध–**पार्थिव**
पृथ्वी को धारण करने वाला–**भूधर**
बायें हाथ से तीर चलाने वाला–**सव्यसाची**
माता की हत्या करने वाला–**मातृहंता**
मृदु बोलने वाला–**मृदुभाषी**

रात में विचरण करने वाला–**निशाचर**
राह दिखाने वाला–**पथ प्रदर्शक**
लौटकर आया हुआ–**प्रत्यागत**
वस्तुओं (नदियों) का मिलन–**संगम**
विष्णु का उपासक या विष्णु से संबद्ध–**वैष्णव**
व्याकरण जानने वाला–**वैयाकरण**
विदेश में रहने वाला –**प्रवासी**
शक्ति का उपासक–**शाक्त**
शत्रु को मारने वाला–**शत्रुघ्न**
शब्द द्वारा जो व्यक्त नहीं हो सके–**अनिर्वचनीय**
हमेशा रहने वाला–**शाश्वत**
शिव का उपासक–**शैव**
सब कुछ खाने वाला–**सर्वभाषी**
सब जगह मौजूद रहने वाला–**सर्वव्यापी**
सहन करना जिसका स्वभाव हो–**सहनशील**
साँझ और रात के बीच का समय–**गोधूलि**
सिर से पैर तक–**आपादमस्तक**
सुनने योग्य–**श्रव्य या श्रवणीय**
शाक, भाजी, फल-फूल खाने वाला –**शाकाहारी**

सार्थक जीवन जीने की कला

–रोमी सूद

लगभग आधी सदी का परिदृश्य हमारे सामने है। इस बीच भारतीय जीवनशैली में तेजी से बदलाव आया है। उपभोक्ता संस्कृति और बाज़ारवाद ने लोगों के जीवन को ही मूल्यहीन बना दिया है। पश्चिम से आयातित सभ्यता और संस्कृति के अंधानुकरण ने भारतीय मूल्यों और परंपराओं को क्षतिग्रस्त कर दिया है। यह सांस्कृतिक पतन भीषण है। हर कोई उधार की जिंदगी जी रहा है। उसकी स्थिति त्रिशंकु की तरह हो गई है। संक्रमण के इस काल में यह आवश्यक हो गया है कि आधुनिक जीवन के अच्छे-बुरे पक्ष को हम भली-भांति समझें। 'सार-सार' को आत्मसात करें और जो 'थोथा' है, उसका तिरस्कार कर दें। आइए! बेहतर और उन्नतिशील जीवन जीने की कला में पारंगत हो जाएं।

- ◆ पुस्तक के आरंभ में दी गई जांच प्रश्नोत्तरी आपको यह पहचान कराएगी कि वास्तव में आपमें कितनी कमियां और कमजोरियां हैं।
- ◆ यह एक ऐसी प्रयोगशाला साबित होगी, जो आपमें संपूर्ण सुधार करके जीवन जीने का तरीका सिखाएगी।
- ◆ हर अध्याय के अंत में प्रण और प्रतिज्ञाएं दी गई हैं, जो पाठक को हर हाल में सच्चा और अच्छा आधुनिक बनाएंगी।
- ◆ इसमें दिए गए साक्षात्कार, वार्ताएं, काउंसलिंग, टिप्स और जीवन-प्रसंग पुस्तक को अधिक उपयोगी और व्यावहारिक बनाने में सक्षम हैं।

डिमाई आकार • पृष्ठ : 123

निराशा छोडो सुख से जिओ

–हरेन्द्र 'हर्ष'

व्यक्ति अचानक आई विपत्ति या मामूली अवरोध से ही घबरा जाता है। इससे उसके हाथ से बहुत से अवसर जाते रहते हैं। अतएव आशा की डोर कभी मत छोड़ें, इसके साथ डटे रहें, फिर देखें आपके जीवन में खुशियां आएंगी। आप उन्नति के लिए आशा की ज्योति जलाकर सतत प्रयास करते रहें। इस कार्य में इस पुस्तक के विचार ही नहीं, उद्धरण, प्रसंग और घटनाएं पग-पग पर आपका मार्गदर्शन करके आपके विकास में सहायक सिद्ध होंगी।

आशा उत्साह की जननी है। आशा में तेज है, बल है, जीवन है। आशा ही समूचे संसार की संचालक शक्ति है। आशा मनुष्य के लिए अमृत है। जैसे सूर्य से पेड़-पौधों को जीवन प्राप्त होता है, वैसे ही आशा से मनुष्यों में जीवन-शक्ति का संचार होता है। निराशा कभी भी आपकी उन्नति नहीं होने देती और सदा आपके लक्ष्य में बाधक सिद्ध होती है। मनुष्य की सम्पूर्ण उन्नति और सफलता बेहतर जीवनशैली से ही संभव है। इसलिए निराशा को कभी पास मत फटकने दें।

जाने-माने लेखक हरेन्द्र 'हर्ष' की सुलझी हुई लेखनी द्वारा रचित यह पुस्तक **'निराशा छोड़ो, सुख से जिओ'** विश्व विख्यात लेखक स्वेट मार्डेन के विचार, चिंतन और लेखन शैली को आगे बढ़ाती है।

डिमाई आकार • पृष्ठ : 136

NEW RELEASES BOOKS

V&S PUBLISHERS
School Atlas
SCHOOL ATLAS

R. M. Onkar
Know your Personality
Discovering your personality
Mental domains of personality
Physical Appearance of Personality
Role of Personality in Performance and Success
Destiny Hidden in your Personality
A Self-Guide for Sharpening Your Competitive Edge to Achieve

71 Famous Scientists

EXC-EL SERIES
BUSINESS ENGLISH
A Complete Reference Manual for Effective Business Communication
Excellence in English Language

SELF-IMPROVEMENT/PERSONALITY DEVELOPMENT

Also Available
in Hindi

Also Available
in Hindi

Also Available
in Kannada, Tamil

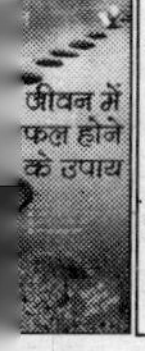
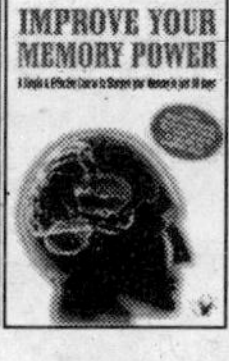

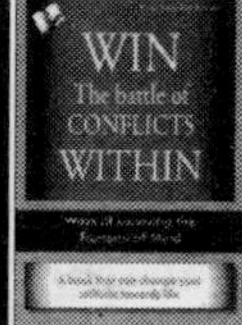

Also Available
in Kannada

Also Available
in Kannada

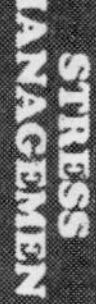

All books available at www.vspublishers.com